Hitler and Stalin

'Coming from one of the world's experts on the Second World War, this is an important and original – and devastating – account of Hitler and Stalin as dictators. A must-read'
Professor Robert Service, author of *Stalin*

'Laurence Rees brilliantly combines powerful eyewitness testimony, vivid narrative and compelling analysis in this superb account of how two terrible dictators led their countries in the most destructive and inhumane war in history'
Professor Sir Ian Kershaw, author of *Hitler*

'In this fascinating study of two monsters, Rees is extraordinarily perceptive and original'
Sir Antony Beevor, author of *Stalingrad*

'A brave and remarkable work. Revelatory, gripping and hugely relevant, it shows Hitler and Stalin as you've never known them. Truly a story of our time, with so many lessons for the troubled world we inhabit today, it will revolutionize your understanding of these two foremost tyrants'
Damien Lewis, author of *The Nazi Hunters*

'Presenting this complex history with his usual clarity, his latest study is an enthralling read, weaving many fresh eyewitness accounts into the narrative, offering new insights and commanding his reader's attention despite the huge scope of his task'
Julia Boyd, author of *Travellers in the Third Reich*

'A vivid and terrifying portrait of the twentieth century's two most brutal tyrants. His mastery of the subject shines through on every page. Provocative, gripping and full of fresh insights, *Hitler and Stalin* is narrative history at its very best'
Henry Hemming, author of *Churchill's Iceman*

Hitler and Stalin

The Tyrants and the Second World War

LAURENCE REES

VIKING

an imprint of

PENGUIN BOOKS

VIKING

UK | USA | Canada | Ireland | Australia
India | New Zealand | South Africa

Viking is part of the Penguin Random House group of companies
whose addresses can be found at global.penguinrandomhouse.com.

Penguin
Random House
UK

First published 2020

001

Copyright © LR History Limited, 2020

The moral right of the author has been asserted

The list of illustrations on p. xi constitutes an extension of this copyright page

Set in 12/14.75 pt Bembo Book MT Std
Typeset by Jouve (UK), Milton Keynes
Printed and bound in Great Britain by Clays Ltd, Elcograf S.p.A.

A CIP catalogue record for this book is available from the British Library

HARDBACK ISBN: 978–0–241–29520–5
TRADE PAPERBACK ISBN: 978–0–241–42267–0

To Benedict

Contents

List of Maps   ix

List of Illustrations   xi

Preface   xv

Introduction   xix

1. The Pact   1

2. Eliminating Poland   22

3. Opposite Fortunes   47

4. Dreams and Nightmares   74

5. Hitler's War of Annihilation   91

6. Invasion   107

7. Desperate Days   131

8. A World War   150

9. Hunger   176

10. Stalin's Overreach   194

11. Across the Steppe   214

12. Struggle on the Volga   234

13. Fighting On   255

14. Fiction and Reality   283

15. Mass Killing   305

16. Collapse of the Centre   324

17. Dying Days   350

18. Victory and Defeat   379

Contents

Afterword   395

Acknowledgements   403

Notes   405

Index   465

List of Maps

p. 23:   Invasion of Poland, 1939

p. 56:   Winter War, 1939–40

p. 70:   Operation Yellow, 1940

p. 109: Invasion of the Soviet Union, 1941

p. 219: Operation Blue, 1942

p. 326: Operation Bagration and the assault on Berlin, 1944–45

p. 365: Movement of Poland's borders, 1945

p. 388: Iron Curtain, 1949

List of Illustrations

1. Joseph Stalin in 1919.
2. Adolf Hitler as a German soldier in the First World War.
3. Stalin with Vladimir Lenin in 1922.
4. Stalin relaxing with his comrades in the 1920s.
5. Hitler as leader of the Nazi Party.
6. Hitler with his girlfriend, Eva Braun.
7. Bodies in the street during the Ukrainian famine of the early 1930s.
8. Soviet prisoners build the White Sea–Baltic Canal during the early 1930s.
9. Inside a hospital for prisoners working on the White Sea–Baltic Canal.
10. Prisoners at Dachau concentration camp in 1933.
11. Guards at Dachau in 1933.
12. Joachim von Ribbentrop signing the Nazi–Soviet pact in 1939.
13. Three military commanders, Grigori Shtern, Khorloogiin Choibalsan and Georgy Zhukov, in 1939.
14. Stalin and Marshal Kliment Voroshilov.
15. Hitler watching German troops invade Poland in 1939.
16. German and Soviet soldiers collaborate in the division of Poland.
17. Finnish soldiers during the Winter War against the Soviet Union in 1939–40.
18. French prisoners, captured by the Germans, in 1940.
19. Hitler in Paris in June 1940.
20. Heinz Guderian.
21. German soldiers in 1941 with a captured portrait of Stalin.
22. A German soldier during Operation Barbarossa.
23. Hitler visits his troops on the eastern front in the summer of 1941.

24. Hitler with Wilhelm Keitel, Franz Halder and Walther von Brauchitsch.
25. Red Army soldiers taken prisoner by the Germans.
26. German soldiers advance on Moscow in December 1941.
27. Red Army soldiers parade in Red Square on the anniversary of the 1917 Revolution.
28. Stalin giving a speech in Moscow's Red Square on 7 November 1941.
29. A boy begging for food during the German occupation of Ukraine.
30. One of the most infamous images of the Holocaust, known as the killing of 'the last Jew in Vinnitsa'.
31. The Germans uncover evidence of a Soviet war crime at Katyn.
32. The first meeting of the so-called Big Three at Tehran: Winston Churchill, Stalin and Roosevelt.
33. President Franklin Roosevelt in a cheerful mood.
34. German soldiers during the battle of Kharkov in May 1942.
35. Soviet partisans operating behind the German front line.
36. Women serving as snipers in the Red Army.
37. Hitler in a pensive mood alongside his military commanders.
38. Red Army soldiers during the battle of Stalingrad.
39. Vasily Chuikov.
40. Friedrich Paulus.
41. Stalin, photographed at the end of 1943.
42. Hitler, photographed in late 1942 or early 1943.
43. Resistance fighters of the Polish Home Army during the Warsaw uprising in 1944.
44. Stalin and Churchill at the Yalta conference in February 1945.
45. Victorious Red Army units during Operation Bagration in 1944.
46. Hitler talking to Luftwaffe officers towards the end of the war.
47. German soldiers examine the victims of the Red Army attack on Nemmersdorf in 1944.
48. One of the last photographs taken of Adolf Hitler.
49. Hitler's bunker in Berlin after the Red Army had captured the city.

50. Winston Churchill, Harry Truman and Joseph Stalin at the Potsdam conference in 1945.

51. The Nazi concentration camp of Bergen-Belsen.

52. Inside a hut in a Soviet prison camp in 1945.

53. Stalin after his death in March 1953.

The photographs come from: 1, Topfoto; 2, 7, 13, 19, 29, 30, private collections; 3–6, 12, 24, 28, 41, Alamy; 8, 9, 14, 17, 26, 27, 31, 32, 38, 44, 48–50, 52, 53, Getty; 10, 11, 15, 20, 23, Bundersarchiv; 16, 22, 33–6, 39, 40, 43, 45, 47, 51, AKG; 18, Adoc-photos; 21, 25, BPK Bildagentur; 37, 42, 46, Ullstein Bild. Every reasonable effort has been made to trace copyright but the publisher welcomes any information that clarifies the copyright ownership of any unattributed material displayed and will endeavour to include corrections in reprints.

Preface

The origin of this book is easy to explain. I've spent the last thirty years making documentaries and writing books about the Third Reich, Stalinism and the Second World War. As a consequence I've met hundreds of people who experienced life under Hitler's and Stalin's rule – not just those who suffered, but those who enthusiastically supported the dictators as well. It was my encounters with these first-hand witnesses, and the intriguing things they said, that made me want to write this book.

Fourteen years ago, for instance, I was in the Moscow apartment of the most famous Soviet cartoonist of the Second World War, Boris Yefimov.[1] He revealed that his work had been so strictly monitored that Stalin needed to approve personally any cartoon he drew on a sensitive topic. When pressed on how it felt to be an artist who could not practise self-expression but instead had to create state-sanctioned propaganda, Yefimov replied that artists had to realize the responsibility they possessed 'not to do harm to their own people' and 'country'.[2]

It was, of course, a totally different perspective on the role of the artist from the one that we possess today in the west. And as he talked I remembered similar views I had heard years before, when I met film directors who had worked for the infamous Nazi propagandist Joseph Goebbels.[3] They too spoke about the need for their artistic work to serve the state. So, in this respect at least, the two regimes sounded alike.

In contrast, the experiences of those people I met who personally encountered Hitler and Stalin on a regular basis could hardly have been more at odds. It was most certainly not the same thing to walk into a meeting with Stalin as to walk into one with Hitler. As individual personalities the two tyrants were far apart.

Over the years I started thinking more and more about this comparison between the two leaders and their regimes. What were the key differences? In what ways were the regimes similar? And, perhaps most crucial of all, to what extent did Stalin and Hitler shape the times they lived in, and to what extent did the times shape them?

After much thought, I decided to focus this work on the period

1939–45. That's because these were the years during which Hitler and Stalin had a direct relationship, first as colleagues in an alliance of sorts, and then not just as mere adversaries but as the two most powerful warlords the world had ever seen. Even though they never met, each of them was very much aware of the other. They even admired each other's ruthlessness.[4] Hitler and Stalin were linked together for nearly six years, and I believe it's that connection that makes this comparison particularly striking.

An emphasis on the war years is one way this book differs from the best-known previous attempt to compare the two dictators – Alan Bullock's *Hitler and Stalin: Parallel Lives*.[5] I've also benefited from the wealth of scholarly research that has taken place on this subject since Bullock wrote his book nearly thirty years ago. But perhaps the biggest difference between this work and *Parallel Lives* is the way I've been able to draw on millions of words of original eyewitness testimony. So much so that most of the interview material quoted here has never been published before.

It's been one of the great privileges of my professional life that, together with my various production teams, I was able to travel across the former Soviet Union and meet people who had never felt able to talk publicly about this history before. Over many years, and for a variety of projects, we travelled from Siberia to Ukraine, from Kalmykia to the Barents Sea and from Lithuania to the River Volga. We met retired members of the secret police, villagers who had suffered at the hands of both German soldiers and Red Army partisans, veterans of gigantic battles like Stalingrad and Moscow, even Stalin's former telegraphist who revealed how the Soviet dictator had nearly fled the capital in the dark days of October 1941. If the Berlin Wall had not fallen, and the Soviet Union had not subsequently collapsed, these witnesses to epic events could never have talked of their experiences without fear of retribution. Their stories would have been lost for ever.

This primary source material is especially valuable in the context of a comparison between the two dictators, because Hitler and Stalin made decisions in warmth and comfort that resulted in the torment of millions, and it's vital that ordinary people who suffered at their hands have a voice.

It's important to treat eyewitness testimony with particular care, and I've written elsewhere of how we checked the authenticity of the material we obtained, and of the nuanced way in which it must be used.[6] But notwithstanding these caveats, and after years of experience dealing with personal testimony, I've concluded that it is a mistake to think that individuals speaking after the event are somehow inherently less 'reliable' than documents of the time. This point was first brought home to me with great force thirty years ago, when I was making a film featuring the testimony of members of a Slovenian unit called the Domobranci, who were handed over to Marshal Tito's men by British forces in the summer of 1945.[7] These eyewitnesses spoke of the brutal way that Tito's soldiers had treated them, and of how the British had seen their suffering. But a report in the archives, written by a British officer at the time, offered a radically different perspective. It spoke of how well Tito's men had treated their prisoners, saying, 'They were kindly and efficiently handled, and provided with light refreshments . . .'[8]

This could be taken to demonstrate the primacy of documents over testimony. But when I interviewed the British officer who had written the report he confirmed the evidence of the Domobranci, and said that he had been told at the time by his superior officer to lie. He expressed surprise that anyone could believe the words he had written in his report, since he had been deliberately ironic. How could anyone, he said, possibly think that Tito's forces would have offered 'light refreshments' to their enemies in such a situation?[9]

I mention this not to suggest that eyewitness testimony is somehow better than contemporaneous material, merely to point out that historians must treat every single source with scepticism.[10] Nor, especially in the context of this history, would I dispute the enormous importance of archival evidence. Many times the discovery of a document that has been hidden for years has reshaped our understanding of the period. Think, for example, of the piece of paper Stalin signed early in the war which authorized the killing of thousands of Polish officers, and which only came to light after the fall of communism in the Soviet Union.[11]

Notwithstanding my decision to focus this work on the period of the Second World War, I also discuss key events that occurred before these years when an understanding of them is helpful for the narrative. For example, I look at the impact of the Red Army purges of the 1930s in the context of the Soviet Union's protracted war with Finland.

Introduction

Hitler and Stalin both came from outside the mainstream. Stalin entered the world in December 1878 in Georgia, 1,300 miles from the heart of Imperial Russian power in St Petersburg. Hitler, metaphorically if not physically, came even further from the centre of German political life. He was born in April 1889 not in Imperial Germany but in neighbouring Austria, in the border town of Braunau am Inn. Both came from ordinary families. Hitler's father was a customs inspector. Stalin's father – a cobbler – was considerably poorer. Both fathers drank and beat their sons.

All this is true, but potentially misleading. That's because we need to remember that large numbers of others at the time were brought up in much the same way, and they didn't go on to terrorize millions. We also need to guard against the temptation to think that even individuals as dominant as Hitler and Stalin were somehow destined to achieve great power. They weren't.

Hitler and Stalin were catapulted into prominence only in the wake of an epoch-shattering event over which they had no control – the First World War. In July 1914, just before the war began, no one would have predicted that Hitler, then twenty-five years old, would go on to become one of the most infamous leaders in the history of the world. He was not even pursuing a career as a politician, but was struggling to earn a living as a painter in Munich, having travelled there from Vienna. He was perceived as an oddity, with a tendency to harangue people about art or literature and blame the world for his failures. 'There was no end to the things, even trivial ones, that could upset him,' remembered Hitler's flatmate from his time in the pre-war Austrian capital.[1] 'Altogether, in these early days in Vienna, I had the impression that Adolf had become unbalanced. He would fly into a temper at the slightest thing.'[2] If you had met this pre-First World War Hitler, most likely you would have agreed with the subsequent judgement of one of his comrades in the trenches – there was 'something peculiar' about him.[3]

By 1914 Stalin, unlike Hitler, was already a revolutionary. Fifteen years before, he had abandoned the seminary where he had been training to become a priest, and embarked as a committed Marxist on a mission to overthrow the state. As the guns of the First World War started to fire, he was in exile in Siberia with a history of crimes behind him – most notably his role in organizing a violent robbery in Tiflis (today's Tbilisi) in Georgia in 1907. Despite his ardent belief in revolution, and his rejection of his birth name of Iosif Jughashvili and his adoption of the dramatic pseudonym 'Stalin', meaning 'Man of Steel' in Russian,[4] there seemed little prospect of his revolutionary group ever gaining power.

The First World War changed both men's fortunes. In the wake of food riots at home and a disastrous campaign on the front line, the Russian Tsar Nicholas II was forced to abdicate in March 1917. But this didn't mean that the Bolsheviks, the group of Marxist revolutionaries to which Stalin belonged, would inevitably come to power. It took a calamitous decision by the Provisional Government after the Tsar had departed, combined with a general disintegration of political and economic institutions, to precipitate that decisive event. In the summer of 1917 the Provisional Government ordered the Russian Army on to the offensive. It was a moment the Bolsheviks, under the leadership of Vladimir Lenin, were ready to exploit. Shortly after battle had been joined with Austro-Hungarian troops in Western Ukraine, the army started to mutiny as Bolshevik revolutionaries embedded in individual units turned the soldiers against their leaders. A few months later, after the October Revolution, Lenin and his Bolsheviks were in power.

If it's hard to see how all that could have happened without the events of the First World War, it's impossible to imagine how Hitler could ever have become the leader of a political party, let alone Chancellor of Germany, without the circumstances of Germany's defeat in November 1918. It was his disgust and anger at the loss of the war, together with his desire to find scapegoats for that loss, which propelled him into politics. He joined a small extremist group called the German Workers' Party in Munich in September 1919. Two years later he was their leader, with the party renamed the National Socialist German Workers' Party, subsequently known as the Nazis for short.

By the 1920s, Hitler and Stalin were already very different from each other in how they saw their role in the political worlds they inhabited. Hitler, unlike Stalin, was the archetypical 'charismatic leader' – a concept originally defined by the German sociologist Max Weber. Charismatic leaders rely primarily on the power of their own personalities to justify their office. They don't fit well into bureaucratic structures and project an almost 'missionary' aura.[5]

'Everything came from the heart, and he struck a chord with all of us,' recalled Hans Frank, who heard Hitler speak in 1920 and subsequently became a leading Nazi. 'He uttered what was in the consciousness of all those present and linked general experiences to clear understanding and the common wishes of those who were suffering and wishing for a programme . . . But not only that. He showed a way, the only way left to all ruined peoples in history, that of the grim new beginning from the most profound depths through courage, faith, readiness for action, hard work, and devotion to a great, shining, common goal . . . I was convinced that if one man could do it, Hitler alone would be capable of mastering Germany's fate.'[6]

Frank's statement that Hitler 'uttered what was in the consciousness of all those present' offers an important insight into his appeal. Charismatic leaders like Hitler are effective only if the audience is receptive to their beliefs. If you disagreed fundamentally with Hitler in the 1920s then you would almost certainly have been impervious to his 'charisma'. His oratory, for example, did not convince a man like Herbert Richter, a German veteran of the First World War. Richter, who was not predisposed to support Hitler, thought he talked in a 'scratchy' voice and had a tendency to 'shout . . . really, really simple' political ideas.[7]

In contrast, Stalin was the antithesis of Weber's model of the charismatic leader. Not only was he a less than inspiring orator, but far from shunning the demands of bureaucracy he embraced them. Throughout his political life he had a profound understanding of the power of committee meetings. In that respect he was fortunate that his own personality exactly matched what the new structures of the Soviet state required. He would preside over a gigantic expansion in the number of people working as administrators within the Soviet system – from fewer than four million in 1929 to nearly fourteen million by 1939.[8]

Stalin was appointed General Secretary of the Communist Party at the Eleventh Party Congress in April 1922 and, as a consequence, had control over vast swathes of communist bureaucracy, including decisions about personnel. This administrative empire became his power base. He was helped by the desire of Lenin and other leading Bolsheviks to centralize power – a goal symbolized by the creation of committees like the Politburo and Orgburo. Significantly, Stalin was the only person to be a member of both the Orgburo and the Politburo as well as the party Secretariat.[9]

So much did Stalin work away from the spotlight in these years that historians still argue about the precise moment at which he became the pre-eminent figure in the country. After Lenin's death in 1924 he was just one of a number of senior figures who ran the newly created Soviet Union. It wasn't until the early 1930s that he managed to shoulder his way to the front. Even then, he never became head of state – that role was fulfilled by another Bolshevik revolutionary, Mikhail Kalinin. But Kalinin had little power within the system. So little, indeed, that Stalin demonstrated his dominance by having Kalinin's wife, Ekaterina, arrested and tortured in Lefortovo prison in 1938.

If the exact moment that Stalin attained power remains opaque, the same can never be said of Hitler. On 30 January 1933 he became Chancellor of Germany and on 2 August 1934, on the death of President Paul von Hindenburg, he was appointed head of state and Führer of the German people. All the world knew, from that point onwards, that Hitler was the central figure who would chart the destiny of Germany. And just as it was providential for Stalin that his own character suited what the new Soviet system required, so Hitler benefited from the fact that his own personality appealed to millions of Germans during the economic chaos of the early 1930s. Qualities that would have excluded him from power in more settled times were now perceived by many as strengths rather than weaknesses: his lack of political experience was seen as refreshing, given the failure of conventional politicians to fix the crisis; his inability to listen to others' points of view and reach a compromise was viewed as a positive, since many now wanted a 'strong man' to take control; his hatred of democracy was embraced, because it seemed that the democratic system had been instrumental in creating the mess in which Germany now wallowed.

This dichotomy, between Hitler the charismatic orator and Stalin the man of many committees, is a crucial one, and a thread that runs through this whole history. It was a distinction that informed, for instance, their differing attitudes to the role of the political parties they oversaw. Even though Stalin, over time, allowed the NKVD secret police and certain economic commissariats to rival the power of the party, it was inconceivable that he would ever have tried to destroy the Communist Party completely – he always remained, at least in theory, its devoted servant. Hitler, in contrast, was always suspicious of any institutional attempt to restrict him. He did everything he could to dismantle any centralized structure that could potentially usurp him. To that end he allowed the German cabinet to atrophy – indeed, the cabinet never met again after 1938. He might even have thought the Nazi Party he had helped create was potentially disposable. According to Hans Frank, at a dinner in 1938 Hitler said that he would be 'the first to throw a burning torch' and 'radically destroy' the Nazi Party if he thought it was no longer needed.[10]

Membership of the Nazi Party was much less exclusive than membership of the Soviet Communist Party. Around five million people carried a Nazi Party card in 1939, compared to fewer than two million card-carrying Bolsheviks – despite the Soviets outnumbering the Germans by more than two to one. Stalin saw the party as an elite institution. And though Hitler continued to value the Nazi Party, he was never quite as committed.

It was the presence of the mighty Gauleiters – Nazi district leaders – that was symptomatic of the way Hitler wanted to run Germany. The forty or so Gauleiters owed their authority entirely to the Führer.[11] He could meet with them, one by one, and ensure they stayed true to his vision. Such was their autonomy under Hitler that they could even ignore instructions from the sinister Heinrich Himmler of the SS. On occasion, they could go as far as to joke about him. Albert Forster, Gauleiter of Danzig–West Prussia and a particular bête noire of the SS leader's, once remarked, 'If I looked like Himmler I wouldn't talk about race.'[12] It is inconceivable in the Soviet system that any of Stalin's subordinates would have openly ridiculed Himmler's equivalent – Lavrenti Beria, head of the NKVD.

Just as the ways in which they approached the process of government were very different, so was the experience of meeting Hitler and Stalin in private. Typical, for the committed Nazis, are the memories of Fritz Darges, a member of the SS who became one of Hitler's adjutants during the war. 'I was very impressed by his bright eyes,' said Darges. 'I had a feeling that the Führer's mind shone right through me. At the same time I had a feeling that I could trust him . . . Even then during our first encounter, I felt that he exuded trust and confidence and never did I feel frightened, nor was I ever inhibited in his presence. I would speak to him as to somebody I trusted and knew well.'[13]

Karl Wilhelm Krause, who was Hitler's valet in the five years leading up to the war, agreed that the Führer was a 'nice person' and 'only wanted the best for the German people'. After the war, like many former supporters of the regime, Krause clung to the erroneous belief that other people around Hitler were responsible for the horrendous crimes of the Nazis, rather than the leader himself. In Krause's eyes, Hitler was 'not guilty'. Moreover, said Krause, he was 'no tyrant, no, he wasn't. He was angry sometimes, who isn't?'[14]

Foreign statesmen could also succumb to the supposed allure of Hitler's presence. The Canadian Prime Minister Mackenzie King met Hitler in 1937 and thought that his eyes had 'a liquid quality about them which indicate[s] keen perception and profound sympathy'. King believed that Hitler was 'really one who truly loves his fellow-men, and his country, and would make any sacrifice for their good'.[15]

Once again, however, this was a case of an individual meeting Hitler who already had at least partial sympathy for his views. Just after his encounter with Hitler, Mackenzie King had lunch with the German Foreign Minister, Neurath, and listened without protest to his analysis of why it had been necessary to curb the alleged power of the Jews. The following year King fought hard against admitting Jews to Canada in the wake of the German takeover of Austria.[16]

For statesmen who were not so predisposed to be enamoured of Hitler, first impressions of the German dictator could be very different. When the British politician Lord Halifax met Hitler for the first time at his house in the mountains of Bavaria, he allegedly mistook the almighty Führer for a footman and was about to hand him his coat before being alerted to his error.[17] The British Prime Minister, Neville Chamberlain, also found Hitler unimpressive when they met in 1938, and later described him as ' "the commonest looking little dog" he had ever seen'.[18]

Many people – Halifax and Chamberlain included – thought not only that Hitler was undistinguished as an individual, but that he was a crude and blustering rabble-rouser who refused to listen to reason. This was not a new trait – he had been like this since his youth. August Kubizek, who knew him before the First World War, said that when Hitler was talking about a book he had just read, he didn't want to hear anyone else's opinion.[19] Indeed, one of the dangers of taking a meeting with him – as Benito Mussolini discovered – was that it could be hard to get a word in yourself. 'Hitler talks, talks, talks, talks,' recorded the Italian Foreign Minister, Count Ciano, in his diary after a meeting in April 1942.

'Mussolini suffers – he who was in the habit of talking himself, and who, instead, practically has to keep quiet. On the second day, after lunch, when everything had been said, Hitler talked uninterruptedly for an hour and forty minutes. He omitted absolutely no argument: war and peace, religion and philosophy, art and history.'[20] Thus – depending on your point of view – Hitler was either a crashing bore or an inspirational visionary.

It would be hard to come away from a meeting with Joseph Stalin feeling either of such extremes. In this respect he was the reverse of Hitler. For the most part, he wanted other people to talk. He was an aggressive listener, and an even more aggressive watcher. 'Stalin was by nature very attentive,' said Stepan Mikoyan, who grew up in the Kremlin in the 1930s, 'and he watched people's eyes when he was speaking – and if you didn't look him straight in the eye, he might well suspect that you were deceiving him. And then he'd be capable of taking the most unpleasant steps.'[21]

Vladimir Yerofeyev, an interpreter who translated for Stalin, remembered how stealthily the Soviet dictator moved: 'Stalin comes in, I'm sitting with my back to the door, I can't hear him enter. But nevertheless I can feel a new presence in the room.' He also experienced Stalin's economy with words: 'if he touched upon a certain subject he would make a statement, say what he had to say then listen to what people had to say to this . . . It wasn't entirely safe to work with him because if he didn't like something, there would have been no forgiveness.'[22]

Moreover, unlike Hitler, it was almost impossible to know what Stalin was thinking. Grigol Uratadze, who was incarcerated with Stalin in Georgia before the First World War, recalled that 'he was completely imperturbable. We lived together in Kutaisi Prison for more than half a year and not once did I see him get agitated, lose control, get angry, shout, swear or – in short – reveal himself in any other aspect than complete calmness. And his voice exactly corresponded to the "glacial character" which those who knew him well attributed to him.'[23]

One of the keys to Stalin's character, according to Stepan Mikoyan, was that he was 'very suspicious . . . he was capable of cheating and betraying others and he suspected other people of behaving likewise . . . He'd sense it if you were lying to him. The most terrible thing was to lie to him . . . [or] if you told him the truth and then someone else told him something different, Stalin would think you'd lied to him. And that for him was the greatest crime of all.'[24]

It's hard to overestimate the importance of this insight. Stalin appears to have treated everything and everyone with suspicion. The dominant question in his mind was always: who could be about to betray me? Memorably, he remarked to a military officer as he walked down a passageway in the Kremlin that was lined with guards, 'See how many of them there are? Each time I take this corridor, I think, which one? If this one, he will shoot me in the back, and if it is the one around the corner, he will shoot me in the front.'[25]

Stalin's niece, Kira Alliluyeva, agreed that Stalin was inherently suspicious, but thought that 'he was born with that quality.'[26] That might be so – we can never with certainty know the cause of this kind of characteristic – but the fact that he had spent years living as a revolutionary on the run, never knowing for sure whom he could trust, must surely have contributed to Stalin's suspicious nature.

Hitler did not possess this level of personal wariness. He tended to trust those in his immediate circle until they demonstrably did something to betray him. If he had not been this trusting, the attempt on his life by Count von Stauffenberg in July 1944 would almost certainly never have happened. Indeed, it's significant that while there were a number of attempts on Hitler's life, there is not one recorded attempt on Stalin's. An intensely suspicious nature clearly has its benefits.

We should also recognize how the technology of the period influenced the public perception of both Hitler and Stalin. That's because they were two of the first individuals in history to have created personas that existed independently of themselves in propaganda films. Previous leaders had used a variety of other media to project their image – via coins, statues or paintings – but this was different. Via the medium of film Hitler and Stalin could be seen and 'known' by millions of people who never actually met them. There they were on the screen, their every action edited for maximum effect.

Inevitably, this could sometimes lead to a disconnect between the propaganda image and the reality. Just as Lord Halifax could think Hitler in the flesh more resembled a servant than the demi-god shown in Goebbels' newsreels, so Stalin in real life could sometimes fail to live up to expectations. When the British Army officer Hugh Lunghi met Stalin during the war he was shocked, because 'in front of me was an elderly little gentleman, even smaller than me and I'm not very tall . . . and he looked rather like a kindly old uncle, and then when he opened his mouth I got another shock because he spoke with this Georgian accent, quite a strong rather marked Georgian accent, perfect Russian, excellent Russian, but with this accent, and he kept his voice very low so it was rather difficult for one to hear what he was saying without a strain.'[27]

To the American diplomat George Kennan, Stalin appeared as a 'low-slung, smallish figure', but 'there was also a composed, collected strength, and a certain rough handsomeness, in his features. The teeth were discolored, the mustache scrawny, coarse, and streaked. This, together with the pocked face and yellow eyes, gave him the aspect of an old battle-scarred tiger. In manner – with us, at least – he was simple, quiet, unassuming.'[28]

Others in the western alliance concluded that Stalin, unlike Hitler, was not just down-to-earth in manner but ultimately unknowable. 'I found him better informed than Roosevelt, more realistic than Churchill, in some ways the most effective of the war leaders,' recalled the suave American statesman Averell Harriman. 'At the same time he was, of course, a murderous tyrant. I must confess that for me Stalin remains the most inscrutable and contradictory character I have known . . .'[29]

Stalin and Hitler each dressed modestly – Hitler in the 1930s often in a brown military-style jacket and Stalin in a grey workers' tunic.[30] This was not an accident. They would have been conscious of the ostentation of the monarchs who had recently ruled their respective states. Tsar Nicholas II and Kaiser Wilhelm II had possessed a whole selection of glittering outfits to choose from, though they had done little to deserve these fancy clothes other than to be born to the right parents. Hitler and Stalin, by dressing simply, demonstrated not just their connection to the ordinary people, but their distance from the monarchs who had preceded them.

Both Hitler and Stalin despised the institution of monarchy. In a conversation in March 1942, Hitler remarked that 'there were at least eight kings out of ten who, if they'd been ordinary citizens, would not have been capable of successfully running a grocery.'[31] As for the Soviet leader, Stalin sought to build a state whose values were diametrically opposed to those of an hereditary monarchy – it was after all Bolsheviks who had murdered Tsar Nicholas II and his family in 1918. It's ironic, therefore, that both Hitler and Stalin ruled until the last moment of their lives – just as monarchs aspire to do. The grip Hitler and Stalin had on their respective nations was relinquished only when their hearts stopped. Given their characters and the political structures around them, it's all but impossible to imagine that either of them would ever voluntarily have stepped aside. In that respect, they had more in common with monarchs than they would have admitted.

There's another similarity between the two tyrants. Neither was married at the start of the Second World War. Stalin had been married twice. His first wife died of illness in 1907 and his second committed suicide inside the Kremlin in 1932. His relationship with his three legitimate children was strained – one son attempted suicide, another became an alcoholic and Stalin sent his daughter's boyfriend to a Gulag. He had no relationship of consequence with any of his several illegitimate children. As for Hitler, he had never married, had no children – illegitimate or otherwise – and saw his girlfriend, Eva Braun, only sporadically. He was not to marry her until the last moments of his life in April 1945.

It's also interesting to note that not only did Stalin's second wife kill herself – and it appears that his treatment of her played a part in driving her to this extreme – but many of the women who had close dealings with Hitler also either committed or attempted suicide. For instance, Eva Braun tried to kill herself twice during the 1930s; Maria Reiter, a shopgirl in Berchtesgaden who became entranced by Hitler, tried to hang herself in 1928; and Hitler's niece Geli Raubal shot herself in Hitler's apartment with his revolver in 1931.

There has been much lurid speculation about Hitler's and Stalin's sex lives – especially Hitler's – but the central point is almost always missed. By 1939 and the start of the Second World War, both men were essentially alone. Neither appeared to possess an intimate confidante.

However, all these similarities are as nothing compared to the one vital quality that Hitler and Stalin shared – by far the most important connection between them. They both believed they had uncovered the secret of existence. They were not like ordinary dictators who resemble Mafia bosses. No, these two actually believed in something outside themselves. They weren't even similar to the religiously driven European monarchs of the past who had faith in a Christian God. On the contrary, both of the dictators abhorred Christianity. In private, Hitler remarked that 'Christianity is an invention of sick brains'[32] – though for pragmatic reasons he largely concealed his true opinion on the subject from the German public.[33]

They were both profoundly post-Enlightenment figures. They believed not only that God was dead, but that he had now been replaced by a fresh, coherent ideology. Moreover, millions of those who followed the two dictators also subscribed to this new reality.

Hitler and Stalin, of course, believed in different things. The secret that Hitler proselytized was most certainly not the same as the one Stalin lived by. Equally, neither Hitler nor Stalin originated the ideologies that they thought revealed the truth about the nature of life; both adapted them from the work of others.

For Hitler the starting point was 'race'. The core of his belief system was the assertion that the way to assess people's value was by examining their 'racial heritage'. This was an idea that came to prominence in 1855 when the diplomat Arthur de Gobineau published his *Essai sur l'inégalité des races humaines* (Essay on the Inequality of the Human Races), in which he claimed that the 'lesson of history' was that 'all civilizations derive from the white race, that none can exist without its help, and that society is great and brilliant only so far as it preserves the blood of the noble group that created it . . .'[34]

It followed for Hitler that preserving the 'purity' of the race was crucial, so it was necessary to sideline the 'racially inferior'. Once again, this wasn't a new concept. Dr Alfred Ploetz, in a book published in 1895, had even suggested that doctors should decide which babies should live or die depending on racial worth.[35] Twenty-five years later, in 1920, Professor Alfred Hoche called for the killing of the 'incurably ill' and the 'mentally dead', asserting that these deaths would be 'desirable for the general welfare' of the state.[36]

This idea that 'race' was the key to understanding the nature of existence was also proclaimed by a number of different German political groups. For example, in November 1918, Rudolf von Sebottendorff – the leading light in the Munich-based Thule Society – claimed that political unrest in Germany was 'created by inferior races in order to corrupt the Germanic peoples'. Around this time, in the *Münchener Beobachter,* a newspaper edited by Sebottendorff, an article appeared which called for Germans to 'Keep your blood clean . . . Purity of race means public health. When all elements of the people are steeped in purity of the blood, then the social question is solved . . .'[37] For groups like the *völkisch* Thule Society there was an anti-Semitic dimension to all of this. In his speech in November 1918, Sebottendorff had declared that chief among the racial dangers that Germany faced was the 'Jew', who was 'our mortal enemy'.[38]

Sebottendorff hadn't invented the canard that the Jews were racially dangerous. In the late 1890s, the philosopher Houston Stewart Chamberlain had written in his *Foundations of the Nineteenth Century* that the 'Aryan' race – which encompassed most Germans – was locked in a battle with the Jews. In Chamberlain's view, this was because both the 'Aryans' and the Jews took pains not to breed outside of their own racial groups, and so consequently they were each involved in a fight for supremacy.[39]

Without acknowledging his debt to the vast majority of those who had voiced such ideas before him, Hitler stated his vision of the world in *Mein Kampf*, a book he composed in prison after the failure of his coup attempt in Munich in 1923. For him life was a never-ending battle. 'Those who want to live,' he wrote, 'let them fight, and those who do not want to fight in this world of eternal struggle do not deserve to live.'[40] In this permanent struggle the Jew was the greatest enemy. The Jew, he asserted, 'remains the typical parasite, a sponger who like a noxious bacillus keeps spreading as soon as a favourable medium invites him'.[41] According to Hitler, the Jews were also responsible for the 'doctrine of Marxism' – an ideology that he said was a demonstrable threat to Germany, since there had been socialist uprisings, which had been subsequently crushed, in Berlin and Munich in the immediate aftermath of the First World War.[42]

None of these racial ideas, claimed Hitler, was mere theory. They were fact – a reality borne out by the self-evident truths of the world around us. As Hitler saw it, this 'planet once moved through the ether for millions of years without human beings and it can do so again some day if men forget that they owe their higher existence, not to the ideas of a few crazy ideologists, but to the knowledge and ruthless application of Nature's stern and rigid laws'.[43]

For Hitler, disagreeing with 'Nature's stern and rigid laws' was as futile as arguing that the earth was flat. And a number of equally dogmatic conclusions flowed from this reality. One of the most consequential was that what mattered in assessing the worth of a particular country was not just conventional economic measures like Gross National Product, but measuring the racial composition of the population. This warped reasoning led Hitler to conclude that America was potentially a more dangerous rival to Germany than the Soviet Union. In his posthumously published *Second Book*, which he wrote in the late 1920s, he claimed that the United States was inhabited by 'people of the highest racial quality' and that 'only a deliberately ethnic racial policy could save the European nations from losing the power of the initiative to America.'[44] On the other hand, in the Soviet Union – or Russia as he persisted in calling it – the 'population is not accompanied by such an intrinsic worth that this [huge] size could become a danger for the freedom of the world. At least not in the sense of an economic or power-political domination of the rest of the world, but at most in the sense of an inundation with sickness-causing bacteria, which are currently found in Russia.'[45]

Hitler foresaw catastrophe for Germany if the racial composition of the country was altered, either by breeding with different races or by the emigration – particularly to America – of the racially most prized human specimens: 'This gradual removal of the Nordic element within our people leads to a lowering of our overall racial quality and thus to a weakening of our technical, cultural, and also political productive forces.'[46]

If you accepted Hitler's racist premise, his vision was coherent. The purpose of life was to strengthen the racial community via any means possible – by controlling who bred and, if necessary, by acquiring more land so that the best racial elements could flourish. Might is always right. To assert otherwise was to go against 'Nature's stern and rigid laws'.

There's one final statement contained in Hitler's *Second Book* that offers another notable insight into his worldview. 'Beginning with the birth of the human until his death,' wrote Hitler, 'everything is doubtful. The only thing that seems certain is death itself. But that is exactly why the final commitment is not the most difficult, because it will one day be demanded in one way or another.'[47]

Hitler is arguing something fundamental here. Instead of focusing on trying to postpone our deaths for as long as possible, we have to understand that it is only a matter of detail whether death comes to us in the next second or in fifty years' time. Death comes regardless.

It follows that life should be about taking risks. That's because death comes to the boring and cautious as much as it does to the daring and the courageous. As a veteran of the First World War, and a witness to countless violent and sudden deaths, Hitler knew all about the arbitrariness of existence.

It was this cocktail of passionately held beliefs that led Hitler to subscribe to the views of those like Dr Ploetz who advocated killing 'racially unwanted' children. Incredibly, one might think, in a speech in 1929 he said that the murder of 70–80 per cent of all newly born German children might be beneficial. 'If Germany gained 1 million children annually,' said Hitler, 'and eliminated 700,000–800,000 of the weakest, then in the end the result would probably even be an increase of force. The most dangerous thing is that we cut off the natural process of selection . . .' He spoke with approval of the 'strongest racial state in history, Sparta', which he said had 'implemented these racial laws systematically'. He warned that, since 'criminals have the possibility of reproduction' and 'degenerates are being laboriously coddled in an artificial way', the consequence was that 'we slowly grow the weak and kill the strong.'[48]

Shortly after he became Chancellor, Hitler pushed through legislation that authorized the sterilization of Germans who suffered not just from diseases like schizophrenia but also from conditions like 'severe alcoholism'. The Nazis sought to justify this step by pointing to the laws of the animal kingdom. The short propaganda film *Das Erbe* (Heritage), released in 1935 and intended to promote the value of forced sterilization, starts with a scene in which a well-meaning but naive student suggests that the insects that are being studied in the laboratory would have 'lived quietly' had they been left in the forest. She is gently chided by her professor, who tells her that 'a quiet life can't be found anywhere in nature' and that animals 'all live in a permanent struggle whereby the weak are destroyed'.[49]

Hitler's violent anti-Semitism fitted seamlessly into this worldview. He subscribed not to the religion-based anti-Semitism of the past but to a 'modern', racially based hatred. The Jews were inherently dangerous, he believed, because of their 'blood'. His desire to persecute the Jews was such that by 1939 German Jews suffered under a whole series of cruel and restrictive measures. The largest pre-war attack on German Jews occurred on 'Kristallnacht', the night of 9 November 1938, when Jewish property was destroyed, synagogues were burnt to the ground, more than ninety Jews were murdered and around 30,000 were taken to concentration camps.

As for the 'Aryan' members of the 'ethnic community', they were told that they were better than anyone else and that their most precious possession was their own racial purity. 'We bear a holy obligation', wrote SS man Joseph Altrogge, in a note contained in his personnel file, 'to keep our blood pure and pass it on to our children and grandchildren.' It was this 'holy obligation' that offered the chance of eternal life – not the traditional promises of the Church: 'Every one of us is merely a link in the chain of the hereditary stream that runs from us to our most distant grandchildren. If we don't cut this hereditary stream, we will live on in our children and grandchildren and will be truly immortal. We don't want to be the weakest link in the chain or interrupt it by staying celibate or childless.' The 'struggle' to achieve this goal, he wrote, had just started, and 'our children and grandchildren will continue it, so that one day the objective, the Trinity of the Reich, the Volk [the People] and the Faith, will be accomplished.'[50]

It also followed that since there was no everlasting life except through your offspring, there was no need to be concerned about any 'day of judgement' after you died. This was a belief that an SS man like Joseph Altrogge had in common with the atheistic Bolsheviks in the Soviet Union.

Like Hitler, Stalin had also been convinced by the work of others. The most influential was Karl Marx. It was primarily Marx's teachings that had drawn him away from the seminary and into the world of revolution. Marx, in a series of works such as the *Communist Manifesto* (written with Friedrich Engels and published in 1848) and *Das Kapital* (published in 1867, with two more volumes published after Marx's death in 1883), laid bare the problems that confronted working men and women in the light of the Industrial Revolution. He declared that working people – whom he called the 'proletariat' – were alienated from productive life. Instead of work being, as it should be, a way for people to feel fulfilled, life in the grim factories of the nineteenth century was destructive of the human spirit. Workers were alienated in several ways: they were alienated from the products they created – since workers in production lines never had the satisfaction of creating something themselves, as they were merely cogs in a giant machine; they were alienated from their own humanity – because they were perceived to have worth only as a result of the products they created for the factory owners; and they were alienated from each other – not least because in the modern factory work is seldom collaborative.[51]

Marx also emphasized the inherent unfairness in the relationship between the workers and the owners of the factories. How could it be right that workers gave up much of their lives to creating products, and yet the profit generated flowed to the rich – merely because they owned the buildings in which the workers were enslaved? The owners could sit around, enjoy themselves and live off the sweat and torment of the alienated workers. How could such a situation be tolerated?

It was a compelling analysis of nineteenth-century working life. And even though Marx's views seemed to apply more to the sweatshops of Manchester than to the agricultural lands of the Russian Empire, Stalin was convinced by them. A sense of the injustice of this world – in which rich peasants, the kulaks, appeared to live off the work of their poorer neighbours – stayed with him to his dying day.

The trouble was that, while Marx was brilliant at analysing the problem, the solution he proposed was not necessarily so convincing. One difficulty was that he asserted that history was destined to move through certain phases. For instance, there was an imperial phase, a feudal phase, a capitalist phase, a socialist phase and a communist phase.[52]

At the time Marx wrote his analysis, he was primarily concerned with the capitalist phase, which was the one he felt he was living through. But he believed the world would move forward, eventually, to communism. In that ultimate endgame of history there would be common ownership of the means of production, no exploitation of anyone, a totally fair society and no need for government, since the state would inevitably 'wither away'.

Arguments raged among followers of Marx about exactly what the great man had meant by certain predictions and theories, and what was the best way of implementing them. Marxist followers denounced each other for corrupting Marxist teachings, much as medieval Christians had attacked each other for 'heresy'. It was this kind of dispute that had led to the formation of the Bolsheviks in the first place. Vladimir Lenin, a revolutionary follower of Marx, had published a book in 1902 called *What is to be Done?* In it he amended Marx's prediction of what needed to happen to escape the capitalist phase of history. Instead of the workers rising up on their own, Lenin said that once the oppression of capitalism became too great a group of dedicated revolutionaries would be needed to lead the world on to socialism. This, and other issues he raised, led to conflict within the Marxist group, the Russian Social Democratic Labour Party. In 1903 there was a split. The followers of Lenin were in the majority, and they became known as Bolsheviks (*bolshinstvo* means 'majority' in Russian), those who disagreed were called Mensheviks (from the Russian word for 'minority').

Stalin, who first met Lenin two years after the split in 1905, was decidedly a Bolshevik. Like Lenin, he believed in professional revolutionaries leading the seismic change necessary to reshape society.

Moreover, Stalin was also clear that the working class could only supplant the rich bosses by force. 'Communists do not in the least idealise methods of violence,' he said in an interview with H. G. Wells in 1934. 'But they, the Communists, do not want to be taken by surprise; they cannot count on the old world voluntarily departing from the stage; they see that the old system is violently defending itself, and that is why the Communists say to the working class: Answer violence with violence; do all you can to prevent the old dying order from crushing you, do not permit it to put manacles on your hands, on the hands with which you will overthrow the old system.'[53]

Lenin, for his part, recognized Stalin as a man of action – his role in the bank heist in Tiflis in 1907 guaranteed that. But it wasn't until 1913, when he wrote *Marxism and the National Question*, that Stalin was seen as a Marxist thinker of any note.

Nationalism was a tricky political issue because Imperial Russia contained a large number of potential 'nations', not least Stalin's native Georgia, and the Bolsheviks needed an unambiguous policy on the matter. Stalin's premise was simple. He said it ought to be 'readily understandable that the nation like any historical phenomenon has its own history, its beginning and its end'.[54] Individual 'nations' within the new Bolshevik state might be permitted to have an element of self-rule, but this was only a temporary solution since Marxist theory dictated that eventually all nations would disappear. Lenin approved of Stalin's work and appointed him head of the People's Commissariat for Nationalities after the revolution.

There was thus an obvious gulf between Hitler and Stalin in the way each viewed the world. One was a devout racist, the other a man who thought the environment primarily shaped individuals. One was a believer in the laws of 'Nature', the other a dedicated follower of Karl Marx. What was more, they each passionately hated the other's belief system. Hitler feared and despised Bolshevism and Stalin detested Nazism.

In this context, the fact that Hitler led the National *Socialist* German Workers' Party has caused confusion among those who aren't that familiar with the history. Wasn't Stalin, they say, also a believer in socialism as a route to communism? So weren't Hitler and Stalin both much the same? The answer is no. They weren't. Stalin was committed to destroying what he saw as the absolute evil of capitalism. He was open about this, saying that 'Without getting rid of the capitalists, without abolishing the principle of private property in the means of production, it is impossible to create [a] planned economy.'[55] Hitler never held such views. Indeed, he came to power with the help of powerful business figures. But it was useful for the Nazis to say they were socialists in propaganda terms, since they thought it made them more appealing to German workers.

The word 'socialism' also symbolized the Nazis' desire to eliminate all class divisions in German society. Hitler wanted to create what he called a *Volksgemeinschaft* – a 'people's community' – in which every 'true' German pulled together for the good of the nation, and big business was required to cooperate towards this goal as much as every other group. As Hitler declared in a speech in April 1922, 'we said to ourselves: there are no such things as classes: they cannot be. Class means caste and caste means race . . . with us in Germany where everyone who is a German at all has the same blood, has the same eyes and speaks the same language, here there can be no class, here there can be only a single people and beyond that nothing else.'[56]

But even in the 'classless' Germany envisioned by Hitler, where everyone was the same 'race', there was still plenty of room for capitalists to make money from the toil of the workers. Hitler, despite leading the National Socialist German Workers' Party, never came close to imposing the kind of controlled economy that Stalin favoured, and he was certainly no socialist himself.

There was also a chasm between the two dictators in terms of their ultimate goals, with the communist aim of a stateless society presenting a sharp contrast to Hitler's idea of a giant empire based on violent racism. This distinction informs how the two ideologies are perceived today. The type of racial hatred that was at the core of Hitler's thinking is rightly condemned – indeed, expressing such beliefs is illegal in many countries – whereas there are still a number of people who proudly proclaim they are Marxists. But, in the context of Stalin's leadership, there is a problem with this analysis, because the harmonious goal of the Bolsheviks – of a state in which government 'withered away' – was not realistically achievable under Stalin. And even Stalin came close to admitting as much.

In his address to the Eighteenth Congress of the Communist Party in March 1939, Stalin admitted that Marx and his collaborator Friedrich Engels had not always been right, and that 'certain of the general propositions in the Marxist doctrine of the state were incompletely worked out and inadequate.' Specifically, when Engels had said that once 'there is nothing more to be repressed' then the state 'withers away' he had omitted to mention the 'international factor'. The problem, said Stalin, was that because other countries were not on the road to communism, the Soviet Union needed 'at its disposal a well-trained army, well-organized punitive organs, and a strong intelligence service' in order to defend itself.[57] In other words, get used to the 'well-organized punitive organs' sticking around, because there was no prospect of them leaving unless the whole world went communist, and who seriously thought that would happen in the foreseeable future?

Finally, we need to recognize one overarching similarity between Hitler and Stalin − both of them offered a vision of a future utopia. They were different utopias, of course, but utopias nonetheless. The road to get there would be hard − even, as Stalin admitted in 1939, taking longer than you could possibly imagine − but a wonderful goal lay ahead regardless. Both offered a vital purpose in life, in a world that could seem meaningless without religious belief.

For Nikonor Perevalov, born in 1917, the year of the Russian Revolution, the reason for his existence could not have been clearer: 'I was aware that the Communist Party had been created in our country in order to build initially a socialist society, and then in future to build communism, and that this society could be built only by conscientious people. This is why I joined the party, in order to be a conscientious person, to lead the masses to this awareness of the need for the victory of socialism and communism ... We wanted to improve the life of the peoples of Russia.'[58] Perevalov subsequently tried to 'improve the life of the peoples of Russia' by joining the NKVD and organizing mass deportations to Siberia.

Johannes Hassebroek, Commandant of Gross-Rosen concentration camp, gained a similar purpose in life from his membership of the SS: 'I was full of gratitude to the SS for the intellectual guidance it gave me. We were all thankful. Many of us had been so bewildered before joining the organization. We did not understand what was happening around us, everything was so mixed up. The SS offered us a series of simple ideas that we could understand, and we believed in them.'[59]

One of the 'simple ideas' offered by both of the ideologies preached by Hitler and Stalin was staunch opposition to the values of liberal democracy. Both rejected outright the principles that constitute 'freedom' today. Both condemned free speech, both attacked human rights at every level. Crucially, both sought to destroy your ability to be an individual. You had no right to be the self you chose. You conformed to the new value system or you were persecuted. Ultimately, this was the reason why the utopias Hitler and Stalin sought could never be free from tyranny – because even if the Promised Land had been reached, anyone who was contrary enough to say they didn't like this new paradise would be punished.

As I hope this book demonstrates, oppression could never be excised from either system. It was the system.

1. The Pact

In August 1939, Hitler and Stalin – the greatest of ideological enemies – did something truly extraordinary. They agreed a pact of friendship. And to many of their supporters, it was an arrangement that seemed to go against all logic.

'We couldn't make sense of it,' said Karl-Hermann Müller, then a young German sailor. 'On the one hand, communism was fought against – at least it should have been – and on the other hand a pact was made with the communists . . . There was no sense in it.'[1]

It's easy to understand Karl-Hermann's confusion – and the bewilderment of millions of others. Hitler had been railing against the Soviet Union for years. As far back as 1924 he had written in *Mein Kampf* that 'the rulers of present-day Russia are common blood-stained criminals' and 'the scum of humanity', who 'overran a great state in a tragic hour, slaughtered and wiped out thousands of her leading intelligentsia in wild blood lust' and once in power operated 'the most cruel and tyrannical régime of all time'.[2]

Hitler, as one who saw the world almost entirely in racial terms, believed race was the key to understanding the action of the Bolsheviks: 'these rulers belong to a race which combines, in a rare mixture, bestial cruelty and an inconceivable gift for lying, and which today more than ever is conscious of a mission to impose its bloody oppression on the whole world.'[3]

As if that wasn't enough, Hitler then offered in *Mein Kampf* the final – and, for him, devastating – reason why the Soviet Union was so dangerous. 'Do not forget', he wrote, that 'the international Jew' 'completely dominates Russia' and 'regards Germany, not as an ally, but as a state destined' to suffer the same fate as Imperial Russia had at the hands of the communists. Moreover, control of the Soviet Union, claimed Hitler, was just the first step for the Jews: 'In Russian Bolshevism we must see the attempt undertaken by the Jews in the twentieth century to achieve world domination.'[4] Any political deal with the Soviet Union was thus unthinkable as far as Hitler was concerned. He explicitly said in *Mein Kampf* that 'you do not make pacts with anyone whose sole interest is the destruction of his partner.'[5]

Hitler's wild theories about the Soviet Union were accepted by his supporters not just because many of them were either overt or latent anti-Semites, but also as a consequence of Germany's defeat in the First World War. In order to deal with the humiliation of the loss, many people – particularly those in nationalistic parties on the right – had looked for scapegoats. They blamed 'the Jews' for plotting behind the lines to bring about German defeat, and Jewish 'democrats' for negotiating the hated peace treaties after the war – most notoriously the treaty of Versailles. And when there were attempted revolutions in Munich and Berlin in 1919, they claimed that Jews, as the force allegedly behind Bolshevism, were attempting a takeover of Germany.

By cherry-picking facts, they tried to defend their claims. Had not a number of Jews led the revolution in Munich which established a short-lived 'Soviet' republic in Bavaria in 1919? Had not Jewish politicians, like Otto Landsberg, taken part in discussions about the Versailles treaty? Were not leading Bolsheviks like Leon Trotsky Jewish? Indeed, had not Marx himself been born a Jew?

However, like all statements of prejudice, the arguments behind these assertions collapse under examination. Yes, a small number of Jews had been involved in the Munich revolution, but the vast majority of German Jews led law-abiding lives and abhorred violent insurrection. Yes, Otto Landsberg had discussed the Versailles treaty, but he was so opposed to it that he subsequently resigned. Yes, Leon Trotsky had been born into a Jewish family, but many other leading Bolsheviks – Stalin and Molotov to name but two – were not. Finally, while Marx had Jewish ancestry he was never a practising Jew. In fact, his father converted to Christianity.

None of those details mattered to Hitler. Throughout his political career he never let the facts impede him, and his blind hatred of the Soviet Union helped him make sense of the world. Indeed, it is hard to think of any single foreign policy belief that Hitler held more passionately in 1924 than his loathing of 'Russian Bolshevism'. His vast prejudice against the Soviets brought together the key strands of his ideological thinking: his racism, his anti-Semitism and his fear of the corruption of German 'blood purity' by a people who sought to destroy their enemies with 'lies and slander, poison and corruption'.[6]

Hitler also openly admitted that he wanted Germany to steal territory from the Soviet Union. He wrote in *Mein Kampf* that he had decided to 'stop the endless German movement to the south and west, and turn our gaze toward the land in the east'.[7] He explicitly said that his 'gaze' rested on territory in 'Russia and her vassal border states'. He could scarcely have been clearer. He sought to create a new German Empire in the west of the Soviet Union; and he said this not in a secret meeting, conspiring with his closest confidants, but in a book published to the world.

In popular myth, this desire to seize land in the Soviet Union is often cited as one of the first examples of Hitler's megalomania. How unbalanced does a human being have to be, so the argument goes, to want to conquer Russia? As Field Marshal Montgomery said, 'Rule One' of war is 'don't march on Moscow.'[8] But that's not how it was seen at the time.

Hitler was aware, as he wrote *Mein Kampf* in 1924, that just six years before the Bolsheviks at German insistence had surrendered vast swathes of land and a third of the population of pre-revolutionary Russia. Under the treaty of Brest-Litovsk, agreed early in 1918, the Bolsheviks gave up the Baltic States, Ukraine and much else besides. The Germans thus discovered in 1918 that invading 'Russia' could be a very profitable enterprise indeed.

Lenin agreed to this humiliating treaty because he wanted out of the First World War. He needed to concentrate on consolidating the revolution at home, and this was the price he had to pay. He wrote in March 1918 that while Brest-Litovsk could be considered an 'obscene peace', the reality was that if the Bolsheviks did not escape the war then 'our government would be swept aside.'[9] He later compared the peace treaty with a deal made with criminals. 'Imagine that your car has been stopped by armed bandits,' he wrote. 'You give them your money, your identity papers, your revolver and the car itself. In exchange you are excused their pleasant company . . . Our compromise with the bandits of German imperialism was just such a compromise.'[10]

The Germans had not been impressed with the calibre of the Bolshevik representatives who had arrived to discuss the deal. 'I shall never forget the first dinner we had with the Russians,' wrote Major General Max Hoffmann, a member of the German delegation. 'Opposite me was the workman, who was evidently caused much trouble by the various implements that he found on his table. He tried to seize the food on his plate first with one thing and then with another . . .' Hoffmann also noticed that a Bolshevik representative, when asked whether he would like 'claret or hock', replied that he would 'prefer' to have whichever was the 'stronger'.[11]

The Brest-Litovsk treaty did not survive long – it was dismantled after Germany's defeat in November 1918 – but when Hitler wrote *Mein Kampf* the memory of the original deal was still fresh.[12] So, at the time, it was not unreasonable to suppose that a deal the Bolsheviks had accepted in early 1918 might one day be forced upon them again. Had the Bolsheviks not already shown their weakness – almost, it might be thought, their cowardice?

One can accuse Adolf Hitler of many things, but lack of consistency in his ideological vision is not one of them. In 1936, for instance, in one of the few broad policy memos he ever wrote, he once again voiced his obsession with the danger of 'Bolshevism'. 'Since the outbreak of the French Revolution,' he wrote in almost apocalyptic terms, 'the world has been moving with ever increasing speed towards a new conflict, the most extreme solution of which is called Bolshevism, whose essence and aim, however, is solely the elimination of those strata of mankind which have hitherto provided the leadership and their replacement by world-wide Jewry. No state will be able to withdraw or even remain at a distance from this historical conflict. Since Marxism, through its victory in Russia, has established one of the greatest empires in the world as a forward base for its future operations, this question has become a menacing one . . .'[13]

Lest anyone be uncertain exactly what Hitler meant with these words, Hermann Göring made their meaning plain at a cabinet meeting in September 1936, when he declared that the Führer's memo started 'from the basic premise that the showdown with Russia is inevitable'.[14] And while Hitler was no longer open in his speeches to the general public about his intention to snatch land in the east, he did reiterate the immense danger posed by the existence of the Soviet Union. In a speech at Nuremberg in September 1937 he talked about the struggle against Bolshevism in epic terms. Never afraid of hyperbole, he described it as a 'colossal event in world history' and the Bolshevik threat as 'the greatest danger with which the culture and civilization of the human race have been threatened since the collapse of the states of ancient times'.

Hitler emphasized that the conflict with Bolshevism was all

encompassing. Everything was under threat – German spiritual life, the economy 'and all other institutions which determine the nature, character and life' of the state. Hitler also reminded his audience yet again that the Jews were behind Bolshevism. He painted a terrifying picture of the threat this posed. He claimed that the Jews – 'an inferior race, through and through' – pursued a policy of exterminating the 'intellectual classes' of the people they ruled. They had to do this, he said, because otherwise they would be defeated by 'superior intelligence'. Summing up, Hitler asserted that there existed in the Soviet Union 'an uncivilized Jewish Bolshevik international guild of criminals' whose aim was to 'reign from Moscow over Germany'.[15]

Notice that Hitler wasn't saying that it was necessary to invade the Soviet Union simply in order to gain more land for Germany. On the contrary, he claimed that Germany was threatened by the desire of the Bolsheviks to pursue 'world revolution'. He positioned himself as the prophet who was warning against an existential threat. This was a clever tactical position, given his ultimate goal – because it followed that one, as yet unspoken, way to prevent the Bolsheviks' own alleged expansionist plans was to attack them before they moved on Germany. The Germans would thus gain all the land they needed in the east not because they were imperialists, but as an 'unintended' consequence of an act of self-defence.

Stalin's attitude to Hitler during the 1930s was nothing like as straightforward. In July 1932, less than a year before Hitler became Chancellor, he ordered that the German Communist Party concentrate not so much on the threat from the Nazis as on the danger posed by other socialists within Germany. A group of German communists went to see Stalin to try to convince him to change his mind, but he dismissed their concerns, saying to one of them, Franz Neumann, 'Don't you think, Neumann, that if the nationalists come to power in Germany, they'll be so completely preoccupied with the West that we'll be able to build up socialism in peace?'[16]

Stalin seems to have believed that the Nazis' well-publicized attack on the 'November Criminals', who had signed the hated Versailles treaty at the end of the First World War, meant that Hitler would be focused on trying to change the restrictive terms of the agreement with the western powers. To a degree, he was right. While Hitler's ideological enemy was always the Soviet Union, in the short term Germany's relationship with France, Britain and the United States mattered more. These were the countries that had primarily been responsible for the crippling reparations, loss of territory and limits on the size of the German armed forces that had been imposed on Germany post-Versailles.

This is not to say that Stalin was ignorant about Hitler's designs on the Soviet Union. He was a keen reader of *Mein Kampf* and marked key passages in his private copy with a coloured pencil.[17] But he knew that geographical reality also meant that Hitler posed no immediate physical threat, because other countries – principally Poland – stood as a barrier between Germany and the Soviet Union. So for all of Hitler's desire to seek land in 'Russia and her vassal states', in practical terms how could he achieve that end?

Nor was the Soviet Union currently pursuing, as Hitler claimed, 'rule over Germany' and 'world revolution'. While it's simplistic to say that Stalin had rejected Bolshevik support for revolution in other countries, it's also the case that he showed little enthusiasm for this goal during the 1930s. True, he did not disband the Comintern – the organization of international communist groups established in 1919 – but as we've seen in his instructions to the German communists in 1932, his primary focus was on crushing other groups on the left that he believed were a threat to the Soviet experiment in socialism.

Only on rare occasions did Stalin approve of Soviet involvement in foreign conflicts. And even when he did, his actions were not straightforward. While, for instance, he sent money and guns to help in the war against General Franco in Spain, he always remained concerned about the exact nature of the groups he was helping. In particular, he wanted the answer to one vital question: did they support the man he hated almost more than any other – Leon Trotsky?

Stalin had managed to outmanoeuvre Trotsky, a fellow revolutionary, during the 1920s. Trotsky's charismatic personality and intellectual gifts had been no match for Stalin's patient cunning. Stalin had expelled him from the Soviet Union in 1929, and Trotsky had been causing trouble for him ever since. From exile, Trotsky – unlike Stalin, a gifted writer – had been criticizing not just Stalin's policies but Stalin the man. Above all, he claimed that Stalin had betrayed the revolution by refusing to embrace the call for world revolution. Instead, he maintained,

Stalin had built a stifling bureaucratic structure in the Soviet Union in pursuit of his own power base. Consequently, he called for Stalin's removal. In 1933 he wrote that the 'Proletarian vanguard' needed to eliminate the Stalinist 'bureaucracy' by 'force' in order to make Stalin hand over power.[18] Four years later, in 1937, he went even further and said in an interview that the only way to oust Stalin, whom he accused of placing himself 'above all criticism', was by assassination.[19] That same year his devastating polemic *The Stalin School of Falsification* was published in English. 'You can juggle quotations, hide the stenographic reports of your own speeches, forbid the circulation of Lenin's letters and articles, fabricate yards of dishonestly selected quotations,' Trotsky declared in the book's conclusion, attacking what he believed was Stalin's attempt to rewrite the history of the revolution. 'You can suppress, conceal and burn up historic documents. You can extend your censorship even to photographic and moving-picture records of revolutionary events. All these things Stalin is doing. But the results do not and will not justify his expectations. Only a limited mind like Stalin's could imagine that these pitiful machinations will make men forget the gigantic events of modern history.'[20] But, sadly for Trotsky, it was the man he thought possessed a 'limited mind' who triumphed over him in the end. After Stalin had ordered Trotsky's murder, a Spanish communist called Ramón Mercader attacked him with an ice axe in Mexico on 20 August 1940. Trotsky died of his injuries the following day.

The surprising truth was that during the 1930s Stalin feared not so much that Bolshevik revolution would fail to break out in other countries as that the wrong sort of revolution – one led by 'Trotskyites' – would succeed. It was a concern that explains much of his behaviour, as his anxiety about Trotsky fuelled his intensely suspicious nature. Who, he demanded, were the 'Trotskyites' working in secret within the Soviet Union? As we shall see, the search for the answer to that question would lead, at Stalin's instigation, to many thousands of bloody deaths.

This then was the background against which Stalin made an important foreign policy speech in the spring of 1939. On 10 March, at the Eighteenth Party Congress, he said that it was 'incredible, but true' that 'non-aggressive states' like America, Britain and France had made 'concession after concession' to the 'aggressor states' (by which he meant Germany, Italy and Japan). Perhaps, he added, the 'non-aggressive states' were pursuing a policy of appeasement because they feared that if there was another war a revolution might break out in their countries. After all, everyone knew that the Bolshevik Revolution had happened in Russia during the 'first imperialist world war'. Or, alternatively, said Stalin, it was because they had abandoned the idea of 'collective security' in favour of 'neutrality' – a policy that only helped 'the aggressors in their nefarious work'.[21]

Stalin went further, and even suggested that the 'non-aggressive states' had a secret agenda against the Soviet Union. He pointed out that they had offered only a feeble response in the face of German aggression against Austria and Czechoslovakia, and yet published 'lies' in the press about 'the weakness of the Russian army' and 'the demoralization of the Russian air force'. They were thus 'egging the Germans on to march farther east, promising them easy pickings, and prompting them: "Just start war on the Bolsheviks, and everything will be all right." '[22] It was during this speech that Stalin made his famous statement that the Soviets would 'not allow our country to be drawn into conflicts by warmongers who are accustomed to have others pull the chestnuts out of the fire for them'.[23]

Stalin's speech sufficiently troubled Winston Churchill, who was not yet back in government, for him to ask the Soviet Ambassador in London, Ivan Maisky, if this meant that Stalin was not ready to 'cooperate with the democracies'. Maisky replied that it was more a call for the democracies to be 'prepared to fight against the aggressors and not just chatter about it'.[24]

This all occurred as Hitler was making a decisive move, one which revealed his true nature and intentions. In March 1939 he orchestrated the dismantling of Czechoslovakia by creating a subservient new country – Slovakia – in the east, and by sending German troops into the remaining western territory in order to establish the Protectorate of Bohemia and Moravia.

This was immensely significant, in part because of what had happened the year before. In March 1938 the Germans had first invaded Austria and then subsequently threatened Czechoslovakia. In order to avert European war Hitler had been forced to shelve his plans to occupy the whole of Czechoslovakia and, after the Munich conference of September that year, agree merely to taking the border area of the Sudetenland, which was largely occupied by ethnic Germans. This last point was crucial to his case, because he had publicly maintained during the 1930s that he was only pursuing the aim of uniting all German-speaking people under his rule. There was some international sympathy with this position, or at least a lack of enthusiasm to go to war over it. As Sir Frank Roberts of the British Foreign Office put it, 'public opinion [in Britain] would not understand getting involved as an ally of France in a war with Germany in Europe, to prevent Germans being attached to other Germans.'[25]

This insouciant attitude was about to change, as Hitler dismembered the rest of Czechoslovakia. And the manner in which he went about this task in March 1939 tells us a great deal not just about the brutal way he felt able to conduct his foreign policy, but also about the extent of his contempt for weaker nations. It was a contempt, as we shall see, that Stalin shared.

Slovakia, territory in the east of Czechoslovakia, had been granted special status by the Czechs after the Munich agreement, and a Catholic priest, Jozef Tiso, had been appointed Prime Minister of the Autonomous Slovak Region. But early in March 1939 the Czech President, Emil Hácha, removed Tiso from office. He was concerned that the Slovaks led by Tiso would declare independence, something the Nazis were trying to engineer. But Tiso was uncertain what to do, until he met Hitler and listened to his threats. The Führer told him that he was going to move into the Czech lands regardless of what the Slovaks decided. The only question for the Slovaks now was whether they preferred independence or for the Nazis to agree to Hungarian designs on their territory. As Hermann Göring had brutally phrased it, when he met a Slovak delegation the previous month, 'Do you want to make yourselves independent? [Or should] I let the Hungarians have you?'[26]

On 14 March, the day after meeting Hitler, Tiso returned to Bratislava for a crisis meeting of the Slovak parliament. One of the politicians present, Martin Sokol, summed up the tense atmosphere: 'No one really wanted to take on the responsibility before history [for declaring independence], because who knew . . . what would happen with Slovakia by the afternoon . . .'[27] Nonetheless, the Slovaks determined that, on balance, independence was the least dangerous way forward and immediately created the Slovak state.

The evening of the same day, Tuesday 14 March, President Hácha of Czechoslovakia arrived in Berlin for talks with Hitler. It would turn out to be a meeting that was less a discussion between statesmen than an

exercise in ritual humiliation. Hitler first kept the sixty-six-year-old
Hácha waiting – this after the sickly Czech President had endured a
lengthy journey from Prague. The urgent business that prevented him
from seeing Hácha consisted of watching a film called *Ein hoffnungsloser
Fall* (A Hopeless Case), a German romantic comedy. He only got round
to meeting Hácha at about one o'clock in the morning, and immediately
launched into an angry rant. The only way to protect the Reich, he said,
was for Germany to occupy the Czech lands at once. If Hácha didn't
place an urgent call to Prague and order Czech forces to offer no resistance to the invading Germans, bloodshed would result. Göring, who
also attended the meeting, added that his planes were ready to bomb
Prague that very morning. At this point Hácha collapsed.

Manfred von Schröder, a young German diplomat, witnessed what
happened next: 'We needed a doctor, and that was my task . . . the famous Professor Morell [Hitler's own doctor] was around, so I called him
and he came and made an injection. People later said he gave him an
injection to do everything Hitler wanted, but I think it was quite a normal injection he gave him in the arm . . . Hácha [once he had recovered]
went back to sign the surrender of Czechoslovakia.'[28]

After Hácha had left, broken by the night's events, Hitler told his
secretaries, 'This is the happiest day of my life. What has been striven
for in vain for centuries, I have been fortunate enough to bring about. I
have achieved the union of Czechia with the Reich. Hácha has signed
the agreement. I will go down as the greatest German in history.'[29]

Hitler had achieved the 'happiest day of [his] life' by ruthless bully-
ing. He believed that in the 'eternal struggle' of life, a small country,
seemingly without friends, could be made to do whatever a bigger,
more powerful neighbour wanted. It was a harsh political and geographical reality that Stalin understood in precisely the same way.

However, Hitler faced a problem as a result of his occupation of the
Czech lands and the creation of a Nazi vassal state in Slovakia. He had,
without question, broken the promise he had made just the year before
that the Sudetenland was his 'last territorial demand'. And since Czechoslovakia was demonstrably full of people who did not consider
themselves German, his claim that he only wanted to unite German-
speaking people was shown to be a lie.

Sir Alexander Cadogan of the British Foreign Office wrote in his
diary, on 20 March 1939, that 'we have reached the crossroads'. As long

as Hitler only tried to gain territory occupied by German-speaking people the British 'could pretend that he had a case', but if he 'proceeded to gobble up other nationalities, that would be the time to call "Halt!"'[30]

Hitler's actions were especially damaging to the British Prime Minister, Neville Chamberlain. Not only had he signed up to the Munich agreement, which had now obviously been broken, but in a crass misjudgement of the situation he had told journalists just days before Nazi tanks moved on Prague that 'The foreign situation is less anxious and gives me less concern for possible unpleasant developments than it has done for some time.'[31]

After the swift Nazi takeover of the Czech lands, Chamberlain believed there was nothing that could be done to restore Czech independence. Instead, now was the time to prevent further German expansion, particularly into Poland. Hitler had said for years that he wanted to recover German territory lost to Poland as a result of Versailles. So Chamberlain, anxious to send a signal to the world, told the House of Commons on 31 March that 'in the event of any action which clearly threatened Polish independence, and which the Polish Government accordingly considered it vital to resist with their national forces, His Majesty's Government would feel themselves bound at once to lend the Polish Government all support in their power.'[32]

The Labour MP Arthur Greenwood asked Chamberlain if he would attempt to bring the Soviet Union, among other countries, 'into this arrangement' – that is, to guarantee the safety of Poland. Chamberlain answered that Lord Halifax, the Foreign Secretary, 'saw the Soviet Ambassador this morning' and 'I have no doubt that the principles upon which we are acting are fully understood and appreciated by that Government.'[33] This was, however, a disingenuous response.

Ivan Maisky, the Soviet Ambassador, recorded in his diary details of the meeting with Lord Halifax that morning. He wrote that Halifax had handed over a copy of Chamberlain's statement and then asked if it was permissible for the British government to say, in a few hours' time, that the Soviets approved of it. Maisky replied that as this was the first time he'd seen it, and obviously his government hadn't yet read the statement either, 'under such circumstances' how was it possible to say the Soviet Union approved of it? Halifax was 'embarrassed' and replied, 'You may be right.'[34]

Halifax's cursory treatment of the Soviets reveals how much the British were wary of Stalin and his regime. To his cabinet, Chamberlain was open about his feelings, saying on 5 April that he 'had very considerable distrust of Russia, and had no confidence that we should obtain active and constant support from that country'.[35] Moreover, he thought that it was a 'pathetic belief' to look to 'Russia as the key to our salvation'.[36]

It's easy to imagine why some members of the British governing class, including Chamberlain and Halifax, felt this way. They knew how the Bolsheviks had murdered the Russian Imperial Family after they came to power. The British upper class and royal family could expect to be treated in just as bloody a way if there was a communist revolution in the United Kingdom. Moreover, hadn't the Bolsheviks said they wanted their 'world revolution' to spread?

On the other hand, these were desperate times and the immediate threat came not from the Soviet Union but from Germany. So the British and French suggested that Stalin offer guarantees to Poland similar to the ones they had just promised. The Soviets replied on 17 April, and proposed a wide-ranging military alliance between Britain, France and the Soviet Union. They suggested not only that each of the three countries would support the others if one was attacked, but that all three countries should commit themselves to assisting the eastern European states that bordered the Soviet Union in the event that they were also invaded.

It was an idea that immediately made the British suspicious. 'We have to balance the advantage of a paper commitment by Russia . . .', wrote Cadogan in an advisory document at the time, 'against the disadvantage of associating ourselves openly with Russia. The advantage is, to say the least, problematical . . .' The reason the proposed alliance was 'problematical' was self-evident to the British. For, as Cadogan wrote, how could the Soviets 'fulfil that obligation without sending troops through or aircraft over Polish territory? That is exactly what frightens the Poles.'[37] Lord Halifax put the Poles' anxieties even more bluntly. 'An intelligent rabbit', he said, 'would hardly be expected to welcome the protection of an animal ten times its size, whom it credited with the habits of a boa constrictor.'[38]

This concern about possible Soviet incursion into Polish territory would not be resolved over the succeeding months of discussion. Indeed, it's hard to see how it could ever have been. How could the Poles be expected to believe that Red Army soldiers would ever leave their country after they had entered Poland to fight the Germans, especially given that the Poles had fought a bitter war with the Bolshevik regime over territorial questions twenty years before? Matters were further complicated by the British offer of additional guarantees to two new countries – Romania and Greece. So they too would have to be consulted about the Soviets potentially coming to their aid.

Nor did the British seem to think the Soviet armed forces were up to much. In April 1939, the Chiefs of Staff reported that while the Red Army was undoubtedly large, there were many weaknesses in its structure and leadership. Chamberlain agreed, saying that in his opinion 'the Russian fighting services were at present of little military value for offensive purposes.'[39]

However, this was not the whole story. Despite the problems they identified with the Red Army, the British Chiefs of Staff thought that the sheer size of the Soviet military offered one advantage. It meant that 'even if the war went so badly for the Allies as to result in Poland and Rumania [sic] being overrun the Russians would still contain very substantial German forces on the Eastern front.' Prophetically the Chiefs of Staff also spotted one enormous risk the British would take if they did not engage with the Soviet Union: 'We should perhaps draw attention to the very grave military dangers inherent in the possibility of any agreement between Germany and Russia.'[40]

Meanwhile, Stalin's suspicious nature continued to make him see potential plots everywhere. What if the British and the French were conspiring together to make the Soviets fight the Germans on their own? In practical terms, wouldn't that be the consequence of any alliance the Soviets entered into with Britain and France, since the Soviets were the only ones who could offer immediate help to the Poles on the battlefield? The British and French, for all the fine words of their Polish guarantee, could only stand by as the Wehrmacht marched on Warsaw. Even worse, what if the British and French were plotting some kind of secret deal with the Germans that would leave Hitler free to attack Poland, and subsequently the Soviet Union, once the two countries had a common border? Had not Chamberlain shown himself all too willing to appease Hitler at Munich? Why wouldn't he do the same thing again?

All of this makes it hard, if not impossible, to know what Stalin's precise intentions were in proposing a military alliance to the British and the French. He must have realized that the Polish question would be all but impossible to resolve. Most likely he just wanted to keep all his options open. He did not want to 'pull the chestnuts out of the fire' for the British and French, but at the same time he was wary of isolation.

As for the British, they were uncertain what to do. One faction remained intensely distrustful of Stalin. Sir Alexander Cadogan at the Foreign Office even described Stalin's proposal for a military alliance as 'mischievous'.[41] Chamberlain also remained suspicious of the Soviets. If it had been left to him there would have been minimal engagement with Stalin. Not only did he regard 'Russia' as 'a very unreliable friend', but the memory of the run-up to the First World War was on his mind, and he feared that if blocs of alliances were put in place, as they had been in 1914, then it could precipitate rather than prevent a conflict.[42]

But others in the cabinet disagreed, and gradually their view came to predominate. For them, the dangers of a neutral Soviet Union, or – worse – a Soviet Union in alliance with Hitler, outweighed the difficulties of establishing a deal. Consequently, by the end of May the British had decided to engage with the Soviet dictator. It's worth noting the significance of this decision, not so much because the British changed their minds, having initially rejected Stalin's proposal for a military alliance, but because it demonstrates one fundamental difference between democracies and dictatorships. Hitler and Stalin made the major foreign policy decisions themselves. While they did not act in utter isolation – they always had to consider the various factions around them and, to a certain extent, broader public opinion – ultimately they themselves chose the way forward. As we shall see, in 1939 it was Hitler, and Hitler alone, who decided that Germany should invade Poland in September. And it was Stalin, and Stalin alone, who decided to enter into a pact with Nazi Germany. Yet in May 1939 Chamberlain agreed to discuss a possible deal with Stalin against his own instincts. Unlike the two dictators, he was directly answerable to his colleagues, and so Britain pursued a policy that its Prime Minister disliked.

Discussions between the British and the Soviets continued over the following weeks, culminating in a decision at the end of July to send a military mission to Moscow. Having thought initially that this was 'an extraordinarily important' development, Maisky, the Soviet Ambassador, became 'seriously alarmed' when the members of the British mission came for lunch at the Soviet embassy before leaving for the Soviet Union. The leader of the delegation, with the quadruple-barrelled name of Sir Reginald Aylmer Ranfurly Plunkett-Ernle-Erle-Drax, told Maisky that they had decided not to fly to Moscow because it would be 'uncomfortable' in the aircraft and they had 'a lot of luggage'. Maisky described as 'incredible' the news that the mission was instead travelling to the Soviet Union by slow freight steamer. 'Does the British Government really want an agreement?' he asked himself.[43]

At the same time as the British prepared their slow-motion mission to Moscow, there were the first indications that the Germans might consider a deal with the Soviets. On 26 July, the week before the ineffectual Admiral Drax and his team lunched at the Soviet embassy, German and Soviet officials met in Berlin, under the guise of trade discussions. Following on from this, on 2 August, Joachim von Ribbentrop, the German Foreign Minister, discussed the 'remoulding' of 'German–Russian relations' with the Soviet diplomat Georgii Astakhov. Ribbentrop even went so far as to say that 'from the Baltic to the Black Sea, there was no problem which could not be solved to our mutual satisfaction.'[44]

In contrast to the British approach, the Germans moved swiftly to try to reach an agreement with the Soviets. Crucial was Ribbentrop's enthusiasm for the deal. According to the British agent Group Captain Malcolm Christie, Ribbentrop had been keen for years on an alliance between Germany, Italy, Japan and the Soviet Union.[45] Ribbentrop, however, was Hitler's subservient creature, and he would never have progressed discussions with the Soviets without his Führer's blessing.

There had been a clue to Hitler's own attitude in his speech on 28 April 1939, not in terms of what he said, but rather in terms of what he didn't say. Despite the wide-ranging nature of the speech, and its international importance, he barely mentioned his well-publicized hatred of the 'Bolsheviks'.[46] Instead he emphasized his desire for 'close Anglo-German friendship and cooperation'. He also stated his belief in 'the importance of the existence of the British Empire', notwithstanding the fact that the British had 'very often' used 'the most brutal violence' to create it – though he added, 'I am nevertheless aware that no other empire came into being by any other way.'[47] But, as a result of recent British actions, he had been 'forced' to come to the conclusion that

'Britain will always make a stand against Germany,' something he 'deeply' regretted.[48]

This was also the speech in which Hitler gave his infamous reply to President Roosevelt's request that he declare that Germany did not intend to attack a whole host of named countries. Hitler was at his most cutting and sarcastic in his response, ridiculing Roosevelt's attempt at mediation and pointing to the President's hypocrisy, as 'the United States has undertaken six cases of military intervention since 1918 alone.'[49]

The speech marks a watershed in Germany's relationship with the United States. Beginning with Roosevelt's initiative in the spring of 1938 to convene a conference about the plight of the Jews in Austria and Germany, one eventually held at Évian a few months later, Hitler had come to see America as a growing threat. It made little difference that the Évian conference had proved ineffectual and that few Jews had been helped – that only fuelled Hitler's sense that the rest of the world were hypocrites when it came to the 'Jewish question'. What mattered to him was that Roosevelt had shown his sympathy for the Jews. Ever since his first speeches in the early 1920s, Hitler had asserted that the Jews were so duplicitous that they sought to control both Bolshevism and capitalism. So here, in his eyes, was confirmation of that belief, as the leader of the largest capitalist state was allegedly bending to their will.

However, the fundamental ideological reality remained. Hitler was moving towards what, for him, was the wrong war. For years he had wanted an alliance with Britain, and his flattering remarks about the British Empire in his April 1939 speech showed how much he still admired the British. Yet now they had rejected him. So he was forced to arrange a pact with a country he had always wanted to invade, and fight a country he had wanted as a friend. It was hardly a foreign policy triumph. Still, it demonstrated a central truth about Hitler's political acumen. He was able to form a long-term vision – in this case the desire to create an empire in the Soviet Union – and could respond swiftly to short-term crises – here the need to protect his eastern flank so as not to fight a war on two fronts. What he couldn't do was link his short-term responses with his long-term vision. This middle ground of coherence was lacking, and the result would be bewilderment among many of his supporters.

As for Stalin, in August 1939 he appeared to be in an exceptionally strong position, since both the British and Germans were courting him. But this strength was to a large extent an illusion. There were, for instance, doubts about how serious the British and French mission to Moscow really was.[50] The members of the delegation finally arrived in the Soviet capital on 11 August, and showed no desire to pursue a deal with any urgency. This wasn't by accident. Admiral Drax had been told 'to go slowly and cautiously'. Indeed, confirmed Drax, Chamberlain hadn't even wanted the approach to Stalin to be made at all.[51]

Hitler's political ambitions, unlike Chamberlain's, demanded that an agreement be reached in a hurry. He wanted to move on Poland before the autumn rains, and an arrangement with Stalin would secure his eastern border after Poland had been destroyed. On 11 August, the same day Drax arrived in Moscow, Count Ciano, the Italian Foreign Minister, met with Ribbentrop. 'The decision to fight is implacable,' records Ciano. 'He rejects any solution which might give satisfaction to Germany and avoid the struggle.'[52] The next day Hitler told Ciano that 'the great war must be fought while he and the Duce are still young.'[53]

Nonetheless, Hitler remained frustrated that he had to consider a deal with Stalin in order to pursue the German attack on Poland. The day before he met Ciano, on 11 August, Hitler spoke with Carl Burckhardt, the League of Nations Commissioner in Danzig, and told him, 'everything that I undertake is directed against Russia; if the West is too stupid and too blind to understand this, then I will be forced to reach an understanding with the Russians, smash the West and then turn all my concentrated strength against the Soviet Union. I need the Ukraine, so that no one can starve us out again as in the last war.'[54] In ideological terms, Hitler thus remained as consistent as ever.

On 22 August Hitler met his military commanders at Berchtesgaden in the Bavarian Alps to enthuse them about the war ahead. And the contrast between this meeting and the discussions that would take place the following day in the Kremlin involving Ribbentrop and Stalin is revealing. Both Hitler and Stalin, in their respective meetings, demonstrated key aspects of their personalities. In his address to his generals, Hitler was at his most preening and self-obsessed. He announced at the start that 'essentially all depends on me, on my existence, because of my political talents,' but acknowledged that he could be 'eliminated at any time by a criminal or a lunatic'. Later in his talk he reminded his audience that 'No one knows how much longer I shall live. Therefore, better a conflict now.' It's a remarkable moment – a glimpse of his bloated ego. For Hitler was saying that one reason for millions to be drawn into war was his anxiety about his own longevity.

Another factor, he said, was the ability of other countries to confront Germany. The 'favourable circumstances' that existed at the moment would 'no longer prevail in two or three years' time'. He emphasized that 'it is easy for us to make decisions. We have nothing to lose; we have everything to gain.' But he also issued a warning: 'We are faced with the harsh alternatives of striking or of certain annihilation sooner or later.' This last sentence was typical of the way he structured his arguments. One of Hitler's standard rhetorical tactics was to pose dramatic alternatives – 'either/or' – and he only ever offered extreme options.

The idea that Germany was facing 'annihilation' unless Poland was attacked was grotesquely hyperbolic. While it was certainly the case that the economy was approaching crisis point, that was a situation Hitler had created himself by demanding that money be poured into armaments rather than consumer goods. But perhaps the 'annihilation' that Hitler had on his mind was not Germany's but his own. He was, like all mortals, most definitely en route to physical 'annihilation' at some point in the future, and he was concerned that he would die before the great empire he craved in the east had been gained.

Paradoxically, what Hitler was frightened of at this precise moment was not that there would be war, but that there would be peace. 'I am only afraid', he said, obviously thinking of the Munich agreement the year before, 'that at the last moment some swine or other will yet submit to me a plan for mediation.'[55]

Later that same day he emphasized that Germany was involved in a 'life and death struggle' and that 'a period of peace would not do us any good.' He openly admitted that he would give a false or 'propaganda' reason for 'starting the war' since 'the victor will not be asked afterwards whether he told the truth or not.' As he ended his address, he told his audience to 'close your hearts to pity' and 'act brutally'.[56]

It used to be argued that a major step change in Hitler's attitude towards the nature of war occurred with his decision to invade the Soviet Union in 1941, a conflict he openly called a 'war of extermination'. But in this August 1939 speech he reveals the same bloodthirsty nature. Hitler was calling, from the first moment of the war, for his generals to 'act brutally' and put aside traditional notions of chivalry and honour.

The very next day, Wednesday 23 August 1939, Joachim von Ribbentrop met Stalin and Vyacheslav Molotov, the Soviet Foreign Minister, in the Kremlin. From the first, Stalin was down to earth and cynical. When Ribbentrop, at the start of the meeting, proposed that the non-aggression treaty should be for a hundred years, Stalin replied, 'If we agree to a hundred years people will laugh at us for not being serious. I propose the agreement should last ten years.'[57]

Stalin did not speak using pseudo-philosophical maxims, as Hitler often did, but preferred to talk in purely practical terms – hence the speed with which the meeting with Ribbentrop moved to a discussion of 'spheres of interest'. Without defining exactly what this term meant, Stalin, Ribbentrop and Molotov cheerfully divided up large chunks of the Europe that lay between them. The only sticking point was Latvia. Ribbentrop argued that Germany should keep part of the country in its own 'sphere of interest' but Stalin wanted it all for himself. After one call to Hitler back at Berchtesgaden, and Hitler's acquiescence to Stalin's demand, the deal was done. Significantly, even though the Germans had not yet invaded Poland – and Ribbentrop only hinted at the possibility, saying 'the Führer is determined to resolve the German–Polish disputes without delay' – they agreed that the eastern part of Poland should be in the Soviet 'sphere of influence'. Despite the vagueness of the term, and the lack of any explicit mention of Nazi plans to attack Poland, everyone in the room knew what was being discussed. Each of them had chosen which countries they would dominate. The exact form that dominance would take was a secondary matter. The important thing was that the two most powerful nations in the region had agreed in advance of any military action how to divide the spoils. It was the clearest possible sign of the gangster mentality they both shared.

Once everything had been agreed, Stalin was presented with a draft communiqué about the talks to issue to the world. He read the grandiloquent language used to describe the new relationship between the two countries and then raised an objection. He asked Ribbentrop whether they shouldn't 'pay a little more attention to public opinion in our countries?' After all, said Stalin, their propagandists had been denigrating each other for 'many years' and yet 'now all of a sudden are we to make our peoples believe that all is forgotten and forgiven? Things don't work so fast.' Following Stalin's comments, the language used in the press release was toned down.[58]

Afterwards, there was something of a party. Stalin wandered round clinking glasses with members of the German delegation, and even toasted the health of Hitler. When, in the early hours of 24 August, photographers were allowed in to memorialize the signing, Stalin asked that 'the empty bottles should be removed beforehand, because otherwise people might think that we got drunk first and then signed the treaty'.[59] The Soviet leader seems to have found the incongruity of the occasion entertaining. 'Let's drink to the new anti-Cominternist,' he said as the celebrations continued – 'Stalin!'[60]

He was well aware of the cynical nature of the arrangement. He knew that the ideological chasm between the two sides had been crossed only by a narrow bridge of self-interest. Immediately after the Germans had left the Kremlin, he told Nikita Khrushchev, then head of the Communist Party in Ukraine, that 'there's a game going on here to see who can best outwit and deceive the other.' According to Khrushchev, Stalin was in a 'very good mood' and understood that Hitler wanted to 'trick' the Soviet Union.[61]

The contrast between the way Stalin conducted negotiations with Ribbentrop and Hitler's bombastic address at Berchtesgaden the day before was pronounced. Where Hitler was loud and vainglorious, Stalin was quiet and watchful. Where Hitler boasted about his own self-importance, Stalin was careful to include Molotov in the meeting and give the false impression that decisions were made collectively in the Soviet state. Where Hitler preached his ideological vision, Stalin dealt in practicalities. He was even prepared to laugh at himself, something Hitler never did.

Even though the Nazi–Soviet non-aggression pact initially shocked the world, the immediate benefits to both sides were obvious. Hitler had managed to ensure that Germany would not be trapped between the Soviet Union in the east and the British and French in the west. And Stalin had achieved his goal of sitting on the sidelines and watching as Hitler and the other western states weakened each other with war. Moreover, as a result of the secret protocol to the non-aggression pact, he gained the possibility of extending Soviet-dominated territory at little or no military cost.

It had always been extremely unlikely that the Soviet Union would, instead of reaching an agreement with the Nazis, have come to an arrangement with the western powers. The question of Red Army access to Poland in the event of a German invasion guaranteed that. But the British, and Chamberlain in particular, also contributed to the destruction of any possible chance of an Anglo-French–Soviet military treaty. As for Hitler, he had still not entirely given up the idea of a settlement with the British. On 25 August, the day after the pact had been signed, he met the British Ambassador to Berlin, Sir Nevile Henderson, and put forward one last proposal for peace. He demanded that 'the German–Polish problem' be immediately resolved, and – once it was – offered the prospect of a comprehensive alliance with Great Britain.

These conditions could never be acceptable to the British, since the only way of solving the 'German–Polish problem' to Hitler's satisfaction was for Poland to capitulate and voluntarily hand over territory. Nonetheless, the very fact of the meeting on 25 August demonstrates once again that Hitler ideally wanted an alliance with the British. 'It is no exaggeration to say that he assiduously courted Great Britain,' wrote Henderson of Hitler, 'both as representing the aristocracy and most successful of the Nordic races, and as constituting the only seriously dangerous obstacle to his own far-reaching plan of German domination in Europe.'[62]

Given that the British would never have agreed to participate in such an alliance with Hitler, the pact with Stalin was scarcely surprising. The Soviet and Nazi governments may have been far apart in their ideological and political goals, but in the practical mechanics of oppression they were closely linked. While Hitler could not understand why Sir Nevile Henderson would not act in what he considered to be British interests and toss aside an agreement made with weaker states, Ribbentrop had a meeting of minds in Moscow with Stalin. Once they sat down together and talked, they found they could easily understand each other and at least pretend to become friends.

2. Eliminating Poland

Despite the ideological gulf between them, in the autumn of 1939 there was one issue on which Hitler and Stalin were in complete agreement. They both loathed Poland. And just a few weeks after the signing of the Nazi–Soviet pact, each of them separately ordered an invasion of this country they so despised. As a consequence millions of Poles would suffer in one of the most brutal occupations in history.

Hitler was angry not just that German territory had been incorporated into Poland after the First World War, but that the Poles had refused his diplomatic attempts to reach an accommodation during the 1930s – a deal that would inevitably have meant the Polish government surrendering part of Poland to Germany.

As for Stalin, his hatred was more personal. Most likely it had been his own experience with the Poles twenty years before that had been the catalyst for his special dislike of the Polish nation. He had played a part as a commissar in the war between Poland and the embryo Soviet state just after the First World War, and had been blamed for not authorizing the transfer of troops when they were needed elsewhere.

The Polish adventure ended in humiliation not just for Stalin, but for the whole new-born Bolshevik state. By the time the war was over in 1921, the Polish government had control of land in the east that contained not just Poles but large numbers of Ukrainians and Belorussians as well. The Poles saw this territory as their ancestral homeland, but the Soviets held a very different view, and that is the perceived wrong they claimed their action in 1939 was designed to put right.

The first to invade were the forces of the Third Reich. On 1 September five German armies – around one and a half million men – attacked Poland. Then, just over two weeks later, on 17 September, more than half a million soldiers of the Red Army moved against Poland from the opposite direction. Polish resistance was soon crushed, and within six weeks the Germans and the Soviets had swallowed up the entire Polish nation. Poland was an independent country no more.

★

Invasion of Poland, 1939

German Army movement,
1 September 1939

Soviet Army movement,
17 September 1939

Final demarcation line

Superficially, each of the invasions appeared different in character. The Nazis, unquestioningly, were engaged in a war of conquest – one, moreover, that was racist to its core. Not only did soldiers of the German Army and local German militia units commit atrocities against Polish civilians, but several thousand members of special units called Einsatzgruppen accompanied the Wehrmacht across the border into Poland. They were tasked with attacking Poles considered especially dangerous – including selected members of the Polish intelligentsia, Jews and priests. Hostage taking also became a preferred method of subjugation and hostages were murdered in the event of any perceived resistance from the Poles.[1] One former member of an Einsatzkommando remembered his commander saying that any Poles 'who make themselves suspect in any way' were to be immediately shot.[2] As a result, within the first few weeks of the invasion, around 16,000 Poles were murdered.[3]

The Soviet invasion, on the other hand, was portrayed altogether differently. In his diary, Ivan Maisky, the Soviet Ambassador to London, described it as a philanthropic gesture, motivated by the desire of the Red Army 'to protect the population's lives and property'.[4] Back in Moscow, Molotov agreed, saying it was a rescue operation to protect the 'blood brothers' of the Soviet people. But all this was just a pragmatic excuse. Days before the Soviet invasion, Molotov had admitted to the German Ambassador to Moscow that this was merely a 'pretext' for the occupation of eastern Poland.[5]

By the time units of the Red Army closed on the agreed demarcation line near Lwów,[6] the Germans had already occupied some of the territory assigned to the Soviets under the secret protocol. There was even the occasional incident of 'friendly' fire between them. But the Germans soon withdrew to the line agreed in Moscow a few weeks before. When they did so, Franz Halder, Chief of the Army General Staff, described the day as one of 'disgrace for German political leadership' given that the Wehrmacht had conquered the territory first.[7]

As the Red Army soldiers entered Polish towns and villages, many of the inhabitants were shocked at their appearance and behaviour. 'They were a rather uneven gang, as my grandmother would have said,' recalled Nina Andreyeva, who lived in Rovno in eastern Poland. 'And straight away they spread out through the houses.' The soldiers would walk into any house they fancied and requisition it, often confining the legitimate owner to a small part of their own property. They would say, according to Nina Andreyeva, 'Right, you are going to live over there. And we will live here.' She remembered how 'They would bring in a machine gun, they would drag a few other things in . . . right on to the parquet floor. Everywhere. It was awful.'[8]

'Compared to the Polish Army, they were very badly dressed,' remembered Anna Levitska, who lived in Lwów. 'They smelt rather odd. I cannot compare it with anything. It was a kind of distinctive sharp smell.' She also recalled that, as soon as they arrived, some of the Red Army soldiers started to steal: 'They used to take people's watches and rings off them in the street and earrings and crucifixes and crosses. They loved watches, I don't know why. Maybe they didn't wear watches or something.' Worse still, it was 'terrifying to go out into the street, because they tried to come on to the young girls. Such a thing happened to me. I was walking along the street near the main post office. [A soldier was] coming towards me, he was drunk of course, that was obvious. He grabbed me by my arm and began to pull me towards him. I began to get frightened and I started screaming. Men were walking by because it was a busy street. They said, "What are you doing, what are you doing to this girl?"' Thanks to the intervention of these passers-by, Anna was released, but 'After that I was frightened to go out into the street for a long time.'[9]

As for the Soviets, they were often shocked by what they found in Poland. For even though they had been told that they had been sent to 'protect' the inhabitants, they noticed, as air force officer Georgy Dragunov said, that 'they did not need such help whatsoever, [and] that this looked more like occupation.' The disparity between what Dragunov had been told he would find in eastern Poland and the reality in front of his eyes weighed heavily upon him. 'We saw things that we were envious about,' he said. 'Some of the soldiers were children of ordinary workers and peasants and they asked us questions as to why they saw such a dramatic difference in the living standard [between the Soviet Union and eastern Poland].'[10]

Even though the inhabitants of occupied Poland clearly possessed material things the Soviets did not, Dragunov did his best to cling to his previous beliefs: 'I had been raised in the spirit of believing that everything in the country [the Soviet Union] was the best . . . If I could see that something was better [in eastern Poland], yes it made me think, but it didn't make me change my mind immediately. We had been told that their country was in crisis, that Poland was falling apart and that we were bringing new order. At the time it was impossible to change your mind so quickly . . . my views were shaped by society, I cannot separate myself from my environment.'

It's easy to understand why Georgy Dragunov felt this way. Even more than Nazi Germany, the Soviet Union was a closed country. Soviet beliefs, value systems and culture were to a large extent self-referring. Virtually no one saw foreign films or newsreels or read foreign books or newspapers, and you learnt quickly as a child to believe in the ideology you were taught. To do anything else was dangerous. So the shock of discovering that the inhabitants of eastern Poland appeared to have a richer existence than people in the Soviet Union could be deeply disturbing. It invited the question, if the Soviet regime had concealed the truth about this, what else had they lied about? Stalin, for his part, was acutely aware of the danger posed by contact between Soviet citizens and foreigners. His suspicions reached almost paranoiac levels when it came to trusting anyone after they had spent time abroad.

Soviet propaganda had not just emphasized the need for soldiers of the Red Army to rescue their 'blood brothers' who lived in Poland, but also – up until a few months before – projected a wholly negative view of the Nazis. Mikhail Timoshenko, who was one of the Soviet officers charged with liaising with the Germans, remembered his initial encounter with them. 'It was the first time that I'd seen them in the flesh, in their German uniforms,' he said. 'We'd heard all about their peaked caps and about a few other things like the German "style" . . . that they considered themselves the [most] superior race on earth. The cleverest, the best organized race. The most cultured race. That all other people, [in] Russia especially, were plebs. They were people who were only fit to be their slaves. I sensed that very well.'[11]

While the Soviets and the Germans tried to forge a new relationship of cooperation on the ground, Stalin decided to try to alter the 'sphere of interests' agreement that had been reached with the Nazis. He told the German Ambassador to Moscow, Count von der Schulenburg, that he wanted to reopen discussions with Ribbentrop, and on 27 September the German Foreign Minister arrived in the Soviet capital once again. Unlike the first, almost furtive visit a month before, Ribbentrop was now treated to a lavish welcome ceremony. Swastika flags flew from the airport terminal building and a guard of honour awaited the Nazi delegation.

Later that same day, Ribbentrop was back in the Kremlin for further discussions with Stalin and Molotov. Stalin told him that he now wanted to swap a small part of Soviet-occupied Poland for the section of Lithuania that the Germans had previously claimed. In response Ribbentrop expressed interest in the forest of Augustów on the border of East Prussia and Lithuania. In this convivial atmosphere, they traded other people's territory between them.

In the course of the meeting, Stalin made one remarkable statement. 'The fact is that for the time being Germany does not need foreign help,' he said, 'and it is possible that in the future they will not need foreign help either. However, if, against all expectations, Germany finds itself in a difficult situation, then she can be sure that the Soviet people will come to Germany's aid and will not allow Germany to be suppressed. A strong Germany is in the interests of the Soviet Union and she will not allow Germany to be thrown down to the ground.'[12]

Stalin was all but promising military aid to the Germans in the event they needed it. And while we can't know the extent to which he meant what he said, it is still notable that he was prepared to go this far in the meeting with Ribbentrop.

There was then a pause in the talks so that Ribbentrop, Stalin and their entourages could enjoy a luxurious meal together in one of the Kremlin's imperial banqueting halls amid the unBolshevik trappings of fine porcelain and golden cutlery. Stalin, once again in a jokey mood, introduced Lavrenti Beria, the notorious head of the Soviet secret police, as 'our Himmler'.[13] Molotov later drank a toast to Hitler, and Ribbentrop returned the compliment and drank to Stalin. It was all remarkably friendly. So much so that Albert Forster, the Gauleiter of Danzig–West Prussia, who was part of the Nazi delegation, later remarked that he had almost felt he was among 'veteran [Nazi] Party members'.[14]

While the Germans took a break to attend part of a performance of *Swan Lake* at the Bolshoi, Stalin and Molotov were busy threatening one of the countries that had been allocated to them under the secret protocol to the treaty. They met with a delegation from Estonia and demanded the right to station Red Army troops on their territory. There was little the Estonians could do about the Soviet request, as they knew Germany would not come to their aid. For Stalin, this was just the start. By the middle of October 1939, all three Baltic States – Latvia, Lithuania and Estonia – had been pressured into allowing the Soviets to base military units on their territory.

Back in Poland, Soviet and German commanders put aside whatever misgivings they may have had about each other and started cooperating over matters like prisoner exchange. The Soviets even gave up a number of German communists to the Nazis.[15] Stalin was no doubt glad to be rid of them, given his suspicion of foreigners in general and foreign communists in particular.

One of the German communists who suffered this fate, Margarete Buber-Neumann, was told by Soviet officials that the five-year sentence she was already serving in a labour camp had been converted to expulsion from the Soviet Union. In February 1940 she was taken by train to Brest-Litovsk and handed over to the SS. She was then sent to Ravensbrück concentration camp, where she was held until April 1945. After the war she wrote of her experience in *Als Gefangene bei Stalin und Hitler* (published in English as *Under Two Dictators: Prisoner of Stalin and Hitler*). It's a remarkable book, one which demonstrates in graphic terms the horror of prison life in both systems.

Not only did Buber-Neumann experience personally how the penal regimes of the Nazis and Soviets were cruel almost beyond belief, but each of her interrogators – both Soviet and German – wanted her to confess to an alternative reality of their choosing. The Soviet secret police demanded she reveal details of her non-existent 'counter-revolutionary' activities, and the Gestapo insisted she agree with the fantasy that she was a communist secret agent sent by Stalin to spy on them. 'Don't be impudent,' her Soviet interrogator said to her – although these sentiments could just as easily have come from her Gestapo tormentor. 'Don't think we haven't got ways and means of making you talk. If you don't come round to reason, you'll stay where you are for months – years if necessary.'[16] No wonder Buber-Neumann later wrote that 'In imprisonment one forgets what life in freedom is like really. There remains only a vague picture.'[17]

The Nazis and Soviets worked harmoniously together not just on prisoner exchange, but also on the practical matter of the exact delineation of the new border between them in Poland. By October 1939 the relationship had grown so cordial that a celebration lunch was held in Warsaw. The head of the Soviet delegation said that 'The atmosphere in which these negotiations have been conducted reflects the spirit of cooperation for the benefit of the German and Soviet peoples – the two greatest nations in Europe!'[18] Hans Frank, who hosted the lunch as Nazi ruler of this part of Poland, said to a member of the Soviet delegation,

'You and I are both smoking Polish cigarettes, to symbolize the fact that we have thrown Poland to the winds.'[19]

The two sides were also focused on subjugating their respective sections of Poland. How they went about this task tells us a great deal about the nature of the regimes. And though there were differences in approach, in certain fundamental ways they were remarkably similar. Both, for example, made free use of torture. In Nazi concentration camps established in Poland, a whole variety of tortures were used on inmates – the majority of whom, at this stage in the war, were Polish political prisoners. The SS, for instance, tied the hands of prisoners behind their backs and then suspended them from hooks. 'I just felt', said Jerzy Bielecki, who suffered this punishment in 1940 – 'Jesus Mary – it was terrible pain! I was moaning . . . the sweat was pouring down my nose and it's very hot and I'm saying, "Mummy!" '[20] Outside of such formalized torture, individual Germans felt free to torment any Poles they encountered, particularly Polish Jews. At one workplace in Warsaw, according to Emmanuel Ringelblum, the Germans 'divide the workers into groups, and have the groups fight one another . . . I have seen people badly injured in these games.'[21]

The Soviet authorities – most notoriously the secret police, the NKVD – also practised torture on a wide scale. Olga Popadyn, a member of an underground youth organization in Lwów, was arrested by Soviet security forces just weeks after they invaded Poland. The interrogators first used their fists to beat her, then a rubber truncheon, and finally, after she had been in the prison several weeks, they made her perform endless physical exercises until she was exhausted and disorientated. Another common torture, linked to this method, was sleep deprivation. 'By the end of it,' said Olga, 'I was half dead.'[22]

Both Stalin and Hitler knew, and approved, of the use of such methods. Before the war, Hitler had even personally called for a particular child murderer to be tortured.[23] And in January 1939 Stalin had written, 'It is known that all bourgeois intelligence services apply physical coercion with regard to representatives of the socialist proletariat, and in the ugliest forms. One might ask why the socialist intelligence service must be more humane with regard to inveterate agents of the bourgeoisie.' Thus, as far as Stalin was concerned, 'physical methods' were completely justified.[24]

★

However, this wasn't the most important similarity between the two regimes during their occupation of Poland. By far the most remarkable was the way each of them used mass deportation as a technique for reordering the country. Indeed, so great was the commitment of both sides to the policy of uprooting innocent families and sending them to suffer far away from their homes that Poland became the site of one of the most horrific acts of ethnic cleansing in the history of the world.

Hitler's overarching plan for Poland was based on the principle of expelling those the Nazis considered 'racially undesirable' and replacing them with the 'racially desirable'. By the autumn of 1939 he had called for German-occupied Poland to be divided into a district in the east – known as the General Government – which would become the destination for the racially 'undesirable', and territory in the west which would be 'Germanized' and home to racially 'superior' specimens. It was also accepted, at least in the short term, that some of the racially 'undesirable' population would have to remain in the Germanized areas in order to provide slave labour in the fields, factories and coalmines. That was one of the reasons why Auschwitz was established as a concentration camp in the spring of 1940. The camp was located in Upper Silesia, an area of Poland designated to become part of the Reich, and intended primarily as a place of punishment for any Pole who was not sufficiently submissive.

Hitler appointed Himmler, head of the SS, to oversee the massive movement of people needed to reshape Poland, and in early October 1939 he was given the portentous title of Reich Commissioner for the Strengthening of German Nationality. Himmler's attempt to implement his Führer's vision would lead to misery, murder and suffering on an enormous scale. It would also cause administrative chaos. The Nazi Propaganda Minister, Joseph Goebbels, recognized this fact, writing in his diary in January 1940: 'Himmler is presently shifting populations. Not always successfully.'[25]

One of the most urgent problems facing Himmler was the question of the fate of the ethnic Germans living in the Baltic States. We have seen that Latvia, Lithuania and Estonia had been forced to accept Red Army troops on their territory in the wake of the second Ribbentrop meeting in Moscow in late September 1939. A few days later, on 4 October, the German Minister in Latvia had written to the Foreign Ministry in Berlin with the warning that 'outright paralysis of the government [in Latvia] appears imminent' and that some 60,000 ethnic Germans were 'in immediate danger of their lives'.[26]

In neighbouring Estonia, where several thousand ethnic Germans lived, Irma Eigi and her parents had a visit from 'representatives of the German cultural office' and were told: 'We have two options: We can stay there and become Russified and probably be deported to Siberia. Or we can all leave Estonia en masse as ethnic Germans, just to stay German. For those of us [living] on the Russian border – I was born in Narva – for those of us there, Stalinist Russia was a terrifying prospect. We were very scared of falling under Russian rule. So the German group decided that so as to remain German, which you no longer could be in Estonia, we will all emigrate together.'[27]

Just days later, sixteen-year-old Irma Eigi and her parents found themselves on a German ship pulling out of Tallinn harbour. Though they had always considered themselves 'German' they had thought of Estonia as 'our homeland' and were devastated to leave. 'It was like standing next to yourself,' she said of her feelings as she watched the coast of Estonia disappear into the distance. 'It happened, you didn't quite grasp it. It was a bit like being in a state of shock. It also happened very, very fast . . . The older ones were very sad, very downcast. Some of them were crying. The young ones – well, you have to imagine how young people are – despite leaving home and despite the pain, young people always have a certain thirst for adventure, naturally. They said, "Home to the Reich." So, of course, we thought that meant the Reich is Germany.'[28]

The Eigis, and hundreds of thousands of ethnic Germans like them, were in for a surprise. Because though the Nazi rallying cry had indeed been 'Home to the Reich' – 'Heim ins Reich' – Hitler and Himmler had a very different geographical definition of the Reich from that of the incoming settlers. For these Baltic Germans were to be colonizers of the 'new' Reich – previously, until September 1939, known as Poland.

On 24 October, as the Baltic Germans steamed towards the Polish coast, Himmler explained the Nazi vision to civil administrators in Poznań[29] in western Poland. 'As early as 3,000 years ago and during the following period Teutons lived in the eastern provinces [that is, this part of western Poland, renamed the Warthegau by the Nazis] in which we now find ourselves,' said Himmler. 'Despite the poor transport conditions of those days and the other primitive conditions that existed, it was possible to settle Germans . . . What was possible then must be even more feasible today.'[30] He imagined that 'in fifty to eighty years' some twenty million German settlers would be living in this area, of whom ten million would be peasants with large numbers of children. 'If there is no more land to be distributed then,' announced Himmler, 'as is always the case throughout history, new land will have to be got with the sword.'

Himmler claimed that this grandiose vision had been thought through in detail, from the security of the settlers – on the borders of this new territory a group of 'military peasants' would offer protection – to the way in which the houses should be built – 'two or three stone courses thick and with good foundations'. As for the Poles who currently inhabited this land, they would be removed, apart from a number of 'Polish workers' who would be forced to 'provide the cheap labour for settlement and for ploughing the fields'.

It was often the case with Hitler and the Nazis, as here, that the breadth of their vision far outstripped their ability to realize it, and there were problems from the start. On arrival families like the Eigis discovered that they were not to be settled in the Old Reich, as they had believed, but in occupied Poland instead. They were outraged. 'We hadn't reckoned on that at all,' said Irma Eigi. 'When we were told we were going to the Warthegau, well, it was quite a shock, I can tell you.'[31]

When the Eigis were allocated a flat in Poznań they 'opened the door with the key. And we came into a room, it was dark. If I am not mistaken the blinds were all down . . . It was really chaotic in this room. You noticed there had been people here who had had to leave very quickly . . . Some of the cupboards stood open. The drawers were open. On the table were the remains of food. And then the unmade beds, messed up.'[32]

The Eigis thought this 'horrible'. They had previously had 'no inkling' that Poles had been forced from their homes to release housing for the Baltic Germans. So they went back to the allocation office and said they wouldn't stay in the flat. But when they were told that if they didn't take this accommodation they would be returned to the transit camp, they decided to stay – at least until another flat became available after Christmas. 'You tell yourself, it's got to be,' said Irma Eigi. 'You don't have any other choice. We didn't want to go back to the camp.'[33]

Other Baltic settlers, like Jeannette von Hehn, were allocated whole estates in the Polish countryside. 'We arrived in manor houses that Poles had been forced to leave,' she wrote. 'Everything bore witness to the unexpected departure of the former owners. Often, they had been fetched away at night – the bedrooms were still untidy, or you could still find remains of a suddenly abandoned meal on the dining table! Everywhere there was foreign furniture; pictures that didn't belong to us stared at us from the walls, and in the wardrobes and dressers all the things that are counted among the most personal life of a human being were to be found!'[34]

In November 1939, in Poznań – the same city in which the Eigis made their new home – the Nazis arrived to throw Irena Huczyńska, a Polish girl of sixteen, and her family out of their flat. 'They [the Germans] wandered around and plundered,' said Irena, 'everybody trembled and burst into tears . . .'[35] Irena's sister, Anna, remembered that her parents had to give the Nazis 'everything they had'. Her mother even had to hand over her wedding ring. Anna was 'terribly upset' for her mother, and her 'younger brother was crying, he was very delicate, started vomiting violently, it simply affected him more than it did me, he was two years younger than me. I thought the worst, I thought they were going to shoot us all.'

As they were forced downstairs they found that the corridor of their apartment block 'was already crowded by our neighbours who were being deported, thrown out their homes . . . terrible panic, noise, screaming, darkness, we could not understand what was going on . . . The surprise of deportation, of being thrown out, leaving your home, and leaving everything behind – it seemed like the end of the world . . . We children, we worried most about our father and mother, that nothing should happen to them, that they should be with us, for if we were separated, well, it would be an even greater tragedy.'[36]

The family was taken to a transit camp where they slept on straw. Here they struggled to survive the cold Polish winter without heating and with very little to eat. Five months later they were put on a train and transported to the south-east of Poland and the area the Nazis called the General Government. This was to serve as the Nazis' dumping ground for unwanted Poles.

'When we arrived', remembered Irena, 'some Jewish people, who were good-hearted, greeted us with tea . . . I even made friends with Jewish women there – they are normal people and I don't know what the world wants from them.' But the Nazi authorities in the General Government insisted on strict separation between Polish Jews and the rest of the Polish population. Irena recalled how 'one young man' handed some bread to a Jew, 'and the next day a poster appeared with his name on it, announcing that he had been shot for breaking the law forbidding giving food to the Jews.'

Irena and her family now found themselves abandoned. They had nowhere to go and nowhere to stay. But then, luckily, an old Polish man felt sorry for them and offered them a room in his house. It was still a long way from the relative comforts of home – there was no running water and they had to sleep on the floor – but it was something. As Anna discovered: 'You can get used to anything . . . They say even hell is not bad once you get used to it.'

What is remarkable about the experience of Anna, her siblings and their parents is not just the appalling cruelty of their treatment but the chaotic manner in which the deportation was organized. As they experienced personally, whole trainloads of Poles were taken to the General Government in the east of Poland and left to fend for themselves. Almost as surprising is the refusal of the Nazis to acknowledge the scale of the task they had set themselves, given that in German-occupied Poland there were around twenty million people.[37]

There wasn't even agreement among the Nazi rulers of Poland about how the process of ethnic reorganization should work. The ruler of the General Government, Hans Frank, did not want his area to be turned into the so-called dustbin of the Reich and protested about the disorganized nature of the operation. As early as January 1940, the Higher SS and Police Leader of the General Government, Friedrich-Wilhelm Krüger, claimed that of the 110,000 Poles already sent to the General Government, more than a quarter, around 30,000, had been dispatched without appropriate arrangements having been made beforehand.[38]

None of that altered Himmler's blithe optimism about the task ahead. This was not an accident. Himmler knew that Hitler valued radical thinking in his subordinates. In the popular parlance of today, he wanted them to think big. Indeed, one of the reasons why Hitler supported people like Himmler and Ribbentrop was because they always came across as both positive and radical. Ribbentrop in particular was despised by many leading Nazis, especially Hermann Göring, and mocked for his pomposity and stupidity. But, like Himmler, he understood one key thing about the

German leader. He knew he should never go into a meeting with Hitler and appear negative.

Himmler set out his own wildly ambitious plans – all the more unachievable in the light of the complaints from his fellow Nazi Hans Frank – in a memo he submitted to Hitler on 25 May 1940, entitled 'Some Thoughts on the Treatment of the Alien Population in the East'. In terms that were consistent with the racist, visionary speech he had given in Poznań back in October 1939, Himmler insisted that Poles should not be taught reading in school, only that it was 'God's commandment to be obedient to the Germans and to be honest, hard working, and well-behaved'. He also outlined how Polish children who were racially acceptable to the Nazis should be snatched from Poland and raised as Germans. As for the General Government, his intention was that over the next ten years the population would 'inevitably consist of an inferior remnant' of people, who would be available as 'a leaderless labouring class'.

After Hitler had read the memo he pronounced it 'very good and correct'. This was the way that crucial policy decisions could be reached in the Third Reich. There was no referral to interested parties, no consideration by a committee, no detailed planning, no consultations, no real discussions of any kind. It was sufficient for a man like Himmler, who had access to Hitler, to write a memo and then note that Hitler approved of it. Stalin, bureaucratic creature that he always was, would have been appalled by this lax method of conducting government business.

Himmler's memo also made one mention of the Jews. Significantly, here too the talk was of deportation. But what Himmler had in mind for the Jews was something far more radical than simply transporting them to a different part of Poland. He imagined a 'large-scale emigration of all Jews to Africa or some other colony', an operation that would lead to the term 'Jew' being 'completely eliminated'.[39] Sending the Jews to Africa had long been a fantasy for anti-Semites. In the nineteenth century Paul de Lagarde had suggested they be transported to the island of Madagascar off Africa's south-east coast. Now, knowing Hitler's penchant for radical imaginings, Himmler was suggesting the same kind of idea. Consequently, in the summer of 1940 after the German victory over France, the Nazis would briefly investigate the practicalities of their own 'Madagascar plan'.[40]

Whether it was to Madagascar or somewhere else, the idea of

deporting Jews had long been one of the central components of Nazi anti-Semitic policy. Hitler had told the Polish Ambassador to Berlin in September 1938 that he had 'in mind an idea of settling the Jewish problem by way of emigration to the colonies'.[41] And earlier that year, in the wake of the German takeover of Austria, Adolf Eichmann of the SS had set up an administrative process in Vienna which allowed the Nazis to rob the Jews of their wealth and then expel them. The problem, from the Nazi perspective, was that few countries wanted to take the Jews – especially after they had been stripped of their assets.

Just a few weeks into the German occupation of Poland, Eichmann had been instrumental in another attempt to solve this Jewish 'problem' when he organized the deportation of several thousand Jews, including some from Vienna, to the Nisko district in the General Government. Little had been done to prepare for the arrival of the Jews, and they suffered – and many died – in the depths of eastern Poland in conditions that were even worse than those the Polish deportees endured. This chaotic and ill-considered scheme was quickly abandoned.

As a short-term measure, the Nazis decided to confine Polish Jews in ghettos, with the first large-scale ghetto in the city of Łódź in the Warthegau sealed by spring 1940. Conditions for the 164,000 Jews imprisoned in the ghetto were predictably appalling, and the death rate soon started to rise. The attitude of leading Nazis to this kind of suffering was summed up by Hans Frank of the General Government, in a speech he had made a few months earlier, in November 1939: 'What a pleasure, finally to be able to tackle the Jewish race physically. The more that die, the better.'[42] But quasi-genocidal as the Nazi actions towards the Jews in Poland were during the first year of the war, this was not yet a policy of mass extermination. The 'solution' the Nazis envisioned for their Jewish 'problem' was still one of imprisonment in ghettos and then brutal deportation. What remained to be resolved was just where and when the Jews could be sent.

At the same time as all this was happening in the Germans' section of Poland, Stalin was presiding over a policy of mass deportations in Soviet-occupied eastern Poland. Unlike the Nazis, Stalin was able to draw on a national history of deporting those citizens considered undesirable. In part, that was because the Soviet Union was so much bigger than Germany, and large areas in the east were both inhospitable and underpopulated. In particular, the tsars had long sent political prisoners – Stalin had been one of them under Tsar Nicholas II – to exile in Siberia.

Once he was in power, Stalin came to embrace the policy of deportation on a much greater scale and in a much more ruthless way. As part of his attack on the kulaks, the rich peasants, in the early 1930s, more than two million had been sent to Siberia and other remote areas.[43] A few years later, when large numbers of Soviet citizens were arrested as 'enemies of the people', many of those who were not immediately killed were similarly deported to the wildest and bleakest parts of the Soviet Union.

Soviet security units now employed these same tactics in eastern Poland. Consider the case of Boguslava Gryniv and her family, for example. On 27 September 1939, after they had settled down to supper in their flat in Lwów, they heard a knock at the door. It was a Soviet official, who told her father that he had been 'invited to go and see the temporary government'. He was taken away to a local prison where he was 'in very good spirits, because he said "They are only accusing me of being a member of the Ukrainian National Democratic Alliance"'. Since this group had been legal under the Poles and wasn't anti-Bolshevik he thought he was safe.[44]

He was wrong, and he subsequently disappeared within the Soviet penal system. Boguslava and the rest of the family prayed each night in front of an icon for him to be returned to them, but to no avail. Nonetheless, her mother never gave up hope – so much so that when the NKVD came in April 1940 to deport all of them to Kazakhstan, she immediately said to her children, 'We are going to your father, this will demonstrate our love for your father.'

Boguslava, her brother and her mother were persecuted just because they were related to someone considered an opponent of the regime. This policy did not originate in Poland. Within the Soviet Union it had not been unusual to target the partners of 'enemies of the people', following an NKVD regulation of 1937, and many of the wives of those arrested were deported and imprisoned in a camp in the Soviet republic of Mordovia.[45]

As for Boguslava and her family, they now travelled by train for several weeks – first east to Novosibirsk and then south-west to Kazakhstan. On the long journey they tried to make sense of the Soviet policy of arrests and deportations. But it was impossible. 'Whereas we perceived

[what had happened to us] as being in some way patriotic and political,'
said Boguslava, 'our neighbour was [just] a very good landowner. They
took him away simply because he had four cows, and some other things.
During the first year, he died from a heart attack that was brought on by
having lost everything that he had worked all his life for.'[46]

When they finally arrived at a collective farm called Red Kazakhstan, they had to sleep on wooden boards in a hut, and walk a mile each
day to labour in a potato field. They suffered particularly during the
'constant snowstorms' of the winter of 1940–41. 'If you don't know
what the snowstorms are like on the steppe,' said Boguslava, 'then
[imagine] a wind full of small snowflakes, which is so dense that you
can't see the person standing in front of you.'

In Kazakhstan, Boguslava received devastating news about her
father: 'They said, "Nobody else will be coming here. You are special
migrants. And he was arrested, so he will be in a concentration camp
somewhere." ' But since 'hope is the last thing to die' her mother
remained certain that he 'would suddenly turn up somewhere'. Unfortunately, she died 'without knowing the real and bitter truth. Because
the truth did not emerge until 1990.' This 'real and bitter truth' was that
Boguslava Gryniv's father had been killed by the NKVD within a few
months of his arrest.

Despite her own suffering, and even though she was not able to return
home for six years, Boguslava said that 'I do not consider the war and
being deported to Kazakhstan as having been the tragedy of my life. I
consider the tragedy [of my life] to have been my father's murder. The
murder of a very just and very noble man, who was not charged with
anything and [for whom] there was no justice.'[47]

It's important to recognize the emotional pain Boguslava and her
family endured because of the refusal of the Soviets to acknowledge the
death of her father. They were allowed to believe that one day, even
long after the war, he would walk through the door and they could be
a happy family once again. For the rest of her life, each time the door-
bell rang, her mother thought it might signal the return of her husband
at last.

Many other families suffered this torment of hope. Hiding the true
fate of those who had been executed was commonplace within the
Soviet Union. Maya Berzina, for instance, whose father was arrested
in Moscow in 1937, was told that he had been sentenced to 'ten years

[in prison] without the right of correspondence'.[48] This, it later transpired, was a euphemism for execution. But it meant that, just like the
Gryniv family in Poland, Maya Berzina was beset by terrible uncertainty about her father's fate.

The default position of Soviet administrators was concealment. The
emotional consequences of this for the families of those who had been
killed were immense – not least, a lifetime of hope. And hope, we discover from this history, can sometimes be corrosive to the spirit. To
know the truth, to mourn, in time to move forward – all that was
denied to these people.

Nor must we forget the additional suffering that this policy caused
for those who were sentenced to death as 'enemies of the people'. They
were forced to die anonymously, without public acknowledgement,
without a last farewell to their loved ones. There was no funeral, no
memorial stone, no urn of ashes. They were turned to nothing.[49] The
Nazis, as we shall see, would also commit mass murder in secret as part
of the extermination of the Jews – having pioneered this policy of killing innocent people in the shadows during their 'euthanasia' action
against the disabled.

No one knows exactly how many people the Soviets deported from
their section of Poland. But one Russian historian calculates that just
over 100,000 were sent from eastern Poland to the forced-labour camps
of the Gulag, and more than 300,000 into exile in remote areas of the
Soviet Union like Kazakhstan.[50]

Because similar actions had previously taken place inside the Soviet
Union, Red Army officers like Georgy Dragunov didn't consider what
was happening in Poland as anything special. Even though the deportations 'looked horrible' they were 'nevertheless not surprising to us
because we have seen all this before'. He considered it all 'part of the
norm', especially since he had been 'raised to believe that those targeted
were enemies of the people and they had to be deported. Only now
with the benefit of hindsight, I know that those were the best people,
but you have to live your life to understand it.'[51]

Several months before the deportation of Boguslava Gryniv and the
other relatives of the murdered 'enemies of the people', Beria had written a secret report for Stalin about another group of Poles considered
dangerous. These were the so-called Osadniks – retired Polish soldiers
who had been given land near the former border between Poland and

the Soviet Union. This combination of their proximity to the border and their previous military background made them special targets. Beria said they represented 'favourable soil for all types of anti-Soviet actions' and asked Stalin for permission to deport them and their families – a consent he swiftly gave.[52]

In Rovno, in the east of occupied Poland, Nikolai Dyukarev was one of the NKVD officers ordered to deport the Osadniks. In a procedure that would be used many times subsequently in deportations during the war, his unit first carried out a detailed reconnaissance of the area and compiled a list of names. Subterfuge was considered essential for this task. Dyukarev posed as an 'agricultural expert' and chatted to the villagers about their farms, while noting carefully 'all the members of the family'. Once identified, the Osadniks, their wives and children were taken from their homes, put on trains and deported east.

For Dyukarev his work was straightforward: 'We had an order to resettle them and that's what we did.' However, he admitted that 'it's really hard to take the children away when they're really small and, when you come to think of it, it's not very good,' but 'I knew that they were our enemies, enemies of the Soviet Union, and they had to be "recycled" . . .' The fact he had been told that Stalin had personally ordered the deportations was crucial. 'Stalin was much like a god for everybody,' he said. 'And all of his words were the last word on any subject.'[53]

Both the German and Soviet security forces also made a special effort to target those who had volunteered to fight clandestinely in the Polish underground, known as the Home Army. Tadeusz Ruman experienced personally just how keen the Germans and Soviets were to eliminate any resistance from this quarter. He served as a courier for the Home Army in early 1940, delivering messages from Lwów to various locations across the border in German-occupied Poland. He was nearly caught a number of times before he finally came to the attention of Soviet security forces in the spring of 1940.

On the night of 10 April he took shelter in a safe house in German-occupied Poland, close to the Soviet demarcation line. In the house, waiting to cross, were a young Polish woman – also a courier for the underground – and a Polish professor from Kraków. As an intellectual he was at particular risk from the Nazis, since they were attempting to destroy the 'leadership class' in Poland. He had only narrowly escaped the infamous Nazi action against university staff at the Jagiellonian University in Kraków in November 1939.

Normally, Tadeusz travelled alone, but he was persuaded by the desperate pleas of the young woman and the professor to take them with him. So that night they all crossed together into the Soviet zone. Next morning, tired of the long walk through the forest, and several miles into Soviet-occupied Poland, Tadeusz's companions convinced him to break with his normal practice. Now, instead of travelling through the countryside parallel to the road, they walked along the road itself. This made their journey easier, but much more risky.

After a few miles they came upon a Soviet roadblock. A sentry stopped them and they were all arrested. Shortly afterwards Tadeusz was sentenced – without a trial – to fifteen years' hard labour. His two companions were also imprisoned, one of them the professor who had previously evaded the Nazis. Tadeusz came to the conclusion, as a result of his experience, that 'Communism is the worst disease the world ever had.'[54]

Like Tadeusz Ruman, Gustaw Herling was arrested in 1940 as he tried to cross the border – in his case the one between Soviet-occupied Poland and Lithuania. He was twenty years old at the time, and a committed member of the Polish resistance. After he had received a sentence of five years' incarceration, he was transported across the Soviet Union to a labour camp outside Archangel that was part of the infamous Gulag system.

Two of Gustaw Herling's experiences once he was in the camp allow us to make a striking comparison with the suffering of his fellow Poles in Nazi concentration camps. The first relates to Herling's observations about the Urkas – the criminal gangs who were imprisoned alongside the political prisoners in the Gulag. The Soviet authorities used these Urkas as a terrifying method of supervision and control. Herling described the Urka as 'the most important person after the commander of the guard' because 'he judges the working capacity and the political orthodoxy of the prisoners in his brigade.'[55] Moreover, 'no guard would have dared to show himself inside the barracks after dark, even when the horrible moans and cries of political prisoners who were being slowly murdered [by the Urkas] could be heard all over the camp.'[56]

Herling first encountered the Urkas on the train to the Gulag. After one of them had lost a game of cards, he approached another prisoner, a Polish officer, and demanded that the Pole hand over his coat. The Urka said that he had 'lost it [the officer's coat] at cards'. When the officer seemed reluctant to give the coat up, the Urka threatened to 'poke' his 'eyes out'. In the face of these threats, the Polish officer surrendered his coat. Herling discovered that a common pastime of the Urkas was to gamble with other prisoners' belongings. After the game was over, the Urka that lost had to steal – using violence if necessary – whatever had been staked.[57]

The use by the Soviet authorities of these criminals to control and intimidate political prisoners mirrors in many ways the decision by the Nazis to employ German Kapos in Auschwitz concentration camp in occupied Poland. The very first prisoners sent to Auschwitz in late spring 1940 were not Poles, but thirty German criminals, transferred from Sachsenhausen concentration camp north of Berlin. These Kapos led work details and effectively had the power of life and death over those in their particular work 'commando'. Some became notorious for their cruelty, like Ernst Krankemann who ran the penal commando. Prisoners under his control had to pull a giant roller through the camp, flattening the ground, while Krankemann sat on the harness of the roller, armed with a whip. Jerzy Bielecki, a Polish political prisoner, witnessed how Krankemann ordered the prisoners to use the roller to crush one of their comrades who had collapsed from exhaustion. 'I had got used to seeing death and beatings,' said Bielecki, 'but what I saw then just made me cold. I just froze.'[58]

If Kapos in any of the Nazi camps ever stepped out of line, then they knew their fate. As Himmler put it: 'As soon as we are no longer satisfied with him, he is no longer a kapo, and returns to the other inmates. He knows that they will beat him to death his first night back.'[59]

In the Gulag, the use by the Soviet authorities of the Urkas as a tool of oppression was never as institutionalized as that of the Kapos in the Nazi camps. Nonetheless the Urkas terrorized the inmates in similar ways. And just as the Kapos spared the SS from much of the dirty work of controlling and disciplining the rest of the prisoners, so the Urkas performed the same function for the Soviet guards.

The second comparison between the Nazis and Soviets that Herling's experiences offer us is similar to the one that Margarete Buber-Neumann observed.[60] Herling recognized that the penal system in the Soviet Union was designed 'not to punish the criminal, but rather to exploit him economically and transform him psychologically'. The whole process aimed at the 'complete disintegration' of the prisoner's 'personality'. Crucially, wrote Herling, a 'prisoner is considered to have been sufficiently prepared for the final achievement of the signature [on his confession] only when his personality has been thoroughly dismantled into its component parts.' This aim was accomplished largely by forcing the prisoner to agree with the lies that the interrogator propagated. As a consequence, said Herling, 'Gaps appear in the logical association of ideas; thoughts and emotions become loosened in their original positions and rattle against each other like the parts of a broken-down machine . . .'[61]

One of the original aims of the Nazi concentration camps was similar, since the SS sought to change the mentality of the inmates. As Hermann Göring disingenuously put it, 'We had to rescue these people, to bring them back to the German national community. We had to re-educate them.'[62] A vital part of this process of 're-education' was making the prisoners understand that the SS had absolute power over their future. For Nazi concentration camps were not 'normal' prisons where the inmates served a sentence determined by a judge. On the contrary, no one sent to a concentration camp ever knew how long his or her imprisonment would last. 'The uncertainty of the duration of their confinement was something with which they could never come to terms,' wrote Rudolf Höss, Commandant of Auschwitz, in his memoirs after the war. 'It was this that wore them down and broke the strongest wills . . . On this account alone their life in camp was a torment.'[63] Höss was referring to the practice in pre-war concentration camps like Dachau, where – though the SS killed some prisoners – the majority were released after serving an average of around eighteen months in the camp.

Auschwitz, from the outset more murderous than Dachau, was first conceived along much the same lines as the pre-war German camps. Before Auschwitz became an instrument of mass extermination, part of its function, at least in the minds of the authorities in the camp, was to demonstrate to the Poles that the Germans were now their masters. In the process of that 're-education' over half of the 23,000 Poles initially sent to Auschwitz were dead within twenty months.[64]

In the Gulag, even though the prisoners were given a determinate sentence, this could be altered at any time. One of the most heartbreaking episodes described by Herling relates to the experience of an 'old railwayman from Kiev, called Ponomarenko', who had been counting down the days of his ten-year sentence, only to be told just before his supposed release that he was now to be held 'indefinitely'. Shortly after he received the news he killed himself. He had discovered, as Herling put it, that 'hope contains the terrible danger of disappointment.'[65]

There were also key differences between the Nazi concentration camps and the Gulag during this period. The most important was the contrast in ideological approach. The Nazis were seeking to 'reorder' Poland according to their racial theories. Though they might think that some of the Poles they sent to Auschwitz in 1940 could be terrorized into not causing them trouble again, they believed that these Poles could never be altered sufficiently to become anything other than obedient slaves. According to the Nazis, the essential precondition for real change was outside any individual's control: the blood that flowed in your veins was the decisive factor in determining your worth. Deadly consequences followed from this belief. Friendly contact between Germans and Poles was banned, and any sexual interaction was considered particularly abhorrent. Polish men who had sex with German women were imprisoned or executed.[66] As for German men who had sex with Polish women, 'In serious cases,' ordered Gauleiter Arthur Greiser in the Warthegau, 'especially when an individual belonging to the German community has seriously injured the German interests of the Reich by relations with Poles, he will be transferred to a concentration camp.'[67]

In contrast, the Soviets focused their attack on the Poles on class, not race. Nikolai Dyukarev, the NKVD officer involved in deporting Poles, put it this way: 'Of course there were different [sorts of] people [in eastern Poland]. We cannot treat the population as a whole. There were rich people, there were poor people, there were cities and there were small villages. For the rich people there was nothing good in it [the Soviet occupation] of course, but for the poor people I think we did improve something and we improved their life.'[68] And while it's arguable how much the invasion of eastern Poland improved anyone's life, it remains significant that this is how Dyukarev perceived the role of the Soviet occupiers. He and many of his comrades believed their task was to take from the rich and give to the poor. Or as they would have said at the time, they wanted to redress the perceived imbalance between the bourgeoisie and the proletariat.

Another difference between the respective occupation policies was the way in which the two leaders, Hitler and Stalin, sought to control what was happening on the ground. In Poland, while Hitler set the broad vision, the detail of policy implementation was left to his Gauleiters. In what was one of the most insightful statements of his leadership technique, Hitler told them that they 'had ten years to tell him that the Germanization of their provinces was complete, and he would ask no questions about their methods'.[69] He recognized that 'mistakes are inevitable,' but that was a small price to pay for a successful programme of Germanization carried out by 'a new type of man, a race of rulers, a breed of viceroys'.[70]

Hitler's desire to allow his 'race of rulers' in Poland the chance to exercise their own personal initiative led to confusion and chaos. The infighting between two neighbouring Gauleiters, Albert Forster of Danzig–West Prussia and Arthur Greiser of the Warthegau, became notorious, with Greiser accusing Forster of 'Germanizing' Poles without the necessary care in order to complete the process quickly.[71]

Stalin, by contrast, permitted no such initiatives. Not only did he personally read the principal documents and endorse the details of any policy, but a shrewd courtier like Lavrenti Beria of the NKVD learnt to start many documents to Stalin with the words 'in connection with your instructions',[72] thus giving the impression that he was merely an instrument of Stalin's will.

This method of governance meant that Stalin's name is on an infamous document in 1940 ordering the murder of many thousands of Poles. The background to this crime was the imprisonment of around a quarter of a million captured Polish soldiers after the occupation of eastern Poland. The officers were separated from their men and incarcerated in special camps, along with selected members of the intelligentsia from eastern Poland. These officers were never considered to be prisoners of war. Instead they were treated as 'counter-revolutionaries'.

During the last months of 1939 they were questioned and attempts were made to get them to convert to the Soviet cause. But most, according to NKVD interrogators, were incorrigible. As a consequence, Stalin – along with several other members of the Politburo, including

Molotov – signed a document on 5 March 1940 which called for the prisoners to be 'examined by special procedure' and, if still thought objectionable, to be shot. The 'special procedure' turned out in most cases to be merely a swift read of their file. Only a few hundred of more than 20,000 people targeted by this order survived.[73]

Why Stalin took this drastic step has never been conclusively explained. Perhaps his hatred of Poland finally erupted and he decided he would kill the Polish elite rather than continue to incarcerate them. Or maybe he knew of and admired the brutal policies the Nazis were pursuing in their section of Poland. We can't be sure. What we do know is that he was responsible for ordering the crime. Soviet documents show that nearly 22,000 people were murdered as a result of this decision. The killings were spread across three killing sites, one of which was the Katyn forest.

Hitler signed no such document in connection with the Poles or the subsequent extermination of the Jews.[74] The 'visionary' system of government over which he presided meant he didn't have to. But he was just as responsible for his crimes as Stalin was for Katyn, although in Hitler's case the guilt has to be demonstrated – as it conclusively has been by numerous historians – without the help of such obviously incriminating evidence.

During their ideologically driven reorganization of Poland, Hitler and Stalin caused the suffering of millions of people. But ambitious and far-reaching as these policies were, their prime focus – as we shall see – was elsewhere.

3. Opposite Fortunes

Two surprising events in the first year of the war offer us an important insight into the difference between Hitler's and Stalin's leadership. Each of the dictators launched an ambitious military action, and while one was an extraordinary triumph, the other was a national embarrassment.

Stalin's military adventure was directed against Finland. In theory this should have been the easiest of missions for the Red Army. Not only was Finland tiny compared to the Soviet Union – fewer than four million Finns compared to more than 160 million Soviet citizens[1] – but the Red Army was immensely more powerful than Finnish forces, bene-fiting from a huge expansion during the 1930s. By 1939, for example, Soviet factories were producing more than 10,000 planes a year, com-pared to less than a thousand in 1931. During the same period tank production increased fourfold.[2]

The problem for Stalin was that human beings were needed to oper-ate all this equipment, and he was predisposed to distrust them. In particular, he feared that a talented general might launch a counter-revolution against his rule. There was historical precedent for just such an event. Had not the French Revolution been subverted by an ambi-tious soldier called Napoleon Bonaparte? As a consequence, to accuse a Soviet commander of Bonapartist tendencies was to call him a traitor to the Bolshevik cause. And the question that was in Stalin's mind was just how many potential Bonapartists were out there?

In addition to that constant anxiety, Stalin's adversary Leon Trotsky was not only alive and well during the 1930s but publishing attacks on the Soviet leader from the apparent safety of the west. Trotsky had helped create the Red Army, and had been appointed People's Commissar of Army and Navy Affairs in March 1918. To a man like Stalin, liable to be suspicious even when there was no cause to be suspicious, this was good reason to distrust any number of Soviet commanders.

On top of all this, Stalin knew that he was replaceable. How could he not be aware of this disturbing fact, when as he looked out over Red

Square he saw the granite mausoleum of the true creator of the revolution, Vladimir Lenin? Stalin, like Trotsky and all the other leading Bolsheviks, had merely been a follower of Lenin. And followers are never indispensable. Only Lenin lived on for ever, lying embalmed in his necropolis just yards from Stalin's office. Hitler, of course, never had this problem, because he, like Lenin, had led the revolution himself.

In the late 1930s, all of Stalin's suspicions suddenly erupted, and he instigated a bloodletting that would become known as the Great Terror. He had always believed that establishing communism would be 'a complicated, long and violent process . . . a struggle, a painful and a cruel struggle, a life-and-death struggle'.[3] But the killings he now authorized were without precedent in a modern state.

Though the repression was not confined to the armed forces, military leaders were particularly targeted. Out of nearly 145,000 officers, more than one in five — 33,000 — were dismissed from their posts and 7,000 of this number were subsequently murdered. The further up the chain of command, the greater the proportionate destruction, with more than 150 of the top commanders removed — over 80 per cent of the total.[4]

Most notoriously, Marshal Mikhail Tukhachevsky was arrested in May 1937 and executed the following month. Tukhachevsky had been instrumental in modernizing the Red Army during the 1930s, but his brilliance as a military theorist, combined with his overconfident personality, led to his downfall. Ominously, Stalin had referred to him as a Napoleonchik, a 'little Napoleon'.[5] Like many of his fellow officers, Tukhachevsky had been tortured into 'confessing'. His statement of 'guilt' was subsequently found to be stained with blood.[6]

Stalin's destruction of much of the Soviet officer corps was not the only cause of the disaster that was to follow. Other factors, such as the way in which the army had been modernized, especially the bizarre decision not to embrace wholeheartedly techniques of communication such as radios, also played a part. But the persecution of military commanders was the main reason why the Soviet forces were so damaged. Even the officers left alive were rendered less effective by the bloodletting. Not only had many of their most talented colleagues disappeared, but the officers that survived realized that initiative and fresh thinking were now potentially fatal attributes.

For example, it was inevitable that during the testing of new military equipment accidents could happen. But now — according to Stepan

Mikoyan, a pilot in the Soviet Air Force – it could be said that any crashes were 'due to saboteurs . . . then you could be accused of not having taken the correct precautions, of being thoughtless, of being a bad manager and thus not "one of us"'. The atmosphere of suspicion was so pervasive that people totally unconnected with the incident could be accused. 'There were cases when someone held a grudge against someone else and wanted revenge,' said Mikoyan. 'He could simply report him: "This man did this incorrectly and badly because he's an enemy."'

There remained, for those dealing directly with Stalin, the challenge of telling him bad news about a military test without being blamed for it oneself. Such people, said Mikoyan, 'always had to bear in mind that they were taking Stalin's line on something. And if they had to communicate with him directly, then [you had] always to tell the truth, but at the same time in such a way that you didn't make him angry!'[7]

Mark Gallay, a young test pilot in the 1930s, also remembered the 'heavy and oppressive effect' of the purges. 'Literally two or three times a week . . . we'd gather for meetings where we mostly discussed the so-called enemies of the people.' At these meetings one or more people would be denounced, sometimes even 'someone present in the room'. But, he said, the vast majority were undoubtedly innocent.

Not surprisingly, according to Gallay, this atmosphere did 'not do good to a person's productivity and creativity. Whatever is oppressive binds a person's initiative.' Gallay was a devoted communist – 'for many years after that, I continued to believe the teachings of Lenin to be invincible and totally justified' – but what he witnessed during the terror convinced him that Stalin 'did colossal harm to the country, at every level, in every sphere, for many years afterwards'.[8]

In this atmosphere of suspicion, one in which talent was undervalued and blind loyalty prized, some truly terrible military commanders were able to prosper. Chief among them was Kliment Voroshilov. An uneducated, unsophisticated former manual worker who liked to drink, Voroshilov was made People's Commissar for Defence in 1934 and enthusiastically supported Stalin during the Great Terror. Tukhachevsky, who worked for Voroshilov, despised him. Another Red Army commander considered that Voroshilov was a 'dilettante in military matters and never knew them deeply and seriously'.[9] Yet Stalin never turned on Voroshilov, who died peacefully in 1969 at the age of eighty-eight. Incompetence was not necessarily a hindrance to high office in the Soviet state. Indeed, it could be a blessing, since a genuinely incompetent general could never be a Napoleonchik.

In October 1939, just one year after the Great Terror had subsided, Stalin decided to confront the Finnish government. He was motivated by one factor above all – geography. As far as he was concerned, Finland was just too close to the Soviet border. Finnish territory, at the time, lay just 20 miles or so away from Leningrad (today called St Petersburg), the Soviet Union's second city and birthplace of the revolution. What if the Germans, or even the western Allies, formed an alliance with the Finns and threatened to invade? It would be easy for an enemy to attack the Soviet Union from Finland. Leningrad might fall in days – its vulnerability obvious to the world.

Molotov invited a Finnish delegation to Moscow for discussions in early October. The Soviets had recently bullied representatives of the Baltic States into agreeing to Red Army bases on their territory. Now it was Finland's turn to be threatened. However, it was not clear that Stalin saw the Finnish case as exactly analogous with the Baltic ones. In the case of the Baltic States, Stalin's demand for Red Army bases turned out to be the first step in total domination – in 1940 the Soviets would move to occupy all of this territory. But Stalin's interest in the Finns seems to have been different. He did not appear to crave the total occupation of Finland.

There were two major differences – once again geographical – between the Finnish situation and that of the Baltic States. To the west of the Baltic States lay the sea, to the east the Soviet Union. The Baltic people were thus trapped. But to the west of Finland lay a lengthy land border with Sweden, a country that had remained neutral during the war. And even though the population of Finland was small, its land area unlike the Baltic States' was large. So why would Stalin want the Red Army to occupy this desolate wasteland? What need did the Soviets have for mile upon mile of forest? They had all the trees they required in Siberia. Much better, Stalin likely thought, to force the Finns into handing over sufficient territory adjacent to the Soviet border so that Leningrad could be protected.

At the first meeting with the Finnish representatives in Moscow, Stalin was straightforward, and apparently honest, in his request. 'We cannot do anything about the geographical situation,' he said.

'Leningrad and its surroundings have about 3.5 million inhabitants, almost as many as Finland. Since we cannot relocate Leningrad, we have to move the border.'[10] Stalin and Molotov wanted this new border to be almost 40 miles further back inside Finland. They also wanted the Finns to give up other territory, including several islands in the Gulf of Finland. In compensation, the Soviets offered to exchange some territory in Eastern Karelia. This amounted to nearly twice as much land as the Finns were losing. But strategically and economically the land the Soviets were prepared to give up was of little value.

During the ensuing negotiations the Finns tried to bargain with Stalin, but never came close to offering him what he'd asked for, even after he slightly moderated his own demands. Eventually, when they arrived for a meeting on 3 November, the Finns were confronted in the Kremlin just by Molotov. Stalin's absence was a bad sign.

Molotov, as we shall see later in this history, was never able to make a deal of substance on his own. Without Stalin present, his default position in diplomatic discussions was either to ask a lengthy series of detailed questions or simply to repeat the Soviet position over and over again. As the Yugoslav politician Milovan Djilas observed, Molotov was 'impotent without Stalin's leadership' and 'his mentality remained sealed and inscrutable.'[11]

Understandably, negotiations with Molotov went nowhere, and the Finns prepared to leave Moscow. But just before they left, on 4 November, they were called back to the Kremlin. This time they faced not just Molotov but Stalin as well. The Soviet leader made one last attempt to reach an agreement and toned down his demands still further.[12] But the Finns once again refused an accommodation. While they were prepared to give up some territory, their own concessions were insufficient to satisfy the Soviets. The Finnish delegation finally left Moscow on 9 November.

Given what was to happen, it seems surprising that the Finns did not manage to come to an arrangement with Stalin. On the face of it the Soviets appeared sincere, although we can never know for sure whether Stalin did ultimately desire to take the whole of Finland. But, significantly, there had been no such lengthy negotiations with representatives from the Baltic States. Nor had there been discussions with them about altering the borders. The Soviets had bluntly insisted on placing military bases on their territory.

Some leading Finns thought that a deal should be done with Stalin. Most notably Marshal Carl Gustaf Mannerheim, who had played a key part in securing Finland's independence at the end of the First World War. Mannerheim was one of the most remarkable figures of the twentieth century – not as well known outside Finland as he deserves to be, the penalty no doubt for belonging to an underpopulated country on the periphery of Europe. When he was a young man Finland had been part of the Russian Empire and, coming from an aristocratic background, he joined the Imperial Russian Army, rising to become a lieutenant general in 1917. After the October Revolution he led Finnish forces against the Bolsheviks and subsequently served as Regent of Finland until losing the first election for the presidency of Finland in 1919.

When Finnish politicians consulted Mannerheim about the Soviet proposals he advised them to reach a settlement. But his advice was rejected. He was now an old man of seventy-two, and perhaps his fellow countrymen thought he had lost the will to confront Stalin. But Mannerheim spoke a great deal of sense. Finland could never win a fight against the Soviet Union.

The Finns who opposed Stalin's demands sought to protect themselves with hope and motivate themselves with fear. They hoped that Stalin's talk was just bluster. Would he really want to start another war at such a delicate moment in his country's history? Even if he did, they hoped that the Finns wouldn't have to confront Stalin on their own. Perhaps Germany or Britain or their neighbour Sweden would offer them help. They also feared that, even if they gave Stalin everything he wanted, this would not be the end of the matter. This was certainly the view of Lieutenant General Harald Öhquist, a Finnish commander, after he'd looked at the Soviet proposal. He thought that 'No officer with modern training could take seriously' what was requested. 'More likely,' he said, 'what they are demanding now is only the preparation for further, far-reaching demands.'[13]

While, as we have seen, it's impossible to be certain whether Öhquist's fears were justified, what is clear is that the Soviets gave every indication of being surprised that the Finns would not accept their proposals. Nikita Khrushchev, the leading Ukrainian communist, thought 'it would be enough to tell them [the Finns] loudly that if they didn't listen, we would fire one shot from our cannons, and then the Finns would throw up their hands and agree to our demands.'[14] In London, the Soviet

Ambassador, Ivan Maisky, was also shocked that the Finns had not signed an agreement with Stalin, telling Lord Halifax on 27 November 1939 that the Finns were not prepared to face up to 'reality' and lived in 'a world of incomprehensible fantasy'.[15]

Although a Soviet military offensive against the Finns had been planned in principle, it had not been expected in reality. So Stalin now not only had to call for greater military preparation, but had to arrange a political contingency plan for Finland, to sit alongside the imminent military action. To that end he decided to make a Finnish communist called Otto Kuusinen head of the new 'democratic' Finland, a country that did not yet exist and which Stalin planned to create by defeating the Finns in battle.

This enabled *Pravda* to announce on 1 December, the day after the Red Army invaded Finland, that the Soviet Union was taking action because the new Finnish Democratic Republic, led by Otto Kuusinen, needed help to liberate the country from the current government. It was thus not necessary for the Soviet Union to declare war on Finland, since the new – and in Stalin's eyes 'legitimate' – government of Finland under Kuusinen had asked for assistance. Stalin subsequently announced that 'We have no desire for Finland's territory. But Finland should be a state that is friendly to the Soviet Union.'[16]

Stalin's words are important – or rather, one specific word: 'friendly'. This is the first time in this history that we have come across this particular adjective in the context of one of the countries in which the Soviets had an interest, but it will not be the last. Stalin was fond of saying that he wished relations with a particular state to be 'friendly'. The word sounds so innocuous, and yet it gave him the power to act as he wished. That's because 'friendliness' is impossible to define.

Stalin, unlike Hitler, was particularly fond of these vague concepts. No one knew, for instance, exactly what was meant by a 'kulak'. Was this specific peasant wealthy enough to be classed as a 'kulak' or not? It was all a matter of opinion. Similarly, Stalin never defined precisely what was meant by 'enemy of the people'. Beria's view, which he said came from Stalin, was simultaneously nebulous and yet potentially all encompassing. 'An enemy of the people is not only one who makes sabotage,' Beria told one of his colleagues in state security, 'but one who doubts the rightness of the party line. And there are a lot of them among us, and we must liquidate them.'[17]

How could anyone defend themselves against the charge that they had 'doubted the party line'? At what point did your constructive criticism of what was happening make you an 'enemy of the people'? It was this deliberate imprecision, something no state upholding the rule of law would tolerate, which meant that at the meetings Mark Gallay attended during the Great Terror anyone present could be denounced as an 'enemy of the people'. The absence of any legal definition meant that it was merely a matter of individual perception. No one could protect themselves from potential doom.

Meanwhile, Stalin was so confident that the Red Army could easily defeat the Finnish forces that he endorsed a strategy of a whole series of offensive thrusts into Finland, and so dissipated the power of the attack. He also took it for granted that the military action would be over quickly. When Nikolai Voronov, head of the artillery, suggested that the operation might last 'two or three months' he was told by a senior officer to 'base all your estimates on the assumption that the operation will last twelve days.'[18]

After a superficial analysis of the situation, Stalin and his fawning acolytes would have assumed that Finnish resistance would soon be crushed. The Finns were not just massively outnumbered – the Finnish Army was less than half the size of the Soviet invasion forces – but most of the Finns' equipment was antiquated and apparently no match for the modern Soviet hardware. But the Finns possessed one advantage in this fight, one the Soviets seem to have forgotten. For just as the reality of geography was the reason for Stalin's actions, so the reality of geography was now entirely on the Finnish side.

The Soviets faced two problems. First, Finland is not just huge but also one of the least populated countries in the world. This allowed the Finns to pull back and draw the Red Army into a wasteland of forest and snow. Second, and just as significant, most of Finland is flat. And since there were many more trees than people, this meant that as Soviet soldiers travelled along narrow roads through seemingly endless forest, all they could see were the trees that surrounded them. Paradoxically, even though they were in a large, relatively uninhabited country, they were liable to experience claustrophobia. 'Tall pines stand all together in the snow like paintings,' said Captain Shevenok, who fought with the Red Army in Finland. 'Above are branches and down below it is bare, as if you are standing not in groves but in some sort of grotto with pillars.'[19]

This problem was compounded by the fact that, unlike the Finns –
almost all of whom had been skiing since they were children – Soviet
soldiers felt uneasy if they left the road and ventured into the forest. In
addition, both Soviet equipment and uniforms were ill suited to the
Finnish climate. Soviet commanders had even neglected to issue sufficient white winter clothing for their troops and to camouflage the
trucks and tanks. As a consequence men and machines stood out easily
against the snow. In contrast, the Finnish soldiers wore camouflaged
winter-weather gear and were regularly supplied with warm food and
dry clothing. The Finns were also superbly led by Gustaf Mannerheim
who had volunteered to lead Finnish defence efforts as soon as the country was threatened.

The main Soviet force attacked as the Finns had expected, north-
west of Leningrad across the Karelian Isthmus, the territory that lay
between the Gulf of Finland and Lake Ladoga. Here the Red Army
quickly came up against fortifications known as the Mannerheim Line.
Cleverly constructed, using wherever possible natural barriers such as
forests and rivers, the Mannerheim Line proved a tough obstacle for the
Soviets. 'We can't even put our noses out of the trenches,' wrote Politruk Oreshin, who was with a Red Army unit fighting just north of the
main Finnish fortifications. 'Our men have launched several attacks
but have always been beaten back. The barbed wire is man-high. Tank
obstacles are everywhere. The marshes and splendidly camouflaged
posts around us make the Finns invulnerable.'[20]

However, it was in the middle of Finland, far from the Mannerheim
Line, that the brilliance of Finnish resistance would gain headlines
around the world. The Soviets had launched an offensive from the east
that was intended to split the country in two, from north to south. But
the difficulty the Soviets encountered was that the Finns decided not to
face them head on, but to attack them from the side as they travelled on
a single road through the wilderness of forest and snow. As a result, the
Finns managed to cut the first of the Red Army units, the 163rd Division, into a number of separate pieces, so that each was isolated from
the others.

Mikhail Timoshenko served in a unit attached to the 44th Division,
the force that was sent to rescue the 163rd. He and his comrades advanced
along a road through the forest 'so narrow that it was difficult for two
vehicles to pass each other ... Technically, it was impossible to

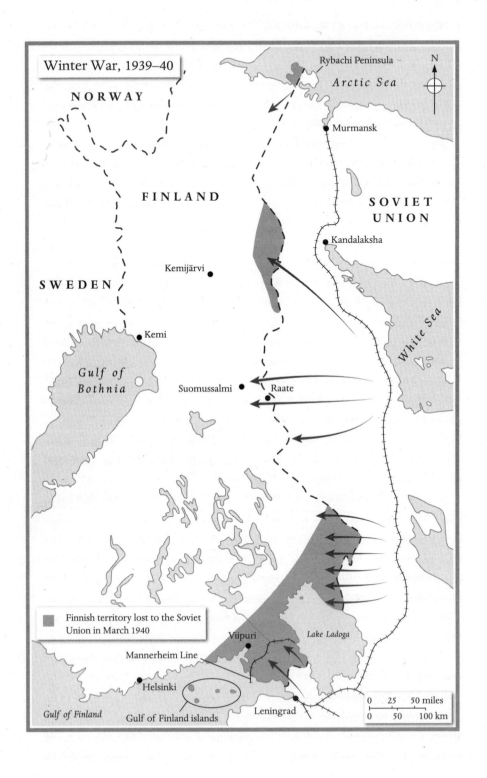

Winter War, 1939–40

NORWAY

Rybachi Peninsula

Arctic Sea

N

FINLAND

Murmansk

SOVIET UNION

SWEDEN

Kemijärvi

Kandalaksha

Kemi

White Sea

Gulf of Bothnia

Suomussalmi   Raate

Finnish territory lost to the Soviet Union in March 1940

Viipuri   *Lake Ladoga*

Mannerheim Line

Helsinki

Gulf of Finland   Gulf of Finland islands   Leningrad

0   25   50 miles

0   50   100 km

manoeuvre. It was even difficult on foot . . . It was like being in the jungle, you had to make a path for yourself. The artillery couldn't turn back, the armoured vehicles stayed where they were and just froze . . . So we realized that the higher command hadn't worked out any of this, there was no plan of action for our division, we'd simply been sent there to cope with whatever we saw.'

Because of the cold, the Red Army soldiers 'could only keep warm, dry their uniforms and prepare food by the bonfires . . . everything along the road was on fire. There were bonfires everywhere, continuous bonfires, as if the road [itself] was on fire . . . It looked to me as if the division was simply "burning" its way through the forest.' But there was an unintended consequence of the fires – they made Timoshenko and his comrades easily visible to the Finns concealed nearby.

'We understood that our army was very strong,' said Timoshenko, 'that it was unbeatable, that it was capable of truly huge feats. And when I saw what was going on there, I just couldn't understand it and nor could many of the officers. What were we meant to be doing, against whom were we meant to be fighting? There were no enemy soldiers. There was no front. There were no installations. There were simply these small groups of Finns who were impossible to catch . . . It was as if the forest itself was shooting at us.'

One night the soldiers were handed 'three or four cases of vodka . . . to give them strength. The soldiers were tired and freezing. They got drunk that evening. They cooked food in their mess-tins to drink with the vodka and then they fell asleep by the bonfires.' The next morning, Timoshenko saw that many had 'frozen to death'.

Timoshenko was certain who was responsible for this disaster: 'The main cause was, without a doubt, the ineptitude of the command. All the soldiers and officers who were there were people devoted to the homeland, the type of people who did their duty conscientiously. But the conditions that had been created for them didn't allow them to carry out their duty honourably.'[21]

The commander of the 44th Division, Alexei Vinogradov, was subsequently held responsible and shot, along with a number of his comrades. But Timoshenko did not blame his own leaders for the catastrophe: 'we knew that none of those men were guilty, none of the officers, nor the division commander . . . nor the commander of the regiment and a few of the others who were punished.' The guilt, as far as he was concerned, lay with those who had sent the soldiers into Finland with equipment ill suited for the task, and who had forced them to abide by such a flawed plan of attack.

However, although Mikhail Timoshenko loyally defended his commander, it was evident that Vinogradov's leadership of the 44th Division was weak. It's questionable whether he made a concerted effort to reach the 163rd Division trapped ahead of him, and he may even have panicked under fire.[22] But it's also the case that the troops of the 44th Division were asked to perform a task for which none had been properly trained. How, for instance, could they pursue and capture the Finns in this snow-filled wilderness when virtually none of the Soviet soldiers could ski?

The battle of Suomussalmi, as the encounter between the Finnish forces and the Soviet 163rd and 44th Divisions became known, was the most famous Finnish victory of the war. Fewer than 12,000 Finnish troops had vanquished an enemy that was four times their size. It was a triumph that fired the imagination of the west. The Americans, for instance, embraced the idea of the gallant and outnumbered Finns fighting on their skis against the brute force of the Bolshevik machine (a romantic notion that reflected only part of the reality, since most of the fighting was on the Mannerheim Line, where dashing skiers were not much in evidence). A national Finland Day was announced in America for 17 December 1939 and a well-known preacher, Henry Emerson Fosdick, wrote a special prayer to be said for the Finns, which included the lines 'We ask for mercy, human and divine, on the people of Finland . . . The families that ruthless violence puts in jeopardy, may our generosity assist; and the hapless victim of hunger and homelessness, may our plenty supply.' There was even a pro-Finland rally in Madison Square Garden in New York on 20 December attended by 15,000 people.[23]

In Britain the enthusiasm for the Finns was almost as great. Not only were there calls in the press to provide assistance to the Finns, but Winston Churchill spoke in a broadcast on 20 January 1940 in almost mythic terms about the example the Finns were setting for the world. 'Only Finland – superb, nay, sublime – in the jaws of peril – Finland shows what free men can do,' said Churchill, who was now back in the government as First Lord of the Admiralty. 'The service rendered by Finland to mankind is magnificent. They have exposed, for all the world to see, the military incapacity of the Red Army and of the Red Air Force. Many illusions about Soviet Russia have been dispelled in these few fierce weeks of fighting in the Arctic Circle. Everyone can see how Communism rots the soul of a nation; how it makes it abject and hungry in peace, and proves it base and abominable in war.'[24] It's also important to note how this narrative of the outnumbered 'free men' of Finland defending themselves valiantly against Bolshevik aggression confirmed the pre-existing views held by senior figures in the British administration that Stalin's armed forces were of little practical value.[25]

All this was a major problem for the Soviets. Stalin had imagined a swift, surgical strike against the Finns both to punish them for their intransigence and to force them to accede to Soviet territorial demands. Instead, the Red Army was suffering humiliation before the world. It was clear that the longer the war dragged on, the more dangerous the situation would become. What if the Americans and British sent not just financial and military aid to Finland but actual troops? What would then become of Stalin's policy of sitting out the war and letting the enemies of Bolshevism fight against each other?

In London, Ivan Maisky, the Soviet Ambassador, understood this threat all too well. Less than two weeks into the war, on 12 December 1939, he wrote that the lack of Soviet progress in the war was resulting in a 'frenzied anti-Soviet campaign' in Great Britain.[26] Two months later, in February, he was even more concerned, saying that he feared that the Soviet Union might be 'drawn into a major war'.[27]

Stalin faced another difficulty. His political scheme to pretend that this was a 'liberation' had been exposed as a cynical ploy. Almost no Finn rushed to embrace the new 'democratic' government of Finland led by Otto Kuusinen. Notwithstanding Finland's tradition of working-class socialism, when it came to a choice between Stalin's puppet and the nationalist – but aristocratic – Gustaf Mannerheim, the Finns found the decision easy to make.

According to Khrushchev, Stalin was 'furious' about the failure of the Finnish campaign. 'Those were dreadful months', wrote Khrushchev, 'from the point of view of both our losses and our long-term prospects . . . A feeling of alarm grew in the Soviet leadership . . . It was as though the halo of invincibility around the Red Army had been dimmed.' The glaring question recent events raised was: 'If we can't deal with the Finns, and we obviously have a much more powerful enemy [in Hitler], how in the world are we going to deal with him?'[28]

Stalin ordered Marshal Semyon Timoshenko to rethink the Finnish campaign and attack in greater numbers on a narrower front – the very strategy the Soviet dictator had rejected just weeks before. Tactics changed as well. Earlier in the campaign Soviet tanks had often become detached from the infantry that attacked with them, making them vulnerable to mobile units of Finns armed with explosive devices. Now, in one of the first signs that the Soviets were learning from bitter battlefield experience, the tanks would stay close to the infantry.

In early February 1940, after a gigantic artillery bombardment, the Soviets began their new offensive. Given the power and focus of the Soviet assault, it was inevitable that the Finns would struggle to cope. On 9 March, Mannerheim ordered General Erik Heinrichs to approach Finnish commanders and ask them to assess the viability of their units. Heinrichs' subsequent report was blunt: 'the present state of the army is such that continued military operations can lead to nothing but further debilitation and fresh losses of territory . . . The commander of the Second Army Corps, Lieutenant General Öhquist, has expressed the opinion that if no surprises take place, his present front may last a week, but no longer, depending upon how the personnel, especially the officer corps, is used. The commander of the Third Army Corps, Major General Talvela, expressed his view by saying that everything is hanging by a thread.'[29]

Both the British and French offered military help to the Finns at this desperate point, but it was uncertain just how serious the offers were. One vital question was the practical ability of the western Allies to deliver any aid, since the Swedes would not allow foreign forces to cross Swedish territory and compromise their neutrality.

Having considered their limited options, the Finns decided they had to negotiate a peace treaty with the Soviets, and the war finally came to an end on 13 March 1940. In the final agreement the Finns were forced to give up more territory to the Soviets than Stalin had originally demanded. But, notwithstanding this 'victory' for the Red Army, an element of humiliation still remained. How could it have taken the Soviets so long to crush such a small nation? And why did it take so many Soviet lives – well over 100,000 – to accomplish that goal?

Stalin had been preparing scapegoats even while the war was taking place. Chief among these was his faithful toady Marshal Voroshilov. But – incredibly – as Stalin lambasted him over dinner for the performance of the Red Army in Finland, the normally acquiescent Voroshilov suddenly snapped and confronted him. 'You are to blame for this,' he said. 'It was you who destroyed our military cadres.' After Stalin had argued back, Voroshilov picked up a plate on which lay 'a boiled suckling pig' and 'smashed it against the table'.[30]

It was a remarkable scene. Few people ever dared to confront Stalin, and even fewer survived the encounter. But while Voroshilov was sacked as Commissar for Defence, he was only shoved to the periphery and sidelined, not murdered. He seems to have been one of only a handful of people that Stalin actually felt something for – perhaps just a faint glimmer of affection. There may well have been qualities in this incompetent soldier that Stalin found amusing. Most essential of all, he was never any threat.

There remained the question of what to do with the sham Finnish government led by Otto Kuusinen. The very existence of this bogus administration had complicated the peace negotiations, since the Soviets had ultimately been forced to make a deal with the real Finnish government – the one they had maintained since the start of the war was illegitimate. Stalin's solution was to create a new republic of the Soviet Union, one that merged some of the territory gained from the Finns with existing Soviet land. Kuusinen was then appointed leader of this latest Soviet construct, which was called the Karelo-Finnish Republic.

Kuusinen knew from personal experience how dangerous it could be to hold a prominent position under Stalin. When his wife and son were arrested on a pretext, he pleaded with Stalin to help, only for the Soviet leader to reply that he could do nothing because many of his own relatives had been detained as well. This comment was probably an example of Stalin's sense of humour.[31]

Many Germans took the war as evidence that the Red Army was no match for the Wehrmacht. Typical were the remarks of Joseph Goebbels, who wrote in his diary on 11 November 1939, 'Russia's Army is not worth much. Poorly led and even more poorly equipped.'[32] The following month he recorded, 'Moscow is still not making any progress in Finland. Embarrassing situation!'[33]

However, Goebbels was also aware of a difficulty that had occurred as a result of the Soviet invasion of Finland. 'The German Volk is completely disposed to be pro-Finnish,' he wrote on 6 December. 'We should not allow this to spring up.'[34] A report by the SD, the intelligence arm of the SS, also confirmed that while 'Finland's attitude is described as unwise and incomprehensible . . . people frequently feel sorry for the Finnish people'.[35] This was a problem for the Nazis because Finland had been allocated to Stalin's 'sphere of influence' under the secret protocol to the non-aggression pact.

Hitler, however, was not one of those who felt sorry for the Finnish people. He held a grudge against the country, in part because he felt Germany's actions during the Finnish Civil War in early 1918 had never been properly acknowledged. He would later write, in a letter to Mussolini on 8 March 1940, that 'The Finnish state owes its existence entirely to a sea of blood from German soldiers, German regiments and divisions, and its subsequent independence is also due to German units . . .' and yet, 'In appreciation of this Finland later took sides against Germany on every occasion, and so far as it was possible took active part in every repressive measure against Germany.' Consequently, 'we have no cause to champion Finland's interests.'[36]

In order to counter the popular support for the Finns within Germany, Goebbels organized a propaganda blitz against them. The Nazis complained that the Finns had not welcomed 'joyfully' the appointment of Adolf Hitler as Chancellor. Instead, they had 'subjected almost every step towards German independence and every action of the Führer towards the removal of the Versailles Treaty to unscrupulous criticism'. Consequently, it was said in an article in the *Völkischer Beobachter*, 'It is at once naive and sentimental to expect that the German Volk in its struggle for its future shall suddenly support all the small states which previously were busy maligning and denouncing Germany . . . We reap what we sow.'[37]

But it does not appear that Hitler shared the view of Goebbels and others in Germany that events in Finland demonstrated the incompetence of the Red Army. In the letter he wrote to Mussolini on 8 March, Hitler said that he believed the Soviet Union (or Russia as he continued to call it) 'never intended to take up this fight, for otherwise she would have chosen a different season of the year; and in that event there is no doubt in my mind that Finnish resistance would have been broken very quickly. The criticisms which have been made of the Russian soldiers in consequence of the operations to date are not borne out, Duce [the Italian term for Mussolini as leader], by reality and the facts. During the World War we fought the Russians so long and so bitterly that we can permit ourselves an opinion on that. Taking into consideration the available supply facilities, no power in the world would have been able, except after the most thoroughgoing preparations, to achieve any other results at 30 to 40 degrees below zero [Centigrade] on such terrain than did the Russians at the very first.'[38]

This was a nuanced view. And while we cannot necessarily accept it at face value – Hitler might well have been pursuing his own agenda with Mussolini – it demonstrates that the German leader was aware that fighting in the bitter cold needed 'the most thoroughgoing preparations'. This was advice that he did not subsequently follow in his own war against the Soviet Union.

While the Red Army had been fighting the Finns, Hitler had been plotting a military campaign that dwarfed Stalin's in terms of both scale and impact. For he had decided to invade western Europe. To do so, naturally enough, he needed the cooperation of his military commanders, and it is here, in this relationship, that we can see a key difference between Stalin's and Hitler's leadership technique at this stage in the war. Partly this variation was to do with the character of each of the leaders, but it was also both cultural and structural.

To understand this fundamental dissimilarity between the two, first consider the distinct ways in which their ruthlessness functioned. Superficially, the willingness of both Stalin and Hitler to kill people who got in their way seems similar. When in 1934 Hitler had ordered the murder of the leader of the Nazi stormtroopers, Ernst Röhm, together with other opponents, Stalin had remarked, 'What a great fellow! How well he pulled this off!'[39] Stalin demonstrably felt a kinship with a fellow dictator who was prepared to eliminate those who stood against him – in this case around a hundred people in the Nazis' infamous 'Night of the Long Knives'.

But there is a crucial difference between Hitler's action in 1934 and Stalin's Great Terror later in the 1930s. It's not just a question of numbers – Stalin targeted many more people – it is the thinking behind the attacks. Hitler turned on Röhm reluctantly. In the end he acted only because he felt he had no alternative. Röhm threatened the delicate political arrangements Hitler had put in place, in particular his alliance with President von Hindenburg and Vice-Chancellor Franz von Papen. Worse, from Hitler's point of view, Röhm wanted the stormtroopers to rival the army as a military force, an idea that Hitler could not tolerate. He wanted to put his trust in trained soldiers, not in Röhm's beer-hall brawlers.

Unjust and murderous as the Night of the Long Knives undoubtedly was – especially for those like the wife of former Chancellor Kurt von Schleicher who was shot as she came to the aid of her husband – there was nonetheless a coherent strategy behind the action. It was one, moreover, that others at the time found rational in terms of both targets and scale. President von Hindenburg praised Hitler for the killings, saying that he had 'saved the German nation from serious danger',[40] and General Werner von Blomberg, the Minister of Defence, declared that Hitler had acted with 'outstanding courage'.[41]

Unlike Stalin, who had been part of a revolution that had dismantled the pre-existing structures of the state, Hitler was to a large extent still functioning within an established framework. While he had, for example, established concentration camps within weeks of coming to power in 1933, they operated in parallel to the existing German penal system. And even though he was committed to reshaping Germany based on his racist and anti-Semitic beliefs, he had not instigated a Stalin-like mass purge of the police or army to punish every individual who might previously have been against him.[42]

General von Blomberg was an avid supporter of Hitler, but there were other leading military figures who were not. General Ludwig Beck, for instance, who was Chief of Staff of the German Army for much of the 1930s, questioned in a note he wrote at the end of 1937 Hitler's signature policy of *Lebensraum*, the gaining of 'living space' in the east. He maintained that the Nazis had not 'thought through' the idea of trying to snatch land from others.[43] It's hard to imagine one of Stalin's military leaders questioning in writing any of the basic tenets of Bolshevism, and surviving.

Hitler did over time seek to replace those generals who were less than enthusiastic about his ideas, and – after a barrage of criticism from the German leader – Beck felt compelled to resign in the summer of 1938. But, significantly, Hitler did not have Beck imprisoned, tortured or executed. Instead Beck merely retired. Indeed, Hitler might, from his point of view, have been better off if he had treated Beck in a more Stalinesque manner, given that six years later Beck was one of the leading plotters in the July 1944 attempt on his life.

Some of Hitler's military commanders even felt able to criticize the actions of Nazi units in Poland. In the autumn of 1939, Johannes Blaskowitz, commander of the German Eighth Army, registered his profound opposition to the brutal treatment of Poles by the SS and other special forces. But even though Hitler railed against him, saying you could not fight a war with 'Salvation Army methods',[44] Blaskowitz still carried on serving in the army, although his career did not prosper as it might have done had he been more compliant.

However, the clearest example of how Hitler had to manage the military commanders around him in a way Stalin did not, was his attempt to persuade them that his vast ambitions were achievable. On 10 October 1939 he read a statement of his intentions to his leading commanders. He told them he wanted the army to prepare and execute, as swiftly as possible, the conquest of France and the Low Countries. His generals were appalled. Franz Halder, who had replaced Beck as Army Chief of Staff, recorded in his diary in early November that 'none of the higher Hq. [Headquarters]' thought that the proposed offensive 'has any prospect of success'.[45] Halder was so shocked that there is evidence that he might even have been plotting to remove Hitler. Just four days after the 10 October meeting at which the Führer had stated his military desires, Halder wrote in his diary, 'Three possibilities: attack, wait, change.' By 'change' it's almost certain Halder meant sidelining Hitler and removing him from the decision-making process, the fate Kaiser Wilhelm II had suffered during the First World War. Nothing like this happened under Stalin's rule. There was no conspiracy by his military leaders against him. As far as we know, all of the life-threatening 'plots' aimed at Stalin during the Great Terror were fictitious.

This does not mean that Hitler was somehow a weaker leader than Stalin, merely that he recognized the particular structural environment in which he operated. Indeed, one of the most revealing remarks that he ever made was 'My whole life can be summed up as this ceaseless effort of mine to persuade other people.'[46] And now he needed to gain the cooperation of his generals, a number of whom were not committed Nazis. While almost all of them approved of many of Hitler's broad aims, especially the rebuilding of the German armed forces and the 'righting' of the so-called 'wrongs' of the Versailles treaty, they were certainly not prepared to accept his plans without question. By whatever means, Hitler had to persuade them that the attack on France was the right way forward.

On 5 November 1939 Hitler met with Walther von Brauchitsch, the head of the army. Brauchitsch told him that the army was not prepared for an invasion of the west, and that the campaign against Poland had revealed a number of problems within the armed forces. He handed Hitler a memo which detailed his claims. He alleged that German soldiers had been 'over-cautious and insufficiently attack-minded' during the Polish invasion and that questions had been raised about discipline.[47]

Hitler was furious. He raged about the 'spirit of Zossen' (the army headquarters was based near the village of Zossen outside Berlin). It was a remark that could also be taken to mean that he suspected the loyalty of his senior officers. He vowed to eliminate this alleged negative attitude among the troops. If necessary, he said, he would travel to the front and question the soldiers himself. Then, in the most terrible fury, he left his office in the Reich Chancellery and slammed the door behind him. Brauchitsch – never the most resolute of men – was utterly shaken by the encounter and said afterwards that he wished to have nothing to do with any attempt to remove Hitler.[48]

Imagine how Stalin would have reacted to a meeting like this. Here was the head of the army objecting to a policy that was central to the leader's plans. Most likely Stalin would immediately have asked Beria to take the man away and torture him to reveal who else was behind this insubordination. Ironically, if at this point Hitler had taken that course of action he would probably have uncovered a genuine conspiracy, or at least the beginnings of one. But he did not act as Stalin would have. Instead he decided that he needed to make yet another effort to persuade his generals that he was right.

At midday on 23 November 1939, Hitler spoke at length to his Wehrmacht commanders at the Reich Chancellery. It was a remarkable oration, combining his own personal philosophy with the reasons behind his determination to launch an attack on the west. He claimed that 'the moment is favourable now' and that if the attack was delayed Germany's enemies would only get stronger. While Russia was currently 'not dangerous' there was no guarantee that this situation would last much longer. The pact with Russia meant nothing as treaties 'are kept [only] as long as they are useful'. But Russia could not be attacked before the danger from the west was eliminated. Hitler's logic was thus straightforward – first attack the west and then attack Russia.

Hitler referred obliquely to the meeting with Brauchitsch just over two weeks before, stating that he could not 'bear being told that the Army is not in good order . . . I can do everything with the German soldier when he is led well.' By implication, he compared the hesitant leadership of the General Staff with his own absolute determination to 'fight and fight again'. He added, 'In fighting I see the destiny of all beings. Nobody can escape fighting if he does not want to go under . . . Basically I did not set up the Wehrmacht in order not to strike. The decision to strike was always in me.' Moreover, since 'the fate of the Reich depends only on me' the time to act was now, before a successful attempt on his life could be made. All this led to his 'irrevocable' decision to attack France and Britain as soon as possible.[49]

Many of the generals who heard Hitler's speech understood it, as Hitler no doubt intended, as an attack on their lack of confidence in him. Fedor von Bock, who was to command Army Group B in the forthcoming operation, noted in his diary that 'the Führer knows that the bulk of the generals do not believe that attacking now will produce a decisive success.'[50]

The military commanders who opposed Hitler's plan were now in a difficult position. The consensus was that the attack on France was doomed, but almost all felt that removing Hitler was politically impossible. His popularity among the mass of the German people was high, especially in the wake of a failed attempt on his life made by Georg Elser at the Bürgerbräukeller on 8 November, just days before his speech to his generals. On 13 November the SD reported that Elser's actions had 'strengthened the notion of togetherness within the German population . . . [and] love for the Führer has grown even more'.[51]

The only way forward for the generals, it seemed, was to accept Hitler's decision. That meant searching for a miraculous way of defeating the western Allies in France and the Low Countries. In this respect Hitler was much more flexible than Stalin. He had made the 'unalterable' decision to attack the west – that choice could not be questioned. But he was prepared to listen to his military experts in order to find the best method of achieving this end. This was in direct contrast to the way Stalin had behaved over the Finnish operation. Stalin, as we have seen, had insisted on an invasion on a broad front and had dictated the way the invasion should be conducted, having previously purged the army of thousands of commanders and in the process demonstrated that anyone who showed initiative was a potential traitor.

Hitler, on the other hand, was excited by the possibility of military daring, and he didn't care who came up with a practical way of achieving his vision. Consequently, a radical plan did emerge – indeed, one of the most radical in the history of war. As is often the case with successful ideas, the authorship was subsequently disputed, with many people trying to claim credit. What's certain, though, is that General Erich von Manstein played an important part in the creation of the audacious new offensive.

Manstein argued that of the two forces that were to attack the west – Army Group A through the forest of Ardennes and Army Group B further north – greater emphasis should be placed on the former. The plan was that when Army Group B attacked, the Allies would believe this was the main force, one that was behaving in a logical and predictable way. Once battle commenced in the north, Army Group A would secretly make its way through the forest of the Ardennes, and then emerge and cross the River Meuse. Armoured units would subsequently head west across the plain of France to the sea, and trap Allied forces between the two German army groups and the English Channel.

It was a plan of immense audacity. If it succeeded the war in the west might be won in a matter of weeks, rather than degenerate into stalemate as it had in the trenches of the First World War. But the element of risk involved is impossible to overestimate. If the Allies discovered the German tanks as they lumbered through the narrow forest roads of the Ardennes, and destroyed them when they were at their most vulnerable, then at that very instant the Germans would almost certainly lose the war.

Hitler immediately championed the plan. The Manstein option appealed to his all-or-nothing approach. It also helped that the plan came from Manstein, who was one of a younger breed of commanders. Another was Heinz Guderian who in 1937 had written *Achtung – Panzer!* which called for the bold use of tanks in attack. Both Manstein and Guderian would become famous under Hitler's patronage. Unlike Stalin, Hitler was not afraid of promoting talent.

He had predicted, back in October 1939, that 'the systematic French and the clumsy English' would not be able to respond adequately to a swift, surprise attack.[52] Events were to prove Hitler right. That's because the main reason the Germans won in the west was the ponderous way in which the Allies reacted to the invasion. Contrary to popular myth, the Germans didn't possess superior equipment in this campaign. In fact, the British and French had more tanks than the Germans. The Germans just used theirs more imaginatively.

From Hitler's perspective there was another reason why he was confident of victory, one that demonstrates his heartlessness. Like Stalin, he was prepared to lose enormous numbers of dead in order to gain his objectives. 'The Führer said in my presence on 29 September', wrote the German diplomat Ernst von Weizsäcker, 'that this offensive might cost him a million soldiers, but that would be the same for the enemy [the British, the French and their allies], who could not bear the loss.'[53]

When the Germans attacked on 10 May 1940, the Allies responded in a predictable way. As the Germans had anticipated, the bulk of Allied forces moved north to confront the Wehrmacht in the Netherlands and Belgium. The Allies did not notice that seven German divisions were advancing in four columns in the south, on winding roads through the forests of Belgium and Luxembourg. Each of these columns was strung out for miles – an easy target for Allied air power.[54] But the Allies did not react to this incursion until too late. The Germans managed to burst out of the forest intact, and by 14 May had crossed the Meuse, the last natural obstacle before a clear run across the centre of France. When he heard what had happened, the French General Alphonse-Joseph Georges broke down and cried.[55] Early the next morning, Prime Minister Paul Reynaud of France rang Winston Churchill, who had been appointed the leader of the British government just days before. 'We have been defeated,' said Reynaud. 'We are beaten; we have lost the battle.'[56]

That same day, 15 May, the Soviet Ambassador to London asked Lloyd George, who had been Prime Minister of Britain during the First World War, if he thought the Allies would lose this new conflict. After complaining that the Ambassador put the question 'too brutally', Lloyd George replied, 'The Allies cannot win the war.' The best they could hope for was to attempt to contain the Germans for the next few months and 'then see'.[57]

By 20 May, just ten days after the attack had been launched, units of Army Group A reached the English Channel and the mouth of the River Somme. Allied soldiers were now trapped. They fell back on Dunkirk, and though more than 300,000 troops were rescued, their military equipment was almost all left behind.

The Germans had just won the largest encirclement battle in the

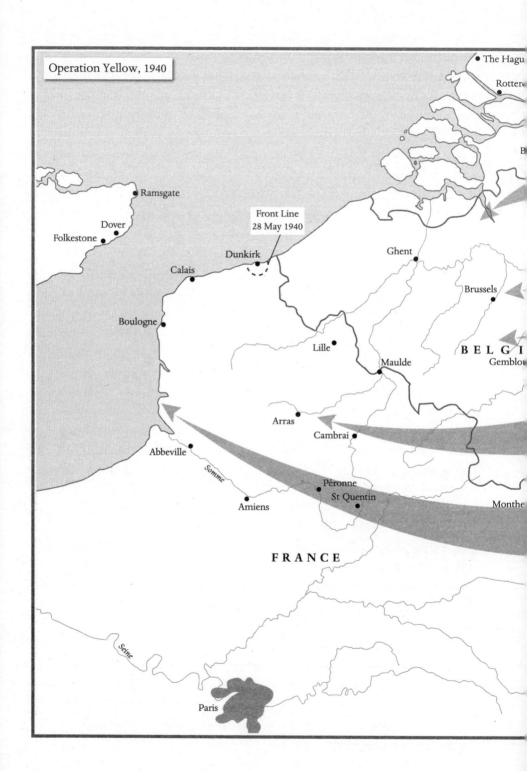

Operation Yellow, 1940

Front Line
28 May 1940

The Hagu
Rotter

B

Ramsgate

Dover

Folkestone

Ghent

Dunkirk

Calais

Brussels

Boulogne

B E L G I

Lille

Maulde

Gemblo

Arras

Cambrai

Abbeville

Somme

Péronne

St Quentin

Monthe

Amiens

F R A N C E

Seine

Paris

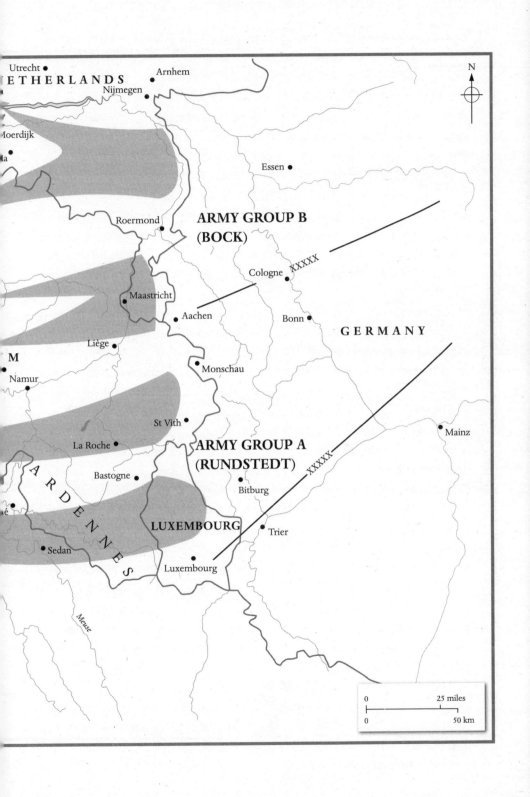

N

Utrecht •

ETHERLANDS

Arnhem •

• Nijmegen

Moerdijk

la •

Essen •

Roermond •

**ARMY GROUP B
(BOCK)**

Cologne • XXXXX

Maastricht •

Aachen •

Bonn •

GERMANY

Liège •

M

• Namur

Monschau •

St Vith •

La Roche •

**ARMY GROUP A
(RUNDSTEDT)**

XXXXX

Mainz •

Bastogne •

Bitburg •

A
R
D
E
N
N
E
S

LUXEMBOURG

• Trier

é •

• Sedan

Luxembourg •

Meuse

| 0 | 25 miles |
| 0 | 50 km |

history of the world. As we shall see, giant *Kesselschlachten* or 'cauldron battles' would be a feature of the war against the Soviet Union, particularly in the summer and autumn of 1941. But it is often forgotten that the biggest *Kesselschlacht* victory of all was achieved in May 1940. The area in which Allied forces were enclosed was huge – 120 miles by 80 miles – and trapped within this massive 'cauldron' were 1,700,000 troops.[58]

The German victory over the Allies was an astonishing triumph. General, soon to be Field Marshal, von Bock, a sober Prussian military man not given to hyperbole, issued a proclamation to his troops that read, 'we have won a victory whose beauty and scope is unsurpassed in history . . . The distress and disgrace that descended over our people after the [First] World War has been blotted out by your loyalty and bravery!'[59]

In order to understand what happened next, we need to try to imagine how men like Bock felt at this moment. Bock, together with the majority of the other senior commanders in the German Army, had fought in the First World War across the very same land that they had now conquered. That war had lasted four bloody years and cost two million German dead, and Germany had not just lost but suffered, as Bock put it, 'distress and disgrace'. In contrast, this war had lasted six weeks, at a cost of fewer than 50,000 German dead, and the Wehrmacht had taken more than one and a half million Allied prisoners. It was tantamount to a miracle – all the more so because, as we have seen, the Chief of Staff of the German Army had stated back in November that 'none of the higher Headquarters' thought the proposed offensive had 'any prospect of success'.

It was hard, almost impossible, not to believe that Hitler was the person ultimately responsible for this extraordinary victory. He had been the one who had insisted on the invasion of western Europe in the face of the negativity of his military commanders. Over a period of weeks he had persuaded them to cooperate in this adventure. And he had also been open to their suggestions for the best way of achieving success.

He had done all of this while knowing that a number of his key generals were not ardent Nazis. Bock, for instance, was an enthusiastic monarchist. In the middle of the campaign he had tried to visit the former Kaiser, who was living in exile at Doorn in the Netherlands, but had been forbidden to see him.

Hitler clearly valued the military ability of these men more than he valued their commitment to Nazi ideology. Imagine if he had 'purged' these generals in a similar way to Stalin. Is it conceivable that this victory would ever have happened? Hitler certainly believed that Stalin's actions during the Great Terror were a mistake, telling Goebbels in July 1937 that 'Stalin is probably sick in the brain otherwise you can't explain his bloody regime.'[60]

By the summer of 1940, and the signing of the armistice with France, the contrast in fortune between Hitler and Stalin was dramatic. Hitler, hailed by Wilhelm Keitel, Chief of the Armed Forces High Command, as 'Grösster Feldherr aller Zeiten' (the greatest commander of all time) and Stalin, confronted by Marshal Voroshilov after the Finnish debacle and told 'You are to blame for this.'[61]

To an extent, the difference between the two during this period is explicable not just by their own character and ideology, but also by their own ambition. Hitler wanted to obtain an empire for Germany. Of necessity that meant he needed the most professional army possible. Stalin had no such desire. His primary focus was on ensuring the survival of the Soviet Union. The conquests he made were largely opportunistic and occurred as a direct consequence of his agreement with the Nazis. He saw a way of gaining territory without much risk – crucially land that made his borders more secure – and he took it.

Stalin did, however, have one major advantage over Hitler in the summer of 1940. He was not at war. Hitler, despite the victory on the mainland of western Europe, still was. And it was a war he did not seem sure how to win.

4. Dreams and Nightmares

Stalin realized immediately that Hitler's victory over France not only changed the whole course of the war, but impacted directly on him. And not in a positive way.

His strategy had been to let the Nazis and the western Allies battle against each other while he watched from the sidelines. Now that plan lay in ruins. And after he heard that the Germans had taken Paris his frustration was obvious. In Khrushchev's hearing, Stalin asked why the Allies couldn't 'put up any resistance at all'.[1] He was 'very quick tempered and irritable', said Khrushchev. 'I had rarely seen him like that.' The reason why Stalin was so disappointed by the Allied performance was self-evident. The Soviet Union could not now escape the conflict. 'War against us', wrote Khrushchev, 'was inevitable.' Stalin had always thought that confronting the Germans might be necessary at some point. But the defeat of the Allies in France meant that 'this moment was drawing near.'[2]

Stalin's confidence in the Red Army's ability to fight the Germans once this 'inevitable' war happened had also been dented by the Winter War in Finland. Consequently, he did his best to ensure that such a humiliation could not happen again. As we have seen, one change was glaringly necessary, and was soon made. Marshal Voroshilov was sacked as Commissar for Defence and moved to an innocuous post dealing with 'cultural' matters. But Stalin took other measures that were less predictable, especially given his past behaviour. Several thousand Red Army commanders, for example, were released from imprisonment, most notably a forty-three-year-old colonel called Konstantin Rokossovsky. He had been jailed in 1937 and charged with a variety of almost certainly fictitious offences. Most likely his Polish origins and his admiration for the ideas of the disgraced Marshal Tukhachevsky had told against him. In prison he had been tortured, but had never agreed to sign a confession.

After his release, Rokossovsky would go on to a glittering career in the Red Army, and yet he would never betray any bitterness towards Stalin, the man behind his suffering. Perhaps his patriotism and commitment to Marxist ideology dwarfed his sense of individual pain. Or maybe he recognized that in the Soviet state injustice was everywhere, and to complain would simply be to ask for more suffering.

Alongside the release of officers from imprisonment came a raft of promotions. One of those elevated was Georgy Zhukov, the man who would become the most famous Soviet commander of the war. He had recently shown his ability as a military leader during the border conflict with the Japanese in Manchuria and Mongolia.

He owed his career entirely to the Bolshevik Revolution. He was the son of a cobbler, born in 1896, and had been raised in extreme poverty before starting an apprenticeship as a furrier. Conscripted into the Imperial Army in 1915 as an ordinary soldier, he joined the cavalry and proved to be a brave warrior, although he scarcely seemed en route to a glittering military career. But the revolution of 1917 transformed his fortunes.

Stalin's rule created many problems and caused many deaths, but it's also important to note the benefits that a policy of increased education and opportunity brought, not just to Zhukov but to millions of others. One measure of change was the literacy rate, which increased dramatically within the Soviet Union. In Soviet Uzbekistan, for instance, in 1926 less than 4 per cent of the population were literate, but by 1939 that figure had shot up to just under 68 per cent.[3]

On 2 June 1940, Stalin ordered Zhukov to a meeting, and asked him about his experiences in the Far East. 'Stalin's appearance,' wrote Zhukov later, 'his soft voice, the depth and concreteness of his judgement, his knowledge of military matters, the attention with which he listened to my report – all this had impressed me deeply.' Only after the fall of communism were the extra words he had originally written following this statement restored to the text: 'if he was like this with everyone, then why was there all this talk about him being such a terrible person?'[4]

Zhukov was certainly not a toady like Voroshilov, and yet Stalin appointed him to command the Kiev Special Military District – a key position, and one until recently held by Marshal Timoshenko, who had just been promoted to Voroshilov's old job of Commissar for Defence. It was a sign that Stalin understood that, in deciding promotions in the current febrile situation, the balance between abject loyalty and ability had to be somewhat recalibrated.

During May 1940, an attempt was also made to listen to criticisms about the army's conduct during the Winter War. In the ensuing discussions,

Kirill Meretskov, who had been one of the senior commanders during the war, voiced his view that the involvement of political commissars in the decision-making process had been a mistake. 'Our people are afraid to say anything directly, they are afraid to spoil relations and get in uncomfortable situations and are fearful to speak the truth.'[5] These were trenchant views, and yet Meretskov wasn't punished for speaking out. On the contrary, he was subsequently made Chief of Staff of the Red Army.

However, this increased tolerance was merely a temporary expedient. It didn't mean that the fundamental injustices of the Soviet system had been addressed. They remained in place, as Meretskov found shortly after the Germans invaded the Soviet Union when he was one of a number of commanders arrested for 'conspiracy'. He was beaten and urinated on by NKVD soldiers and made to 'confess'. Beria later admitted that his 'treatment . . . had been sheer butchery'. Out of operational necessity, Meretskov was reinstated shortly afterwards and subsequently given command of the 4th Army. Stalin greeted him on his return to favour by saying, 'Good day, Comrade Meretskov, and how are you feeling?'[6]

Notwithstanding this unpredictable atmosphere, Marshal Timoshenko did manage to implement a number of reforms in the wake of the Winter War. The authority of officers to command was strengthened, and military training was restructured.[7] Even junior officers like Mikhail Timoshenko, who had suffered on the front line in Finland, believed they had learnt something from their experience. 'When the war was over,' he said, 'I came to the conclusion that the Finns had taught me a lot about how to act in a time of war.' He pointed to the tactical use of machine guns and mortars as something he and his comrades learnt from the Finns: 'The Finns had taught us . . . In every company there was [now] a mortar unit, which we didn't have during the Finnish war. It was good [military] science.'[8]

Stalin did his best to push the borders of Soviet territory further west. He did this not just, as we have seen, by securing territory from Finland and moving against the Baltic States, but by demanding in June 1940 that the Romanians give up the most eastern area of their country – Bessarabia – which had previously been part of the old Russian Empire. Stalin also took the opportunity to snatch the nearby territory of Northern Bukovina from the Romanians. This meant that the Soviets were even closer to the Romanian oilfields, something that concerned Hitler, who knew how much the Nazis needed that oil.

In Britain, the new Prime Minister, Winston Churchill, tried to rally the country after the defeat of France. It was not an easy task, even given the successful rescue of over 300,000 troops at Dunkirk, for the unpalatable reality was hard to hide. The Wehrmacht had proved to be a better fighting force than the British Army. As General Sir Alan Brooke, one of the British corps commanders in France and later Chief of the Imperial General Staff, wrote in his diary on 23 May, 'the success they [the Germans] have achieved is nothing short of phenomenal. There is no doubt that they are the most wonderful soldiers.'[9]

Britain, in the foreseeable future, could not defeat Germany. On the contrary, Britain itself might be conquered. Only three obstacles prevented an immediate German invasion – the fighters of the RAF, the British fleet and, most valuable of all, the English Channel.

Stalin's man in London, Ivan Maisky, was one of a number of observers who thought that Hitler's triumph in the west was epoch changing. 'We are witnessing the fall of the great capitalist civilization,' he wrote on 20 May, 'a fall similar in importance to that of the Roman Empire. Or, perhaps, even more important . . .' Even the titans of 'capitalist civilization' seemed worried. When Lord Halifax, the Foreign Secretary, met the Soviet Ambassador on 10 July, he asked what would happen to the 'landlords' if there was a revolution in Britain. Would they suffer 'the same fate' as the rich peasants had in the Soviet Union? Maisky was non-committal in his reply, though he did point out that since Britain was an industrial country 'here it is not the landlords but the bankers and industrialists who play the key role.' Halifax seemed relieved, and said that while he felt landlords might be heavily taxed, he didn't think there would be an 'agrarian revolution' in Britain. He added, 'I'm sure, for instance, that everybody in my village would be sorry if something happened to my family.'[10] It's a remarkable exchange. Here was Lord Halifax reduced to asking the Soviet Ambassador what would happen to his own family in the event of a Bolshevik takeover in Britain.

In Germany, the mood was very different. 'Ninety-nine percent of the German people have turned off thinking for themselves,' wrote civil servant Friedrich Kellner, a critic of the regime, in his diary in July 1940. 'A boundless arrogance can be seen in all layers of the population – an indestructible faith in the power of weapons.'[11] Otto Klimmer, then a child in eastern Germany, remembered that 'all this was happening with such lightning speed . . . we almost felt like victors ourselves. Accordingly, that was the mood among [us] friends. We were somebody! We were the great victorious people!'[12] Maria Mauth, a schoolgirl from central Germany, confirmed that 'everyone was carried away ... We would listen to the news flashes and were incredibly proud and moved, and frequently many people would shed tears of pride. You have to imagine it. I cannot understand it today, but it was just like that.' She also recalled that 'those who came back from France brought lots of stuff with them, entire lorry loads, and they said they had "bought" it. They never bought it in a million years! It was magnificent somehow. We enjoyed life too, I have to say.'[13]

But for Hitler there still remained the problem that Great Britain had not yet exited the war. Britain was an aggravation – an enemy, certainly – but the country was not a compelling strategic target. From Hitler's perspective Britain offered neither extensive 'living space' for German settlers nor large amounts of raw materials. Ideological reasons also told against directing a major campaign against Britain. Hitler had always admired the British Empire and for years had wanted Britain as a friend, not a foe. Although he self-evidently now wanted to defeat Great Britain, he was worried that other countries might benefit as the British Empire disintegrated, and that would not necessarily be to Germany's advantage.[14] Then there were military reasons why an invasion of Britain was deeply problematic. Strong as the German Army undoubtedly was, more than 20 miles of sea lay between it and Britain, and the German fleet was no match for the British Navy.

While Hitler had his doubts about the wisdom of an attack on Britain, he had no such reservations about the country that had always been his primary target – the Soviet Union. The fact that he was temporarily in a relationship with the Soviets did not change that basic reality. It didn't matter either that the Soviets were helping his war effort with the delivery of raw materials; nor that they had made the conquest of France possible, since it was only because the Germans were secure on their eastern front that they had been able to turn west. All this, to Hitler, was merely the product of short-term expediency. And it was time for that to end.

A difficulty many people have with fully understanding this period in history is that we know what happened – the Soviet Union turned out to be the graveyard of Nazism. Since we know the extent of the disaster for the Nazis, it's hard not to think the decision to invade was utterly irrational. An appreciation of why it was actually considered by many to be a good idea at the time – a much better idea, indeed, than the invasion of France had been – is not helped either by the number of German generals who, after the war, claimed they had always been against the campaign. General Halder, for instance, subsequently said that he had believed back in the summer of 1940 that Hitler was a 'fool' to think of turning on the Soviet Union.[15] But this self-exculpatory talk can't be taken at face value. In Halder's case, he wrote in his diary on 3 July 1940 that the 'primary' problems Germany faced were now Britain and 'the east' and that the 'latter must be viewed chiefly with reference to the requirements of a military intervention which will compel Russia to recognize Germany's dominant position in Europe'.[16]

Less than four weeks after Halder made that entry in his diary, Hitler asked his military planners to examine the possibility of moving against the Soviet Union that very autumn. Alfred Jodl, Chief of the Operations Staff of the Wehrmacht, quickly replied that such swift action was impossible.[17] Hitler's request followed meetings earlier in the month with both Halder and Grand Admiral Erich Raeder about the practicalities of invading Britain. Halder noticed at this meeting, on 13 July, that while Hitler was 'greatly puzzled by Britain's persisting unwillingness to make peace' he believed that the British were acting in this way because they placed their 'hope on Russia'.[18] Six days later, in a speech to the Reichstag, Hitler publicly voiced his regret that Britain and Germany were not at peace, and made 'an appeal to the sense of reason in England', saying that 'I am still sad today that despite all my efforts I have not succeeded in gaining this friendship with England which, I believe, would have been a blessing for both peoples . . .'[19]

It was against this background that leading military commanders attended a briefing on 31 July at Hitler's retreat in the mountains of southern Bavaria. To begin with, Admiral Raeder gave a gloomy assessment of the chances of crossing the English Channel with an invasion fleet. Nonetheless, he offered one possible plan. Barges, carrying soldiers, would be towed across the Channel by fishing boats, with the landing planned for dawn. This meant crossing the Channel at night, and at least a 'half moon' was needed. The earliest dates were 22–26 September, but that fell 'into the bad-weather period'. It was all so problematic that Raeder suggested postponing the invasion until the following spring. Hitler – and this was almost a first for him – actually seemed to sympathize with a senior officer bringing him bad news. He also raised an additional problem himself, warning about 'weather conditions against which human effort is unavailing' such as 'storm tides'. The conclusion he reached was that the air war should start immediately and only if that succeeded should an invasion be considered. Even so, he still worried about the vast disparity between the two navies, with Germany possessing only '8 percent' of Britain's destroyer strength.[20]

None of this should have been surprising. Hitler had shown no affinity with seaborne warfare. He was very much a central European, he loved the mountains, not the ocean. That was one reason he had wanted to split the world between the British and Germans. Britain was a sea power – Britannia 'ruled the waves', not the land – which was fine, as far as Hitler was concerned, because he wanted to create a new German Empire on the landmass of eastern Europe, one that was reachable from Germany by autobahn and rail, not by boat.

At the meeting, Hitler was much more enthusiastic about another idea – invading the Soviet Union. His reason was simple. 'Russia', he asserted, was 'Britain's last hope'. Significantly, he did not mention the overwhelming ideological reasons that he believed justified such an attack. There was no talk of the dream of *Lebensraum* or of crushing both the Bolsheviks and their supposed Jewish masters. Instead, speaking to these hard-headed military men, he used the most practical reason he could come up with. Britain relied on Russia, so eliminate Russia and Britain – at last – would quit.

As a justification it did not hang together. As events currently stood, the Soviet Union had a fractious relationship with the British. So much so that Britain had come close to sending troops to fight the Red Army in Finland just months before. Britain seemed more likely to be at war with the Soviet Union in the near future rather than to rely on the Soviets for help.

Britain's 'last hope' wasn't Russia but the United States – a country that the Germans could do nothing about. Once he became Prime Minister, Churchill's priority on the diplomatic front had been to convince President Roosevelt to offer as much help to Britain as possible. And while Hitler did acknowledge that Britain had 'hope' in the United States as well, he also said that eliminating Russia would destroy the British faith in America. But why? He gave no reasons for this bizarre assertion.

Almost certainly, Hitler was dissembling. While it's possible he believed there was an element of truth in what he was saying, he nonetheless didn't mention his two main reasons for wanting to confront the

Soviet Union. The first was practical. He had the world's best army at his disposal. And if he was not to invade the Soviet Union with this superb fighting force, what was he to do with it?

The second reason was ideological. As Stalin knew, Hitler had been dreaming of attacking the Soviet Union since he wrote *Mein Kampf* back in the 1920s. Not only would the conquest of large tracts of Soviet land provide more 'living space' and resources for the Germans, but it would deal with the greatest racial threat Hitler believed Germany faced – given that the majority of Soviets were, in his eyes, either Slavs or Jews or Bolsheviks, or a combination of each. And Hitler hated all of them.

One common objection, heard often after the war and sometimes during it, was that the sheer size of the Soviet Union meant that it was impossible to conquer. But Hitler never intended to occupy the whole country. The senior commanders of the German forces – and Hitler himself – had all witnessed during their lifetimes how victory could be achieved in the east without capturing every piece of Soviet territory. As we have seen, the treaty of Brest-Litovsk proved exactly that fact. This agreement had subsequently been dismantled after the end of the First World War, but the memory of it remained. The Germans had forced Lenin to give up some of the best land in the Soviet Union; why couldn't the Nazis do the same to Stalin – and in the process gain even more territory?

The truth is that turning on the Soviet Union was seen by many of Hitler's generals as a more sensible option than invading Britain. It was certainly a more practical one. Less than a week after Hitler's 31 July conference, Halder noted that the navy was 'full of misgivings' about launching an attack on Britain and the air force was 'very reluctant' to take part in such an operation.[21] However, this doesn't necessarily mean that the Soviet Union was perceived as an easy alternative target. As Hubert Menzel, then a major working at German Army headquarters in the Operations Department, put it, 'we approached this task of invading the Soviet Union with considerable reservations and with extreme caution. But we had no other alternative. From long experience [we knew] that it takes about four years for an army – at least in modern times it does – to develop from the status quo to be able to attack in a major offensive. We knew that the Russians had basically slaughtered their entire officer corps in 1938, so they would need about four years, that is up to the end of '42, early '43 . . . We had realized during the

Finnish campaign that the Russians were hardly capable of managing large-scale operations. During the Polish campaign, we had seen how difficult it had been for the Russians even to move at a fortnight's notice. So there were genuine opportunities, tangible opportunities, within one or two years, to at least weaken the Russians to such an extent that they would be unable to wage war for years.'[22]

Ostensibly, Hitler adopted a twin-track strategy that summer and autumn, with his planners working on proposals for an invasion either of Britain or of the Soviet Union. But for Hitler it must only have been a single track. His initial lack of enthusiasm for a campaign on the British mainland had if anything deepened still further by the middle of August. Immediately after a ceremony at which he awarded field marshals' batons to his victorious commanders, he told them that he was 'considering a landing in England only as a last resort, if all other means of persuasion fail'.[23]

Two of the most senior military figures in Germany – Halder and Brauchitsch – were considering a third option: attack the British in the Mediterranean and strengthen the Nazi empire within Europe. In September, Admiral Raeder, head of the German Navy, added a twist to this plan by suggesting that the Wehrmacht should move on the Middle East to gain the oil there, and even consider subsequently invading the Caucasus, the oil-rich area of the Soviet Union, from the south. But Hitler showed little enthusiasm for either option. He remained focused on a frontal assault on the Soviet Union.

All of which makes what happened next so strange, because Hitler permitted Ribbentrop to invite the Soviet Commissar for Foreign Affairs, Vyacheslav Molotov, to Berlin for talks. Ribbentrop's motive for the invitation was straightforward. He had come up with a plan of his own, and sought to sell it to Hitler. He wanted to solve the growing problem of Germany and the Soviet Union squabbling over the smaller countries of central Europe by convincing the Soviets to look to the south-east for their new conquests. Instead of Europe, the Soviets should attack India. This bizarre scheme fitted into Ribbentrop's vision for a new world order, whereby the Nazis would control Europe, the Soviet Union India and the Persian Gulf, Japan the Far East, and Italy the Mediterranean and parts of Africa.

No one could ever fault Ribbentrop for lack of radical ideas, and this was as radical as they came. Plenty of people, however, did fault him for his lack of intelligence. William Shirer, an American correspondent in Berlin, described him as 'one of the most truculent and stupid of the Hitler gang, and a mean little liar to boot!'[24] Count Ciano, the Italian Foreign Minister, remarked that 'The Duce [Mussolini] says you only have to look at his head to see that he has a small brain,' and the consensus among those Nazis who worked for Ribbentrop was that he was 'pompous, conceited and not too intelligent'.[25] Reinhard Spitzy, a German diplomat and committed Nazi, remembered that when Hitler tried to defend his Foreign Minister to Hermann Göring, by saying that Ribbentrop 'knows quite a lot of important people in England', Göring replied, 'Mein Führer, that may be right, but the bad thing is, they know him.'[26] Göring also referred to Ribbentrop as 'Germany's no. 1 parrot' because of his tendency to repeat Nazi slogans over and over again.[27]

Ribbentrop had found himself sidelined in the early days of the war. His coup of the non-aggression pact was long behind him, and the proposed Molotov meeting was an obvious attempt to shoulder his way back into Hitler's favour. Hitler's motives, however, are harder to read. Consider two statements he made to General Halder just three days apart. On 1 November, Hitler talked of Molotov's proposed visit to Berlin and said that he hoped he could 'bring Russia into the anti-British front'.[28] But on the 4th Hitler referred to 'Russia' once again, saying to Halder that it 'remains the great problem of Europe. We must do our utmost to be prepared when the great showdown comes.'[29]

The most persuasive explanation of Hitler's attitude is that, while he was prepared to see what Molotov had to say, it would have taken something quite extraordinary for him to change his mind about moving on the Soviet Union. We know this because on 12 November Hitler made his intentions clear in a directive to his military commanders. 'Political discussions for the purpose of clarifying the attitude of Russia in the immediate future are being started,' it read. 'Regardless of what outcome these conversations will have, all preparations for the East already orally ordered, are to be continued.'[30]

Just a few days before, back in Moscow, Stalin had revealed the immense pressure he was under. The stress of worrying about the ability of the Red Army to defend the country against an attack broke through at a lunch on 7 November, attended by Georgi Dimitrov, head of the Comintern, and many other senior figures – including Molotov, who was just about to leave for Berlin. Stalin bemoaned the state of the

Soviet military, and claimed he was 'the only one dealing with all these problems. None of you could be bothered with them. I am out there by myself . . . Look at me: I am capable of learning, reading, keeping up with things every day – why can you not do this? You do not like to learn; you are happy just going along the way you are, complacent. You are squandering Lenin's legacy . . . But I will show you, if I ever lose my patience. (You know very well how I can do that.) I shall hit the fatsos so hard that you will hear the crack for miles around.'[31]

It was a disturbing mix of self-pity and threat. Georgi Dimitrov, who recorded Stalin's tirade in his diary, wrote that he had 'never seen and never heard' the Soviet leader behave in such a way before.[32] And with Stalin's admonishment ringing in his ears, Molotov left for the German capital, arriving at the Anhalter station in Berlin on 12 November – the very day Hitler ordered that 'preparations' be continued for the invasion of the Soviet Union.

In Molotov's entourage was a young interpreter called Valentin Berezhkov, who subsequently wrote of the similarities he observed between the two regimes. In particular, he pointed out the 'same idolization of "the leader", the same mass rallies and parades where the participants carried portraits of the Führer and little children presented him with flowers. Very similar, ostentatious architecture, heroic themes depicted in art much like our socialist realism.' And when he saw that 'women lifted their babies for him [Hitler] to touch,' he later realized that 'Stalin was like that.'[33]

After settling into their luxurious accommodation at the Bellevue Hotel, the Soviet delegation were taken to Ribbentrop's office in what had formerly been the Reich President's palace. Ribbentrop explained that he wanted to brief Molotov before the meeting with Hitler. He began by asserting that Britain had already been defeated. The only question now was when the British would acknowledge this fact. Indeed, claimed Ribbentrop, Germany's position was so powerful that the Nazis were no longer focused on how to win the war, but were concerned merely with how to end a war they had already won. Next, he launched into his epic plan for 'spheres of influence' throughout the world – though he pretended that Hitler had come up with the idea. Talking of specifics, he asked if the Soviets would consider a move south in order to gain free access to the sea. Molotov, who so far had merely listened to Ribbentrop's monologue, now enquired what sea Ribbentrop meant.

The German Foreign Minister said he had been referring to the 'Persian Gulf and the Arabian Sea'. Molotov, according to notes of the meeting, said nothing in reply. Only after listening to Ribbentrop talk about Turkey and China did Molotov finally respond. He said that precise definitions of concepts like the new 'sphere of influence' were necessary, and the proposal would in any case subsequently need to be discussed in Moscow. He also raised one practical point, and it had nothing to do with Ribbentrop's fantastic notion of a possible Soviet advance to the Arabian Sea. He said that he wanted to talk about the situation in Finland at this summit – a subject Stalin had told him to raise.[34] Stalin was particularly concerned about Finland because the Germans had recently started supplying arms to the Finns. This was especially troubling as Finland had been assigned to the Soviet 'sphere of influence' the previous year. Indeed, we know, thanks to the discovery of Stalin's instructions for Molotov, that the main point of the mission from the Soviet perspective was not to negotiate some all-encompassing new deal, but to gain intelligence about Germany's foreign policy goals.[35]

Later that day, Hitler met Molotov for the first time. Berezhkov, who accompanied Molotov, thought the German leader was 'haughty and arrogant' and that 'in this respect he was the complete opposite of Stalin, who amazed everyone with his ostensible modesty and total lack of desire to impress.' When he shook Hitler's 'cold and damp' hand, Berezhkov felt as if he was 'touching a reptile'.[36]

At the start of the meeting Hitler remarked on how much the relationship between Germany and the Soviet Union over the past year had benefited both parties. Neither had got everything they wanted – that never happened in negotiations – but each had emerged stronger. If they quarrelled then only third parties would benefit.

In response, Molotov said that Hitler had talked in 'general' terms and in 'general' he agreed with him. But, as he had warned Ribbentrop hours before, he wanted to raise the specific issue of Finland. He also said that the Soviets were keen to know Germany's intentions towards 'Bulgaria, Rumania [sic], and Turkey'. Hitler, speaking once again in broad terms, said that indeed much needed to be resolved.

So the first day of discussions ended. It was already plain that the two sides were far apart, not just in the specifics that each of them wanted from the conference, but in the overall manner in which they approached the meetings. Molotov wanted to know detail. Hitler preferred to speak in the most grandiose terms.

Most notably, the underlying fissure between the Soviet Union and Nazi Germany had been exposed. The Soviets were anxious to learn the exact German intentions towards a range of countries in Europe, at precisely the moment the Nazis wanted them to look elsewhere for territorial plunder.

The next day the split became even more apparent when Hitler dealt head on with the question of Finland. He reminded Molotov that Germany had not intervened in the Soviet invasion of Finland, and stated that he still recognized that Finland was in the Soviet 'zone of influence'. On the other hand, Germany was 'very greatly interested' in the supply of 'nickel and lumber' from Finland. There was also a 'purely psychological factor' at work here, which was that the Finns 'had gained the sympathies of the world' by the courageous way they had fought – so much so that in Germany the population was 'somewhat annoyed' at the position his government had taken over the issue. Hitler followed this up by saying that he felt the Germans had been short-changed by the Soviets the previous year, when they had agreed with Stalin's request to swap territory in the Baltic States for the Lublin area of Poland. He then criticized the recent Soviet occupation of Northern Bukovina, particularly as this territory, taken from the Romanians, contained a number of ethnic Germans.

Molotov disagreed with Hitler's version of events, saying that if the Germans had not wanted the territory swap then the Soviets would not have pressed forward with their plans, and that Bukovina was 'not of very great importance'. He also made a pointed reference to the contribution the pact with the Soviet Union had made to the defeat of France, saying that 'the German–Russian agreement had not been without influence upon the great German victories.'

Hitler ignored this remark and insisted that he did not want the Soviets to invade the rest of Finland. This would inflict 'such a strain' on the German–Soviet relationship that it must be avoided. Molotov said this was not currently an issue. Hitler answered that 'it would be too late for a decision when it became so' – by which he meant that if the Soviets did invade Finland it would precipitate such a crisis that it would be hard to unpick the situation by diplomatic means.

One wonders if Molotov, and subsequently Stalin, stopped to think why Hitler was so keen that the Red Army didn't occupy the rest of

Finland. The excuses Hitler gave at the meeting did not justify the vehemence of his feelings. After all, why couldn't the Germans still get their nickel and timber from Finland after the Soviets had conquered the country? But there was an alternative, much more credible explanation for Hitler's position. If Germany was planning an attack on the Soviet Union, it was very helpful for Finland not to be occupied by the Red Army.

There are two useful insights into Hitler's negotiating tactics that we can gain from this exchange over Finland, techniques Stalin was also fond of using. The first was that when Hitler stated a goal that was an absolute priority – in this case his desire that the Soviet Union should not invade Finland – he was utterly inflexible about it. By remaining intransigent he forced Molotov either to back down or to risk a major dispute between the two countries.

Stalin was later to act in the same way towards the Allies over his primary goals, most notably his desire to hold on to the territory he had gained as a result of the Nazi–Soviet pact. Even when it would have avoided a good deal of conflict in his relationship with the Allies if he had moderated his demands, he stood firm. He, like Hitler, knew he could do so because he had an absolute understanding of another vital truth, one that is the second insight we can gain from this Molotov meeting – the power of physical threat. Hitler was, in effect, threatening Molotov that if the Soviets advanced further into Finland then there would be harmful consequences. And he could issue this warning only because he was at the head of a powerful army.

This language of force was one Stalin understood very well. For example, when a pre-war French politician told him he wished to curry favour with the Catholic Church and the Pope, Stalin famously asked dismissively, 'How many divisions has *he* [the Pope] got?'[37] A central part of Stalin's character was his contempt for those who did not have the military might to back up their words. He and Hitler would both have agreed with Mao Zedong's dictum that 'Political power grows out of the barrel of a gun.'[38]

After the spat about Finland, Hitler talked once again in generalities. He told Molotov that the imminent collapse of the British Empire would result in a 'gigantic world-wide estate in bankruptcy', and the Soviet Union could share in the spoils. Molotov replied that while he was 'in agreement with everything that he had understood', what was important was first to resolve the future relationship between Germany and the

Soviet Union. Molotov then – yet again – drew Hitler back into specifics. What about the guarantee of protection that the Germans had given to the Romanians? What about the other countries in which the Soviet Union, as a 'Black Sea power', had an interest, like Bulgaria? Hitler brushed these questions aside by saying he would have to talk all this over with Mussolini, as the Italians also had an interest in that part of the world.

It had been a singularly unproductive encounter. The dispute over policy had not been helped by the clash of personality between Hitler and Molotov. Indeed, it would be hard to imagine a man more likely to irritate Hitler than the pernickety Molotov. When Hitler talked in visionary terms, Molotov responded with detailed quibbles. Understandably, given the nature of the meeting, Hitler never saw Molotov again.

However, even in Hitler's absence the conference didn't go much better. Ribbentrop protested that Molotov was questioning him 'too closely' about Germany's intentions. And instead of answering Molotov, he preferred to read out a proposal for the Soviet Union to join the existing tripartite pact – the agreement between Germany, Japan and Italy signed in September 1940. He also offered the Soviets an expansion route towards India as part of the grand plan he had previously outlined. But for his part Molotov could not be shifted from his position that 'all these great issues of tomorrow could not be separated from the issues of today and the fulfillment of existing agreements.' The inability of the two sides to form any mutual understanding was illustrated – famously – by this last conversation between them, which took place as they sheltered from an attack on Berlin by British Bomber Command. 'You say that England is defeated,' remarked Molotov. 'So why are we sitting here now in this air-raid shelter?'[39]

Hitler professed to be positive about the failure of the Molotov talks. Immediately afterwards he said to his army adjutant Major Gerhard Engel that he was now 'really relieved', because the relationship between the Soviet Union and Germany would 'not even remain a marriage of convenience'. Molotov, claimed Hitler, had 'let the cat out of the bag' about Soviet plans – presumably by focusing the discussion on countries like Finland and Bulgaria. 'To let Russia into Europe', said Hitler, 'would be the end of Central Europe; even the Balkans and Finland were dangerous flanks.'[40]

Yet the very next day, 16 November, Halder had the impression that 'Russia has no intention of breaking with us' and 'Russia wants to be a partner.'[41] However, even if Russia did still want to 'partner' with Germany, the reality was that leading Nazis like Joseph Goebbels still found the Soviets repulsive. Shortly after the Molotov visit Goebbels wrote in his diary about a meeting he had recently held with a member of his senior staff in the Propaganda Ministry, Leopold Gutterer, who had experienced life in Moscow. 'It confirms my views,' wrote Goebbels, 'it is bleakness elevated into a system. No culture, no civilization, only terror, fear and mass paranoia. Appalling!'[42] Just days before, Goebbels had observed Molotov in the Reich Chancellery and pronounced him 'shrewd', but also 'very reserved' with a 'face of waxy yellowness'. The Soviet delegation accompanying Molotov contained 'not a single man of any stature. As if they insist on confirming our theoretical insight into the nature of Bolshevist mass ideology . . . Fear of each other and inferiority complexes are written all over their faces.'[43]

At the end of November, Stalin finally revealed the conditions under which the Soviets would agree to join the tripartite pact. And his reply was not the one Ribbentrop had wanted to hear. Stalin insisted that the Germans cease their contact with Finland and confirm once again that the country was in the Soviet 'sphere of influence'. The implication was obvious – Germany needed to understand that the Soviets could act towards Finland as they wished. The Soviets also wanted to place military bases in Bulgaria and Turkey.

Assuming Stalin hoped to agree a deal with Hitler, he had just made a major mistake. He had overplayed his hand and demonstrated to Hitler that the Soviets were not prepared to walk away from their claims to European territory. Not that Stalin had many options. He was ever conscious of the fact that the Wehrmacht's victory on the mainland of western Europe had massively strengthened Germany's position. Consequently his own negotiating stance, one of trying to appear strong but from a weakened standpoint, was fraught with risk. He did have some leverage over Hitler – the trade relationship – and he had shown earlier in the year that he was not averse to using it, when the Soviets had delayed the delivery of promised raw materials until the Germans had fulfilled a variety of demands, including handing over examples of Luftwaffe planes for them to examine.[44] But the stakes were now higher given the Germans' recent stupendous military successes. In any case, Stalin's tough stance over the trade deal only served to provide Hitler with a further reason for the Wehrmacht to attack the Soviet Union. As

Walther Funk, Nazi Economics Minister, put it, Germany could not be 'dependent upon forces and powers [that is, Stalin and the Soviets] over whom we have no influence'.[45]

Regardless of Ribbentrop's futile efforts to sign Stalin up to the tripartite pact, Hitler clearly felt a renewed sense of purpose after the fiasco of the Molotov visit, because just a month later, on 18 December, he signed the war directive for the attack on the Soviet Union. We can only imagine how much pleasure the opening sentence of the order must have given him: 'The German Wehrmacht must be prepared to crush Soviet Russia in a quick campaign (Operation Barbarossa) even before the conclusion of the war against England.'[46]

Without question, Hitler wanted this war. The truth had always been that any lengthy relationship with the Soviet Union was bound to fail unless Hitler abandoned his fundamental ideological aim – the pursuit of *Lebensraum* and the creation of a new German Empire in the western Soviet Union. And he could no more abandon that goal than he could stop breathing.

But having the vision was easy. The problem Hitler faced now was to make it happen.

1. Joseph Stalin in 1919, two years after the Bolshevik victory in the Russian Revolution. A fellow prisoner, incarcerated with him in Georgia before the First World War, remarked that Stalin had a 'glacial character'.

2. Adolf Hitler as a German soldier in the First World War. In the words of one of his wartime comrades, there was 'something peculiar' about him.

3. Stalin with Vladimir Lenin, the father of the Russian Revolution, in 1922. Even after Lenin's death two years later, Stalin would never entirely escape his shadow.

4. Stalin, on the far left of the photograph, relaxing with his comrades in the 1920s. Seated next to him is his wife, Nadezhda Alliluyeva. She would commit suicide in Moscow in 1932.

5. This is the image Hitler sought to project as leader of the Nazi Party – a man who was married to destiny and abstained from worldly pleasures.

6. Unknown to the German public, Hitler had a girlfriend, Eva Braun. Here she is watching over her dozing boyfriend at Berchtesgaden in the Bavarian mountains.

7. Bodies lie in the street during the Ukrainian famine of the early 1930s. Stalin's policy of forced collectivization was a major factor in causing the deaths of nearly four million people in Ukraine.

8. Soviet prisoners build the White Sea–Baltic Canal during the early 1930s. When the canal was completed it was found to be too shallow for large-scale maritime traffic.

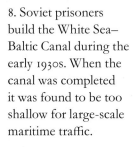

9. A rare photo inside a hospital for prisoners working on the White Sea–Baltic Canal. Thousands of labourers from the Gulag died while toiling on this major construction project in the north-west of the country.

10. Prisoners at Dachau concentration camp flatten a road by pulling a heavy roller. Dachau, which was to be the model for subsequent Nazi concentration camps, opened shortly after Hitler came to power in 1933.

11. Guards at Dachau in 1933. Many of the SS who committed terrible atrocities during the war were trained at Dachau – most infamously Rudolf Höss, Commandant of Auschwitz.

12. (*Left*) Joachim von Ribbentrop, the German Foreign Minister, signs the Nazi–Soviet pact in Moscow in the early hours of 24 August 1939. Stalin, standing behind him, is clearly very happy.

13. (*Middle*) Three military commanders in 1939. On the left Grigori Shtern of the Red Army, who was shot as a traitor two years later, in the middle Khorloogiin Choibalsan, Marshal of the Mongolian People's Army and a devoted follower of Stalin, and on the right Georgy Zhukov, who would go on to become the most famous Soviet Marshal of the war.

14. Stalin and the scarcely competent Marshal Kliment Voroshilov. Despite Voroshilov's many failings as a military commander, Stalin stuck by him.

15. Hitler watches German troops taking part in the invasion of Poland in 1939. The Germans, in collaboration with the Soviets, would swiftly defeat the Poles.

16. German and Soviet soldiers collaborate in the division of Poland. On 1 September 1939 the Germans had invaded Poland from the west, and on 17 September the Red Army had invaded from the east.

17. Finnish soldiers on skis during the Winter War against the Soviet Union in 1939–40. Even though they were hugely outnumbered by the Red Army, the Finns thwarted Stalin's desire to gain a swift victory.

18. A long column of French prisoners, captured by the Germans during their offensive in western Europe, May–June 1940. The German triumph left Stalin shocked and concerned.

19. Hitler in Paris in June 1940. Having fought against the French in the First World War – and lost – this was a moment of immense triumph for him.

5. Hitler's War of Annihilation

The Germans were planning a war without parallel. They envisaged not just launching the single largest invasion in history, but devastating the territory they conquered in ways that almost defy the imagination. At a gathering of SS leaders at the castle of Wewelsburg just days before the attack on the Soviet Union began, Heinrich Himmler remarked that '30 million' people would die in the area that the Nazis wanted their forces to occupy.[1]

But while the vision – though appalling – was clear, the means by which it could be achieved were anything but. This disconnect between vision and implementation would never be adequately resolved by the Nazis and was one of the reasons why they were to lose the war. It also tells us a great deal about Hitler's technique of leadership and how it contrasted so starkly with Stalin's.

The whole idea of Operation Barbarossa – named after Emperor Frederick Barbarossa who led the third crusade in the twelfth century – was awash with unknowns. Exactly how far should the Germans penetrate into Soviet territory? What precisely were the depths of Soviet reserves? Most of all, how quickly could the war be won, since the goal was to achieve a swift victory? These were questions to which Hitler didn't know the answers. According to his adjutant, Major Engel, Hitler remained uncertain about 'Russian strength' on the very day he issued the Barbarossa directive in December 1940.[2]

However, Hitler didn't let his lack of knowledge get in the way of his expansive aims. When in early January 1941 he talked to his generals about the objectives of the campaign, he emphasized that after the Red Army had been surrounded and destroyed the Germans should capture the industrial centres of the Soviet Union and occupy Baku in the Caucasus, the heart of Soviet oil production. He reminded his military commanders that this 'gigantic Russian area holds immeasurable resources'. But while it's easy to see why Hitler wanted all this to be achieved, it's harder to grasp how he thought it was possible in practical terms. Baku, for instance, was nearly 2,000 miles from Berlin.[3]

On 20 February, General Georg Thomas, head of the Office of the War Economy, delivered a report in which he emphasized the importance of 'getting hold of the oil-producing area of the Caucasus in undamaged condition'.[4] But this only highlighted the very problem that no one in a position of power seemed to want to confront. While it was clear that one of the main reasons the Germans were about to invade the Soviet Union was to gain resources – chiefly oil – that they didn't currently possess, what remained unanswered was this key question: did they have the resources they needed in order to get the resources they wanted? In short, did their desires exceed their ability to fulfil them? Ultimately, Hitler never acknowledged this flaw inherent in the Barbarossa plan. He wanted a swift war to gain access to land and raw materials, but the raw material that he most craved – oil – was an enormous distance away.

When Thomas met with Hermann Göring on 26 February, the Reichsmarschall agreed that 'the oil-producing area of Baku must be acquired' but then breezily added that 'like the Führer' he was 'of the opinion that the whole Bolshevist state would collapse when German troops invaded the country'.[5] It was not so much a strategic plan, more a statement of faith. In the light of this insouciant attitude, it's not surprising that subsequent, more negative reports written by Thomas most likely never reached Hitler. Those closest to him knew there was no point in showing such thinking to him.[6]

Field Marshal von Bock experienced personally how much Hitler disliked any critical assessment of Operation Barbarossa when he visited him on 1 February 1941. Bock said that the Germans would 'defeat the Russians if they stood and fought', but he questioned whether they could be forced to make peace. By implication, Bock was asking how the Soviet Union could be conquered if the Germans accepted from the beginning that they could never occupy the whole country. Hitler dismissed the objection, saying that if the Soviets didn't make peace after the capture of Ukraine, Leningrad and Moscow then 'we would just have to carry on.' Bock noticed that the Führer 'sharply rejected any idea of backing down – without my having suggested it to him'. Hitler was unequivocal. 'I will fight,' he said. 'I am convinced that our attack will sweep over them like a hailstorm.'[7] Bock didn't question Hitler further. He was well aware that he was speaking to the man who had overseen the triumphant conquest of western Europe less than a year earlier. As Bock himself had written in his diary, two months before, he believed that Hitler 'sees the bright and dark sides of the big picture calmly and clearly'.[8]

Hitler had been similarly optimistic at a military conference he had hosted at the Berghof, his mountain retreat near Berchtesgaden, on 9 January. He had once again voiced the opinion that the British were carrying on the war only because they hoped that the Soviet Union and America would one day come to their aid. It was 'out of the question' to imagine that the British on their own were capable of invading continental Europe. Once the Soviet Union had been destroyed, and the Japanese were able to turn against the Americans in the Far East, then the British would surely make peace. If they didn't, they knew they would lose their empire. Hitler also gave an insight into his view of Stalin, saying that the Soviet leader was 'very smart' because while he was unwilling to 'openly stand against Germany' he 'would increasingly create trouble in situations that are difficult for Germany'. This was one of the reasons that 'Russia needs to be smashed.'[9] Once again, Hitler was spinning a story to his military commanders that justified moving against the Soviet Union not on ideological grounds, but out of practical necessity.

Ten days later, on 19 January, Hitler met Mussolini. While the Führer did not reveal his plan to invade the Soviet Union, the Italian leader found him both 'very anti-Russian' and reluctant to launch a cross-Channel operation against the British. 'It is no longer a question of landing in England,' wrote Count Ciano, after Mussolini reported on his conversation with the German leader.[10] Ciano also noticed, without knowing the reason why, that Ribbentrop lacked his normal 'bravado'. When Ciano asked his German counterpart how long he thought that the war would carry on for, Ribbentrop replied that it wouldn't be over before 1942.[11] It's likely that Ribbentrop was still feeling deflated after the collapse of his grand plan to draw the Soviet Union into the tripartite pact.

Hitler's confidence in the likely success of the forthcoming attack on the Soviet Union was shared by many of his military experts. General Jodl, head of the Operations Staff of the Wehrmacht, memorably remarked that 'the Russian colossus will prove to be a pig's bladder, prick it and it will burst.'[12] And the final invasion plan, which was devised with input from both Hitler and his military planners, reflected that over-optimistic attitude. It was agreed that the main thrust should be in the centre of the Soviet Union, on the Minsk–Smolensk–Vyazma–Moscow axis that went directly to the Soviet capital. Two other army groups – one to the north and one to the south – would head respectively for the Baltic States and Leningrad and for Ukraine and Kiev. Hitler emphasized once again that one of the main objectives of the operation was to destroy the Soviet armed forces, as well as ensure that the Baltic and Leningrad were secured. The capture of Moscow itself was 'completely immaterial'.[13] This last point was a matter of some dispute. Leading figures in the army, like Brauchitsch, disagreed with Hitler and wanted to target the Soviet capital in an attempt to destroy the command and administrative centre of the country. Bock, who would lead Army Group Centre, had noted in his diary an 'especially interesting' Swiss newspaper article about the importance of the fall of Paris during the French campaign, quoting from it the line 'After the loss of Paris, France had to become a body without a head. The war was lost!'[14] The view these generals plainly held was that the same thing would almost certainly happen in the Soviet Union once Moscow fell.

Historians still argue about whether the focus from the beginning of Barbarossa should have been on reaching Moscow, or whether Hitler's view that capturing the resources the Germans so badly needed was more important. On balance, however, the argument is probably in Hitler's favour. It is no accident that many of the generals who argued for the Moscow option – the way that Napoleon had tried to conquer Russia – had held staff roles during the First World War. It's questionable how much they fully understood the immensity of the change in the nature of warfare since then. In that respect Hitler and the younger German commanders were more attuned to the demands of a modern mechanized war. They understood that machines need fuel – and lots of it.

What's strange, given this background, is that Hitler did not make Army Group South stronger. This was the thrust that was first headed towards the fertile land of Ukraine and was then tasked with moving on to capture the oil of the Caucasus. On the other hand, altering troop disposition in this way would have meant risking being unable to destroy the large numbers of Red Army units that lay to the north, and so might have left the Germans vulnerable to a flank attack. Hitler, for once, was not prepared to take an all-or-nothing tactical gamble.

While the German leader finalized the details of the invasion, Stalin made a series of decisions that shaped the way in which the Soviet Union would respond to the German attack, and in many respects these decisions were lamentable. That was certainly the judgement of Winston Churchill, who wrote after the war – at a time when his relationship with Stalin was one of distrust – that 'it may be doubted whether any mistake in history has equalled that of which Stalin and the Communist chiefs were guilty when they . . . supinely awaited . . . the fearful onslaught which impended upon Russia . . . Stalin and his commissars showed themselves at this moment the most completely outwitted bunglers of the Second World War.'[15]

Once again, however, we have to be careful not to let hindsight cloud our view of Stalin's actions. It's easy, once you know what happened, to say that people should have acted differently. At the time, before events unfold, options can seem very different, not least because the fundamental problem with intelligence gathering always remains – can you believe the information you are given? And if you do believe it, what conclusions should you draw? But even if we make the most generous allowance for the predicament in which Stalin found himself, Churchill's condemnation of Stalin was still justified. Notwithstanding our knowledge of subsequent events, Stalin demonstrably made the wrong choices, and placed his country in great peril.

One reason was the way Stalin ran the Soviet Union. His suspicion of others was such that he wanted to read as much as possible of the intelligence himself. Before the German invasion on 22 June, the Soviet military alone compiled 267 intelligence assessments of which 129 reached the Soviet leadership.[16] Many of these reports tracked German troop movements towards the eastern border of German-occupied territory. But what did they mean? Were German units merely training in this territory to prepare for an invasion of Britain, for instance? Perhaps they were encamped there so as to be far away from British air attack? And even if the Germans did plan on threatening the Soviet Union, why would they invade without warning? Maybe the Germans just wanted the Soviets to think they were in danger, so as to extract further concessions from them over trade or territory? It was to be expected – and this was a common belief not just among the Soviet leadership but elsewhere – that the Germans would issue an ultimatum first.

Stalin, as we have seen, had thought since the defeat of France that the Soviet Union was in a perilous position, but he seems at times during the weeks preceding the invasion to have tried simply to wish away the immediacy of the threat. His suspicious nature was so deep rooted that the more clear-cut the data was, the more he was capable of seeing it as deceitful. Molotov later explained Stalin's attitude this way: 'I think that one can never trust the intelligence. One has to listen to them but then check on them. The intelligence people can lead to dangerous situations that it is impossible to get out of. There were endless provocateurs on both sides.'[17]

Stalin faced an additional problem. Assuming the Germans were genuinely planning to invade, what could he do about it? One answer was to demonstrate to the Nazis just how strong the Soviets would be as an opponent. To that end the Soviet authorities allowed German engineers to examine their aircraft-manufacturing plants. This turned out to be a mistake. For when the German visitors learnt of the vast potential of the Soviet aviation industry, the knowledge just fuelled Hitler's desire to confront the Soviet Union as soon as possible. 'Now you see how far these people have got,' said Hitler. 'We must start at once.'[18]

Stalin was also undoubtedly to blame for presiding over a mistaken military strategy by endorsing the view that the Red Army should retaliate immediately if the Soviet Union was attacked. The plan was to concentrate military units near the border and then, if Germany started a war, to push the invaders back and fight on their territory. This fitted well with the notion that the Soviets were not 'defeatist' in approach. They would not retreat into their own country, giving up land to the enemy, but would move forward against the enemy as soon as the initial advance had been contained. The philosophy behind this strategy was taught even to relatively junior officers like air force pilot Mark Gallay. 'Our work was always based on the assumption that we would be fighting on enemy territory,' he said. 'We were prepared for the scenario that if we were attacked, we would immediately respond with a strong blow.'[19]

This proactive reaction to any attack – which was to prove catastrophic during the first weeks of the German invasion – was also the reason why, some years ago, it was suggested that Stalin had intended a pre-emptive strike against Germany. Extensive research since has demonstrated that this was not the case. We know this, in part, because of what happened in May 1941. At a speech he gave on 5 May to graduates of the Soviet Military Academy, Stalin said that 'In fully defending our country, we are obliged to act offensively. We must move from defence to a military policy of offensive action. We must reorganize our propaganda, agitation, and our press in an offensive spirit. The Red Army is a modern army, and a modern army is an army of attack.' This certainly could be interpreted as a desire to confront the German forces massing on the border of Soviet territory at some point in the future. Indeed, Marshal Timoshenko and Zhukov – now Chief of Staff of the Red Army – considered just such an offensive plan. But they had monumentally misjudged their boss's true intentions. 'Have you gone mad,' Stalin said to them, 'do you want to provoke the Germans!' He then added the threat, 'If you provoke the Germans on the border, if you move forces without our permission, then bear in mind heads will roll.'[20]

This misunderstanding demonstrates a key difference between Stalin and Hitler. Unlike Hitler, who was offering an unwavering vision to his military commanders, Stalin was delivering a whole variety of mixed messages. To graduates of the military academy he promised an 'army of attack', yet he was furious when his senior military commanders interpreted this as a desire to confront the Germans pre-emptively. To one audience inside the Soviet Union, Stalin wanted to appear strong, to another he didn't want to appear provocative. To the Nazis he tried to present an attitude that was resolute yet simultaneously friendly. But by wallowing in this mess of contradictions all he managed to do was to appear weak – astonishing given that his reputation was based on ruthlessness. 'Stalin and his people remain totally passive,' wrote Goebbels in his diary on 7 May. 'Like a rabbit with a snake.'[21] Two days later he added that 'Stalin is apparently afraid.'[22]

There was an obvious reason for Stalin's mental state – the demonstrable power of the German armed forces. As if the conquest of France and the Low Countries in 1940 had not been proof enough, in April 1941 the Germans invaded Yugoslavia and mainland Greece and conquered both in less than a month. In contrast, Stalin knew not just that the Red Army had performed badly in the Winter War, but that war games held in January 1941 had shown that Soviet forces were unprepared for a major conflict. After that chastening episode Stalin had sacked Meretskov as Chief of Staff and appointed Zhukov.

On the German side, as the date of the invasion of the Soviet Union grew near, the ideological nature of the forthcoming struggle surfaced more and more. As we have seen, Hitler had been careful in his early discussions with his military commanders to highlight why the fight against the Soviet Union was necessary in strategic terms, as a way of forcing Britain out of the conflict. But now he emphasized that this was to be a different kind of war. This was – as he said to 200 officers on 30 March – a 'war of extermination'. Moreover, he called for the 'extermination of the Bolshevist commissars and of the Communist intelligentsia'.[23]

Perhaps not all of the officers present would have agreed with the radical nature of Hitler's views, but many certainly acknowledged that the Soviets offered a very different type of threat from that posed by the French or the British.[24] Consider the views of a young officer such as Rüdiger von Reichert. He was twenty-four years old in 1941 – too junior to be present at the meeting of 30 March – but he articulated a common view. He came from an aristocratic family with a military background, and his father had been opposed to Hitler. Nonetheless, Rüdiger von Reichert and his father shared a 'deep-rooted fear of the Bolshevization of Central Europe'. They remembered how immediately after the First World War there had been socialist revolts in both Berlin and Bavaria. Now, as Rüdiger von Reichert prepared to fight on the eastern front, he accepted that this would be 'a different kind of battle, a much more bitter battle, a battle in which everybody's survival was at stake, literally, because to us Germans, according to what we imagined, captivity could very easily mean death . . .' He felt there was a 'primeval fear of the east' stretching right back to the days of the 'Turks in front of Vienna' in the seventeenth century and the 'raids of the Huns' more than a thousand years before that. There was also the nature of Bolshevism to consider, which he saw as 'economically incompetent', so much so that he believed that the Soviet regime had 'resulted in the pauperization of the people'. He also disliked the fact that the Bolsheviks had 'an anti-religious tendency'. Another consideration, he confessed, 'albeit not a decisive one to our mind', was 'that it was said that there was a strong Jewish influence [behind Bolshevism]'.[25]

Despite these views, Rüdiger von Reichert saw himself as an honourable officer and claimed he did not approve of the atrocities committed by German units during the war in the east. While one might question the extent to which hindsight clouded his recollections, the reality is that in the aftermath of the war he was not judged to be guilty of any crimes. He subsequently became a general in the West German Army, and was awarded the Grand Cross of Merit of the Federal Republic of Germany.

More ideologically committed German soldiers voiced their opinions about the forthcoming conflict in much more strident terms. For instance, Colonel General Erich Hoepner said in an order of 2 May to the Fourth Panzer Group that the war against the Soviet Union was 'an essential phase in the struggle for existence of the German people. It is the ancient struggle of the Germanic people against the Slavs, the repelling of Jewish Bolshevism.' In this war there had to be an 'iron will' to 'exterminate the enemy completely'.[26] Days earlier, Colonel General Georg von Küchler, commander of the Eighteenth Army, had written to remind his divisional commanders that 'There is a profound abyss that separates us from Russia ideologically and racially . . . The present-day Russian state will never distance itself from its objective of world revolution, long-term peace with present-day Russia is impossible. It will always strive for expansion to the west . . . If Germany wants to have some peace for generations, from the threatening danger in the east, this cannot be about pushing Russia back a little – even if it is a hundred kilometres – but the aim must be to destroy European Russia, to dissolve the European Russian state.'[27]

Küchler also warned that 'In the case of Russian troop units who lay down their arms, one should be aware that we are fighting against racially alien soldiers.' Furthermore, 'the political commissars' within the Red Army were to be treated not as ordinary combatants but as criminals. This last reference was in support of the infamous 'Commissar Order', which was finally issued by the Army High Command on 6 June. This called for any political officers of the Red Army who were captured to be shot at once. There was no widespread opposition among the army leadership to the imposition of this murderous instruction. And while Field Marshal von Bock, now confirmed as Commander-in-Chief of Army Group Centre, the most powerful of the three army groups, did question the correctness of similar orders which allowed troops to shoot any Soviet they thought was a partisan, he did so because he feared that letting soldiers effectively kill anyone they wanted was bad for discipline.

What Bock's diary reveals is that he was concerned less with the proposed exterminatory nature of the forthcoming war and more with the military mechanics of the invasion. Commanders like Bock were focused on trying to win the war on the battlefield. They broadly accepted that this was a 'war of extermination' but thought detailed 'political' questions could be left to others. Bock hinted at his own attitude to the regime when, in the entry for 7 June, he described how he had felt unable to protect an acquaintance who had previously come to him afraid of arrest, saying he 'could not meddle in political matters'.[28]

The idea that the Wehrmacht largely fought a 'clean' war in the Soviet Union, while the 'dirty' tasks were left to the SS and other committed Nazis is a falsehood that flourished after the war when many German generals tried to airbrush their actions in their memoirs. Take the case of General Erich von Manstein, famous for his part in the drafting of the invasion plans for the 1940 campaign in the west, and now about to command a panzer corps in Operation Barbarossa. In his autobiography published in 1955 he wrote that he had informed his 'superiors that the Commissar Order would not be implemented by anyone under my command'.[29] But, on the contrary, his units did follow the Commissar Order. Indeed, at his trial after the war Manstein was found guilty of exactly this offence.[30]

Despite managing to lie in his autobiography about the Commissar Order, Manstein could not resist voicing in the same work what must surely have been his true opinion of these Soviet political functionaries. He claimed that the commissars were 'certainly not soldiers', instead 'their task was not only the political supervision of Soviet military leaders but, even more, to instil the greatest possible degree of cruelty into the fighting and to give it a character completely at variance with the traditional conceptions of soldierly behaviour.'[31] Manstein once again omits a vital truth – that it had been the German leadership, not the Soviets, that had planned on this being a war fought 'at variance with the traditional conceptions of soldierly behaviour' before the first shot was even fired. And after the war in the east had started, Manstein himself issued the following statement: 'This struggle against the Soviet army will not be solely fought according to the customary European laws of war.'[32]

The truth is that the nature of the forthcoming conflict was all too apparent to Hitler's generals. For instance, just over a week before the invasion began, Bock listened as the Führer – drunk on overconfidence as he contemplated the forthcoming campaign – talked about how to supply the '65–70 [German] divisions' that would remain in the Soviet Union after the war had been won. Hitler was adamant that they must be fed 'off the land'. It thus followed that they had to live by stealing food from the local population. Bock, according to his own diary, raised no objection.[33]

It was no surprise that Hitler raised that issue because the basis of this war was the despoiling of the Soviet Union. On 2 May, at a planning meeting attended by army officers as well as administrative officials, it was concluded that millions of Soviet citizens would die of starvation.[34] As mentioned earlier, Himmler and others subsequently mentioned they were expecting a figure of thirty million dead.[35]

Starvation was to be a central feature of the forthcoming war. It was an idea that was built into the very conception of the operation. For German planners, like Herbert Backe, under secretary at the Reich Ministry of Food and one of the architects of a 'Hunger Plan', the priority was always to ensure that there was no repeat of the collapse in food supply that had so crippled the German war effort towards the end of the First World War. Göring would pithily express this same view in August 1942 at a meeting of senior Nazi leaders: 'This everlasting concern about foreign peoples must cease now, once and for all. I have here before me reports on what you are expected to deliver. It is nothing at all, when I consider your territories. It makes no difference to me in this connection if you say that your people will starve. Let them do so, as long as no German collapses from hunger.'[36]

There was to be no compassion shown towards the population of the Soviet territory that was about to be occupied – only callousness. 'Poverty, hunger and thrift have been the lot of the Russians for centuries,' says a document signed by Herbert Backe prior to the invasion. 'Their stomachs are elastic – so let us have no misplaced pity.'[37] Alfred Rosenberg, who would become Minister for the Occupied Eastern Territories, was similarly brutal in a speech he made two days before the invasion:

'Feeding the German people undoubtedly heads the list of demands that Germany will make upon the East in the coming years . . . We do not accept that we have any responsibility for feeding the Russian population as well from these surplus-producing regions. We know that this is a harsh necessity, which has no truck with pity or sentiment.'[38]

In their determination to ravage the Soviet Union and steal food, the Nazi policymakers were motivated not just by the historical knowledge of what had happened in the First World War and the ideological drive to settle in the east, but by a sense of practical necessity. The meat ration for ordinary Germans had been lowered from 500 to 400 grams at the start of June 1941, and there was an awareness that the willingness of the German population to support the war was partly determined by the food supply.[39] As Goebbels said in his diary on 29 March, 'The Ukraine is a good bread-basket. Once we are sitting there, then we can hold out for a long time.'[40]

For these leading Nazis, the invasion of the Soviet Union potentially solved a whole host of problems. It removed the threat of Stalin withholding supplies in order to put pressure on the regime; it destroyed the British 'hope' of eventual Soviet aid; it made the Nazis masters of continental Europe; it meant that Germany gained access to an enormous amount of raw materials, and – most importantly – it created *Lebensraum* for the German people. It was a seductive package. Even the knowledge that in the process they would kill thirty million people was not sufficient to dissuade them. After all, hadn't Hitler written in *Mein Kampf* nearly twenty years before that 'Those who want to live, let them fight, and those who do not want to fight in this world of eternal struggle do not deserve to live'?[41]

It is in the context of these radical – and exterminatory – ideas that we need to place the decision made before the invasion to target specific groups of Soviet Jews. The Jews, as we have seen, were perceived as offering a particularly dangerous threat in the forthcoming conflict, because the common Nazi prejudice was that the Jews were running the Bolshevik state. Hitler had said as much, over and over again, and his followers now parroted his belief. 'Jewish-Bolshevism, you see, that was the big enemy,' said Carlheinz Behnke, an SS soldier about to take part in the coming war. 'These were the people to fight against because they meant a threat to Europe, according to the view at the time . . . The Jews were simply regarded as the leadership class or as those who were firmly in control over there in the Soviet Union.'[42] The Jews, of course, were not 'firmly in control' of the Soviet system, but this was nonetheless a lie that was widely believed.

We've seen how Jews were already suffering in the Nazi state. In Poland, for instance, thousands had already been shot in the aftermath of the invasion and many others had been forced into ghettos where they were living – and dying – in appalling conditions. But what was planned now was different. This was a systematic mass-murder plan from the start. Reinhard Heydrich, Himmler's closest subordinate, had created four Einsatzgruppen – special task forces – of around 3,000 people. These units would follow immediately behind the army groups and, as he made clear in a document dated 2 July 1941, murder 'Jews in the service of the [Communist] Party or the State'. They were also ordered to encourage the locals to rise up and attack Jews.[43]

It was not a coincidence that it was against the background of the war against the Soviet Union that the Holocaust was born. For Hitler, the conflict against Stalin would be a kind of liberation, a chance at last to confront the enemies he most hated.

As the war grew ever nearer, Stalin's position was parlous. The flight to Britain on 10 May by Hitler's deputy, Rudolf Hess, only added to his sense of misgiving. According to Khrushchev, Stalin was sure that Hess had been sent by Hitler on a mission to make peace with Britain so that Germany would have a free hand in the east.[44] In reality Hess had made a wholly unauthorized attempt to negotiate with the British on his own initiative. But the timing made Stalin even more suspicious, especially when combined with remarks the British Ambassador to Moscow, Sir Stafford Cripps, had made the previous month. On 18 April, Cripps had written to the Soviet leadership warning that Britain could, at some point in the future, be tempted to arrange a separate peace with Nazi Germany. Cripps made this extraordinary statement because he thought it might help prevent the Soviet Union moving closer to the Nazis. It was a crass move on his part and only fed Stalin's deep fear that the British were untrustworthy.[45] Shortly afterwards, when Cripps passed Stalin a warning from Churchill about an imminent German invasion, the Soviet leader refused to take it at face value.

Stalin was right to have doubts about the British. It was not that they were planning a separate peace with Germany, but that many in the

British elite felt nothing but disdain for the Soviet leadership. For example, Sir Alexander Cadogan, permanent secretary of the Foreign Office, wrote in his diary in January 1941 after the appointment of Anthony Eden as Foreign Secretary, that he was glad to find that Eden was 'quite alive to [the] uselessness of expecting anything from these cynical, blood-stained murderers'.[46] Yet Cadogan was the man called upon less than a week before the invasion to brief the representative of these 'blood-stained murderers' – the Soviet Ambassador to London, Ivan Maisky – on detailed British intelligence that appeared to prove the Germans were about to attack.

On 18 June, two days after Cadogan had passed on comprehensive information about 'this avalanche, breathing fire and death' that 'was at any moment to descend' upon the Soviet Union, Maisky had dinner with Cripps, now back in London.[47] He listened as Cripps confirmed that Hitler had nearly 150 divisions ready to invade the Soviet Union. Maisky refused to believe that the Germans would make the catastrophic mistake of starting a war with the Soviet Union. Perhaps Hitler was just using the threat of an invasion to heighten the tension and to negotiate a better deal for gaining raw materials from the Soviets.[48]

Stalin possessed the same mindset. Just like Maisky, when presented with what appeared to be unequivocal evidence he rejected it. On 17 June, he received a report from Commissar Merkulov saying that a 'source, working in the headquarters of German aviation [the Air Ministry], informs us: 1. All military measures by Germany in preparation for an armed attack on the USSR are fully complete, and an attack may be expected at any moment.' Stalin scrawled across the report: 'To Comrade Merkulov. You can tell your "source" from the German Air Headquarters that he can go and fuck his mother. This is not a "source", but a disinformant.'[49]

Hitler, by comparison, would never have spent his time studying all of the intelligence information that Stalin did, but even if he had would never have written obscenities on such a document. His sense of his own special status would have prevented him from using the language of the street.

Given their environment in the Kremlin, it's no wonder that the ambitious courtiers around Stalin were tempted to tell him what he wanted to hear. Most notable in this respect was Lavrenti Beria, whose career in large part had been based on pandering to his boss. 'A lot of functionaries have recently fallen prey to shameless provocation and the sowing of unrest,' he said to Stalin on the day before the invasion. 'We have to reduce [those] secret agents . . . to the dust of concentration camps, as aids to international provocateurs wishing to bring us into conflict with Germany.' Beria also reassured Stalin that 'my people and I . . . are staunchly maintaining your view: Hitler will not attack us in 1941.'[50]

Stalin was not, however, in a state of absolute denial. When on 20 June reports reached him that German merchant ships were leaving Soviet waters without waiting to load their cargoes, and officials in the German embassy in Moscow appeared to be burning their documents, he authorized an increase in air-defence readiness in the capital. But he still balanced any potentially aggressive actions with a desire to avoid provoking the Germans. Even now, as reports from German deserters came through saying that the attack was imminent, Stalin thought that perhaps this was just the German military acting without orders from their political leadership.

While Stalin dithered, in Germany there was a sense of optimism among many of those who knew of the impending offensive. 'The enemy will be annihilated outright,' wrote Goebbels on 16 June. 'The Führer estimates that the campaign will take four months, I estimate fewer. Bolshevism will collapse like a house of cards. We face an exceptional triumph . . .'[51] Many ordinary soldiers shared this sense of inevitability about the forthcoming war. 'We assumed that it would all happen quite quickly,' said Carlheinz Behnke of the Wiking Division of the SS, 'as had been the case throughout France; that we would definitely manage the stretch up to the Caucasus so as to then fight against Turkey and Syria. That's what we believed at the time. Not just myself, my fellow soldiers did too.'[52]

Abroad, many of Germany's adversaries had little confidence in the ability of the Red Army to hold back any German attack. As soon as they heard of the invasion, officials at the British War Office warned the BBC not to give the impression that the Soviets would be able to carry on the fight for longer than six weeks.[53] As for Germany's close ally Italy, Count Ciano thought it 'possible' that 'calculations in Berlin' were correct and the war would 'all be over in eight weeks'. But he presciently asked 'what if this should not be the case? If the Soviet armies should show the world a power of resistance superior to that the bourgeois countries have shown, what results would this have on the proletarian masses of the world?'[54]

Churchill, as we have seen, described Stalin and his close comrades as 'bunglers' because they ignored warnings of the imminent German attack. But the subsequent focus on Stalin's errors has overshadowed the fact that Hitler was as much, if not more, of a bungler. Stalin's mistakes were to prove calamitous in the short term, most notably his decision to leave so many units of the Red Army close to the border with Nazi territory and yet not placing them on full combat readiness, together with the atmosphere he created in which his commanders feared taking the initiative. All this would place the Soviet Union in danger, and all this was Stalin's fault. However, Hitler's errors, in the long term, would prove to be worse. He let his ideological prejudices blind him to the possibility that the Soviets might offer more resistance than he anticipated. It should have been clear to him at the planning stage that the Germans' own lack of resources made the initial goals of the invasion – in particular the oil of the Caucasus – all but unattainable. But just as Beria toadied to Stalin, so Hitler's generals – Halder, Brauchitsch and Keitel – went along with what their Führer wanted. All of these subordinates either suppressed their genuine opinion or made an even more disastrous error and thought the judgements of their respective leaders were correct.

Ultimately, both Hitler and Stalin made the same mistake. Both fooled themselves into believing that they could think into existence what they wanted to happen. To an extent, they lived within their own universe of alternative facts. In Stalin's case he asserted that the Germans were not planning to invade, and so this became – to him – the truth. Hitler maintained that the Soviet system would collapse under pressure, and so that became his reality. Famously, the Germans were so confident that they would win this war before winter that hardly any of their soldiers were issued with cold-weather clothes.

Neither Hitler nor Stalin understood the conceptual error they were making. Neither of them was in control of the events they imagined into existence, and yet they counted on the correctness of their predictions. Neither of them had a plan B. It was plan A or catastrophe.

In the early hours of the morning of Sunday 22 June 1941, as the German attack commenced, Goebbels wrote in his diary: 'One can hear the breath of history. A great, wonderful time in which a new Reich is born.'[55]

He could not have been more wrong.

6. Invasion

As Albert Schneider advanced into Soviet territory on the morning of Sunday 22 June, he witnessed a bizarre sight: 'Prisoners of war were coming towards us, in underpants, in nightshirts, perhaps 5 per cent of them were wearing a uniform and that was only half put on. So I gleaned from that we had managed to surprise them . . . they had been taken out of their beds.'[1]

There is perhaps no better image of the inadequacy of the Soviet response than Schneider's revelation that Red Army soldiers were – quite literally – caught with their trousers down. Schneider, who served in a German assault gun unit, entered Soviet territory a couple of hours after the first attack. And the spectacle of Red Army troops surrendering in their underwear fuelled his belief that the war would be won quickly and 'we will all be back home in a year at most.'

The Soviets had only heard confirmation that the Germans had launched an invasion shortly after four in the morning, when the German Ambassador, Count von der Schulenburg, arrived at the Kremlin. He told Molotov that the Germans had entered Soviet territory because units of the Red Army were massed so close to the border that they posed a threat. The Nazis had often used a faked pretext in an attempt to justify their aggression, but this excuse was so transparently deceitful that it was as if they had ceased even to try to concoct a plausible one. Molotov, who – according to one of the Germans who accompanied Schulenburg – was 'visibly struggling with deep inner excitement', replied that Germany had attacked without reason, adding plaintively, 'Surely we have not deserved that.'[2]

After they had learnt of the initial German incursion across the Soviet border, at around 3.30 in the morning, Timoshenko and Zhukov had insisted that Stalin be woken at his dacha. Once raised from his bed, Stalin had hurried to the Kremlin and met with a small group of advisers, including Beria and Zhukov. Stalin was still desperate to believe that this wasn't really a full-scale invasion. Prior to Schulenburg's confirmation that this was war, Stalin had suggested that it might all be a 'provocation' from senior figures in the Wehrmacht. Perhaps, he claimed, Hitler had nothing to do with it.[3]

Over the previous few weeks Stalin had been drinking more than usual, and according to Zhukov he was depressed that morning. Understandably so, as the Soviet leader was witnessing the collapse of his entire strategy. From the moment that the Nazi–Soviet pact had been signed nearly two years before, he had sought to stay out of the fight between the Germans and the Allies.

Significantly, it was Molotov, not Stalin, who spoke to the Soviet people on the day of the invasion. Molotov, as we have seen, was someone who possessed a kind of anti-charisma. An aura of lassitude hung over him, and his speech that day reflected his overwhelming dullness. He discussed the German betrayal of the Nazi–Soviet pact – something that was all but irrelevant now – and called on the population to gather round the Bolshevik Party and the 'great leader' Stalin. It would have been impossible for ordinary Soviet citizens to hear Molotov's speech without asking the question – where was Stalin's rallying cry? It was a question that remained unanswered for nearly two weeks.

In the early days of the invasion, Stalin's failure to prepare Soviet forces to face the Germans, combined with his desire to keep large numbers of Red Army units close to the front line, resulted in mayhem. 'We saw a lot of aeroplanes, [and] exploding bombs,' said Georgy Semenyak, who served in a Red Army unit at the border. 'For the first time in my life, I saw people dying.' After four days his unit started to fall back. 'We also did not understand . . . why we had to begin to retreat. It was incomprehensible. It was a dismal picture. During the day, aeroplanes continuously dropped bombs on the retreating soldiers. The retreating men moved in vast columns. They were all young men – twenty, twenty-two years old – who were armed with only rifles, hand grenades and gas masks.'[4] The officers abandoned their men, jumping on board passing vehicles in a bid to escape. And so, 'as we approached Minsk, our section was left with virtually no commanders. And without commanders, our ability to defend ourselves was so severely weakened that there really was nothing we could do.' Shortly afterwards, Semenyak was captured by the Germans.

The Germans achieved this breakthrough not because their army was fully mechanized and the Soviets were backward in technology. In fact, enormous amounts of money had already been spent by the Soviet state on new equipment for the Red Army. The Soviets possessed better

Invasion of the Soviet Union, 1941

Front lines 1941
— 21 June
···— 1 September
‒ ‒ ‒ 30 September
•••• 4 December
→ German attack

SWEDEN

FINLAND

Helsinki

Gulf of Finland

Baltic Sea

Tallinn

ESTONIA

Narva

Lake Ladoga

Leningrad

Novgorod

LATVIA

Kalinin

Moscow

LITHUANIA

Vyazma

ARMY GROUP NORTH
(Leeb)

Königsberg

Vitebsk

Smolensk

ARMY GROUP CENTRE
(Bock)

Minsk

BELORUSSIA

Tula

Białystok

SOVIET UNION

Warsaw

Brest-Litovsk

Kursk

GENERAL
GOVERNMENT
(POLAND)

Pripet Marshes

Kiev

ARMY GROUP SOUTH
(Rundstedt)

Lwów

Vinnitsa

Kharkov

Dnieper

SLOVAKIA

Carpathian Mts

Dniester

UKRAINE

HUNGARY

Odessa

Sea of Azov

ROMANIA

Bucharest

Sevastopol

Danube

Black Sea

N

| 0 | 100 miles |
| 0 | 100 km |

artillery than the Germans, and while the Germans had a greater number of trucks than the Red Army, the Soviets had more tanks and
planes.[5] Aware that his country might well face an external threat, Stalin had expanded the size of the armed forces over recent years. So much
so that the Red Army had almost quadrupled between 1937 and 1941 –
from 1.1 million soldiers to 4.2 million.[6]

The fundamental reason why the Soviets faced calamity as the Germans attacked was that the Red Army was sclerotic. Commanders did
not just fear taking the initiative, but had to endure interference from
'military illiterates' – as the war correspondent and poet Konstantin
Simonov described them – such as Stalin and Lev Mekhlis, the vicious
character who ran the Main Political Administration of the Red Army.[7]
For some Soviet officers the resulting stress was all too much. In
Ukraine, Khrushchev watched as a commander committed suicide in
front of him. 'Such incidents occurred with other commanders as well,'
wrote Khrushchev. 'That's what the situation was like. And yet we
hadn't been at war for even ten days.'[8]

Strategically, the idea that the Red Army should attack into enemy
territory as soon as the Germans advanced was shown to be disastrous,
while at a practical level the Red Army was hampered by the Soviet
suspicion of radio as a secure means of communication. With phone
landlines easily cut by the Germans, Soviet front-line units were soon
out of touch with the commanders behind them. It was a problem exacerbated by the tactics employed by the Germans. Motorized units would
attack on a narrow front – often not much more than one road – and
pierce through the Soviet defensive line. Their attack would be coordinated by radio between tanks on the ground and air support above.
Once the motorized units were through the line, infantry would follow.
The key was speed. Motorcyclists would advance even more quickly
than tanks once the line was breached and at night they would launch
flares far behind the Soviet forces. As a result Red Army units thought
they were surrounded – even before they really were. Panic was often
the consequence.

Fyodor Sverdlov, a Red Army soldier opposing German Army
Group Centre, remembered his unit retreating hundreds of miles in the
first months of the war. 'We were marching at night and fighting during
the day,' he said. 'When our company stopped at one of the villages late
at night, we wanted to have three or four hours' rest, but we were woken

up by the noise of the German motorcyclists and tanks and we had to jump out of the window and run like rabbits to the nearest wood.'[9]

In the Baltic, Mikhail Timoshenko, veteran of the Winter War, also noticed that after the Germans' 'tank armada broke through our defences, they began to send small groups of saboteurs into our rear. And they started firing into our rear. It had a big effect on morale. People started shouting, "We're surrounded!"' Timoshenko watched in amazement as 'the Germans advanced along the roads and our army from the Baltics – whole groups of men – simply threw down their weapons and their equipment and were retreating. The entire forest was crammed full of soldiers, while the Germans were advancing along the roads. They were singing songs and nobody was there to stop them. I was in shock, I didn't understand it. I asked them [the Red Army soldiers]: "Where are you going? Why have you abandoned your weapons?" They all answered the same thing: "We're surrounded!"'[10] Vasily Grossman, the Soviet war correspondent, observed the same phenomenon, writing in his notebook: 'Stories about being cut off. Everyone who has escaped back can't stop telling stories about being encircled, and all the stories are terrifying.'[11]

If the Soviets were hampered in their attempts to resist the Germans by the inadequacies of the leadership of the Red Army, the Wehrmacht benefited enormously from the way in which their leaders, often sergeants and below, were empowered to make decisions on the battlefield. The use of this *Auftragstaktik* (mission command) meant that while soldiers were told what was expected of them, they could to a large extent decide how to accomplish the objectives themselves. 'The independence of the lower-level leadership was simply marvellous,' said Peter von der Groeben, a major with an infantry division within Army Group Centre. 'The ordinary lance corporal or the NCOs, the platoon leaders, lieutenants and so on, the individual company commanders, you didn't have to tell them a lot.' Groeben considered the success of the German Army during this early period 'an astonishing achievement' and long after the war was over still had 'the highest regard for the ordinary people who did this'.[12]

A week into the invasion, and still before he had talked to the general public, Stalin learnt that Minsk, the capital of the Soviet republic of Belorussia, was in imminent danger of capture. When he confronted Zhukov, Chief of Staff of the Red Army, about this calamitous situation, Zhukov – the hardest of hard men – had tears in his eyes. Stalin

then stormed out of the room, uttering the words, 'Lenin founded our
state and now we've fucked it up!'[13] Exactly what happened next is in
dispute. Khrushchev alleged that Stalin was 'completely paralysed,
unable to act, and couldn't collect his thoughts', and that he now
retreated to his dacha having announced, 'I am giving up the leadership.' Khrushchev based this on what Beria and Malenkov subsequently
told him.[14] But doubt has been cast on the idea that Stalin could not
cope in the days immediately after the invasion. While it's true that
he retreated to his dacha on 29 June, it's uncertain exactly why. Was it
because he had emotionally collapsed or merely because he was working
on a speech and taking stock of the situation?[15]

Anastas Mikoyan memorably wrote about the visit which he and
other members of the Politburo made to the dacha to coax Stalin out.
Mikoyan claimed he had 'no doubt' that Stalin thought 'we had come to
arrest him.'[16] This was a view that Beria also held, according to his son.[17]
However, the delegation had not arrived to remove Stalin, but merely to
ask him to become head of a Committee of State Defence. Stalin agreed,
and by 1 July he was back once more in his office in the Kremlin.

The most persuasive interpretation of this incident is that, while Stalin was under enormous stress in the aftermath of the invasion, he had
not psychologically collapsed. He carried on with his work until he
decided to retreat briefly to his dacha after the meeting with his military commanders about the impending fate of Minsk. However, even
though it is unlikely that he had suffered an emotional breakdown, this
does not mean that Mikoyan and Beria were wrong about his reaction
to their arrival at his dacha. Most likely he did have suspicions that they
had come to arrest him.

The idea, sometimes put forward, that Stalin was performing a
Machiavellian trick – allegedly learnt from Ivan the Terrible – whereby
he feigned weakness in order to see if anyone was prepared to attack
him, is attractive but implausible. First, he was genuinely feeling the
pressure, so he would hardly have thought that this was the time for a
secret loyalty test. Second, why would he take the risk that his colleagues might genuinely turn against him? It would scarcely have helped
him to say, 'I was only testing,' as Beria's secret police led him away.

What's more significant, and something that's not discussed as much
as the dacha-breakdown theory, is why Stalin's close comrades did not
try to remove him now that he was at his most vulnerable. One reason

is self-evident – fear. In order to turn on Stalin they would have had to conspire, and who would risk conspiring, even at this darkest moment, in case the person you approached informed on you? But there's also a less blatant, and more important, reason why they couldn't act. For years the central message of Soviet propaganda had been the genius of Comrade Stalin. At the time of his birthday celebration in December 1939, for instance, *Pravda* described the Soviet leader in these laudatory terms: 'There is no similar name on the planet like the name of Stalin. It shines like a bright torch of freedom, it flies like a battle standard for millions of labourers around the world; it roars like thunder, warning the doomed classes of slave owners and exploiters . . . Stalin is today's Lenin! Stalin is the brain and heart of the party! Stalin is a banner of millions of people in their fight for a better life.'[18]

Now, at the most desperate time in the history of this young country, who could undo all these assertions and declare that 'the brain and heart of the party' could not cope? Even if the Politburo had pretended Stalin was ill, or dead, what effect would his absence have had on the morale of the general population? Wouldn't there have been a call for an immediate humiliating peace to be agreed with the Germans – one that would make Brest-Litovsk look generous?

While these political machinations worked their way through in Moscow, on the front line there were instances of Red Army soldiers fighting with determination against the Germans and offering effective resistance – notably at the fortress of Brest, in the very city where the Brest-Litovsk agreement had been signed just over twenty years before. But overall the picture remained bleak. In only five days the forward units of Army Group Centre had closed around Minsk, nearly a third of the way to Moscow. Heinz Guderian, the panzer commander, called this swift advance the 'first great victory of the campaign'.[19] On 3 July, a few days after Minsk had fallen, General Halder, Chief of Staff of the German Army, wrote in his diary that it was 'probably no overstatement to say that the Russian Campaign has been won in the space of two weeks'.[20]

Around this same time back in Germany, civil servant Friedrich Kellner heard one lady remark, 'The successes are simply fabulous,' and a man say, 'The Russian armies will be captured in eight days.'[21] The Germans weren't alone in this optimism. Maisky, the Soviet Ambassador to London, noted that officials at the War Office in London didn't think the Soviets would hold out 'more than 4–6 weeks'.[22] It was a view shared by George Orwell, who wrote in his diary on 23 June that the British were anticipating that communists would soon flee the Soviet Union and become émigrés 'just like the White Russians' who had previously escaped the revolution. 'People have visions of Stalin in a little shop in Putney,' he wrote, 'selling samovars and doing Caucasian dances, etc., etc.'.[23] In America, the Secretary of War wrote to President Roosevelt that after consulting military experts he had found 'substantial unanimity' of opinion. Their conclusion: that 'Germany will be thoroughly occupied in beating Russia for a minimum of one month and a possible maximum of three months.'[24]

In determining their own public response to the invasion, the British and American governments had to walk a delicate line, not just because they believed that the most likely outcome was that Stalin would soon be defeated, but also because both governments had roundly condemned communism in the past. In a statement issued on 23 June, Sumner Welles, acting Secretary of State, emphasized that 'the principles and doctrines of communistic dictatorship are as intolerable and as alien' to Americans as 'the principles and doctrines of Nazi dictatorship. Neither kind of imposed overlordship can have, or will have, any support or any sway in the mode of life, or in the system of government, of the American people.' However, because of the aggressive nature of the Nazi regime, 'any defense against Hitlerism, any rallying of the forces opposing Hitlerism, from whatever source these forces may spring, will hasten the eventual downfall of the present German leaders.'[25] In other words, the Americans hated both regimes, but since one was an immediate threat they should consider supporting the other. It was not exactly an offer of wholehearted support, and this grudging statement was not even issued by the President himself.

Churchill's response was altogether more sophisticated. He too emphasized, in a speech he gave on the day of the invasion, that 'The Nazi regime is indistinguishable from the worst features of Communism' and that he would 'unsay' nothing that he had previously said about the nature of Stalin's regime. But then, in a great rhetorical flourish, he talked of the '10,000 villages of Russia, where the means of existence was wrung so hardly from the soil, but where there are still primordial human joys, where maidens laugh and children play'. He went on to picture this idyll under the 'hideous onslaught' of the 'Nazi war machine'. Cleverly, he diverted his listeners' sympathy towards the ordinary Soviet people, and while implying that Stalin and his gang might be despicable, he emphasized that what mattered now was the fate of the Soviet peasants. Churchill also argued, much as the Americans had done, that 'the Russian danger' was 'our danger' because Hitler was now a common enemy.[26]

In Moscow, Stalin did his best to respond to the difficulties that beset the regime, and his immediate actions were characteristic in two ways. First, as his colleagues had suggested, he formed a committee. Stalin always felt comfortable with committees, and he now became head of the most powerful one in the Soviet state – the Stavka, the Committee of State Defence. Second, he searched for scapegoats. Again, this was his standard response in a crisis. His default reaction was to seek to blame someone – and, whoever was held responsible, it could never be Stalin himself. In this case, the military commanders were blamed. One of the most high profile of those targeted was General Dmitry Pavlov, who had commanded units that faced the maelstrom that was German Army Group Centre. Pavlov was arrested in early July and executed before the end of the month. Many of his subordinate officers were killed along with him, including his chief of communications. For good measure Pavlov was also charged with involvement in a plot against the Soviet state dating back to the 1930s. It was not thought necessary to explain why someone guilty of such a crime could possibly have been allowed, five years later, to command large elements of the Red Army.

Pavlov was not exactly a dynamic leader – one of his axioms was 'Never mind – those at the top know better than we do.' But many others had also been responsible for the calamity at the front.[27] Indeed, there is some truth in the statement Pavlov made after he had been accused: 'I am not a traitor. The defeat of the forces that I commanded took place for reasons beyond my control.'[28] Pavlov had been ordered, in accordance with the flawed Soviet strategy of fighting an offensive form of defence, to attack the Germans – and this had only made it easier for the Germans to surround his forces. But the architects of this disastrous strategy were never held to account – just those who tried to carry it out.

As part of this vengeful response to the crisis, the Soviet security forces turned on those internal enemies they considered a threat. For instance, at Brygidki prison in Lwów, in Soviet-occupied Poland, the NKVD murdered around 4,000 political prisoners as the Germans approached.[29] Olga Popadyn, who was in the prison hospital at the time of the killings, remembered seeing 'a number of dead bodies' by the prison gates, and that in the heat of the summer a terrible smell soon pervaded the area.[30] Up to 10,000 more prisoners were killed elsewhere. Others were deported east – around 750,000 prisoners – and many died en route.[31]

Nor was it only prisoners who suffered. Just prior to the invasion, thousands of people considered 'enemies of the Soviet state' had been deported from the Baltic States, together with their partners and children. On 13–14 June, about 18,000 were deported from Lithuania alone.[32] The lie that the 'Jews' were behind this crime would subsequently be spread by the Nazis and others, a calumny that was especially cruel since a number of Jews had been among those deported from the Baltic States by the Soviet security forces.[33]

However, these responses – the formation of a special committee and the murder and punishment of 'enemies of the people' – were not the only ones Stalin employed. Intriguingly, he also did two things that were new. First, on 3 July he finally spoke to the Soviet people, more than a week after the invasion. Famously, he started his speech by saying, 'Comrades, citizens, brothers and sisters. Men of our army and navy. I am addressing you, my friends.'[34] At the time this was a remarkable – indeed a radical – opening. The reference to 'brothers and sisters' and 'my friends' offered a level of intimacy that had not been present in any previous Stalin speech. It was as if he had decided to assume the role of father of the Soviet people – independent of Bolshevik principle. It was almost a return to a more traditional, nationalist approach. Many Soviet citizens would remember the 'warmth' of this greeting for years.[35]

The rest of his speech was less impressive and altogether more prosaic. Stalin lied and said that the 'finest divisions' of the German Army had already been defeated – a statement that fitted badly with his subsequent assertion that 'a grave danger hangs over our country'. He also felt compelled to justify the signing of the pact with the Nazis, saying that any other 'peace-loving' state would have acted the same way.[36] But none of this really mattered alongside the power of his opening words.

The second surprising action Stalin took in those early days of the war related to religion. Despite the fact that the regime had closed the majority of churches and persecuted many priests, Stalin allowed religious leaders like Patriarch Sergius of the Orthodox Church to make a rallying cry, calling on the Soviet population to fight back against the Germans. This was a considerable reversal of policy. The Church had suffered appallingly under Stalin. By the spring of 1938 only five churches were open in Leningrad.[37]

Stalin likely acted this way because the Soviet persecution of Christians was an obstacle in his pursuit of better relations with countries like America – nations that he now wanted on his side. But it was also an attempt to unite as many Soviets as possible behind the resistance cause.[38] Stalin knew that it had not been possible, so far, for the godless Bolsheviks to eliminate Christian belief within the Soviet Union. Although many churches had closed, a number of those that had remained open were well attended. Now he could capitalize on that reality, as long as he accepted that this was a time to take a more pliable attitude towards enforcing his ideological beliefs.

But while Stalin demonstrated an element of flexibility, Hitler remained as uncompromising – and annihilatory – in his ideological aims as ever. The German leader was now ensconced at the Wolf's Lair, his military headquarters in a forest a few miles from the East Prussian town of Rastenburg. Here he talked to his close associates about the nature of the conflict he had just unleashed. Two weeks into the war, he said that 'Bolshevism must be exterminated . . . Moscow, as the centre of the doctrine, must disappear from the earth's surface, as soon as its riches have been brought to shelter.'[39] A few weeks later he was reminding his dinner guests that 'The Slavs are a mass of born slaves, who feel the need of a master.'[40] He was also scathing about Ukrainians, saying that he had 'no interest' in establishing an independent Ukraine and that he thought it 'better' not to 'teach them to read'.[41]

Many of those outside the Nazi elite did not realize at first that Hitler's intentions were so draconian. For instance, Carlheinz Behnke, of the SS Wiking Division, thought that Ukraine would have a privileged status in the east: 'Since we knew of the special relationship with Ukraine – already during the First World War, Ukraine had been independent for a brief period – we assumed that once Ukraine had been occupied, it would become an independent state and the soldiers [from Ukraine] would probably fight on our side against the rest of the Bolshevists.'[42]

Many Ukrainians felt the same way. 'The Germans who fought against the Soviet Union were perceived by us as allies, especially since everyone was hoping that they would immediately set up a Ukrainian state,' said Aleksey Bris, who started to work for the Germans as an interpreter after they had arrived in Ukraine. 'In the beginning everybody thought that the war would really end with a total defeat of the Soviet Union . . . we lived in an environment in which we were creating Ukrainian culture . . . [for] the young people, it was all very exciting and beautiful.'

Bris did not think he had done anything wrong in collaborating with the Germans. 'If you are part of any system at all, irrespective of where it is, you have to live within that system. You can either make your way up within that system, or slide down within it. The system surrounds you and you swim along with all the rest.' Above all, he emphasized, he and the others who collaborated had been driven by the 'hope that the Germans would come and set up a Ukrainian state'.[43]

One of the main reasons Ukrainians wanted to be rid of Soviet rule was the appalling suffering they had endured less than ten years before – suffering for which Stalin was largely responsible. Nearly four million Ukrainians had died in a famine that was linked both to Stalin's desire for the collectivization of agricultural land and to his insistence that food should be taken from Ukraine to feed the rest of the Soviet Union. The push towards collectivization – a policy which meant that peasants lost control of their own farmland and livestock – was linked to Bolshevik theory. Peasants who sold their produce and made decisions about managing their own smallholding were, in Bolshevik terms, akin to capitalists. More than 100,000 kulaks, the wealthier peasants, were sent to the Gulag in the early 1930s and in excess of two million more peasants were deported to remote regions of the Soviet Union like Siberia.[44]

To make matters worse, government officials scoured the countryside checking that peasants were not concealing food from the state. One Ukrainian, Olha Tsymbaliuk, recalled that these Soviet officials snatched 'flour, cereals, everything stored in pots, clothes, cattle. It was impossible to hide. They searched with metal rods . . . they searched in stoves, broke floors and tore away walls.'[45]

By stealing food from the peasants in the early 1930s, these Bolsheviks foreshadowed the Germans' actions in 1941. The Ukrainians – living in one of the most fertile regions on earth – were thus to suffer two appalling periods of starvation, precisely because powers from outside coveted their agricultural riches. In the early 1930s they starved because of decisions made by Stalin and his followers, and in the early 1940s they starved because of decisions taken by Hitler and his followers.

Given the events of the 1930s in Ukraine, it was not surprising that so many Ukrainians initially wanted to help the Nazis. In doing so, many of them sought not just to take part in an independent Ukraine within the Nazi empire, but to punish those they scapegoated for the crimes of the Bolsheviks – most notably the Jews. In a series of pogroms in Lwów, Ukrainian locals supported by German Einzatzkommandos murdered at least 4,000 Jews.[46] Carlheinz Behnke, then in the Waffen SS, witnessed the bloody action of the Ukrainians in the Lwów area. The reason the Jews were targeted, he believed, was because 'of the mass murders by the retreating Red Army', in particular the killing of prisoners at Brygidki prison in the city. He remembered that he and his comrades 'thought it was justified, that's clear, that's what we thought. The initiators of the acts which the Red Army committed, well, now it was their turn and they were being shot too . . . I always have to stress that at the time, given our education, we didn't see anything else and were incredibly trusting and simply believed it . . . as an ordinary soldier, eighteen years of age, you didn't worry about things being unlawful, not at all.'[47]

The idea that the Jews whom the Ukrainians and Germans were killing in Lwów had actually been responsible for the deaths of prisoners at Brygidki was ludicrous, since the prisoners had been killed by members of the NKVD who had now fled the city. But the murder of so many innocent Jews demonstrated once again the elision of Bolshevism and Judaism that was so commonplace in Nazi thinking.

There were many more instances, in other parts of German-occupied Soviet territory, of locals killing Jews, encouraged and helped by the Germans. In Lithuania, for example, German figures suggest that 3,800 Jews were killed in the city of Kaunas alone, and large numbers of Lithuanians murdered Jews alongside the Nazi killing squads across the country.[48] In one notorious incident outside a garage in Kaunas, a Lithuanian man used an iron bar to smash the heads of forty to fifty Jews. A crowd gathered to watch, and one of the Germans who witnessed the murders later remarked that 'The conduct of the civilians, among whom there were women and children, was unbelievable. After every blow of the iron bar they applauded.'[49]

While these killings were taking place, German soldiers continued to advance into Soviet territory. But there were soon worrying signs for the German planners that the Wehrmacht was not making as much progress as anticipated. German soldiers discovered, for instance, that their

tanks were using much more fuel on the bad roads than had been
expected. And both air crews and infantry were suffering from exhaustion. This all meant that the territory which they had anticipated
conquering within twenty days had not been subjugated within forty.[50]

In addition, even though enormous numbers of Red Army troops
had been killed or captured, Soviet reserves were greater than the
Germans had previously believed. 'The whole situation makes it
increasingly plain that we have underestimated the Russian colossus,'
wrote General Halder in his diary on 11 August. 'At the outset of
the war, we reckoned with about 200 enemy divisions. Now we have
already counted 360.' Even though Halder believed that these units
were not up 'to our standards', the truth was 'there they are'. Another
problem Halder identified was that as Red Army soldiers were pushed
back German supply lines became more stretched, while the Soviets
were getting 'near their own resources'.[51]

Shortly after Halder wrote these words there was a major dispute
between Hitler and his generals. Units of Army Group Centre were
engaged in a battle for Smolensk, a city on the central axis of attack towards
Moscow. Though the Germans would eventually win this battle in early
September, Soviet resistance was stronger than expected and every day the
struggle continued German forces fell further behind the original invasion
schedule. The question now – a question that had been fudged before
the invasion began – was straightforward. Should the Germans press on
towards Moscow, or pause at Smolensk while different units of Army
Group Centre headed north towards Leningrad and south to aid their
colleagues fighting to capture the resources of Ukraine? Halder and
Brauchitsch both wanted to push on to Moscow. Hitler disagreed, so much
so that he put the reasons for his disagreement in writing – something, as
we have seen, he rarely did. While he accepted that the Germans had been
successful so far because 'individual army groups or armies' had been able
to 'make their own decisions' about how to defeat the enemy, he emphasized that this freedom was only acceptable as long as it did not interfere
with his 'master plan'. And Hitler's 'master plan' most certainly did not
involve moving immediately on Moscow, but focused instead on destroying the Soviet military and gaining valuable resources for the Reich.[52]

Hitler was not in good shape when he wrote this note. We know this
because Goebbels visited him around this time and found him 'rather
exhausted and in poor health'. This was understandable, concluded

reds of thousands had already
ie infamous Order 270, which
ather than be captured. Com-
targeted. If they surrendered,
eir families could be arrested.[65]
ow in the chain of command,
it to the death. It was an order
s, because it made command-
ir troops. A tactical retreat to
sensible decision taken under
idered a betrayal.
rian's command, managed to
nber. It was now obvious that
ge numbers of Soviet troops.
ient as Chief of Staff, warned
s should pull back, but Stalin
authorize a minor reposition-
rponos, in command of the
or lines of retreat and start
istance.'[66]
cov, Kirponos' chief of staff,
g. Stalin called this a 'panic-
ad and restraint'. He wanted
without looking back'.[67] But
eality. Finally, on 16 Septem-
draw. But General Kirponos
iving it in writing. Who can
previous messages and the
ving day, 17 September, Red
3ut it was too late. The Ger-

a gigantic scale. More than
vas the biggest defeat yet for
can be laid at Stalin's door.
best form of defence, which
war, had not been devised
oorted, the decision not to

Goebbels, as the 'responsibility for an entire continent sits on his shoulders today'. Hitler felt he had been 'fooled' over the capabilities of Soviet forces, as they were much stronger than he had been led to believe. He even told Goebbels that he thought 'maybe the moment will come when Stalin will ask us for peace.' If that happened then Hitler might possibly be tempted to accept as long as the Germans gained 'extensive' amounts of territory and the 'Bolshevik army' was destroyed 'to the last gun'.[53]

Goebbels' encounter with Hitler in the gloomy surroundings of his military headquarters was a remarkable one. The Führer – who normally demonstrated complete confidence in his judgement – was wavering. He told Goebbels that, instead of destroying Bolshevism, the Nazis could be 'indifferent' towards its fate, as 'without the Red Army, Bolshevism is no threat to us.'[54]

It's not hard to comprehend why Hitler might have been feeling this way. The greatest gamble of his career – even bigger in scale than his decision to attack western Europe the previous year – was not going as he had expected. He would shortly recover, but this low point in his fortunes, witnessed by Goebbels, was the first crack in Hitler's carapace of self-confidence about the struggle ahead.

But if this was a bad moment for Hitler, it was also a bad moment for Stalin. He had not just made a series of strategic blunders before the war began that had helped the Germans in their advance, but he was still making strategic decisions which damaged the Red Army's chances of mounting a successful defence. Not that he was allowing this anxiety to show to those who worked for him – at least according to Nikolay Ponomariev, a member of Stalin's communications staff in the Kremlin. He met Stalin for the first time in the summer of 1941. 'I was very nervous,' said Ponomariev. 'Maybe I only survived the experience because I was young, I was twenty-four years old and I'd never been so close to Stalin before, only [seen him] during parades when he'd been up on the podium, but now he was only about a metre away from me.' Ponomariev was impressed by Stalin's grasp of the situation. 'At that time, I was doing a great deal of work, handling all kinds of talks with the big commanders, but nobody was as articulate as he was. From then on, a great weight lifted from my mind and I realized that I would be able to work with him.'

Rather like Hitler's valet, who thought his boss was a 'nice person',[55] Ponomariev was keen to point out that he thought from his own

personal experience that there was another side to the leader h
one that historians have neglected. 'I think it was on the secor
came in, greeted me, shook my hand and turned out to be a c
different person from when I'd seen him the first time [wh
been so serious]. He was pleasant, interested in things, enjoy
What was more, 'in my view, he was . . . how shall I put it . .
kind. Attentive. In five years, not once did I hear him raise h
anyone or offend anyone or behave in an unpleasant way – no
That's why I respected him, and I'll say it straight, I loved h
poise, which made it easy for me to handle the talks and get al
him], so to speak, to feel at home with and close to him.'[56]

This is a side of Stalin that is not often remarked upon. I
we run away with the notion that he was a 'kind' person, w
contextualize Ponomariev's remarks. Ponomariev was a jun
within the Kremlin hierarchy, just as Hitler's valet was withir
system. For a young soldier like him it was a life-changing ev
be in the same room as Stalin. He was massively predisposed, I
all of the pressures of the cultural environment he inhabite
Stalin impressive. A half-smile from the Soviet leader, one sy
word – actions which in someone else might have gor
unnoticed – suddenly become magnified into essential charac

Despite his supposed 'articulacy' and 'poise', the disasters ke
for Stalin that summer. In late August, he presided over the big
disaster in either Soviet or Russian history. Over 200 ships –
of warships and merchant transport vessels – attempted to
of the harbour at Tallinn, in Estonia, and make for the Sovi
Kronstadt to the north-east. By this point Tallinn was surro
German forces, and because Stalin and his military comma
delayed the exit of the fleet as long as possible, they had allc
for the Germans to lay nearly 3,000 mines in the path of the
ships.[57] A combination of these mines and attacks by Germa
wreaked havoc on the fleeing Soviet forces. 'Erupting out c
huge pillars of flame and black smoke signalled the loss of figh
and transport vessels,' said Admiral Kuznetsov, the Commis
Navy. 'With nightfall, the hideous roar of Nazi bombers sub
this didn't mean that the crews could relax, because of the d
threatening from the water. In the darkness it was difficult
moored mines, now floating amongst the debris of smashed li

Red Army soldiers surrendering, as hun
done. On 16 August he put his name to
instructed units of the Red Army to die
manders and commissars were particular
they would be considered deserters and tl
But every single soldier, no matter how
was told to insist that their unit should fi
that would have unintended consequenc
ers frightened of pulling back to save th
allow a unit to regroup and fight again –
battlefield conditions – could now be co

The Second Panzer Group, under Gu
cross the River Desna at the start of Sept
the Germans were seeking to encircle la
Marshal Shaposhnikov, Zhukov's replac
Stalin and suggested that Red Army un
refused. Even though he did subsequentl
ing of some troops, he told General I
South-Western Front, to 'Stop looking
looking for lines of resistance and only r

On 13 September Major General Tup
reported that 'catastrophe' was approach
ridden dispatch' and demanded a 'clear
Red Army units to 'put up a stubborn fig
mere words could not change the militar
ber, the Red Army was authorized to w
wouldn't implement the order without re
blame him, given the content of Stali
threatening nature of Order 270? The fol
Army units at last attempted to pull bac
mans had encircled them.[68]

It was a disaster for the Soviet Union
600,000 troops were killed or captured. I
the Red Army, and it was a calamity tl
While the Soviet doctrine of attack as tl
had caused so many losses at the start of
by Stalin but merely enthusiastically s
retreat from Kiev was entirely his.

Jews. It was a massacre of innocent civilians without parallel – so far – in the war.

Dina Pronicheva was one of the few who managed to escape Babi Yar. Having first been ordered – like the other Jews – to take off her clothes, she dropped into the murder pit just before she was shot and pretended to be dead. Amid the maelstrom of shooting, and with naked bodies all around her, she lay undetected. Later that day, as she tried to make her escape, she saw near by that 'seven or so Germans brought two young Jewish women [who were still alive]. They went down lower to the ravine, chose an even place and began to rape these women by turns. When they became satisfied, they stabbed the women with daggers . . . And they left the bodies like this, naked, with their legs open.'[83]

It is only relatively recently that the crimes of sexual violence committed by the Germans and their collaborators have been subjected to the kind of scholarly analysis that these atrocities merit. This work gives the lie to the idea that the occupying forces were restrained from committing such atrocities by the ideological strictures of Nazism. The truth is that this was a vile and dirty war in all possible ways.

Sexual contact between Germans and either Jews or Slavs was officially strictly forbidden. But this rule was not enforced rigorously. For example, Carlheinz Behnke confessed after the war that while serving with his SS unit he had had sex with a 'pretty young Ukrainian or Russian woman' in a town east of Kiev. He wrote in his diary that he 'mounted' her, together with 'many comrades'. Behnke's 'punishment' for this 'race crime' was merely not to be promoted for six months.

Behnke claims that the woman consented to sex – although how consent was possible in such circumstances is impossible to imagine. 'We heard there is this house,' he said, 'and there it could be done. So four or five of us went there. Well, and one after the other. As one did in one's youthful carelessness. Without thinking anything of it.' He maintained that he and his comrades gave the woman 'chocolate' in payment for the sex. 'To this day I can smell her perfume, and whenever I smell a perfume like it, I say: "That smells like a Russian tart!" Maybe harsh words, but I still remember that smell. And we found out that the Russian or the Ukrainian women weren't "subhuman creatures", but that they were just as beautiful as our own women, you see. Not really coarse, but a bit more sturdily built, but beautiful women.'[84]

In Kiev, Viktoria Ivanova and her mother heard about the massacre at Babi Yar within hours of it happening. 'Everyone knew that shooting had taken place,' she said. 'You cannot hide such a fact. The knowledge spread around the city very quickly.' She and her mother immediately went into hiding, and were passed between various friends. In one flat they hid in a room concealed from the rest of the apartment by a large wardrobe, 'So when the Germans were looking into that room they would only see five or six people sleeping together, and they couldn't see that there was another room beyond it. So in this state of fear we lived. All this horror we had to survive. Of course, being a child, I was shivering and I was clinging to my mother and I knew that every minute they could penetrate into our room and they would immediately shoot us and the people who were hiding us. It went on for three years.'

Ivanova was well aware of the contrasting way in which non-Jewish Ukrainians acted during the war: 'There were people among Ukrainians who were saving Jews and there were some who were betraying Jews, because the population divided into two parts.' Her own mother was subsequently killed by the Germans because a neighbour informed on her. 'Naturally, I had a double kind of feeling,' she said, 'because I was saved by Ukrainians . . . [but] I hated those who were betraying our people. I can't respect such people.'

More than anything, however, Ivanova blames the Germans for visiting all this horror upon Ukraine in general and Ukrainian Jews in particular: 'I thought they were beasts, like dogs. I associated them with their hounds. We used to call them German Shepherds, because a person who can kill another person is like a dog that is trained to capture people and to kill them.'[85]

Hitler did not personally kill Viktoria Ivanova's mother and the other Jews of Kiev, any more than Stalin had watched as Ukrainians starved to death in the famine of the early 1930s. But both of them were responsible for their respective crimes. All the suffering they created was the product of the ideologies they proselytized. Stalin ruthlessly pursued his policy of restructuring Soviet agriculture even though he knew of the deaths that were occurring as a result, and Hitler's worldview meant that Jews in the Soviet Union had to be eliminated in one way or another.

An ideology is only words, but the suffering that can result is very real. And in the Soviet Union, that suffering was about to get much worse.

7. Desperate Days

The autumn of 1941 was a turning point in the lives of Hitler and Stalin. One of them would publicly declare that victory had almost been won, while the other would make what was arguably the single most important decision of his life.

In early autumn Hitler was full of confidence. The Red Army had been not just defeated at Kiev, but utterly crushed. This was the kind of victory that Hitler had been counting on since the moment he had decided upon the invasion. 'He is exceptionally pleased with this development and positively exudes joy,' wrote Goebbels after meeting him on 23 September. 'The spell has been broken. We can anticipate great new victories again within the next three to four weeks.'

The sick and dispirited Hitler that Goebbels had encountered back in August was no more. Now Hitler talked of getting quickly to Stalingrad and denying the 'Bolsheviks' access to 'their coal and armaments production'. All his dreams of seizing Soviet resources seemed possible once again. He also told Goebbels of his plans for Leningrad. He wanted this great metropolis to 'vanish' from the face of the earth. Bolshevism, he said, had originated here and 'in this city Bolshevism will ultimately be smashed.' He had no plans for German troops to capture the city as 'we would not be able to feed the mass of 5 million [people] herded together there.' The plan was to starve them to death and 'destroy' the city by blasting it out of existence. 'The most dreadful city drama history has ever seen will show itself here,' wrote Goebbels. 'Bolshevism, which began with hunger, blood and tears, will [become] extinct in hunger, blood and tears.'

Hitler boasted to Goebbels that 'The actions that are currently being undertaken are his very own work.' He said that his military 'experts', such as Brauchitsch, had opposed his wish to move troops south and attack Kiev. Moreover, he had even been 'forced to record his actual intentions in a detailed memo to convince the generals of the rightness of his operational measures. In fact, this is a deplorable sign of lack of boldness in our military authorities' train of thought. Of course, today everybody is convinced of the rightness of these measures, since there is success. But this isn't hard to do; what is hard is to predict successes correctly. It is easy to honour successes that have already been achieved.'[1]

It was an archetypal Hitlerian performance. Many of his characteristics as a leader were on show. The absence of magnanimity towards those he had defeated – indeed, has there ever been a crueller conqueror? The grandiose plans that were wildly overambitious – how could the German Army possibly reach Stalingrad, more than 600 miles away across the steppe, before winter made the terrain virtually impassable for German tanks? And his conceited, grotesquely egotistical urge to boast that he had been right all along. It wasn't enough that victory had been won at Kiev, he wanted to humiliate the 'experts' who had contradicted him.

We see all this showing off and inhumanity as hugely negative. But Goebbels, along with many other Nazis, didn't perceive Hitler's words that way. The killing of millions of 'Bolsheviks' was regarded as necessary, given that they were thought to be 'subhuman' and the Germans wanted their land. The notion that, with winter approaching and their supply lines stretched, the Wehrmacht could advance hundreds of miles across the steppes was seen as a wonderfully aspirational goal. What could be more exhilarating than ambitious objectives that once reached would make all of them famous for eternity? As for Hitler's criticism of his generals, did not that just prove yet again – reassuringly – that the Führer was always right?

On 17 September, a few days before he met Goebbels, Hitler had been boasting of his brilliance to a different set of cronies. In one of his after-dinner monologues he reiterated that he had needed to 'throw all my authority into the scales' to enable the Kiev operation to happen. He then cynically remarked, 'I note in passing that a great part of our successes have originated in "mistakes" we've had the audacity to commit.'[2]

That same night he revealed how he approached the making of key decisions. 'The spirit of decision does not mean acting at all costs,' he said. 'The spirit of decision consists simply in not hesitating when an inner conviction commands you to act.' It's a useful insight into Hitler's mentality as a leader. As we have seen, he did not follow the conventional rule of management – first consult as wide a range of views as possible and then decide. More often than not, he consulted no one but himself. At crucial moments in the history of the Third Reich he merely announced to his underlings what he had decided. He then relied on his lack of self-doubt and considerable powers of persuasion, allied to the authority of his office, to push through what he wanted.

This did not necessarily mean that Hitler was always decisive. As General Halder had noted during the French campaign, he was sometimes 'terribly nervous' and 'afraid to take any chance'.[3] But his comments on 17 September explain why this was so. Hitler always found it necessary to wait for his 'inner conviction' before making a major decision. If such a feeling was absent, then he did not know for sure what to do. The fate of Germany was thus in the hands of a man who was controlled by the emotions of his 'inner conviction' – a sensation which he could not call upon when needed, but for which he was forced to wait.[4]

The contrast between Hitler and Stalin that autumn was glaring, not just in terms of the way the war was progressing – Stalin was as anxious about events as Hitler was confident – but also in manner of leadership. While it was certainly true, as we have seen in the context of Kiev, that Stalin was capable of making inept decisions entirely on his own, he did not rely on 'inner conviction' to tell him what to do. Most often he first consulted with his comrades and then acted. Take the communication he sent to the Bolshevik leaders in Leningrad after he had learnt that the town of Shlisselburg, just over 20 miles east of the city, had fallen to the Germans on 9 September. Unlike Hitler, who would issue 'Führer directives' in his own name, Stalin most of the time signed his instructions along with several of his colleagues – in this case Molotov, Malenkov and Beria. 'We are disgusted by your conduct,' the telegram said. 'All you do is report the surrender of this or that place, without saying a word about how you plan to put a stop to all these losses of towns and railway stations. The manner in which you informed us of the loss of Shlisselburg was outrageous.'[5]

But though there appeared to be a gulf in leadership style between the two dictators, the idea that Stalin was part of a collective decision-making process was an illusion. Though four people signed the document sent to the leadership of Leningrad, the sentiment in the telegram was authentic Stalin. He believed in creating a blame culture that was all pervasive. What he feared was loss of control, and the way he felt his overarching control could best be maintained was by naked threat.

At the same time as Stalin was raging about the fate of Leningrad, he was instructing his Ambassador to London, Ivan Maisky, to warn Churchill that if he didn't authorize the equipment and other material the Soviets demanded there was the 'risk' that the Germans would win the war in the east. Moreover, Maisky, on Stalin's behalf, wanted the British either to cross the Channel and fight the Germans in France or attack the Nazi state via the Balkans. Once again, Churchill warned that the British would only achieve 'certain defeat' if they followed such a course.[6]

In this same meeting, Churchill also said that Britain could not provide the military aid the Soviets needed in the narrow timescale that Stalin demanded. 'Only God, in whom you don't believe,' said Churchill, 'can help you in the next 6–7 weeks.' In any case, he added, even if the desired equipment was authorized immediately, it wouldn't arrive in the Soviet Union for several months.

Stalin replied to Churchill just over a week later, asking the British to send '25–30 divisions' to the Soviet Union to fight 'side by side' with the Red Army. Once again Churchill turned the request down, saying it was 'sad' that he could not send the troops Stalin asked for, 'but, unfortunately, that's how it is.'[7] He took this line despite warning in a note to Roosevelt at the start of September that 'we could not exclude the impression that they [the Soviets] might be thinking of separate terms.'[8] But not even the possibility that Stalin might try to exit the war and make peace with Hitler could change the reality of the British position.

In early October the British and Americans did, at least, manage to conclude an agreement that offered some additional aid to the Soviet war effort – although Stalin was underwhelmed by how the deal worked out. Under the 'First Protocol', Churchill and Roosevelt agreed to send several hundred aircraft and tanks every month to the Soviet Union. But fewer than 500 British tanks were delivered in 1941, along with just over two dozen American ones. Moreover, the Soviets were unhappy with the quality of the British tanks they received. The Matilda and Valentine tanks were considered both slow and vulnerable.[9]

Stalin's desperate desire for outside assistance reflected a worrying truth for the Soviets – Hitler's forces appeared to be better led, better trained and altogether superior to the soldiers of the Red Army. A flavour of this crisis in Soviet confidence was caught by the war correspondent Vasily Grossman, when he witnessed the interrogation of a captured

Wehrmacht motorcyclist in September 1941. 'He is Austrian,' wrote Grossman, 'tall, good-looking. Everyone admires his long, soft, steel-coloured leather coat. Everyone is touching it, shaking their heads. This means: how on earth can one fight people who wear such a coat?'[10]

Soviet forces were about to face an even bigger challenge. After the victory at Kiev, Hitler authorized Operation Typhoon, the advance on Moscow. In preparation for the attack, Field Marshal von Bock's Army Group Centre had been strengthened to create a force of more than 1,500 tanks and almost two million soldiers. No German commander in history had ever had such an instrument of war at his disposal.

Guderian's panzers launched the offensive on 30 September and soon gained a spectacular victory. In just four days his tanks travelled more than 120 miles and captured the city of Orel. The Soviets were taken completely by surprise. When the first units of the 6th Company of the 4th Panzer Division arrived in the city they saw the trams rumbling through the streets.[11] 'City life was still in full swing,' recalled Arthur Wollschlaeger, commander of 6th Company. 'When the citizens of Orel saw us, they fled into the buildings and side streets, white as ghosts. Rattling and swaying, a streetcar tried to exercise its right of way, even ringing its bell.'[12] Famously, when Vasily Grossman's editor 'angrily' asked him 'why didn't you file anything about the heroic defence of Orel?' he replied, 'Because there was no defence.'[13]

Orel was the first of a series of German victories over the next few weeks that made many of those around Hitler convinced that the war in the east was effectively won. 'It seemed', wrote Nicolaus von Below, Hitler's Luftwaffe adjutant, 'that an open road to Moscow lay before us.'[14] Amid this glow of optimism, Hitler returned to Berlin from the Wolf's Lair to give a speech at the start of the Winter Relief programme. This speech, at the Sportpalast on the afternoon of 3 October, is one of the most important that Hitler ever gave, not because he said anything new about his fundamental ideology, but because in the course of the address he made one of the greatest mistakes of his political career – a mistake that was devastating for a charismatic leader.

Hitler, talking not just to the audience in front of him but to the German people via radio, stated categorically that 'everything' had 'gone as planned' and 'this enemy is already broken down and will never rise again!'[15] These were words which many people took to mean that the war in the east had been won and the Red Army defeated. As a result, there

was an intense, short-term benefit for the regime – one amplified by the
fact that this was the first time Hitler had talked in public since the start of
the war against the Soviet Union. 'Internally the Führer's speech has
worked like a wonder,' wrote Goebbels in his diary on 5 October. 'All
criticism, all pessimism, even all the anxiety has vanished completely.'
But Goebbels, a sophisticated propagandist, also expressed 'concern' in his
diary that 'public opinion' might rise 'too high' as a consequence.[16]

Six days later on 9 October, Otto Dietrich, Hitler's press secretary,
held a briefing for journalists and was just as overconfident as his Führer
had been, if not more so. 'For all military purposes,' proclaimed
Dietrich, 'Soviet Russia is done with.'[17] The next day the German press
was triumphant. 'The military power of Bolshevism is shattered for
ever,' said the *Preussische Zeitung*. 'Victory in the east dashes England's
hopes for a two-front war.'[18] The *Völkischer Beobachter* was just as cele-
bratory, crowing that 'The campaign in the east' was 'decided' and that
this moment marked the 'military end of Bolshevism'.[19]

Goebbels was now seriously concerned. 'Dr Dietrich comes back
from the Führer's headquarters and speaks in front of the press,' he
wrote in his diary on 10 October. 'He gives a picture of the military
situation which is extremely positive and optimistic, almost too positive
and too optimistic. When, for example, the headline "The war is
decided!" is issued to the press, it's certainly going too far.' Goebbels
worried that there were still 'tough days ahead' and that all this overconfidence could return to haunt them. 'I hope to God', he wrote, 'that
the military actions will keep developing in a way that we don't suffer a
psychological setback.'[20]

Reassuringly for the Nazis, at the moment that Goebbels wrote those
words there seemed little immediate chance of such a 'setback'. On the
contrary, the Germans were winning spectacular victories. Army Group
Centre managed to create two giant encirclements, one at Vyazma and
another south at Bryansk. When the Germans entered Vyazma – only 60
miles west of Moscow – they nearly captured the Soviet commander,
General Rokossovsky. It was the Mayor who broke the news to him that
panzers could be seen from the belfry of the church in the city centre.
Rokossovsky escaped only because he dodged down a side street to avoid
an advancing German tank.[21]

Hundreds of thousands of Soviet troops were trapped in the Vyazma
pocket. Walter Schaefer-Kehnert, an officer with the 11th Panzer,

remembered the scenes as they tried to escape from the encirclement. Schaefer-Kehnert saw Red Army soldiers 'walking on like a herd of sheep' towards the German line. At night, 'mostly drunk, [because] they'd distributed all the vodka they had before . . . shouting "Hooray", they're storming [towards the Germans] by the thousands . . . This gave a completely different feeling from any battle we had seen before.'[22]

Schaefer-Kehnert recalled that sometimes a German machine-gun company would be overwhelmed by the sheer number of Red Army troops pouring forward, and, having shot enormous numbers of Soviet soldiers, were finally killed themselves. 'You can imagine', said Schaefer-Kehnert, 'what feelings their replacements had, waiting the following night for more Soviet soldiers to rush towards them.' He also recalled 'very funny stories . . . You see if they had no ammunition any more, of course, our infantry men were also withdrawing. They were then running through the night and one said to the other, "What unit are you from?" and then realized he was running together with a Russian! Both were running east, you see, with the Russian wanting to get out, and he [the German] wanted to get back to the supply dumps.'

Inside the 'cauldron', conditions for the Red Army soldiers soon became all but unbearable. 'The situation of the encircled forces has worsened sharply,' reported Lieutenant General Lukin on 10 October. 'There are few shells, bullets are running out, and there is no food. They eat that which the population can provide and horseflesh. Medicines and dressing materials are used up. All tents and dwellings are over-flowing with wounded.'[23]

Viktor Strazdovski, an eighteen-year-old private with the Soviet 32nd Army, was one of the Red Army soldiers suffering at Vyazma. All he and his four comrades had between them were two rifles and a few rounds of ammunition: 'Everything [else] had been destroyed and was in flames. Naturally our mood was such that . . . on the one hand we couldn't disobey our orders, while on the other we knew that we were doomed and that there wasn't really anything that we could do with our rifles if we did run into the Germans.' He and a small group of his comrades managed to find a way out of the encirclement, but 'we were lucky, in that at the crucial moment, we avoided colliding with them [the Germans] . . . but that was sheer chance, it was simply fate.'[24]

Vasily Grossman, the Soviet war correspondent, witnessed the massive numbers of Soviet civilians who were trying to escape east, away

from the danger of German encirclement. 'I thought I'd seen retreat,' he
wrote in early October, 'but I've never seen anything like what I am seeing now, and could never even imagine anything of the kind. Exodus!
Biblical exodus! Vehicles are moving in eight lanes, there's the violent
roaring of dozens of trucks trying simultaneously to tear their wheels
out of the mud . . . This isn't a flood, this isn't a river, it's the slow movement of a flowing ocean, this flow is hundreds of metres wide. Children's
heads, fair and dark, are looking out from under the improvised tents
covering the carts, as well as the biblical beards of Jewish elders, shawls
of peasant women, hats of Ukrainian uncles, and the black-haired
heads of Jewish girls and women. What silence is in their eyes, what wise
sorrow, what sensation of fate, of a universal catastrophe!'[25]

Stalin was well aware of the threat the German advance posed. And
at this decisive moment in October he allegedly wanted to seek peace
terms with the Germans. According to a Russian academic, Professor
Viktor Anfilov, who interviewed Marshal Zhukov in the 1960s, Zhukov overheard Stalin talking to Beria on the phone that October, saying
'get in touch through your agents with the German intelligence service,
find out what Germany is going to want from us if we offer to sign a
separate peace treaty.'[26]

It's possible that Zhukov might have been mistaken about the nature
of the conversation. However, Stalin had once before suggested discussing a peace deal with the Germans in a moment of crisis. A few months
earlier, in July 1941, Pavel Sudoplatov, an NKVD agent, was told by
Beria – acting on Stalin's orders – to contact the Bulgarian Ambassador
to Moscow. Sudoplatov then tried to use the Ambassador as a go-
between to see what terms the Germans would be prepared to accept
in order to end the war. Would they, for example, 'be happy with the
handing over of such Soviet lands as the Baltic States, the Ukraine,
Bessarabia, Bukovina and the Karelian peninsula?' Not only did Sudoplatov subsequently write about this meeting with the Bulgarian
Ambassador, but archival documents from 1953, at the time of Beria's
trial, also support his story.[27]

The Russian historian Dmitri Volkogonov offers a different version
of this incident with the Bulgarian Ambassador. He quotes a conversation he had after the war with Marshal Moskalenko, who told him:
'Stalin, Beria and Molotov discussed in private the question of surrendering to Fascist Germany, agreeing to hand over to Hitler the Soviet

Baltic republics, Moldavia, a large part of the Ukraine and Belorussia. They tried to make contact with Hitler through the Bulgarian ambassador. No Russian tsar had ever done such a thing. It is interesting that the Bulgarian ambassador was of higher calibre than these leaders and told them that Hitler would never beat the Russians and that Stalin shouldn't worry about it.' According to Moskalenko, Molotov even remarked that giving up this Soviet territory would be 'a possible second Brest Litovsk Treaty', and that 'if Lenin could have the courage to make such a step, we had the same intention now.'[28]

Inevitably, since there could have been few issues more secret at the time than an attempt to make peace with the Germans, the evidence for these peace feelers is uncertain and, in places, contradictory. This applies not just to the question of whether Stalin was directly involved himself, but even to whether he was wholeheartedly behind the idea. Sudoplatov later claimed that Beria told him that the attempt to use the Bulgarian Ambassador as a go-between was part of a ploy to disconcert the Germans, and that there was never any serious desire to make peace. But that's exactly what the official line would have been up to the very moment any peace deal was signed. In particular, the conversation that Zhukov said he overheard in October 1941 between Stalin and Beria sounds less like an attempt to confuse the Germans and more like a genuine attempt to find out what terms Hitler wanted to bring the war to an end.

Regardless, it's hard to imagine the circumstances in which Hitler would ever have agreed to make peace with Stalin at this stage of the war. For the Nazis, as we have seen, this was not just an ideological war, but a fight to gain resources – not only the wheat fields of Ukraine, but the oil of Baku as well. And the idea that Stalin would have acquiesced to these demands, especially when the Nazis were a thousand miles away from Soviet oilfields, is surely fanciful.

The significance of these accounts lies more in the insight they offer into Stalin's attitude at this decisive time. They remind us that it was not inevitable that the Soviets would fight on. Stalin was wavering. That makes this an inconvenient part of the history for those who wished, after the war, to portray the Soviet leader as uniquely steadfast under pressure.

On 13 October the tanks of the 1st Panzer Division drove into Kalinin, north-west of Moscow. The German advance appeared – superficially at least – to be inexorable. In the capital there were not just signs of unease, but over the next few days evidence of genuine panic, as Muscovites feared they too would soon be under direct attack. The situation was made still more febrile by Stalin's decision to authorize the evacuation of key ministries to Kuibyshev on the River Volga, more than 500 miles south-east of Moscow. On 15 October, a secret document of the Stavka, the State Defence Committee, stated that it had been decided 'to evacuate the Presidium of the Supreme Soviet and the top levels of Government . . . (Comrade Stalin will leave tomorrow or later, depending on the situation) . . . In the event of enemy forces arriving at the gates of Moscow, the NKVD – Comrade Beria and Comrade Shcherbakov – are ordered to blow up business premises, warehouses and institutions which cannot be evacuated, and all underground railway electrical equipment.'[29]

Maya Berzina, her husband and their three-year-old son were among those who tried to flee Moscow after they saw that government officials appeared to be abandoning the capital. They tried to leave the city by river, fearing that the roads out were blocked and that soon 'the Germans would take Moscow.' On their way to the southern port she heard rumours that Germans had been seen on trams in the city, and that some Muscovites were preparing signs welcoming the Germans into the Soviet capital. There were also stories that shops were being looted. 'I was frightened for my life,' she said, and full of 'anxiety for the future'.[30]

A Moscow medical student called Tatyana Tsessarsky returned to the dormitory in which she lived to find that the majority of her fellow students had fled: 'They had run away and left everything . . . Not everyone felt patriotic. There were a lot of people who felt aggrieved. Most forgot those feelings once the fighting started, but not everyone.' Outside the dormitory she saw that someone had painted a large swastika on a fence.[31]

At least one observer, N. K. Verzhbitskii, believed that the 'masses' were acting in this way because 'they began to remember and count up all the insults, oppression, injustices, pressure, bureaucratic machinations of officialdom, contempt and self-puffery of party members, draconian orders, deprivations, systematic deception of the masses, the newspapers' braying self-congratulations . . . It is terrible to hear. People speak from the heart. Can a city really hold out when it's in such a mood?'[32]

Grigory Obozny, a nineteen-year-old soldier who helped the police try to control the panic, remembered that a number of Muscovites were accused of 'subversion' and giving 'signals to the planes by flashing lights'. But he did not believe that most of his fellow citizens were turning on the regime. The problem, as he saw it, was that when the bosses left and the factories closed 'people just didn't know what to do with themselves.'[33] Without leadership, they were unnerved.

Even the ultimate symbol of strong leadership – Joseph Stalin – was ordering some of his comrades to leave Moscow. On 15 October, Georgi Dimitrov, head of the Comintern, talked with Stalin, in the presence of Molotov. 'You have been told that you have to evacuate?' said Stalin to Dimitrov. 'It has to be done if you are to continue functioning.' Stalin explained that Moscow 'cannot be defended like Leningrad'. This was a reference to the fact that Leningrad, now under siege from the Germans, could still be supplied from outside the city via a perilous route from the north east. 'As we took our leave,' wrote Dimitrov, Stalin told him, ' "Have to evacuate before the day is out!" – which he said as if he were saying *"Time for lunch!"* '[34]

On the evening of the next day, Thursday 16 October, Stalin's personal telegraphist, Nikolay Ponomariev, was ordered to disconnect the equipment in his Kremlin office and collect his personal belongings: 'Thirty minutes after I'd packed away the apparatus, one of Stalin's personal bodyguards came to see me. I knew all the bodyguards. "Are you ready?" he asked. I said: "I'm ready. Where are we going?" "You'll know when we get there! Let's get ready to go." There was a car outside, we got in and drove off.'

They travelled through the blacked-out city, as the autumn rain lashed against the car. It was, he said, 'a difficult situation, in the streets it was almost primitive'. Moscow was 'usually a noisy city, a happy city. Now so few people remained . . . those who did looked strange . . . a look of fear, you know, as if expecting something unpleasant.'[35]

Eventually they reached their destination – the station where Stalin's armoured train was waiting. 'I sat down in a compartment,' said Ponomariev, 'but I felt bad that we were leaving, that Moscow would be surrendered . . . what was it all about? It isn't difficult to imagine what kind of a tragedy, what kind of misery the Soviet people were going through. That's why I, both as a human being and as a Muscovite, also felt that it was terrible, awful.' Looking out on to the platform,

Ponomariev saw Stalin's personal bodyguards. It was clear that Stalin was expected at any moment.

Ponomariev was present at one of the single most dramatic moments in the history of the war – arguably in the history of the twentieth century. The question that would be resolved that night was straight-forward, but of enormous importance. Would Stalin board the train and flee the capital or would he stay, even though much of the government had already left?

It was a desperately difficult decision for him to make. The situation in Moscow was undoubtedly grim for the Soviets. But the Germans faced numerous problems as well. One was a direct consequence of their recent success. While large numbers of Red Army soldiers had been captured, some had managed to escape the encirclements at Vyazma and Bryansk and now hid in forests behind the German lines. In the vast expanse of western Russia, the Germans could not hope in the short term to eliminate the threat these enemy troops posed to their lines of communication.

Another difficulty was the weather. October had brought rain, which made the unpaved roads of Russia all but impassable for the mechanized units of the Germans. 'I don't think anyone has ever seen such terrible mud,' wrote Vasily Grossman. 'There's rain, snow, hailstones, a liquid, bottomless swamp, black pastry mixed by thousands and thousands of boots, wheels, caterpillars. And everyone is happy once again. The Germans must get stuck in our hellish autumn, both in the sky and on the ground.'[36]

Grossman was right, as no less a figure than Field Marshal von Bock, commander of Army Group Centre, confirmed. 'The Russians', Bock wrote in his diary on 21 October, 'are impeding us far less than the wet and the mud!'[37] At the end of the month, when 'the Führer asked for a detailed [personal] account of the battle conditions', Bock concluded that Hitler had made the request because 'he probably refused to believe the written reports, which is not surprising, for anyone who hasn't seen this filth doesn't think it possible.'[38]

The weather was also a factor in one of the most fundamental prob-lems the Germans now confronted – the question of supplies. It was proving difficult to deliver adequate replacements of military hardware and other provisions to the fighting units. At the start of November, Army Group Centre was struggling to function as desired. Only sixteen supply trains a day of the required thirty-two were reaching the soldiers on the front line.[39]

However, it wasn't just a question of getting supplies to the front. There was an even larger underlying issue – the German industrial base simply wasn't big enough to sustain the objectives that Hitler had set. The steel allowance for the army, for example, was reduced on 25 October 1941 to 173,000 tons a month, and it had not been that low for more than three years. It was impossible to give the army what it needed. But this was a reality that Hitler just would not accept. As the armed forces' Defence Economy and Armament Office stated, Hitler 'refuses to believe that there are not enough raw materials. After all, he has conquered all of Europe. The armed forces must be given what they demand.'[40]

Hitler's private conversations during this critical month of October reflect this disconnect between the reality on the front line and his own perception of the war. On 17 October, for example – several days after the autumn rains had started – he was spinning an ambitious fantasy about building 'windmills all over the place' in Ukraine, and planting 'fields, gardens, orchards' in the fertile soil. 'What a task awaits us!' he said. 'We have a hundred years of joyful satisfaction before us.'[41] Later that night he was speaking in more annihilatory terms, saying that he had 'no feelings about the idea of wiping out Kiev, Moscow or St Petersburg'.[42] Four days later, he gave further evidence of his megalomaniacal mindset when he claimed that 'Berlin will one day be the capital of the world.'[43]

That same night, 21 October, Hitler did make one reference to his leadership of the German armed forces – words that offer us another insight into his mentality. 'A war-leader is what I am against my own will,' he said. 'If I apply my mind to military problems, that's because for the moment I know that nobody would succeed better at this than I can.'[44] These sentiments demonstrate why Hitler could carry on believing that 'we have a hundred years of joyful satisfaction before us' at the exact same time his own military forces were stuck in the mud. He would almost certainly have thought that this was merely a temporary setback, and remembered the times before in his career when he had been written off, only to triumph in the end – not just with the conquest of France in 1940, but more recently when his military 'experts' had been against the move on Kiev.

While the invasions of western Europe and the Soviet Union were different in scale and scope, they were the same in one vital respect – both were enormous gambles. But the fact that the gamble had succeeded in France did not necessarily mean it would succeed in the Soviet Union. Hitler thus failed to appreciate the truth every gambler should know – no one's luck lasts for ever.

In both the invasion of western Europe and the war against the Soviet Union the Germans had planned a short, furious war to overwhelm the enemy. This approach not only suited Hitler's character, but was to a large extent forced upon the Germans by their inability to fight a long-drawn-out conflict. Once again it came down to resource allocation. The Germans could not sustain a war of attrition. For example, in 1941 the Soviet Union produced just over 6,500 tanks, compared to the German output of 5,200. In 1942 the figures would change dramatically (for reasons that we shall consider later)[45] with the Soviet Union turning out over 24,000 tanks and the Germans fewer than 10,000. Add in the American resources behind the British war effort, and the scale of the problem the Nazis faced was all the more daunting.[46]

Hitler was not ignorant of the problem. He just chose to minimize it. What else could he do? His personality was the glue holding the whole German war edifice together. If he projected an air of defeatism it would have had a devastating effect not just on those around him but on the morale of the troops on the front line.

The more intriguing question is this – despite these fundamental difficulties, did Hitler really believe that victory was still achievable? The answer to that is most likely yes. In October 1941, it was still just about objectively possible, even given the practical problems, to believe the Germans could win the war. That was primarily because of the existence of one person – Joseph Stalin. So far in this war, Stalin's mistakes had cost hundreds of thousands of lives. As the catastrophic defeat at Kiev had demonstrated, he could single-handedly lose the Soviets a battle, even though they possessed more troops and tanks on the ground than the Wehrmacht.

All this was hidden from the Soviet population at the time. They knew nothing of Stalin's incompetence as a military commander. As a result, he was still seen as an inspirational figure – the father of the nation. Consider the views of Vyacheslav Yablonsky, for example. As a nineteen-year-old student he helped build the defences just outside

Moscow in October 1941, and to a large degree Stalin inspired him in his efforts. Stalin was 'the one I loved and I loved him until he was dead. Why did we love Stalin? Well, we just loved him as a person who cared about us.'[47]

Enormous numbers of other Soviet citizens felt the same way. The cry, as Red Army soldiers went into battle, 'For the Motherland, for Stalin!' was commonplace. So imagine if now, on the evening of 16 October 1941, Stalin had boarded his armoured train and abandoned Moscow. What would that have done to the morale not only of Muscovites, terrified of the German advance, but of soldiers fighting for their lives at the front?

We can't know the answer for sure. That's because Stalin didn't flee the Soviet capital that night. He decided to stay and continue to lead the struggle from his office in the Kremlin. But not everyone agreed this was the sensible option. When three days later, on 19 October, senior Soviet figures waited in the anteroom outside Stalin's office for a meeting with their leader, 'Beria set about persuading everyone that we should abandon Moscow,' wrote V. S. Pronin, President of the Moscow Soviet. 'He argued that we should give up Moscow and set up a defensive line on the Volga. Malenkov supported him, Molotov mumbled his disagreement. In fact, I particularly remember Beria's words: "But how are we going to defend Moscow? We have absolutely nothing at all. We have been overwhelmed and we are being shot down like partridges." Then all of us went into Stalin's office. Stalin came in as usual with his pipe. When we had settled down, Stalin asked: "Are we going to defend Moscow?" Everyone was silent. He waited a moment and then repeated his question. Again no reply. "Very well [said Stalin], we will ask individually." Molotov replied first: "We will defend [Moscow]." All, including Beria, answered the same: "We will defend [Moscow]."'[48]

As a picture of what it was like to work for Stalin, this episode is particularly revealing. For instance, notice how despite Beria's certainty before the meeting that he and the rest of the Politburo should evacuate Moscow, he was instantly cowed in Stalin's presence – not by argument or tantrums from the Soviet leader, but by a simple question. What's also apparent is that everyone present at the meeting knew what Stalin expected them to say. Stalin's subordinates owed their lives to the fact that they could anticipate what was required of them, and they demonstrated just that ability here.

It's inconceivable that Hitler would ever have conducted a meeting in such a way. He never asked his subordinates for their advice on important questions, even disingenuously as Stalin did here. Asking advice was utterly inconsistent with his vision of a leader as someone who first listens to his 'inner conviction' and then persuades others to go along with the decision that resulted. But since the Bolshevik ideal was consensual government by the party, Stalin understood that he had to cloak his own views behind a smokescreen of communality.

Make no mistake, however. It was Stalin and Stalin alone who decided to stay in Moscow. What's more, he never shared the reasons why he had resolved not to leave the capital. All the signs on 16 October were that he was planning to go. In many ways, as Beria so graphically pointed out, that would have been the safe course of action. The consequences for the Soviet war effort of Stalin's death or, worse still, capture would likely have been catastrophic. On the other hand, the benefits of Stalin staying in the capital as a figure of defiance were also potentially enormous.

Most likely, Stalin was influenced by Zhukov's view that Moscow could be saved.[49] Zhukov had already shown in the previous months that he was prepared to voice his genuine opinions – or at least as much of them as he judged he could and still keep his life. Significantly, on 20 October, Stalin insisted that a photograph of Zhukov was published the next day in both *Pravda* and the *Red Army News*. This was the very first time that such publicity had been given to an individual military leader. David Ortenberg, editor of the *Red Army News*, later said that Zhukov had told him that the use of the photograph had been ordered so as to enable him to be scapegoated if Moscow fell. That might indeed be one reason for Stalin's action, but it's also probable that he wanted to communicate the news that a gifted commander was leading the defence of Moscow.[50]

We also need to remember that the Germans never planned on occupying the Soviet capital. Instead, they intended to use a combination of artillery and air bombardment to erase the city completely. The example of Kiev had demonstrated to the Nazis the dangers of capturing a major urban centre, and Moscow was too big to be taken street by street without enormous losses, especially given the defences that were now in place.

The fact that the Germans intended to surround Moscow makes

Stalin's decision to stay all the more vital, because in such circumstances the morale of the trapped population was crucial. Muscovites would surely have lost much of their will to hold out if they had seen their supreme leader desert them. Stalin was, as we have seen, like a stern and unforgiving father. But respect for such a figure is based on strength. Fathers are supposed to offer protection. They can be forgiven a great deal, but if they cease to protect their children – if instead they run away when their children are in mortal danger – then their authority collapses.

Stalin, in short, would have found it hard to be a credible leader of the Soviet Union if he had left Muscovites to their own devices. And the consequences for the Soviet war effort could have been calamitous. Indeed, had Stalin run from Moscow the Soviet Union might well have lost this war. If May 1940 and the decision to fight on was Churchill's moment of destiny, then October 1941 and the decision to stay in Moscow was Stalin's.

One of Stalin's first acts after he had resolved to stay in the capital was to announce new measures to secure the city. Notably, in the light of his decision to raise the profile of Marshal Zhukov, he began State Defence Committee Decree no. 813 on 19 October by declaring that the 'defence of the capital' west of Moscow 'has been entrusted to the commander of the Western Front, General of the Army Comrade Zhukov'. He also name-checked the man responsible for the 'defence of Moscow on its approaches . . . Lieutenant General Artem'ev'. It was, perhaps, another indication of the people who would be held responsible if the Germans were not beaten back.

The decree also called for the 'introduction of a state of siege in the city of Moscow and areas adjacent to the city from 20 October 1941'. This involved both the imposition of a curfew between midnight and five in morning and the implementation of the 'strictest security regimen in the city', to be policed by the NKVD and others. Moreover, 'provocateurs, spies and other enemy agents calling for the violation of the order' were 'to be shot on the spot'.[51]

Vladimir Ogryzko commanded one of the NKVD units charged with restoring order to the capital, and candidly recalled his own role in targeting 'traitors': 'We'd been carrying out our duties in doorways of buildings, in various districts, on mobile patrols, when suddenly a woman came running towards us shouting: "Look, over there, they're firing off flares!" Our job was simple. We surrounded the house and eliminated them on the spot. What is "maintaining law and order" all about? It's about being quick on your feet and quick off the mark . . . you have the evidence, you make the right manoeuvres and you act immediately. That is the sort of dynamic, active duty that we were carrying out. During a state of siege, there's great power over all the inhabitants. Great power. There can be no mercy. Otherwise falsehood, crime, desolation and whatever else you want will triumph. The order determines that nobody will even contemplate breaking the law during a state of siege. Break it and you're for it! That was the law. It was an inexorable law.'

Ogryzko and his men were called to a vodka distillery where there had been a break-in. 'Masses of people', he said, 'were already drunk. They were breaking open barrels, breaking glasses, they took bottles which were already open. It was a dreadful sight. The only way of putting an end to it was by using force.' As he examined the scene, Ogryzko saw that 'Some of them were sober and they were inciting the others to drink – we eliminated them . . . Once we had restored order, however, we then sorted through the drunks . . . looking at each person, and found out who was who and what was what. You get the picture?'[52]

On the streets of Moscow, Ogryzko operated a straightforward rule: 'Whoever wouldn't obey the command "Stop or I'll shoot!" Whoever resisted. That would be it.' By such uncompromising measures, in a few days order was restored to Moscow. And Ogryzko was not alone in praising Stalin's leadership at this decisive time and in believing that 'excellent decisions were taken'. He and his comrades took inspiration from Stalin's perceived strength and the knowledge that he commanded the war from the Kremlin in the heart of the city – a view they could hardly have held if Stalin had left Moscow for the safety of Kuibyshev on the Volga.

Stalin, for all his dour demeanour, understood the power of symbolism, and at this moment he was the symbol of Soviet resistance. No more so than at the annual parade on 7 November in Red Square to mark the anniversary of the 1917 revolution. General Artem'ev, in charge of security in Moscow, had wanted to cancel the celebration. Imagine if there was a German air attack during the parade. But Stalin had insisted the march-past take place as usual. It was an act of defiance that showed how far he had come from the man who kept silent in the immediate aftermath of the invasion.

At eight o'clock on the morning of Friday 7 November, Soviet tanks and troops emerged into Red Square, moved alongside the Kremlin walls and travelled on past St Basil's Cathedral.[53] In the speech he gave at the parade, Stalin compared the present situation to the difficulties the Bolsheviks had endured in 1918. 'The spirit of the great Lenin inspired us at that time for the war against the interventionists,' he said. 'And what happened? We defeated the interventionists, regained all our lost territories and achieved victory . . . The spirit of the great Lenin inspires us for our patriotic war today, as it did twenty-three years ago.'[54] Across Red Square, Stalin could see two giant portraits of equal size on the office building opposite. The portraits were, of course, of Stalin and Lenin.

Academic research has demonstrated the immense importance of Stalin's actions during this period. Out of more than two and a half million pieces of mail that were reviewed by military censors during the first half of November, three-quarters showed an increased confidence as a result of listening to Stalin speak. Stalin was something of a dreary orator – he sounded more like a bureaucrat than a warrior – but his low-key, calm approach offered the Soviet people the reassurance they needed at this desperate time.[55]

As Soviet troops marched through Red Square on 7 November, the Germans launched their final assault on Moscow. 'It has begun to freeze,' Field Marshal von Bock had written in his diary two days earlier, 'which makes movement easier.'[56] But while the cold conditions allowed Bock's armoured units to advance more freely, it also made life harder for the German soldiers, most of whom did not have proper protection from the snow and ice.

Both Hitler's Wehrmacht and Stalin's Red Army were already weakened by more than four months of bloody conflict. Now they would fight not just each other, but the bitter weather as well.

8. A World War

Just as certain dates were sacred to Stalin and the Bolsheviks, so certain dates were sacred to Hitler and the Nazis. Each regime sought to create new traditions, and honouring major events in their recent histories was vital to them. The past mattered to Hitler and Stalin – now more than ever.

Despite the risk of a German attack, Stalin had recognized how important it was that he stand in Red Square on 7 November to commemorate the anniversary of the 1917 revolution, and now Hitler understood that he needed to rally the nation as a whole, and the Nazi Party in particular, on 8 November, the eighteenth anniversary of the start of the Beer Hall Putsch in Munich. So, despite all the demands on him at his wartime headquarters in East Prussia, he made the long journey to southern Germany so that he could be present for the commemoration of the anniversary of the failed Nazi uprising in 1923. Once he arrived in Munich, he had to deliver a difficult speech. Just a month before he had promised that the Red Army would 'never rise again'. Yet now, as winter closed in on the eastern front, the Red Army was still fighting.

Hitler's default position when events did not work out as he had predicted was to blame someone else. Nothing was ever his fault. Such behaviour is hardly uncommon. Stalin acted the same way, and large numbers of politicians today continue to blame others for their own mistakes. What was unusual about Hitler was that he almost always said the same people were behind all of Germany's problems – the Jews.

When he stood up to speak at the Löwenbräukeller on the evening of Saturday 8 November, Hitler revealed to his audience of old party comrades that 'I knew behind this war was that arsonist who has always lived off the dealings of nations: the international Jew.' Moreover, 'I came to know these Jews as the arsonists of the world.'[1]

It was, to an extent, familiar material. As we have seen, Hitler had been blaming the Jews for Germany's ills for years. And because he relied on conspiracy theories – the Jews were often accused of operating secretly in the shadows – it didn't matter that he could not prove his outlandish claims were true. In fact, the lack of any evidence that the Jews were responsible for the current problems could be turned into a plus point. The absence of proof served only to demonstrate how clever the Jews were at hiding their tracks.

In his speech, Hitler used the Jews both as the reason for continuing the fight against the Soviets and – by implication – as a justification for why the war now presented such a challenge. It was the Soviet Union, he said, that was 'the biggest servant of Jewry'. Only 'mindless, prole-tarianized subhumans' remained on Soviet territory and 'above them, there is the huge organization of the Jewish commissars – in reality, slaveowners.'

'The most awful type of slavery that has ever been in the world', said Hitler, 'exists in the Soviet Paradise – millions of frightened, oppressed, depraved people, half-starved . . . It will be a real salvation for Europe not only if this danger vanishes, but also if the fertility of this soil bene-fits all of Europe.' In reality the 'soil' of the Soviet Union, of course, was destined in Hitler's mind to benefit not 'all of Europe' but Germany alone.

Hitler singled out Stalin for attack as a man who was 'nothing other than an instrument in the hands of this almighty Jewry'. Once again, he claimed, the Jews were controlling events from behind the scenes. 'If Stalin is on the stage', he said, then behind the 'curtain' lay Jews who, 'in ten-thousandfold ramifications, control this mighty empire'.[2]

Hitler ridiculed Stalin for falsely claiming in his speech the day before that Germany had lost 'four and a half million people' in the war. He asserted that 'what this potentate in the Kremlin says is really very Jewish.' It was yet another example of how Hitler ascribed anything negative to the Jews. If you lied, you were speaking in a 'very Jewish' way.

Significantly, Hitler ended the speech by referring back to the First World War and declaring, 'We were cheated out of victory at the time.' His audience did not need to be reminded – he had said it so many times before – of his claim that the Jews had plotted to bring about Germany's defeat in 1918. But, he promised, 'This time, we will make up for what we were cheated out of. Point by point, position by position, we will put it on the account and cash it in. The hour will come when we will go up to the graves of the soldiers killed in action during the Great

War and be able to say: Comrades, you did not die in vain . . . Comrades, you triumphed after all!'[3]

So that was what was at stake here – nothing more or less than total redemption for the German defeat in the First World War. It was an idea that would have resonated with his audience. The greatest humiliation of their lives had been the peace of 1918. Now Hitler was telling them that all this past suffering would be put right. And, as long as you accepted his premise, it followed that this meant an inevitable reckoning with the Jews. This time, he implied, the Jews would not profit from the war and bring about Germany's destruction, as the Nazis claimed they had done before. No, this time, as Hitler had 'prophesied' in his speech in January 1939, the Jews risked 'extermination' if they brought about a world war.

Hitler's all-encompassing charges against the Jews seem so ludicrous that it's worth asking if he actually believed what he was saying. To the vast majority of people today, his views are not just anathema but absurd. Yet all the signs are that, to the depths of his being, Hitler was sincere in his beliefs. He lived in a subculture that nurtured these fantasies about the imagined Jewish 'threat', and he surrounded himself with people who were just as convinced that the Jews were a 'problem' that had to be 'dealt with'.

It had been accepted from the planning stage of Operation Barbarossa that Jews in the Soviet Union would be specially targeted. Killing squads accompanied the army groups as they advanced into Soviet territory, tasked with murdering Jews. Initially they killed 'Jews in the service of party and state', though it was also clear from the start that this was the bare minimum of Jews that were supposed to die. In July, just a few weeks after the launch of the invasion, the killing squads had been reinforced, and over the summer and autumn of 1941 Jewish women and children in the occupied Soviet Union were also shot.

However, it was not just the Germans who were committing mass murder. Many others helped them – especially the Romanian Army. The Romanians had invaded the Soviet Union alongside the Germans, primarily in order to regain territory previously lost to the Soviets. The Romanian leader Ion Antonescu had assured Hitler just days before the invasion that 'Because of its racial qualities, Romania can continue to play a role as an anti-Slavic buffer for the benefit of Germany.'

The Romanian leadership were not just anti-Slav (they said that they themselves were 'Latin'), they stated they were anti-Semitic as well. Later in 1941, the Romanian Foreign Minister told Goebbels that Romanians were 'antisemites by birth and conviction'.[4]

On 16 October, immediately after occupying the city of Odessa on the Black Sea, Romanian forces started murdering thousands of Jews. Subsequently, following the destruction of their military headquarters on 22 October, Romanian units intensified the attacks. More than 20,000 Jews who had been taken to the village of Dlanic, just outside Odessa, were imprisoned in warehouses and murdered. 'One by one, the warehouses were riddled with machine gun and rifle fire,' stated a report written just after the war, 'doused with gasoline and ignited, except for the last warehouse, which was blown up. The chaos and the horrifying sights that followed defy description: wounded people burning alive, women with their hair on fire coming out through the roof or through openings in the burning storehouses in a desperate search for salvation . . . Others tried to escape, climbed on to window ledges or on to the roof amidst the flames, and begged to be shot.'[5] More than 30,000 Jews were murdered in Odessa; and across the Soviet territory claimed by Romania hundreds of thousands more would die.[6]

The Romanians were not committing these crimes because the Nazis forced them to. On the contrary, there is evidence that they felt they were leading the way. 'The die has been cast,' wrote the editor of the Romanian newspaper *Porunca Vremii* in the summer of 1941, 'the liquidation of the Jews in Romania has entered the final, decisive phase . . . To the joy of our emancipation must be added the pride of [pioneering] the solution to the Jewish problem in Europe . . . present-day Romania is prefiguring the decisions to be made by the Europe of tomorrow.'[7]

At a cabinet meeting on 13 November 1941, Antonescu proclaimed, in the context of the massacres in Odessa: 'I have a responsibility toward history. Let the Jews of America sue me, if they will. We must not show mercy to the Jews, because, given the chance, they would show us no mercy – neither to me, you or the nation . . . Therefore, don't be lenient with the Jews. Be assured that, given the chance, they will take their revenge. In order to ensure that no Jew is left to take revenge, I shall make sure to destroy them first.'[8]

Antonescu's words could just as easily have come from Hitler's mouth. And they matter in the context of an examination of the relationship between Hitler and Stalin because they demonstrate how others also subscribed to Hitler's vision of a 'crusade' against Stalin, Bolshevism and Judaism. The Romanian action in Odessa shares a number of traits with Nazi attacks on the Jews. Like the Nazis, the Romanians often killed Jews in retaliation for attacks on their soldiers. They also believed, as did the Nazis, that the Jews were inextricably linked to Bolshevism. This, it bears repeating, was a lie. Indeed, anti-Semitism was not uncommon in the Soviet Union. In Odessa, for instance, at a rally against Jews in September – before the Romanians entered the city – the crowd shouted, 'Beat the Jews and save Russia!'[9]

Nonetheless, this belief that the Jews were 'behind' any action that the Soviets took – especially anything considered underhand – was widespread among the invading forces, and was most clearly expressed in the way the Germans linked Jews and 'partisans' together. By the late autumn of 1941 there were thousands of Red Army soldiers behind German lines, often troops who had hidden in forests in the wake of one of the giant encirclement actions. These soldiers, together with other specially trained partisan fighters, posed a serious threat to German supply lines, and were treated as spies who should be shot on sight.

The automatic – and false – linkage between the partisan threat and the Jewish 'threat' was common among German soldiers. Take the order issued by Walther von Reichenau, commander of the Sixth Army, on 10 October: 'The main aim of the campaign against the Jewish-Bolshevist system is the complete destruction of its forces and the extermination of the Asiatic influence in the sphere of European culture. As a result, the troops have to take on tasks which go beyond the conventional purely military ones . . . soldiers must show full understanding of the necessity for the severe atonement being required of the Jewish subhumans. It also has the further purpose of nipping in the bud uprisings in the rear of the Wehrmacht which experience shows are invariably instigated by Jews.'[10] Reichenau thus makes explicit the supposed connection between partisan actions 'in the rear' and Jews. It was a linkage that Himmler wholeheartedly endorsed, so much so that killing 'partisans' became a camouflage term for killing Jews. For instance, when he met Hitler in December 1941, Himmler cryptically wrote in his desk diary by the words 'Jewish question' the comment 'to be exterminated as partisans'.[11]

At the same time as Jews were being killed in the Soviet Union – not just as supposed 'partisans' but also in large numbers simply for being Jews – Hitler was considering the fate of Jews elsewhere in the Nazi empire. And the decisions he took in the latter part of 1941 offer us an insight not just into the role of the war in the shaping of his murderous thinking, but also into the unwitting part Stalin's own actions may have played in influencing the German leader.

Hitler had been asked by Goebbels as far back as the summer of 1941 to authorize the deportation of German Jews. Goebbels, in his capacity as Gauleiter of Berlin, told him on 19 August that he felt it was unacceptable that 70,000 Jews still lived in the capital at the same time as German soldiers were dying in the east. But having listened to Goebbels' entreaty Hitler decided against deporting the Berlin Jews. He did, however, authorize another measure against them. From 1 September all Jews over the age of six in the Old Reich and incorporated territories had to wear a yellow star on their clothing.

But just a few weeks later Hitler changed his mind. Not only would the German Jews have to wear the yellow star, but they would also be deported. We don't know exactly why he made this volte-face. But it's possible that he was influenced, at least in part, by an idea brought to him on 14 September by Otto Bräutigam, who worked for Alfred Rosenberg, Minister for the Occupied Eastern Territories. Rosenberg suggested that all the Jews of central Europe should be deported in response to Stalin's recent decision to target the ethnic German population of the Volga region.[12]

Stalin, suspicious as ever, had been concerned about the loyalty of these Soviet citizens of German descent. In August the 'autonomous region' in which the Volga Germans lived was administratively eliminated, and at the start of September more than 600,000 of them were deported to the wilds of the Soviet Union where they endured terrible suffering. There 'is nothing but grey emptiness', wrote one Volga German. 'We live in a hut. The sun burns terribly; when it rains the hut leaks, all our things are wet. We sleep on the ground. We work all day till we fall. We have been forced to work on the dungheaps, mixing dung by hand with fertilizer eight hours a day, even during the worst heat.'[13]

Given these conditions, thousands of Volga Germans died. They were one of the first of the ethnic groups within the Soviet Union to suffer internal exile during the war – they would not be the last.

However, it's unlikely that Hitler authorized the deportation of the German Jews entirely as a result of Stalin's actions. Rosenberg's idea was just one of a number of proposals about the Jews he received around this time. For instance, on 15 September Karl Kaufmann, Gauleiter of Hamburg, wrote to the Führer asking for the Jews to be removed from the city because he wanted to give their houses to other Germans who had lost their homes in Allied air raids.

Although Goebbels, Rosenberg and Kaufmann all gave different reasons for wanting the Jews deported, they shared the same motive – vindictiveness. Germans were suffering and the Jews should be made to pay the price. These leading Nazis all believed Hitler's lie that the Jews had lived in comfort in Germany during the First World War while loyal troops died on the front line. This should not be allowed to happen again – despite the fact it had never happened in the first place.

But even though in the autumn of 1941 Hitler authorized the deportation of Jews living within the boundaries of the Old Reich, that is not to say that he had detailed plans about what should happen to them once they arrived at their destinations. Something quasi-genocidal, certainly, but whether it was immediate execution or a more prolonged death from mistreatment appeared, at this stage, to be up to his underlings. Some Jews from Germany, for example, were sent to the overcrowded and disease-filled Łódź ghetto in Poland, while others were transported directly to the occupied Soviet Union where they were shot.

At the same time as the Jews were sent east, soldiers of the Wehrmacht continued to advance towards Moscow in Operation Typhoon. And as they did so the disconnect between what they could actually achieve and what they were told to achieve grew ever larger. On 13 November Guderian's chief of staff attended a meeting at Army Group Centre and was told by senior commanders that the target of their panzer army was Gorky, a city '250 miles *east* of Moscow'. It was a ludicrous goal, given the available supplies and the worsening weather. 'This was not the month of May,' said Guderian's chief of staff, 'and we were not fighting in France.' Guderian, when he heard the plan, remarked that the goal was simply 'impossible'.[14] But what's most noteworthy about this episode is that army professionals, including General Halder, were party to this 'impossible' proposal.[15]

Operation Barbarossa was now weeks behind schedule, but Hitler still remained positive. As late as 22 November, Goebbels reported the Führer's undiminished ambition: 'If the weather keeps being favourable to us, he still wants to attempt to encircle Moscow and thereby condemn it to hunger and complete devastation.' What's more, when Goebbels asked him if he thought Germany would win this war, Hitler replied that 'If he had believed in victory in 1918 when he lay without help as a half-blinded corporal in a Pomeranian military hospital, why should he not now believe in our victory when he controlled the world's most powerful army and almost the whole of Europe was at his feet?' It was an unfortunate comparison. The 'half-blinded corporal' may well have believed in victory in 1918, but that did nothing to prevent Germany's humiliating defeat. As for the dangers of the approaching winter, Hitler appeared to will them away as well. 'World history', he told Goebbels, 'is not made by weather.'[16]

A week later, despite increased problems on the eastern front caused by bad weather and lack of supplies, Hitler remained upbeat. It didn't matter, he told Goebbels, that the Germans had just been driven back from Rostov, since he planned on withdrawing 'just far enough that he can still bomb it' and 'in doing so, a bloody example should be made. For that matter, the Führer has always taken the view that one should not capture big cities of the Soviet Union . . . Moscow and Leningrad are not to fall into our hands as cities; they must be destroyed, and later be put under the plough . . .'[17]

It's as if Hitler was convincing himself by convincing his audience – in this case his Propaganda Minister, Joseph Goebbels. Rationally, it must have been hard for Goebbels to believe that events would turn out as Hitler predicted. But listening to Hitler was never entirely about rationality. As Konrad Heiden, a journalist who witnessed the rise of the Nazis, reminds us, Hitler's speeches often ended 'in overjoyed redemption, a triumphant, happy ending; often they can be refuted by reason, but they follow the far mightier logic of the subconscious, which no refutation can touch'.[18]

Hitler's problem was that while it was easy for him to spin wondrous stories to Goebbels, it was another matter altogether to 'refute' cold facts when they were laid before him. And astonishingly, the very same day that he was showering Goebbels in optimism, he met with men who told him some very harsh truths indeed. The industrialist Walter

Rohland, who oversaw the production of German tanks, informed him not only that the Soviets were producing effective weapons en masse, but that such was the industrial potential of the Americans that Germany would lose the war if they became involved in the conflict. The discussion took an even more depressing turn for Hitler when Fritz Todt, the Armaments Minister, told him unambiguously that 'the war is not winnable by military means.' Hitler then asked 'how else should I end this war?', only to be told by Todt that a political solution was necessary. Hitler replied, 'I can scarcely see a way of ending it politically.'[19]

Many aspects of this encounter are worthy of note. Perhaps the most important, in the context of a comparison with the Soviet leader, is that both Rohland and Todt were prepared to be honest in front of Hitler and tell him news he did not want to hear. They could do this only because they believed it was safe to do it – in contrast to those who served Stalin. As we saw in the last chapter in the context of the decision whether or not to leave Moscow, members of the Politburo such as Lavrenti Beria felt they could voice their genuine beliefs only outside the meeting. Once in Stalin's presence they crumbled.

It's also significant that Hitler sailed on once again, despite hearing news that was so devastating that it would likely have crushed a statesman with a normal mentality. This is all the more remarkable because, like Stalin, he had no close confidant, no one to whom he could express his own innermost fears, anxieties and desires. But the fundamental difference between the two of them in this respect was that Stalin created a world around him in which his subordinates feared telling him harsh truths. That was not the case with Hitler.

At the front, units of Army Group Centre edged towards Moscow. But the nearer they came, the harder the Red Army fought. The panzer officer Walter Schaefer-Kehnert remembered that there was 'very heavy resistance' as they neared the Soviet capital. 'I personally saw, going through a small road through the forest, three other soldiers walking in front of us – 100 to 150 metres in front of us – and [there was] an explosion and you see only the pieces of flesh hanging in the trees to the right and to the left, just blown up there.'

Despite the strength of Soviet resistance, by early December the closest German reconnaissance unit had reached a point just 12 miles from the centre of Moscow. Schaefer-Kehnert and his comrades were some miles further back, but nonetheless realized that they were within artillery range of the Soviet capital. 'I measured this distance to the Kremlin and said, "Well, if we had a long-range cannon, we could shoot at the Kremlin."' He and the other soldiers were excited by this revelation and subsequently spent the whole night firing their artillery at the centre of Moscow.

But the cold made conventional fighting almost impossible. 'This night already was when the temperature dropped below 30 degrees below zero,' said Schaefer-Kehnert, 'and our machine guns were not firing any more . . . this is the worst for the infantry men, you have a machine gun that doesn't shoot. This really makes you afraid, then you have no means more to defend yourself, and the same happened with vehicles to get them started. Then the personal equipment – the leather boots – we had huge losses when soldiers during the night had no opportunity to warm up somewhere, they got frozen toes and fingers, so our losses were much more than wounded [in battle], there were those with frozen fingers and feet . . . I still remember the battalion commander we had in the first phase, he was a young officer in the Ludendorff General Staff during the First World War, and he always said, "If you want to make war, you have to equip yourself properly for it."'[20]

The Germans had reached the end of the line. They would advance no further towards Moscow. On 3 December the commander of 4th Panzer, General Hoepner, wrote: 'The offensive combat power of the Corps [XII, XL Panzer, XLVI Panzer, LVII Panzer] *has run out* . . . Any further offensive may lead to sapping the strength of units and make the repulsion of Russian counterattacks impossible.'[21]

Hoepner's words were prescient. Just two days later, on 5 December, the Red Army launched a massive counter-attack. A total of twenty-seven Soviet divisions crashed into the Germans outside Moscow. Unlike the German equipment, Soviet armaments were designed for this harsh weather. As Bock put it succinctly in his diary on 5 December, 'Our own tanks are breaking down, while those of the Russians are better suited to winter conditions.'[22]

Alfred Rubbel, a tank commander in a panzer unit in front of Moscow, remembered fighting that December as a 'terrible experience . . . the war had changed completely'. Instead of feeling pride in German technology he and his comrades were now 'quite envious' of Soviet equipment such as the T34 tank, which was 'a big shock for everybody. We didn't know anything about the T34. They fit very well to what the

Russians needed. The Russians tended to simplify technology, and against us they had pressurized air – that's the way they started their motors. It had wider tracks so it could go over mud. We couldn't.' The sheer persistence and resilience of the Red Army soldiers was also having an effect on their opponents. 'We understood how much the Russians were willing to suffer,' said Rubbel, 'and how hard they could be, that they were asked to do things that would have been impossible to ask us to do, and that Russian soldiers tolerated that. We were not told about this [before the invasion].'[23]

Rubbel was now opposed by soldiers like Vasily Borisov. 'During the counter-attacks there was man-to-man fighting,' said Borisov, who served in a Siberian unit. 'We had to fight the Germans in the trenches. The fitter ones survived and the weaker ones died . . . We had bayonets on our rifles and I was very strong – I could pierce him [the German soldier] with a bayonet and throw him out of the trench . . . they were wearing coats like us, so the bayonet went through. It's the same as piercing a loaf of bread – no resistance . . . It's a question of either/or. Either he kills you or you kill him. It's a real bloody mess . . . Our infantry joined in and we pushed them away further to the next line. Our guys were strong. Red Army soldiers. They were strong enough to fight like that.'[24]

Faced with men like Borisov, Rubbel felt that, 'sort of suddenly, our idea of superiority started to fade away in view of these soldiers, whose leadership by the way also started becoming better . . .'[25] On 7 December, two days into the Soviet counter-attack, the notoriously laconic Bock wrote, 'Difficult day. The right wing of Panzer Group 3 began withdrawing during the night.'[26]

But the evening of that same day – Sunday 7 December – would bring still more momentous news for Hitler and the Germans. The Japanese bombed the American naval base at Pearl Harbor in a surprise attack, and shortly afterwards the United States of America was at war with Imperial Japan. On the face of it, this should have been a potentially devastating development for Hitler. He had previously said that it was necessary for Germany to have 'solved all problems in Europe' before America joined the war. If that goal could not be achieved, then 'woe betide us if we're not finished by then.'[27]

Germany was already in a relationship with Japan via the tripartite pact, but there was no necessity under the terms of this treaty for the

Germans to declare war on America, because it had been the Japanese who had initiated the conflict. Yet, four days later, on 11 December, Hitler announced that Germany was now at war with the United States. To many people, this seems an astonishing decision to have made. Why – voluntarily – bring about a war with an economic powerhouse, thousands of miles away? A country, moreover, that Germany could never hope to conquer?

Far from dwelling on these questions, Hitler appeared pleased that Japan had attacked America. 'We can't lose the war at all,' he said. 'We now have an ally which has never been conquered in 3,000 years.'[28] Many of those around Hitler seemed equally delighted. After they heard the news of Pearl Harbor 'the entire Headquarters [of the supreme command] . . . seemed to be caught up in an ecstasy of rejoicing,' wrote General Warlimont.[29] It was a sense of elation that was shared by the German Foreign Minister, Ribbentrop. 'A night telephone call from Ribbentrop,' recorded Count Ciano, the Italian Foreign Minister in his diary; 'he is joyful over the Japanese attack on the United States. He is so happy, in fact, that I can't but congratulate him, even though I am not so sure about the advantage. One thing is now certain: America will enter the conflict, and the conflict itself will be long enough to permit her to put into action all her potential strength.' Even Mussolini was 'happy' at the news because 'for a long time now he has been in favor of clarifying the position between America and the Axis.'[30]

There were several reasons, seen from the perspective of Hitler and those around him, for this apparently strange reaction to the news that America was now fighting in the war. The first was that America had already been helping the British war effort for some considerable time. The previous year the Americans had promised to exchange fifty destroyers for the right to use several military bases in British territory. A few months later Roosevelt had suggested a more extensive Lend-Lease arrangement under which the British would receive a whole panoply of military and other supplies. Most recently, there had been a series of incidents between American warships and German U-boats in the North Atlantic. So for Hitler, and military commanders like Admiral Raeder, the German declaration of war on America merely allowed the Kriegsmarine to fight back in a war the United States had already half declared.

The second immediate advantage of the current situation, as Hitler

saw it, was that the Americans and the British would now be distracted
from the war in Europe by the conflagration in the Pacific. Important
British bases were not just under threat but would soon be captured
by the Japanese – Hong Kong surrendered on Christmas Day 1941, and
Singapore followed less than two months later on 15 February 1942.

Finally, there was an ideological dimension. Hitler had become
increasingly convinced that the Jews were behind Roosevelt – a man he
had publicly branded a hypocrite back in 1939 – and now there was a
chance to confront this perceived danger out in the open. America, Hitler believed, could never have been Germany's friend.

Hitler had agreed with the Japanese just before Pearl Harbor that
Germany would declare war on the United States after the Japanese
attack. The fact that Hitler would be the one to declare war mattered
hugely to him. He could have waited for America to do so, or held off
until the situation in the Atlantic worsened from the German perspective. But that would have made it obvious that he was not in control of
events. And appearances mattered to him.

Hitler decided to return to Berlin and give a major setpiece speech to
members of the Reichstag on 11 December. It was a remarkable occasion, because the German audience – whether listening to him in person
or on the radio – were well aware of the history of the First World War,
and knew how harmful the intervention of the Americans on the Allied
side in 1917 had been to the German war effort. Yet Hitler now spent
much of his speech explaining how and why, in his opinion, Germany
had been drawn not just into the war in 1939 but also into the fight
against the Soviet Union in 1941. His alternative history focused on
how 'British diplomacy' had 'forced' the Germans into war in 1939, and
how the British had prevented the conflict ending in the summer of
1940 by the 'rejection' of his 'peace offer'. As for the war against the
Soviet Union, that had occurred because Hitler wanted to prevent
Stalin attacking Europe and if the Germans had not acted when they
did then 'Europe would have been lost.'[31]

Hitler then explained – almost plaintively – how, in his view,
Roosevelt and America had been acting against Germany and helping
the British, despite the Germans never 'inflicting any suffering' on the
United States. As for the reason Roosevelt had turned on Nazi Germany, that was easily explained. Roosevelt was 'reinforced' by the
'satanic malice' of the Jew. Moreover, the fact that Roosevelt had not

understood that the Jews were 'interested only in disruption and never in order' demonstrated that the American President didn't just have 'mental imbecility' but must be 'insane'.[32]

Roosevelt and Churchill, said Hitler, ought to concentrate on their own problems: 'Instead of stirring up wars, these gentlemen, who live in socially backward states, should have looked after their unemployed. There is enough need and hardship in their countries to keep them occupied, in terms of the distribution of foodstuffs.'

The Germans, claimed Hitler as he summed up, had been the victim of an international conspiracy. It was therefore necessary for Germany to stand united with Italy and Japan and fight against 'the United States of America and England'. Hitler was 'unshakeably resolved' to pursue this war to 'a victorious end'.[33]

The central theme of the speech was typical Hitler. He presented the current situation as one in which there was no alternative to fighting on. It was once again a case of either/or. Germany would either be victorious or annihilated. This way of presenting events was characteristic. From his very first moments as a politician in the aftermath of the First World War he had dealt in extremes. One of the first clues that he saw the world in these terms came at the end of the presentation of the twenty-five-point Nazi Party programme at a meeting at the Hofbräuhaus beer hall in Munich in February 1920. The last words of the document read, 'The leaders of the Party promise to work ruthlessly – if need be to sacrifice their very lives – to translate this programme into action.'[34] This was plainly not a conventional manifesto of a run-of-the-mill political party. For what 'normal' manifesto ends with a commitment from the party leaders that they will die if necessary to reach their goals?

The same extremist way of looking at events was inextricably bound into Hitler's way of perceiving the war against Stalin. He had deliberately set out to make this conflict one which would lead either to victory or to destruction. His insistence that this was a war of 'extermination' all but guaranteed that the Soviets would want to take horrendous revenge on the Germans if they triumphed in the end. But Hitler saw this as a positive. In the letter he wrote to Mussolini on the eve of the war he said that he felt 'spiritually free' now that Germany was about to attack the Soviet Union.[35] And that freedom was based on the knowledge that this was an epic conflict in which he – and Germany – would either win or face destruction. As he said to Goebbels on 16 June 1941, 'we must gain the victory, no matter whether we do right or wrong. We have so much to answer for anyhow that we must gain the victory because otherwise our whole people . . . will be wiped out.'[36] The stakes were not just high, they were absolute, and that is how he wanted it.

Hitler's speech on 11 December was a public statement of defiance. But just how did he think 'a victorious end' was to be achieved, given that 3,000 miles of ocean separated America from Europe, and Germany had never been much of a naval power? He had been nervous about invading England across the Channel, so how could he defeat America?

The answer is that it's unlikely that Hitler was looking that far ahead. His priority remained the war against Stalin. It would take time for the Americans to increase their armament production and transport their troops and their hardware across an Atlantic patrolled by German U-boats. Hitler told Goebbels just before Pearl Harbor that while 'He does not underestimate the United States' he 'still doesn't regard an entry into the war as an acute threat. They cannot change the situation on the continent. We are firmly in control in Europe . . .'[37] The Americans would also now be engaged in fighting the Japanese thousands of miles away. So if the Germans could defeat the Soviets in 1942, and if Soviet resources – particularly the oil – could be captured intact, it might be possible to hold out for a stalemate in which Britain and America eventually accepted the new status quo.

This was verging on a fantasy scenario, not least because of the numerous 'ifs' involved. But it was one that Nicolaus von Below, Hitler's Luftwaffe adjutant, appeared to share. He thought there was still 'a chance' to destroy the Soviet Union before the United States 'with all her enormous potential' was able to make an impact on the battlefield. This was also, he believed, his Führer's judgement. Hitler 'was certain he would defeat Russia in 1942'.[38]

But while Hitler was projecting an image of utter confidence in public, behind the scenes he knew that his commanders were struggling to keep their own optimism intact. Take the case of Ernst Udet, a German fighter ace from the First World War. He had been made Director of Luftwaffe equipment by his old wartime comrade Hermann Göring, and it was a job for which he was utterly unsuited. Udet loved flying, drinking and having fun, and yet he was now bogged down in administrative matters he could not solve. Worse still, Göring, when attacked by Hitler for the failures of the Luftwaffe, tried to pass the blame on to Udet. This chain of Hitler placing unattainable goals on the shoulders of Göring, and then Göring transferring the overambitious objectives on to a subordinate, would cost Udet dearly. He shot himself on 17 November 1941.

Around this time, other German commanders also left the scene. But they did not need to kill themselves – their own bodies turned on them. On 10 November, a week before Udet shot himself, Field Marshal von Brauchitsch suffered a heart attack. On 16 December, Bock, who – with Army Group Centre – had led the single greatest concentration of military power in the history of the German Army, wrote in his diary that his health was 'hanging by a silk thread'.[39] Two days later he was removed from command.

A number of other senior military leaders who were not quitting because their health demanded it were sacked because they proposed retreating to more defensible positions in the face of the renewed Soviet threat. Field Marshal von Rundstedt, for example, who was commander of Army Group South and one of Hitler's most loyal military leaders, was removed when he pulled back further from Rostov than the Führer wanted. In a pattern that would be repeated later in the war, the man Hitler chose to replace him, Walther von Reichenau, subsequently had to ask to retreat to the position that Rundstedt had suggested, and Hitler now agreed. For all his belief in the 'triumph of the will', Hitler could not 'will' the military reality to be different. As for Reichenau, he did not survive long at the head of Army Group South. A few weeks after his appointment he suffered a stroke and died.

These senior commanders all supported Hitler's aims. The problem they faced was a purely practical one. They discovered that when they presented logical reasons to Hitler for why they needed to do something, he might simply refuse to agree. They thus came face to face – perhaps for the first time – with his alternative reality. This realization could be devastating.

The most blatant example of this phenomenon came on 20 December 1941, when Hitler met with one of his favourite commanders – the panzer leader Heinz Guderian. By now Hitler had decided on a replacement for Brauchitsch as head of the army. He had resolved, the day before he met Guderian, to appoint the only man in the Reich that he considered up to the job – himself.

Guderian arrived at Hitler's headquarters in East Prussia, hopeful that 'our Supreme Command' was prepared to listen to 'sensible propositions' from a 'general who knew the front'.[40] But he was in for a 'surprise'. Hitler greeted him with a 'hard unfriendly expression in his eyes', and so Guderian assumed that an enemy of his must have briefed against him. The general explained that his troops were withdrawing to a position agreed with Brauchitsch a few days before. When he heard this news, Hitler shouted, 'I forbid that!' But Guderian explained that the withdrawal was already in progress and to halt it now would leave the troops exposed. Hitler said they should dig in where they were. When Guderian said that was impossible because the ground was frozen, Hitler replied, 'In that case they must blast craters with the heavy howitzers. We had to do that in the First World War in Flanders.'

Guderian explained, at length, how this was impractical, but Hitler was intransigent. Guderian repeated that halting the troops where they were would cause a needless loss of life, only for Hitler to reply, 'Do you think Frederick the Great's grenadiers were anxious to die? They wanted to live, too, but the king was right in asking them to sacrifice themselves.' Hitler also told Guderian that he had 'too much pity' for his troops and that he should distance himself from them. As he left the meeting, Guderian overheard Hitler say to Keitel, head of the Armed Forces High Command, 'I haven't convinced that man!'[41] Six days later, on 26 December, Guderian was told that he had been relieved of command of the Second Panzer Army.

In his memoirs Guderian presented this as an example of an out-of-touch politician refusing to understand the realities of war. But that is a simplistic way of interpreting what happened. While it's certainly the case that by now Hitler was often making unreasonable demands of his military commanders, that does not necessarily mean that they were always right and he was always wrong. Hitler – as we have seen – had insisted on pushing forward with the invasion of western Europe in 1940 against the advice of many of his senior commanders. And his judgement had been proved triumphantly correct. So who was to say that he might not have been correct in this instance? If he had given the impression to his generals that they could pull back to any position that they felt was suitable, who knows where they might have gone? By communicating that his first response was always to tell them to hold firm, at the very least he made them more reluctant to retreat.

Nor is it the case that Hitler was always as irrationally intransigent as Guderian paints him. For instance, another – more junior – German officer, Günther von Below, attended a meeting in December 1941 at the Wolf's Lair and encountered a different Hitler. 'It was very calm,' remembered Below; 'Hitler asked a few questions and then the telephone went. It was Field Marshal von Kluge.' The field marshal explained that he wanted to withdraw some units from their forward position. 'So the army corps', said Hitler, 'will retreat from a position which is not good . . . back into the snowy waste.' He then 'discussed the question with Kluge for some time, and eventually he said: "Well, Field Marshal, you bear the responsibility, you carry it out." So he was completely calm . . .'[42]

But while the details of how the Germans should have dealt with the Moscow crisis are still argued over by historians, one significant point is often overlooked. This marks the moment when Hitler's sense of absolute conviction – which was regarded as a massive strength immediately after the victories of summer 1940 – came to be seen by Guderian, and some others, as a tremendous weakness.

At the same time as he was dealing with these military matters, Hitler was making decisions about a subject which he considered of equal, if not greater, importance – the Jews. As we have seen, in his speech on 11 December, Hitler claimed that the Jews were behind not just Stalin and Bolshevism, but President Roosevelt and the American decision to help the British war effort. And the role that he perceived the Jews to be playing in this war was a subject that was still very much on his mind the next day, when at the Reich Chancellery he met a group of around fifty Nazi leaders.

In one of his most noteworthy diary entries, Goebbels recorded what Hitler said: 'As regards the Jewish question, the Führer is resolved to clear the air. He prophesied to the Jews [in a speech in January 1939] that if they were to bring about another world war, they would experience their own extermination. This was not a hollow phrase. The world war is here, the destruction of the Jews must be the inevitable consequence. The question must be seen without sentimentality. We are not here to take pity on the Jews, but only to feel sympathy with our own German people. Since the German people has once again sacrificed around 160,000 fallen in the eastern campaign, those who initiated this bloody conflict will have to pay with their lives.'[43]

At this moment, as Goebbels reveals, a number of different strands came together – the war in the east, the fate of the Jews, the entry of America into the war and the vindictive cruelty of Hitler's vision of the world. The Jews were to die because they were 'behind' this 'world' war and because it was unconscionable that they should live while German blood was being shed in the war against Stalin. Those were the immediate reasons why this crime should happen. But the long-term 'cause' of the extermination of the Jews remained in Hitler's mind – which was that they had to be 'dealt with' in order for the perfect racial state to be achieved.

However, just because Hitler had called for the 'destruction of the Jews' it didn't mean that it was currently possible in practical terms to murder millions of people within the Nazi state. Once again, Hitler's expressed desires exceeded the current ability of his underlings to achieve them. In this instance, this was scarcely surprising, since he was asking them to commit mass murder on a scale never before attempted in history.

Hans Frank, the ruler of the General Government in Poland – an area that contained a large number of Jews – offered an insight into the atmosphere in which Hitler had made his statement about the Jews, in a speech he gave himself on 16 December 1941. Frank, who had attended the 12 December meeting, said to his own staff that he had been told 'in Berlin' to 'liquidate them [the Jews] yourselves!' Moreover, he said, he had his 'own ideas' on how to destroy the Jews. It was, once again, an example of how Hitler's leadership worked. He had the vision – in this case the destruction of the Jews – and others had to devise ways of achieving it.[44]

While this is not the way that Stalin worked, the similarities between Hitler's action against the Jews and Stalin's decision to order the deportation of an entire ethnic group, the Volga Germans, just a few months before, do appear – superficially at least – to be strong. The targets in each case were distinct groups of people, and the punitive measures were taken against the group as a whole, regardless of any perceived individual 'blame'. The groups were also both removed from their homes and transported to locations where they would suffer en masse.

There were also, however, crucial differences. While Hitler explicitly talked of the 'destruction' of the Jews, Stalin did not appear to think in such absolute terms. Though large numbers of the Volga Germans who were deported did die – perhaps a quarter or a third of those exiled – there was no plan in place to kill them all. Nor, as previously discussed, did Stalin believe in the kind of racial theories that were central to Hitler's worldview. He targeted groups like the Volga Germans because he thought they were a potential threat and, in the particular circumstances of the war, might work against the state. He did not believe that they were 'inferior' or inherently different from other Soviet citizens. He would have thought Hitler's talk of 'blood' determining destiny simply laughable.

However, in the ruthless way in which he directed military operations, Stalin was more than equal to Hitler. Already in this war he had demonstrated his monumental disdain for the suffering of his troops. When, for example, Army Commissar Stepanov had requested permission to pull his soldiers back from his position near Moscow, Stalin had merely asked him if he and his soldiers had spades. When Stepanov replied that they did, Stalin said: 'Comrade Stepanov, tell your comrades that they should take their spades and dig their own graves. We will not leave Moscow.'[45]

Fyodor Sverdlov, a commander of a rifle company who took part in the December offensive, heartily approved of Stalin's lack of compassion. 'You can't feel pity,' he said, 'you shouldn't feel pity for the soldier who can get killed any minute. If you feel pity for him, it means that you run the risk of surrendering a big part of the country to the Germans who would execute thousands of people.'

Sverdlov developed his own theory of war that December – one Stalin would have supported. Attack whenever possible. 'Those who were advancing, who were going on, survived,' said Sverdlov. 'Because if you move on, if you get closer to the enemy, it seems incredible, but you are in the so-called dead zone which is not vulnerable to the enemy's artillery . . . It means that, from this short distance you are sure to destroy the enemy with your fire. This was our tactics.'[46]

Sverdlov was also prepared to be just as ruthless as Stalin. He personally killed, 'without thinking twice', a soldier who tried to run away from combat. 'War is a cruel business,' he said. 'Our war was not like the Franco-German war, when an armistice was signed soon and which was followed by a party in which both Germans and the French were taking part. That was the last-century business. The war we were fighting was a matter of life and death. The life of the whole country and the whole nation was at stake.'

Just as Sverdlov was inspired by Stalin's leadership, so he and his comrades focused much of their hatred on Adolf Hitler. 'I remember a liaison officer running up to me,' recalled Sverdlov, 'and saying "Commissar Kulish is killed." I ran to the left flank and I saw he was still alive, but he was bleeding and I could see he was wounded in the lungs. He was such a witty man. When I asked him, "Nikolai, how are you?", he answered, "I hope Hitler feels the way I do now." And he died the same day.'

The war didn't just change the lives of soldiers on the front line, it also had a profound effect on many Soviet citizens back home. The composer Dmitri Shostakovich wrote that before the war 'one had to cry silently, under the bedspread. Nobody must notice it. Everybody was afraid of everyone.' Now, even though the war 'brought incredible suffering and misery', it also meant that 'the secret, isolated grief became everyone's grief. One was allowed to talk about it, one could cry openly, openly mourn for the dead. People needed no longer be afraid of their tears.' The poet Yevgeny Yevtushenko felt much the same way, writing that the war 'lightened the Russians' spiritual burden, for they no longer needed to be insincere'.[47]

Stalin was an exception to this rule, as he continued to feel the need to be insincere, no more so than in his dealings with Poland – a country, as we have seen, that he especially disliked. Poland had, through no desire of its own, become an ally of the Soviet Union in the wake of Operation Barbarossa. But it was impossible to forget the recent history between the two countries. Not only had the Soviets appropriated eastern Poland in September 1939 and deported hundreds of thousands of Polish citizens to the wastes of the Soviet Union, but Stalin had personally signed the order that condemned to death thousands of Polish officers. This was something that, naturally, Stalin omitted to mention when he held a meeting in the Kremlin on 3 December 1941 with General Sikorski, the Prime Minister of the Polish government in exile, and General Anders, a Polish officer who had been imprisoned by the Soviets earlier in the war.

Instead of taking the Polish request for information about the missing officers seriously, Stalin first insisted – ludicrously – that they had been released, and then suggested that they might have 'escaped'. When General Anders asked where several thousand Polish officers could possibly have escaped to, Stalin replied, 'to Manchuria'.[48]

Stalin seemed to be playing with the two distinguished Polish generals. He knew that he possessed the power in this relationship, and so

felt able to joke about the fate of thousands of people that he had previously ordered to be murdered. The Poles knew he was lying – how
could thousands of Polish officers possibly have escaped Soviet captivity and travelled to Manchuria? And Stalin must have been aware that
the Poles knew he was lying. But he didn't care. He had to take this
meeting with his new 'allies', but he didn't have to behave himself
during it.

While Stalin was not normally so contemptuous towards more powerful allies like Britain and America, his behaviour still remained crude, at
least in diplomatic terms. In November 1941, for instance, he sent a message to Churchill in which he brusquely said he wanted to know British
plans for post-war Europe. He demanded immediate 'clarity' in Anglo-
Soviet relations. He also complained that the armaments the British were
sending to the Soviets were arriving 'inefficiently packed' and so sometimes 'reach us broken'.[49] When Churchill read Stalin's words he became
angry. Maisky, the Soviet Ambassador, thought Churchill was 'obviously enraged' by the 'tone' of Stalin's message.[50]

The following month the British Foreign Secretary, Anthony
Eden, made the tortuous journey to the Soviet Union on board a
British warship in an attempt to improve the relationship. He met
Stalin in the Kremlin on 16 December, the same day that Hans Frank
was telling his subordinates in Kraków that they had been told to
'liquidate' the Jews. On arrival the British delegation were surprised
to learn the topic that Stalin wanted to discuss above all others – post-
war borders. With the Germans so close to Moscow they had expected
the Soviet leader to focus on the question of how best to win the war.
But Stalin was demonstrating once again his understanding of how
raw power works. He knew that the Red Army was bearing the
brunt of the German threat, and he felt that the Allies should pay for
all this spilt Soviet blood. The immediate price was an agreement
that the Soviets could keep the territory they had gained under the
terms of the Nazi–Soviet pact.

Matters came to a head at the second meeting, held at midnight on 17
December. Stalin looked over some drafts that the British had prepared
and remarked that while they were 'certainly interesting' he was 'much
more interested in the question of the USSR's future frontiers'. He
demanded once again that the British recognize the 1941 borders. The
British refused. Stalin persisted, saying that the 'question of Soviet

frontiers' was 'of exceptional importance to us', and given that the Soviet Union was 'bearing the brunt of the war on its shoulders', why was the British government still not prepared to 'recognise the Soviet western frontier?'

Stalin then brought up the question of the Baltic States, territory the Soviet Union had snatched prior to Operation Barbarossa. 'Our troops may take hold of the Baltic States again in the immediate future,' said Stalin. 'Well, will Great Britain refuse us recognition of these frontiers in that case?' Eden replied weakly that 'for the British Government, the three Baltic States do not at present exist' since they were occupied by the Germans.

At times during the meeting, it seemed that Stalin was ridiculing Eden – humiliating him as he had humiliated the Polish generals who had asked about their missing colleagues. 'Perhaps tomorrow', said Stalin facetiously, 'Britain will declare that she does not recognise the Ukraine as part of the USSR.' He summed up by saying that he was 'greatly surprised' by the British attitude – a 'highly ridiculous situation had come about' and 'presumably, one ally must support another ally.' Eden was so browbeaten that he remarked that, while he 'did not have the power to recognise the Soviet's western frontier immediately', a solution 'only requires time, a measure of postponement'. But Stalin continued to berate him, protesting that it 'looks as if the USSR has to ask Britain for a favour'.[51]

It was a bravura performance from Stalin. By focusing on one point – the need to agree the post-war western borders of the Soviet Union – and relentlessly pressing it home, he pushed Eden into a corner from which he could not escape. Eden could not say he agreed to the borders without consulting Churchill, and he could not say what the British would do if the Soviets occupied this territory after they drove the Germans out. He thus not only appeared weak but, as Stalin pointed out, found himself in a 'highly ridiculous situation'.

Eden's trip ended with a dinner at the Kremlin on 20 December, with the British delegation finally leaving the festivities at five in the morning. By this time, according to the Foreign Office permanent secretary Sir Alexander Cadogan, Stalin, who had been relatively 'tight' – or drunk – during the dinner was 'sober'. Cadogan 'marvelled' at this, since he believed that Stalin had drunk 'pretty consistently' for '7 hours'.[52] What the British diplomat did not realize was that Stalin often drank less than it appeared, in order to observe his guests while they were inebriated. Not all of Stalin's colleagues, however, were so abstemious. Marshal Voroshilov became so drunk that he ended up wrestling with a junior diplomat from the British embassy. By four in the morning he was so far gone that he had to be carried away.[53] Stalin would never have let himself get into such a state. As for Hitler, nothing like this could have happened to him, since he abhorred both alcohol and smoking.

This December encounter between the British and the Soviets was memorable in a number of ways. The first is that Anthony Eden found it hard to reconcile Stalin's reputation with the reality of Stalin the man. He later said that he had done his best to imagine the Soviet leader 'dripping with the blood of his opponents and rivals, but somehow the picture wouldn't fit'.[54]

Stalin's shrewdness, his calmness, his lack of histrionics, all meant that he did not conform to the conventional image of a dictator. Like Eden, Sir Alexander Cadogan was disconcerted by Stalin's demeanour. 'Difficult to say whether S. [Stalin] is impressive,' he wrote in his diary. On the one hand he was an all-powerful ruler; on the other it would be hard to 'pick him out of a crowd'. His 'twinkly eyes' and his 'stiff hair' made him look 'rather like a porcupine'. Above all, he was 'very restrained and quiet'.[55]

Eden subsequently came to the conclusion that Stalin was one of the most impressive political operators he had ever encountered. 'Marshal Stalin as a negotiator was the toughest proposition of all,' he wrote after the war. 'Indeed, after something like thirty years' experience of international conferences of one kind or another, if I had to pick a team for going into a conference room, Stalin would be my first choice. Of course the man was ruthless and of course he knew his purpose. He never wasted a word. He never stormed, he was seldom even irritated.' Instead, added Eden, Stalin was 'hooded, calm' and never raised his voice.[56] British politicians had previously had dealings with Hitler, most notably at the time of the Munich crisis in 1938. And Hitler – unlike Stalin – not only seldom kept quiet for long periods during a meeting, but was liable to harangue foreign politicians at length.

Stalin's less histrionic approach certainly proved to be effective with Eden in December 1941. The British Foreign Secretary left Moscow convinced that Stalin saw the question of the post-war Soviet borders as the 'acid test of our sincerity'. But Eden also recognized that this was a delicate matter, because point two of the Atlantic Charter – the agreement Churchill had reached with Roosevelt in the summer of 1941 – called for any 'territorial changes' to be made only according to the 'freely expressed wishes of the people concerned'. Nonetheless, in a note he wrote to Churchill in early January 1942, Eden made as powerful a case as he could for giving Stalin what he wanted.[57]

Eden's suggestion produced a tirade from Churchill. The territories Stalin wanted at the end of the war, Churchill wrote, 'were acquired by acts of aggression in shameful collusion with Hitler'. Moreover, the Soviets had 'entered the war only when attacked by Germany, having previously shown themselves utterly indifferent to our fate and, indeed, they added to our burdens in our worst danger'. There should be 'no mistake' about the position of the government he led, which 'adheres to those principles of freedom and democracy set forth in the Atlantic Charter'.[58]

It was confirmation of the immense gulf that existed between Britain and the Soviet Union. The Soviet leader saw nothing wrong in large countries plotting to take land from small countries. As a result he wanted to come to an arrangement with the British similar to the one he had reached with the Nazis. At his first meeting with Eden he had even raised the possibility of agreeing a 'secret protocol' with the British that would guarantee the post-war borders of the Soviet Union. A similar 'secret protocol', as we have seen, had been arranged with Ribbentrop in 1939. Eden dismissed the idea as 'impossible'.[59]

As for Churchill, his words about the importance of democratic 'principles' were fine and noble. But, as we shall see, he would not live up to them.

9. Hunger

Hitler and Stalin, different in so many ways, both understood one immense truth – the power of hunger. They knew from personal experience that the giving or withholding of food was a devastatingly effective method of control. Each of them, during the First World War and in its immediate aftermath, had witnessed how hunger had played a part in political insurrection. And once they had gained power themselves, they used that knowledge, with dreadful consequences. Each of them was responsible for the deliberate death of millions of men, women and children by starvation. It was a crime so terrible that it should always be considered a major part of their legacies.

The most infamous example of mass death by starvation in the war occurred in Leningrad – today's St Petersburg – during the nearly 900 days of the German siege of the city. No one knows exactly how many people died during this period – perhaps 700,000 to 800,000, though some estimates suggest a million or more.[1]

In the first weeks of Operation Barbarossa, in the summer of 1941, Army Group North advanced quickly towards Leningrad. 'Early on we started to hear about the number of towns taken by the German Army,' said Lev Razumovsky, a Leningrad student at the time. 'We were all shocked. How could it happen that we were losing ground so easily? We were supposed to fight the enemy on his territory and finish the war with little bloodshed.'[2]

Army Group North was so successful that by 8 September Leningrad was surrounded. The city was now cut off from the rest of the Soviet Union, apart from a precarious route over Lake Ladoga. For weeks before this disaster occurred, Stalin had been criticizing the leadership in the city. 'We have never known of your plans and undertakings,' he said on 22 August, in a letter to the city's leader, Andrei Zhdanov. 'We always learn by chance that something or other is intended, that something or other is planned, and then there is a gap. We cannot put up with this. You are not children and you well know that there is no need for forgiveness. Your justification of being overworked is laughable. We are no less overworked than you. You are simply disorganized and you feel no responsibility for your acts, as a result of which you act as if you were on an isolated island, without considering anyone.'[3]

On 29 August, after learning that the town of Tosno, close to Leningrad, had fallen to the Germans, Stalin sent a telegram to Molotov and Malenkov who were visiting the city as part of a 'special commission'. 'If things go on like this I am afraid that Leningrad will be surrendered out of idiot stupidity,' he wrote, 'and all the Leningrad divisions fall into captivity. What are Popov [commander of the Leningrad Front] and [Marshal] Voroshilov doing? They don't even tell me how they plan to avert the danger. They're busy looking for new lines of retreat; that's how they see their duty. Where does this abyss of passivity of theirs come from, this peasant-like submission to fate? I just don't understand them.'[4] In another telegram sent to Molotov around the same time, Stalin voiced his suspicion that a traitor was in their midst: 'Doesn't it seem to you that someone is deliberately opening the road to the Germans?' He concluded that 'The uselessness of the Leningrad command is so absolutely incomprehensible.'[5]

Stalin's telegrams can only have hindered any exercise of initiative by the Leningrad authorities. The Soviet leader uttered no words of encouragement, no practical help, just threat. He also offered, with the sentence 'we are no less overworked than you' two insights into his character. First his propensity to self-pity and self-justification in a crisis, and second – by his use of the first person plural – the way in which, once again, he sought to conceal himself behind others. But with Stalin the collective was almost always just a smokescreen. Eden, for example, might meet with Stalin and Molotov in December 1941, just as Ribbentrop had done in September 1939, but in each case the idea of collective decision-making was an illusion. There was only one decision-maker on the Soviet side – and his name was Joseph Stalin.

No contingency plans had been put in place to evacuate the civilian population from Leningrad before the siege began, and this oversight would have catastrophic consequences. Though several hundred thousand did escape by train, around two and a half million civilians were left inside the city, together with more than 300,000 in the immediate environs, still within the German encirclement. The reasons behind this blunder were complex, and certainly included mistakes by the Leningrad authorities, but Stalin must take most of the blame. He showed little concern for the safety of the population of Leningrad, and never gave orders for a concerted evacuation of non-combatants. His focus on the military defence of the city was coupled with an inability to deal with the speed at which events were happening.

After they had surrounded Leningrad, the Germans discussed among themselves what their next step should be. And the deliberations of the High Command of the Wehrmacht, expressed in a document dated 21 September, illustrated the brutal mentality of all those involved. The occupation of the city was ruled out, because the Wehrmacht would have to feed the population – something that must have been anathema to them given the dictates of the Hunger Plan. Another possibility was isolating the city behind an electric fence, 'to be guarded with machine guns', but this was problematic for a number of reasons, not least that 'it is doubtful whether we can expect our soldiers to fire at escaping women and children.'

One of the most bizarre ideas was for President Roosevelt to be allowed either to supply the civilians inside Leningrad or to take them away after the city had surrendered. Presumably the possibility of the American President's involvement was raised because he was perceived by the Nazis as someone who had sympathy for the Jews – and by extension other people enduring suffering – given that he had convened the ineffectual Évian conference before the war. However, the Germans knew that it wasn't practical for Roosevelt to help, and the offer, had it been made, would have been mere propaganda. A more realizable option was to 'first isolate Leningrad hermetically and, as far as possible, pound it to dust with artillery and air attacks'.[6]

Just before the High Command voiced these brutal views, the Army Chief of Staff, General Halder, had given his opinion, and it too was a heartless one. He wrote in his war diary that 'the situation [in Leningrad] will remain tight until such time when hunger takes effect as our ally.'[7] Ten days later, Hitler pronounced his own judgement. Leningrad, he said, was to 'disappear from the face of the earth'. The city should be encircled and levelled to the ground by artillery fire and air raids. Any attempt by the civilians to surrender should be rejected 'because we cannot and should not solve the problem of housing and feeding the population'.[8]

Shortly before this instruction was officially issued, Hitler had spoken privately of his decision: 'I suppose that some people are clutching their heads with both hands to find an answer to this question: "How can the Führer destroy a city like St Petersburg [as Hitler called Leningrad]?" Plainly I belong by nature to quite another species.' He went on to explain that though he would prefer 'not to see anyone suffer' he had to act when 'the species is in danger'. He added – in one of the clearest explanations for his actions that he ever gave – that if he hesitated to act now then sacrifices would be demanded in the future. Thus, for the sake of the utopia of tomorrow, many must die today.

It was no accident that just before he uttered those words Hitler had talked about the First World War, the pivotal experience of his life. He had entered that conflict 'with feelings of pure idealism' only to see 'men falling around me in thousands'. As a consequence, he learnt not just that 'life is a cruel struggle, and has no other object but the preservation of the species,' but that 'the individual can disappear, provided there are other men to replace him.'[9] To be wholly accurate, he should have added that he also believed that one particular individual could never be replaced – himself.

On 21 September, just before Hitler spoke in those annihilatory terms about Leningrad, Stalin had been talking in the same kind of way. He wrote to the Leningrad authorities in response to news that the Germans might attempt to force Soviet civilians to walk in front of their troops as human shields. 'They say', wrote Stalin, 'that among the Bolsheviks in Leningrad there are those who don't consider it possible to use weapons against messengers such as this. I consider that if there are such people among the Bolsheviks, then they should be exterminated straight away, as they are more dangerous than the German fascists. My advice: don't get sentimental, but smash in the teeth of the enemy and their helpers, whether voluntary helpers or not. War is pitiless, and it brings destruction, first of all, to those who show weakness and permit wavering . . . There must be no mercy, either to the filthy Germans, or to their delegates, whoever they may be.'[10]

'War is pitiless . . . There must be no mercy' was another belief about which Hitler and Stalin were in complete agreement. Indeed, Stalin's words are remarkably similar to the final instruction Hitler gave his generals just before the invasion of Poland, when he told them to 'close your hearts to pity' and 'act brutally'.[11] It is this attitude, shared by both tyrants, that in large part explains the level of suffering that this war would create. Stalin's ruthlessness had already extended to executing generals who did not perform as required and employing 'backstop' units to shoot any Red Army soldiers who retreated. His view that Soviet civilians, forced to walk in front of German troops, should also be mown down without pity was part of this same mentality.

Unlike Hitler, Stalin was reacting to an existential threat. His country was at risk, and in desperate situations leaders tend to do desperate things. However, what differentiates Stalin from other leaders who are prepared to contemplate radical measures in self-defence is that he displayed this same brutal mentality long before his country became involved in a war for survival. As we have seen, several million people starved to death in Ukraine in the early 1930s as a consequence of his political decisions, and about a million more died a few years later in the Great Terror. Moreover, Stalin's past history – just like Hitler's – demonstrated that he was merciless primarily for ideological reasons. Both leaders were trying to remake the consciousness of an entire country, and both thought that this goal justified the creation of the most appalling suffering along the way.

Inside Leningrad, the question of how much food should be given to each citizen became a vital one – a genuine case of life and death. In this respect, it is a common misconception to suppose that the essence of Bolshevism was equality. Lenin, for example, did not preach that each citizen deserved equal sustenance. At the time of the famine during the civil war in 1921, he declared that food 'distribution must be thought of as a method, an instrument, a means for increasing production. State support in the form of food must only be given to those workers who are really necessary for the utmost productivity of labour. And if food distribution is to be used as an instrument of policy, then use it to reduce the number of those who are not unconditionally necessary, and to encourage those who are.'[12]

Those at the very top – Stalin and other prominent members of the party – were never short of food during the war. 'Here we are starving to death like flies,' wrote Leningrader Elena Mukhina in her diary in December 1941, 'and yesterday Stalin in Moscow gave another dinner in honour of Anthony Eden. It's a disgrace. They are gorging themselves there while we can't buy a piece of bread like normal human beings. They're organizing dazzling receptions there, while we live like cavemen.'[13]

Just as Stalin and his colleagues in Moscow had enough to eat, so did the leadership inside Leningrad. Communist Party members fared best of all, along with those deemed essential to the running of the city, such as senior engineers and industrial managers. 'You could not imagine more inequality than we have now,' wrote another Leningrader, Irina Zelenskaia: 'it is clearly written on people's faces, when you see side-by-side the terrible brown mask of a malnourished employee being fed in accordance with that wretched second category, and the florid face of some person in authority or "girl from the canteen".'[14]

As Zelenskaia pointed out, it wasn't just functionaries who benefited from above-average food rations, but also many of those who worked in food distribution. Anna Ostroumova-Lebedeva, a book illustrator, was all too conscious of this new reality. 'Anastasia Osipovna came to see me,' she wrote in her diary in May 1942. 'She had recently been to the public baths and was completely astounded by the large number of well-fed Rubenesque young women with radiant bodies and glowing physiognomies. They are all workers in bakeries, cooperatives, soup kitchens, and children's centers. In bakeries and cooperatives they cheat the unfortunate inhabitants. They divide the best food among themselves; for example, they leave the hind quarters for themselves. In the soup kitchens and children's centers, they simply steal. The same thing goes on, I think, at the highest level of the food-distribution system.'[15]

Children were particularly at risk during the siege, not just because those caring for them in orphanages or children's homes could take their food, but also because it was relatively easy to steal from children as they walked the streets. The younger the child, the more vulnerable they were, especially after their parents had died. One woman entered a flat to see a small girl holding on to her dead mother's hand, saying 'Mummy, I'm hungry,' while another child stared 'mindlessly, his swollen face that of an old man, and saying nothing'. Elsewhere, another visitor to a flat found two toddlers sharing a bed with the 'gnawed corpse of a woman'.[16]

Even for older children, the loss of a parent during the siege could be all but paralysing. 'Lord, I'm surrounded by strangers, strangers, only strangers, no family or friends,' wrote teenager Elena Mukhina in her diary in April 1942, after the death of her mother. 'Everyone walks past indifferently, nobody even wants to know me. Nobody cares about me at all. Spring is here, we had the first thunderstorm yesterday, life goes on, and nobody but me notices that Mama is not here. That terrible winter carried her away.'[17]

A combination of the appalling winter of 1941–2, one of the coldest for years, together with lack of food, inadequate healthcare and German bombardment brought misery and death to Leningrad. It also brought another horror – cannibalism. 'I saw it with my own eyes,' said Viktor Kirshin, who lived through that winter. 'There was this woman lying for several days in our yard – with her breasts cut off. I saw this boy, a young child, dismembered . . . It's frightful.' Lack of food tormented the inhabitants of the city and had driven them to this extreme. 'It's impossible to communicate that feeling of hunger,' said Kirshin. 'It's the most terrible thing in the world. You have the feeling that some sort of animal has climbed inside you. Some savage beast. And he's scratching you, gouging you with his claws, tearing your insides, ripping everything. He demands bread, bread, demands food, demands to be fed.'[18]

Leningraders became used to the sight of despoiled bodies on the street. 'With his back to the post, a man sits on the snow, tall, wrapped in rags, over his shoulders a knapsack,' wrote Vera Kostrovitskaia in April 1942. 'He is all huddled up against the post. Apparently he was on his way to the Finland Station, got tired, and sat down. For two weeks while I was going back and forth to the hospital, he "sat" 1. without his knapsack 2. without his rags 3. in his underwear 4. naked 5. a skeleton with ripped-out entrails[.] They took him away in May.'[19]

There was also another, still more sinister side to the practice of cannibalism in Leningrad – murdering fellow human beings for their meat. The NKVD files reveal that a whole variety of people were driven to commit murder in order to survive. From the mother who killed her eighteen-month-old daughter so as to obtain meat for her other children and herself, to an out-of-work plumber who murdered his own wife so that his son and other relatives could be fed.[20] But while the line between eating the flesh from the body of a person who has already died and killing in order to gain that flesh seems clear to us today, it would not necessarily have appeared so distinct at the time. Hastening an inevitable death in order to provide food for children dying of hunger may well not have been seen as an obvious case of murder.

It's impossible to be certain how widespread cannibalism was during the siege. One NKVD report said that just over 2,000 people had been arrested for the crime by the end of 1942, but since it was relatively easy to hide the offence given the vast numbers who were dying of starvation, this is almost certainly an underestimate of the true number of cannibalistic acts.[21]

The destruction of the dignity of death during the siege had another consequence. Since life literally depended on possession of a ration card, there were cases where bodies were stored in flats so that relatives could carry on using the dead person's card. One Leningrader returned to her former flat to discover three bodies lying in her bedroom. 'Evidently the neighbors have set up a morgue in my room,' she wrote in her diary. 'Well, then, let them: corpses don't bother me.'[22]

Much of the testimony of those who suffered in the siege focuses on how individuals were tested by the experience, and in the process discovered aspects of their character they never knew existed. 'I think that real life is hunger, and the rest a mirage,' wrote the Leningrad scholar Dmitry Likhachev. 'In the time of famine people revealed themselves, stripped themselves, freed themselves of all trumpery. Some turned out to be marvellous, incomparable heroes, others – scoundrels, villains, murderers, cannibals. There were no half-measures.'[23]

Elena Kochina discovered this same truth as early as October 1941. 'Before the war many people, showing off, would adorn themselves with bravery, fidelity to principles, honesty – whatever they liked,' she wrote in her diary. 'The hurricane of war has torn off these rags: now everyone has become what he was in fact, and not what he wanted to seem. Many have turned out to be pitiful cowards and scoundrels.'[24]

The tragic reality that Elena Kochina believed she had discovered was that 'each of us struggles silently with his own sufferings. There's no way we can help one another . . . We realize now that man must be able to struggle alone with life and death . . .'[25] As she tried to come to terms with this revelation, she concluded a few weeks later that 'There is evidently some measure of physical suffering beyond which a person becomes insensitive to everything except himself. Heroism, self-sacrifice, the heroic feat – only those who are full or who haven't been hungry long are capable of these.'[26] In this judgement she was partly wrong and partly right. Wrong because there were undoubtedly individual acts of self-sacrifice during the siege that demonstrated the best of the human spirit. But right because such nobility was hardly widespread.

Hitler, his military commanders and the ordinary German soldiers who besieged Leningrad knew that they were creating this suffering. Indeed, as we have seen, they deliberately set out to cause these lingering deaths because they did not want to risk their own lives in taking the city. Nor did they want to have any responsibility for the inhabitants if they managed to conquer it. Such thinking was part of a broader pattern. As we saw earlier, plans devised before the invasion called upon the German troops to live off the land as far as possible, which inevitably meant stealing food from the people who lived there.

Albert Schneider, a soldier with a Wehrmacht assault-gun battalion, remembered that 'when we spent two or three months in front of Moscow people were systematically robbed of everything . . . the cellars were searched to see if there were potatoes and so on, without any consideration as to whether the people might starve to death themselves.' He witnessed how one peasant was shot when he objected to German soldiers stealing his pig, because 'it was assumed right from the start that these were "subhuman creatures". They have no other purpose in life than to serve us and when we have no more use for them, they can be thrown on the scrap heap. That was the propaganda message at the time and it proved sufficiently effective . . . I think that was when I actually realized that human beings are nothing more than wild animals. I am still of the opinion today that human beings are wild animals.'

Schneider was not against the invasion of the Soviet Union in principle. 'I was definitely opposed to the Bolshevists,' he said. 'I still am today.' Moreover he felt it legitimate that those in positions of power or influence in the Bolshevik Party should be targeted: 'It did not seem all that terrible to me . . . that party officials – who encouraged others to murder people – that they had to be punished too.' His objection was that no effort was made to win the ordinary Soviet people over to the Nazi cause.

In Ukraine, in the early days of the invasion he met a local woman who 'spoke German because she was a language teacher' and 'she had a very German attitude, pro-German attitude. On this occasion she also told me that she was glad to be freed from Bolshevism now . . . She explained it by saying that Stalin had allowed many people to starve to death or had them executed – millions at the time – and that she was now hoping that the Germans would defeat Bolshevism and they would be free. That's what they were all counting on that we – the Germans – would liberate them. And liberate them we did, but we liberated them from everything else as well!'[27]

The German Army weren't just starving Soviet citizens by besieging

Leningrad and stealing food from villagers as they advanced, they also made concerted efforts to deprive the population of food once they occupied urban areas. In the eastern Ukrainian city of Kharkov, for instance, Field Marshal von Reichenau had told his soldiers to 'increasingly live off the land' because this 'was not only a war of weapons but also an economic war'. Following this logic, German authorities decided that only those in Kharkov who were working for the occupying forces would be given food – the rest should be left to starve to death.[28]

Inna Gavrilchenko, who was fifteen years old when the Germans entered Kharkov in the autumn of 1941, remembered the invaders marking their arrival with 'some three or four days of incessant robbery'. They stole 'food' and 'clothes'. She was particularly upset when a soldier took 'the dream of her life', a pair of 'black gloves with embroidered cuffs' that her aunt had given her. 'I was so shocked,' she said, 'I couldn't believe that it had really happened . . . it seemed to me so inexplicable, unpardonable.'[29]

Just as in Leningrad, the Kharkov winter of 1941–2 was 'very severe, very bitter'. Soon, with the Germans stealing food from the inhabitants of the city, many started to starve. As she walked along the street, Inna Gavrilchenko saw people lying face down in the snow, but 'you never knew' if they were 'dead or dying or just had fainted'. Few people tried 'to kneel or to bend' down beside those who had collapsed because 'they were not sure they would have been strong enough to get up themselves.'

After Gavrilchenko's own father died on 1 May 1942, she lived alongside his corpse for eight days, 'Because I couldn't possibly do anything about it. I couldn't bury him . . . on the one hand I was too weak, on the other hand I had no money to pay for the grave.' Soon she began to feel 'stupefied' and a visitor to the flat saw her speaking to her father's corpse – 'he was cold already, but I kept talking to him.' When a neighbour brought her a piece of bread, Inna asked her dead father to eat it. 'I showed it to him and said "Look, you haven't seen bread for a long time, look it's nice real bread, just have a mouthful, just have a piece of it." And he wouldn't.'

The neighbour who brought Inna the piece of bread had the food only because she knew a German soldier. It was perhaps inevitable in such circumstances that some Germans found it hard to watch Ukrainians they knew personally starve to death, and so gave them scraps to eat. Indeed, this was the fundamental problem for the German authorities with the implementation of the Hunger Plan in places like Kharkov. If those who were to be starved were physically separated from the Germans – either besieged in Leningrad or behind the wire of a ghetto – it was easier to let them die. Living alongside someone who was dying of hunger could create emotional complications.

German Army propaganda recognized the danger that some troops might show compassion, and attempted to eliminate it. 'Each gram of bread or other food that I give to the population in the occupied territories out of good-heartedness, I am withdrawing from the German people and thus my family . . .' ran one such piece of propaganda. 'Thus, the German soldier must stay hard in the face of hungry women and children. If he does not, he endangers the nourishment of our people. The enemy is now experiencing the fate that he had planned for us. But he alone must also answer to the world and history.'[30]

As for Inna Gavrilchenko, she survived by eating tree bark and leaves, and later by getting a temporary job in a meat factory. She even drank the dirty water in which the dishes had been washed in a German canteen, because bits of food still remained in it. Sometimes, she admitted, she resorted to stealing. She lived day to day, hoping the war would soon be over. 'I don't remember myself thinking about the future,' she said. 'You see the thing is that when the war began, we didn't think it was going to last long. We thought it was going to last a month. At most two months, three months. Nobody thought that it was going to last four years.'[31]

Horrendous as conditions were in Leningrad and Kharkov, the greatest number of deaths by starvation in the early months of the war occurred somewhere else entirely – in the prisoner-of-war camps containing Soviet soldiers. Incredibly, only 1.1 million of the 3.35 million Soviet prisoners captured by the Germans in the first months of the war were still alive by December 1941. Many thousands who died were shot as a consequence of the Commissar Order, which called for all Soviet political officers to be killed on capture. The rest had mostly perished of disease or starvation – or a combination of both.[32] When General Wagner, Quartermaster General of the Army, was told in November 1941 that Soviet prisoners were starving to death in German captivity, he responding by saying, 'Non-working war prisoners . . . are supposed to starve.'[33]

That same month, Göring told the Italian Foreign Minister, Count Ciano, that armed guards were no longer needed to direct columns of

Soviet prisoners: 'It is enough to put at the head of the column of prisoners a camp kitchen, which emits the fragrant odor of food; thousands and thousands of prisoners trail along like a herd of famished animals.' Earlier in the same conversation, Göring had mentioned that the Soviet prisoners were not only 'eating each other' but had also 'eaten a German sentry'.[34]

The German Army even tried to prevent Soviet civilians from giving what little food they possessed to the POWs, as Anatoly Reva, a child in Kharkov, discovered. A camp containing Soviet prisoners backed on to their family home: 'And my father, through the kindness of his heart, went there, and threw food over the fence: potatoes, beetroot, whatever there was, to help them, so that they would have something to eat. He was deaf and dumb . . . They [the German soldiers] started shouting at him – "Go away", "Go away", and he couldn't hear, so they shot him. One, two shots and that was it. They had killed him . . . With them, the slightest act of disobedience meant death, death, death. Whether you did something or failed to do something.'[35]

Georgy Semenyak was one of the minority of Soviet soldiers captured by the Germans in 1941 who survived to the end of the year. He was taken prisoner just weeks into the conflict and incarcerated, together with thousands of his comrades, in a massive camp – little more than a giant field enclosed by barbed wire. The Germans denied all the prisoners adequate food and left them to starve.

'We all sat under an open sky,' said Georgy Semenyak. 'Nowhere to hide. What we tried to do during the night time was dig holes in the ground, and tried to sleep there . . .' He and his fellow captives were well aware that they were victims of a terrible crime. 'Of course, we were sure that it was unjust,' he said. 'No international law would allow such behaviour towards prisoners of war.'[36]

An unknown number of Soviet prisoners never even made it to the camps, but were shot as they tried to surrender or shortly after capture. Many of these soldiers were not commissars, but ordinary rank-and-file troops. One 'justification' sometimes given by German veterans for these killings is that they were acting in retaliation for Soviet atrocities against captured Germans. But though there were undoubtedly such cases, this is not a sufficient explanation. That's because there is evidence that a number of Soviet prisoners were shot on capture in the early days of the war, before such a 'revenge' claim could be made. This order, for example, was issued by General Joachim Lemelsen, commander of a panzer corps, on 25 June, just three days into the war: 'I have observed that senseless shootings of both POWs and civilians have taken place. A Russian soldier who has been taken prisoner while wearing a uniform and after he put up a brave fight, has the right for a decent treatment. We want to free the civilian population from the yoke of Bolshevism and we need their labour force . . . This instruction does not change anything regarding the Führer's order on the ruthless action to be taken against partisans and Bolshevik commissars.'

But his words appear to have had little effect, since he was compelled to write five days later that 'still more shootings' were occurring. 'This is murder!' said Lemelsen. 'The German Wehrmacht is waging this war against Bolshevism, not against the united Russian peoples. We want to bring back peace, calm and order to this land which has suffered terribly for many years from the oppression of a Jewish and criminal group. The instruction of the Führer calls for ruthless action against Bolshevism (political commissars) and any kind of partisan! People who have been clearly identified as such should be taken aside and shot only by order of an officer . . .'[37]

In theory, Lemelsen's instructions were unambiguous – but not in practice. On the one hand he called for 'decent treatment' for ordinary Soviet POWs, while on the other he wanted Hitler's 'ruthless action' to be enforced against partisans and commissars. For soldiers on the front line the distinction could be hard to make, especially when the war as a whole was said to be a war of 'extermination' against 'subhumans'. Consider, for example, the attitude of a German like Wolfgang Horn, who at the battle of Vyazma encountered a group of Soviet soldiers as they lay huddled on the ground, terrified, with their hands and arms covering their heads. He shouted out 'hands up' in Russian, and when they didn't immediately respond, he and his comrades killed them. 'When they don't surrender,' he said, 'we shoot them. It was natural for us to do . . . They are cowards – they didn't deserve any better, anyhow.'[38]

Against this background, it's perhaps surprising not that a majority of Soviet prisoners died at the hands of the Germans in 1941, but that a substantial minority survived. And for each prisoner who did make it through to the end of the war, there is a different story of personal endurance. Pavel Stenkin, for instance, put his survival down to Stalin's policy of forced collectivization. Stenkin was captured in the first few hours of the war and taken to 'a huge field surrounded by barbed wire' in German-occupied Poland. He and the rest of the prisoners were fed with weak soup – and that only occasionally. As a result, his comrades started to die of starvation. It was then that he noticed that those 'who came from good families, where they were used to being well fed, they were dying first of all'. But thanks to collectivization Pavel Stenkin had had plenty of experience of feeling hungry. 'Collective farms were a disaster at the time,' he said, 'cattle were dying . . . everything was dying.' Consequently, since he 'was always feeling hungry', he had adapted during his childhood to living off scarcely any food.[39]

In October 1941, Pavel Stenkin and several thousand of his comrades were sent to Auschwitz concentration camp in southern Poland. They were not the first Soviet prisoners to arrive in Auschwitz. Three months before, in July, several hundred Soviet commissars had been transported to the camp. They were some of the many thousands of commissars who had managed to evade detection after they had been captured, only for their status to be discovered once they had been transported to a POW camp for ordinary Soviet prisoners. Rather than murder the commissars on site, the German authorities decided to send them to concentration camps to be killed. Some were transported to camps like Sachsenhausen within the pre-war boundaries of the Reich, others to Auschwitz.

At Auschwitz, the treatment of the Soviet commissars became notorious: in a camp already known for its brutality, other inmates were shocked at their suffering. 'They were pushing these wheelbarrows full of sand and gravel whilst running,' said Jerzy Bielecki, a Polish political prisoner who witnessed the commissars labouring in a gravel pit. 'It was very difficult. The planks they pushed the wheelbarrows over were sliding from side to side. It was not normal work; it was a hell that the SS men created for those Soviet prisoners of war . . . There were four or five SS men with guns. And those that had a gun from time to time would load it, look down, take aim and then shoot into the gravel pit. Then my friend said, "What is that son of a bitch doing?" And we saw that a Kapo was hitting a dying man with a stick. My friend had army training and he said, "Those are prisoners of war. They have rights!" But they were being killed while working.'[40]

However, Pavel Stenkin and his comrades were not commissars, and their arrival a few months later marked a change in the configuration of Auschwitz. In September 1941, Himmler had decided on a vast expansion of the camp. Up until now there had only been one Auschwitz – Auschwitz main camp, modelled on pre-war camps like Dachau. But now Himmler ordered the immediate construction of an immense new camp, a mile and a half from the existing Auschwitz, at a village the Poles knew as Brzezinka and the Germans called Birkenau.

Auschwitz Birkenau, which was subsequently to play an infamous part in the extermination of the Jews, was not originally built as a mechanized killing factory. Instead it was supposed to house Soviet prisoners of war. The plan was for the camp to hold 100,000 people, making it the biggest in the whole Nazi system, and for the Soviet prisoners to be forced to work not just within the camp but in various industrial enterprises near by. The question of how such a vast edifice could be built on marshy fields, in the midst of a war that was already causing a shortage of resources, was easily solved. Ten thousand starving Soviet prisoners like Pavel Stenkin would be made to build the camp themselves. And their terrible fate has still not received the public attention it deserves.

Kazimierz Smoleń, a Polish political prisoner, remembered the arrival of the Soviets that autumn. 'It was already snowing – extraordinary to have snow in October,' he said. Even so, the Soviet POWs 'had to give all their clothes away and jump into barrels with disinfectant, and naked they went to Auschwitz [the main camp]. Usually they were completely emaciated.'[41] Pavel Stenkin recalled with horror how the SS humiliated the new arrivals. 'To start with we were undressed. It was a sanitary check,' he said. 'They were hosing us either with cold or hot water, either cold or [scalding] hot [and] the mockery started. So we were totally lost . . .' He felt that the existing prisoners in the camp were not well disposed towards the Soviet POWs either. The Poles 'didn't like us' because 'they were like our colony . . . Simply all nationalities didn't like us. Just as they didn't like fascists in Europe, in the same way they didn't like communists.'[42]

Rudolf Höss, the Commandant of Auschwitz, wrote that on arrival the Soviet prisoners of war were in 'very poor' condition. This was primarily because they had been starved, both in their previous camp and on their forced march to Auschwitz. Their guards had given them 'hardly any food' and 'during halts on the way' the prisoners had been 'turned out into the nearest fields and there told to "graze" like cattle on anything edible they could find'. Höss, writing after the war, mentions their condition not out of compassion but to express his annoyance at the quality of the human material he had been given with which to build Birkenau. 'Their weakened bodies could no longer function,' he said. 'Their whole constitution was finished and done for.' Höss described how the starving Soviet prisoners resorted to eating each other, because the camp administration – which he oversaw – denied them adequate food. 'When the foundations for the first group of buildings [at Birkenau] were being dug,' he wrote, 'the men often found the bodies of Russians who had been killed by their fellows, partly eaten and then stuffed into a hole in the mud.'[43]

Pavel Stenkin soon realized that 'nobody was going to leave alive, everybody was expecting to die or to be killed . . . we knew our place – a grave. I am alive now, and in a minute I am finished, this was the constant feeling. They could kill me any minute, and you would not know why.'[44] Out of the 10,000 Soviet prisoners of war who were taken to Auschwitz to build the camp at Birkenau, more than 9,000 were dead by the spring of 1942. Stenkin survived only because he and a handful of his comrades managed to escape from their guards when they were on a work detail outside the barbed wire of the camp.

The SS at Auschwitz also used starvation as a punishment. When a prisoner escaped, a group of other inmates would be selected from the barrack or work detail that the escapee belonged to. These prisoners would then be taken to Block 11 in the main camp and locked into 'starvation' cells, where they would be left to die.

Auschwitz, at the time of the starvation cells and the building of Birkenau, was not yet a place where Jews were sent en masse. But elsewhere, in ghettos and camps across many parts of German-controlled territory, the Nazis were systematically starving large numbers of Jews. As early as the summer of 1940 there had been a food demonstration in the Łódź ghetto in Poland, with Jews shouting 'We want bread, we're dying of hunger.'[45]

The food crisis in Łódź had been caused by the use of starvation as a weapon of extortion. After the ghetto had been sealed in spring 1940, the Jews had been forced to give up their valuables at inflated rates for food, with desperate women even handing over their wedding rings in exchange for bread. Arthur Greiser, Governor of the Warthegau, saw this as the most effective way of robbing the Jews. Only after the death rate rose to record levels – with 1.5 per cent of the ghetto population dying in July and August 1940 – were the Nazis satisfied the Jews no longer possessed anything of value. It was only at this point that the decision was taken to allow Jews to work in substantial numbers in factories within the ghetto, in order to produce goods which the Germans would exchange for food.[46]

However, this change did not mean that there was now sufficient food for everyone. There were still food shortages – a situation made worse by the arrival in the autumn of 1941 of thousands of Jews from within the pre-war borders of the Reich. 'People had changed in three months of hunger,' wrote Oskar Rosenfeld, who had been deported to Łódź in a Jewish transport from Prague. 'Almost all had bent backs, shaky legs. Illnesses slipped their way in. Pneumonia even in young people. Thousands tossed on their plank beds, deprived of sleep, since their bones hurt when they lay down, and dreamed of food . . . Three months of undernourishment have put thousands in danger of dying.'[47]

Even before the arrival of Jews from outside Poland, Nazi administrators had known that many of the Jews currently in the ghetto would likely die of hunger in the months ahead. Rolf-Heinz Höppner, an SS officer based in Poznań in the Warthegau, told Adolf Eichmann in July 1941: 'There exists this winter the danger that all the Jews can no longer be fed. It should be seriously considered if it would not be the most humane solution to dispose of the Jews, insofar as they are not capable of work, through a quick-acting agent. In any case it would be more pleasant than to let them starve.'[48]

This is a key document. It recognizes the fundamental difficulty the perpetrators faced in implementing their starvation policy, one we have already seen in the context of Kharkov. It was not very 'pleasant' for the Nazis to stand by and watch people starve to death. But, equally, there was no acknowledgement that this was a situation they had created themselves. Just as Rudolf Höss at Auschwitz did not accept that he was responsible for the hunger and cannibalism of the Soviet prisoners in his charge, so Höppner did not question the validity of the policy that had brought the Jews to the brink of starvation. The immediate solution to the 'problem' of the starving Jews was to feed them adequately, not murder them by a 'quick-acting agent'. But that did not occur to Höppner any more than it occurred to Rudolf Höss at Auschwitz. Both of them knew that the ideology proselytized by Adolf Hitler prevented such a humane solution, as the Jews were dangerous and the Soviet prisoners were subhuman. It was vital, as the army propaganda urged, to 'stay hard' in the face of starvation.

The pursuit of a starvation policy was much easier for Hitler and Stalin than for the people they led. Hitler never visited the ghettos and camps of Poland and Stalin never undertook a tour of the camps within the Gulag system. Both men were emotionally insulated from the suffering they caused. Indeed, Hitler emphasized the value of distancing oneself from this kind of individual torment when he met General Guderian in December 1941 and criticized him for his emotional attachment to his soldiers. 'You feel too much pity for them,' said Hitler. 'You should stand back more.'[49] They are words that could just as easily have come from the mouth of Joseph Stalin – a man no one ever accused of 'too much pity'.

As previously discussed, Stalin was responsible for one of the most monstrous episodes of mass starvation in history, when nearly four million Ukrainians perished in appalling circumstances in the early 1930s.[50] But many Soviet citizens also died elsewhere of hunger during the period of his leadership – particularly in the Gulag. The Soviet authorities estimated in 1939 that as many as 60 per cent of all inmates suffered from malnutrition or diseases associated with lack of food.[51]

One Gulag official revealed in a letter to Beria in 1941 how he approached his work: 'Our task is to wring out [*vyzhat'*] of the camp population the maximum quantity of marketable commodities.'[52] Consequently, prisoners who could not work or who failed to reach their work quota were considered of little value, and so received reduced rations. They were then caught in a spiral of decline. Antoni Ekart, a Pole who survived the Gulag, expressed it this way: 'Less work equals less food, less food equals less energy, less energy equals less work, and so on until the final collapse.'[53]

Another Pole, Gustaw Herling, who was arrested by the Soviets in 1940, saw hunger wreak havoc within the camp in which he was imprisoned. He wrote that 'Hunger is a horrible sensation, which becomes transformed into an abstraction, into nightmares fed by the mind's perpetual fever.' He concluded 'that there is nothing, in fact, which man cannot be forced to do by hunger and pain'. Moreover he became 'convinced that a man can be human only under human conditions, and I believe that it is fantastic nonsense to judge him by actions which he commits under inhuman conditions . . .'[54]

Herling witnessed how a prisoner supervisor, who wanted to have sex with a woman inmate, set about breaking her will by depriving her of food. The supervisor bet Herling that the woman would succumb. 'About a month after we had agreed on the bet,' wrote Herling, 'he came one evening to my barrack, and without a word threw a torn pair of knickers on my bunk.' After this, Herling saw that the woman started having sex with 'whoever wanted to . . . have her' until eventually he found her 'on a pile of potatoes with the brigadier of the 56th, the hunchbacked half-breed Levkovich'.[55] In the light of his experience, Herling delivered this admonishment: 'If God exists, let him punish mercilessly those who break others with hunger.'[56]

It's a sentiment that Wiesława Saternus would agree with. She was deported from Poland with her family to Siberia and made to work in a logging camp. Like many deportees, she was not technically a prisoner in the Gulag system, but she still experienced periods of starvation. 'The hunger was horrible,' she remembered, 'and it's a strange experience, hunger. It can't be understood by anybody who hasn't experienced it. Real hunger damages a human being – a man becomes an animal.'[57]

But perhaps Pavel Stenkin is the person most qualified to talk about how both Hitler and Stalin presided over cultures that caused the death of millions from hunger, because after escaping from Auschwitz Birkenau he was subsequently imprisoned by the Soviet authorities in a Gulag. As a result of his capture by the Germans, and based on no evidence, he had been accused of 'spying'. This was a common charge the NKVD made against Red Army POWs. It didn't matter that Stenkin had been unconscious when the Germans took him prisoner on the first day of the war. He had still betrayed the motherland by allowing himself to be captured.[58] Having been starved in a German camp, he now found that he was permanently hungry in a Soviet camp. Only on his release in 1953, after Stalin's death, could he start 'to eat my fill'.

Having experienced both systems, Pavel Stenkin formed the view that 'Fascism and Communism were the same. One may agree or disagree with this, but this is my opinion. I know this better than all.'[59]

10. Stalin's Overreach

In the first few months of 1942, Stalin lived with the consequences of two decisions. One could have cost the Soviets the war, while the other helped them win it. Yet, ironically, both were made possible by the same feature within the Soviet state – the centralization of power.

The first decision related to one of the most important wartime factors of all – resources. In theory the Soviet Union should have been in desperate trouble at the start of 1942 as the Germans occupied the heart of Soviet industrial and agricultural production. From the coalmines of Kharkov to the wheat fields of Western Ukraine, the Germans controlled it all. And it was not just land that had been lost, but valuable human resources as well. In 1940 the Soviet Union possessed 8.3 million industrial workers, but by 1942 that number had been reduced to 5.5 million.[1] Yet despite all this loss an apparent miracle took place in the Soviet Union. In 1942 the Soviets massively outproduced the Germans in military equipment. They made 10,000 more aircraft than the Germans, 15,000 more tanks and an incredible 115,000 more artillery pieces.[2]

This achievement was possible only because, just days after the Germans invaded, a Council for Evacuation had been created under the guidance of the ruthless Lazar Kaganovich. The plan was to transport as much industrial infrastructure as possible to the east, far away from the German advance. Factories were dismantled and workers and their families evacuated. By the end of 1941 over 2,500 industrial units had been shipped to safety. No wonder Zhukov believed that 'The heroic feat of evacuation and restoration of industrial capacities during the war . . . meant as much for the country's destiny as the greatest battles of the war.'[3]

The pre-war years of rapid industrialization had given workers valuable experience in fulfilling an agreed plan as swiftly as possible. As a consequence, the whole of Soviet society was used to obeying instructions from the centre. In this enterprise – unlike on the battlefield – the ability to use one's initiative was not essential and centralization of decision-making a positive advantage. Moreover, the tasks required of the workers were straightforward. Once factories were reassembled, far from the front line, they were ordered to mass-produce immense numbers of relatively unsophisticated weapons.

Stalin understood that, in a modern war, the battle was fought in the factory just as much as on the front line. In November 1941 he had predicted that the side 'who will have the overwhelming superiority in the production of motors will win the war'.[4]

Stalin was the perfect leader to oversee the operation. He believed in planning from the centre and managing through trusted servants who would not deviate from their instructions. And no servant was more willing to follow the dictates of his master than Lazar Kaganovich, the man who had previously helped organize the collectivization of agriculture in Ukraine that had resulted in the deaths of millions. Known as 'Iron' Lazar, in the 1930s he had inflamed the atmosphere of paranoia during the Great Terror with his speeches, striving to make Stalin happy. Though Kaganovich soon found it necessary to hand over chairmanship of the Evacuation Council to a deputy, he continued to play a major part in the relocation of the factories as Commissar for the Soviet railway system.[5]

Within the relocated Soviet factories, workers were called upon to labour for long hours, and also to produce vast numbers of identical guns and tanks. The controlled economy of the Soviet state meant that administrators at the centre could determine at will the balance between the manufacture of military equipment and the manufacture of consumer goods. And at this desperate moment the production of the latter all but vanished as a priority.

There was no equivalent of this centralized armaments structure in Germany. Various ministries competed to select which weapons to develop. Presiding over all this rivalry was Adolf Hitler, a man deeply suspicious of any integrated structures. His own factotum in charge of the Economic Four Year Plan was Hermann Göring, a dilettante who had greeted economic experts lined up to meet him with the phrase 'Of course, I know nothing about economics, but I have an unbridled will!'[6]

But there was a paradox. Stalin's desire to centralize power, which made possible the successful movement of industry to safety in the east, also hindered Red Army soldiers when it came to fighting the Germans. We've already seen how the initiative-based decision-making of German units on the front line – the so-called *Auftragstaktik* – contrasted dramatically with the inability of Red Army commanders to decide for themselves the best way of achieving their objectives. That weakness in Soviet strategy continued into 1942 and, when combined with the impulsive demands of a leader who was an amateur in military matters, would once again prove disastrous for Soviet forces.

In January 1942 Stalin ordered the Red Army to attack the Germans in a variety of places across the front. Buoyed by the successful Soviet counter-attack outside Moscow, he believed that the Germans were near collapse. But just as Hitler had grotesquely underrated the Red Army's resilience prior to the invasion of the Soviet Union, so Stalin was to make the same mistake now about the Wehrmacht.

Stalin was so overconfident that he wanted to focus not on one single operation but on a wide-ranging offensive. 'The day is not far', he said in a speech in February, 'when the Red Army with mighty blows will throw the brutal enemies from Leningrad, will clean them out of the towns and villages of Belorussia and the Ukraine, of Lithuania and Latvia, of Estonia and Karelia, and will free the Soviet Crimea, and in the whole Soviet land red banners will again wave victoriously.'[7]

It was a ludicrously overambitious commitment, almost as foolhardy as Hitler's promise the previous autumn that the Red Army would 'never rise again'. Stalin's error soon became manifest in the fate of the Second Shock Army — a story so calamitous that it was erased from Soviet history for many years. Stalin demanded in early January that Marshal Meretskov launch an attack on Army Group North in front of Leningrad. Meretskov asked for a delay so that he could organize his forces, but Stalin refused.[8] Red Army units moved forward, only to find themselves almost entirely encircled — with no more than a narrow, perilous corridor of land connecting them back to their own lines. The troops inside the pocket soon became desperate. 'We were completely helpless,' said one of the soldiers, 'since we had no ammunition, no petrol, no bread, no tobacco, not even salt. Worst of all was having no medical help . . . The main problem, though, was hunger. Oppressive, never-ending hunger. Wherever you went, whatever you were doing, the thought of food never left you . . . Once somebody found an old potato, buried among the ashes of a hut. We cut it up and each got a tiny piece. What a feast! Some men licked their piece, some sniffed it. The smell reminded me of home and family.'[9]

In scenes reminiscent of the Finnish war, Red Army units were isolated and left to die, either of starvation or from German bombardment. The soldiers of the Second Shock Army perished in conditions that one German eyewitness said were 'almost indescribable . . . There is no forest left . . . Everything is shot to pieces and ripped up. Crater lies next to crater, and countless dead Bolshevists cover the battlefield. Hundreds, no, thousands of dead enemies, in mud and dirt, alongside and on top of each other.'[10] From a Soviet perspective, the operation had been a disaster. Out of 326,000 soldiers committed to the various actions, just over 300,000 had been lost – either killed, wounded or captured.[11]

For the Germans it was a welcome success after the setback in front of Moscow. 'The account of the winter battles of the Volkhov cauldron [encirclement] has now, after only a few months, become a heroic song that rings out to us as from days gone by,' said a lyrical German account published later in 1942. 'Step by step, the cauldron was annihilated. The space in which the once proud Soviet shock army, Stalin's hope, the liberation army of Leningrad, was huddled together became increasingly tight. One enemy force after another was surrounded, cornered and annihilated, until the last resistance had been broken, the last Bolshevist had been killed in action or captured.'[12]

'You can be proud to have gained this victory!' General Lindemann told soldiers of the German Eighteenth Army. 'Not only have you proved your superiority to the Soviet hordes, but you have also braved the icy cold of the winter and the impenetrable mud of the spring. The homeland will be eternally grateful for your readiness to make sacrifices, and your deeds will never be forgotten in Greater Germany's history!'[13]

In the centre of the front, the Soviet offensive in the area of Rzhev-Vyazma did succeed in pushing back the Germans so that Moscow was no longer immediately threatened, but the underlying strength of Army Group Centre remained and the losses for the Soviets were severe. As a result, Marshal Rokossovsky was subsequently highly critical of the decisions made by Stalin and the Stavka that January – so critical that the section in his memoirs in which he talked about these actions was not published until after the fall of communism. Rokossovsky described the military action taken by the Soviets in early 1942 as 'pointless', since it was obvious that the Germans still remained a powerful adversary and the Red Army was not up to the task of defeating them head on. What was needed was a period of delay so as to give Soviet forces time to regroup and wait for reinforcements. Instead, the attacks against the Germans, who were now well dug in and protecting a defensive line, just exhausted Soviet forces. Rokossovsky's devastating conclusion was that Stalin and the Stavka had made 'the most crass mistake'.[14]

Even Stalin, at the time, acknowledged that there were 'failings' in the Red Army's use of tanks in the offensive. 'Up to now co-operation between infantry and tank formations and units is poorly organised,' he wrote in an order sent at the end of January. Problems included infantry commanders 'failing to establish concrete objectives' and 'in retreat even failing to warn commanders of tank units of the changed situation'. Moreover, 'Field commanders are extremely hasty in the deployment of tank units' and were not conducting 'even the most elementary reconnaissance of the area and enemy positions'.[15] Once again, it was everyone's fault but Stalin's. Yet it had been his overconfidence and military ignorance that had been in large part responsible for the failure of Soviet soldiers on the battlefield.

But none of these issues, nor the problems Red Army units were having more generally in engaging the Germans in the early months of 1942, made Stalin want to pause to regroup. Instead, after consulting with Marshal Timoshenko and Nikita Khrushchev, he agreed a major offensive in the south, around Kharkov in Ukraine. Cooler military minds – including Zhukov – saw the idea as needlessly risky and were against it. Nonetheless, Stalin dismissed their concerns and ordered the General Staff 'not to interfere on any question concerning' the Kharkov attack. Stalin, it would transpire, had made another terrible mistake.[16]

Boris Vitman, a Red Army intelligence officer who took part in the Kharkov campaign, remembered the mood of optimism as the attack was planned. 'A lot of American and British equipment was arriving,' he said. 'I remember a big number of English shoes, boots, being brought. And the arriving units were getting those English boots and a lot of military equipment was arriving too.' There was even talk among the troops that the Soviets would soon win the war.

Early in the morning of 12 May 1942, as Vitman and the rest of the Red Army soldiers waited for the attack to begin, they heard an immense barrage from Soviet artillery. This too gave the troops a feeling of confidence. Who could survive such an onslaught? Immediately after the end of the hour-long bombardment, six Soviet armies advanced towards the German lines. But when Vitman reached the first German defence works, he was surprised to see that they had been abandoned. Anticipating an assault the Germans had pulled back. Vitman and his comrades continued marching on, still encountering little resistance. 'Occasionally we were met by mortar salvoes,' he remembered, but 'we could see no Germans, only dead civilians.'[17]

In places the Red Army managed to advance 30 miles, and this success made Stalin remark that he had 'grounds for sending a sharp rebuke to the General Staff', because as a result of their lack of enthusiasm 'he had nearly cancelled the operation which was developing so successfully'.[18] The rapid Soviet advance supported his assessment, made in Order Number 55 back in February, that 'The element of surprise gained by the German–Fascist forces has been completely expended, eliminating the unequal conditions of war under which we have been fighting. Now the fate of the war will be decided not by the element of surprise, but by factors constantly in force: rear stability, the army's morale, the quantity and quality of divisions, armaments, and the organizational capabilities of the army's leadership.'[19] But Stalin could not have been more wrong in his belief that the 'element of surprise' had been eliminated, as several hundred thousand of his Red Army soldiers were about to discover.

'The Germans were luring us into a trap,' said Boris Vitman. 'On the outskirts of Kharkov, all of a sudden our attack faced very strong resistance from the Germans. The Germans had prepared in advance a very powerful defence line . . . There were a lot of warehouses around with very strong basements and they were very advantageous firing points. Some of our tanks were blown up. In the outskirts of Kharkov the tanks were losing their manoeuvrability and went out of action. In this way our offensive choked.'[20]

The swiftness of the Soviets' advance was to be their undoing, as the Germans closed behind the Red Army units in a classic manoeuvre of entrapment. Joachim Stempel, an officer with the 14th Panzer Division, remembered that 'we were in quite a euphoric frame of mind, and our aim was to encircle these, the best of the Russian troops, and destroy them.'

Stempel also witnessed the inability of the Soviet commanders to react quickly to this new situation: 'Had things been handled differently, had they immediately changed direction and, using their troops that were still intact, attempted to force a breakthrough, it might have proved considerably more difficult to keep a hold on the encirclement.'

It was a triumph that was all the greater for the Germans because they were outnumbered by the Soviets. Stempel believed that his unit's 'lack of men and equipment, in the face of being outnumbered by the Russians, was translated by the flexible German leadership into [the tactic of] rushing from one focal point to the next, being strong not everywhere, but just at the decisive points.'[21]

This powerful German response had been made possible not just because of the 'flexible German leadership' but because Soviet forces had attacked directly into an area where large numbers of German units had gathered in preparation for an offensive to the south-east. In a catastrophic failure of intelligence, the Soviets had not known of their presence. This ignorance was partly a result of Operation Kreml, a deception operation mounted by the Germans to make the Soviets think that their main attack that summer would once again be directed against Moscow. But Stalin was also at fault. Since the German deception plan coincided with his own assessment, he had been all too willing to accept it.[22]

Nine days into the offensive, Boris Vitman visited the headquarters of the Soviet 6th Army. It was in chaos. Officers were packing up documents and running about, waiting to be surrounded. Shortly afterwards the Germans attacked. 'The worst thing was when we could no longer offer any resistance,' said Vitman, 'when we had run out of ammunition completely. The fire was coming from all around, from machine guns and from mortars. They didn't even have to aim carefully. There were so many people . . . you know into such a group of people you can always hit somebody without taking aim. After the planes had dropped bombs, the shelling began. Then when the shelling stopped, the planes arrived and began to drop bombs [again] and it all turned into a bloody mess.'[23]

Vitman was captured by the Germans as they closed on the encirclement. He was one of over 250,000 Red Army soldiers lost as a result of the Kharkov operation. In captivity he survived largely because he had learnt German at school, and so could act as an interpreter. Speaking German meant he was treated better than other prisoners, because the Germans didn't consider him to be as 'inferior' as those of his comrades who spoke only Russian.

The battle of Kharkov was of huge significance for both sides. For the Germans, it was a welcome reassurance that victory might still be possible. 'The army had regained their inner security after the heavy burden of the defensive battles,' wrote Colonel Selle of the German Sixth Army. 'Their sense of superiority to the enemy had been strengthened anew.'[24]

The sheer scale of the destruction left unforgettable memories for many of those Germans who participated in the fight. 'The rising sun throws its rays on a dreadful battlefield,' wrote Lieutenant Colonel Soldan in an article in the *Völkischer Beobachter* in June 1942. 'Officers who have seen the conflict of 1914–18 assert that the cruelty here exceeds everything seen so far . . . Masses of the enemy who wanted to surrender were driven back under the pistol fire of their officers and commissars like a herd of sheep . . . Infantry soldiers who hesitated to follow tanks – they did not have any ammunition left! – were clubbed forward . . . In contrast, there are reports of the purposeful initiative of our officers, of the wonderful bravery of our troops, of brilliant achievements of entire regiments and individuals.'[25]

Herbert Rauchhaupt, a German war correspondent, wrote not just about the aftermath of the battle – 'wherever one goes in the encirclement south of Kharkov, there are Soviet tanks, disabled, flame-covered, abandoned' – but also boasted about how a 'ridiculously small' German force had won an epic victory over 'an overwhelming enemy force'.[26] Consequently, armed with the knowledge that they could beat the Red Army even when outnumbered, many German soldiers – like Joachim Stempel – left the battlefield of Kharkov in high spirits and confident of their ability to deal with whatever lay ahead.

For the Soviets, it was easy to understand why the battle had been lost. What was hard, once again, was for the guilty men – and one guilty man in particular – to accept responsibility for their mistakes. Stalin was most obviously at fault. He had shown himself yet again to be an amateur in military matters. Not only was the whole offensive incompetently overseen, but he had refused to listen to those experts, like Zhukov, who had warned against the plan in the first place. But others were responsible for the disaster as well. Soviet intelligence operatives had failed spectacularly, allowing the Red Army to advance unwittingly into an area where some of the best German units had congregated. Timoshenko and Khrushchev had also made calamitous errors – especially Timoshenko, who had reacted too slowly to events and allowed the offensive to continue even after the danger of encirclement became apparent.

The allocation of responsibility for the Kharkov debacle became a major controversy after Stalin's death. Khrushchev, once he became leader of the Soviet Union, asserted that he and Timoshenko had both wanted to abandon the operation earlier, but Stalin had refused[27] – a claim Zhukov disputed. Other heavyweights from the war, like Marshal Vasilevsky, also weighed in with their versions of events.[28] But all this personal bickering hid a bigger issue. It was Stalin who had created the culture that had made the disaster of Kharkov possible. Who, for instance, would want to be a Soviet general asking Stalin for permission to retreat? Hitler normally allowed generals he lost faith in to retire on a pension; Stalin was capable of having them shot.

It wasn't even as if Stalin was improving as a military decision-maker. Kharkov showed that he was just as inept a commander in spring 1942 as he had been in the summer of 1941. 'Everyone always knew that you had to learn from your enemy,' said Makhmut Gareev, an infantry officer during the war, and a man who would subsequently rise to high military office in the post-war Soviet Union. 'In the Red Army we followed Lenin's slogan, and Stalin supported it, that the army who doesn't want to master all the enemy's strategies and tactics is a criminal army. Everyone realized that you always had to take heed of all the enemy's strong points and learn from them, but not everyone was very attentive about these things.'[29] And one person who was certainly not 'attentive' was Joseph Stalin.

Stalin, predictably, accepted none of the blame for Kharkov. Instead he held Timoshenko and Khrushchev responsible. 'Battles must be won not with numbers but with skill,' he told them. 'If you do not learn to direct your troops better, all the armaments the country can produce will not be enough for you.'[30] He subsequently admonished Khrushchev and sidelined Timoshenko. Khrushchev had feared for his life when called in to see Stalin, knowing that his leader 'was a treacherous person. He was capable of anything except admitting he had made a mistake . . . Everything that Stalin said was supposed to be a product of genius. Everything that Stalin spoke against was worthless and insignificant, and people who insisted on something that Stalin was opposed to were dishonest and perhaps even enemies of the people.'[31]

But Stalin did not hand Khrushchev over to Beria and his NKVD torturers. There was, perhaps, something about the bluff Khrushchev that amused him. For whatever reason, Stalin contented himself with humiliating him, toying with him almost, so that whenever Khrushchev left Stalin's office he could never be certain what fate awaited him.[32]

It wasn't just Stalin who spent the early months of 1942 refusing to accept responsibility for his own actions. Hitler behaved in exactly the same way. In the aftermath of the German setback outside Moscow, he once again blamed the familiar scapegoat of the Jews for the problems Germany faced. He proclaimed that the Jews were the reason why Germany was now at war with America, and why Churchill had not made peace. Moreover, he declared, the Jews still lurked behind Stalin, directing his every action.

What was different now was that Hitler's rhetoric on the subject was consistently exterminatory. In his New Year message, Hitler promised that 'The Jew will not exterminate the European peoples, but will be the victim of his own plot.'[33] And on 30 January, in a speech on the ninth anniversary of his appointment as Chancellor, he explicitly stated that 'We are well aware that this war can only end either in the extermination of the Aryan peoples or in the disappearance of Jewry from Europe . . . And the hour will come when the most evil world enemy of all time will be finished with for at least a millennium.'[34]

'One must act radically,' said Hitler at a private gathering where Himmler was present, a week before his speech at the end of January. 'When one pulls out a tooth, one does it with a single tug, and the pain quickly goes away. The Jew must clear out of Europe.' But he also demonstrated that by 'clear out' he meant something sinister, by comparing the Jews to Soviet prisoners of war in German camps, where 'many are dying'. None of this, he added, was his 'fault' since the Jews had provoked the war.[35]

One of the many intriguing aspects of Hitler's behaviour during this period is that he was also beginning to have doubts about the loyalty of the Germans as a whole. Just four days after he compared the Jews to Soviet POWs, he warned in private that the entire population of Germany might not measure up to his expectations – in which case they too did not deserve to live: 'if the German people were no longer inclined to give itself body and soul in order to survive – then the German people would have nothing to do but disappear!'[36]

As we have seen, from the moment that he announced in 1920 that the leaders of the Nazi Party were prepared to kill themselves if their party programme was not adopted, most important decisions for Hitler had been either/or – either we triumph or we perish. So in that respect it might seem characteristic that he was musing in this way at the start of 1942. Nonetheless, this does mark a significant moment. While Hitler had warned before that the German people faced catastrophe if they did not follow the course he prescribed, this statement is one of the first in which he implied that Germans *deserved* to 'disappear' if they lost 'faith'. Though he had written in the early 1920s in *Mein Kampf* that 'the world is not for cowardly peoples' and that 'the race which cannot stand the test will simply die out, making place for healthier or tougher and more resisting races,' that was all theoretical talk.[37] And even if it followed logically that the Germans themselves would die out if they were not strong enough as a 'race', was not that fate supposed to be avoided if you followed Adolf Hitler? Indeed, was not the very point of supporting Hitler that his leadership would ensure victory? Yet here he was – in private admittedly – stating that notwithstanding his own leadership Germans might deserve to 'disappear'.

This was one of the unintended consequences of following Adolf Hitler. There was no escape from his statement that if a 'race' collectively failed then their destruction *ought* to follow. The trouble for many of Hitler's supporters was that, while they might have lapped up the propaganda saying they were better than everyone else, they hadn't thought through what would happen if another 'race' proved superior. In such circumstances, by the self-same logic they supported, they themselves were unworthy of life. In contrast, even though core Marxist beliefs were as certain a reference point to Stalin as racial theory was to Hitler, it's all but impossible to imagine Stalin – even in private – ever conveying a sense that the entire Soviet people deserved to 'disappear'.

Moreover, Hitler does not seem to have appreciated that it was possible for his troops on the front line outside Moscow to give themselves 'body and soul' to the cause and yet still fail. In a modern war, what did the 'faith' of the individual soldier count for if his opponent's machine gun worked in the cold and his own didn't?

As well as blaming the Jews, and potentially the whole German people, Hitler had two other targets in his sights in early 1942. The first was an 'evil' which he said was 'gnawing our vitals'. This 'evil' was 'our priests'.[38] Hitler's relationship with Christianity had been problematic ever since he entered politics. He had felt compelled in some of his early speeches in the 1920s to pay lip service to 'our saviour' in order to keep on his side Nazis who were Christian. But subsequently he preferred to talk not about Jesus but about a vague mystical idea he called 'Providence'. The reality was, as he made explicit in private in the early months of 1942, he despised Christianity.

In April 1942 he remarked that he disapproved of the Catholic Church because it was a 'school of pessimism' and kept human beings in line only by the threat of hell. He spoke of how hard it was to 'free the human soul' from the 'haunting terror of Hell which the Catholic Church impresses' on children during their 'most tender years'. He took exception to the illogicality of the whole idea of hell, asking how it was possible for someone to be 'roasted and tortured' after their body no longer existed.[39]

Hitler also disliked the notion that 'fighting men' should be 'pestered with religious precepts which ordain abstinence of the flesh'. If warriors were prepared to give their lives for their country then they should be allowed to enjoy sexual intercourse – 'the greatest joy that life has to give' – without the criticism of priests.[40]

Hitler was aware as he voiced these complaints that the previous year he had faced problems because of the Church. In Bavaria, an attempt by Nazi officials to remove crucifixes in schools had resulted in waves of protest. 'You wear brown shirts on top,' read a typical letter of criticism to local Nazis, 'but inside you're Bolsheviks and Jews.'[41] Following a barrage of disapproval, the policy was reversed.

Even worse, from Hitler's perspective, had been a sermon by the Bishop of Münster in August 1941 attacking the Nazi policy of killing selected disabled people. Have these 'unproductive people' really 'forfeited the right to live', asked Bishop Clemens August von Galen?[42] Once again, the Nazis were forced to alter their policy in the face of public protests.

Though all this was frustrating for Hitler, events were not quite how they seemed. He largely escaped blame for the crucifix debacle, as Nazi underlings were the target of the criticism, and Galen's intervention only stopped the transportation of the disabled to specific killing centres, not the murder of selected disabled patients in individual hospitals. Nor did Galen seek to undermine the regime in other fundamental ways. He wrote a letter in September 1941 supporting the war in the east, parroting the Nazi line that 'for decades the Jewish-Bolshevik rulers from Moscow have been trying to set not just Germany but the whole of Europe in flames.'[43]

Nonetheless, in the early months of 1942 Hitler was angry with the Church. The question was, what could he do about it? The answer was not a great deal. Just like Stalin, he recognized that it would be a tactical mistake to pick a fight with the institution of the Church at this critical moment in the war. 'I can't at present give them the answer they've been asking for,' he said in February 1942, 'but it will cost them nothing to wait. It's all written down in my big book. The time will come when I'll settle my account with them, and I'll go straight to the point.'[44]

Hitler was not just irate about the 'pessimism' of the Church and about the impact on German morale of protests like the one Galen made from the pulpit; he was troubled by a more fundamental issue. As he saw it, priests were always trying to do the one thing that most contravened the law of nature. They wanted to protect the weak. That was the reason he was furious about Bishop von Galen's intervention. He felt it was unconscionable that the weak should live while the strong had to die protecting Germany. As Dr Hermann Pfannmüller, an enthusiastic supporter of the 'euthanasia action', put it: 'The idea is unbearable to me that the best, the flower of our youth must lose its life at the front in order that the feebleminded and irresponsible asocial elements can have a secure existence in the asylum.'[45]

It was this belief that there were forces at work which sought to protect 'enemies' on the 'home front' – whether Jews or any of the many other groups the Nazis targeted – that enraged Hitler. 'If one permitted the filthy swine at home to be treated leniently and to be thus preserved,' he said in private on 22 May 1942, 'while a large number of idealists die at the front, then one would pave the way for a negative selection, demonstrating that one had not understood the lessons of the war years 1917–18.' Hitler felt 'personally responsible for preventing the creation of a home front of villains as in 1918, while the heroes die in the war.'[46]

It followed that anything which promoted the 'lenient' treatment of offenders and thus might cause 'negative selection' was a danger to the Nazi state – especially at this most testing time. And while Hitler thought he could do little about Church interference, he could attack another institution that he felt was similarly dangerous – the legal profession. He railed against the way in which 'our judicial system bends lovingly over individual cases, amuses itself by weighing the pros and cons and in finding extenuating circumstances . . .'[47] The result, he argued, was that 'filthy swine' were treated much more leniently than they deserved.

Hitler, as he often did,[48] came to pin his argument on one single case. In March 1942 a German shipyard worker called Ewald Schlitt was convicted of beating up his wife, who eventually died. He was sentenced to five years in prison, which was considered appropriate given that Schlitt had acted in a sudden bout of anger rather than with premeditated cunning. Hitler thought the leniency outrageous. Immediately after learning of the sentence he rang the acting Minister of Justice, Franz Schlegelberger, and angrily told him that things must change. In Hitler's view this was exactly the kind of case that illustrated how the 'judicial system bends lovingly' to help 'filthy swine' as brave Germans lost their lives on the front line.

Schlegelberger immediately did all he could to appease Hitler. He wrote to the German leader saying 'I share your desire for the harshest punishment of criminal elements . . .' and ensured that the Schlitt case was reassessed.[49] The judges at the new court hearing called for Schlitt to be executed, and on 2 April 1942 he was guillotined. Without doubt, Schlitt lost his head because of Hitler. There could be no greater example of the extent to which he could interfere in the German legal system. But, for Hitler, it was not enough.

Little more than three weeks after Schlitt's death, Hitler gave a speech to the Reichstag in which he called for the assembled deputies to confirm that he possessed 'the legal right to require anyone to fulfil their duties or, if the case dictates, to sentence to a dishonourable dismissal those who, in my view, fail to perform their duties conscientiously, or to relieve any person from office and position, regardless of who he is or which acquired rights he has'. He explicitly stated that, if in the future he didn't like any decision taken in court, he'd sack the person who had made it. 'From now on,' he said, 'I will remove from office judges who obviously fail to recognize the orders of the moment.'[50] After Hitler had spoken, Göring called upon members of the Reichstag to designate their Führer 'Supreme Law Lord'.

The Reichstag did as requested, passing the law unanimously. Goebbels wrote that there was 'passionate applause' from the assembled deputies in support of Hitler and that the German leader was 'very happy to have got this off his chest'. But even though Goebbels said in the immediate aftermath of the speech that the address was 'one of his best',[51] just two days later he was less certain. Enemy countries, he wrote, had taken the speech as 'the cry of a drowning man' and 'the dressing down which [the system of] Justice received is exaggerated into a huge internal rebellion.' As for the audience within the Reich, there was a problem. People wondered 'why the Führer had to be given new powers in the first place'.[52]

Goebbels was astute enough to realize that Hitler's call to be appointed 'Supreme Law Lord' had backfired. Among other roles, Hitler was already Chancellor, Führer of the German People and head of the army. Didn't that make this new title unnecessary? Why therefore had he demanded the job – especially when the very fact that he was able in effect to gift himself the role demonstrated that he didn't need it?

One reason was Hitler's fear that unrest might develop on the home front. Rations had recently been cut and every German was aware that the war in the east was not going as planned. Now the whole population knew that they could expect no mercy from the Supreme Law Lord, Adolf Hitler. But there was more to Hitler's move than merely wanting to threaten his people into submission. His actions reflected a core part of his ideological belief. As he said in his Reichstag speech on 26 April, 'nobody can in this period insist on acquired rights; instead, he must know that today there are only duties.' It was another sign that to him the individual meant nothing except as part of the collective. You had no absolute right to anything. All of the liberal freedoms – of free speech, religion, rule of law, individual self-expression – were worthless in the face of the demands of the state. And who articulated the demands of the state? An individual called Adolf Hitler. So while the catalyst for Hitler's desire to confirm himself as Supreme Law Lord may well have been the way the war was going in spring 1942, the underlying cause was his continuing commitment to the kind of Germany he wanted to build – a racial state in which the people had to conform to his will.

A month after Hitler had been declared Supreme Law Lord, a converted Soviet bomber landed at Dundee airport in Scotland on a secret mission. Vyacheslav Molotov – the man who had negotiated with Adolf

Hitler in Berlin eighteen months before – had come to negotiate with the western Allies. Though Churchill had wanted to publicize his presence, Stalin demanded that no one should know Molotov had visited the west until he returned safely to Moscow.

Molotov and his entourage were escorted south to the Prime Minister's country residence at Chequers, where Molotov had a strange encounter with a member of the Churchills' household staff. When she knocked on Molotov's door in the early hours of the morning to ask him to pull his curtains tight because of the blackout, Molotov opened the door holding a pistol. While the problem with the curtains was swiftly resolved, it was, as Churchill later said, an encounter that 'reveals one aspect of the gulf between the Soviet way of life and that of the Western powers'.[53]

Churchill also learnt, as Hitler and Ribbentrop had before, that Molotov was a man impenetrable to charm. When, for example, the British Prime Minister commiserated with Molotov after Soviet military personnel had been killed in a crash involving a British plane, Molotov responded by saying that this 'was a very sad fact, but accidents in aviation were always possible' and then moved straight on to business.[54] Sir Alexander Cadogan of the Foreign Office came to the conclusion that 'Molotov had all the grace and conciliation of a totem pole.'[55]

Molotov had arrived in Britain not for a feel-good exploratory chat, but with two familiar demands. First he wanted the British to agree that at the end of the war the Soviets could keep the territory they had gained in their pact with the Nazis, and second he sought an agreement for a swift Allied invasion of western Europe – the so-called second front. Both requests were problematic for the British. How could they allow the Soviets to keep half of pre-war Poland, especially when, as Churchill had said to Eden a few weeks before, Stalin had gained this territory 'in shameful collusion with Hitler'?[56] As for the second front, the British still believed it was impracticable to arrange a cross-Channel invasion in 1942. The Allies had neither the troops needed for the attack nor the means to get all of them safely across the Channel.

Understandably in the circumstances, the talks dragged on without agreement. When the British suggested a draft treaty that was vague on the question of the post-war frontiers, Molotov forwarded it to Stalin on 24 May with the comment: 'We consider this treaty unacceptable, as it is an empty declaration which the USSR does not need.' In response Stalin said something extraordinary: 'We do not consider it an empty declaration but regard it as an important document.' The lack of detail about frontiers was 'not bad perhaps' as it 'gives us a free hand'. In any case future borders 'will be decided by force'. Molotov quickly responded: '. . . I believe that the new draft treaty can also have positive value. I failed to appreciate it at once.'[57]

It was a reminder of just how dangerous it could be to work for Joseph Stalin. Molotov had told his boss what he thought he wanted to hear, only for Stalin to contradict him. The underlying panic in Molotov's response reverberates through the years. But there is a bigger question. Why did Stalin soften his attitude to the western Allies? One reason must surely have been the timing of the exchange. As Stalin considered his reply to Molotov, the Red Army was in the process of losing hundreds of thousands of men at the battle of Kharkov.

Back in December 1941, when Stalin had met with the British Foreign Secretary, Anthony Eden, and insisted that the Soviets retain after the war the territory they had gained under their pact with the Nazis, the military situation had been very different. Even though the Germans were close to Moscow, the Red Army had just launched a successful offensive. But now, five months later, the failure at Kharkov demonstrated the extent of Soviet vulnerability. So now was not the time to argue about the detail of post-war borders. Now was the time to focus on the second front. Above all else, Stalin wanted the western Allies to launch D-Day in a matter of months in order to relieve the pressure on the Red Army.

There is, however, another likely reason why Stalin was not insistent about the border question. We know today that the alliance between the so-called Big Three – the Soviet Union, America and Britain – held together until the end of the war. But in 1942 no one knew for sure that it would be sustained. Stalin's intensely suspicious nature might well have made him think that if the Red Army was badly defeated in the south of the Soviet Union, perhaps the western Allies might seek an accommodation with Hitler. It would have gone against all the available diplomatic and military evidence, but – as we have seen – Stalin was capable of reading into an event the reverse of the reality. The same reasoning applied to the actions of the other members of the Big Three, only more logically. Neither the British nor the Americans could ever be sure that Stalin would honour the alliance. Perhaps he might suddenly want to exit the war and make peace with Hitler. After all, he had signed a pragmatic deal with the Nazis before, so why not again?[58]

As Stalin had requested, Molotov signed an anodyne treaty with the British and travelled on from Britain to America, where Roosevelt awaited his arrival in Washington with a massive amount of self-confidence in his ability to manipulate his Soviet guest. 'I know you will not mind my being brutally frank', Roosevelt had written to Churchill in March, 'when I tell you that I think I can personally handle Stalin better than either your Foreign Office or my State Department. Stalin hates the guts of all your top people. He thinks he likes me better, and I hope he will continue to do so.'[59] And for Roosevelt the first step in 'handling' Stalin would be to 'handle' Molotov, his representative.

The process by which Roosevelt hoped to manipulate Molotov began within hours of his arrival on 29 May.[60] As soon as the visiting Foreign Minister had settled into the White House, he and the American President held talks in general terms about the war, including the prospect of a second front. Later in the evening, Roosevelt raised his idea of a world 'police force' of Britain, the Soviet Union, China and America. It was a notion dear to Roosevelt's heart and would eventually morph years later into the creation of the United Nations. Molotov was non-committal about the plan, but agreed that it was an 'important issue',[61] and that's where discussions ended for the day. Roosevelt had not raised any of the Soviet requests in detail, saying that he awaited the presence of his military experts next morning. This delay was not an accident, as Roosevelt had not ended his attempt to 'handle' Molotov that evening.

According to documents from the former Soviet archives, shortly after eleven o'clock that night Molotov heard a knock at the door of his bedroom in the East Wing. It was the President's special adviser Harry Hopkins. He asked Molotov if he could come in for a private word. 'I can tell you that President Roosevelt is a very strong supporter of a second front in 1942,' Hopkins told him. 'But the American generals don't see the real necessity of the second front. Because of this I recommend you paint a harrowing picture of the situation in the Soviet Union so that the American generals realize the seriousness of the situation.'[62] Hopkins added that Molotov should tell Roosevelt that he intended to follow this strategy next morning, before the meeting started. Molotov agreed.

The details of this encounter emerged from the Soviet archives only after the fall of communism. There is no reference to the talks in the contemporary American sources, only confirmation that Hopkins 'went in for a moment' to talk to Molotov.[63] It's not hard to see why Roosevelt and his confidants would have wanted Hopkins' approach kept secret. The American President was trying to demonstrate that he was Molotov's 'friend' – so much so that he was prepared to brief against his own generals. More than that, using Hopkins as an intermediary meant that there was an easy exit strategy for Roosevelt in case the plan backfired. He could say there had been a misunderstanding about the contents of the message, or that Hopkins had exceeded his brief or even acted without the President's knowledge. It was a devious tactic, but potentially effective.

The next day, in the presence of both General George Marshall, the US Army Chief of Staff, and Admiral Ernest King, head of the navy, Molotov followed Hopkins' advice and held nothing back. He emphasized that while it might appear that the sensible course of action was to delay the second front until 1943 in order to make better preparations for an invasion of France, that strategy could well be unwise. The western Allies, he said, 'cannot count' on the Red Army holding the Germans back. By 1943 Hitler could have control of the 'oil-producing areas' of the Soviet Union. 'Therefore,' he concluded, 'to delay the second front until 1943 is fraught with risk for the USSR and great danger for the USA and Britain.' It was an astonishing admission of potential Soviet weakness.

Roosevelt then directly confronted his military experts. He said that he wanted to open a second front in 1942. Could they make it happen? General Marshall gave a politician's answer, saying that discussions were under way about the practicalities of such an operation and 'Should this preparatory work be concluded successfully this year, the establishment of the second front will be possible in 1942.'[64]

After the meeting, General Marshall told Roosevelt that he wanted to prevent any definite commitment being made to the Soviets and 'urged that there be no reference to 1942' in the post-summit statement.[65] But to no avail. Roosevelt insisted, and the wording used in the communiqué at the end of the talks appeared at first glance to offer just such a promise. But on closer inspection it retained an element of ambiguity. 'In the course of the conversations,' read the communiqué, 'full understanding was reached with regard to the urgent tasks of creating a second front in Europe in 1942.'[66]

Roosevelt explained his reasoning in a note he sent to Churchill on

31 May. The American President said that he was 'more than ever anxious' to have a cross-Channel operation in 1942. 'I have a very strong feeling that the Russian position is precarious and may grow steadily worse during the coming weeks,' he wrote. Moreover, he was 'especially anxious' that Molotov 'carry back some real results of his Mission and that he will give a favorable account to Stalin. I am inclined to think that at present all the Russians are a bit down in the mouth.'[67]

Roosevelt wanted to do all he could to charm Molotov, and he seems to have been nervously wondering how his attempts compared to Churchill's. Molotov revealed in a telegram to Stalin that after their first dinner together Roosevelt had talked with him in a 'more intimate setting' on a sofa in the White House drawing room. 'Roosevelt asked me', said Molotov, 'whether Churchill had received me like this, hinting at the unaffected and candid style of his reception.' Molotov replied diplomatically that he was 'very pleased' with both Roosevelt's and Churchill's hospitality.[68]

It was another sign of how Roosevelt appeared to feel in competition with Churchill for Soviet favour. He had already asserted, even though he was yet to meet the Soviet leader, that Stalin 'liked' him better than the British, and now he was fishing for Molotov's praise. But Roosevelt knew that the exercise of his legendary charm would only get him so far with the tough men of the Soviet Union. He also needed to deliver what they wanted. And Stalin wanted nothing from the Americans at this perilous moment more than a definite commitment to launch an invasion of western Europe in 1942. So Roosevelt decided to give the impression that he would provide the longed-for relief.

While it was true that the commitment made by the Americans after the Molotov talks was slightly vague – what exactly did a 'full understanding' about the second front in 1942 actually mean? – the evidence is that, although Molotov remained sceptical about the President's assurance, Stalin thought Roosevelt was promising that he would endeavour to launch an invasion of France that year. And yet the President knew that almost certainly such an operation wouldn't happen in 1942[69] – not least because his chief military adviser, General Marshall, had told him of the difficulties involved.[70]

Stalin believed the word of one of the most powerful men in the world. But he had made a mistake. Roosevelt had deliberately misled him, and once Stalin found out, the consequences for the western Allies would be considerable.

11. Across the Steppe

June 1942 was a month of great optimism for the Germans. In North Africa, Rommel and the Afrika Korps were pushing Allied forces back, culminating in the capture of Tobruk on the 21st. In the Arctic, the U-boats of the Kriegsmarine and the warplanes of the Luftwaffe were mounting devastating attacks on Allied convoys. And in the south of the Soviet Union the Germans were still basking in the glory of their comprehensive defeat of the Red Army at Kharkov.

For Joseph Klein, a German paratrooper whose unit had only recently arrived on the eastern front, it was obvious that victory was in sight: 'I must say we were all very sure of winning, and everybody believed this would carry on the same way as it had during the first battles in Russia. Nobody thought this would have a bad end, not at that time . . . I never doubted Germany for one moment in those days. I also believed we were on the right side because one thing is for sure. If the Russians had succeeded in breaking through the German lines then Europe would be communist today.'[1]

Helmut Walz, a young soldier fighting with Army Group South, agreed that all this 'encouraging news' meant that belief in the power of the Führer was 'unbroken'. He and his comrades felt 'superior' to the enemy because 'the Russians lagged behind us as far as their entire development was concerned. In general you had the feeling that National Socialism was very much superior to Bolshevism.'[2]

Stalin, suspicious and worried about Hitler's intentions in the wake of the humiliating loss at Kharkov, was convinced that the Germans were planning a new attack on Moscow. But on 19 June, when a German Fieseler Storch plane crashed behind Soviet lines, he received a shock, because the Storch contained not just a German officer called Major Joachim Reichel but a complete set of German battle plans. These documents revealed that the forthcoming offensive would not take place around Moscow as Stalin had predicted, but in the south towards the River Don and the Caucasus beyond. It was unwelcome news, insofar as it contradicted the judgement of the Soviet leader. So Stalin simply disregarded it. Once again he dismissed accurate intelligence as disinformation. But the German offensive – codenamed Operation Blue – was indeed to be in the south, and it would be launched on 28 June, just nine days after the Soviets had captured the battle plans from Major Reichel. And while we can't fault Stalin for looking on the Reichel documents with suspicion – they could, after all, have been part of a deception plan – what is blameworthy is his insistence that he was right. No proper contingency plans were drawn up to deal with the possibility that Reichel's battle plans were genuine.

Hitler, who from the planning stage of the invasion had always wanted to snatch Soviet resources, staked everything on this offensive. 'If I do not get the oil of Maikop and Grosny,' he told the commanders of Army Group South just before the attack, 'then I must end this war.'[3] Major Hubert Menzel, who had helped plan the initial attack on the Soviet Union the previous year, was also well aware that Operation Blue was a final gamble. 'We knew that we had to bring about a decision regarding the war in the east by the end of '42,' he said. 'At Moscow things had gone wrong and things were no longer working out. So the decision was taken, where can we confront the Russians still in '42? So that they really have to confront us . . . because we knew that from '43 onwards, we'd have to reckon with involvement from the West.'[4]

Operation Blue began just as Reichel's plan had predicted, and German units pushed forward in the south of the Soviet Union. Initial reports were encouraging for the German High Command. Although the forces involved had been depleted by a year's struggle on the eastern front – the vast majority of vehicles lost, for instance, had not been replaced[5] – it seemed as if this was to be a repeat of the glory days of the summer of 1941. Joachim Stempel of 14th Panzer remembered that 'Our initial impression was that the Russians were fleeing.'[6]

'It was a proud experience', said Gerhard Münch of the 71st Infantry, 'having succeeded in advancing that far to the east, further and further and further . . . We felt that our equipment was superior and that we were also better trained than the Russians. The Russian senior leadership had not yet been trained to the level where they were able to handle mechanized units . . . The Russians gambled with people, whereas our training [focused on] sparing people.'[7]

What particularly struck the Germans as they advanced further east was the immensity of the space. 'The steppes were bleak, barren, just endless expanse up to the horizon,' said Joachim Stempel. 'Not like in Germany, where you can see the next town after every bend in the road, but here there was nothing. You could look through binoculars, just nothing – dust, sand and the burning heat. We said to ourselves, hopefully we won't have to experience this in winter. But we were so optimistic and euphoric that these thoughts only lasted a few seconds.'[8]

Helmut Walz remembered that 'the wormwood grass stood maybe 30, 40 centimetres high, and with each step we took, we encountered countless gnats. Incredible! That in itself was quite a strain, and it can become a considerable hindrance. Furthermore, the sun was glaring. The land was as flat as a pancake, scattered with small hollows in which there are some kind of green ponds.'[9]

Franz Halder, Chief of the Army General Staff, was confused about what exactly the swiftness of the advance signified. 'The actual picture of the enemy situation is not yet clear to me,' he wrote in his diary on 6 July. 'There are two possibilities: either we have overestimated the enemy's strength and the offensive has completely smashed him, or the enemy is conducting a planned disengagement or at least is trying to do so in order to forestall being irretrievably beaten in 1942.'[10] In reality, it was a little of both. While Stalin was more willing now to allow units to pull back when tactically necessary, there were also instances of panic.

'We felt desperation and anger,' said Anatoly Mereshko, who led a group of officer cadets against the advancing Germans, 'because of our helplessness, and also we wondered, why do they not let us properly fight the enemy? Why do we have to keep withdrawing . . . As for our [other] retreating units, they were really completely demoralized people. They didn't know where they were going and they didn't know where to look for their units. For example, they were told to reassemble in Marinovka, but where was Marinovka? About five or six soldiers would turn up and ask: "Where is Marinovka?" So they just walked and walked, carrying their weapons with them because without weapons they would be interrogated.'[11] Even though new armaments had been handed to some Red Army defenders, the overall picture for Mereshko and his men remained bleak. 'If there were a hundred and twenty people in the company only about forty, forty-five had all the right weapons, and they had rifles dating back to 1890 . . . Also we had so-called self-charging rifles, but they were such rubbish that we had to give them up after the first combat. After the first specks of dust got in, they no longer worked.'[12]

On 19 July, as the Germans advanced towards Rostov with the road to the Caucasus open beyond, Ivan Maisky, the Soviet Ambassador to London, wrote in his diary that the Soviets faced an 'extremely grave' moment in their history and a 'deadly danger . . . to the revolution, and to the entire future of humanity'.[13] The week before, Maisky had discussed with Churchill why it was that the British had experienced such defeat in North Africa. Churchill had replied that the German Army was fighting the war 'better' than the British. In addition, British soldiers 'lack the "Russian spirit"' which was one of 'die but don't surrender'.[14]

However, the reality was not as straightforward as either Maisky or Churchill perceived it. Yes, the Germans had made great progress in the south of the Soviet Union and had indeed 'waged war' in Africa better than the British, but behind the scenes all was not well. For years there had been an underlying tension between Hitler and many of his generals, not just about their different attitude to risk – with Hitler almost always more of a gambler – but also about broader questions concerning the way a warrior should be, and the manner in which such a man (and, to Hitler, warriors were always men) should hold himself. Reinhard Spitzy, a committed Nazi who served in the German Foreign Office, recalled Hitler's view that 'My generals should be like bull terriers on chains, and they should want war, war, war. And I should have to put brakes on the whole thing. But what happens now? I want to go ahead with my strong politics and the generals try to stop me. That's a false situation.'[15]

In the summer of 1942 Hitler most definitely did not think his generals were like 'bull terriers on chains'. Quite the contrary. On 13 July he sacked Field Marshal von Bock, the commander of Army Group South, because he wasn't making progress quickly enough. This was the second time Bock had been dismissed by Hitler. He had previously, in December 1941, lost his job as commander of Army Group Centre. He maintained that this latest removal was purely the result of Hitler's 'impatience'.[16] He would not be the last gifted commander to be dismissed in the course of this operation.

Ten days later, at Hitler's new forward headquarters in Ukraine, the German leader issued the wildly optimistic Directive Number 45. The opening sentence set the tone: 'In a campaign of little more than three weeks, the broad goals I had set the south wing of the eastern front have been essentially achieved.' He then listed a series of new objectives.

Instead of Army Group South accomplishing its tasks sequentially, one part – Army Group A – would now proceed directly to the Caucasus, and another – Army Group B – would move east towards Stalingrad and 'occupy the city'.[17] Up to now, taking Stalingrad had never been a goal of this operation.

As a consequence of Hitler's decision, it was now as if Army Group A and Army Group B were fighting totally different campaigns – one down towards the Caucasus, the other across the steppe towards Stalingrad. Such were the immense distances involved that German units were more like ships journeying through the ocean than armies on land. The contrast with the swift advance across France in 1940 was stark. Here, on the vast steppe and in the high mountains, the problems of supplying the fighting troops grew exponentially.

The same day that Hitler issued the directive, General Halder wrote in his diary that at a military conference the German leader had erupted into a 'fit of insane rage' and hurled the 'gravest reproaches against the General Staff'. The trigger for this outburst was a row about the disposition of forces around Rostov, but the broader reason was Hitler's sense that his generals were once again demonstrating timidity. Halder, unsurprisingly, had a different perspective. 'This chronic tendency to underrate enemy capabilities is gradually assuming grotesque proportions and develops into a positive danger. The situation is getting more and more intolerable. Here is no room for any serious work. This so-called leadership is characterized by a pathological reacting to the impressions of the moment and a total lack of any understanding of the command machinery and its possibilities.'[18] But Hitler was in a hurry, and could not have cared less about the 'command machinery'.

Shortly after Hitler had issued Directive Number 45, Rostov fell to the Germans, with Red Army units retreating in disarray. And as Army Group A began the march south towards the oilfields of the Caucasus little of the discontent at headquarters was shared by the troops on the ground. 'Clearly we were cheerful,' said panzer commander Alfred Rubbel; 'we drove and drove, and suddenly we came to a cornfield and there we stood guard. Then we fuelled up and we continued. It was almost frivolous, like the seven hundred kilometres [advance] in autumn of '41. So the roads were good. We got enough to eat. We talked about the carnival in Aachen. We didn't see the enemy. [Instead] We think the sun is shining. I was thinking of [the legend of] Prometheus, who had

20. Heinz Guderian, one of the most famous German commanders of the war. The advance of his panzer units towards Moscow in the early days of Operation Barbarossa was one of the swiftest in history.

21. German soldiers near Minsk in July 1941 proudly display a captured portrait of Stalin. The speed with which the Germans reached Minsk, capital of Belorussia, surprised and appalled Stalin.

22. A German soldier uses a flamethrower during Operation Barbarossa. From the beginning, the Germans fought a 'war of extermination' against the Soviets.

23. Hitler visits his victorious troops on the eastern front in the summer of 1941. In those early weeks of the invasion, it appeared that his gamble of invading the Soviet Union might succeed.

24. Hitler and his key military leaders during the decisive month of October 1941. From left to right, Hitler, Wilhelm Keitel, Franz Halder and Walther von Brauchitsch.

25. The Germans took more than three million Red Army soldiers prisoner in the first months of the war. Over two million of them were dead by December 1941.

26. Soldiers from German Army Group Centre advance on Moscow in December 1941. The German failure to win the battle for Moscow would prove to be a decisive moment in the war.

27. On 7 November 1941, Red Army soldiers parade in Red Square on the anniversary of the Revolution. Even though the Germans were close to Moscow, the parade still went ahead.

28. Stalin, who had considered leaving Moscow just weeks before, gave a speech to his soldiers in Red Square on 7 November and assured them that the German invaders were facing disaster.

29. A boy begging for food during the German occupation of Kharkov in the east of Ukraine. The Germans planned on starving millions of Soviet citizens to death.

30. One of the most infamous images of the Holocaust, known as the killing of 'the last Jew in Vinnitsa'. A member of a German murder squad is about to shoot a Jewish civilian in Ukraine in 1941.

31. In the spring of 1943 the Germans uncovered evidence of a Soviet war crime – the massacre of thousands of Polish officers in the forest of Katyn outside Smolensk.

32. Winston Churchill sits between Stalin and Roosevelt for a meal at the Tehran conference at the end of 1943 – the first meeting of the so-called Big Three.

33. President Franklin Roosevelt in a cheerful mood – as he often was. He prided himself on his ability to 'handle' people. He thought he could 'handle' Stalin. He was wrong.

34. German soldiers during the battle of Kharkov in May 1942. Their decisive victory at Kharkov made many of them think it was still possible to defeat the Soviet Union.

35. A group of Soviet partisans operating behind the German front line. As the war progressed, so did the effectiveness of the partisans, and Hitler was keen to deal with them as brutally as possible.

36. Women served in the Red Army in a variety of combat roles, such as tank crew, fighter pilots and – as here – snipers.

37. Hitler in a pensive mood alongside his military commanders. Staring at the camera on the left is General Jodl, next to him in the coat with fur collar is General Guderian and half hidden behind Hitler's right shoulder is Field Marshal Keitel.

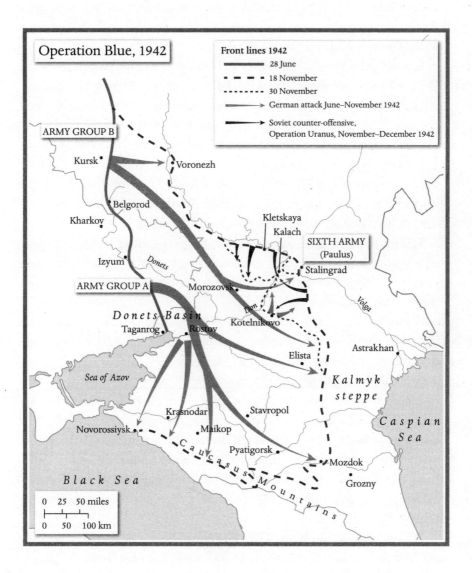

Operation Blue, 1942

Front lines 1942

———— 28 June

– – – 18 November

········· 30 November

———→ German attack June–November 1942

———→ Soviet counter-offensive, Operation Uranus, November–December 1942

ARMY GROUP B

Kursk

Voronezh

Belgorod

Kharkov

Izyum

Donets

ARMY GROUP A

Morozovsk

Kletskaya

Kalach

SIXTH ARMY (Paulus)

Stalingrad

Volga

Donets Basin

Taganrog

Rostov

Don

Kotelnikovo

Astrakhan

Elista

Kalmyk steppe

Sea of Azov

Caspian Sea

Krasnodar

Maikop

Stavropol

Novorossiysk

Caucasus Mountains

Pyatigorsk

Mozdok

Grozny

Black Sea

0   25   50 miles

0   50   100 km

stolen the fire . . . [It was as if] Prometheus came out. Then it started to become warm, and this amazing scenery of the Caucasus, wonderful fruits, tomatoes, mandarins.' Rubbel remembered that summer advance as 'wonderful, it was not war . . . Our wives often ask us, why do you look so cheerful [in photos of this time] – was it so much fun to wage a war? It's difficult to explain to them. I then came up with this explanation. Good friends together, that is something special.'[19]

It was in this buoyant atmosphere that on 21 August troops from the Wehrmacht's mountain division climbed Mount Elbrus, the highest peak in the Caucasus, and placed a swastika flag on the summit. They could not have imagined Hitler's reaction. He was not merely displeased, he was beside himself with fury. Such an indulgence was almost criminal, he thought, at a time when every moment mattered.[20] It's certainly hard to imagine soldiers of the Red Army taking time off to pursue similar aims without the approval of the Soviet leader. Stalin's displeasure could have been extremely dangerous for them.

Hitler's desire to gain the resources of the Caucasus as quickly as possible was understandable, given a meeting he had held ten days before on 11 August. Together with Albert Speer, Paul Pleiger of the Reich Coal Association and other industrialists, he had discussed the problems of coal supply along with iron and steel production. Hitler had attacked Pleiger at the start of the meeting, claiming that American workers produced three times as much coal as German ones. If that was the case, why couldn't Pleiger deliver more coal? But Pleiger 'persistently' refused to accede to Hitler's demand to increase production. It just wasn't possible. 'Then,' according to one of those present, 'Hitler said very calmly and determinedly: "Herr Pleiger, if due to a lack of coking coal the output of the steel industry cannot be raised as intended, then the war is lost." All of us were thunderstruck. There was profound silence. Finally, Pleiger said: "My Führer, I will do everything humanly possible to achieve the aim." '[21]

It's a significant moment. After Hitler had been told it was impossible for him to have more resources, he had admitted that Germany would lose the war. It was shocking news from a leader who almost always tried to put a positive spin on events when talking to anyone outside his innermost circle. In addition, by attempting to increase existing output merely by an act of will, a small but nonetheless distinct gap opened up between Hitler and reality. While it was all very well for Pleiger to agree to do his best to provide the coal Hitler wanted, trying to make his Führer's wishes happen in practice was a very different matter. As it transpired, despite the emotion of the encounter, coal deliveries never reached the level Hitler had demanded.

The meeting also demonstrated Hitler's awareness that events were slipping away from him. In the background he knew the Americans were lurking, not yet making a decisive contribution to the war, but gearing up to deliver one. It was all the more reason for the campaign in the south of the Soviet Union to be won as quickly as possible – certainly more quickly than his generals said was achievable. Like Pleiger they needed to be ordered to do the impossible.

Not that any of these issues affected Stalin's mood at the time – which was both angry and worried. The fall of Rostov at the end of July marked a particular low point. The Germans had first conquered the city in November 1941, and after the Red Army had managed to retake it shortly afterwards there had been great celebrations. For the Soviets, Rostov had become the symbol of the turning of the tide. Yet now the German wave had washed over them once again.

After the loss of Rostov, Stalin issued a new command – Order 227. And he didn't try to hide his fury: 'Elements of the Southern Front, following the lead of panic-mongers, gave up Rostov and Novocherkassk without putting up serious resistance and without orders from Moscow, drenching their banners in shame.' He emphasized that the idea that the Red Army should withdraw in order to regroup was fatally flawed: 'Every commander, Red Army soldier and political worker should understand that our resources are not without limits . . . To retreat further means to ruin oneself together with our Motherland.'

The conclusion Stalin drew from this worrying state of affairs was dramatic. 'Not a step back! Such should now be our principal call. We must stubbornly defend every position, every metre of Soviet territory to the last drop of blood, cling to every last scrap of Soviet soil and hold our ground until all other possibilities have been exhausted.'[22]

For Fyodor Bubenchikov, a junior officer and a committed communist, 'The good thing about Order 227 was that it told the truth. It was read in full to every company, to every battalion, every soldier knew it. We were children of our time. At that time an order signed by Stalin which told the truth touched the heart of every man from the commander to every soldier. Units were brought from the front line and every soldier had to swear an oath, to be sworn in again. I think it's a change in the attitude of everyone towards the war. The question in 1942 was "To be or not be?", whether the Soviet Union was going to be or not be.'[23]

Order 227 became famous. The words 'Not a step back!' came to symbolize Soviet resistance. But it was a curious document, because it's hard to see in practical terms what was new. As we have seen, Stalin's Order 270, issued in August 1941, had already branded as 'betrayers of the Motherland' those soldiers who surrendered to the Germans or retreated without authorization.[24] Equally, the formation of so-called blocking detachments to shoot any soldiers who attempted to flee the battlefield had been tried before. Stranger still was the fact that the order was issued around the same time that Stalin was allowing commanders to pull back their troops to avoid encirclements. Just a few weeks before, for instance, he had authorized troops to withdraw 100 miles south-east, from close to Millerovo to the River Don.[25]

German soldiers, advancing east towards the Don, spotted that some Red Army units were pulling back not out of fear but for reasons of strategy. 'The Russians just sort of retreated in an orderly fashion and resisted us,' said Gerhard Hindenlang, an infantry officer. 'They did this very well. We had very few contacts with them until we got to the Don salient. At the time they very cleverly used the vastness of the terrain and we were further and further removed from our supply depots.'[26]

So Order 227 was not all it seemed. Indeed, it's possible that Stalin wanted this draconian statement made at precisely the moment he was becoming more flexible about permitting Red Army units to withdraw. He must have felt that the real danger now was that some commanders would use this new development to pull back without authorization. He realized that a managed withdrawal could easily turn into a rout. Order 227 was designed to prevent that happening.

It's also ironic that an order designed to quell panic had the smell of panic about it. The sentiments in Order 227 are those of a desperately worried man – so worried that, around the time he issued the order, Stalin demonstrated that he was prepared to reverse a number of previously held beliefs. At the end of July, shortly after he issued Order 227, he created new medals solely for officers. The Orders of Nevsky, Kutuzov and Suvorov were awarded to commanders who showed particular skill or bravery. Remarkably, the orders were named after warriors who all predated the revolution. This was a blatant appeal to a patriotism that transcended any Marxist belief structure. Later in the year, in a further retreat from Bolshevik practice, the role of the political officers, the commissars, was downgraded and regular officers were given sole right to command.[27]

The lowering of the status of commissars was a particularly popular decision, as they were widely disliked.[28] Vasily Borisov, for instance, said that he and his comrades in a Siberian division 'liked their commanders but hated the commissars because they abused power. For example, a commander would come to the trench when the soldiers were digging the trenches and make sure that everyone was looked after – well fed and so on. Whereas when commissars came they were very rude.' Early in the war 'during a counter-attack, a very young inexperienced soldier felt too scared to get out of the trench. And I saw with my own eyes a political officer shoot this soldier in the head as a deserter. I saw it with my own eyes . . . Yes, he [the young soldier] felt scared but he wasn't a traitor he was just a coward. He could have been sent to a penal battalion, but the commissar wanted to set an example, to show others. I felt disgusted. I felt I hated the commissar. It left a strong imprint.'[29]

There's one last sign that Stalin was prepared to change in the face of increased danger. At the end of August he promoted Zhukov to First Deputy Commissar of Defence. This made him Stalin's effective deputy in military matters. Coming from someone who had previously had concerns that a new Napoleon would arise from within the armed forces to challenge his authority, it was a brave appointment. Stalin realized that now was not the time to focus on potential rivals. With the Germans advancing into the heart of the Soviet Union, it was the moment to promote talent.

However, some aspects of Stalin's leadership technique had not changed, as Nikolai Baibakov, Deputy Minister for Oil Production, discovered when he met the Soviet leader in August 1942. Stalin ordered Baibakov to 'go by plane to the northern Caucasus' and, if he judged that the Germans were about to capture the oil, destroy the drilling infrastructure. So far, so normal. But then Stalin added his own spin to the request, telling Baibakov that if he wrecked the oilfields and the Germans didn't reach them, he would be killed. Equally, if he didn't destroy the installations and the Germans did manage to reach them, he would also die. Baibakov, who had met Stalin several times before, did not find this overt threat out of the ordinary. 'It was quite natural,' he said, 'because the oil was feeding [that is, necessary for] the whole of the country. What he did was fully justified . . . What can I say? It was a calm situation. He was sitting on his chair, I was sitting on my chair and we had that conversation. I didn't feel any fear.'

Baibakov believed that Stalin was 'a great man. Not everyone will agree with me. Even people of my generation will not all say the same but I have only positive feelings about him. Of course he made mistakes but people criticize him too much now.'[30]

In August 1942 both Hitler and Stalin were facing moments of crisis. Yet their approach to motivating their subordinates could hardly have been more at odds. Hitler appealed to Paul Pleiger – pleaded almost – to attempt the impossible. He piled on emotional pressure until Pleiger, seemingly helpless to do anything else, agreed to try to do as his Führer requested. Stalin, in contrast, was uninterested in playing emotional games. He believed in the power of threat. While he had shown that he was capable of appealing to Soviet patriotism, beneath his words always lay the blunt reality of his vision of life – a primitive world in which human beings responded best to violent intimidation. Perhaps the most extraordinary aspect of this leadership technique is that a man like Baibakov, having been brought up in such a culture, thought it all perfectly normal.

This was an exceptionally difficult time for Stalin, not just because of anxiety about the fate of the oilfields of the Caucasus, but also because of problems in the relationship with Churchill that dated back to earlier in the summer. At the start of July the British had suffered one of the greatest naval catastrophes in their history. The Arctic convoy PQ17, en route to the Soviet Union, had been attacked by the Germans and twenty-four of the thirty-nine ships destroyed.

The British Chiefs of Staff had recommended in May that the sailing of PQ16, the convoy before PQ17, be suspended because of the danger of attack, but Churchill had insisted that it proceed. 'Not only Premier Stalin but President Roosevelt will object very much to our desisting from running the convoys now,' wrote Churchill in a note to his chief military adviser General Ismay that reveals the extent to which political, rather than just military, considerations influenced his decision. 'The Russians are in heavy action and will expect us to run the risk and pay the price entailed by our contribution.' This was so, he admitted, even though the 'price' might be considerable. 'My own feeling mingled with much anxiety is that the convoy ought to sail on the 18th [May]. The operation is justified if a half get through. The failure on our part to make the attempt would weaken our influence with both our major allies. There are always the uncertainties of weather and luck which may aid us. I share your misgivings but I feel it is a matter of duty.'[31]

Six of the thirty-six ships in PQ16 were sunk on the way to the Soviet Union. To Churchill this level of loss was politically acceptable – hence his giving permission for PQ17 to leave. But the loss of so many ships on PQ17 made him rethink future British policy, and he decided to cancel all upcoming convoys. Telling Stalin about their cancellation would not be easy, especially since he had not only to give the Soviet leader this bad news, but also to confirm that the British didn't think there could be a second front until 1943. It was a double dose of disappointment at the exact moment that the Wehrmacht was advancing swiftly across the steppes of southern Russia.

In his message to Stalin, sent on 17 July, Churchill did his best to explain the context of his decision about the convoys. He went into detail about the danger posed by 'heavy [German] surface forces' and asserted that 'My naval advisers tell me that if they had the handling of the German surface, submarine and air forces in present circumstances, they would guarantee the complete destruction of any convoy to North Russia.' Consequently, he said, 'we have reached the conclusion that to attempt to run the next convoy, P.Q. 18, would bring no benefit to you and would only involve dead loss to the common cause.'[32]

As for the delicate issue of the second front, Churchill mentioned it almost as an afterthought, and even then tried to put a positive gloss on the news that the invasion of France was not happening in 1942. He said that cancelling the convoys to the Soviet Union meant that British warships were free to protect Atlantic convoys, which in turn allowed more American soldiers to be sent to Britain to build up for a 'really strong second front in 1943'.

Stalin's reply, on 23 July, was icy. 'I received your message of July 17,' he began. 'Two conclusions could be drawn from it. First, the British Government refuses to continue the sending of war materials to the Soviet Union via the Northern route. Secondly, in spite of the agreed communiqué concerning the urgent tasks of creating a Second Front in 1942, the British Government postpones this matter until 1943.'[33]

It was an archetypical response from Stalin – no diplomatic pleasantries, no attempt to understand the British position. Just sharp displeasure. He wanted British convoys, and he wanted a second front in 1942. Now Churchill had denied him both. And the way in which he questioned Churchill's decisions verged on the offensive. Stalin said his 'experts' found it 'difficult to understand' why the merchant ships of PQ 17 had been sunk in such large numbers, and he lectured Churchill about the realities of battle, saying 'in war no important undertaking could be effected without risk or losses.' He also pointedly reminded him that 'of course, the Soviet Union is suffering far greater losses.' As for the second front, he thought this issue was 'not being treated with the seriousness it deserves'.

When Maisky, the Soviet Ambassador, handed over Stalin's note, Churchill was 'depressed and offended at the same time'. Maisky even thought that Churchill might have believed that this was a precursor to the Soviet Union leaving the war, and so he quickly reassured him this was not so. The following day he wrote in his diary that Churchill was a 'hot tempered character'.[34] The contrast with the cold-hearted Stalin was all too evident. Yet, just like Roosevelt, Churchill seems to have believed that the problem wasn't that Stalin did not want to form a close relationship with him, but merely that he hadn't yet had a chance to experience the power of his personality. For Stalin, however, this was a dispute about practical matters – it was immaterial to him whether he had a 'relationship' with Churchill or not.

The British Ambassador to Moscow, Sir Archibald Clark Kerr, warned his colleagues in London that Stalin and those around him did not think 'we are taking the war seriously'. In a cable he sent just two days after Stalin's blunt note to Churchill, Clark Kerr wrote that 'they set up their own enormous losses against our (by comparison) trifling losses in men and material since the close of 1939.'[35] Shortly after he sent this cable, Clark Kerr suggested that Churchill should come to Moscow and meet Stalin to discuss matters with him personally. Churchill quickly agreed, and so one of the most intriguing encounters of the war was hurriedly arranged.

After an arduous plane journey via Egypt, Churchill and the first cohort of the British delegation landed at Moscow airport on 12 August 1942. The talks began that very evening, in the dingy surroundings of Stalin's office in the Kremlin – a place which reminded one of the British visitors of 'a railway waiting room'.[36] Stalin immediately told Churchill that there was bad news from the front, and claimed that virtually all the German forces in Europe were concentrated against the Red Army. He followed this assertion with a not so subtle jibe about the 'trifling' contribution he believed the British had made so far to the war. Churchill replied by explaining why the second front was impossible in 1942 but assured Stalin that the 'British and American Governments were preparing for a very great operation in 1943.'[37]

Up to this point the meeting had proceeded on predictable lines. But when Churchill told Stalin that there were twenty-five German divisions in France ready to oppose any landing, Stalin snapped back, 'A man who was not prepared to take risks could not win a war.' It was tantamount to accusing the British of cowardice. But Churchill pressed on and launched into an enthusiastic description of the RAF bombing campaign against Germany. He emphasized the willingness of the British to target civilians and promised that 'if need be, as the war went on, we hoped to shatter almost every dwelling in almost every German city.'

By now Churchill was not just using his rhetorical gifts but also his artistic ones, as he drew a picture of a crocodile to demonstrate that Africa was the vulnerable underside of the German reptile. For that reason, he argued, the campaign in Africa should be regarded as a second front. With Stalin now rather less sullen than he had been at the start of the encounter, the discussion ended.

Churchill thought the meeting had gone well for a first encounter. In the official note he sent back to London after he had left Stalin, he wrote, 'I expect I shall establish a solid and sincere relationship with this man.'[38] But in private the British Prime Minister was prepared to be less diplomatic. 'Unfortunately,' wrote Air Chief Marshal Tedder, who was concerned about the listening devices that were almost certainly installed at their dacha, Churchill 'rather let himself go' in his description of the Soviet leader, 'speaking of Stalin as just a peasant, whom he, Winston, knew exactly how to tackle'.[39]

The next day would prove that Churchill had overestimated his ability to 'tackle' the Soviet leader. First Stalin sent the British a note in which he once again suggested the British had reneged on the promise of a second front. Then, at a meeting that evening, he was even more overt in his suggestion that the British were refusing to mount the second front out of cowardice. After launching into a spirited defence of the British position, Churchill returned once more to his dacha.[40]

The following day began a little better, but culminated in a gala

dinner at the Kremlin that Churchill attended in a bad mood and left
relatively early, saying to his friend and doctor Sir Charles Wilson that
Stalin 'didn't want to talk to me' and 'the food was filthy'.[41] The next
morning Churchill was all for leaving Moscow, certain that Stalin had
taken against him. It took the combined efforts of Wilson and Clark
Kerr to convince him to turn up at a final meeting with the Soviet leader.
To begin with, the encounter ran along familiar and unproductive lines,
but then something different – and to Churchill significant – happened.
Stalin asked Churchill to a late-night dinner of suckling pig in his private
apartment in the Kremlin. The two of them, along with Molotov, stayed
up drinking into the early hours. And when Churchill returned to his
dacha at three in the morning he was euphoric, claiming he 'had cemented
a friendship with Stalin'.[42] He left Moscow later that day enthused about
the possibilities of working with the Soviet leader.

It was an extraordinary turnaround within twenty-four hours.
Churchill had moved from wanting to cut short the visit because it was
so unproductive to believing that a huge amount had been accomplished –
even though nothing of substance had actually been achieved. Stalin,
for instance, hadn't bothered to hide the bloodthirsty nature of his
regime, openly admitting to Churchill during their drink-fuelled night
together that the kulaks had all been 'killed' and joking that Molotov
was a 'gangster'. Yet Churchill was still entranced.

Stalin was an exotic figure to western statesmen. He was one of the
most powerful people in the world, but someone that no western leader
knew much about in personal terms. And now Churchill was getting
drunk with him. Surely that must mean something? But it didn't. This
was a mistake that others had made before. Sir Archibald Clark Kerr, for
example, wrote in a letter to Stafford Cripps in April 1942 that 'with
Stalin I like to think that I clicked. We fraternized over pipes and we
were amused by each other's jokes. Indeed I found him to be just my cup
of tea.'[43] But, as Clark Kerr subsequently discovered, while he may have
felt he had 'clicked' with Stalin, there is little evidence that Stalin felt he
had clicked with him.

Air Chief Marshal Tedder witnessed two incidents that August that
demonstrated how Churchill tried to establish an emotional relationship
with Stalin, and how he failed each time. The first was during one of the
difficult meetings at the Kremlin, when Churchill said he had journeyed
to Moscow 'in the midst of my troubles . . . hoping, hoping, I said, to

meet the hand of comradeship . . . and I am bitterly disappointed. I have not met that hand.'[44] Stalin ignored the entreaty. The second was at the Kremlin banquet, when Churchill asked Stalin if he had 'forgiven' him for his support of the Russian royalists during the revolution. 'It is not for me to forgive,' said Stalin; 'it is for God to forgive.'[45] A response that had a special subtext, given that Stalin was an atheist.

We've already seen, in the context of Hitler, that 'charisma' exists only in a relationship between people. The same truth, naturally enough, applies to Stalin. And the tendency to project a series of qualities on to the person one is meeting, coupled with an exaggerated sense of one's own attractiveness, can lead to grotesque misunderstandings. That's surely part of the explanation for what happened here. Both Churchill and Clark Kerr had monumental egos. Both thought they were tremendously impressive people. Moreover, their predisposition to think they were all but irresistible was likely heightened by their relative contempt for Stalin, a man of humble origins. To Churchill, Stalin was 'just a peasant', to Clark Kerr he was a 'possum that you would get very fond of (against your better judgment), but would have to keep a sharp eye on, lest he nip you in the buttocks out of sheer mischief'.[46]

Before their boozy dinner, when it had been apparent that Stalin was not succumbing to the power of Churchill's personality, Clark Kerr told the Prime Minister that, while 'he was an aristocrat and a man of the world', Stalin and the Soviet leadership 'were straight from the plough or the lathe. They were rough and inexperienced. They didn't discuss things as we discussed them.' Consequently, Churchill shouldn't be 'offended by a peasant who didn't know any better'.[47]

But the prize for the most contemptuous assessment of Stalin goes to Colonel Ian Jacob, military assistant secretary to the war cabinet, who observed the Soviet leader at the gala dinner in the Kremlin and wrote in his diary, 'It was extraordinary to see this little peasant, who would not have looked at all out of place in a country lane with a pickaxe over his shoulder, calmly sitting down to a banquet in these magnificent halls.'[48]

There seems to have been little acceptance on the British side that Stalin had a reasonable point of view. But any objective observer would have acknowledged that he did. The Soviet Union was in a desperate position in the summer of 1942, yet at this very moment of crisis the British had cancelled the Arctic convoys. What was more, having been led to believe – at least by Roosevelt – that there would likely be a second front in 1942, Stalin had just been told that no such offensive would be mounted. In such circumstances, who wouldn't be angry?

However, at least one member of the British delegation did give credit to the Soviet leader. Sir Alan Brooke, Chief of the Imperial General Staff, was immediately 'much impressed by his astuteness, and his crafty cleverness. He is a realist, with little flattery about him, and not looking for much flattery either.' Brooke also spotted the vast difference in character between Churchill and Stalin: 'The two leaders, Churchill and Stalin, are poles apart as human beings . . . Stalin is a realist if ever there was one, facts only count with him . . . but he is ready to face facts even when unpleasant. Winston, on the other hand, never seems anxious to face an unpleasantness until forced to do so. He appealed to sentiments in Stalin which do not I think exist there.'[49] That last sentence is one of the most perceptive remarks ever written about the relationship between Stalin and the other western leaders. Both Churchill and Roosevelt would indeed persist in the years to come in trying to appeal to sentiments which simply did not exist in Stalin.

Brooke astutely summed up Stalin by saying that while he was an 'outstanding man' with a 'quick brain and a real grasp of the essentials of war', at the same time he possessed the ability to send 'off people to their doom without ever turning a hair'.[50] It was an assessment that was a great deal more accurate than the one Churchill left Moscow with, which was that the Soviet leader was no longer an awkward peasant, but a 'great man' alongside whom it was a 'pleasure' to work.[51]

Three weeks after Churchill's visit to Moscow, a new crisis occurred at Hitler's forward headquarters at Vinnitsa in Ukraine caused by the German leader's continuing obsession about the progress of the summer offensive – or the lack of it. He had already lost his temper once before, late in August, and accused senior military commanders of 'intellectual conceit, mental non-adaptability, and utter failure to grasp essentials'.[52] Now there was to be a major row with Jodl, Chief of the Operations Staff of the Wehrmacht. This was quite an achievement, since Jodl was the most sycophantic of Hitler's commanders.

Jodl journeyed to visit Field Marshal List, commander of Army Group A, at Stalino on 7 September. List told Jodl that the German advance down into the Caucasus had been hindered by a combination of unreliable supply lines, mountainous terrain and increased Soviet resistance. It was becoming obvious that the capture of the oilfields of Baku was beyond the capabilities of the German troops under his command. And List, it should be remembered, was one of Hitler's most gifted military commanders. While not as flashy a personality as Manstein or Guderian, he nonetheless had played a leading role in both the conquest of France and the astonishing German success in Yugoslavia and Greece, just before the start of Operation Barbarossa.

Jodl listened to List's complaints, returned to Vinnitsa and related what he had heard to Hitler. The result was an unparalleled outburst from the German leader. Among other insults, he attacked his generals for 'lack of initiative'. Jodl then did the unthinkable and answered him back. He told Hitler that List was merely obeying the orders that he had been given. This only exacerbated matters, as Hitler now said that his previous statements were being twisted and thrown back at him. Feeling betrayed, he turned his back on Jodl and left the room.[53]

Nicolaus von Below, Hitler's Luftwaffe adjutant, had been away from headquarters when the argument occurred, but returned shortly afterwards to find the place 'plunged in gloom'. He discovered that 'the situation conferences were no longer being held in the Wehrmacht Command Staff house but in the large study at Hitler's quarters.' Moreover, Hitler would not shake hands with his military staff when they entered, as had been his custom, and 'dined alone in his bunker'. He also insisted that everything he said at his military conferences should now be recorded by 'two female Reichstag stenographers' to ensure that his words could not subsequently be distorted.[54]

Hitler complained to Below that 'the mass of older generals were past their best and must be replaced by younger officers.' The first to fall victim to this new thinking was the man whose plain speaking had been the catalyst for the Führer's outburst – Field Marshal List – who was sacked the day after the row with Jodl. General Halder, Army Chief of Staff, was next. Hitler told Below that Halder was 'dispassionate and dry' and while he could spot problems developing, he couldn't solve them.[55] Halder was dismissed on 24 September, and noted in his diary that Hitler had said that it was necessary to educate the senior command in 'fanatical faith in The Idea'.[56]

The new Army Chief of Staff – and someone who appeared to possess 'fanatical faith in The Idea' – was General Kurt Zeitzler. While he lacked Halder's strategic experience, he could be guaranteed to be more deferential to Hitler. Even more revealing was Hitler's choice of a replacement commander for Army Group A. Out of all of the talented military minds available to him, he chose the individual he considered to be the best possible candidate – himself. It was as if he believed not just that he was the only person who mattered, but that he was able to do everyone else's job better than they could. It was just a shame that there was only one of him.

Incredibly, Hitler was now in day-to-day command of an army group more than 600 miles away, fighting on the east coast of the Black Sea. He had thus inserted himself at four different levels of the military hierarchy – as commander of an army group, as Supreme Head of the Army, as Supreme Head of all the Armed Forces and as head of state. Even more bizarre was his assessment that such a fractured and confusing structure could ever possibly work.

While it's a common belief among megalomaniacs that the best possible solution to any problem would be if they could only do all the important jobs themselves, few actually act upon that idea. Hitler was the exception. It was an especially surprising development given that previous successes – like the conquest of France – had occurred when he had set the vision but allowed commanders on the ground maximum flexibility. The initiative of generals like Guderian and Rommel had been instrumental in winning that campaign. How did Hitler think such military creativity could flourish in Army Group A, when its new leader was hundreds of miles away from the troops he commanded?

All this upheaval was part of Hitler's response to the realization that the oil of the Caucasus would not be captured by the Germans as planned – something which he had said had to be achieved or else he would have to 'end this war'. There was further confirmation of the parlous condition of the German war effort when General Friedrich Fromm, head of armaments supply for the army, presented a devastating memo to Hitler at the end of September. Fromm laid out, with the help of 'attached documents', the detailed reasons why a war on 'two to three fronts' would not be 'bearable' in the long run, not least because of the likely 'intervention of the Americans and the beginning of the air war [the bombardment of German cities]'. But Fromm did more than point out that the Germans would inevitably lose the war if they carried on fighting, he suggested they immediately seek a way out of the conflict. Hitler should 'disengage' from leadership of the Wehrmacht to 'address' the 'foreign policy problems'.[57] The task of the armed forces should now 'merely consist in preventing any serious setbacks until the negotiations would have reached a satisfactory close'. The aim was not to gain a 'victory', but to 'avert a disaster'.[58]

Hitler's reaction to this depressing report was predictable. He criticized the messenger. But Fromm was not removed from office. Hitler must have realized after his recent spate of sackings that his supply of experienced military administrators was not inexhaustible.[59]

By the time he read Fromm's memo, Hitler was concerned not just about Army Group A and its stalled advance towards the Caucasus, but about the progress of Army Group B and the Sixth Army under General Paulus. While the journey across the flat steppe between the River Don and the Volga had been relatively easy going for the Germans, as they neared Stalingrad the resistance of the Red Army had intensified. 'The Russian field fortifications which were staggered west of Stalingrad', said Joachim Stempel of the 14th Panzer Division, 'had been prepared and extended in such a way that they really did represent a huge obstacle.' In particular, Stempel and his men feared powerful 'Russian flamethrowers' because they inflicted 'the most gruesome burns and injuries on our side'.[60]

Anatoly Mereshko, commander of a unit of officer cadets, confirmed that 'Nearer to Stalingrad there were better-equipped trenches, various fire positions, observation points, and defence was properly organized in accordance with laws of military art.' But the casualty rate in his unit was still high. 'The worst was to look at the [German] tanks driving across the trenches with our cadets in them. And then those tanks turned round and again moved back, crushing everything, burying our soldiers alive . . . Those who say that they never felt fear at war are lying. Everyone feels fear. No one wants to die, but in this respect the commander is in a more advantageous position. He has to set an example to his subordinates. We Russians have a saying, "In public death is beautiful." In other words, if your hundred men look at you, you behave differently. It's frightening, but you suppress fear. You know that you can get killed.'[61]

Despite Soviet resistance, the Sixth Army reached the outskirts of Stalingrad at the end of August 1942. This city, which at the start of the campaign had been perceived by the Germans as a sideshow compared to the main offensive directed towards the Caucasus, would now become the site of one of the defining struggles of the war. It was to be a battle not just between Nazi Germany and the Soviet Union, but between the two protagonists – Adolf Hitler and Joseph Stalin.

12. Struggle on the Volga

On the afternoon of Sunday 23 August 1942, eleven-year-old Valentina Krutova was picking berries not far from her home in Stalingrad when she heard a rumbling noise. She looked up and saw wave after wave of warplanes, black against the sky. Moments later a series of explosions ripped through the city. Flames rose from the large industrial plants and oil tanks near the River Volga, and closer by women and children fled in panic from their burning wooden houses.

It was the start of several days of bombing by the Luftwaffe that resulted in the deaths of up to 25,000 people.[1] The casualties were high because more than half a million civilians were still living in the city. 'It was Stalin's order,' said Valentina, 'which said we won't surrender Stalingrad. People were not allowed to leave . . . There was a lot of faith in Stalin, and that's why everyone hoped that the city would not be surrendered.'[2]

Fourteen-year-old Albert Burkovski also witnessed the attack. He was down at the Volga, fetching water. 'We didn't think the Germans would come,' he said. 'But when the bombing began it was really horrible. I can still remember the planes, the noise they were making, and it became real hell. I don't know how people managed to bear it.' When he returned home he discovered that his house had been destroyed: 'There's nothing. I can only hear the groaning, screaming. I dumped this water and burst out crying. I couldn't do anything. I cried in the hope that somebody would come to the rescue. But what could you do, even if you had shovels? We came two days later and could still hear some noises. The children had not suffocated yet. I was left all alone. Burnt house, dead people, everything is mixed up . . .'[3] Albert Burkovski's grandmother, and everyone else in the house, had been killed in the largest air attack yet mounted on the eastern front.

Just a few days later, on 3 September, Joachim Stempel stood on raised ground close to the Volga and looked out over Stalingrad as it burnt beneath him. 'It was a very impressive thing to be standing on the border with Asia and being able to say – we're at the Volga! . . . It was an inspirational feeling . . . We thought it can't take much longer now – we're here.'[4]

It's not hard to imagine why Stempel believed that he and his German comrades had reached their final goal. Though the ultimate geographical objective of Operation Barbarossa had never been explained to them, they believed that Stalingrad on the River Volga, 1,400 miles from Berlin, was as far east as they needed to advance. It was a feeling confirmed by the view Stempel saw in front of him. Beyond the wide Volga, there was nothing 'but forests, more forests, plains and the endless horizon'. In short, east of them, there was nothing worth conquering.

None of them realized that not only had they not reached the end, they were only at the beginning. Ahead of them lay a brutal struggle for control of the burning city below them. Over the months to come Stalingrad would become famous as a symbol of Soviet resistance. The irony was that, as we have seen, the capture of Stalingrad had never been part of the original German plan of Operation Blue. It was only after the offensive began that Hitler had demanded that the Sixth Army take the city, instead of merely destroying its industrial infrastructure.

Some officers within the Sixth Army, like Günther von Below, thought that for Hitler the city came to have 'a symbolic significance, because of its association with his enemy Stalin, so taking Stalingrad was, for him, some kind of ideological victory over Bolshevism. I'm sure that somehow contributed to his decision.'[5] Originally called Tsaritsyn, the city had been renamed Stalingrad in 1925 in honour of Stalin's presence there during the revolution.

Geography appeared to favour the attacker. Stalingrad stretched in a narrow line along the west bank of the Volga for more than 20 miles, but was seldom more than a few miles wide. It was an unusual shape for an urban centre – the plan dictated by the presence of the giant river. And with the Germans surrounding the city on three sides, the only route for supplies was across the Volga from the east bank, a perilous crossing under German artillery fire.

The officer tasked with taking the city was Friedrich Paulus, commander of the Sixth Army, a tall scholarly-looking man in his early fifties. 'He came across as being very cool and superior,' said Gerhard Hindenlang, a battalion commander at Stalingrad. 'He was an outstanding General Staff officer, but he wasn't a commander of troops. He lacked heart for that. He was a ditherer.'[6] Field Marshal von Bock shared this opinion. A few months earlier he had thought Paulus had been slow to exploit the Soviet weakness at the battle of Kharkov.[7]

Paulus met with Hitler at Vinnitsa, his field headquarters in Ukraine, on 12 September to discuss the Stalingrad operation. He had arrived at a particularly fraught moment. Field Marshal List, commander of Army Group A, had just been sacked and General Halder, Army Chief of Staff, would be fired in a few days. Hitler had also recently lost his temper with Jodl, accusing him of misreporting his views. General Warlimont, who arrived at Vinnitsa shortly after all this trauma, gave an insight into the atmosphere: 'Instead of greeting me when I entered the log cabin, Hitler fixed me with a long malevolent stare and suddenly I thought: the man's confidence has gone; he has realized that his deadly game is moving to its appointed end, that Soviet Russia is not going to be overthrown at the second attempt and that now the war on two fronts, which he has unleashed by his wanton arbitrary actions, will grind the Reich to powder. My thoughts ran on: that is why he can no longer bear to have around him the generals who have too often been witnesses of his faults, his errors, his illusions and his day dreams; that is why he wishes to get away from them, why he wishes to see people around him who he feels have unlimited and unshakable confidence in him.'[8]

Paulus was exactly the kind of general who fitted into Hitler's new world. The combination of his training as a meticulous military planner together with his indecisive character meant that he lacked both the courage and the inclination to challenge the German leader. But while Paulus served a purpose for Hitler in the immediate short term, the fact that he was the antithesis of buccaneering generals like Rommel, Manstein and Guderian would soon prove counter-productive.

Initially, however, none of this seemed a problem. Capturing Stalingrad didn't appear to be a particularly challenging task. When the Germans launched a major offensive towards the city on 14 September they made good progress. They advanced towards Mamayev Kurgan, the strategically vital hill overlooking the centre of the city, as well as the railway station and the river landing stages. But the further the Germans got into the city, the more difficult their task became. All of the tactical advantages they enjoyed on the open steppe vanished in the claustrophobic atmosphere of street-to-street fighting. It wasn't just the difficulty of clearing the rubble and burnt-out buildings of the enemy, it was that in this environment raw courage counted for more than tactical sophistication. In the most famous Soviet example of this, on 14 September, the 13th Guards Rifle Division crossed the Volga under heavy fire and ran straight into the thick of the fighting. By the next day 30 per cent of the division were dead or wounded, and by the end of the battle little more than 300 of its original strength of 10,000 men were still alive.[9] But their sacrifice prevented the Germans reaching the banks of the river.

The determination of the defenders was epitomized by the commander of the 62nd Army, Vasily Chuikov. What he lacked in broad strategic thinking, he made up for in sheer toughness. Fond of alcohol – Stalin had initial doubts about giving him the 62nd Army since he thought Chuikov would 'make a mess of this army with his drinking'[10] – he also had a forceful way of showing his displeasure with subordinates. 'He went as far as beating people with his fists or with a stick, for which Stalin told him off,' said Anatoly Mereshko who served with Chuikov.[11]

Not that Chuikov was the only commander to beat up those who served in his unit. Vasily Grossman, the Soviet war correspondent, wrote of two Red Army officers who each 'has his own chain of command of punching. They are both huge, massive men, with fat, meaty fists. Actions have been brought against both of them in the Army Party Commission, but they aren't deterred. They give promises, but are unable to keep them, like drunkards. They blow their top every time.'[12]

Mereshko remembered Chuikov as 'a man of strong will. Very brave. I would even say recklessly brave. Army commanders don't need to be that recklessly brave. For example he always liked to reach the front line, [and] he demanded from us that we always reach the front line. He always caught you out on your lies if you hadn't been to the front line but said you had . . . He would just ask all minute details . . . He was very tough on control.'

According to Mereshko, Chuikov was not a 'great strategist', but he was nonetheless 'good at tactics', someone who 'could sense well the course of the battle, and could take timely decisions and in spite of all the obstacles carry out his decision. This was his main quality – perseverance . . . I can understand why Paulus couldn't understand Chuikov's tactics, because Paulus was used to strategic thinking, and you didn't need any strategic thinking there. You had to know the tactics of street-fighting.'[13]

Chuikov's character, if not his supposed heavy drinking, would undoubtedly have appealed to Stalin. Like Zhukov, he was interested in the end much less than the means. And if the means meant ruthlessly using the human resources at his disposal then so be it.

However, it would be a mistake to suppose that all of the Red Army soldiers in Stalingrad were prepared to sacrifice themselves for the greater cause. A number of them shirked their responsibilities, and consequently were treated without pity. More than 13,000 people died at the hands of the Soviet authorities during the battle. This kind of draconian discipline was inconceivable in the armies of the western Allies.

Paradoxically, the geography of the city, which initially had seemed to favour the Germans, benefited the Red Army in one key respect. There was nowhere to retreat. With the Germans in front and the river behind, the default position for the Soviet troops had to be to stand and fight. Chuikov's declaration 'there is no land beyond the Volga' became the motto of the defenders.

Many in the Sixth Army just couldn't understand the determination of the Soviets to carry on the struggle. In an echo of Hitler's incomprehension in the summer of 1940 when the British did not give up fighting, one soldier in Stalingrad wrote to his loved ones back home, 'We often think that Russia should capitulate, but these uneducated people are too stupid to realize it.'[14]

As the German offensive stuttered to a halt, a bitter fight ensued for individual buildings – one for which the soldiers of the Wehrmacht were ill prepared. 'We were fighting for the stairwell,' remembered Gerhard Münch of the 71st Infantry Division. 'We were on the first floor and the Russians were in the basement. Only hand grenades were thrown, other than that nothing happened – nothing else was possible since the Russians were in the basement of the same house, we were above them . . . the army hadn't been trained for this style of house-to-house fighting, not at all, it had never been practised.'[15]

'House-to-house fighting was dreadful,' confirmed Joachim Stempel. 'The soldiers were all confronted with a very different [situation] at that point. When we were standing in front of the factories – the tractor factory, the armaments factory, the metallurgical factory and, last but not least, the bread factory – you could no longer ascertain what was what, because previously unnoticed enemy [soldiers] were suddenly firing from all sides and so [we were] attacked from behind . . . We had never experienced fighting of this kind.'[16]

Those September days were fraught not just for the soldiers in Stalingrad, but for their respective leaders, Hitler and Stalin. For Hitler a sense of desperation was growing. On 11 September, when presented with a report that showed not only that Stalin still had two million soldiers available to fight in the south, but also that the Soviets were producing more than a thousand tanks a month, he turned on the speaker 'with foam at the corner of his mouth, and with clenched fists' said he would not 'tolerate such idiotic twaddle'.[17] The German leader just could not bear to listen to this kind of bad news – especially given that he had come so close to his goal. The Sixth Army had almost managed to clear Stalingrad of the Red Army, just as the soldiers of Army Group A had almost managed to reach the oil wells of the Caucasus. But almost was not good enough.

Hitler travelled to Berlin at the end of September and gave a speech to thousands of junior officers. 'That was the only time that I saw him close up during the war, the speech to the officer cadets at the Sportpalast,' said Carlheinz Behnke of the Waffen SS. 'At the time we were still impressed, he was wearing a field-grey uniform, the Iron Cross first class was the only decoration.' Like Behnke, each member of Hitler's audience had grown up within the Nazi state and had been educated from an early age to believe in their Führer's almost mystical power. Above all, they had been told to have 'faith' in Adolf Hitler. So it's not surprising that Behnke and many of his comrades were still 'unconditionally prepared to pledge ourselves to the Führer'.

Timing was also part of the reason for their continued confidence. They were largely ignorant of the fundamental problem of lack of resources, and so from their perspective it still seemed that victory might be in sight. And Hitler promised them no ordinary victory, but a gigantic colonization of the east – one that offered them all glory. 'He developed a vision which was inconceivable,' said Behnke. 'It was a utopian view. We were fascinated . . . The fact that *Lebensraum* was being moved towards the East in a common Great Europe. At the time I thought that was right. Without giving a thought to all the things associated with it, killing people and so on and so forth . . . And nowadays we sometimes say in jest, we can be glad that we lost the war, because otherwise I would be a regional commander, a gauleiter, somewhere and be performing my duties somewhere far away from home . . . I think we simply felt superior somehow, you see. Superior to the Slavonic peoples. It seems naïve today when you think about it. This huge empire!'[18]

The second speech that Hitler delivered on his brief visit to Berlin was more problematic for him. This was an address to mark the start of the annual charitable campaign for 'Winter Relief'. Not only did this remind the German people that another winter was approaching with the Wehrmacht still fighting in the east, but the previous year Hitler had spoken as if the war against Stalin was almost won, and the newspapers had come close to proclaiming victory in the east. Demonstrably, that hadn't happened. And the subsequent entry of America into the war now prompted the question – how could the Germans ever be victorious?

In that respect, the battle for Stalingrad was emblematic. This city, which at the start of the offensive had been of little consequence, now symbolized the German achievement in the war in the east. And even though Hitler denied that Stalingrad was of interest 'because this place bears Stalin's name', he did admit that it was in a 'strategically important location'. He also made this vow: 'you can rest assured that no one can take us away from this place.' This was an even more definite promise than the one he had reneged on the previous October, when he had assured the Germans that the Red Army 'will never rise again'. This time he staked his reputation on a specific city. His soldiers would not leave Stalingrad. That was his deliberate and unambiguous assurance.

Hitler didn't need to make this promise. He could have omitted that sentence from his speech without a problem. So why did he decide to say it? Most likely it would have been to encourage the German soldiers currently fighting for the city, and reassure their relatives back at home that their sacrifice was worthwhile. But it's also probable that he was indulging in a trick he had practised many times before. By stating this promise with sufficient conviction, he was trying to convince himself and others that it would happen. It was another form of burning his boats – a variant on the either/or portrayal of events that had been his preferred method of rhetorical discourse for years.

Above all else, Hitler was keen to show that progress was being made, and that this fight was not stagnating as the First World War had done. Significantly, he said during the speech that 'at a time when seemingly nothing is happening, enormous things are still being created.'[19] One reason for this reassurance was obvious – the increased suffering of the German people at home from Allied bombing raids. Hitler admitted that Churchill, 'the man who has invented bomb warfare against an innocent civilian population', had recently promised that the bombing campaign would be 'greatly increased'. But he immediately saw this threat as the work of Jews who he claimed were 'behind' both Churchill and 'the

great warmonger Roosevelt'. In a chilling reference to the extermination of the Jews that was currently under way, he promised that the
Jews will soon not 'feel like laughing any more'.

However, for a large proportion of the ordinary German population
living under the threat of Allied bombing raids, what mattered most
was whether or not their houses would be destroyed. So Hitler's words
demonstrated his own priorities. He couldn't stop the bombing, but he
could kill the Jews.

One other reference he made in his long and often tedious speech is
worth mentioning. In contrast to Stalin, who had recently introduced
awards like the Order of Suvorov specifically for senior officers, Hitler
gloried in the fact that the Knight's Cross could be won by a soldier of
whatever rank – the only criterion was that the recipient was a 'brave
man who is fit to be a leader of his people'. That Germany's highest
award for valour could be received by anyone in the army demonstrated,
he said, 'the collapse of an old world'.

For many Germans, Hitler's emphasis on the elimination of the class
structure was a major reason for his appeal. 'Some things will remain for
ever,' said a captured German officer, secretly taped by the British. 'They
will last for hundreds of years. Not the roads [the Nazis built] – they are
unimportant. But what will last is the way in which the state has been
organised, particularly the inclusion of the working man as part of the
state. He [Hitler] really has made a place for the working man in the state
and no one has ever done that before . . . This principle of everyone
working for the common cause, the idea that the industrialist is really the
trustee for the capital represented by German labour and for the other
capital, all sounds so easy, but no one managed it before.'[20]

But in this classless Nazi utopia there would not be equality of the
sexes. A woman's primary function was to care for her husband and
children, with the image of the German mother almost deified in Nazi
propaganda. Though several hundred thousand women served as auxiliaries in the Wehrmacht, they worked as secretaries or nurses or in other
non-combat roles. The idea of women fighting at the front line was
totally anathema to Hitler. However, Stalin took a very different view.
Many of the more than a million women in the Red Army served in
combat roles, as tank commanders, snipers or fighter pilots.

Wilhelm Roes, a member of the SS Leibstandarte, fought against T34
tanks manned by Soviet women. After observing them as POWs, he

concluded that 'They were so hard, so fanatical, these women. I mean they were probably all volunteers. If you looked at their eyes, if looks could kill they would have killed us on the spot. They were put on a truck and taken to the rear – I don't know what happened to them. We talked about this for a long time [afterwards] within our tank. First people said [to me], "You stop [being part of our crew], we'll have a young girl in here instead, so we'll have more fun." That's the way we started talking about this.' He and his comrades 'couldn't really understand' why the Soviets permitted women to fight in combat as 'in the Third Reich our women were placed on a pedestal. The mother is the one who bore the children and I always had a great respect for women. My mother was just a wonderful person.'[21]

Roes and his comrades thought women serving in combat roles was 'typical of a communist regime. They do everything to get the foe out of their land.' In a way, he was correct. The extensive use of women in Soviet forces was a result, in part, of the perilous situation in which the country found itself. As Tamara Kalmykova, who fought at Stalingrad as a communications officer, said: 'A woman in fighting is a rare phenomenon. But here the fighting was so hard that I couldn't stand aside. How can I not be revengeful, if twenty-eight people bearing my name [her relatives] died and seven returned [home] crippled, or if some of my people died in concentration camps, or were burnt alive. Any woman of any nationality will, if she is put in my place, behave the same.'[22]

However, the widespread participation of women in the Soviet war effort also reflected a philosophical difference between the two regimes. Hitler did not allow women to bear arms and serve in the front line even towards the end of the war, as the Red Army advanced into Germany, whereas women had played an active role in the creation of the modern industrialized Soviet state during the 1930s. The Nazi notion that women should focus on the 'three Ks – *Kinder* (children), *Küche* (kitchen) and *Kirche* (the Church)' was anathema to the Soviet Communist Party. But that does not mean that Soviet women did not suffer discrimination. For instance, the use of 'campaign wives' – the practice of a commander selecting a Soviet woman to be his sexual companion – was tolerated within the higher reaches of the Red Army. So much so that the war correspondent Vasily Grossman described the use of campaign wives as 'our great sin'.[23] These women were often junior in rank to the man who desired them, and so pressure could be placed on them to comply.

Women in the Red Army faced other difficulties. 'I must say, conditions were really very hard,' said Ekatarina Petluk, a tank driver with the 3rd Tank Army. 'For me, a woman, the worst time was my monthly period. There was seldom enough cotton wool or bandages. I had to improvise and use whatever I could find. You must understand, I was young and very shy. I had to keep my dignity and my femininity, surrounded by so many men.'[24]

Every soldier in the Red Army – whether male or female – was expected to endure the most difficult of conditions. In Stalingrad, for instance, Albert Burkovski remembered communication teams living in sewers: 'It was very humid, very damp, and also the smell was unpleasant. They were short of oxygen there . . . But they were safe. Because no mines, no grenades could break through such thick walls. They stayed in the sewage till the very end.' To amuse themselves in the sewers, when not on duty, the soldiers played 'lice races'. And 'whoever's louse was the first to reach the end won.'[25]

The ability of Red Army soldiers to put up with such privation was a crucial advantage in their struggle against the Germans. Vasily Grossman wrote that while Russians were 'brought up to hardship . . . Germans, on the other hand, are prepared for easy victories that would be based on technological superiority, and they give in to the hardship caused by nature.'[26]

Chuikov demanded that those under his command stay as close as possible to the Germans on the front line. This not only negated the Germans' ability to use artillery against the Red Army, but also forced them to fight the Soviets on their own terms – often hand to hand. Helmut Walz, a private with the 305th Infantry Division, remembered how he and his comrades tried to adapt to this unfamiliar method of combat. 'At one time or another, we all had to make use of the spade. At the time we received the new spades – which were folding [models] and you had to screw them together – but they could also be a terrible weapon . . . it takes only a second, you could hit someone over the head or hit him in the stomach or somewhere else when there was nothing else to be done.'[27]

On 14 October the Germans mounted another offensive against the Red Army in Stalingrad. Once again the defenders buckled under the pressure, but did not break. There were even rumours that Stalin had arrived in the city to support them personally – false, of course, but nonetheless symptomatic of the powerful, almost mystical, figure that the Soviet leader had become for those fighting for the motherland.[28]

Far from exhorting the troops on the front line, Stalin was safe in his office in the Kremlin, letting his suspicious mind run wild. 'All of us in Moscow have formed the impression that Churchill is intent on the defeat of the USSR in order to then come to terms with . . . Hitler . . . at our expense,' he wrote in a dispatch to Maisky, his Ambassador in London, on 19 October. Stalin believed that 'without such a supposition' it was 'difficult to explain' why Churchill had refused to launch the second front, was 'progressively reducing' arms shipments to the Soviet Union and had recently decided not to try Rudolf Hess until after the war. Stalin's suspicions about the fate of Hess, Hitler's deputy, who had been in British hands since May 1941, verged on the pathological. Stalin also asserted 'on the question of the systematic bombing of Berlin' that 'Churchill proclaimed . . . in Moscow' he would do this in September, but he had not fulfilled this 'one iota, despite the fact that he could undoubtedly do it'.[29]

Churchill, of course, was not plotting to take Britain out of the war, and Stalin's words are mostly revealing about his profound sense of anxiety. But there was, however, an underlying truth behind his message. The reality was that the western Allies were not doing that much to help the Red Army deal with the German onslaught on the eastern front.

Moreover, Stalin's telegram to Maisky also demonstrates that Stalin thought the fate of the Soviet Union was still in the balance. It's a useful reminder not to assume from the victory they gained several months later at Stalingrad that Red Army soldiers were somehow destined to succeed.

The Germans' October offensive, like their previous efforts to take the city, ground to a standstill. 'With hindsight,' said Gerhard Münch, a German infantry officer who fought in Stalingrad, 'the whole thing seems quite insane, because there is no longer any point to it, you see. There is no longer any intention to change [the situation] because of the lack of the resources that could bring about such a change. We were running out of people and, in any case, a shock troop leader cannot be found just like that. It is pointless being allocated soldiers who have been trained for ten weeks back home, and being asked to post them among the rubble at Stalingrad; it's not even worth attempting, I might as well just send them back home again . . . By the next morning, they'll all be dead anyway, because they just don't have the experience, they lack the right instincts, you see.'[30]

The daily losses were such that German officers could work out how long it would take before there were no Wehrmacht soldiers left in the city.[31] And it appeared that back at his headquarters Hitler might well have been performing similar calculations. His Luftwaffe adjutant noticed that he 'often seemed unduly pensive and far away . . . Did he truly believe even now that the war could end in a German victory? The question was surfacing for the first time. The answer could not be fathomed.'[32]

Hitler was concerned not just about Stalingrad, but about a possible landing by Allied troops in North Africa. It was a possibility that became a reality on 8 November, when 100,000 Allied soldiers, including Americans for the first time, invaded Algeria and French Morocco. The timing could scarcely have been worse for the German leader. This was the anniversary of the Beer Hall Putsch, and Hitler had travelled to Munich to give his traditional commemorative speech that evening. But what could he say about the Allied invasion? Every German knew that the arrival of the Americans in France in the First World War had marked a low point in their country's fortunes. Now here they were fighting the Germans on the battlefield once again. As Goebbels wrote in his diary: 'we are standing at a turning point of the war.'[33]

Although in private Hitler did not 'underrate the American initiative',[34] in public he pretended that the subject wasn't worth discussing. In his lengthy speech at the Löwenbräukeller in Munich he made just one brief reference to the invasion, saying that if Roosevelt – 'this old gangster' – was claiming that the attack was to 'protect' North Africa from the Germans then 'there is no need to say a word on this untruthful claim.' For the rest, it was familiar stuff. Once again he reminded his audience that he had been laughed at when he prophesied that the Jews would be 'exterminated' if they caused another world war, but countless numbers of those who had laughed at the time 'don't laugh any more'. And he assured his audience that the Germans were preparing a devastating response to the Allied bombing campaign.

However, despite this bluster, he could not conceal his inability to deliver on the promises he had previously made. Stalingrad, he had to admit, had still not been taken, though he claimed 'there are only a few tiny places [of resistance] left'. But it didn't really matter, he said, that the city had not fallen, because ships were no longer travelling on the Volga.

Hitler must have realized how lamely he was coming across because towards the end of his speech he said that it was better if the German armed forces spoke for him on the battlefield. In the future he planned to speak 'only on rare occasions'. He ended the address on a predictable note, saying that his audience must always remember that 'this war will decide the existence or non-existence of our Volk'.[35]

The whole speech smacked of weakness and excuse. Hitler just could not hide the fact that Germany appeared to be losing the war. Indeed, the situation was so bad that some of those close to him were even talking about trying to make peace with the Soviet Union. As Hitler's train had travelled towards Munich, two days before his speech, it had stopped briefly at Bamberg in Bavaria so that he could meet with Ribbentrop. The German Foreign Minister proposed that an approach should be made to Stalin via Soviet diplomats in neutral Sweden in order to end the war in the east. Hitler rejected the plan, saying that 'A moment of weakness was not the proper time to negotiate with an enemy.'[36]

The pressure on Hitler was mounting – and not just as a result of the way the war was going, but because he was not used to regular working hours. Prior to the war he had led the life of a dilettante, often not getting up until late in the morning. According to Fritz Wiedemann, his personal adjutant in the 1930s, Hitler even 'disliked the study of documents'. Wiedemann said that he had 'sometimes secured decisions' from Hitler, 'even ones about important matters, without his ever asking to see the relevant files. He took the view that many things sorted themselves out on their own if one did not interfere.'[37] But these laissez-faire days were behind him, replaced by the strain of holding regular military conferences and often feeling isolated and under attack by those who attended.

Hitler now retreated to the Berghof in the mountains above Berchtesgaden for a holiday of sorts. The Berghof symbolized the good old days of country walks and cream teas. But it was one of the worst places he could have chosen at this precise moment, given that he insisted on controlling the detailed strategy of his troops nearly 1,500 miles away. For on 19 November, while Hitler was resting on the Obersalzberg, the Red Army launched one of the most formidable attacks of the war.

The offensive, codenamed Operation Uranus, had its origins in a meeting between Stalin, Zhukov and Aleksandr Vasilevsky, Chief of the General Staff, back in September. As Stalin was examining a map he overheard Zhukov and Vasilevsky talking about 'another solution' to the Stalingrad problem. Instead of berating them for not focusing on his own views, he asked the two to spend time developing their idea. When they returned Zhukov and Vasilevsky presented Stalin with a radical plan – an attempt to encircle the Germans and their allies by cutting into their supply lines far west of the city. Stalin was initially concerned that the attack would be too far away from the fighting in Stalingrad – one thrust would be more than a hundred miles north-west of the city – but after some persuasion he accepted the idea.[38]

This is a key moment in the history. It wasn't just that the plan was so adventurous. What was at least as intriguing was Stalin's new willingness to encourage his generals to come up with creative solutions themselves on such a vast scale. Stalin's growing trust in Zhukov appears to have been the principal reason for this fresh development. A study of the messages sent between the two men in the autumn of 1942 reveals a change in tone from the Soviet leader. He was now writing 'What are you planning?' and 'Do you think?' rather than dictating what should be done and moving swiftly to criticize. It wasn't that he had suddenly turned into a caring person. He could still be just as scathing to other generals as he had been in the past. But Zhukov was treated differently. Stalin, the man who had built his career on trusting no one, appeared to be trusting this son of a cobbler from the province of Kaluga.[39]

Though there is some controversy about the exact date of the meeting between Stalin, Zhukov and Vasilevsky, there is no question about the substantive issue – Stalin listened to his generals and placed special confidence in Zhukov. The contrast with Hitler's actions at the same time could hardly have been greater. For at precisely the moment that Stalin was displaying an element of collegiateness, not only was Hitler interfering in the detailed decisions of his military commanders, but in Paulus he had appointed a man who demonstrably lacked initiative. And while no one can pretend that these were the only reasons for what was about to happen, they were certainly essential preconditions for the disaster that would shortly befall the German Sixth Army.

The attempt to encircle the Sixth Army in Stalingrad would primarily target the Romanian forces protecting the rear areas to the west of the city. Romanian units were not as well motivated, as well led or as well armed as their German allies. But this was not the only astute part of the idea. Even though the offensive employed more than half of all the available tanks the Soviets possessed, the scale of the operation was successfully concealed from the Germans by a massive deception plan. Fake bridges were built far away from the actual direction of the offensive in order to mislead the German reconnaissance effort. Military units were camouflaged during the day and then moved into position under cover of darkness. Bridges that were to be used in the attack were constructed a foot or so underwater so as to make their existence hard to detect from the air.

But perhaps the single greatest innovation was the way Soviet armour was to be coordinated with infantry. 'Previously tank units were used mainly as a support for infantry,' said Ivan Golokolenko, an officer in a tank unit who took part in Operation Uranus. 'But this new idea was very different. At some narrow stretch of the front the defence would be broken and then through this narrow gap two tank corps would be introduced. The objective of the tank corps was to bypass the enemy's fortified areas and points of resistance and go deeper and deeper to capture the really important points like bridges or city towers. Infantry was supposed to follow the progress of the tanks and clear up whatever was left – this was the new thing.'[40]

Fyodor Bubenchikov, a battalion commander, was also learning fresh skills: 'At the courses you were taught new tactics . . . We were taught to be flexible, not to fight the enemy in the straightforward way, but to be able to encircle, to strike from the flanks, to use artillery. We were told to teach the soldiers not to be afraid of the enemy's tanks and planes. The main thing was not to run away, not to be afraid.'[41]

Zhukov and Vasilevsky presented their final plans to Stalin in mid-November. Zhukov said the Soviet leader was in a 'good frame of mind' and 'listened to us intently. Because he did not rush to smoke his pipe, [but instead] stroked his moustache and did not once interrupt our report, it was obvious that he was pleased.'[42]

Early in the morning of 19 November, just before the start of the offensive, a message from Stalin was read to the waiting troops. Ivan Golokolenko felt the words were 'fatherly . . . parental' and they brought him 'close to tears . . . I felt a real upsurge, a spiritual upsurge.' And while we can't be certain how common this kind of reaction was, the evidence is that many other soldiers were similarly affected.[43] Once again, Stalin had made a patriotic appeal to his troops. In that respect his job was more straightforward than Hitler's. It was easy for Soviet citizens to understand why they should resist. The Germans had invaded their land and were trying to kill them.

From the very first day of the offensive it was apparent that Operation Uranus would succeed. 'You can't say that we went on without facing the enemy's resistance,' said Ivan Golokolenko, 'but it was easier than it used to be. The enemies were not as active. They seemed to be more at a loss. They didn't seem to have prepared any fortified areas, they hadn't prepared their positions.'

Golokolenko's unit quickly seized the headquarters of a Romanian corps, along with their storage depot: 'we captured a lot of warehouses with ammunition and food supplies. We helped ourselves to the food that we found in their warehouses. There were things that the Soviet soldiers had never seen in their lives: liquorice, chocolates, and sausages and cheeses and wines and pickles and – amazing things. It was only natural that we had a binge. My friend, who was the commander of a tank company, could hardly wake up his driver because the driver got so drunk.'[44]

Hitler, who was still in southern Bavaria, learnt of the start of Operation Uranus when General Zeitzler got in touch from headquarters in East Prussia. Hitler ordered that the 48th Panzer, under General Heim, push the Red Army back. But Heim's forces were inadequate for the task and failed. As a consequence, Hitler subsequently sentenced Heim to death. This absurd attempt to assign personal blame to one general for a catastrophe that had many causes was later corrected and the sentence commuted, but it demonstrated the German leader's state of mind at the time. He was reacting as Stalin had in the early, panic-filled days of the summer of 1941, with General Heim initially treated like the hapless General Pavlov.

Although the Soviets had broken through Romanian forces guarding the flanks of the German position, Hitler still refused to believe that the Sixth Army in Stalingrad was in peril. According to Below, his Luftwaffe adjutant, while he accepted that the Sixth Army could be temporarily surrounded, he believed the Germans would soon be able to organize a successful rescue mission.[45]

Just three days after the launch of Operation Uranus, Red Army units from the north met up with those coming from the south and the Sixth Army was encircled. Ivan Golokolenko and his comrades saw this as a turning point in the war. The encirclement showed that 'we were

capable of beating the enemy and this operation stands out in my memory as the brightest and most memorable event in my military career.'
For Golokolenko it wasn't just the fact that the Germans and their allies
had been pushed back that was satisfying, it was that the Red Army had
humiliated their enemy as a result of superior tactical skill: 'We had been
trained to advance at night . . . It was deep night, two or three a.m. perhaps. We were going into [village] houses and waking up Germans. I
went into one house and saw a German officer lying in bed with a Russian woman. He got up and started to get dressed in our presence.'[46]

By now Hitler was travelling back to his headquarters in East Prussia.
The journey took much longer than usual as he kept stopping the train in
order to call his military commanders. And his message at each stop could
not have been clearer – the Sixth Army was forbidden to attempt a break-
out. 'The army is temporarily encircled by Russian forces,' Hitler declared,
with the emphasis no doubt on the word 'temporarily', and 'The 6th
Army must know that I am doing everything to help it and to relieve it.'[47]

Despite the sudden encirclement, the mood in the Sixth Army was
relatively positive. As Gerhard Münch, still fighting in Stalingrad, put
it: 'The prospect of an army being encircled for any length of time or of
an entire army being given the order to stay put was inconceivable. The
possibility never even occurred to us.'[48]

Hubert Menzel, another German officer trapped in Stalingrad, had
been flown into the city just days before the Soviet offensive, after his
appointment as chief of operations of the 16th Panzer Division. Like
many German soldiers he knew that Wehrmacht units had been rescued
from encirclements before, most notably earlier in the year at Demyansk.
But, in a way, that knowledge – and their trust in Hitler's promise to
come to their aid – created an atmosphere of passivity that ill served the
soldiers of the Sixth Army. Like a number of post-war military experts,
Menzel came to the view that the only way they could possibly have
been saved would have been to act fast: 'Had the supreme command been
able to send something to help the Stalingrad army to fight their way out
at that point, then it could have been done.'[49] Whether that would have
worked is impossible to know for sure, although it's hard to imagine how
the malnourished soldiers in Stalingrad could have fought their way to
safety without a relief column close to them. But such discussions are
purely academic: Hitler would never have permitted such an early break-
out attempt to be made, because he appeared convinced the situation

could be resolved without the German troops leaving Stalingrad. When Paulus asked Hitler a few days into the encirclement if he could try to escape the Soviet ring, he was told to stay where he was.

Hitler, despite objections from others, was persuaded by Göring that it would be possible to supply the Sixth Army from the air. It was a ridiculously optimistic idea. A combination of the winter weather and Soviet anti-aircraft guns meant that the daily target of 500 tons of supplies could never be met over a sustained period.

As they sat it out, waiting for the crisis to be resolved, Menzel marvelled at the ability of his men to cope: 'It was an incredible performance when lying in a crater, just in the snow, unable to sleep, very little food and [yet] still to say, I won't give up . . . Night after night they'd lie in an icy hole, very badly fed, decreasing [in numbers] all the time, and they'd still hold out, fire at once if the Russians approached. They held out for one and a half months, being outnumbered umpteen times. Once an icy hole had been lost, they mounted a counter-attack immediately and regained the hole in the snow. So it was an incredible achievement.'[50]

Conditions for the Soviet civilians trapped inside the German-occupied section of Stalingrad also grew worse after the encirclement, and unlike the soldiers around them they did not even have meagre rations to eat. 'The winter was very harsh,' said Valentina Krutova, who was eleven years old at the time, and who tried to survive alongside her elder brother and younger sister. 'All three of us slept in one bed. We had nothing to heat the house with. We had nothing to wear. One day my brother went to look for food but didn't find anything. One day he climbed into the attic of one of the houses, where he found either some cowhide or horsehide. He didn't know what to do with it. It was too hard to be cut with a knife, and he had to use a saw to cut it . . . and we roasted this hide on the fire. We couldn't chew it but we could suck it. The salt that was in it somehow satisfied our hunger. This is how we survived. By the end, when we ran out of this food, we thought it was the end. We were just lying in bed without getting up.'[51]

A rescue attempt – Operation Winter Storm – was finally launched under the command of Field Marshal von Manstein on 12 December. But despite making good initial progress, German units soon began to bog down. The problem was not just the bad weather, but that Manstein's troops faced being trapped themselves. The Soviets had powerful forces in the surrounding area, ready to take part in another offensive, Operation

Saturn, which aimed to cut off the Germans' Army Group A to the south. The potential destruction of the Sixth Army was bad enough, but this new threat – both to Army Group A and to Manstein's soldiers – was worse.

In the light of all this, Manstein realized he could not progress much further, and so called for the Sixth Army to fight its way out of Stalingrad in an attempt to reach his relief force, but Hitler rejected the idea. The deterioration in the battle readiness of the Sixth Army since the encirclement, partly the result of the failure of Göring's Luftwaffe to supply it adequately from the air, meant that any attempt to leave Stalingrad would have been almost suicidal. On 23 December, Manstein's relief effort was abandoned.

The Soviets knew they were about to win an enormous victory, but they underestimated the scale of their forthcoming triumph. They thought there were fewer than 90,000 people caught within the encirclement.[52] In fact, more than a quarter of a million Germans and their allies now awaited their inevitable fate at Stalingrad.[53]

The atmosphere among the trapped soldiers was predictably grim. For instance, after learning that officers in his artillery regiment had committed suicide, Gerhard Münch discussed with his 'own company commanders' whether they should 'all shoot ourselves together'. They decided against the idea only because 'as long as soldiers had to be led under our command, we did not have any moral right to commit suicide.'[54]

On 12 January 1943, in an attempt to ensure that Hitler knew the true plight of the Sixth Army, Paulus ordered Captain Winrich Behr, a decorated panzer officer on the intelligence staff, to fly out of the encirclement and report personally to the German leader. Once in Hitler's presence Behr insisted on telling the brutal truth. In front of the Führer and two dozen other senior officers, he recounted how the soldiers of the Sixth Army were not only starving and disease ridden, but were holding out with ever diminishing supplies of ammunition. Hitler insisted that a great relief operation was imminent – something Behr, who had met Manstein before his encounter with the Führer, knew was untrue. But still Hitler attempted with his rhetoric to create a mirage of approaching redemption.[55] As for Behr, he believed that the German leader 'had lost touch with reality. He lived in a fantasy world of maps and flags . . . It was the end of all my illusions about Hitler. I was convinced that we would now lose the war.'[56]

Once again, one can only marvel at Hitler's capacity for self-deception. Just like Stalin in the run-up to the launch of Operation Barbarossa, he appeared to be living in a self-constructed reality – one that did not conform to the facts. Did he really think that the Sixth Army could still be rescued? It's hard to believe. What was essential, he must have felt, was to ensure that the soldiers in Stalingrad did not lose hope. A mass surrender would be humiliating. Far better for propaganda purposes that all the soldiers of the Sixth Army should die fighting.

Around this time, Below – Hitler's Luftwaffe adjutant – was astonished by the ability of the German leader to hold himself together and never betray 'a sign of weakness' nor show 'that he saw any situation as hopeless . . . he contrived to put a positive value on setbacks and even succeeded in convincing those who worked most closely with him'. As a consequence, even Below – who saw himself as more realistic than others – still 'did not believe that we would actually lose the war'.[57]

As Behr attended his fruitless meeting with Hitler, the Red Army was several days into Operation Ring, the attempt to liberate the city of Stalingrad itself. The Germans and their allies offered fierce resistance, helped by the knowledge that there was no point now in husbanding resources of fuel and ammunition. They all knew that this was their last stand.

As the battle thundered around him, battalion commander Gerhard Münch was ordered to fly out of the city and take dispatches to headquarters more than a hundred miles to the west. 'This was such an inconceivable idea,' recalled Münch, who did not want to leave his unit at this most terrible moment. 'My initial reaction was that it was impossible.' But the order was very real, and he could not question it.

Münch was driven to the only operative airfield within the encirclement. Here, under fire from Soviet artillery, he saw two planes coming in to land 'after some toing and froing'. Immediately after the planes had reached the ground, he 'witnessed such a gruesome scene, because from the snow, from holes everywhere, an enormous number of soldiers emerged. Soldiers who were wounded, not wounded, fleeing soldiers, and they all stormed towards the planes.' One of the pilots managed 'to get some order into the crowd so as to avoid the plane becoming overloaded and then he said: "Come on, get into the cockpit with me." '

Münch's plane taxied down the snow-covered runway with several soldiers clinging to the outside of the fuselage, 'in the hope of escaping that way'. But their presence endangered everyone on board the plane.

So once the pilot had taken off he twisted the aircraft one way and then another and the soldiers fell away into the snow.

Just a few hours later Münch was back in the relative safety of head-quarters. He never shook off the 'trauma' of leaving his troops behind: 'It stays with you. The soldiers believed in me and there existed between the soldiers and their commander that relationship of trust which is at the core of any military operation, and then, in the end, I was flown out.'[58]

On the same day that Münch escaped Stalingrad, Paulus asked Hitler if he could surrender the Sixth Army. It was obvious that further resist-ance was pointless. But Hitler dismissed the request. It went against the narrative of martyrdom he was building. And as part of that myth he promoted Paulus to field marshal eight days later. It was a sign for Paulus to commit suicide since no German field marshal had ever been cap-tured before. But Paulus refused to kill himself, and was taken alive by the Soviets as they entered the city.

Hitler was beside himself when he heard the news about Paulus. And the transcript of the situation conference at which he vented his fury offers a revealing glimpse into his mentality. 'It hurts me so much', he said, 'because the heroism of so many soldiers is destroyed by a single spineless weakling . . . What does that mean, "Life"? . . . the individual indeed has to die. What remains alive beyond the individual is the people. But how one can fear this moment – through which he (can free) himself from misery . . . !' Yet Paulus had rejected the idea of gaining 'national immortality' in favour of being eaten by 'rats' in a Soviet prison.[59]

The fundamental problem, said Hitler, was that among Germans 'the intellect is cultivated too much and strength of character not enough'. It was vital that this situation be reversed and 'strength of character' taught at the expense of the intellect. If this didn't happen, 'then we never will get that species which alone can stand the heavy blows of fate. That's decisive.'[60] For Hitler it was easy to see what course of action German soldiers should take if they were surrounded: 'you gather yourselves together, build an all-round defence, and shoot yourself with the last cartridge.'[61]

He was clear in his own mind about the need for self-sacrifice if vic-tory was not achieved. But how many of his followers agreed with him?

13. Fighting On

If you are the successful, charismatic leader of a major power you enjoy many benefits: the public adore you to the point of quasi-worship, you can make momentous decisions entirely on your own and – above all – you possess the knowledge that you are an epic figure who will be remembered by history. But there is one gigantic potential downside. If things go wrong it's hard to escape the blame. And that was the problem that Adolf Hitler faced in the wake of the German defeat at Stalingrad.

Hitler's solution was straightforward – stay out of sight. And though Stalin had also retreated from view during the disastrous early days of Operation Barbarossa, Hitler's motivation in the face of similar calamity was not quite the same. In early 1943 he almost certainly felt he was more securely in power than Stalin did back in the summer of 1941, even in the face of the loss of the Sixth Army. For a variety of institutional and personal reasons that we shall explore later, he was hard to dislodge. But as leader, particularly one who relied on his charismatic authority, he understood that it was immensely damaging to his prestige to be associated with failure.

So it was Hermann Göring who had the thankless task of giving the speech on 30 January 1943 to mark the tenth anniversary of Hitler's appointment as Chancellor. Göring tried to portray the annihilation of the Sixth Army as an heroic sacrifice, akin to Leonidas and the outnumbered Spartans who had fought the Persians at Thermopylae. But it wasn't the most effective historical parallel. The Spartans hadn't been encircled at Thermopylae by the superior tactics of their enemy. Nor had the Spartans surrendered en masse as the Sixth Army had done, although the Nazis did their best to keep that fact hidden from the German people, claiming instead they had all fought to the last.

Göring argued that because 'Providence' had allowed a 'simple fighter' like Adolf Hitler to attain greatness, then this was a guarantee of 'victory'. How was it possible, he asked, that 'all this is supposed to be meaningless?' As for the victors at Stalingrad, he claimed that the Soviets were now down to their 'last reserves' and the Red Army consisted of 'tired old men and sixteen-year-old boys'.[1] It was an assertion that was totally at odds with the reality, as this motley crew had just crushed the mighty Sixth Army.

It was not Göring's finest moment. But then his finest moments were long behind him. His current impotence was symbolized by the appearance that day of Allied bombers over Berlin – which meant his speech had to be delayed an hour. It was a humiliating demonstration of his own failure as head of the Luftwaffe, especially as he had previously promised that the German capital would never be attacked.[2]

The same day that Göring tried to put a gloss on the German defeat at Stalingrad, Joseph Goebbels read out a proclamation from Hitler. The statement made only the most oblique reference to Stalingrad – referring to an 'heroic struggle' on the Volga. Instead it focused on the 'Central Asian–Bolshevik wave' which now threatened to 'break over' Europe.[3] This, it was claimed, was the main reason why the Germans had to keep on fighting. From now until the last moments of the war, Hitler would try to terrify the German people by warning of what lay ahead for them if they surrendered. Unspoken, but understood because everyone knew the nature of the war in the east, was also the message that since a brutal war had been fought on Soviet soil by the Germans the Red Army would be seeking vengeance. There was thus no alternative but to hold out to the last.

Goebbels built on this message just over two weeks later in the most famous address he ever gave, his Total War speech. 'The goal of Bolshevism is Jewish world revolution,' he said. 'They want to bring chaos to the Reich and Europe . . . A Bolshevization of the Reich would mean the liquidation of our entire intelligentsia and leadership, and the descent of our workers into Bolshevist–Jewish slavery.'

How should the Germans confront this danger, asked Goebbels? By adopting 'equivalent, though not identical, methods' to the Bolshevists was his answer. This meant pursuing a policy of 'Total War'. Night clubs, bars, luxury shops were all to close and the German people had to work longer hours. He ended his speech by posing a series of rhetorical questions, such as 'Do you agree that those who harm the war effort should lose their heads?' and 'Is your confidence in the Führer greater, more faithful and more unshakable than ever before?'[4] Even though Goebbels' ecstatic audience consisted of supporters of the regime, it was still a bravura performance.

In private Goebbels was nothing like as confident. According to

Albert Speer, Minister of Armaments, he was speaking not just of a 'leadership crisis' but of a 'Leader crisis'.[5] Part of the problem, argued Goebbels, was the influence Martin Bormann, head of the Party Chancellery, had over Hitler. He was increasingly the gatekeeper to the German leader – a development many of the old guard resented.

Goebbels and Speer wanted to sideline Bormann, and gain more sway over Hitler themselves by creating a new advisory committee. The plan was for Hermann Göring to chair this new group and for Speer and Goebbels to be prominent members. In retrospect, Göring seems an odd choice for the role, but his legacy in the Reich remained a powerful one, both as head of the Four Year Plan and as one of the original fighters for the Nazi cause.

However, there was a problem with the attempt to enlist Göring's support. He was furious with Goebbels, in part because his favourite Berlin restaurant, Horcher, had been closed as a consequence of the Total War austerity drive. So Speer travelled to see Göring at his house on the Obersalzberg, in the mountains of southern Bavaria, in an attempt to make peace. When he met Göring, Speer 'was astonished' by his appearance. The Reichsmarschall had 'lacquered fingernails' and an 'obviously rouged face, although the oversized ruby brooch on his green velvet dressing gown was already a familiar sight to me'. As Göring listened to Speer, he 'occasionally scooped a handful of unset gems from his pocket and playfully let them glide through his fingers'.[6]

The meeting went well. Göring agreed that Bormann had accumulated too much power and that something should be done about it. He also seemed prepared to forgive Goebbels. So the Propaganda Minister immediately hurried to the Obersalzberg, writing in his diary that Göring 'received me most charmingly and is very open-hearted. His dress is somewhat baroque and would, if one did not know him, strike one as almost laughable. But that's the way he is, and one must put up with his idiosyncrasies . . .'[7]

Goebbels explained that he wanted Göring to lead a new Ministerial Council for the Defence of the Reich. Once again, Göring was receptive to the idea.[8] But even though Goebbels later told Speer that 'this is going to work' and that Göring 'has really come to life again',[9] Goebbels was sufficiently perceptive to see that Göring tended to look at events a 'little naively'. For example, Göring couldn't 'understand how the British plutocracy' could make such a 'close an alliance with

Bolshevism' – something Goebbels thought demonstrated Göring's inability 'to differentiate between expediency and real conviction'. Göring also asked 'in despair where Bolshevism still gets its weapons and soldiers [from]' – a question Goebbels dismissed as 'unimportant'. What mattered was that the Red Army 'always manages to get more'.[10]

Once they had Göring's agreement to their plan, Speer and Goebbels travelled to Ukraine to sell the idea to their Führer. At his forward headquarters at Vinnitsa, they met a volatile Hitler. He was 'very angry at the Italians' because 'they are actually doing nothing. They are no good for the Eastern Front; they are no good for North Africa; they are no good for submarine warfare; they aren't any good even for anti-aircraft at home. The Führer is right in asking why they are in the war anyway!' He was also angry at his generals: 'The Führer's judgment of the moral qualities of the generals – and that applies to all arms of the service – is devastating . . . They all cheat him, fawn upon him, furnish him statistics which any child can contradict, and thereby insult the Führer's intelligence.'[11]

Goebbels didn't think this was the most suitable atmosphere in which to persuade Hitler to adopt his plan, so he decided to wait until later in the trip. But matters didn't improve at dinner either, as news came through that Nuremberg, the city that had hosted Nazi Party rallies since the 1920s, had been subjected to a large Allied bombing attack. In a fury, Hitler ordered Karl Bodenschatz, Göring's Luftwaffe representative, to be dragged from his bed and brought to him. Hitler then harangued Bodenschatz about the deficiencies of German air defence in general and the leadership of Hermann Göring in particular.[12] Not surprisingly, Speer and Goebbels eventually decided not to mention their plan at all during their visit to Vinnitsa.

Speer subsequently had second thoughts about Göring's suitability for a major new leadership position. At a conference about the steel industry held at Obersalzberg a few weeks after the Hitler meeting, he watched as Göring arrived 'in a euphoric mood, his pupils visibly narrowed' and first ranted to the industrial experts about 'blast furnaces and metallurgy', before proceeding to utter 'a succession of common-places' such as the need to 'produce more' and 'not shun innovations'. After 'two hours' of this, 'Göring's speech slowed and his expression grew more and more absent. Finally, he abruptly put his head on the table and fell peacefully asleep.'[13]

The black comedy of this failed attempt to influence Hitler matters, because it tells us a great deal about how the Third Reich functioned in the weeks immediately after Stalingrad. While leading Nazis had tried since the formation of the party to manoeuvre themselves into positions of influence, what was happening now was of a different order of urgency.

Notably – for all Goebbels' talk of a 'Leader crisis' – there was no attempt to confront the central problem: Adolf Hitler. He was the primary reason that events were working out so badly. The only hope of radical change was for Hitler to stand aside. Yet Goebbels and Speer made no attempt to remove him, and never seemed even to have asked themselves how diminishing Bormann's influence over Hitler and replacing him with the plainly inadequate figure of Hermann Göring would have solved anything.

However, it was Göring, in his original discussion with Goebbels, who offered one of the most valuable insights into why leading Nazis were so reluctant to move against Hitler. 'Göring realizes perfectly what is in store for all of us if we show any weakness in this war,' wrote Goebbels. 'He has no illusions about that. On the Jewish question, especially, we have taken a position from which there is no escape. That is all to the good. Experience shows that a movement and a people who have burned their bridges fight with much greater determination than those who can still retreat.'[14]

Goebbels knew very well what was going on in the east. As he wrote in his diary in March 1942, a 'rather barbaric procedure, that is not to be spelt out, is applied here, and there is not much that remains of the Jews themselves. All in all, we can say that 60% of them have to be liquidated, whereas only 40% can still be used for work . . . We must not let sentimentality rule in these matters. If we didn't ward off the Jews, they would destroy us. It is a life-and-death struggle between the Aryan race and the Jewish bacillus.'[15] Against the background of their support for this heinous crime, Goebbels and Göring must have felt they had few alternative options – except to carry on and hope for victory.

But what was happening here was more than mere resignation in the face of events. At Vinnitsa, Goebbels had sat talking with Hitler until three in the morning. It was a 'long and intimate exchange of views' that gave him 'all sorts of hope for the future'.[16] He left his Führer's presence having 'gained a large measure of strength'. Speer, who witnessed this transformation in Goebbels, wrote that 'afterward, he no longer spoke of a "Leader crisis". On the contrary, it even seemed as if he had recovered his old confidence in Hitler.'[17]

Goebbels – probably the most intelligent of the Nazi elite, and certainly the most witheringly sarcastic – was not an emotional pushover. Yet Hitler seemed almost to have worked a magical trick on him. And not for the first time. In 1926, at a Nazi conference in Bamberg in northern Bavaria, Goebbels had been so disappointed with Hitler's views on policy that he wrote in his diary that he was in 'despair' and 'could not entirely believe in Hitler any more'.[18] Yet two months later, after Hitler had asked Goebbels to come to Berlin and spend time with him, the Propaganda Minister had completely regained confidence in his Führer. He wrote, 'Adolf Hitler, I love you because you are great and simple at the same time. This is what one calls a genius.' Policy differences now appeared insignificant, what mattered was to have faith in the leader.[19]

Goebbels was far from the only person that Hitler affected in this way. 'I experienced examples of it,' said Ulrich de Maizière, a General Staff officer who attended meetings with Hitler in the last part of the war, 'of men who came to tell him it could not go on any longer – and even said that to him. And then he talked for an hour and then they went and said, "I want to give it another try" . . . Well, he had an enormously strong will, you know, and he had powers of persuasion that could gloss over any rational arguments . . . if he ordered the attack on the Caucasus and the logistics expert told him that there wasn't enough fuel then he would say, "then just seize the petrol. I don't care, it will be done." '[20]

But while, as de Maizière said, Hitler undoubtedly had strong 'powers of persuasion', we have also to understand that these 'powers' worked effectively only on those who were predisposed to be persuaded – people who were desperate to believe that there was a way out of Germany's predicament. They would have remembered how in the past Hitler had been proved right when others doubted him. Who could forget, for instance, the victory in France that many had thought impossible? So now they hoped for a similar transformation. As Hitler said, back in 1927, 'Be assured, we too put *Glauben* (faith) in the first place and not cognition. One has to be able to believe in a cause. Only *Glauben* creates a state. What motivates people to go and to battle and die for religious ideas? Not cognition, but blind faith . . .'[21] Stalin, by contrast, would never have called for his fellow Soviets to die out of 'blind faith'. He was too much of a rationalist for that.

So it's hardly surprising that Hitler had problems dealing with people who did not support him primarily out of 'faith' – like Field Marshal von Manstein, one of the Wehrmacht's best tacticians. Heinz Guderian later wrote that he had tried to get Hitler to appoint Manstein as head of the Wehrmacht towards the end of the war, but since Manstein 'formed his own opinions and spoke them aloud' Hitler had preferred to stick with Keitel, who tried to 'fulfil Hitler's every wish before it had even been uttered'.[22] It wasn't that Manstein was somehow not fully committed to German victory. It was just that he did not demonstrate 'blind faith' in the supposed genius of Adolf Hitler.

As for Guderian, he experienced personally Hitler's attempt to influence the emotions of those around him when he visited the Führer's headquarters in late February 1943. He had been fired as a military commander just over a year before, after he had complained about the decision not to pull back from Moscow, and hadn't seen the German leader since. He now noticed that Hitler had 'aged greatly' during the intervening period. Hitler said he wanted Guderian to return and become Inspector General of Armoured Troops and that he regretted the 'numerous misunderstandings' that had occurred between them. Crucially, he then added the words: 'I need you.'[23] This kind of personal appeal was typical of him. Peter von der Groeben, chief of operations for Army Group Centre, remembered how 'at the end of every meeting he [Hitler] would always personally turn to the field marshal in charge and say, "But you're not going to abandon me," and he took both his hands and shook them . . . He had an immense ability to manipulate and influence people.'[24]

Guderian said he'd take the job, but only on condition that he would report directly to Hitler. This was agreed, but Guderian subsequently found it impossible to perform his work as powerful Nazis were able to frustrate his efforts. When he met Himmler, for instance, Guderian found that the SS leader was pursuing his own agenda for the Waffen SS, supported by Hitler. As for Göring, he simply refused to meet with Guderian. 'That gentleman', wrote Guderian, 'was too preoccupied with his non-military activities to spare me the necessary time.'[25]

Away from these political machinations, ordinary Germans tried to come to terms with the catastrophe of Stalingrad. It was a task made more difficult by the decision of Hitler and Goebbels to lie about what had happened to the soldiers of the Sixth Army. Despite the Red Army taking more than 90,000 prisoners, the Nazis claimed that every single German had died at Stalingrad – all killed in one huge Götterdämmerung. This deception turned out to be a monumental propaganda mistake, for the predictable reason that it was impossible to keep the real fate of the captured soldiers quiet. 'Not everyone will be able to resist the temptation to try and get news by listening to enemy broadcasts,' warned an official from the Foreign Office's press and information unit. 'In the eyes of the simple masses, "taken prisoner" is very different from "killed", no matter how many times they are told that the Russians murder all prisoners taken.'[26]

The Soviets immediately recognized this propaganda gift and dropped leaflets into German lines naming the prisoners taken alive. One of these leaflets found its way to a German woman who tried to contact the relatives of those listed. When questioned by the Gestapo, she said that she 'wanted to help the affected persons' and 'felt sorry . . . that they did not have any news of their relatives'.

The Gestapo faced a dilemma. The woman was scarcely a subversive – not only had some of her close relatives died in the First World War, she had lost one of her own sons in this current one. Her motivation appeared to be merely compassionate concern for her fellow Germans. Nonetheless, she was disseminating the 'lies' of the enemy. In the end, the Gestapo decided to let her off with a warning. It was exactly the kind of morale-sapping mess that could easily have been avoided if the regime had not told such a transparent lie.[27]

While their families back home were being told they were dead, the Germans captured at Stalingrad languished in Soviet captivity. Many of them, understandably, were utterly disillusioned. Throughout his imprisonment, Gerhard Hindenlang, a battalion commander with the Sixth Army, remembered Hitler's words in the final days of Stalingrad: 'He sent us a radio message, hold on because we will relieve you . . . And we really believed it. We believed it completely . . . Of course I was bitterly disappointed.' Once in Soviet hands Hindenlang was tortured. He recalled that 'they hit me with bits of wood that were used for firing the stove' and, on other occasions, 'they covered my head with a towel and poured water on it, and that is terrible because you can't breathe . . .' He came to the conclusion that Stalinism and Nazism 'were exactly the same. They were both cruel systems. And I never expected that I would ever get home.'[28]

Hubert Menzel, chief of operations of the 16th Panzer Division at Stalingrad, described how his captors 'set upon us and looted, looted, looted . . . they took everything off us, any kind of valuables. Whatever they could find. Incomprehensible to us. And be it a handkerchief, be it a pair of underpants, be it a scarf, to the Russians these were all treasures. We were searched, looted, repeatedly.' Menzel went to great lengths in his attempts to hide his engagement ring, even crawling 'under a heap of corpses' to hide. 'I pulled the corpses on top of me, the dead had already been thoroughly looted, and so I wasn't looted then.' As they were marched further behind the lines 'the looting subsided, because we were out of the battle zone by then. But we got weaker and weaker because there was hardly any food, the cold was very, very bad. And as soon as someone collapsed he was simply shot. There was a bang, a shot through the base of the skull or a shot in the back and he was lying on the ground. So the number of marchers kept on decreasing.' Menzel's situation deteriorated when he was forced to pull a 'sledge loaded with stolen goods which they'd taken from dead soldiers, because the Russians had a use for anything . . . They simply loaded everything on to [the sledge] – a huge thing, it was incredibly heavy. I myself pulled the sledge for a long, long time, was constantly beaten, [and] had my teeth knocked out . . . I was almost done for.'[29]

Eventually Menzel was imprisoned in a camp close to the Ural Mountains. Here, an epidemic of typhus broke out among the prisoners of war: 'Every morning we'd put aside three, four or five dead, and then we tried to position them nicely [in their beds] for another two or three days so that we'd get their rations which would be shared out equally. So we arranged the dead next to us. It's somewhat macabre, but it's the truth. Dying and all that, it was part of the daily routine . . . In that way the dead helped us . . .'

Menzel faced another challenge. Like many German prisoners, he was asked to join the so-called National Committee and state publicly that he was an 'anti-fascist'. In exchange he was told he'd receive better treatment: 'Those who signed were assigned cushy little jobs. The others were up for hard labour. We were told, if you don't sign, you go straight out and work.' But Menzel refused to sign: 'It was obvious what the purpose of it was – it was meant to have an effect on our own lines, to influence [the soldiers] who were still fighting.' He considered that it was his duty not to 'get roped into undermining' his 'own front line'. Consequently he 'was consigned to so-called political isolation, [and] taken to the notorious Block Six, where we were completely cut off until the summer of '45. That was the response to people who weren't willing to submit to this National Committee.' Menzel was finally released from a Soviet camp in 1955, twelve years after his capture in Stalingrad. Looking back, he believed he was able to survive because 'I'm a relatively solid old piece of furniture' and 'able to withstand quite a lot'.[30]

But it wasn't just the ability of the German POWs to 'withstand quite a lot' of mistreatment that affected their chances of survival. Another factor was their rank. As a general rule the Soviets – contrary to any egalitarian principle – treated officers better than rank-and-file soldiers. An incredible 90 per cent of ordinary soldiers from the Sixth Army perished after they had fallen into Soviet hands, compared to just 5 per cent of senior officers. The Soviets clearly saw propaganda value in keeping German generals alive and 'converting' them to their cause.[31] It was this that made more junior German officers like Joachim Stempel so angry. He claimed that just 'minutes' after capture 'the general was no longer with his troops – he was in a heated fast train, with white linen on the bed and table, on his way to the generals' camp in Moscow.'[32]

Walter Mauth, an ordinary soldier in his early twenties with the Wehrmacht's 30th Infantry Division, experienced the kind of treatment that more lowly German captives could expect. Captured in 1944, he was first 'robbed' when a Red Army soldier told him that 'he had to march to Berlin, so he needed good shoes. And he noticed my socks, the Russians did not have socks, they wore footcloths. "Take them off!" [said the soldier]. So I was standing there barefoot.' Shortly afterwards he discovered that 'behind the lines the Russians employed women, so the medical service was mainly left to them. Women came, with guns, they wanted to beat me to death, then a first lieutenant arrived who protected me from these females, and then I said: "I will never marry!" That's what I said at the time: "If females are this violent, I won't get married!" They were furious with us, weren't they, furious . . . [The Germans] had destroyed everything, might have killed their husbands, shot their brothers, I don't know.'

Once imprisoned in a Soviet camp, Mauth described his life as 'bloody awful, brutal and we were hungry, hungry and hungry and more hungry'. Some prisoners were so desperate that they 'killed the forest warden's dog' and 'carved it up in the camp'. Since there were no cooking facilities, 'they must have eaten the meat raw . . . Sure, it is difficult to imagine, but . . . what we know here [today], that is not real hunger, we simply eat because we have an appetite or something like that. Hunger is, if you are lying down and you get up and you fall down again because everything goes black, that's hunger. That's what happened to us. Happened to me personally.'[33]

Walter Mauth was one of the more fortunate German POWs. He was captured after the death rate had peaked in the camps – it had reached a high in early 1943 of nearly 60 per cent.[34] But in the context of this death toll we need to remember the fate of Soviet soldiers captured by the Germans. Out of around 5.7 million taken prisoner during the war, about 3.3 million died. The greatest proportion of the Soviet dead had perished by December 1941, when out of the 3.35 million soldiers captured in the first six months of the war an incredible 2.25 million had lost their lives in German hands.[35] By contrast, of the three million Germans taken prisoner by the Red Army more than two million survived the experience.[36]

As the Soviet authorities processed the vast numbers of POWs taken at Stalingrad, Stalin and his military commanders decided to mount another wide-ranging series of attacks across the front, in an action not so dissimilar from the failed offensive against the Germans a year before that had culminated in the disaster of Kharkov.

This decision to attempt a giant encirclement of the Second Panzer Army, which was the heart of the German forces in the centre of the front, might seem strange, given this past experience, but it's a valuable reminder that history seldom offers simple explanations. It would be easy – and wrong – to think that by allowing Zhukov and Vasilevsky to plan Operation Uranus Stalin had fundamentally altered his behaviour, that from now on the Soviet leader would be both collegiate and aware of his own limitations as a commander. Although it was the case that he had worked out which of his commanders he was prepared to trust – Zhukov in particular – he had not resolved to take a more hands-off approach to the formulation and execution of Soviet strategy. And in the wake of the wildly successful Operation Uranus, Stalin was once again both dominant in military decision-making and over-confident. The mentality that had created the Kharkov debacle had not yet vanished.

This new offensive in the centre of the front was a failure. Marshal Rokossovsky later called it a 'crude error'. He thought that 'appetites' had 'prevailed over possibilities'.[37] While in the south, despite initial success – including the capture of Kharkov – the Red Army soon suffered setbacks. Reinforced with three elite SS divisions, including Hitler's own life guard the Leibstandarte, German forces under Field Marshal von Manstein recaptured Kharkov one month later and drove the Red Army back. Yet again Stalin's leadership had failed. Once again he had been defeated by the superior tactical ability of his enemy.

Such reverses only served to fuel Stalin's anger about the perceived lack of help from his western Allies. While the Allies had not been inactive – they had provided aid to the Soviet Union under Lend-Lease, had engaged Axis forces in North Africa and were bombing Germany – for Stalin the central question remained. When would they start the liberation of western Europe and open a second front? As far as he was concerned, everything else was a sideshow. So the fact that the British and Americans seemed to be misleading him about when this second front would be launched only made him angrier still.

Back in December 1942, Stalin had written to his allies: 'I feel confident that no time is being wasted, that the promise to open a second front in Europe, which you, Mr President, and Mr Churchill gave for 1942 or the spring of 1943 at the latest, will be kept and that a second front in Europe will really be opened jointly by Great Britain and the USA next spring.'[38] After this note, Stalin had continued to press the British and Americans for a definitive date for the second front, writing on 30 January 1943 to Churchill and Roosevelt that it was his 'understanding' that the Allies had set themselves 'the task of crushing Germany by the opening of a Second Front in Europe' and he would be 'very obliged for information concerning the actual operation planned for this purpose'.[39]

Stalin finally received a reply from Churchill on 12 February 1943. 'We are also pushing preparations to the limit of our resources for a cross-Channel operation in August,' wrote Churchill, 'in which both British and US units would participate. Here again, shipping and assault-landing craft will be limiting factors. If the operation is delayed by the weather or other reasons, it will be prepared with stronger forces for September. The timing of this attack must, of course, be dependent upon the condition of German defensive possibilities across the Channel at that time.'[40]

It was obvious to Stalin that Churchill and Roosevelt were still not offering an absolute commitment to open the second front in 1943, and that they had demonstrably failed to deliver on their previous deadline for the invasion of France of 'spring of 1943 at the latest'. Stalin's patience grew even thinner after German reinforcements reached the eastern front in the first few months of 1943. These, he argued, were the very same units that ought at this moment to be fighting the British and Americans in France after the launch of the promised second front.

The Soviet Ambassador to London, Ivan Maisky, outlined in his diary the reason why he thought the western Allies were behaving as they were, a view large numbers of Soviet citizens shared. He wrote on 5 February that 'on the one hand' the 'ruling class' in Britain would like to wait until the Red Army had hugely weakened the Germans before invading France, but didn't want to delay so long that the Soviets could get to Berlin before they did. Consequently, the British and Americans wanted the second front to be launched 'not too early and not too late' but '*just in time*'.[41] It was a view that dismissed all the excuses of London and Washington about the lack of landing craft and other practical problems as mere camouflage, behind which lay a ruthless realpolitik and an utter disregard for the mounting Soviet dead. While this was a cynical view of events, it was one for which there was a good deal of circumstantial evidence. For instance, Senator – later President – Harry Truman had said publicly, just after the invasion of the Soviet Union in the summer of 1941, that 'if we see that Germany is winning, we ought to help Russia and, if Russia is winning, we ought to help Germany, and that way let them kill as many as possible', although 'I don't want to see Hitler victorious under any circumstances.'[42] The *Wall Street Journal* had gone even further, saying around the same time that 'The American people know that the principal difference between Mr Hitler and Mr Stalin is the size of their respective mustaches.'[43]

Times had changed since then. Not only had America entered the war, but the Soviets had fought back more successfully against the Germans than many had believed possible. Nonetheless, in the spring of 1943 and in the context of the delay in the second front, you didn't have to possess Stalin-like levels of suspicion to think that Churchill and Roosevelt were secretly happy to let the Red Army bear the brunt of the fighting, and that the anti-Soviet sentiment of the summer of 1941 still existed in certain quarters.

It wasn't even as if in the current circumstances the British and

Americans were treating the Soviet Union as a full ally. The British refused to share details about a whole range of military equipment with the Soviets. For example, they withheld innovations in radar jamming and bombsights. The Americans were even more reticent. They didn't want the British to tell the Soviets about many other pieces of new technology, such as the latest developments in jet engines.[44]

Oliver Harvey of the British Foreign Office encapsulated in his diary the dilemma many in the western alliance felt. 'The Russians are very tiresome allies, importunate, graceless, ungrateful, secretive, suspicious, ever asking for more, but they are delivering the goods . . . They are winning the war for us.'[45]

Stalin, having closely studied Churchill's dispatch and listened to the British excuses about the second front, expressed his displeasure in a note on 15 March 1943. 'I deem it my duty to warn you', he wrote, 'in the strongest possible manner how dangerous would be, from the viewpoint of our common cause, further delay in the opening of the second front in France.' He even went as far as to express his 'grave anxiety' about the 'uncertainty' emanating from London and Washington on the subject.[46]

But at the same time Stalin did something curious. On the very day he sent this telegram of 'grave anxiety' he sent another note to Churchill, congratulating the British for their recent bombing of several major cities in Germany. Then two weeks later he wrote another effusive dispatch, having just seen *Desert Victory*, a documentary film about the Allied campaign in North Africa. Maisky handed this letter to Churchill on 31 March and noted the Prime Minister was 'deeply touched'; Maisky could even see 'tears' in his eyes. 'You have never brought me such a wonderful message before,' said an emotional Churchill. In particular, he valued Stalin's remark that *Desert Victory* would do much to correct the impression – held by 'rascals' in the Soviet Union – that the British were staying on the 'side-lines' and not fighting.[47]

It was an extraordinary turn of events, not least because Stalin, in accusing the British in the past of not fighting enough, had been the chief 'rascal'. And while he does seem genuinely to have liked the film about the African campaign, the success of the British effort against the German Afrika Korps was already known to him, as was the fact that in terms of scale these battles did not compare to the struggle on the eastern front. Stalin's comments were so astonishing that one official at the

British Foreign Office wondered whether this was a 'leg pull'.[48] Perhaps this was just a private joke? After all, Stalin had shown in the past that he had a black sense of humour. As we have seen, he had mischievously suggested to the Polish leadership that their missing officers, whom he had ordered to be murdered, had escaped 'to Manchuria'. He had also cynically called himself an 'anti-Cominternist' at the time of the pact with the Nazis. So one straightforward explanation for the contradictory tone of his messages to Churchill was that he got a perverse pleasure from messing with other people's emotions.

It's also another example of the power that Stalin possessed because he appeared not to care whether or not he established a personal relationship with Roosevelt and Churchill. This, as we have already seen, was the fundamental reason that Stalin remained a mystery to a deeply emotional character like Churchill. Struggling to explain Stalin's conduct, the Prime Minister wondered if there might be 'two Stalins'. In mid-March, when Stalin had sent two messages on the same day – one friendly, one cold – Churchill had explained it away by saying that the first had been sent by the Stalin who 'was anxious to preserve good relations with me' while the second was the consequence of 'Stalin in council', where the Soviet leader had to endure 'a grim thing behind him' in the form of powerful advisers 'which we and he have to reckon with'.[49]

It was a misjudgement of gigantic proportions. But it's also easy to understand how such a mistake could be made. Churchill had not instigated a bloody purge, or the mass starvation of millions, or any of the many other crimes that Stalin had already been responsible for. Above all, unlike Churchill, Stalin's hold on power depended not on people 'liking' him and voting for him at the ballot box, but on his subordinates fearing him with an intensity that is hard to convey. There was no 'grim thing behind' Stalin. He was the 'grim thing' himself.

But notwithstanding the difficulties Churchill had in understanding Stalin, and the Soviet leader's sniping over the second front, the alliance was not fundamentally in danger of splitting apart. Everyone wanted to see Hitler defeated, and it now appeared that the war had turned in favour of the Allies, even given the setbacks the Red Army had recently suffered. Stalin also showed signs, once again, that he was taking the advice of Zhukov, his most trusted commander. On 8 April, Zhukov had written to the Soviet leader and said, 'It would be better for us to wear down the enemy on our defence, knock out his tanks, bring in fresh reserves, and finish off his main grouping with a general offensive.'[50] In other words, don't attack again until we are properly prepared.

However, this relative calm between the Allies was about to be broken in a way that would test the relationship as it had never been tested before.

It was the Polish question, which had so often proved a problem between Stalin and the western Allies, that was once again to cause the trouble. 'Polish mass graves have been found near Smolensk,' wrote Goebbels in his diary on 9 April 1943. 'The Bolsheviks simply gunned down and then buried in shallow mass graves some 10,000 Polish prisoners, among them also civilians, bishops, intellectuals, artists and so forth. On top of these mass graves they built facilities of various sorts to make any possible traces of their outrageous deeds disappear. The secret of these shootings leaked out through hints from the local inhabitants . . .'[51]

The Germans had found the remains of some of the 22,000 leading figures from occupied eastern Poland who had been murdered by the NKVD in the spring of 1940, at three separate killing centres within the Soviet Union. Though Stalin had been one of several Politburo members who had authorized the crime, the murders had happened because he wanted them to. The blood was on his hands.

It's not difficult to imagine the magnitude of the crisis caused by this discovery. Poland was an ally not just of Britain and America, but of the Soviet Union as well. Now it had been discovered that one ally had most likely murdered thousands of elite citizens of a fellow ally. It focused attention on a question that Churchill and Roosevelt were anxious to avoid – hadn't the British and Americans made an alliance with one mass murderer in order to defeat another mass murderer? If so, why was Allied propaganda pretending otherwise and lauding Stalin?

Goebbels instantly recognized the problems that the unearthing of the bodies caused for the Allies. 'We are exploiting it with all the tricks of the trade,' he wrote.[52] Such 'exploitation' included showing the bodies to 'Polish intellectuals' so as to demonstrate 'what awaits them if their cherished wish of the Germans being beaten by the Bolsheviks should ever come true'. This was deeply hypocritical, of course, since the Nazis had targeted the Polish elite themselves.[53]

One of the villagers who lived close to the Katyn forest, Dmitry Khudykh, remembered how the Germans let the locals view the possessions of the murdered Poles. 'They wanted us to act as witnesses to history,' he said. But Dmitry and his friends were not 'particularly interested' as they had already seen 'death inflicted by the Germans'.[54] More successful, as far as the Nazi propagandists were concerned, was their call for an independent examination of the bodies and the commissioning of a film about the massacre. Many of the Polish officers had carried photos of their wives and children, and the sight of these images in the film was deeply affecting.

Not surprisingly, the leaders of the Polish government in exile, based in London, took a special interest in the discovery. They had been asking about the fate of their officers for three years. Now, it seemed, they had at last learnt what had happened. The Soviets had murdered them.

Stalin's response to this crisis revealed a great deal about his character and his political gifts. That he denied all knowledge of the crime was predictable. What was more audacious was that he coupled this denial with an all-out attack on the Polish government in exile. On 19 April 1943, *Pravda* called them 'Hitler's Polish collaborators' and accused the Polish Minister of Defence of offering 'direct and obvious help to Hitlerite provocateurs'.[55] It was a breathtaking piece of political effrontery. Not only were the Soviets lying about their own responsibility for the crime, but the so-called 'help' offered by the Poles to the Nazis had consisted merely of their suggestion that there might be an independent inquiry into the atrocity.

It was another example of how Stalin believed that power was everything in politics. He knew that the British and Americans needed him. So the fact that they might suspect – might even come to believe for certain – that his regime had murdered these Poles was of no consequence. Instead, he could use this incident to punish the Polish government in exile, a group he had always disliked. Just as during the 1930s, when he had made his old comrades, under torture, deny what they knew to be the truth and swear to any outrageous lie the torturers proposed, so he would now ratchet up the torment of the Poles by accusing them of collaborating with the Nazis just because they wanted to uncover what had actually happened to their comrades.

Shamefully, we might think today, both the British and Americans went along with this black pretence. On 28 April Churchill revealed his own lack of concern for who had perpetrated the crime when he said in a confidential note to Anthony Eden that 'There is no use prowling morbidly around the three year old graves at Smolensk.'[56] A few days earlier he had written to Stalin and told him that he was 'examining the possibility of silencing those Polish papers in this country which attack the Soviet government and at the same time attack Sikorski [the Polish Prime Minister] for trying to work with the Soviet government'.[57]

But Stalin had already realized how much he could turn the Katyn massacre to his advantage, and swiftly replied to Churchill, telling him that the 'interruption of relations with the Polish Government is already decided' because of the 'ingratitude and treachery' of the Poles.[58] It followed, as everyone knew, that this opened the possibility of Stalin creating his own tame Polish government. It was the same tactic he had used at the time of the Finnish invasion. It hadn't worked then because the Red Army had failed to perform as expected on the battlefield. But the situation now was very different. In time, Soviet forces would almost certainly liberate Poland, and given that Stalin had just refused to talk to the legitimate Polish government in exile, the western Allies faced a host of new problems. While the British and Americans fretted about what to do, Stalin could toy with them. He hadn't said he would definitely form a puppet Polish government – Maisky told the British there was no current intention to – but the option remained, no matter what the Soviets might officially say.[59]

The Germans continued to press on with their propaganda advantage. The commission they appointed to investigate the massacre may only have contained one forensic scientist from an area outside Nazi control, but the report it issued was still damning. It was apparent to any fair reader of the evidence that the Soviets had committed the crime. The Polish officers had first gone missing in spring 1940, and the trees on top of the mass graves had been planted at that exact time. In addition, eye-witnesses had heard gunfire coming from the forest around the same period, and stated that the whole area had been under N K V D control.

Sir Owen O'Malley, British Ambassador to the Polish government in exile, examined the evidence and reached much the same conclusion as the investigative commission organized by the Germans. He wrote, diplomatically, that the 'cumulative effect' of the evidence threw 'serious doubt on Russian disclaimers of responsibility for the massacre'. He also pointed to a truth that few in the British and American administrations wanted to hear: 'we have been constrained by the urgent need for cordial relations with the Soviet government to appear to appraise the evidence with more hesitation and lenience than we should do in forming a common sense judgment on events occurring in normal times or in the ordinary course of our private lives . . .'[60]

These were deeply inconvenient truths. Churchill, who felt obliged to forward the report to Roosevelt, called it in his covering note 'a grim, well-written story, but perhaps a little too well-written'.[61] Meanwhile the doyen of the euphemistic put-down, Sir Alexander Cadogan, confessed that 'I had rather turned my head away from the scene at Katyn – for fear of what I should find there,' but having now been forced to consider the matter, he had decided that 'on the evidence that we have, it is difficult to escape from a presumption of Russian guilt.' But he questioned whether 'on the purely moral plane' O'Malley's report offered anything new, asking: 'How many thousands of its own citizens has the Soviet regime butchered?' He concluded that there was nothing to be done about this new Soviet crime.[62]

Many other British diplomats were also keen to make this whole business go away. It was, from their perspective, phenomenally awkward. One of the most forthright in his desire not to find out what had truly happened at Katyn was the British Ambassador to Moscow, Sir Archibald Clark Kerr. In a note to Anthony Eden, he warned against pursuing any inquiry into the killings because 'the anger and unconvincing terms of Soviet denials suggests a sense of guilt' and an independent inquiry 'might show that guilt was there'.[63]

As for Roosevelt, his attitude is easy to deduce. He simply ignored the O'Malley report. It was how he often dealt with unpleasant information he wished he had never been sent. It was the very same tactic the Soviet authorities frequently employed. For instance, Hugh Lunghi, a British officer serving at the embassy in Moscow, remembered that the 'usual' response from Soviet officials to any request was first to say 'we're dealing with it' and then never to mention it again. 'We called it', said Lunghi, 'the "cotton wool" treatment.'[64]

The unease with which the western Allies dealt with Katyn contrasted with the bombastic propaganda approach of the Nazis. But, in private, there was an element of understanding from the Nazis about why the Soviets had committed the crime.

Goebbels, for example, couldn't help but take a swipe at the dead Poles in his diary, saying that 'it was probably their own fault' that they'd been murdered since 'they were the real warmongers.'[65] As for

Hitler, he envied Stalin for the way he had 'got rid of all opposition in the Red Army [by killing people like Marshal Tukhachevsky] and thus ensured there is no defeatist tendency in the army.' He also praised Stalin for introducing political commissars into the armed forces as this had 'benefited the fighting capacity of the Red Army'.[66] It all served to show how Hitler understood – even admired – Stalin in ways that his democratic allies could never do.

Interestingly, many ordinary Germans also seemed to understand why the Soviets had thought it necessary to murder the Poles. The SD, the intelligence section of the SS, reported that 'A large section of the [German] population sees in the [Soviets'] elimination of the Polish officers . . . the radical extinction of a dangerous opponent, unavoidable in war. One could set it on the same plane as the bombing attacks of the English and Americans on the German cities and, finally, also our own battle of annihilation against the Jews.'[67]

For many Germans, this was clearly a war of horrors on all sides.

Churchill and Roosevelt didn't just face difficulties over Katyn, they still hadn't resolved the problem of the second front. They hadn't even agreed a date between themselves when it could be launched. Partly this was because Churchill was still not keen on the idea. When he met Roosevelt in Washington in May 1943 he emphasized the practical difficulties of a cross-Channel invasion, especially in the context of the drain on Allied resources caused by the campaign in North Africa and by the need for landing craft in the war against the Japanese in the Pacific. After days of discussion the British and Americans agreed to postpone the second front yet again until spring 1944. This meant giving Stalin bad news once more.

What's remarkable, however, is that at the very moment that Roosevelt and Churchill were discussing these issues a special emissary of the President's was meeting with Stalin in the Kremlin – and the British Prime Minister knew nothing about the encounter. It's an episode that illustrates the duplicity that could lie behind Roosevelt's practised air of conviviality. The American President had, on his own, decided two things. He needed to meet Stalin personally and he wanted Churchill kept in the dark.

Roosevelt thought that in a one-to-one meeting he could use his famous charm to establish a better relationship with the Soviet leader – a relationship that had self-evidently been damaged by the dispute about the second front. And the first step towards making this happen was to dispatch an envoy called Joseph Davies to Moscow with a personal message for Stalin.

Davies had been the American Ambassador in the Soviet Union in the 1930s, and was sympathetic to the regime. He'd written a book called *Mission to Moscow* which peddled the lie that many of the show trials during the Great Terror had been legitimate. A Hollywood film that lauded Stalin, based on the book, was just about to be released. The film contained several excruciating moments – none more so than the reconstruction of Davies' meeting with the Soviet leader. 'Mr Stalin,' said the actor playing Davies, 'I believe, sir, that history will record you as a great builder for the benefit of mankind.'[68]

The current American Ambassador to Moscow, William Standley, was told nothing about the purpose of Davies' mission. He wasn't allowed into the meeting between the envoy and Stalin, nor was he even permitted to know the contents of the letter from Roosevelt that Davies carried. 'I felt as if I had been kicked in the stomach,' he said. 'A pretty state of affairs!'[69]

With Standley left outside the room, Davies proceeded to tell Stalin about the many deficiencies of their common ally – the British. Not only would Britain be financially 'through' for many years after the war but Churchill and his Foreign Secretary Anthony Eden were 'adherents of an Imperial policy' that was outdated. And while Davies also expressed 'admiration and respect' for Churchill and Eden, it was obvious that he wanted to sideline the British.[70] It was an impression that was confirmed once Davies handed over the letter from Roosevelt. The President wrote that he wanted to meet Stalin without Churchill present, and suggested the summit be held on either 'side of [the] Bering Straits'.[71] Stalin asked why Churchill was not invited, only to be told that Roosevelt and the British Prime Minister 'did not always see eye to eye'.

It was an astonishing insult to Churchill. If the meeting just between Roosevelt and Stalin took place, and deliberately excluded Churchill, the implication would be that the Americans and Soviets were planning a post-war future in which the British would be marginalized.

Stalin must have relished the situation. He certainly understood the diplomatic power that he now possessed as a result of Roosevelt's request. He was evasive over the question of the date of any potential summit, implying in his meeting with Davies that since the Soviet Union was bearing the brunt of the fighting he was a good deal busier than Roosevelt.

Back in Washington, and oblivious to events in Moscow, Churchill discussed with Roosevelt the best way of telling Stalin about the delay to the second front. The solution they came up with was bizarre. They decided not to mention the subject until the last but one paragraph in a long message outlining Allied military strategy.

It's hard to know what they hoped to achieve by behaving in this way. George Elsey, a naval intelligence officer who was present in the White House Map Room as Churchill, Roosevelt and their staff drafted the final note, remembered that 'Roosevelt was very quiet that night', leaving General Marshall, the Army Chief of Staff, to argue out the exact content with Churchill and the British delegation.[72] But whatever the provenance of the final wording, the charmless note they sent Stalin on 2 June verged on the insulting.[73]

Stalin responded, predictably, by saying that 'the opening of the second front in Western Europe which was postponed already from 1942 to 1943, is being postponed again, this time until spring 1944.' This created 'exceptional difficulties' and left the Soviet Union fighting 'almost in single combat with yet [a] very strong and dangerous enemy'.[74]

Churchill, while privately irritated by 'these repeated scoldings, considering that they have never been actuated by anything but cold-blooded self-interest and total disdain of our lives and fortunes',[75] was nonetheless careful not to communicate his true feelings directly to Stalin. Instead, on 20 June he sent a placatory note offering to 'go at any risk to any place that you and the President may agree upon' for a face-to-face meeting.[76] This was – unbeknown to Churchill – an offer that confirmed to Stalin just how much the British Prime Minister had been excluded from knowledge of the Davies mission.

Roosevelt saw his secret dealings with Stalin starting to unravel. Stalin was in no mood to meet with him after the rebuff over the second front, and there was always the risk that Churchill would find out about the Davies meeting. So it was left to the emollient Averell Harriman, another of Roosevelt's special envoys, to tell Churchill about the American President's duplicity. He explained to Churchill that it just wouldn't be possible for Roosevelt to form an 'intimate understanding' with Stalin if Churchill was in the room.[77]

Churchill made his objections plain in a note he sent Roosevelt. 'Averell told me last night of your wish for a meeting with U.J. ['Uncle Joe' – their nickname for Stalin] in Alaska a deux. The whole world is expecting and all our side are desiring a meeting of the three great powers at which, not only the political chiefs, but the military staffs would be present in order to plan the future war moves . . .' Consequently, said Churchill, any meeting excluding him would be a gift for enemy propaganda and thus 'serious and vexatious, and many would be bewildered and alarmed thereby'.[78]

In his response, Roosevelt lied. He said that he had never suggested meeting Stalin on his own, but that the Soviet leader had 'assumed' it. He added, disingenuously, that he did think there were 'certain advantages in such a preliminary meeting', chiefly that Stalin would be more 'frank' than if attending a full-scale conference.[79]

Churchill's attitude subsequently changed after he received another angry communication from Stalin about the second front. 'It goes without saying', wrote Stalin, 'that the Soviet Government can not put up with such disregard of the most vital Soviet interests in the war against the common enemy.'[80] This was a serious escalation. Perhaps Stalin was now so angry that he might be prepared to make a separate peace with the Germans. This was especially worrying given that on 16 June, just days before Stalin sent this note to Churchill, a Swedish newspaper had reported that Soviet and German diplomats had met near Stockholm.[81] It's likely these low-level contacts were of no real significance, especially since Hitler had previously said that he would consider a deal with Stalin only from a position of strength. But the Allies did not know this.

In the light of these concerns, Churchill withdrew his objection to the proposed meeting between Roosevelt and Stalin.[82] What mattered at this moment was placating Stalin. But predictably, given the prevailing atmosphere, the meeting 'a deux' never happened.

These detailed exchanges between the three leaders are revealing, not just because they show the reality behind the propaganda myth of the chummy relationship between Churchill and Roosevelt, but also because they demonstrate once more Stalin's political skill. Unlike Churchill, who could well up with tears at a kind word from Stalin, the Soviet leader remained calm and considered. As Joseph Davies observed, Stalin 'didn't flicker an eyelash' as he listened to the contents of the letter from Roosevelt.[83]

The Soviet leader was seldom prepared to reveal what he thought. Instead he carefully graduated his responses. Witness how he had sent Churchill various levels of displeasure in his different messages about the second front. He knew when to escalate matters and when to offer a hint of praise. He also knew that the most eloquent statement could sometimes be silence. After the row in late June, for instance, Stalin did not reply to any message sent to him by Roosevelt or Churchill until 8 August. He let them both fret for over a month, trying to guess his true mood.

While Stalin toyed with his allies, Hitler was forced to downgrade his military aspirations and deal with the reality that his enemies were getting stronger every day. For the past three years the Germans had launched shattering offensives in the late spring and early summer. The invasion of western Europe in 1940, Operation Barbarossa in 1941 and Operation Blue in 1942. Each of these campaigns had, to begin with, been enormously successful. So what could the Germans offer for the campaigning season in 1943? The answer demonstrated the paucity of their options, and lacked the epic quality of the previous years. Instead of a vast offensive across a huge front, it was an attack on Soviet forces around the city of Kursk, just under 300 miles south-west of Moscow.

Kursk was an obvious target for the Germans. There was a massive bulge in the front here, with territory occupied by the Soviets sticking out into the German front line. Anyone looking at the map would have thought it likely that the Wehrmacht would attack from the north and south in an attempt to encircle large numbers of Soviet troops. And that was the trouble for the Germans. Unlike all three of their previous summer operations, this one was predictable. There were to be no surprises at Kursk.

Hitler's generals were divided about the wisdom of the attack – this was certainly not a case of the German leader insisting on the plan against united opposition. But Hitler compounded the problems inherent in mounting such a forseeable operation by delaying the proposed start date several times. He wanted to wait for the delivery of new tanks like the Tiger and the Panther – General Model, for instance, was keen on adding their strength to the firepower of the Ninth Army.[84] But this too was a mistake, as the Panther, in particular, had teething problems. Guderian, as Inspector General of Armoured Troops, pointed this out to Hitler in early May and questioned why the offensive was being launched at all, declaring it 'pointless'. Was it not more sensible, he argued, to husband resources in order to deal with the inevitable Allied invasion of France?[85]

Guderian was able to talk to Hitler this frankly because he normally came across, in Goebbels' words, as 'a passionate and unquestioning follower of the Führer'.[86] This was a fact Guderian chose not to elaborate on in his post-war writings. According to his memoirs, he even dared to ask Hitler semi-facetiously, 'How many people do you think even know where Kursk is?' and 'Why do we want to attack in the East at all this year?' He claimed that Hitler replied, 'You're quite right. Whenever I think of this attack my stomach turns over.'[87]

But even if Hitler did say exactly that to Guderian, he was probably voicing no more than a momentary doubt. These words did not represent the true Hitler. Throughout his political life he always strove to be proactive. Defensive strategies were for more cowardly leaders. Hitler's preferred view on the forthcoming offensive was contained in an order of 15 April 1943 when he declared that 'the victory of Kursk must shine like a beacon to the world.'[88] In a conversation with Goebbels in late June he asserted that not since 1941 had the Wehrmacht been so strong in the east. He reiterated to Goebbels that the war against Stalin was the 'decisive front' and that even though he accepted that the Germans could not advance to the Caucasus at the moment, the Soviet Union would 'sooner or later' collapse as a result of a 'food crisis'.[89]

It was delusional. The Soviet Union showed no sign of collapsing from starvation or anything else. On the contrary, it was growing stronger. Moreover, how could victory at Kursk offer a 'beacon to the world' when, as Guderian implied, most people didn't even know where Kursk was? But at least the offensive allowed Hitler to take the initiative. This was an increasingly rare occurrence, as the Germans were fighting defensive battles on almost every front.

But the delay in launching the offensive, coupled with the obviousness of the target, meant that Stalin and the rest of the Soviet military command had plenty of time to prepare for the German attack. The evidence they obtained about German intentions was extensive. Not only were the British passing intelligence to the Soviets, but John Cairncross, a Soviet spy working at the codebreaking centre at Bletchley Park, was revealing to the NKVD much of the detailed information the British authorities chose to withhold. As a result the Soviets were able to build a gigantic series of defensive lines within the Kursk salient, exactly in the areas they had learnt the Germans would attack. In places these defence works stretched back nearly 200 miles into Soviet lines.[90]

On the German side, panzer commander Alfred Rubbel remembered that while 'there was a lot of time for preparation . . . we didn't take it that seriously. We went to the theatre. We went to the cinema in Kharkov. I walked my dog.' But over time the lengthy delay in launching the attack started to worry him. He 'didn't sleep very well' and his 'thoughts got darker and darker'.[91]

In an action that symbolized the way the initiative had passed to the Red Army, the battle began not when the Germans started to advance, but when the Soviets fired a gigantic barrage in order to disrupt the Wehrmacht's final preparations. Thanks to their intelligence gathering, the Soviets knew in advance the moment when the Germans planned to attack. Not just that, but the gigantic Soviet force of 1,800,000 soldiers and 5,000 tanks assembled for the battle was roughly twice the size of the German units that opposed them.[92]

Rubbel and his panzer squadron moved forward in the first wave on 5 July 1943, and almost immediately found themselves in a Soviet minefield. Rubbel was annoyed because 'aerial reconnaissance' should have spotted 'that it was not possible for the tanks to get through' in this sector, and he soon came to believe that the whole attack was 'irresponsible' – a waste of German resources. On the battlefield he saw 'tanks from all over the front, from Leningrad to Rostov', all sent to 'show the world' what the Germans could do. 'It could have worked,' he felt, but only if the operation 'hadn't been postponed four times'.[93]

Wilhelm Roes, a member of a tank crew with the SS Leibstandarte, also felt let down by lack of information about the enemy in front of him. 'It's something I still have to reproach our German Luftwaffe [for], their reconnaissance was not very good. You can hide ten [enemy] tanks, but to hide almost eight hundred . . .'

Roes and his squadron were soon fighting their way through the massed Red Army units in front of them. In the process he came upon gruesome sights he had never seen before: 'twenty metres behind us there was a Russian soldier, our tank had driven over his stomach . . . He still had a very pink face, looked at us, his helmet was gone at the back. We [were] told that you never give them water [in such a situation], you must never give them water. [So] what do we do with him?

He's only five centimetres sort of thick in the middle. While we were sitting, all of a sudden his head fell to one side and he died that minute . . . Well, we came back. We sat in the tank. I must admit I trembled. My whole body was trembling. This was my reaction to the battle. That poor boy could have been me. I suddenly realized how close death actually was, and I'd just met him. But the whole day you destroyed tanks, you're aiming at machines, you're not shooting at [people] . . . always the machines you're aiming at.'[94]

Rubbel and Roes were both fighting in Tigers, tanks that were protected by 10 centimetres of steel and armed with 88mm cannon. 'We knew that the Germans in their newspapers and on the radio used to say that the Tigers would destroy the Russian defence like a knife cutting butter,' said Mikhail Borisov, who fought on the Soviet side at Kursk. 'When we saw those tanks for the first time I could see soldiers' hands shaking and what they felt inside themselves you could have guessed.'[95]

'I had an encounter with just such a tank,' said Ivan Sagun, a tank commander with the 2nd Soviet Tank Army at Kursk. 'He fired at us from literally one kilometre away. His first shot blew a hole in the side of my tank, his second hit my axle. At a range of half a kilometre, I fired at him with a special calibre shell, but it bounced off him like a candle . . . I mean, it didn't penetrate his armour. At literally 300 metres, I fired my second shell. Same result. Then he started looking for me, turning his turret to see where I was. I told my driver to reverse fast and we hid behind some trees.'[96]

But Red Army soldiers had prepared well for this battle and they persevered. Their commitment was symbolized by Ekatarina Petluk, one of the female tank crew with the 3rd Tank Army: 'Every minute there were bombs and shells exploding, shrapnel lying everywhere. At any moment the tank could be destroyed and all the crew killed. I was wounded twice during the battle at Kursk – once in my face when a bomb exploded behind my tank. I had heard a bomb whistle towards us, then I saw black smoke, and thought my tank was on fire. If your tank catches fire, you have to get out quickly in case it blows up. I looked out to see if it was burning, and some shrapnel hit me in the face, but luckily none of it went into my eyes. So I tied a bandage round it and drove on into battle.'[97]

The two sides grappled with each other in one of the biggest tank battles ever fought. And while the Red Army may not have possessed tanks as technologically advanced as the Germans', they made up for this disadvantage in sheer numbers. 'We saw a spectacle I have never seen before,' remembered Gerd Schmückle, a battalion commander with the 7th Panzer Division. 'About one mile in front of us we saw hundreds of Russian tanks, they must have been camouflaged before, now they were lined up like in a parade, side by side and in a very deep formation. It was a terrible view for us because our tank regiment was now very small. We had lost a lot of tanks, and suddenly we saw this armada in front of us.'[98]

In one engagement 600 Soviet tanks took on 250 German ones. The Soviets suffered enormous casualties, losing around 400 tanks compared to German losses of seventy panzers.[99] But the Germans were much less able to bear such a sacrifice. Consequently, there was little hope of the two German thrusts meeting up and encircling the Soviets as planned, and Hitler called off the operation in mid-July.

The Soviets had not won a great victory – at Kursk their losses were greater than the Germans'. But the psychological effect of the battle was profound. For the first time the Soviets had held off a German summer offensive. After two gruelling years, the initiative had passed to Stalin and the Red Army.

14. Fiction and Reality

It's not easy to pick the most difficult month that Hitler survived during the war. There are plenty of options: December 1941 and the reverse in front of Moscow, February 1943 and the collapse at Stalingrad, June 1944 and the launch of D-Day, are some of the obvious candidates. But for sheer sudden pressure – much of it unanticipated – July 1943 was perhaps the most demanding of all. How Hitler came through that month, still in power and able to convince those around him to fight on, is one of the most remarkable stories of the whole conflict.[1]

On 10 July Allied troops landed in Sicily, and suddenly Hitler had a whole new set of problems. Though the second front that Stalin had been calling for – the invasion of France – had still not been launched, this was certainly, as Churchill had claimed, a second front of sorts. For the first time the Americans were fighting in Europe, and it was soon apparent that they and their allies were winning. Reports came through of Italian troops throwing away their weapons and surrendering. Would others swiftly follow their example? Were all Italians just going to give up?

Hitler had made disparaging remarks about the Italians' lack of fighting spirit before. In particular, he thought they'd performed badly on the eastern front. So, in an attempt to inject some determination into his wavering ally, he immediately hurried south to meet with Mussolini.

Hitler and Mussolini met at Feltre in northern Italy on 19 July. Here, in the blazing summer heat, Hitler harangued the Italian leader non-stop for more than two hours. The German leader had long been the senior partner in the relationship and during this encounter he did not bother to hide that fact.

Hitler said that both Italy and Germany were involved in an epoch-defining struggle that could not be dodged. It was impossible to leave the fight to the 'next generation', as 'nobody can say if the next generation will be a generation of giants.' He pointed out that Rome 'never rose up again' after its period of greatness in ancient times. Now was the moment to carry on the struggle, not to question the way ahead. But, significantly, he wouldn't give the Italians extra weapons for the fight.

Instead he was only prepared to send more German units to Italy. The implication was clear. Hitler didn't trust his ally.[2]

The relationship between the two dictators was cracking apart. Hitler promised Mussolini over lunch that the Germans were developing wonder weapons that would turn the war around, but the Italian leader was less worried about future armament production and more concerned with getting through the next few days and weeks. Vague promises for an indeterminate future were of little help to him.

Mussolini was unsure what to do. At one point in the conference, the Italian Ambassador to Berlin, together with the head of the High Command of the Armed Forces, asked him privately why he wasn't talking to Hitler about finding a way out of the conflict. In response Mussolini asked if they were ready to 'destroy at a stroke twenty years of Fascism' and 'cancel out the achievements which we have worked so long and so hard to realize'. In any case, he said, 'it is easy to talk about a separate peace. But what would Hitler do? Do you really think that he would allow us to have any freedom of action?'[3]

Mussolini was right – none of his options were attractive. He was trapped between the power of the Allies and the power of Germany. But even he didn't realize how quickly events would turn against him. On the evening of 24 July, just five days after his encounter with Hitler, he attended a meeting of the Fascist Grand Council in Rome. This was not a regular event – the Council hadn't convened in four years. But despite the fact that the meeting was long and fractious, Mussolini left the gathering still thinking he was in little danger.

The next day, 25 July, Mussolini had an audience with the Italian monarch, King Victor Emmanuel III. It was during this encounter that he first learnt that he had been deposed, and as he left the palace he was arrested. Even though his replacement, Marshal Badoglio, pledged to keep Italy in the war as Germany's ally, there was a sense that the end of the fight was near.

Just hours after Mussolini's arrest there were demonstrations on the streets of Italian cities as crowds voiced their hatred for the man who had led Italy for over twenty years. 'Everyone was shouting: "Fascism is finished,"' wrote the young journalist Milena Milani. 'The pavements [in Rome] were awash with waste paper. People seemed to have gone mad. There were party badges underfoot as you walked: everyone was tearing them off their jackets and throwing them on the ground. Some people were burning portraits of Mussolini, others were hacking off fascist symbols. Where were the fascists? I pushed my bicycle through the streets. Via del Tritone was seething with vast screaming crowds. Everyone in the city had abandoned their houses. Windows were lit. Men and women were embracing one another: they thought that the war was over as well. Nobody had given any attention to the words of Badoglio on the radio: "Italy will honour its word" [to Germany].'[4]

Goebbels, observing events from Berlin, was appalled. 'It is incredibly distressing to think that a revolutionary movement that has been in power for twenty-one years could disintegrate in such a way.'[5] Hitler, equally outraged, started discussing with his generals what military options were open to the Germans in order to deal with the developing situation in Italy. But suddenly, little more than two days after Mussolini had been deposed, the Germans had to face a whole new calamity.

On the night of 27–28 July, the city of Hamburg was engulfed in a massive firestorm. This was the single most destructive night during a series of Allied bombing raids that had started on 24 July and did not end until 3 August. The whole campaign had been carefully planned to have a cumulative effect that was devastating. One raid quickly following another so that the German civil defence forces on the ground had no time to extinguish the conflagration. The firefighters were also hampered by the inclusion in the bomb loads of delayed-action explosives, designed to detonate as they were working.

British Air Ministry experts had previously examined data about the flammability and proximity of houses in German cities, in order to determine the most damaging sections to target. Setting on fire the 'terraces of box-like buildings dating from the Middle Ages' in the centre of cities like Hamburg was expected to 'yield good dividend'.[6]

There was also another, technological reason the raid was so devastating. 'The effectiveness of the first Hamburg raid was due to at last getting permission to use something we'd had in the bag for a long time,' said Air Chief Marshal Sir Arthur Harris, head of Bomber Command, 'which was known as "window" – the dropping of clouds of aluminium paper strips, which completely upset not only the German location apparatus but also their gun-aiming apparatus.'[7]

The result was the heaviest bombing losses suffered by a European city during the war, with around 37,000 dead. On 27–28 July, the combination of dry hot weather, the flammability of the area targeted and the fact that buildings were still burning from the previous raids, all came together to create a giant firestorm. The Police President of Hamburg described it as a 'hurricane of fire . . . against which all human resistance seemed vain'.[8] The Gauleiter of Hamburg, Karl Kaufmann, called the effects of the British bombing raid 'a catastrophe of inconceivable dimensions'.[9]

Ben Witter, a resident of the city, recalled how during the raids people had been 'burning like torches'. They leapt into canals only to find that the water was ablaze: 'It was burning because very many small ships had exploded and oil had been released into the water and people who were themselves on fire jumped into it. Some kind of chemical must have been in it because they burned, swam, burned and went under.'[10]

Gretl Büttner, another resident of the city, saw 'Ruins everywhere, as far as the eye could see. Debris on the streets, collapsed house fronts, far-flung stones on kerbs, charred trees and devastated gardens . . . And always the sound of new buildings collapsing and the crackling of the ravenous fires still feeding could be heard. Poor, beautiful, beloved, raped city! One was without words.'[11]

Inevitably, the destruction of Hamburg – combined with the fall of Mussolini – had an effect on civilian morale in Germany. One confidential intelligence report compiled by the SD said: 'The idea that the form of government in the Reich, which was considered immutable, could also suddenly change . . . is very widespread.' In addition, the SD reported that 'there are also some reports of old spiteful jokes such as the one about the Führer's having withdrawn to write a book with the title "My Mistake".'[12]

For some members of the regime it was all too much. The Chief of Staff of the Luftwaffe, Hans Jeschonnek, an ardent supporter of the Nazis, killed himself on 18 August. The catalyst for his decision appears to have been the RAF's raid on Peenemünde, the Germans' secret rocket-development site, but he had previously described Stalingrad as 'trifling' alongside Hamburg.[13]

Goebbels was deeply concerned about the effect of the bombing raids, noting on 25 July that the letters he was receiving from members of the public 'contain an extraordinary amount of criticism'. Ordinary Germans kept 'questioning why the Führer does not visit the areas hit particularly hard by the air raids, why Göring does not show up, and especially why the Führer doesn't talk to the German people and give information on the current situation. I feel it's necessary for the Führer to do this,' Goebbels noted, 'despite his heavy military burdens. One cannot ignore the people for too long; ultimately, they are at the centre of our war effort. If the people ever lost their inner strength and their faith in the German leadership, it would create the most serious leadership crisis we have ever faced.'[14] But Hitler would not heed Goebbels' advice. He was still not prepared to show himself when events were going badly.

Yet despite all of the setbacks he faced during July 1943, and his refusal to use his oratorical gifts to raise morale, Hitler remained securely in power at the end of this disastrous month. So why did he not suffer the same fate as Mussolini? One reason, as we have already seen, was that Germans perceived the threat from the east as existential. No one could expect the occupation of a conquered Germany by the Red Army to be similar to the occupation of Italy by the western Allies. There was no easy way out of the war against Stalin. His soldiers would surely want revenge for the suffering the Germans had inflicted upon their country.

However, this was not the only reason why Hitler survived in power. He was also helped by the way the Nazi state was structured. Hitler, unlike Mussolini, was head of state. There was no monarch above him to criticize or remove him. Nor was there an equivalent to the Grand Fascist Council to call him to account. In addition, Hitler knew he could count on the loyalty of members of the SS. Indeed their very motto, 'Meine Ehre heisst Treue' ('My honour is called loyalty') proclaimed their everlasting support. So, at this time of crisis, it was no accident that Hitler turned for help to Heinrich Himmler, the leader of the SS. Himmler was appointed Minister of the Interior in August 1943, and would now play an ever more prominent role in the suppression of dissent.

Another difficulty faced by anyone who wished to depose Hitler was his inaccessibility. For much of the time he lived in a secure military compound in a remote forest in East Prussia. The only people he regularly came into contact with were Nazi officials or military officers. Consequently, they were the only people with a realistic chance of removing him. Moreover, given that there was no possibility that Hitler would agree to be sidelined, as the Kaiser had been in the First World War, the only certain way of stopping him was by killing him. This raised two further problems: one emotional and one practical. The practical one was straightforward. Assuming someone was willing to attempt an assassination, were they prepared to act as a suicide bomber and kill themselves as well as Hitler, or would they insist on surviving their Führer's death and attempt to kill him remotely, most likely via a timed explosion?

The emotional problem was more intractable. Every soldier had sworn an oath to Adolf Hitler, and for a number of German officers breaking that oath was an impossibility. In addition, they all knew that a 'stab in the back' legend had grown up after the First World War – the fantasy that German forces on the front line had been undermined by Jewish politicians and industrialists back home. If Hitler was killed now, wouldn't a similar myth be created? Who would want to be responsible for that?[15]

Despite all these difficulties, there were German officers who did come forward and volunteer for the task. Unlike Stalin's military commanders, Hitler's officers were ready to turn on their leader. Indeed, by the summer of 1943, several attempts had already been made on Hitler's life. Officers at Army Group Centre had planned to murder Hitler when he visited them in Smolensk in March 1943. They placed a bomb, disguised as a package of liqueur bottles, in the plane taking Hitler back to his headquarters, but it failed to explode.

Just over a week later, on 21 March, another officer, Rudolf Christoph Freiherr von Gersdorff, tried to blow himself up alongside Hitler at an exhibition of captured Soviet weaponry in Berlin. He set off timers on the small bombs he carried in his pockets and followed Hitler round the exhibition. But Hitler hurried by more quickly than expected, leaving Gersdorff to defuse the bombs in a toilet.

Notwithstanding these failed attempts on Hitler's life, there was another issue which hung over many Germans by this point in the war, and which influenced their opinion of Hitler and the regime – the persecution of the Jews. One SD report compiled after the Hamburg raids stated that some Germans were saying 'that now the airmen would come to Würzburg too, given that the last Jew recently left Würzburg'.[16] Another SD report, from December 1942, said that 'news from Russia' about the killing of Jews had reached Franconia in the south of Germany, and consequently people felt that 'if the Jews come again to Germany, they will exact dreadful revenge upon us.'[17] The perceived linkage was plain: the persecution of the Jews would lead to more suffering for non-Jewish Germans. And while it was Hitler and his supporters who had directly ordered the removal and killing of the Jews, large numbers of ordinary Germans had either benefited from their departure or at least done nothing to save them. The uneasy sense of guilt that many Germans felt was something the Italians were spared when they moved against Mussolini. No Jews had yet been deported from Italy.

Even though Hitler knew that the war was going against him in the summer of 1943, he remained adamant that the murder of the Jews was a priority. So it's instructive to see what happened when – on that rarest of occasions – someone challenged him on the subject. Towards the end of June 1943, Hitler had returned to the Berghof in southern Bavaria for a break from the claustrophobia of life at his military headquarters. Two of his guests at the Berghof were Baldur von Schirach, former head of the Hitler Youth and now Gauleiter of Vienna, and his wife Henrietta. As the daughter of Heinrich Hoffmann, Hitler's personal photographer, Henrietta had known the German leader since she was a child. This personal connection no doubt emboldened her to act as she did.

One evening, as they all sat in the great hall of the Berghof, she told Hitler in a soft voice that she had seen Jewish women weeping in the streets as they were deported from Amsterdam. Hitler was furious. He demanded to know why this was any of her business and blamed her for being 'sentimental'. He pointed out that thousands of German soldiers were dying in the war, leaving inferior specimens of humanity still alive. Shortly after this tirade, the Schirachs left the Berghof. Although the encounter was brief, it demonstrated Hitler's unshakeable ideological commitment to a policy of mass murder. For him there was no turning back.[18]

Whether talking to Henrietta von Schirach about the Jews or to his generals about military matters, Hitler was always certain he was right. He believed that all the suffering and death he was creating was not only for the benefit of his Reich, but also in accord with the racial prescriptions of natural law. He was as committed as any religious fanatic.

The propaganda image that Goebbels created around Hitler helped bolster the idea that the German Führer was an almost messianic human being. It showed him as a man who lived the life of an ascetic. A man who was 'married' to the nation, one who had shunned all normal human comforts in order to focus on the cause. But this – at least insofar as it reflected his personal life – was an illusion. During the war, and unbeknown to ordinary Germans, he had a girlfriend.

Hitler had first met Eva Braun in Munich in 1929, after she started work for his photographer Heinrich Hoffmann at the age of seventeen. Hitler took a fancy to this pretty blonde – twenty-three years his junior – and by the time he became Chancellor in January 1933 they were in a relationship, but scarcely a conventional one. Only in the relative isolation of the Berghof did Hitler acknowledge Eva as his girlfriend, and even then she had to be kept hidden from all but Hitler's closest colleagues. Herbert Döring, the manager of the Berghof, remembered that Eva had to leave whenever Hitler held a meeting with outsiders. Once, when a conference went on longer than expected he agreed to sneak her back into the building via 'the kitchen entrance'.[19]

Yet this subterfuge could not hide the fact that Braun and Hitler had adjoining rooms at the Berghof, and so the nature of their relationship was apparent to regular visitors. 'I could only wonder at the way Hitler and Eva Braun avoided anything that might suggest an intimate relationship,' wrote Albert Speer, the Nazi Armaments Minister – 'only to go upstairs to the bedrooms together late at night.'[20]

Though Hitler was never openly affectionate to Eva, there was a certain bantering quality to their relationship. Hitler 'teased her about her [small] dogs, which he said were nothing but a couple of dusting brushes', wrote Traudl Junge, one of Hitler's secretaries, 'whereupon she replied that Blondi [Hitler's Alsatian] wasn't a dog at all but a calf.'[21]

But whatever else Eva Braun was to Hitler, she was not an equal. 'In general Hitler showed little consideration for her feelings,' said Speer. 'He would enlarge on his attitude toward women as though she were not present: "A highly intelligent man should take a primitive and stupid woman." '[22] Consequently, 'Even toward Eva Braun he was never completely relaxed and human. The gulf between the leader of the nation and the simple girl was always maintained.'[23]

The 'gulf' between them was such that in order to get what she wanted – and not incur Hitler's wrath – she occasionally had to enlist the help of staff at the Berghof. 'She always liked to nibble,' said Döring. 'She would eat chocolates. During the war there weren't any, or very rarely. So she came along and talked to me and my wife [who also worked at the Berghof]. We didn't have anything, all the supplies had gone. So I had an idea. I took a letterhead, Berghof, Obersalzberg . . . Hitler was not mentioned in the letter, I would like to emphasize, but I wasn't either, not in the text. And I composed a letter, a very nice letter, and I sent it to a very big chocolate factory . . . Hitler would have forbidden it, Bormann too. Bormann didn't like her anyway, because in his eyes she was a parasite. Bone-idle and so on. So I wrote the letter and after four, five or six days, a parcel arrives, and what a parcel! I don't know whether there were 10, 15 or 20 pounds of chocolates!' Döring paid the enclosed invoice out of the Berghof accounts and hoped no one would ever look too closely into the matter: 'Hitler couldn't be allowed to find out, he would have humiliated Eva and me as well.'[24]

At the same time as Hitler was in a relationship with Eva Braun, there were rumours that Stalin was involved with a woman in an even more discreet way. No one can know for certain, but it appears likely that during the war he had a sexual relationship with one of his servants – Valentina Istomina. She was nearly forty years younger than Stalin and was the housekeeper at his dacha just outside Moscow. Plump, cheerful and homely, she was the antithesis of Stalin's ex-wife, Nadezhda Alliluyeva. Where Nadezhda had been intense and prepared to argue, Valentina was bubbly and submissive.

Stalin never publicly acknowledged any relationship with Valentina Istomina. 'Whether or not Istomina was Stalin's wife is nobody's business,' said Molotov years later. 'Engels lived with his housekeeper.'[25]

So it appears that during the war Hitler and Stalin each chose a sexual partner who was subservient. The contrast with the partners of some of their closest colleagues was marked. Molotov's party-activist wife Polina, for example, had been Minister of Fisheries before the war, and Goebbels' wife Magda was easily her husband's equal in shrewdness and ambition. Molotov and Goebbels demonstrably wanted a great deal more from their wives than their bosses did from their girlfriends.

It's not too difficult to suggest why this was so. Hitler and Stalin both kept a distance from those around them. This was obvious in the case of Hitler – no one could claim to be on intimate terms with him – but less so with Stalin, given the raucous, drunken evenings he spent at his dacha with his entourage. This bonhomie, however, was just a façade. In reality, those around Stalin knew little about what he was really thinking. The only thing they knew for certain was that they could be arrested and tortured at any moment. As Khrushchev said: 'All of us around Stalin were temporary people. As long as he trusted us to a certain degree, we were allowed to go on living and working. But the moment he stopped trusting you, Stalin would start to scrutinise you until the cup of his distrust overflowed. Then it would be your turn to follow those who were no longer among the living.'[26]

Intriguingly, Hitler and Stalin had each been attracted to far more intellectually demanding women in the past. Stalin's second wife Nadezhda Alliluyeva had been opinionated and independent, studying for a time at the Industrial Academy in Moscow.[27] And Hitler had been drawn to the sophisticated Magda Goebbels before her marriage to the Propaganda Minister.[28] But, regardless, by this point in their lives Hitler and Stalin had settled on more deferential companions.

Stalin, unlike Hitler, had children. Yakov, his son by his first wife, was an officer in the Red Army and was captured by the Germans less than a month into the war. He died at Sachsenhausen concentration camp in April 1943. Stalin's relationship with Yakov had always been fractious and he 'bullied' and 'picked' on him.[29]

Stalin's youngest son, Vasily, turned into an alcoholic and spent much of his time womanizing. He would die at the age of forty in 1962. Stalin's daughter, Svetlana, initially had a more positive relationship with her father, but that too went sour when he insisted on controlling her private life.[30]

Hitler would have looked on these problems as inevitable. He was convinced that it was a terrible fate to be the child of a 'great' man. 'Hitler's point of view was, he wasn't going to marry,' said Herbert Döring. 'If he were to marry and have children, they would suffer. He was such a genius, and the children wouldn't amount to anything and they would be ridiculed.'[31]

Both Hitler and Stalin had health concerns during the war. Hitler's stomach problems – which had been with him for years – worsened, and he also developed a tremor in his left hand. Towards the end of the war he may even have exhibited the early symptoms of Parkinson's disease.[32] His prognosis was not helped by the many pills and injections administered by his incompetent doctor, Theodor Morell. As for Stalin, he developed arteriosclerosis and had trouble with his circulation. His smoking would have exacerbated these troubles, and his drinking can't have improved things either.

Against this background, in July 1943, Stalin capitalized on the Red Army's success in holding the Germans at Kursk by ordering a series of offensives. The first, Operation Kutuzov, was aimed at German positions south-west of Moscow, and by early August the city of Orel – scene of a humiliating Soviet defeat in October 1941 – had been liberated.

Problems for the Germans were multiplying. Increasingly, Wehrmacht units had to face not just Red Army soldiers in front of them, but Soviet partisans operating behind their lines. This was no accident. There was a direct relationship between Red Army success on the battlefield – and consequently the belief that the Germans would soon be expelled from Soviet territory – and the overall effectiveness of the partisan movement. The Leningrad headquarters of the partisans, for example, reported that partisan units destroyed just 870 railway trucks in 1941, but a massive 5,374 in 1943.[33] Around Orel in ten days at the end of July 1943, they wrecked railway lines in nearly 7,500 locations. Shortly afterwards about 100,000 partisans were involved in the broader Operation Rail War across a vast area behind the German front line.[34]

The way Hitler and Stalin each reacted to the partisan war was a microcosm of the brutal philosophy at the core of their thinking. Hitler had previously welcomed Stalin's call on 3 July 1941 for resistance behind German lines, because 'it gives us the opportunity to stamp out everything that stands against us' and to 'shoot dead anyone who even looks at us askance'.[35] The following year, on 8 August 1942, Hitler had compared the war against the Soviet partisans with 'the struggle in North America against the Red Indians' and said that 'victory will go to the strong, and strength is on our side.'[36]

When officers like Colonel Reinhard Gehlen, of the Army Intelligence Agency for the East, suggested at the end of 1942 that the local population should be enlisted in the fight against the partisans, Hitler simply reiterated his hard line, arguing that 'Only where the struggle against the partisan nuisance was begun and carried out with ruthless brutality have successes been achieved.'[37] In pursuit of this policy of 'ruthless brutality', German forces shot innocent hostages in reprisal actions, burnt houses to the ground and even used villagers as human mine detectors to clear roads of suspected explosive devices.

Soviet citizens living under German occupation were often placed in an impossible position. If they went along with German rule, they could be accused of collaboration by the partisans. If they helped the partisans, they could be shot by the Germans. They also risked unjust denunciation by their neighbours to either side. Anyone who had a score to settle could have them destroyed.

The situation was made still more dangerous by the practical problems the partisans faced in surviving behind German lines. While occasionally they were supplied from airdrops, most of the time they took food from the locals – by force if necessary. 'Sometimes when we went hungry', admitted Mikhail Timoshenko, who led one partisan group in the north of the Soviet Union, 'we'd take a cow from a collective farm. We'd cut it open and cook it on a campfire.'

In addition to taking food from the locals, the partisans were capable of taking their lives as well. 'We killed any of the population who helped the Germans,' said Timoshenko. 'Let's imagine that you'd betrayed a group and that I know all about it. You're at home, OK? You're not hiding from anyone. You live with your family . . . The traitor wouldn't imagine that someone else knew and had told me. I'd send two men to him at night. They'd open the door and take him. They'd bring him back to us, and we'd begin to question him . . . Many of them wouldn't admit to it of course. It's a very difficult thing to admit to: that you've betrayed your own.'

But this interrogation by a three-man impromptu 'court' was a mere formality, since Timoshenko claimed he always had 'reliable information' beforehand that the 'traitor' had collaborated. As a result, every single person taken for questioning by his unit was subsequently shot in the back of the head: 'I didn't have the right to let a traitor go. Our Soviet laws for the rear stipulated that he had to be tried and sent to prison because he had helped the Germans because he had collaborated with them. But where could we send him? Where could one find a prison there? It was clear that, whether or not you really wanted to, you had no choice but to take the kind of decision that our court took. Certainly.'

Timoshenko operated the same ruthless standard in his dealings with the Germans: 'Our task was as follows: to destroy their manpower, their equipment, blow up the bridges, the railway lines, destroy communications – in other words to destroy everything that could be of use to the enemy. To destroy all of it. Wreck it . . . I'm a very kind person by nature. I can't kill an animal, you understand? Or even hit it across the face. But I felt that I had to kill the Germans, you understand? Not only because of the propaganda, but also because of a feeling inside me that the Germans had come to rape my sister, kill my mother, my daughter. That they'd come to make me a slave.'[38]

Stalin would have approved of Mikhail Timoshenko's ruthlessness – particularly the way he dealt with 'traitors'. Indeed, the Soviet authorities went further. In June 1942 a decree of the State Defence Committee declared that the families of people sentenced to death for collaboration with the Germans should be punished by five years in exile.[39] It didn't matter that the wives, husbands, fathers, mothers or other close relatives of those convicted had done nothing wrong themselves.

Stalin's merciless approach to his own people extended to the battlefield. Though the daily losses, with one or two exceptions like the Battle for Berlin, declined over the last years of the war as the Red Army became more tactically proficient, the basic belief in the expendability of the individual never changed. It's an attitude that was epitomized by the use of penal battalions. These units were composed of soldiers who had been convicted of disciplinary offences, supplemented by prisoners from the Gulag, and were tasked with especially dangerous, often near-suicidal tasks.

Nearly a million Soviet soldiers were found guilty by military courts in the course of the war. Of these over 400,000 were placed in penal units, and the rest sentenced to prison or shot. Around 160,000 Red Army soldiers were executed during the conflict, more than ten times the number of German soldiers who suffered the same fate.[40] Similarly, while the Germans also used penal battalions, the Soviets embraced the concept to a much larger degree.

Vladimir Kantovski was one of the tiny minority who survived service in a Soviet penal battalion. He was sent to prison in 1941 at the age of eighteen for protesting at the arrest of his teacher. Once in the Gulag he responded to a call for 'volunteers', and by the start of 1943 he was a soldier in the 54th Penal Company. Even though he knew the risks, as a 'patriot' he welcomed the chance to fight the Germans. 'For me, the little freedom I had in the penal battalion meant a lot,' he said. 'Can you imagine, understand, what freedom is? For that you have to spend half a year in Omsk prison being completely immobile in the cell, and you can only look into the sky through a slot in the window.'

Like many in the penal battalions, Kantovski experienced only one battle. Near Demyansk, south of Leningrad, his unit was ordered to walk towards the German positions in 'reconnaissance through combat'. Soviet commanders used poorly armed and wholly expendable troops to gain intelligence on the type of forces ranged against them. As the Germans shot and killed members of the penal battalion, the Soviet commanders learnt the location of their guns.

Kantovski felt 'fatalistic' as he advanced. 'I don't think you can feel any patriotism when you are participating in such an attack. I think the overriding feeling is one of bluntness – your feelings are blunted . . . You know what is happening is unavoidable, fatal, and it's like a game of Russian roulette. Well, what's your lot going to be?'

Kantovski soon discovered his fate. He was shot by a machine gun and collapsed to the ground. As he lay bleeding, he worried that his commanders might think he had somehow invited this wound. If they did, he would be executed for cowardice. But realizing that his only choice was between dying on the battlefield and risking death at the hands of his own countrymen, he decided to crawl back to the Soviet lines. In the context of a penal battalion, he was 'lucky'. Though most of those in his unit died that day, his life was spared. But while a number of soldiers wounded in the penal battalions were considered to have 'pardoned' their sins 'through blood' and were transferred to ordinary Red Army units, the Soviet authorities decided to return Kantovski to the Gulag. He was released only in 1951. Throughout this experience he distinguished between his love for his country, his faith in communism and his hatred of Stalin: 'We knew that Stalin's power was not proletarian dictatorship, but it was dictating to the proletariat . . . and it was a cruel dictatorship.'[41]

Fyodor Bubenchikov, who commanded a penal unit in 1943, had a very different perspective on the use of penal battalions. He had been sent to the unit not as a punishment, but to control the recalcitrants who had. 'Part of your job was to keep them together and to send them into battle,' he said. 'They were given weapons only right before the battle. They were trained with dummies . . . In such conditions they were not ordinary soldiers.' Consequently, he argues, it was sensible for him to lead these men not from in front, but from several hundred metres behind: 'You have four hundred men who recently arrived from a colony [that is, the Gulag], who were former recidivists, or thieves or criminals. They were trained in the course of five or six days. You can't get to know people really well in the course of such a short time. Then they are handed out weapons and you run in front of them leading them into the battle? Where is the logic [in that]? We had the right to be behind the soldiers, but we made sure that they were brought food in a timely fashion and received their vodka ration . . .'[42]

As we've seen, both Hitler and Stalin also strove to keep their distance, not only from the soldiers dying on the front line, but from the hardships ordinary citizens endured back home. This is why it is so intriguing that Stalin suddenly decided to visit the front in early August 1943. He travelled by train and car towards the line at Rzhev, west of Moscow. But he spent only four days away from his office, and was still some distance away from the actual fighting. None of that mattered, however, because this trip was all about pretence.[43] It allowed Stalin to be portrayed in the Soviet media as a brave commander who was close to his troops, and to make a point to Churchill and Roosevelt. Neither of them had to repel Germans from their own countries, neither of them had to deal with such momentous battlefield decisions. 'Only now, having come back from the front,' boasted Stalin to Roosevelt on 8 August, 'can I answer your message of July 16th.'[44] He must have revelled in the chance to give the impression that he was all but fighting in the trenches. No wonder he had no time to chat with the Allied leaders. No wonder he was angry at the lack of a second front. Seldom has so much political mileage been gained from such a cursory trip.

Stalin's visit to the 'front' also provided him with immediate leverage on the question of the location of any future summit. In his telegram of 8 August, he directly coupled his duties as a fighting man – peddling the lie that he 'frequently' had to 'go to the different parts of the front' – with a newfound desire to meet with Roosevelt and Churchill. But because of the need to 'submit' everything 'to the interests of the front' he suggested that this meeting be held in the Soviet Union, 'either in Astrakhan or in Archangel'.

Stalin had decided that, while it might be useful for him to meet face to face with Roosevelt and Churchill, that meeting should be held under Soviet supervision. The encounter, if it was to take place, would be on his terms. It was a demonstration of raw power.

For the next few months, the western Allies tried their best to get Stalin to change his mind. Roosevelt, especially, hoped the conference could be held somewhere closer to him. This wasn't just a question of geography. Statesmen understand that appearances matter. Most often, the weak travel to see the strong.

Stalin eventually suggested Tehran as the location for the meeting.

The city was relatively close to the Soviet Union, and the Soviets already had a presence in Iran as a result of their joint invasion of the country with the British in 1941. But Roosevelt was vehemently opposed to the idea. He complained that he couldn't travel to Tehran 'for constitutional reasons'. He had to be able to sign or veto bills from Congress in Washington within a narrow time frame, and planes might not be able to fly out of Tehran because of bad weather. He suggested a whole gamut of alternatives – Cairo, Asmara in Eritrea or 'some port in the Eastern Mediterranean' where each leader could have his own ship.[45]

But Stalin held firm. If the meeting couldn't be held in Tehran then he would send Molotov instead. This was too much for Roosevelt. He had already met Molotov. He wanted to meet Stalin. So in a telegram on 8 November 1943 he relented. Miraculously, he had now 'worked out a method' by which he could fulfil his presidential duties and still fly to Tehran.[46] Thus before the meeting even started Stalin had already asserted his dominance.

By the time the conference convened in late November, Soviet forces were closing on Kiev, having driven the Wehrmacht back across eastern Ukraine. This was in direct contrast to the relative failure of the Allies in Italy. The surrender of the Italians had been so botched – with Mussolini arrested on 25 July and the Italian capitulation not announced until 8 September – that the Germans had managed to disarm the Italian Army and prepare solid defences. Strong German resistance, coupled with difficult terrain, meant the Allies were now finding it hard to make progress.

Nor, just prior to Tehran, was the relationship between the British and American leaders in good shape. The Americans had been concerned about Churchill's attitude to the second front during a meeting in Cairo, just before the delegations left for Iran. On 25 November, Lord Moran[47] met Roosevelt's trusted adviser Harry Hopkins, and 'found him full of sneers and jibes'. Hopkins was angry with Churchill because he felt the British Prime Minister was focused on the war in Italy rather than in planning the attack on France. As a consequence, said Hopkins, 'Some of us are beginning to wonder whether the [cross-Channel] invasion will ever come off.'[48]

'Sure, we are preparing for a battle at Teheran [sic],' said Hopkins in conclusion. 'You will find us lining up with the Russians.' Moran was taken aback: 'What I find so shocking is that to the Americans the P.M.

is the villain of the piece; they are far more sceptical of him than they are of Stalin.' Moran bemoaned the fact that because of this discord the Allies were about to meet Stalin 'without a common plan'.[49]

However, while there was no common plan, there was certainly a Roosevelt plan – and it was a straightforward one. He was determined to form a relationship with Stalin. But the arrogance of the American President, who thought no one was impervious to his charm, combined with the virtuosity of Stalin's negotiating tactics, led to the Soviet leader leaving Tehran with almost everything he wanted. Contrary to popular myth – which places the Yalta conference in February 1945 as the moment when the western Allies bowed to Soviet power – the policy was already on show at Tehran.

Roosevelt demonstrated his desire to ingratiate himself with Stalin from the start of the conference. The President had accepted Stalin's offer that he and the American delegation move into the compound of the Soviet embassy in Tehran. Ostensibly this was because the planned American accommodation was some way from the conference venue and so transportation might not be secure. But Roosevelt was surely pleased to be so close physically to Stalin. Although there was another consequence of the move – the Americans were now under Soviet surveillance. They would have known everything Roosevelt said in private.

The President insisted on meeting Stalin without Churchill present, before the first plenary session of the conference. Roosevelt liked to talk, and as we have seen, unlike most leaders, Stalin liked to listen. So, at least in that sense, they were ideally suited. When they met, on the afternoon of 28 November, Roosevelt discoursed at length on a variety of topics. But there was one constant theme, his attempt to distance himself from the British Prime Minister.[50]

Roosevelt painted Churchill as almost a colonial relic. Hopkins later told Lord Moran that the American President had said to Stalin that 'he hoped Malaya, Burma and other British colonies would soon be "educated in the arts of self-government"'. Roosevelt also warned Stalin 'not to discuss India with the Prime Minister', hinting at Churchill's reactionary views. And, as Moran wrote, 'Stalin's slits of eyes do not miss much; he must have taken it all in.'[51]

At the first meeting of all three leaders, which followed straight after Roosevelt's intimate chat, Churchill joined in the attempt to impress Stalin. Both he and the President spoke in flowery terms about the

special nature of the occasion. Roosevelt waxed lyrical about the symbolism of the leaders sitting together as 'members of the same family'
while Churchill 'prayed that they might be worthy of this wonderful
God-granted opportunity of rendering service to their fellow-men'. In
response, Stalin merely said he hoped they would 'make good use of this
opportunity'.[52]

The Soviet leader was equally straightforward in his comments during the substantive part of the meeting. He first offered a concession. He
agreed that the Soviet Union would join in the war against Japan, as
Roosevelt had craved, but only after Germany had been defeated. He
then reiterated his demand for a second front. That, essentially, was all
he had to say. He gave with one hand and took away with the other. A
simple, coherent message.

Sir Alan Brooke, Chief of the Imperial General Staff, watched the
three leaders at the meeting, and while he dismissed as 'a lot of blah-
flum' the attempt by Churchill and Roosevelt at 'buttering up the
Russians'[53] he 'rapidly grew to appreciate the fact that he [Stalin] had a
military brain of the very highest calibre . . . In this respect he stood out
when compared with his two colleagues [Roosevelt and Churchill].'[54]

Stalin had hardly demonstrated by his actions so far in the war a 'military brain of the very highest calibre', so Brooke's comments are intriguing.
Perhaps Brooke saw in Stalin a character not so very dissimilar to his
own – not in terms of criminal ruthlessness (that trait belonged entirely to
Stalin) but in the ability to recognize what was the central point in any
argument and state it plainly. The two men also shared an intense dislike
of the kind of 'blah-flum' favoured by Roosevelt and Churchill.

Charles Bohlen, Roosevelt's translator, noticed that Stalin had a habit
of 'doodling wolf heads on a pad with a red pencil' and 'never showed
any agitation and rarely gestured', but 'sat quietly, cigarette in hand,
concentrating on the discussion'.[55] When he did speak, he did so to take
the meeting back to the point that mattered to him – the need for an
immediate second front.

Stalin carried this considered and watchful stance into his encounter
with Churchill that night, and Europe is still living with the consequences of what happened between them. For it was during this meeting
that Churchill told Stalin he agreed that the Soviets could keep eastern
Poland after the war – the very territory he had said the previous year
could not be given up without breaking the Atlantic Charter.

Stalin handled the discussion with consummate skill. Churchill tried his best to get the Soviet leader to reveal his views before he outlined his own plan, but to no avail. Stalin merely said he felt no 'need' to speak. Churchill pressed on and said that he imagined the whole of Poland shifting westwards, with the Poles taking German territory to compensate for the loss of land in the east, now to be given to Stalin.[56] Churchill made this offer – one of the most consequential alterations of borders in recent times – without discussing it beforehand with the Polish government in exile. The Poles, allies of both the British and the Soviets, were thus not consulted about the dismemberment of their own country.

Stalin, as we have seen, had been calling for eastern Poland to be given to the Soviets since he first met the British Foreign Secretary back in December 1941. Yet now, incredibly, he hadn't even had to ask for this territory to be given to him. Churchill just handed it over. The British Prime Minister tried to defend his actions in a letter to Anthony Eden a few weeks later, in January 1944. He talked of the 'tremendous victories' of the Red Army and the 'deep-seated changes which have taken place in the character of the Russian State and government' together with the 'new confidence which has grown in our hearts towards Stalin'.[57] But there remains a strong suspicion that this was just more 'blah-flum'. Maybe Churchill had managed to convince himself that the 'changes' for the better he claimed he'd seen in Soviet policy were really substantial. Arguably there were small signs of transformation. It was true, for instance, that Stalin had abolished the Comintern in May 1943 – though he had always been ambivalent about this organization designed to establish communism abroad. This was a minor 'change', however, compared to the crimes of the Soviet regime that Churchill knew about and chose not to mention – Katyn, for example.

So it's likely that Churchill's suggestion that Polish borders be radically changed was simply a case of ruthless realpolitik. He knew that the Red Army would take this territory as it advanced, and the western Allies were not prepared to fight to get it back for the Poles. He admitted as much in another note he sent to Eden in January 1944, when he said that the Poles 'must be very silly if they imagine we are going to begin a new war with Russia for the sake of the Polish eastern border'.[58]

Stalin undoubtedly held a strong hand over the Polish question, but he still played it brilliantly. In contrast with his continual refrain about the second front, he chose to wait and let the western Allies come to him. He knew his soldiers would take Poland before the western Allies, so he was in control. And, as we have seen, the way he had manipulated the Katyn revelations earlier in the year gave him a plausible, if dishonest, excuse not to deal with the Polish government in exile. A less sophisticated political player might have proclaimed his dominance at Tehran and demanded his allies accept his demands. But Stalin kept quiet and waited. He knew time was on his side.

Roosevelt had not been present during Churchill's conversation with Stalin about Poland, but later in the conference he did reveal his own position. Significantly, he chose to do this in secret, away from the formal discussions. He told Stalin that as he was considering running for president again in 1944, he had to take notice of the views of Polish-American voters. He wanted their support, and publicly announcing, prior to the election, a massive reordering of the Polish nation was obviously problematic. But, confidentially, he could tell Stalin that he agreed with Churchill that the Soviets could keep eastern Poland after the war.[59]

How Stalin must have enjoyed this encounter. Not only had the American President agreed to his demands, but by drawing Stalin into his confidence he had placed himself in a position of weakness. If Roosevelt subsequently did not keep his word, then Stalin could leak what he'd said. This was the kind of behind-the-scenes deal that Stalin relished. He had tried to get Eden to agree to a secret protocol about this very issue back in December 1941, only to have his suggestion summarily rejected.[60] How things had changed.

Charles Bohlen, who witnessed Roosevelt's 'secret' conversation with Stalin about Poland, recognized that 'it was a great mistake.'[61] Within minutes it was apparent why. At the next plenary session – held immediately after the 'secret' conversation – the American President suggested that Stalin could discuss the future of Poland with the Polish government in exile. This comment played well with the Polish-Americans back home. But fuelled by the knowledge that Roosevelt had already conceded the key issue of the new borders, Stalin was able to reject the idea immediately. He lied and said that members of the Polish government in exile were 'in contact' with the Germans – virtually implying that they were traitors. Neither the British nor Americans spoke out against this calumny.[62]

Matters were made worse by Churchill subsequently saying that he expected the post-war Polish government to be 'friendly' to the Soviets. The ambiguity over just what the word 'friendly' really meant in the context of a relationship with Stalin would come to haunt not just further negotiations over Poland, but the administration of many eastern European countries after their liberation.

It can be argued that once again Churchill and Roosevelt were just being pragmatic. They were not going to go to war with Stalin over the way he chose to run the countries the Red Army occupied after the war. But that brutal truth was not much comfort to the millions who would now swap the rule of one tyrant – Adolf Hitler – for another – Joseph Stalin. Anyone who still considers the Second World War to have been a wholly moral conflict, a straightforward story of good versus evil, needs to confront this uncomfortable reality.

In the weeks after the end of the conference, Sir Alexander Cadogan voiced his unhappiness about the Soviets in his diary. Not only did he complain about their 'bloody-minded' attitude towards the Poles, but he was utterly outraged by a false allegation, published in *Pravda*, that the British were negotiating a separate peace with Germany. Cadogan was so furious that he wrote in his diary on 17 January 1944 that the 'Russians' were 'the most stinking creepy set of Jews I've ever come across'.[63]

It's important to note Cadogan's resort to an anti-Semitic slur when he was angry. It reminds us that anti-Semitism existed in many places during this period – even among those who were fighting the Nazis. It wasn't the case, as Cadogan must have known, that the Soviet leadership was predominantly Jewish. The two leading figures – Stalin and Molotov – most certainly were not, and Stalin would demonstrate his own anti-Semitism in brutal fashion after the war.

While Cadogan railed against the Soviets, Churchill was sufficiently depressed during the conference to have a late-night vision of devastation. 'I believe man might destroy man and wipe out civilization,' he told Lord Moran, his doctor. 'Europe would be desolate and I may be held responsible.' Moran believed he knew why Churchill felt this way. 'Until he came here, the P.M. could not bring himself to believe that, face to face with Stalin, the democracies would take different courses. Now he sees he cannot rely on the President's support. What matters more, he realizes that the Russians see this too. It would be useless to try to take a firm line with Stalin. He will be able to do as he pleases. Will he become a menace to the free world, another Hitler? The P.M. is appalled by his own impotence.'[64]

By the time of Tehran, Stalin had already demonstrated his willingness to commit crimes – most blatantly by ordering the killings at Katyn in 1940. He had also seen how the British and Americans were prepared to ignore his actions. But he had not stopped committing atrocities. Quite the opposite, because just after the conference ended he was to preside over the deaths of many thousands of innocent men, women and children. And once again the western Allies would do nothing about it.

15. Mass Killing

Hitler, as the world knows, presided over the most horrific crime in history – the Holocaust. But the shadow cast by this terrible event has meant that much less attention has been paid to the enormous number of civilian deaths that Stalin was responsible for at the same time. This lack of focus on Stalin's wartime crimes, combined with the perception that as an ally of the West he was on the side of righteousness during the conflict, has meant that the Soviet leader has largely escaped the level of censure that he deserves.

How many people know, for example, the details of Stalin's horrendous acts of ethnic cleansing that took place during the war? Typical was his action against the population of Kalmykia, launched just after he returned to the Soviet Union from the conference at Tehran. The Kalmyks, an ethnically distinct group of Mongol descent, lived on the barren steppe south of Stalingrad, west of the Caspian Sea. This territory was as far east as the Germans ever reached in the war against the Soviets, and they were a long way from home – Elista, the capital of Kalmykia, is nearly 1,500 miles from Berlin.

After the Red Army had recaptured Kalmykia at the end of 1942, Stalin had to decide how to treat the inhabitants of this obscure part of the Soviet Union. In October 1943 he made his intentions clear.[1] He wanted the entire nation to suffer a punishment deportation, as a result of which many thousands would die. The formal decree authorizing the action, issued by the Presidium of the Supreme Soviet in December, claimed that 'many' Kalmyks had collaborated with the Germans. But while it was true that the Germans had recruited around 5,000 into the Kalmyk Cavalry Corps, a far greater number of Kalmyks – over 23,000 – were serving in the Red Army.[2] And since the Kalmyk Cavalry Corps had retreated with the Wehrmacht, the collaborators weren't even around to be punished.

None of that mattered to Stalin – in part because of the ethnicity of the Kalmyks. Stalin wanted to create a centralized state, and the presence of various ethnic populations within the Soviet Union was hard to reconcile with that ambition. While individual groups like the Kalmyks and Crimean Tatars were permitted to proclaim their ethnic heritage and remain in their traditional homeland, they were carefully watched to ensure that their sense of ethnic identity never developed into a desire for autonomy. Nothing could be more against the principles of the Soviet state than the quest for independence.

It was an issue that was exacerbated by Stalin's wartime focus on the imperial history of Russia. This new emphasis on past glories could be seen in a whole host of ways. For example, as we have seen, in 1942 Stalin created new military awards and named them after Russian military heroes like Alexander Nevsky, Mikhail Kutuzov and Alexander Suvorov. Soviet newspapers also overtly linked the fight against the Nazis with the imperial past. 'Now, in wartime,' wrote one journalist, 'we even more warmly and closely sense our blood tie with the founders and creators of Great Russian culture.'[3] Russia was always portrayed as the dominant member of the Soviet family, the big brother that all minor republics should look up to.[4]

There was a precedent for what Stalin was about to do to the Kalmyks. The ethnic Germans from the Volga region, for instance, had been deported to remote areas of the Soviet Union in 1941, and before the war Koreans living on the far eastern Soviet border had also been sent into internal exile. Altogether during his time in power, Stalin would order the deportation of several million people belonging to a variety of different national and ethnic groups, and around a million of them would die. The Kalmyks were one of the first to be targeted after their territory had been liberated from German occupation, and their treatment was a sign of things to come.

The deportation of the Kalmyks was to be an act of murderous ethnic cleansing: murderous because insufficient care had been taken to feed or house the deportees and so it was inevitable that thousands would die, and ethnically targeted because any Russian living in Kalmykia was exempt from the planned action. There was to be no attempt to assess individual guilt or innocence. Merely being born an ethnic Kalmyk was enough to render you liable for punishment.

On 28 December 1943 the NKVD moved on the Kalmyks in one giant coordinated action. Nineteen-year-old Vera Tachieva was at teacher training college when 'All of a sudden at six o'clock in the morning armed soldiers came in and announced that we were to be evicted.'

She went into shock, and some of her friends fainted: 'Our teachers came up to us and tried to calm us down. At that point, a lorry pulled up. We only had our personal belongings with us to put into the suitcases. They brought us to the railway station, put us into a cargo train wagon and more and more people followed and the wagon got full. We were sitting on that train crying. My friend was leaving her mother behind and she was screaming, where is my mother, how am I going to find my mother? We had the feeling we lost everything.'

The sudden destruction of her familiar world was all the more distressing for Vera because she was an ardent communist and had not even lived in an area of Kalmykia that had been under German occupation. 'We didn't know about any reasons [for the action]. We were brought up in the spirit of communism. We believed in communism. And we were young. When the train set off a panic on the train began. Shouting and noise. Weeping.'

Vera travelled on the train, crammed in with other Kalmyks, for five days. On board, as they journeyed to an unknown destination, they were soon covered in lice. 'One student got ill and then died. He got so much lice that you could see lice crawling all over him. Everyone was getting lice . . . We had to wait until the next station at which they had to remove the dead people. At the end we got used to it. While we were getting close to Novosibirsk [in Siberia], they began to collect all the corpses in the back carriage of the train and these corpses were piled up and then removed at the next stop, because the train had to go on and on . . . Most people were trying to calm each other down. They were saying, "No, no, don't scream." Or "They will sort it out, they will find the guilty party, they can't kill us." Some people had hope.'[5]

Kalmyks were hunted down wherever they were. Aleksey Badmaev was taken from a military hospital where he was recovering from an injury sustained in battle. He had fought on the Stalingrad front and been awarded a medal for valour. But it counted for nothing. All that mattered was that he was a Kalmyk. Like Vera Tachieva, Badmaev was a dedicated supporter of the regime: 'The commanders shouted [as they attacked], "For the motherland, for Stalin!" We were shouting because it was some sort of a protection. We were not afraid when we were shouting . . . the motherland has to be defended. That's how we were taught from the first year in school. We had nothing but our motherland. We were taught to be patriotic. Of course, we knew that there were rats and enemies of the people, but we believed that they were indeed enemies. One man, for example, was arrested and we wondered why, and we were told that he had been saying bad things about Stalin. We thought this was the correct thing to do. He shouldn't have said bad things about Stalin.'

But now Aleksey Badmaev – guilty only of the crime of being born a Kalmyk – was to be deported: 'When I learnt of the Kalmyk deportation, it was a shock for me that I haven't recovered from. What was I fighting for, what was I spilling my blood for, why did my people have to be relocated? My heart ached because of it. I'm telling you, it's crime enough to punish one man who is innocent, but only a sick, mentally ill, an abnormal man can give an order to relocate a whole people.'[6]

The operation was considered a success from the perspective of the NKVD. Beria reported directly to Stalin on 4 January 1944 that 'in all 26,359 families or 93,139 persons were loaded on to 46 special trains' and deported to Siberia.[7] There they had to work – often manual labour in the most appalling circumstances – or starve.

'Those who didn't have anything to swap for food and didn't know Russian, they went begging,' said Evdokiya Kuvakova, who was deported as a child. 'Some [of the locals] gave them some bread, but nevertheless a lot of people died of starvation . . . That deportation made me a sick person. My sister died young because she suffered so much, she experienced so many hardships . . . I still can't take it in.'[8]

Aleksey Badmaev was sent to a labour camp with other Kalmyk soldiers. 'The camp was awful,' he remembered. 'There were some German prisoners of war . . . others were criminals.' Instead of fighting on the front line, he and his Kalmyk comrades were put to work in the forest: 'At first we were pulling out tree trunks, they had to be felled and pulled out. If you failed to fulfil your quota during the day, you didn't receive the food ration of your bread, and people died of starvation very quickly. Out of 200 people, a month later only seventy-two survived. One hundred and twenty-eight died.'[9]

Stalin's approach to these deportations was similar in many ways to the Nazis' attitude towards the Jews during the ghetto phase of their persecution. Just as the Nazis wanted rid of a hated group, so did Stalin. Just as the Nazis watched as Jews in the ghettos starved in front of them, so Stalin by his actions demonstrated that he couldn't care less whether those who were deported died of hunger. 'The rapid dying out of the

Jews is for us a matter of total indifference,' said one Nazi overseeing the Łódź ghetto in November 1940, 'if not to say desirable . . .'[10] And, according to Kalmyk survivors, there were party officials in Siberia who felt the same way about them.

If the Jews had been left in the ghettos, and the Kalmyks in Siberia, it is almost certain that both groups would have been exterminated over time. In the Warsaw and Łódź ghettos, the two biggest in Poland, the death rate exceeded the birth rate not long after the ghettos were sealed, while the Kalmyks were similarly dying out in their new home. Of just over 90,000 Kalmyks deported in December 1943, around 74,000 were alive in 1949 but fewer than 65,000 in 1959.[11] Soviet officials knew that the Kalmyks were en route to extinction as early as July 1946. 'The mortality rate among the Kalmyks is really high,' wrote a Soviet official in Novosibirsk. It 'exceeds the birth rate by 3.5 times'.[12] The Kalmyks as a people were saved from annihilation only by a change in Soviet policy several years after Stalin's death.

Stalin never openly said that he sought to exterminate the Kalmyks. But, in practical terms, was he not slowly committing just that crime? He had ordered them deported away from their homeland to an environment where their death rate hugely exceeded their birth rate. What else was this but a policy of gradual extermination?

Looking back, Aleksey Badmaev was in no doubt about the resemblance between the crimes: 'Like Hitler who wanted to kill all the Jews, it was similar. What wrong did my people do to Stalin and to Beria? I don't know . . . One man, an old man I met on a train station, lost three sons at the front, but [still] he had to be deported, or my mother was deported, whose only son was fighting at the front. This was the essence of the crime. I think there's nothing in the world matching this crime but what Hitler did.'[13]

However, there were a number of differences between Stalin's and Hitler's actions. One that is often overlooked is who, at the time, was held responsible for the crime by those who suffered. For the Jews, it was obvious that Hitler was to blame. He had been shouting anti-Semitic rhetoric for years. But for punished people like the Kalmyks the guilt was less clear. Many of them felt that Stalin – the leader they had been taught was wise and caring – could not possibly have known what was happening. Some even wrote to him, begging him to intervene. 'To the leader and teacher of the peoples of the USSR, comrade

Stalin: Dear and deeply esteemed Joseph Vissarionovich,' began one letter from three Kalmyk party officials, sent in April 1946: '. . . in the immense and bleak Siberia, the Kalmyks are physically dying out, suffering moral and national degradation. This became possible only because among us, the Kalmyks, was found a negligible little gang of traitors, cursed by their people.' But, in contrast, 'Thousands of Kalmyks' sons in a[n] honourable and manly way fought on all fronts, many of them gave their lives for Soviet power – for you, comrade Stalin – and for the happiness of their own people . . . The Kalmyks await a decision on their fate from the government and from you, dear Joseph Vissarionovich. They should be returned to their native land, nationally united, politically rehabilitated and economically reborn . . .' The letter, signed 'with Communist regards', received no reply. While the exact fate of the three individuals who wrote this document is not known, the majority of those who sent letters of complaint to Stalin were transferred to prison camps to pay for the 'crime' of bothering him with their pleas.[14]

Another, more important difference between Hitler's and Stalin's policies is that, after the creation of the ghettos, Hitler presided over not just the mass shooting of Jews in the occupied Soviet Union in 1941, but also the mechanized extermination of Jews in camps like Auschwitz and Treblinka later in the war. But, while this distinction is undoubtedly vital, it is also useful to understand the prior context. A clue to what Hitler's intention for the Jews would have been in 1940 – had the war ended in the summer as the Nazis had anticipated – is offered by the seemingly bizarre Madagascar plan. As we saw earlier, in a memo he sent to Hitler in May 1940, Himmler wrote that he hoped 'completely to erase the concept of Jews through the possibility of a great emigration of all Jews to a colony in Africa or elsewhere'. Hitler, on receiving the memo, declared it 'very good and correct'.[15] And shortly after the defeat of the French that summer, the head of Jewish affairs at the German Foreign Office wrote that 'France must make the island of Madagascar available for the solution of the Jewish question.'[16]

The Nazis thus seriously considered sending the Jews to Madagascar. But this was not to be a homeland for the Jews akin to Israel. No, this was to be the site of their gradual extermination. The island was unable to sustain the lives of millions of Jews, and their life there 'under the administration of the Reichsführer SS'[17] would likely have been even more ghastly than in the ghettos of Poland. The Jews would still have died, just slowly and over a longer period than in the gas chambers. It is significant, given what was to happen, to note that Himmler in his 1940 memo also wrote that actions like forced deportation were 'the mildest and best, if one rejects the Bolshevik method of physical extermination of a people out of inner conviction as un-German and impossible'.[18] Yet within two years Himmler would be organizing a 'physical extermination' that was unparalleled in the history of the world.

Hitler and Himmler envisaged the Madagascar 'solution' to their 'Jewish problem' only for as long as they believed the war would end in 1940. They recognized that there was no possibility of transferring the Jews thousands of miles to Africa while the conflict continued. But even though the Madagascar plan was shelved once it became clear that the British would not make peace, it nonetheless offers us an insight into the comparative mentalities of Hitler and Stalin. That's because the Nazi proposal to send the Jews to Africa was not so very different from Stalin's plan to send punished peoples like the Kalmyks to Siberia. In both cases the property and belongings of the people deported were to be given to others and all traces of their lives in their homeland were to be eradicated. But while we can be certain in the case of the Nazis that the Madagascar plan was quasi-genocidal, it's harder to speak so definitively about Stalin's ultimate intentions for the ethnic groups he deported. Part of the problem is that, unlike Hitler, Stalin never confided his future desires to anyone. Hitler shouted out in his speeches that he wanted to exterminate the Jews. Stalin never said anything comparable, probably in order to keep his options open. As he had shown at the time of the Great Terror in the late 1930s, he was capable of encouraging his secret police to torture and kill, and then subsequently accusing them of going too far.

There is also an apparent paradox in the tyrants' involvement in the killings. While Stalin did not talk much about his intentions towards the groups he wanted to target, and Hitler talked a great deal, the Soviet leader is the one who left a paper trail of guilt behind him. It's easy to prove that he was a war criminal. We know he met with Beria and authorized the punishment deportation of a variety of different ethnic groups. Yet it is much harder – though still possible – to prove Hitler's responsibility for the Holocaust.

However, if you understand the different natures of the regimes and the contrasting personalities of the two leaders, this apparent paradox disappears. Hitler did not need to create a paper trail of written orders for the Holocaust, precisely because he spoke so much about his desire to see the Jews exterminated. It made complete sense to those beneath him that by killing the Jews they were fulfilling their Führer's vision. They didn't need to see a series of legal documents signed by their head of state authorizing the murders. But because Stalin did not speak so extensively in public about his plans and 'visions', those who supported him could never be certain that they were following his precise wishes without seeing his commands in writing.

We can see how the different systems functioned in practice by comparing the experience of two perpetrators – Oskar Groening and Nikonor Perevalov. Groening, an SS man who served at Auschwitz, and Nikonor Perevalov, a lieutenant in the NKVD, had a great deal in common. Both, for example, had volunteered enthusiastically to serve in their respective units, having been brought up as children to support the regimes. As an eleven-year-old, Groening, born into a nationalist family, was excited when Hitler became Chancellor in 1933, and he believed the Nazis would change Germany for the better.

As for Nikonor Perevalov, born just three months before the revolution of October 1917, he became a member of the Communist Party as soon as he could: 'Being a communist meant, like for all young Soviet people who were joining the party, that you wanted to be in the front ranks of our people, and set an example in everything, in all situations, and to educate non-party people, to bring them forward. I always meant this. It was necessary to do this in order to successfully destroy the enemy.'[19]

Both Groening and Perevalov dreamt of serving in an 'elite' organization. In Groening's case that meant volunteering to join the SS, in Perevalov's the NKVD. Each of them also understood the broad aims of the regime. Perevalov wanted to confront the 'enemies of the people' who stood in the way of a communist Soviet Union, and Groening to defeat the external and internal enemies of the new Reich, chiefly the Jews. 'The Jews were actually the cause of Germany's misery,' said Groening, '. . . and we were convinced by our world view that there was a great conspiracy of Jewishness against us.'[20]

Neither Groening nor Perevalov had somehow been hypnotized into their beliefs by the personalities of Hitler or Stalin. They were following Hitler and Stalin not so much as individuals, but as representatives of a system of values and practical policies that would lead to utopia. And they understood that as members of 'elites' they had a crucial part to play in creating this ideal new future.

Each of them was also told that the work he was about to undertake was top secret. Groening could not mention the existence of Auschwitz to 'friends or brothers or comrades or people who were not in this unit . . . we had to march forward individually and sign a statement to this effect.' And Perevalov, when he and his unit were sent to Kalmykia at the end of 1943, initially knew only that 'we had been brought here to carry out a secret mission.'

When Perevalov first heard that his mission was to force the Kalmyks from their homeland he thought the action was justified: 'Of course, I believed that [their] collaboration could have been true . . . I had to deport them.' He and the rest of his unit were read the 'order of the Presidium of the Supreme Soviet' authorizing the deportations. So, secure in the knowledge that the action was sanctioned at the highest level of the state, he prepared to remove the Kalmyks from their homes.[21]

Groening's experience was very different. Even though he had promised to keep knowledge of his forthcoming work at Auschwitz secret, he still believed he was being posted to a conventional concentration camp. It wasn't until after he had settled into his duties in the economic department of the camp that an SS colleague happened to mention casually that this was a special installation – one the Jews never left.

Once he learnt that Auschwitz was a place of mass murder, Groening's ideological beliefs allowed him to understand why this atrocity was happening: 'The necessity of annihilating the Jews was clear to us and justified in our eyes, because we believed that the enemy was not just in the air or at the front line or in England and so on, but that the enemy who had instigated the war were the Jews: this was our political education. Now, if you then go and say that we are at war, we have to do everything we can against those who want to defeat us, and these are primarily world Jewry and Jewish capital who are trying to gain world supremacy for the Jews and for communism – sometimes these things were equated – so . . . this was only a part of the war that we were waging.'[22]

Groening felt he didn't need to hear legal authorization for what went on as he performed his new role. He relied on the values he had been taught as a child. The Jews were a 'problem' that had to be dealt with one way or another. Now, in the life-and-death struggle of the war, an extreme – and top-secret – method of solving that 'problem' had been devised.

Both Groening and Perevalov discovered, however, that while it was one thing to understand in principle why these actions had to take place, it was quite another to make them happen in practical terms. And once their work was under way, both had doubts. For Groening, the first moment of concern came when he attended the arrival of a transport of Jews. This was not normally his job. Usually he spent his time in an office, counting the money taken from the murdered Jews. Only occasionally did he have to watch their arrival and check that their belongings were secured.

When the selection of the Jews had been completed, and the majority had been taken away – either to be admitted to the camp or for immediate gassing – Groening was shocked at what happened to the people left behind. He watched as those too ill to walk, or children who had lost their mother, were treated with appalling brutality. He witnessed one SS man smash a child's head against the side of a truck, while other SS shot elderly Jews and threw them 'on a lorry like a sack of wheat'.[23]

Groening was so outraged by what he saw that he complained to his unit commander. He was told that, while the gassing of the Jews 'couldn't be avoided', these 'excesses' and 'sadistic' acts at the arrival area shouldn't be happening. Reassured that 'if there was a necessity to exterminate the Jews, at least it should be done within a certain framework,' Groening continued to work at Auschwitz.[24]

As for Perevalov, he had doubts about the wisdom of the action against the Kalmyks when he saw that the vast majority of those to be deported were women, the elderly or children: 'I thought, well how can the whole people be sent away? I wondered what our central government was going to do about the Kalmyk communists, about the party activists . . . This is what I couldn't understand. This is what made me feel sorry for all those people, sorry for that group of people whom I saw.'[25]

But, unlike Groening, Perevalov did not mention his doubts to a superior: 'An order is an order, but also, what was more important, the decree was issued by the Supreme Soviet. But I think that both the Supreme Soviet, our main legislature, and the government and the Communist Party, the leaders made this mistake.' Nonetheless, 'it was my duty to fulfil the order. Such were the provisions of the army service. No matter how unwilling I could have felt, no matter what my understanding of the situation was, I was not supposed to think about it and speculate. An order is an order, it has to be fulfilled . . . Disobeying an order in a battle situation was to be court-martialled and punished in accordance with the military rules.'[26]

One difference between their situations was that Perevalov – while causing appalling suffering – was not part of a killing process centred on one location. He could not be certain what would happen to the Kalmyks once they had been deported. Even though it was obvious that there was insufficient food and water for them on the trains taking them to Siberia, he could reassure himself that this was not his concern and that their ultimate fate lay elsewhere. Groening, on the other hand, was working in a facility designed to murder, and admits that he was 'a cog in the machinery, a necessary cog'.[27]

But despite working at Auschwitz, the site of the largest mass murder in the history of the world, Groening was insulated from much of the horror of the killing process and he became habituated to his working life: 'Over years if you're not at the [arrivals] ramp every day which I wasn't – I only did it every three or four weeks to supervise what happened to the luggage – you somehow come to terms with your task. You're aware of other tasks your colleagues do and if they do them in a humane enough way – even if you know that this truck with the people who can no longer walk and the small children, that within the next half-hour they will be dead – this one accepts because these things have become everyday routine.'[28]

The notion that the Jews or others were dealt with 'humanely' at Auschwitz is a calumny that cannot pass without correction. There was nothing 'humane' about Auschwitz, and the testimony of large numbers of eyewitnesses who saw – and in many cases experienced – the appalling suffering at the camp confirms that fact.[29]

Perevalov, unlike Groening, regularly came into contact with distressed civilians. He stood close to them and read out the decree authorizing their deportation. He was feet away from their wailing and screaming. He knew in visceral terms the misery he was bringing into people's lives and thus had no emotional distance from the suffering.

One further reason why Perevalov experienced no such distancing from his task was because, in comparison with the procedure at Auschwitz, the NKVD were honest about the atrocity they were committing. Perevalov told his victims what was about to happen to them. Auschwitz, in contrast, was built on lies. As Groening admitted, the Kapos – prisoners supervising the unloading of transports – 'managed to persuade people to believe that they were only being registered now'. This duplicity continued up to the moment when the Jews were gassed in what they had been told was a 'shower room'. Groening was well aware of the benefits of the deception plan for the SS working at the camp. 'It is easier', he said, 'to throw a hand grenade behind a wall than to kill a man who is in front of the wall.'[30]

Groening and Perevalov, however, did share one conceptual difference in comparison with the leaders of the regimes they served. While Hitler and Stalin had been branded as criminals during the years of their fight for power, Groening and Perevalov believed that they were representatives of the established order – that they were on the side of the law and were punishing the guilty. The idea that they might be criminals themselves would have been incomprehensible to them. This is one of the reasons why both had such problems dealing with the subsequent collapse of the regimes they served. Groening in particular developed a complex and often contradictory way of coming to terms with his past. He passionately believed that 'the victor's always right', and that the Allies operated a double standard. 'We saw how bombs were dropped on Germany,' he said, 'and women and children died in firestorms. We saw this, and said, "This was a war that was being led in this way by both sides."'[31]

Many Nazis, including the Commandant of Auschwitz, Rudolf Höss, also attempted to equate the Holocaust with the bombing of German cities. But it's a false parallel. Though still understandably controversial, the Allied bombing in both Germany and Japan was motivated by a desire to win the war, did not target one group of the population and stopped the moment the war was over. By contrast, the extermination of the Jews was driven by racial hatred, targeted one group purely because of their origins and would almost certainly have carried on even if the Germans had won.

Groening did, however, recognize that what happened at Auschwitz was 'terrible . . . and the fact that I had to be there disgusting'. But he did not feel 'guilty'. He also knew, in the early 2000s at the time he uttered these words in an interview, that the German authorities had not attempted to prosecute him for any crime.[32] But all that changed several years later when he was charged with being an 'accessory' to murder. He was sentenced to four years in prison in 2015, but died in 2018 before starting his jail term, at the age of ninety-six.

There are many Kalmyks who believe that Nikonor Perevalov and his comrades in the NKVD should have been held similarly accountable. 'They remained unpunished and they lived their lives,' said Evdokiya Kuvakova. 'It's a great injustice towards the whole [Kalmyk] people.'[33] Instead of punishment, Perevalov received a pension. He did, however, have to deal, like Groening, with the collapse of the political world that he had served so willingly. After the fall of the Soviet Union in 1991 he developed, again like Groening, a complex way of coming to terms with his past: 'I will put it like this: the deportation of the people was illegal, but it wasn't the fault of the NKVD troops. Our platoon – my men – did not do anything illegal, but it was illegal on behalf of the supreme power . . . This is how I would put it . . . I disapprove [of Stalin's crimes]. But we were living in that time and the whole people believed that that's how it had to be.'[34]

After taking part in the deportation of the Kalmyks, Nikonor Perevalov moved on to play a role in the deportation of an even larger ethnic group, the Crimean Tatars. The operation was, once again, sanctioned personally by Stalin after reading a report from Beria. The Soviet authorities claimed that 20,000 Tatars, out of a population of around 190,000, had collaborated with the Germans during their occupation of the Crimea. Yet, just as with the Kalmyks, the innocent majority of Tatars were to be punished along with the guilty.

On 18 May 1944, Perevalov was one of more than 20,000 NKVD troops who organized the deportation of the entire Tatar people. And just as he had with the Kalmyks, he had doubts about what was happening, especially when he saw an elderly woman carried out of her house on a stretcher and dumped on a truck. 'She was so weak that she didn't utter a single word,' he said. 'She didn't even move. She was very old . . . that old woman wasn't guilty of anything . . . Most people were not guilty of anything. I have to be frank about it.'[35]

Most of the Crimean Tatars were sent to Uzbekistan, where large numbers died – more than a third of those deported.[36] Like the Kalmyks, the Tatars couldn't understand why the innocent were being made to suffer. Surely, they thought, once Stalin realized what was happening this 'mistake' would be corrected. Musfera Muslimova, who was eleven at the time of the deportations, remembered that 'rumours' persisted long into their exile that 'Some of the trains have already gone back, Stalin has had them returned home . . . People constantly vindicated him. "It isn't Stalin, it's someone else, it isn't him." Later on it became obvious that it had been Stalin all along. Without him none of this could have been accomplished, none of it would have happened . . . Of course he was the cruellest of people . . . You can't comprehend it when you are small, but with the years the anger increases.'[37]

Yet despite all the similarities between these two perpetrators, and between the murderous crimes of Hitler and those of Stalin, one crucial difference remains. Hitler may have initially employed methods of killing similar to Stalin, like deportation and starvation, but subsequently he also pursued something entirely new: the mechanized extermination of an entire people. The killing factories of Auschwitz, Treblinka and the other death camps have no parallel in Stalin's Soviet Union. The Holocaust remains a singularly appalling crime. Hitler presided over the creation of factories of death, designed to eliminate an entire group of people in a definite time frame, while Stalin did not. Whatever he may ultimately have wanted for people like the Kalmyks and Tatars, the fact is that the nation survived, and the majority of deportees – after his death – returned home.

On 16 May 1944, just two days before Nikonor Perevalov and the NKVD moved against the Crimean Tatars, the first transport of Jews arrived at Auschwitz from Hungary – a country that had, up to now, refused to send Jews to the Nazi death camps.[38] Special preparations had already been made at Auschwitz for the enormous numbers of Jews due to arrive – more than 400,000. Most notably, a new railway spur had been laid so that transports could proceed directly to Auschwitz-Birkenau. Previously Jews had to be taken to the camp from a siding about a mile away. But, even though the Hungarian Jews had been expected, the murder facilities had trouble coping. The vast majority of the Jews were selected for immediate death, and there wasn't sufficient capacity in the crematoria ovens to burn that many bodies, so giant pits were dug and the bodies burnt in the open. Some Jews were even thrown into the flaming pits alive.[39]

During this intense killing period, Oskar Groening mostly sat in his office counting the money stolen from the arriving Jews. The Hungarian action was something of a gold rush for the SS at Auschwitz. Because the Hungarian deportations had been organized so swiftly, a number of the Jews arrived with their valuables still hidden on their bodies or in their clothes or luggage. Theft was rampant among the SS at Auschwitz and this was a chance for them to get rich.

There was a laissez-faire attitude to discipline among many of the SS. Groening remembered that they would snatch any alcohol carried by the Jews and drink it themselves: 'We didn't feel any sympathy or empathy towards one or other Jewish group from any particular country, unless you were keen on getting a particular kind of vodka or Schnapps.' His abiding memory of the Hungarian action was that 'the Hungarians, for example, had a lovely plum brandy.'[40]

Hitler had long wanted to annihilate the Jews of Hungary, but it had not been easy for him to arrange their destruction. He could not order their deportation with a nod of his head the way Stalin could order the removal of Kalmyks and Tatars. The Soviet leader never had to worry about gaining the help of non-Soviet institutions in order to make his vision a reality. Hitler, on the other hand, often had to use a mixture of persuasion and threat to get what he wanted.

On 18 March 1944 Admiral Horthy, the Regent of Hungary, arrived at Klessheim Palace in Austria for talks with Hitler. The Hungarians had been members of the Axis alliance since November 1940, but had always followed their self-interest rather than the Nazis' ideological goals. Their participation in the war against the Soviet Union, for instance, had scarcely been wholehearted, and now Horthy wanted Hungarian soldiers to be recalled from the eastern front. Hitler, however, had a very different sort of discussion in mind. He told Horthy that he knew the Hungarians were trying to reach a deal with the Allies to get out of the war. Furthermore, by refusing to take radical action against the Jews, the German leader claimed that Horthy was permitting a dangerous and disloyal faction to subvert the war from behind the lines. Hitler said he was no longer prepared to accept such a situation. German troops would occupy Hungary immediately, and the Hungarian leader had to acquiesce.

When the elderly Admiral refused to allow German soldiers across the Hungarian border, Hitler threatened the safety of Horthy's family.

Horthy was outraged and said he wanted to leave at once. Suddenly, there was an air-raid siren and smoke wafted across the castle. Horthy was told that during this crisis all the telephone lines were down with Budapest. In such circumstances, he couldn't leave.

But it was all a hoax. There was no air raid, and nothing wrong with the phones. The smoke had been created by the Nazis themselves. It had all been designed to keep Horthy at Klessheim. And the deception worked. Horthy, trapped in the castle, agreed to let German troops into Hungary and install a government that would be subservient to the Nazis. The Wehrmacht marched into Hungary the very next day, 19 March.[41]

The occupation of Hungary helped the Nazis in a number of significant ways. It was both strategically advantageous as they could now position their troops on the eastern borders of Hungary in case of Soviet attack, and materially advantageous since they could now take whatever goods they wanted from the country. But the great prize, as far as Hitler was concerned, was direct access to large numbers of Jews.

Adolf Eichmann arrived in Budapest soon after German troops had occupied the city and – knowing that it wasn't possible to deport hundreds of thousands of people without the cooperation of the local authorities – began looking for Hungarians who could help organize the mass deportation. He quickly enlisted the help of confirmed anti-Semites within the Hungarian administration, such as State Secretary László Endre and a high-ranking officer in the Hungarian gendarmerie, László Ferenczy.

With the help of the gendarmerie and other Hungarian officials, the action against the Jews was conducted with extraordinary speed. The NKVD had needed weeks of detailed planning to organize the deportation of ethnic groups like the Kalmyks. And they were operating within the borders of their own country. But Eichmann oversaw the forced detention of more than 200,000 Jews in eastern Hungary in less than two weeks. It was inconceivable that this mass selection and movement of people could have been achieved without the willing collaboration of the Hungarian authorities.

Many of these Hungarians were motivated not just by anti-Semitism but also by greed. Like so many of those who persecuted the Jews, they saw an opportunity to get rich. One Hungarian Jew remembered that her family were forced to sell for a pittance everything they had. And the man who had 'bought' their home and business watched 'not with compassion but with glee' as they were marched to the waiting deportation trains.[42]

Israel Abelesz was one of the Hungarian Jews sent to Auschwitz. He remembered that the SS sought to reassure the new arrivals that they had nothing to worry about. Consequently, there were no 'scenes' on the arrival ramp. It was 'like in a factory. It was like on a conveyor belt, and there shouldn't be any hitch in the conveyor-belt system.'

Israel's father, mother and younger brother were selected to be murdered immediately. But Israel was sent to a part of Auschwitz-Birkenau he called a 'labour pool' where prisoners periodically endured further selections – chosen to work as slave labour within the Auschwitz complex of camps or elsewhere. If after several weeks they had not been selected for work, they went to the gas chambers. 'Every day there was rationing of food,' he said. 'It was just not enough, a starvation diet. The overwhelming feeling besides the fear of death is the feeling of hunger. The feeling of hunger is such an overpowering feeling that it covers up any other feeling, any other human feelings . . . [you become] just like a dog who is looking for food.'

Long after the war and his liberation from the camp, Israel Abelesz was still tormented by his experience of Auschwitz: 'I don't know how to deal with it . . . hardly a day passes when I'm lying in bed and I cannot sleep for one reason or another, [I] always look at those faces of the children [selected to die] and my imagination goes: what's happened in their last minute? When they were in the gas chambers and the Zyklon B started and they couldn't breathe any more? And they realized that we are going to get suffocated from the gas. What was in their mind?'[43]

On 26 May, as Hungarian Jews were dying in the gas chambers of Auschwitz, Hitler explained to his generals why the fight against the Jews was so vital. 'By removing the Jew,' he said, 'I have eliminated the possibilities of the formation of any revolutionary nucleus. Of course, you can say to me: "Well, couldn't you have solved this more simply – or not more simply, because everything else would have been more complicated, but more humanely?" Gentlemen, officers, we are in a life-or-death struggle.'[44]

It's a statement of great importance. Not only does it explain why Hitler thought it essential that resources be devoted to killing the Jews at a time when they could valuably be deployed elsewhere, but it also highlights a similarity in approach between Hitler and Stalin. Hitler said that by targeting the Jews he had 'eliminated the possibilities of the formation of any revolutionary nucleus'. These were words that could just as easily have been spoken by Stalin in an attempt to justify the deportation of ethnic groups like the Kalmyks, Tatars and Volga Germans.

Like Hitler, Stalin had a permanent concern. Who could lead a revolution against him? He was at least as focused on the enemy at home as on the enemy on the front line. He had not forgotten that he had been part of a successful revolution on the streets of Petrograd (St Petersburg)[45] over twenty-five years before. He knew from personal experience how swiftly the established order could collapse. So throughout his career – and most especially in wartime – Stalin was hypersensitive to any potential threat from within the Soviet state.

There's one final similarity between them in this context. Both Hitler and Stalin were particularly concerned about the loyalty of people living near the border with other countries, anxious lest they foment dissent close to any potential front line. That partly explains why the population of the Baltic States was persecuted so harshly by Stalin, with tens of thousands deported just before the launch of Operation Barbarossa. It also explains why Hitler was especially keen to attack the Hungarian Jews in March 1944.

But though Stalin found it easier than Hitler to implement his policy of persecution during the war, it was harder for him to judge when such drastic action was necessary. For Hitler the matter was straightforward. It was a question of race, blood and ideology. These were absolutes. He believed the threat from the Jews had to be eliminated. But Stalin, as we have seen, was balancing a number of competing objectives. Though he was always suspicious of ethnic groups within the Soviet Union, he had no ideological imperative to destroy them. They were just another 'problem' he had to deal with. He had to weigh a variety of different factors, not least how easy it was in practical terms to punish an entire section of the Soviet Union. Stalin knew, for example, about the extent of German collaboration within Ukraine. Not only were many of the guards in the death camps of Ukrainian origin, but Ukrainian nationalist partisans were fighting Red Army partisans as well as the Germans. If Stalin thought the Kalmyks deserved to be punished en masse for the collaboration of a minority, surely by that logic every Ukrainian ought to have been deported to the wilds of the Soviet Union as well.

But they weren't. As a policy it was simply impracticable.[46] Ultimately, that fact highlights one final overarching difference between the two tyrants. Stalin, while a mass murderer guilty of the most appalling crimes, always had an eye on what was realistic. But Hitler dreamt of murder on an immense scale – not just the killing of the Jews but the deaths of tens of millions of other people, primarily in the Soviet Union. It was only the defeat of Germany that prevented Hitler and his supporters from implementing this vast scheme of destruction more than they did.

By the spring of 1944, as D-Day neared, that defeat was coming ever closer. But Hitler remained confident. He told Goebbels in March 1944 that when the Allies landed troops in France he was 'absolutely certain' that German forces would throw them back into the sea. Goebbels expressed 'hope' that Hitler was right, but confessed to his diary that 'lately we've been disappointed so often that you feel some scepticism rising inside you.'[47]

Events were about to prove Goebbels' growing 'scepticism' correct, and Hitler's 'absolute certainty' wrong.

16. Collapse of the Centre

June 1944 saw the launch of two devastating offensives against the Third Reich. One of them is famous – D-Day, the long-awaited second front. The other – Operation Bagration – is scarcely commemorated in the west. It's a sign, many Russians still believe, that the scale of the contribution of the Soviet Union to the defeat of Hitler remains unrecognized. And they make a valid point.

Operation Bagration not only dwarfed D-Day in size, but was also much more successful than the initial Allied advance in France. While the western Allies struggled to push through Normandy, Soviet forces were inflicting on the Germans the largest battlefield defeat in their history.

Through the planning and execution of this vast Soviet offensive we can see how far apart Hitler and Stalin had grown as wartime commanders. Hitler was rigid and unimaginative, Stalin creative and flexible. It was as if three years after the launch of Operation Barbarossa they had changed personas.

Stalin gave this new offensive the name 'Bagration' after a Georgian prince who had died fighting against Napoleon. It was another sign of how he was linking the current conflict with past imperial glory. What was unusual was that Stalin had chosen a Georgian aristocrat for this honour, not a Russian one.[1] But then Stalin was a Georgian himself, so perhaps he found the connection just too irresistible.

The Soviet plan was to punch a giant hole straight through Army Group Centre – the pride of the Wehrmacht – and march west. As a consequence of the scale of that ambition, Stalin committed nearly two and a half million fighting personnel to the offensive. What was even worse, from a German perspective, was that the Wehrmacht did not see an attack of this size coming. German intelligence believed that the Soviets still had the bulk of their forces in the south. It was a mirror image of the mistake Stalin and his generals had made at the start of Barbarossa, when they thought the main German attack would come through Ukraine rather than further north.

The whole of Operation Bagration was replete with symbolism. The first assault was planned for 22 June – exactly three years after the start of the German invasion – and brought swift success. Two days later, on 24 June 1944, Marshal Rokossovsky's tanks suddenly emerged from the seemingly impassable Pripet Marshes to confront the Germans. It was reminiscent of the brilliant German advance through the Ardennes four years before. Only this time, it was the Germans' turn to be astonished. The Soviets had managed to lay wooden causeways through the marsh, and German intelligence hadn't noticed.[2]

The way the Soviet thrusts did not pause to regroup but carried on pushing ever further into enemy-held territory resembled the bravura of the early days of the German advance in Barbarossa, and little more than a week after the start of the Bagration offensive, Minsk was recaptured. This was a moment of great significance, as it had been the fall of Minsk, capital of Belorussia, that had caused such panic in the Soviet High Command back in June 1941.

Similarly, just as Stalin by his incompetence had played a vital part in helping the Germans succeed in 1941, so Hitler did the same in the summer of 1944. The most glaring mistake he made was insisting on the creation of so-called Feste Plätze or 'fortified places'. Hitler ordered the building of these static defences so that they would 'fulfil the function of fortresses in former historical times . . . They will allow themselves to be surrounded, thereby holding down the largest possible number of enemy forces, and establishing conditions favourable for successful counter-attacks.'[3] It was an idea so out of date as to be – literally – medieval. Instead of being part of a line of fortifications, these Feste Plätze would be isolated and could be attacked by modern artillery on all sides.[4] General Jordan, commander of the Ninth Army, was scathing about the plan in June 1944, calling Hitler's order for the creation of the Feste Plätze 'particularly dangerous'.[5]

Heinz Fiedler, a soldier with the German Ninth Army, personally experienced the ineffectiveness of these Feste Plätze. He and his comrades were ordered to defend Bobruisk, even after the Red Army had passed by and surrounded them. Soon the Germans were running low on ammunition, and their destruction seemed inevitable. Fiedler remembered that one of his comrades, directing an artillery barrage, 'requested fire on to his own position when the situation had become hopeless. So, rather than falling into Russian hands, he preferred to be killed by German artillery. Those are the real heroes.'[6]

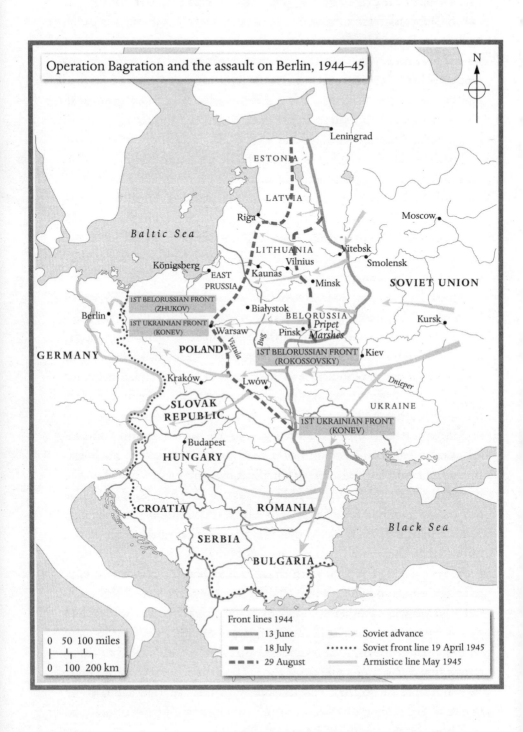

Operation Bagration and the assault on Berlin, 1944–45

N

Leningrad

ESTONIA

LATVIA

Riga

Moscow

Baltic Sea

LITHUANIA
Vilnius
Vitebsk
Smolensk

Königsberg
EAST
PRUSSIA
Kaunas
Minsk
SOVIET UNION

Berlin

1ST BELORUSSIAN FRONT
(ZHUKOV)

Białystok
BELORUSSIA
Pripet
Marshes
Kursk

1ST UKRAINIAN FRONT
(KONEV)
Warsaw
Pinsk
Bug

GERMANY
POLAND
Vistula
1ST BELORUSSIAN FRONT
(ROKOSSOVSKY)
Kiev

Kraków
Lwów
Dnieper

SLOVAK
REPUBLIC
UKRAINE

1ST UKRAINIAN FRONT
(KONEV)
Budapest
HUNGARY

CROATIA
ROMANIA
Black Sea

SERBIA

BULGARIA

0 50 100 miles

0 100 200 km

Front lines 1944
━━━ 13 June
━ ━ ━ 18 July
━ ━·━ 29 August

⟶ Soviet advance
•••••• Soviet front line 19 April 1945
━━━ Armistice line May 1945

Eventually the order came to evacuate, and Fiedler and the few survivors of Bobruisk attempted to reach German lines through territory now held by the Red Army. They tried not to panic, because 'once a crowd has started to run . . . it's as if it were infected,' but the 'primal' screams of the wounded 'still ring in my ears to this day'. He saw one young officer hold up his arms when he was shot, and though 'he was married' he did not call out his wife's name: 'his final scream was "Mother!"' Fiedler witnessed so many horrors inside Bobruisk that 'even today I still sometimes dream [nightmares] about it.' Like General Jordan, he blamed Hitler and his advisers at headquarters for all this suffering.

Fyodor Bubenchikov, an officer in the victorious Red Army, took particular satisfaction in 'Hitler's order to keep the Germans in the fortified areas' because it 'doomed the Germans to death'. He was also astonished by the speed of the Soviet advance: 'We captured Mogilev so quickly that the Germans failed to blow up the bridge and a whole [Soviet] tank corps crossed the river. Near Minsk we encircled a 100,000-man-strong German force. It took us two months to destroy the Paulus army [at Stalingrad], but near Minsk by 3 July the Germans were encircled.'[7] Bubenchikov and his comrades were ecstatic. 'We felt we were flying on the wings of victory,' he said. 'Victory always makes everyone feel like this, from ordinary soldier to commander, and all our units were filled with this sensation.'[8]

Among the soldiers of the Red Army, the thought of Stalin was never far away. Veniamin Fyodorov, a private with the 77th Guards Regiment, remembered how every attack started with the cry 'For the motherland, for Stalin, forward!' But while he also vividly recalled the success of the offensive, at the same time he could not forget the dangers of the battlefield. He believed that the 'first time in battle it's okay, but the next, in the second battle, you feel as if there is no head on your neck, and it's as if your brain is naked. You hear your heart thump, thump, thump, and you think the bullet is going to hit you. It'll hit, it'll hit! You wonder whether you will stay alive. And the same pumping in your temples. It's a horrible thing, because every man wants to live . . . But a bullet is a fool, it can reach anyone.' Even given the risks, Fyodorov thought it preferable to be the first over the top in any advance. 'When you're in the first echelon you don't see anything, but when you're in the second or third echelon, then you walk on the wounded and dead people. It's very frightening.'[9]

Veniamin Fyodorov was an unusual veteran. Not only did he speak frankly about his own feelings of fear on the battlefield, but he was also prepared to talk openly about how some Red Army soldiers tried to injure themselves to escape the fight: 'There were cases of self-mutilation . . . [a soldier] would shoot and the bullet goes through [the hand]. For the doctors it was difficult to find out whether it was a real wound or self-inflicted wound . . . There were such cases. Also there were those who burst out crying, as if they were inhaling some poisonous vapours.'

Fyodorov was one of a minority of soldiers who was able to return to his village at the end of the war: 'In the village there were thirty-two houses. In those thirty-two houses fifty-seven people were called up. Only about five including me came back. All the others had been killed.' And he discovered that life during the war had been almost as hard for those who had remained at home as for those who had fought at the front: 'There was a new law – a new order from Stalin. "Everything for the victory, everything for the front". Everything was requisitioned . . . People had to kill their own cattle and eat all the supplies of potatoes they had . . . A lot of people in our village died. Men and women.' Fyodorov's own father 'starved to death. He had been slaving in the collective farm all his life and then died, starved to death. This motto, "Everything for the front", was wrong. People should have been able to keep some of the harvest.'[10]

Though Veniamin Fyodorov is just one soldier, his voice is important. It's a corrective to the idea that in the summer of 1944 the war suddenly turned around for the population of the Soviet Union. Life remained tough – both on the front line and in the villages. Death still stalked all of them.

As for Hitler, his order to hold fast in Feste Plätze summed up the paucity of his ideas. All he had to offer was that Germans should hang on today and hope for a better tomorrow. 'Our own war leadership, on all fronts, focuses now on gaining time,' said General Jodl in a talk to his own staff on 3 July 1944, voicing Hitler's views. 'A few months can prove simply decisive for saving the Fatherland . . . Our own armaments justify great expectations . . . Everything is being prepared, with results in the foreseeable future. So the demand is for fighting, defending, holding, psychological strengthening of troops and leadership. Nail down the front where it now stands.'[11]

But the soldiers of what remained of Army Group Centre – outnumbered two to one – could not do as Jodl and Hitler asked. The Red Army pushed on through them, reaching Vilnius, capital of Lithuania, on 13 July. The Baltic States, which had been independent countries prior to 1940, were now swallowed up by the Soviet Union. Churchill had written in January 1942 that 'the transfer of the peoples of the Baltic States to Soviet Russia against their will would be contrary to all the principles for which we are fighting this war and would dishonour our cause'.[12] But it turned out that Stalin's guns were more effective than Churchill's 'principles'.

During Bagration the Germans lost more than 300,000 soldiers in two weeks – an incredible number, not seen before in German military history over such a short period.[13] On 28 June, in a vain attempt to stem the Soviet advance, Hitler changed commanders of Army Group Centre. But just swapping Field Marshal Busch, who had loyally enforced Hitler's stand-fast order, with Field Marshal Model, did nothing to alter reality. The Red Army outnumbered the Wehrmacht in both fighting personnel and equipment.

Matters were about to get even worse for Hitler. On 20 July an aristocratic army officer, Colonel Claus von Stauffenberg, took a bomb into a briefing with Hitler at the Wolf's Lair, his headquarters in East Prussia. It was the culmination of a series of failed assassination attempts. We have already seen how Hitler had been lucky a number of times – once when a bomb placed on his plane failed to detonate and once when he shortened his schedule unexpectedly at an exhibition. Henning von Tresckow, chief of staff of the Second Army, and one of the prime movers of the conspiracy, now reasoned that the only certain way of killing the Führer was to gain access to the Wolf's Lair. Stauffenberg's promotion to colonel on 1 July, together with his new responsibilities, meant that he now had just that opportunity.

The idea was that on Hitler's death the plotters would make the head of the reserve army, General Friedrich Fromm, activate a plan codenamed Valkyrie. Originally designed by the regime to be implemented in the event of riot or revolution, the plan could now be subverted and used to render the structures of the Nazi state inoperative. As a consequence, power would fall into the hands of the army. At least, that was the theory.

There were a number of obvious ways the plan could go wrong. One was the character of General Fromm – a man who acted more out of self-interest than principle. He couldn't be relied upon to do what he was asked. Another was the method of killing Hitler. Since Stauffenberg was Fromm's chief of staff, and would be useful to the conspirators back in Berlin after Hitler's death, he had to survive the attack. So the most reliable way of killing Hitler – by suicide attack – just wasn't an option.

On the morning of 20 July, Stauffenberg and Lieutenant Werner von Haeften, his adjutant, arrived at the Wolf's Lair. Haeften and Stauffenberg carried two bombs with them, but were only able to arm one in time for the meeting with Hitler. Stauffenberg placed the armed bomb under the table in the briefing room, made an excuse and left. The bomb went off shortly afterwards, but Hitler survived with minor injuries. He was lucky once again – exceptionally lucky in fact. If Stauffenberg had left the second bomb, even unprimed, in the briefcase with the first, then the combined explosion would have almost certainly killed everyone in the room.[14]

There was initial confusion among the plotters about whether Hitler had died. But once it was clear that he still lived, support for the coup began to waver. The actions of Field Marshal von Kluge in Paris were typical. He walked away from the conspiracy once he knew Hitler had escaped alive. 'If only the pig were dead,' he said. A month later, shortly before he committed suicide, Kluge confessed that he was 'no great man'.[15]

In the face of all this vacillation, the uprising was doomed. The failure was encapsulated by a brief exchange between General Ludwig Beck, the designated new head of state, and General Olbricht, a supporter of the coup, at the headquarters of the High Command in Berlin. Olbricht had placed his soldiers around the building to protect it, and Beck wanted to know if they were prepared to die for him. Olbricht did not know if they would. But, without question, plenty of soldiers were still willing to die for Adolf Hitler. Every German soldier had sworn an oath to obey the Führer, and most had been brought up as children to revere him. How could Olbricht compete?

Within hours the conspiracy had failed, and the leading plotters – including Stauffenberg, Olbricht, Tresckow and Beck – subsequently paid with their lives. But even though, after the war, they would be hailed as heroes, we must not over-romanticize their motives. Consider Stauffenberg. While objecting to the anti-Semitism of the Nazis, he nonetheless was pleased that Germany had conquered Poland and was full of joy at the victory over the French. His final conversion to the cause of resistance came only in 1942 after he learnt that the SS were murdering Jews in Ukraine. But by then he also knew that the Germans had been held by the Red Army outside Moscow, and that America was in the war.[16] Perhaps it's not being unduly cynical to suggest that just as Admiral Horthy would not have wanted to take Hungary out of the war had the Germans still been victorious on the battlefield, so there would also have been less support among German officers for removing Hitler had the Wehrmacht been winning the war against the Soviet Union.

Many ordinary Germans were appalled by the attempt on Hitler's life. According to SD reports, the most common response was 'Thank God, the Führer is alive.' And while it's hard to be certain about public opinion in a totalitarian state where to speak against the regime was to invite retribution, other evidence does support the SD's claim. An examination of 45,000 letters from soldiers serving in the German armed forces, conducted by the censor in August 1944, revealed that 'The treachery of the conspiratorial clique is rejected by all as the greatest crime against the German people.' Though soldiers could be punished for writing negative things about the regime, there was no need to speak out against it. Silence was always an option – and one, for the most part, not taken here.[17]

After hearing about the attack on Hitler, some Nazi Party members even voiced their approval of the brutal measures taken by Stalin against Red Army officers during the Great Terror. The SD heard remarks like 'Stalin is the only clear-sighted one among all the leaders, the one who made betrayal impossible in advance by exterminating the predominant but unreliable elements.'[18]

Hitler now demanded an increase in the 'Nazification' of the armed forces. He appointed Heinz Guderian as Chief of Staff of the Army – a man whom leading Nazis such as Joseph Goebbels regarded as committed to the cause. Guderian insisted that every member of the General Staff should have 'an exemplary stance in political questions'. Guidelines issued on 22 July called for soldiers to be lectured about the 'cowardly murderous strike against the Führer' and for 'symptoms of unsoldierly and dishonourable behaviour' to be immediately identified and denounced.[19] Two months later, on 24 September, Hitler issued a law confirming the central role of Nazi ideology in the armed forces:

'Members of the Wehrmacht have the duty to act in the spirit of National
Socialist ideology, both on duty and off duty, and to advocate it at all
times. It is one of the essential tasks of all officers, non-commissioned
officers and Wehrmacht officials to teach and lead their subordinates in
the National Socialist way.'[20]

There were as many as 47,000 'National Socialist Leadership Officers'
by the start of 1945. In the last months of the war, Walter Fernau, a lieutenant who had fought on the eastern front, was one of them. But while
he was tasked with raising the morale of his men, he felt the material he
received from Nazi officials to use as the basis of his pep talks was not
'suitable': 'For example, it said I was to tell the troops [about] Frederick
the Great's battle at Küstrin [in 1758]. Well I thought to myself, what's
the point of that? What has Küstrin got to do with the German Army
now? So I thought, well, you can put that away.'

Instead of delivering a history lecture, Fernau first created a 'wonderful atmosphere' by getting a soldier to play an accordion and calling on
the troops to sing 'seaman shanties'. Once his audience was in a mellow
mood, he levelled with them about the military situation by saying 'in
simple soldiers' language' that 'it's all shit!'

He 'didn't talk of victory, well that was all nonsense to me, you
know, I would have had to enter the lunatic asylum'. Instead, he called
on the soldiers to trust in Hitler and his ability to make a 'good ending'
to the war. What was the point, he asked, of chucking their rifles away
now when their Führer – who knew much more about the true wartime
situation than they did – might be about to find a way of finishing it?[21]

But a 'good ending' to the war scarcely looked likely for the Germans. Indeed, it hadn't looked likely for some time.

On 20 July 1944, as Stauffenberg was priming his bomb, Red Army soldiers experienced a moment of great significance – one that would result
in Stalin demonstrating his ruthless disregard for humanity once again.
Soldiers of the First Belorussian Front crossed the River Bug and entered
territory that the Soviets recognized as Poland. The question of just
who were the legitimate rulers of this country was now of immediate
practical importance. The following day, 21 July, Stalin gave his answer –
his own puppets were in charge. A 'Polish Committee of National
Liberation' was formed in Moscow and then swiftly signed a series of
agreements with the Soviet government that effectively gave the Red

Army a free hand on Polish territory. Stalin now had the tame Polish administration that he desired. It was a blatant attempt to bypass the Polish government in exile in London.[22]

As part of the scheme, Stalin also created his own Polish armed forces. The 1st Polish Army was formed in July 1944 from previous Polish units already operating under the auspices of the Red Army. Many of the soldiers were Poles who had previously been POWs within the Soviet Union, but a number of Soviets served in these 'Polish' forces as well. Nikolai Brandt, for instance, was an officer with the 1st Polish Army. He dressed in Polish uniform and he claimed to come from a town in Poland. But he was Russian through and through. In 1943, as part of a deception plan, he had been taught Polish and briefed on his 'new' personal history. He was told to say he came from a small town in south-east Poland, and when he asked how he could keep up that pretence since he had never visited the place, he was told 'don't worry, it doesn't exist any more. It was completely destroyed by the Germans through bombardment.'

Brandt trained with Polish soldiers in early 1944, prior to the formation of the 1st Polish Army. 'I was commanding my battalion,' he said. 'We were very well equipped. And they spared us [from the fighting], because we were meant to become the bulk of the future Polish Army so there was not much point in us getting killed.' After July 1944, and now consolidated as the 1st Polish Army, the situation changed and Brandt and his men saw a great deal of action. 'I ran and I shouted in Polish "forward" and the boys ran after me,' he remembered. 'They were good boys. They loved me and they ran and we got hold of the first trenches.'[23]

Brandt rapidly concluded that in war there is no such thing as individual humanity, there is only 'global humanity' – by which he meant that individuals may be called upon to sacrifice their own lives for the sake of others. For example, as an officer he had to select men to participate in 'reconnaissance through combat', a dangerous form of attack also carried out by penal battalions.[24] These soldiers had to attack in small numbers in order to 'help us identify' the sources of 'enemy fire', and consequently 'the majority of these people are doomed.' The idea that it was a Russian masquerading as a Pole who was selecting genuine Poles to die is surely emblematic of the corrupt nature of Stalin's deception plan.

As for Stalin's attitude towards legitimate Polish military units, that soon became all too apparent. Initially, the Red Army accepted the help of the Home Army – Polish resistance fighters, loyal to the government in exile – in liberating Polish cities. But that position changed once the Germans had been defeated. In Lublin, for instance, on 26 July, the Red Army took away the weapons of the soldiers of the Polish 9th Infantry Division, and shortly afterwards arrested their commander, General Ludwik Bittner, and took him to the Soviet Union. The following month Soviet forces imprisoned nearly 3,000 officers and men of the Polish Home Army in the former Nazi camp of Majdanek, in the suburbs of Lublin.[25]

In eastern Poland, the part of Poland that Stalin now claimed as Soviet territory, the attitude of Soviet forces was just as uncompromising. The Polish Home Army under Colonel Filipkowski had played a vital part in the liberation of Lwów in July. Filipkowski's soldiers had managed to disrupt German attempts to defend the city and smoothed the way for the entrance of units from the First Ukrainian Front. But in late July, once the city had been made secure, Filipkowski was told to disband his unit of the Polish Home Army, and that his soldiers could join Stalin's Polish units. Less than a week later, after being duped into attending a 'military conference', around thirty officers of the Home Army in Lwów were arrested and classed as 'criminals and Polish fascists'.[26]

One of the highest-priority targets for the Soviets as they entered Lwów was the Gestapo headquarters in the city. So much so that NKVD units even targeted the building as the Germans were in the process of leaving, because they were desperate to capture the Gestapo files intact. After they had gained the files and had questioned local informants, the NKVD arrested not just collaborators but anyone who appeared as if they might possibly oppose them. 'They [the informers] told us that somebody hated Soviet power and was a threat to us and then we would arrest him,' said Vyacheslav Yablonsky, an NKVD officer who took part in the Lwów operation. 'They could be saying bad things about us or just thinking we were bad.'

The 'normal' sentence for 'saying something bad', said Yablonsky, was 'about fifteen years of forced labour . . . Now I think it was cruel, but at that time, when I was young, twenty-two or twenty-three years old, I didn't . . . Now I understand that it's cruel because I'm older. I don't think it was a very democratic time. Now you can say anything, but at that time you couldn't.'[27]

Anna Levitska was one of those the NKVD targeted in Lwów. She had already lived through the previous Soviet occupation of her beloved city earlier in the war, and had dreaded the return of the Red Army. Now, after the Soviets had consolidated their rule over eastern Poland, she was picked up on the street by two NKVD men and taken to prison. She had been denounced by others who had previously been arrested, and that was enough to condemn her. Her interrogators 'showed me some photographs of different men . . . They said, "You don't know them?" Of course I didn't know them. I denied it.'[28]

Like many who fell into the hands of the NKVD, she was tortured: 'They usually took me for interrogation at night, and you were not allowed to sleep during the day. There was always a guard who would knock on the window and call out "Don't sleep!" When they took me for interrogation at night, there was usually just one investigator. On some occasions a few [other] people would come in and would begin beating me. They sat me on a small stool, the stool was fastened to the floor. I sat on the stool, they would approach me and beat me all over: on my head, in the face, on my back. I would collapse on the floor. Sometimes I lost consciousness. They would throw water over me [to bring her round] . . . and then continue [the beating]. On other occasions, they brought me there and made me sit there for the whole night.'[29]

After nine months of this abuse, and even though she was innocent of the particular charges the NKVD levelled against her, Anna decided to 'sign all the statements . . . just so that I'll get transferred out of here quicker'. She was worried that the Soviet authorities might discover her real 'crime' – that she had given medicines and medical dressings to members of the resistance. Having signed the 'confession' the NKVD created for her, she was sentenced to fifteen years' hard labour. She was released only after Stalin's death.

Anna Levitska experienced both the Soviet and German occupations of her city, and comparing the two experiences she came to some surprising conclusions. While recognizing that the German 'behaviour towards the Jews was terrible', she felt from her own personal perspective that she had been safer during the German occupation than during the Soviet one: 'Of course [under the Germans] there was the curfew hour. You could not walk around the city at night. You couldn't sit in

the same tramcar that the Germans travelled in . . . The trams had separate entrances, one for the Germans, the other for everyone else. There
might be just one person sitting there [in the tram car reserved for the
Germans] or maybe even nobody at all, whereas in the other car there
would be people travelling in large numbers. That went on. But you
didn't feel that same danger [as under the Soviet occupation].' To Anna,
the Germans 'were more cultured . . . In the street, for example, in relation to what I was saying about them being more civilized, they did not
behave like the Red Army soldiers had done.'

When called upon to compare the leaders and their regimes, she
replied, 'In my opinion they were the same. Hitler and Stalin. You
know, although you might say that Hitler's regime and Stalin's regime
were somehow different from one another superficially, in their behaviour or actions, they were not.'

She considered it unjust that, while many former Nazis were held to
account after the war, those who committed crimes on behalf of the
Soviet state were never prosecuted: 'They did not admit that they had
any responsibility . . . for those crimes [committed] during Stalinism.
That of course is unsettling. All those people who were involved in this
[those crimes] are still prospering, they live well . . . and have good pen-
sions. They are able to enjoy life, so to speak . . . I want to see them
punished. It hasn't happened and it is not likely to happen. Maybe when
we are gone.'[30]

As the Soviets sought to crush any dissent in newly 'liberated' Poland,
the government in exile in London could only look on in despair. They
had tried to gain the support of the British and Americans, but with
little result. In June, just weeks before the Red Army crossed into
Poland, Prime Minister Stanisław Mikołajczyk had finally obtained an
audience with President Roosevelt. It was an encounter that deserves to
be better known in the west, because it showed Roosevelt at his most
mendacious. The President has largely escaped censure for the lies he
told during the war. In part that's because he led the most powerful
democratic nation in the world, one that was committed to overthrow-
ing the Nazis. Nonetheless, as we have already seen in this history, he
could deceive and dissemble with aplomb. And at the meeting he held
with Prime Minister Mikołajczyk of Poland he dispensed a cornucopia
of untruths.

Roosevelt appeared to be in a good mood the day he met Mikołajczyk. D-Day had just been launched successfully and the Soviets were about to start their offensive against the Germans in the east. So when Mikołajczyk entered the room he found a playful Roosevelt. 'I have studied sixteen maps of Poland this morning,' said the President. 'In only three hundred years, parts of White Russia have been Polish, and parts of Germany and Czechoslovakia . . . On the other hand, parts of Poland have at times been annexed to these countries . . . It is difficult to untangle the map of Poland.'[31] As a result, he told Mikołajczyk, he couldn't be expected to know 'whether this or that town would be on this or that side of the frontier line' in the future. However, he would do his best to ensure that Lwów – a place of considerable importance to the Poles – stayed a Polish city.

The President said he had formed a positive impression of Stalin, and thought the Soviet leader was 'neither an imperialist nor a communist'. In any case, the Polish Prime Minister should not be concerned about the Soviets, as 'Stalin doesn't intend to take freedom from Poland. He wouldn't dare do that because he knows that the United States government stands solidly behind you. I will see to it that Poland does not come out of this war injured.'[32]

Roosevelt blamed Churchill for bringing up the question of the fate of eastern Poland with Stalin, and for suggesting a new border based on the Curzon Line – a proposed demarcation line between Poland and the Bolsheviks drawn in 1919 under the auspices of Lord Curzon, which would give eastern Poland to the Soviets. The adoption of the Curzon Line as the border would be a disastrous outcome for Mikołajczyk, not least because many of the Polish soldiers fighting the Germans in Italy came from this eastern part of Poland. If the Curzon Line was to be the new frontier, then once the war was won their homes would no longer even be in Poland. They were thus fighting – and dying – for an illusory future. Even victory would not give them back their land.

Roosevelt did not mention that he had already secretly agreed that Stalin could have this territory. He wanted, cynically, to keep quiet about the subject until after the presidential elections later in the year, so that he didn't endanger support from Polish-Americans. Consequently, on this question of vast importance to the future integrity of Poland, he lied to the Polish Prime Minister, blatantly and to his face. It was an appalling betrayal of the ideals of the Atlantic Charter – the agreement that Roosevelt himself had been instrumental in creating – as well as a reminder of how big countries, democracies as well as dictatorships, can ultimately do whatever they want to small, friendless ones.

Roosevelt did at least ask Stalin to meet with Mikołajczyk and the Poles. But Stalin's response was masterly in its display of raw power. He said he would agree to the meeting, but only if the Poles accepted the Curzon Line as the new boundary with the Soviet Union, and thus gave up eastern Poland. He also demanded a change in the composition of the Polish government in exile. He didn't consider it 'friendly' enough to the Soviet Union. So he wanted Mikołajczyk to dismiss the Information Minister, the Defence Minister, the Commander-in-Chief and the President. Stalin, it appeared, now demanded the right to decide the composition of the Polish government in exile. And these were his initial demands, mere preconditions before he would agree to a meeting with the Poles. Not surprisingly, Mikołajczyk couldn't accept them.[33]

This was the background to one of the most tragic episodes of the war – the Warsaw uprising, when the Polish Home Army rose up against the Germans occupying the city. There was obvious political advantage for the Polish government in exile if its own army of resistance fighters liberated Warsaw ahead of the Red Army. It would strengthen the position of the Home Army once the Soviets arrived, especially given that the NKVD had already arrested Polish officers in Lublin and Lwów. If Stalin tried to do the same thing in Warsaw after the liberation, the world would know he was persecuting the saviours of the Polish capital.

The question of the exact timing of the uprising was a matter of life and death for the resistance fighters in Warsaw, as was Stalin's potential response. By the end of July reconnaissance units of the Soviet 2nd Tank Army were approaching the suburbs of the city, though this did not necessarily mean that the Red Army was in a position to launch an immediate assault on the Polish capital. And while bellicose statements from Soviet-controlled radio propaganda stations in late July may have offered some encouragement to the population of Warsaw to rise up, that did not automatically mean the Red Army would help them if they did. Crucially, if Stalin ordered his forces not to move into the city shortly after the uprising began, the Home Army could not hold out against the Germans.

It was this uncertainty about Stalin's reaction that concerned the Commander-in-Chief of the Home Army in London. He thought that rising up without the cooperation of the Soviets 'would be politically unjustified and militarily nothing more than an act of despair'. Mikołajczyk was less certain. He left the decision up to the local commander in Warsaw.[34]

Stalin finally agreed to let Mikołajczyk visit Moscow in late July, without the Polish government in exile meeting all his conditions. His demands had been so outrageous that he must have known they could never be met. But just because he had agreed to let Mikołajczyk and his colleagues into the Soviet Union didn't mean that he necessarily had to meet them. For Mikołajczyk it was important to see Stalin quickly because the uprising was imminent. But he was told by Molotov that he would not be meeting with the Soviet leader at all, but instead with the tame government of Poland the Soviets had established – now known as the 'Lublin' Poles because they were based in that recently liberated Polish city.

The uprising finally began in Warsaw on 1 August, and Polish freedom fighters started battling on the streets of the Polish capital with the Germans. Yet, in Moscow, Mikołajczyk still hadn't managed to see Stalin. It wasn't until two days later, on the evening of 3 August, that the Soviet leader finally consented to meet the Polish Prime Minister and his delegation. Predictably, the encounter did not go well for the Poles. Stalin's contempt was palpable. He kept bringing the subject back to his own personal Polish government, the Lublin Poles. Why hadn't Mikołajczyk talked to them? As for the Warsaw uprising, he questioned how effective the Home Army could be in fighting the Germans. 'What is an army without artillery, tanks, and an air-force?' he said. 'They are even short of rifles. In modern warfare such an army is of little use. They are small partisan units, not a regular army. I was told that the Polish government had ordered these units to drive the Germans out of Warsaw. I wonder how they could possibly do this, their forces are not up to that task. As a matter of fact these people do not fight against the Germans, but only hide in woods, being unable to do anything else.'[35] Stalin's statement oozed derision. His scorn for the Polish delegation was such that he even took several phone calls during the meeting.

How pleased Stalin must have been to humiliate Mikołajczyk and his colleagues. How cleverly he must have thought he had played the whole Polish question. He had not said outright that he refused to help the Poles in Warsaw – he knew that would be unwise, given the views of his western Allies; on the other hand he had not said exactly how and when he would. Once again Stalin, from a position of power, demonstrated the value of ambiguity.

The Soviets would subsequently argue that they had not been in a position to take the Polish capital in the early days of August. 'Frankly speaking,' wrote Marshal Rokossovsky after the war, 'the timing of the uprising was just about the worst possible in the circumstances. It was as though its leaders had deliberately chosen a time that would ensure defeat.'[36] Rokossovsky's troops had already advanced hundreds of miles in just a few weeks, and the Germans had managed to regroup to defend the Polish capital. 'Do you think that we would not have taken Warsaw if we had been able to do it?' Rokossovsky said to a western journalist later in the summer of 1944.[37]

The Red Army may not have been capable of immediately launching a major offensive against Warsaw in early August, but this doesn't mean that they couldn't have done so a few weeks later. Averell Harriman, American Ambassador to the Soviet Union, formed the view by mid-August that 'the Soviet Government's refusal [to help the uprising] is not based on operational difficulties, nor on a denial of the conflict, but on ruthless political calculations.'[38]

Zbigniew Wolak, a nineteen-year-old commander of a Home Army unit, fought on the streets of Warsaw that summer. Like many of the resistance fighters, this was his first experience of combat: 'You remember your first love, [and] you remember your first dead person. On the front if you're an airman or artillery you don't see the people you kill, but if you're an infantryman and you fight in the streets you see the face of that person . . . I shot him [a German soldier] and he fell halfway out the window and he was my age – the helmet fell off his head – he was blond, he was my age, a boy. After some time they pulled him by the legs inside. It's hard to forget . . . You say it's a sense of duty to shoot, but you can't get used to killing, it's very hard to get used to it, that's how it was.'

Wolak witnessed not just Germans dying but also his close comrades in the Home Army. 'My friend says, I want to check what the Germans are doing. He took out a brick [from the fortification] and he put his face there and he was shot in the forehead. Next day we buried him. He was one of the oldest soldiers. He was forty-something, he had a wife and two children.'

Without the help of the Red Army, the Poles were losing the battle. In the summer of 1944, the Germans wreaked havoc in Warsaw as SS units shot children, and raped and murdered women. Zbigniew Wolak found it hard to reconcile the sights of mutilation and death he was witnessing with the image he had formed of the Germans before the uprising. He had previously seen Germans as 'human beings' but now 'when they started carrying out executions and massacres' he saw them only as 'criminals', while they for their part treated the Home Army as 'bandits'. This mutual 'stereotyping', he concluded, made it 'easy to kill one another'. Years later, long after the war, he worked alongside Germans and his view changed once again. 'It turned out they were excellent colleagues,' he said. 'They turned out to be great family men.'[39]

Heinrich Himmler saw positives for the Nazi cause in the destruction of Warsaw. On 21 September 1944 he spoke to a group of officers about his reaction to the news that the uprising had started: 'I went at once to see the Führer. I am telling you about it as an example of how one must react to such news with utter calmness. I said: "My Führer the timing is unfortunate. But from a historical point of view it is a blessing that the Poles are doing that. We'll get through the four and five weeks [it will take] and then Warsaw, the capital city, the brain, the intelligence of this 16–17 million-strong Polish nation will have been obliterated, this nation which has blocked our path to the east for seven hundred years and since the first battle of Tannenberg has always been in the way. Then the historic problem will no longer be a major one for our children, for all those who come after us, and for us too." Moreover, I simultaneously gave orders for Warsaw to be totally destroyed. You may think I am a fearful barbarian. If you like I am one, if I have to be.'[40]

Warsaw was not the only historic European capital to experience an insurrection in the summer of 1944. Eight hundred and fifty miles away to the west, Parisians were about to rise up against their German occupiers. And the contrast between the fate of these two famous cities in 1944 was remarkable. Warsaw was trapped between the armies of Hitler and Stalin, Paris between Hitler and the western Allies – a difference that mattered in a myriad of ways.

To begin with, just as Stalin had problems with Prime Minister Mikołajczyk and the Polish government in exile, so Roosevelt and Churchill had an uneasy relationship with the leader of the Free French, General de Gaulle. Famously – or infamously, depending on your point of view – de Gaulle was a difficult person. 'In the designs, the demeanour and the mental operations of a leader', wrote de Gaulle, 'there must be always a "something" which others cannot altogether fathom, which puzzles them, stirs them and rivets their attention.'[41] Furthermore, 'He [the leader] must accept the loneliness which, according to Faguet [a French academic], is the "wretchedness of superior beings".'[42]

Churchill – who was not a fan of dealing with people who thought they were 'superior beings' – came to the conclusion that de Gaulle was 'an enemy of the English people'.[43] Others shared that decidedly negative view. At a meeting in July 1943, General Sir Alan Brooke listened to a 'long tirade of abuse' from Churchill about de Gaulle that he 'heartily agreed with'. Brooke thought de Gaulle 'a most unattractive specimen' and added that 'whatever good qualities he may have had were marred by his overbearing manner, his "megalomania" and his lack of co-operative spirit . . . In all discussions he assumed that the problem of the liberation of France was mine, whilst he was concentrating on how he would govern it, as its Dictator, as soon as it was liberated!'[44] Lord Moran, Churchill's doctor, wrote in his diary that 'De Gaulle positively goes out of his way to be difficult' and that he was an 'improbable creature, like a human giraffe, sniffing down his nostrils at mortals beneath his gaze'.[45]

But all this invective was as nothing alongside Roosevelt's dislike of the French general. Just before D-Day, the President told Edward Stettinius, the American Under Secretary of State, that 'The only thing I am interested in is not having de Gaulle and the National Committee [a provisional Free French government in exile] named as the government of France.'[46] Roosevelt's intense dislike of de Gaulle was partly personal – he just couldn't stand him as a human being – and partly political – he worried that de Gaulle would pursue colonial policies after the war.

But even though both Roosevelt and Churchill had an aversion to de Gaulle, they did not move decisively against him, despite the fact they could easily have done so. De Gaulle's reputation was built on his access to the radio. It was his wartime BBC broadcasts from London that had made him famous. Consequently, if he had been denied access to the airwaves he would have all but vanished from sight.

Who can doubt how Stalin would have behaved in similar circumstances, with his talk of ensuring neighbouring nations were 'friendly' to the Soviet Union? Or how Hitler might have treated a man with 'superior' airs, but who was nonetheless dependent on him? Yet, difficult as de Gaulle undoubtedly was, the British and Americans continued to tolerate him. Churchill was even capable of empathizing with him, despite all the problems he caused. According to Moran, the Prime Minister admired de Gaulle for not relaxing 'his vigilance in guarding' the honour of France 'for a single instant'.[47]

However, even at this late stage in the war the Americans still did not recognize de Gaulle's Free French movement as the legitimate government of France, and it was by no means certain that he would lead France in the wake of the liberation. But de Gaulle's visit to Bayeux in Normandy on 14 June – just eight days after D-Day – demonstrated the power he possessed by virtue of his personality and reputation. The people of Normandy were not natural de Gaulle enthusiasts. They were currently trying to survive amid the fierce fighting between the Allies and the Germans, and there appeared to be no great desire among them to punish the collaborators of the Vichy regime. One Allied report said that 'even after the invasion, the peasants preferred to sell their butter to the retreating Germans than to our men who were considered suspect.'[48]

Yet, despite all this, when de Gaulle arrived in Bayeux the population welcomed him and around 2,000 turned out to hear him speak. It was this kind of evidence of spontaneous support for the general among the French population that contributed to Roosevelt's decision, on 11 July, to acknowledge the Gaullists as 'the working authority for civilian administration in the liberated areas of France'.[49]

After the Allied breakthrough at Avranches in late July and early August, and the disaster of the failed German counter-attack, the capture of Paris appeared possible. But Paris was of little strategic importance to the Allies, and there was talk of bypassing the city and pushing on towards the German border. At this moment, just as Stalin held the fate of Warsaw in his hands, so the British and Americans held the fate of Paris in theirs.

While the western Allies debated the best way forward, the Germans in Paris under their new commander, General Dietrich von Choltitz, prepared to defend the city. But, unlike in Warsaw, the Germans didn't seem that committed to the task. 'No combat troops, units lacking solid structure . . .', wrote the commander of German troops at Fontainebleau. 'Insufficient armament. AA [anti-aircraft] detachments not equipped with necessary means of observation and signal equipment for ground-fighting . . . In view of the particular difficulties of fighting in a large city and the material superiority of the enemy, any real resistance on the part of the Paris Mil[itary] District could not be expected.'[50]

General von Choltitz, who had only recently been appointed Military Governor of the city, was trying to reconcile two irreconcilable objectives. Hitler wanted Paris defended – and utterly destroyed if necessary – but the German leader hadn't allocated sufficient military forces to make such aggressive actions possible. Choltitz would later claim that he had prevented the destruction of Paris. Yet while it's true that the bridges of Paris and some of the major buildings that had been mined were ultimately saved, the reality was that the Germans did not have the ability to destroy Paris in the way they were currently taking Warsaw apart, brick by brick. Choltitz almost certainly made pragmatic choices, in the knowledge that his actions would help sanitize his reputation. In doing so he joined a long list of Germans who – now that they thought the Nazis would lose – were hurriedly putting the best gloss they could on their war record.

By mid-August the situation in Paris was febrile. Among the different resistance groups in the French capital, it was the communists who were most keen on an uprising. De Gaulle's representative in Paris, Alexandre Parodi, had been told not to order an uprising without co-ordinating with Allied forces. But on 15 August, after the police went on strike, some resistance fighters took to the streets. The Prefecture of Police was occupied by the resistance on the 18th, and the following day Parisians rose up against their occupiers, just as the Polish Home Army had done in Warsaw at the start of the month. And, just like the Poles, the French fighters did so without first consulting the commanders of the approaching army of liberation.

Though the resistance fighters outnumbered the German defenders two to one, the Germans were better equipped, and a sustained fight between them would likely have been bloody and prolonged. A proposed truce between the two sides didn't hold, and by 22 August the French were fighting the Germans on the streets once again. Over the next two days, as the battle intensified, the Grand Palais went up in flames – set on fire by the Germans – and there was a real danger of further destruction.[51] Hitler issued an order on the 23rd that 'Paris must not, or only as a field of rubble, fall into the hands of the enemy.'[52]

Just as in Warsaw, the army outside the capital urgently had to decide what to do. But, unlike in the Polish capital, the resisters in Paris were not left to die on the streets while their potential liberators waited outside the city. On 20 August, de Gaulle paid General Eisenhower a visit, and demanded to know why Allied troops were not advancing on Paris – in particular soldiers of the 2nd Armoured Division, commanded by the French general Philippe Leclerc.

Eisenhower told de Gaulle that the uprising in Paris had started prematurely – it was 'too early' for them to be confronting the Germans openly on the streets. De Gaulle disagreed and said he would order Leclerc to advance on Paris himself if need be – despite the fact that de Gaulle had no authority to do so. Nonetheless, three days later the Allies did as de Gaulle had requested, and Leclerc was told he could move on Paris. His forward units reached the Hôtel de Ville – the symbolic heart of the French capital – on the evening of 24 August. The following day the majority of the 2nd Division, together with some American soldiers, arrived to consolidate the Allied control of the city, and Choltitz surrendered on behalf of the German occupiers that afternoon.[53]

Later that same day, 25 August, de Gaulle became a legendary French hero when he arrived in Paris and spoke his famous words from the Hôtel de Ville – 'Paris humiliated! Paris broken! Paris martyrized! But now Paris liberated!' He added that Paris had 'liberated herself'. This was not strictly true, since without the might of the Allied armies behind the Free French forces, de Gaulle would not have been present in the Hôtel de Ville making his speech.[54]

While the Allies advanced to occupy Paris, the Red Army steadfastly refused to mount a major offensive on Warsaw, and without support from Soviet forces the failure of the uprising was inevitable. At the start of October, the commander of the Home Army in Warsaw, General Tadeusz Bór-Komorowski, surrendered to the Germans. More than 200,000 Poles died as a consequence of the uprising, and many of the survivors blamed not just the Germans but Stalin for this huge loss. 'No one who is not dishonest or blind could have had the least illusion that everything which had happened was always going to happen,' wrote General Anders, commander of the Polish units in the British Army; 'i.e. not only that the Soviets will refuse to help our beloved, heroic Warsaw, but also that they will watch with the greatest pleasure as our nation's blood is drained to the last drop.'[55]

It's hard not to agree with Anders' judgement. For while Stalin had wanted in September to appear to be offering some limited help to the resisters – most notably by allowing soldiers from his 1st Polish Army to land on the west bank of the Vistula – it was all much too little, much too late. The reality of Stalin's position was best expressed in a message the Soviets sent to the American Ambassador in Moscow in the middle of August, which stated that 'the Soviet Government do not wish to associate themselves either directly or indirectly with the adventure in Warsaw.'[56]

It wasn't until January 1945 that the Red Army finally marched into the Polish capital, as part of their Vistula–Oder offensive. 'You should have seen what liberated Warsaw was like,' said Nikolai Brandt, the Soviet officer pretending to be a Pole, serving with Stalin's Polish Army. 'The German sappers had blown up all the buildings, and before that they had been scorched by flamethrowers . . . So Warsaw was just stones. There was no one left in those houses.'[57]

As Brandt walked through the ruins of Warsaw, dressed in his Polish uniform, a woman approached him. 'At last I can see a real Polish officer,' she said. 'How wonderful that is!' Brandt started to chat to her, but saw 'she looked somehow disappointed.' The women asked, 'But why is your accent so bad? You must be from Kraków.' Brandt said no, he was from a small town in the south-east of Poland – as his fictitious backstory required him to say: 'I didn't want to admit I was Russian. It would look bad. A Russian officer in the Polish Army. It would look like a fake army. I felt like, if I had undertaken to be a Polish commanding officer, let everyone continue thinking that I was Polish.'[58]

It's a moment that encapsulates both the immense cynicism of Stalin's attitude towards the Poles and the contrast between what was happening in Warsaw and what was happening in Paris. It wasn't just that Stalin had held the Red Army back until the Polish Home Army in Warsaw had been destroyed, but that when his 'liberators' did eventually arrive, among the soldiers were a number of 'fake' Polish officers like Nikolai Brandt. Yet, when the French 2nd Armoured Division liberated Paris, there had been no 'fake' Frenchmen among Leclerc's officers. France was now set back on the way to democracy and freedom, Poland placed on the road to a new tyranny.

In October 1944, Churchill had tried – and failed – to resolve the conflict between the Polish government in exile and Stalin. He had travelled to Moscow and, during his opening encounter with Stalin at the

Kremlin on 9 October, had described the Polish question as 'the most tiresome' the two leaders faced, although at least, he said, the borders were 'settled'.[59] Stalin would receive eastern Poland after the war, as he had long wanted. But, as we have seen, it was disingenuous of the two leaders to consider the borders 'settled', since the legitimate government of the country that was being dismembered had repeatedly rejected the plan.

Churchill did suggest that the 'London Poles' should be made to come to Moscow at once where they would be 'forced to settle'. The problem, Churchill said, was that while the Poles were brave fighters, they 'had unwise political leaders. Where there were two Poles there was one quarrel.' Stalin agreed, adding that 'where there was one Pole he would begin to quarrel with himself through sheer boredom.'[60]

Just four days later, at Churchill's request, Prime Minister Mikołajczyk arrived at the Kremlin to discuss the future of Poland. The Polish premier cannot have had good memories of his last meeting with Stalin, three months before, when the Soviet leader had toyed with him over the possibility of Soviet help for the Warsaw uprising. It was a memory that must have been made all the more distressing by the knowledge that little more than a week earlier the Home Army had been forced to surrender to the Germans in Warsaw – in large part because Stalin had not ordered the Red Army to take the Polish capital and relieve them.

Nonetheless, Mikołajczyk had to deal with reality. And the reality was that his country was small and powerless compared to the Soviet Union, and that Britain could not do much in practical terms to help the Poles. It was the Red Army that was standing on Polish soil, not the British. The power lay with Stalin, and he knew it.

Stalin once again hid behind the pretence that the other Polish government – the one he controlled – needed to be consulted. But still, he was prepared to state that 'there can be no good relations' between Poland and the Soviet Union unless the Poles agreed to relinquish eastern Poland. Churchill supported Stalin, and said the British agreed that the Soviets should take this territory not 'because Russia was strong but because Russia was right in the matter'. So far, so predictable. Mikołajczyk already knew this was the British position. But at this point the discussion grew ugly – or, from Mikołajczyk's perspective, even uglier. Devastatingly, Molotov suddenly revealed that President Roosevelt had agreed at the Tehran conference nearly a year before to give eastern Poland to the Soviets, but 'did not wish it published at the moment'.[61]

This came as a shock to Mikołajczyk, since just four months before Roosevelt had said no such thing to him. On the contrary, he had led the Polish Prime Minister to believe that he was on his side.

The following day, matters scarcely improved. Churchill lectured Mikołajczyk, telling him, 'Because of quarrels between Poles we are not going to wreck the peace of Europe . . . you are absolutely crazy . . . Unless you accept the frontier you are out of business for ever. The Russians will sweep through your country and your people will be liquidated. You are on the verge of annihilation.' Moreover, if the Poles 'want to conquer Russia we shall leave you to do it. I feel as if I were in a lunatic asylum. I don't know whether the British government will continue to recognize you.'[62] The cumulative effect of all this vitriol on Mikołajczyk is not hard to imagine. He could take no more, and resigned his post on 24 November.

Churchill was doing little more than accepting the unpleasant truth. British public opinion, bolstered by propaganda portraying the Soviets as a valued ally, would almost certainly never have accepted a new war to free Poland from Stalin's grasp. That truth also partly explains why Churchill produced what he called a 'naughty' document at one of the meetings with Stalin. It was this piece of paper for which the October trip to Moscow is chiefly remembered. Churchill had jotted down the percentages of influence that each of the allies should have in various European countries. He wrote: 'Romania: Russia 90%, the others 10%. Greece: Britain (in accord with USA) 90%, Russia 10%. Yugoslavia [and] Hungary: 50/50%. Bulgaria: Russia 75%, the others 25%.'[63]

We shouldn't be too shocked by Churchill's actions. It wasn't so much that he was handing countries like Romania and Bulgaria to Stalin as that he recognized that they had been given away already, as a result of their geography and the success of the Red Army. Arguably, his secret discussions with Stalin about these percentages saved Greece from the threat of communist domination after the war.

What is surprising, however, is the way Churchill continued to delude himself about the nature of his relationship with Stalin. He wrote to the war cabinet in October, saying that he had 'talked with a freedom and beau gest[e] never before attained between our two countries. Stalin has made several expressions of personal regard which I feel sure were sincere.'[64] To his wife he said, 'I have had very nice talks with the Old Bear [Stalin]. I like him the more I see him. *Now* they respect us & I am sure they wish to work w[ith] us.'[65] And just as he had before, Churchill was inclined to ascribe any problems he encountered in his dealings with Stalin to others operating in the shadows, a concern he expressed in his telegram to the war cabinet by saying 'I repeat my conviction that he is by no means alone. "Behind the horseman sits dull care." '[66]

Yet even as Churchill was saying all this, it was obvious how Stalin's security units were behaving in the territory they had just 'liberated'. By the start of October the NKVD had imprisoned around 100,000 former Home Army soldiers and other leading Poles.[67] At the end of the month, just days after Churchill's visit to Moscow, one Home Army commander wrote that 'In the town of Krześlin, Siedlce powiat [county], the NKVD have organized a punishment camp for members of the AK [Home Army] and the Government delegature. Those arrested sit in dug-out holes about 2 metres square with water up to their knees – in darkness. The camp is completely isolated. It contains an estimated 1500 people.'[68]

The truth, which Churchill did not yet accept, was that Stalin only wanted 'to work' with the other allies in order to get what he wanted. And so far, he appeared to be succeeding.

But this was all about to change. For 1945 would bring both victory for the Allies, and – belatedly – a realization of just who Stalin really was.

17. Dying Days

In November 1918, when the First World War ended, the German Army was still fighting on enemy soil. On the western front, the Allies had not even reached Brussels in Belgium. On the eastern front, the Russians – having left the war with the treaty of Brest-Litovsk – were no longer any kind of threat. But this new war, fought in the shadow of the last, would be very different. This time the invaders would battle their way into the heart of Germany. And nothing illustrates Hitler's mentality better than his decision to fight until Red Army soldiers were just yards from his bunker in Berlin.

In the autumn of 1944 both the western Allies and the Soviets crossed into Germany for the first time. In the west, the city of Aachen was captured by the Americans on 21 October, while at the same time the Red Army occupied the East Prussian village of Nemmersdorf. What happened in Nemmersdorf was to become infamous. After the Soviet forces had been pushed back, the Germans found that more than two dozen villagers had been murdered – including thirteen women and five children. At least one woman had been raped. German photographers swiftly took pictures of the bodies, after placing them in horrific poses to suggest violent sexual assault.[1] It was a propaganda gift for the Nazis.

Goebbels wrote in his diary on 26 October that events in Nemmersdorf should convince Germans of what they 'can expect if Bolshevism really gets hold of the Reich'. German newspapers reported more than sixty dead, mass rape and even one case of crucifixion. But the propaganda blitz was not quite as successful as Goebbels had hoped. Though many Germans were undoubtedly traumatized by events in Nemmersdorf, others questioned not just the accuracy of the German stories but their inherent hypocrisy. One SD report from Stuttgart, for example, said that some people thought that the Soviet action was revenge for 'atrocities that we have perpetrated on enemy soil, and even in Germany. Have we not slaughtered Jews in their thousands? Don't soldiers tell over and again that Jews in Poland had to dig their own graves?' The conclusion from all this was clear: 'By acting in this way, we have shown the enemy what they might do to us in the event of their victory.'[2]

The incursion of the Red Army into Germany was just one of the problems that Hitler had to deal with that autumn. He was also witnessing the collapse of his allies. By October, Soviet forces had occupied Romania and Bulgaria, and both countries had declared war on Germany. Hitler prevented Admiral Horthy, Regent of Hungary, from changing sides only by organizing the kidnapping of Horthy's son and blackmailing the Admiral into handing over power to the leader of the Hungarian fascists, Ferenc Szálasi. Hitler would subsequently try to portray these defections as a positive, saying that during 'this mightiest people's struggle of all time, we see those dropping away who are small, cowardly and unfit for life'.[3] But it's hard to believe that he really thought the destruction of his erstwhile allies was a reason for celebration. Perhaps, once again, he was trying desperately to convince himself of an alternative reality.

Even Hitler's most committed supporters started to question the wisdom of carrying on the fight. In September 1944 Goebbels wrote to the Führer about rumours he had heard that Stalin might be willing to consider a separate peace. It 'would not be the victory that we dreamed of in 1941', he said on 20 September, 'but it would still be the greatest victory in German history. The sacrifices that the German people had made in this war would thereby be fully justified.'[4]

Hitler never even replied to Goebbels' suggestion. It wasn't just that it was difficult to see why Stalin would accept a deal with the Germans when the Red Army was winning on the battlefield, but Hitler's whole personality militated against the idea. Victory or annihilation – that was his choice now.

It was in this gloomy atmosphere that the anniversary of the Beer Hall Putsch loomed into view. Perhaps predictably, Hitler decided not to attend the commemorations in Munich that November. There was no good news of any kind with which to leaven his speech. So, just as he had in the wake of the Stalingrad defeat, he called upon someone else to deliver his words. This time, the stooge was Heinrich Himmler, possibly the worst orator in the Nazi Party. But even the most gifted performer could not have made much of the raw material on offer. It was all too familiar. The Bolsheviks wanted to destroy Germany; and the 'democracies' out of 'incomprehensible absurdity' were helping them, even though they 'would immediately be in their graves with the victory of Bolshevism, which would smash the democratic states along with all their ideas against a wall'. As usual, the Jews were to blame. 'The Jew is always behind human stupidity and weakness . . . The Jew is the mastermind in the democracies, as well as the creator and driving force of the Bolshevik world beast.'[5]

Once again Hitler openly fantasized that the Jews were responsible for anything and everything that he opposed and feared. Unlike Stalin, who saw different potential enemies wherever he looked, Hitler saw the same enemy the world over. He had recently told his Luftwaffe adjutant, Nicolaus von Below, that the reason he was not prepared to concentrate all his forces against the Soviet threat was because 'he feared the power of the American Jews more than the Bolshevists.'[6] It's an aspect of Hitler's thinking that is often underestimated. As he saw it, the Jews controlled Stalin and the Jews controlled Roosevelt and the Jews controlled Churchill.

But, for all of his attempts to blame the Jews for his current predicament, Hitler knew that success was the only way to redeem himself in the eyes of the German people. Charismatic leaders – and Hitler, as we have seen, is the archetypal example – are immensely vulnerable once they start failing. Given that their followers have supported them primarily out of faith, there is no bedrock of rational understanding beneath their trust. Once events go against charismatic leaders, it is as if they are standing on quicksand. Only fresh victories can shore them up. Hitler knew this, and so he decided on a new offensive.

The Germans planned on launching an attack on the western Allies in the Ardennes forest, with the aim of pushing the enemy back to the coast and taking the port of Antwerp in Belgium. Hitler's reasoning, when he explained it to his commanders, could not have been more straightforward. 'Wars are ultimately decided by one side or the other realizing that the war as such cannot be won any more,' he told them. 'Thus our most important task is to get this realization across to the enemy.' It was essential to take risks and attack, since 'overlong periods of just defensive steadfastness wear you out in the long run.'[7]

However, the Germans lacked the resources to get this 'realization across to the enemy', even though Hitler committed the best forces he could to the operation. But, at least to begin with, the Germans did have the advantage of surprise. Who would have thought that Hitler would order a large offensive when strategic retreat was what was needed? So when the attack was launched on 16 December it made some progress. The Fifth Panzer Army, for instance, managed to lay siege to Bastogne in Belgium – but this was still more than a hundred miles from Antwerp.

The Germans were also helped in their initial advance by the overcast weather, which made it hard for the Allies to attack from the air. But once these twin initial advantages – surprise and bad weather – had dissipated, the offensive collapsed. By the end of 1944, after General Patton had broken the siege of Bastogne, the Germans were even worse off than they had been before, since they had squandered many of their own scarce reserves.

Hitler, whose ability to remain largely positive about the prospects of victory had been remarkable over the last two years, now showed signs that his confidence was dwindling. Nicolaus von Below saw the initial indications in late November 1944, when – just before he was forced to leave the Wolf's Lair because Soviet forces were approaching – Hitler had remarked that 'the war was lost.' But it was the failure of the Ardennes offensive that tipped him into outright despair. 'Never before or subsequently', wrote Below, 'did I see him in such a state.' 'I know the war is lost,' said Hitler. 'The enemy superiority is too great.' But the conclusion Hitler reached about what this catastrophic situation meant was entirely characteristic. 'We will not capitulate, ever,' he said. 'We may go down. But we will take the world down with us.'[8]

Hitler never voiced these views to ordinary Germans. Instead they were fed a propaganda diet of hope for the future ('wonder weapons' would soon arrive and turn the war around), exhortations from history (hadn't Frederick the Great had dark moments during the Seven Years War and yet won eventual victory?) and the prospect of the alliance between the western democracies and the Soviet Union falling apart.

Committed Nazis had varying degrees of difficulty in reconciling such promises with the reality of the devastation around them. Take the case of Otto Klimmer. He was sixteen years old in 1944 and a devoted National Socialist, whose father was also loyal to the cause. But then, as Germany's fortunes declined during the year, his father said to him, 'Boy, we cannot win this war . . .' This, said Otto Klimmer, was 'something quite amazing to me, if it hadn't been my father I would certainly have been outraged. That conversation, in particular, was a decisive factor for me. I began to view certain incidents happening around me differently, without objecting to them, or doing anything about them, because I was far too convinced despite these things that victory was [still] a given.'

By 1944, many of Klimmer's schoolmates had been drafted into the army. He himself was too young to serve, but he was still desperate to help the regime: 'I addressed several letters to the military district command asking to be allowed to become a soldier, telling them it was the highest honour for me to die for the Führer, nation and fatherland. I really wrote that, I absolutely wanted to be part of it all. This might go some way towards illustrating how mad a time this was.' Educated from the age of three to believe wholeheartedly in National Socialism, supported within a family that gloried in Hitler's early foreign policy triumphs, Klimmer found it all but impossible to rethink his view of the world. 'It was not the case that you saw it as a dictatorship,' he said, 'but you participated in it out of your own free will. You might find this difficult to imagine, but that's what it was like . . . And this is what I have blamed myself for repeatedly during my lifetime, in relation to other things too. Anti-tank ditches were being dug in the centre of town exclusively by inmates of the concentration camp, and I had to pass that spot every day. Do you think I felt any kind of sympathy, any pity? I did not. That was just the way it was, they were political opponents of National Socialism, the fact that they were locked up I considered completely normal at the time, the fact that they were guarded by members of the SS, were yelled at, were pushed around from time to time, I thought that was normal at the time. That just goes to show how twisted we were, that we were hardly a master race but were rapidly becoming inhuman ourselves.'[9]

Hitler's New Year proclamation on 1 January 1945 reconfirmed his own inhumanity. Broadcast on radio, his quavering voice burst through the static to threaten Germans that if 'anyone . . . tries to escape making his contribution or lowers himself to becoming an instrument of foreign powers' he would be eliminated by the 'present leadership'. Germans should fight on because 'Anglo-American statesmen' along with 'Bolshevik rulers and the international Jews who in the end are behind everything' planned on tearing the Reich to pieces and transporting 'fifteen to twenty million Germans to foreign countries'. But, said Hitler, in the knowledge that millions of Jews had already died in the Holocaust, the 'power which we have solely to thank for all this – the Jewish international enemy of the world' – will end the war by bringing about its 'own annihilation'.[10]

Hitler refused to acknowledge that the fundamental problem Germany faced was that its enemies were just too powerful. No, he claimed, the primary reason for the 'collapse' of countries like Italy, Finland, Romania and Bulgaria was 'the cowardice and indecisiveness of their leaders'. But rational listeners would have realized that bravery and commitment were not effective defences against bombs and bullets, and that Hitler had little left to offer them, except threat and hate.

The contrast in mood and demeanour between Hitler and Stalin in January 1945 was immense. Arthur Tedder, the RAF officer who was Deputy Supreme Commander of Allied operations, visited Stalin that month and later offered an intriguing insight into the Soviet leader as victory grew near. After he had been ushered into Stalin's presence, he gave him a present of cigars 'with General Eisenhower's compliments'. Stalin pointed to them and asked, 'When do they go off?' Tedder replied, 'They do not go off until I have gone.' This idea – that the Deputy Supreme Commander of Allied operations was trying to murder the Soviet leader by bringing a bomb into his presence – apparently went down well as a 'small joke'.

Tedder spotted several changes since his last visit to Moscow in 1942, both in the decor of Stalin's office and in the demeanour of the man himself. When Tedder had been in the office two years before, 'the portraits had been those of Karl Marx, Engels, and others.' But now 'they were of four field-marshals from Russian military history, including Suvarov [sic].' This martial theme was reflected in Stalin's change of appearance. In 1942 he had been dressed in a peasant's garb of 'grey smock, breeches, and field boots' but now 'he was in full sail as a field-marshal, suitably hung with red stars and similar appropriate decoration.'[11]

These changes, while outwardly superficial, were actually of great significance. For years Stalin had been careful to present himself as a modest worker. He refused to live in ostentation – apart from the incongruity of the occasional Kremlin banquet. His plain clothes made a vital statement. He was not like the tsars and other monarchs, dressed in a fancy uniform and awash with decorations. But he had now succumbed to temptation and abandoned his previous commitment to simplicity.

Stalin's military uniform appears to have made its first outing at Tehran in November 1943. Sir Alexander Cadogan noticed the change and thought that Stalin appeared 'rather uneasy' in his new oufit.[12]

Why did Stalin suddenly decide to wear a uniform? The biggest clue is the date of the change. He only started to look like a supreme commander when his army was unquestionably winning. In other words, he wanted the credit and, as we shall see, after victory had been achieved he was anxious not to share that glory. Stalin, wrote Tedder, 'had been mentioned in the same breath as Napoleon and Alexander the Great, and did not appear to object to such comparisons'.[13]

As for the change in pictures, the British Ambassador to Moscow, Sir Archibald Clark Kerr, first spotted these alterations after the victory at Kursk in 1943. 'I was interested to notice that over the table at which we sat hung huge portraits of Suverov [sic] and Kutuzov. They had pushed enlarged photographs of Marx and Engels into a corner.'[14] These changes, as we have seen earlier in this history, were part of Stalin's scheme to connect with the military glories of Imperial Russia's past and, now that the portraits were hanging in his office, perhaps also to suggest that in the future he deserved a place among this pantheon of military greats.

After the 'joke' about the cigars, Tedder and Stalin focused on the military situation. Just like Sir Alan Brooke before him, Tedder 'was most impressed by Stalin's knowledge of his subject'. And while the Soviet leader was generally in good humour during the encounter, there was a 'moment when one saw a flash of his awe-inspiring anger'. Stalin turned to General Antonov of the Soviet General Staff and demanded to know why a particular German oil plant had not been bombed: 'Antonov went pale, and rose rather shakily to his feet to reply . . . This incident gave an impressive glimpse of the fear which ruled the régime.'[15]

A few weeks before, in December 1944, Charles de Gaulle had witnessed a similar display of Stalin's leadership technique. At a banquet in the Kremlin, Stalin offered a toast to the commander of the Red Army Air Force, Chief Marshal Novikov. 'He has created a wonderful air force,' said Stalin. 'But if he doesn't do his job properly then we'll kill him.' Stalin then turned to General Khrulev, Director of Supply. 'There he is!' declared Stalin. 'It is his job to bring men and material to the front. He'd better do his best otherwise he'll be hanged for it. That's the custom in our country!' Later in the evening he said to his interpreter, Boris Podzerov, 'You know too much. I had better send you to Siberia.'[16]

This display, it appears, was an example of Stalin enjoying himself. He was in an expansive mood that evening, even though de Gaulle had conducted himself in the discussions about a French–Soviet treaty as he normally did – stiff-necked, without humour and high on the idea of the 'honour' of France. Stalin had deployed all of his skills as a negotiator in an attempt to get de Gaulle to recognize his puppet Polish government, the Lublin Poles, but the Frenchman had resisted.

Nonetheless, Stalin congratulated de Gaulle. 'Well done!' he said. 'I like dealing with someone who knows what he wants even if he doesn't share my views!'[17] This was patently untrue. The list of people who had made clear their views to Stalin and yet had still suffered at his hands was enormous – the Polish government in exile earlier in 1944 and the Finns in 1939 to name but two. Perhaps the impending prospect of victory against the Germans, and the general atmosphere of an evening in which he had amused himself by openly threatening his subordinates with execution, had briefly mellowed him. Possibly he was also conscious of his own mortality that night, as towards the end of the evening he remarked to de Gaulle, 'After all, it is only death who wins.'[18]

De Gaulle later recorded his own impression of Stalin – one that reveals a good deal about both of them. He thought Stalin was 'possessed by the will to power. Accustomed by a life of machination to disguise his features as well as his inmost soul, to dispense with illusions, pity, sincerity, to see in each man an obstacle or a threat, he was all strategy, suspicion and stubbornness . . . As a communist disguised as a Marshal, a dictator preferring the tactics of guile, a conqueror with an affable smile, he was a past master of deception. But so fierce was his passion that it often gleamed through this armor, not without a kind of sinister charm.'[19]

Just after de Gaulle met Stalin, Red Army soldiers began a bitter fight for Budapest, the capital of Hungary. Hitler had declared the city a 'fortified place' – one that had to be defended to the last. In mid-January 1945 the Germans destroyed the bridges across the Danube and prepared to make a last stand with their Hungarian allies in the fortress on Gellért Hill in Buda. It wasn't until the middle of February that the Soviets finally managed to take the whole city.

According to Boris Likhachev, who commanded a Soviet tank unit, the soldiers were 'exhausted' after their victory: 'We wanted to have a good wash, to charge our batteries – to recover. We were very good at recovering.'[20] For some soldiers in the Red Army the form this 'recovering' took in Budapest became infamous. One estimate is that 50,000 women were raped in the capital, and more across the rest of the country.

'The worst suffering of the Hungarian population is due to the rape of women,' said a contemporary report compiled by the Swiss embassy in Budapest. 'Rapes – affecting all age groups from ten to seventy – are so common that very few women in Hungary have been spared.'[21] Even Hungarian communists protested at what was happening. One group in Kőbánya, in the eastern suburbs of Pest, reported that 'Mothers were raped by drunken soldiers in front of their children and husbands. Girls as young as 12 were dragged from their fathers and mothers to be violated by 10–15 soldiers and often infected with venereal diseases.' When the Hungarian communists protested, the Red Army soldiers reacted with 'fits of rage' and 'threaten to shoot us'. That this was an act of vengeance was made clear to the Hungarians. 'And what did you do in the Soviet Union?' the soldiers asked them. 'You not only raped our wives before our eyes, but for good measure you killed them together with their children, set fire to our villages and razed our cities to the ground.'[22]

Finding Red Army veterans prepared to admit to the crimes the Red Army committed was not easy. Boris Likhachev's blithe comments on events in Budapest immediately after the capture of the city were typical: 'There might have been cases of maltreatment, but I don't know of them. But logically there could have been. Logically, because historically the winners always want to look for some benefits for compensation for the hardships.'[23]

So Fiodor Khropatiy of the 2nd Ukrainian Front was unusual, in that he openly admitted that Soviet soldiers carried out rapes as they advanced west towards Germany. He estimated that around 30 per cent of his comrades committed the offence. And even though for Red Army soldiers rape was officially a crime, in his experience all the guilty escaped punishment: 'No one complained, this is why no one was put on trial, I never heard about anyone being put on trial.' He remembered that 'it was more officers than soldiers [who committed rape], because they ate better and they wore better clothes, and they were not as exhausted. This is why they were more enthusiastic, but as to the soldiers, there were stronger soldiers who felt less tired [who] were more prone to getting involved with women . . . I didn't do anything of that kind, but others did, and did it all the time. Such cases were very common, and there was a big spread of VD, officers picked up venereal diseases. They didn't want to turn to doctors and they got injections surreptitiously.' He saw how one officer, a lieutenant colonel, 'got drunk and he wanted a woman, and he sent his aides to find a woman for him. I was a witness of how they were chasing a woman. They found a widow, but she managed to run away, she broke the window and jumped down, they fired at her, but they missed, and she ran away. Everything happened, it was a war, a cruel war. War is a cruel business. I'm sure he got another one, but I was glad this one ran away. I'm sure that his aides continued to look for another woman . . . some people behaved in a gentler way, but others in a rude and rough way. Behind all this is the physiological need, in the same way as the hungry man wants to satisfy his hunger and when he does it, he's happy.'

Khropatiy was keen to set what happened in the context of this bloody and terrible war: 'I remember, in Budapest, I saw a family – husband, wife and their daughter. I remember the column of tanks was passing by and I remember one of the tanks running over the man and killing him, squashing him under itself. After twenty or thirty seconds, this person was just a piece of meat. This was terrible cruelty. I don't know if it was intentional or if the driver couldn't see the man.'

As he looked back on the whole conflict, he felt 'ashamed . . . first of all, because in the beginning of the war, Hitler and Stalin kissed each other, and Hitler fought the whole of Europe, and Stalin, at the same time, was sending everything to help Hitler and leaving his own country unfed and poor. Then, Hitler and Stalin fell out because they couldn't divide [the spoils] equally. I'm ashamed that we allowed our country to have such leaders, who involved our country in this terrible war in which we lost so many millions of people, to say nothing of the emotionally traumatized people.'[24]

Not surprisingly, Stalin took a very different view of the history – so different that had Fiodor Khropatiy openly expressed these sentiments under Stalin's rule he would have been immediately arrested. Unlike Khropatiy, Stalin also appears to have been relaxed about his soldiers raping civilians. Milovan Djilas, a Yugoslavian communist, had protested about rapes committed by Soviet soldiers in Yugoslavia, but when Djilas visited Moscow in late 1944 Stalin complained that he had 'insulted' the Red Army. Couldn't he 'understand' it, he said, 'if a soldier who has crossed thousands of kilometres through blood and fire and death has fun with a woman or takes some trifle?'[25]

The rapes weren't even confined to foreign women. In Poland, the Soviet correspondent Vasily Grossman reported that 'Liberated Soviet girls often complain about being raped by our soldiers. One girl said to me, crying: "He was an old man, older than my father." '[26]

At the end of December 1944, Guderian, Chief of Staff of the German Army, was particularly worried about the impact of the next Soviet attack. He knew from intelligence reports just how strong the Red Army had become. But when he travelled to Hitler's headquarters to tell him of the danger, Hitler dismissed the idea that the Soviets possessed such an advantage. He called it an 'enemy bluff' and the notion they had such resources available to them the 'greatest imposture since Genghis Khan'. He claimed that the Soviets regularly lied about the number of soldiers in each unit. What they called 'tank formations' in reality 'had no tanks'. The ironic dimension of this argument did not escape Guderian, who knew that it was Hitler who was now attempting to deceive everyone about the strength of German forces by performing exactly the same trick. 'Panzer brigades were [now] two battalions,' he wrote, 'that is to say with the strength of regiments.'[27]

Guderian, for all his many deficiencies as a human being, was at least a talented military commander. Yet he was forced to listen to the views of the militarily incompetent mass killer Heinrich Himmler, who sat next to him at dinner that night. 'You know, my dear Colonel-General,' Himmler told him, 'I don't really believe the Russians will attack at all.'[28]

The reason Himmler spoke as he did is not hard to grasp. He owed his entire career to Adolf Hitler. And since Hitler had led the Nazis through dark times before, who knew what he might turn up now in these desperate moments? It was delusional thinking, but from Himmler's perspective it made a kind of sense.

Guderian had not given up hope that Hitler would listen to reasoned argument and devote greater resources to counter the forthcoming Soviet offensive. So he made another attempt to persuade Hitler, on 9 January 1945. Armed with 'maps and diagrams' prepared by army intelligence, he demonstrated the danger the Germans faced. Hitler responded by saying that the man responsible for this information should be locked up in a 'lunatic asylum'. A furious row followed, in which Guderian said that since he also believed this intelligence he should be 'certified' as a 'lunatic' as well.[29]

Three days later the Soviets launched their massive Vistula–Oder offensive. Hitler's response was to order that a number of senior officers be 'interrogated' and even arrested over the decisions they had made as the Red Army advanced. Guderian, seeing – as any rational person would – the gravity of the situation, visited Ribbentrop in an attempt to convince him to persuade Hitler to make peace in the west, so that all efforts could be directed at holding back the Soviets. Ribbentrop refused, saying that he knew his Führer wouldn't countenance such an idea. When Hitler heard about the meeting he accused Guderian of committing 'high treason'. But it was an empty threat, as he never had Guderian arrested as a consequence.[30]

Guderian and German military intelligence had been right. The Soviets had an enormous material advantage during the Vistula–Oder offensive: about five times as many troops, at some vital offensive points even more than that. Given the weakness of the opposition, the Red Army made swift progress, advancing around 300 miles in just three weeks.

What's remarkable, once again, is the similarity between Hitler's conduct during this period and the way Stalin acted in the spring and summer of 1941: the contempt for military intelligence that accurately predicted an attack but that, in doing so, went against the preferred picture of events in the dictator's mind; the desire to arrest officers who failed to do the impossible and halt the waves of enemy troops; the sense that betrayal was imminent and that those close by were plotting against their leader.

Stalin had recovered from that low point, but there was no realistic hope that Hitler could do the same. The German leader merely repeated that, whatever happened, November 1918 would not be repeated. He would die sooner than capitulate.

Earlier in this history we saw how the fledgling Nazis had presented their party programme in 1920 at the Hofbräuhaus in Munich, declaring in the last sentence of the document that the leaders of the party were prepared 'to sacrifice their very lives . . . to translate this programme into action'.[31] Now, twenty-five years later, Hitler was moving ever closer to fulfilling that promise – he would soon 'sacrifice' his life.

In February 1945, Stalin basked in the success of the Vistula–Oder offensive as he made his way to the Crimea to meet Roosevelt and Churchill for the Yalta conference. Here, just as he had at Tehran, he would prove himself a master negotiator. Even before the talks began, he had once again won the battle of the location of the conference. This time Roosevelt and Churchill had agreed to trek all the way to Yalta on the Black Sea. Stalin, who never travelled to Britain or America during the war, had at last made both his allies visit him on Soviet soil.

Stalin was 'full of beans', according to one eyewitness – words that could not be used to describe President Roosevelt's appearance.[32] When the American President emerged from his plane at Saki airfield, onlookers were stunned. 'His face was waxen to a sort of yellow,' said Hugh Lunghi, a member of the British delegation, 'waxen and very drawn, very thin, and a lot of the time he was sort of sitting, sitting there with his mouth open sort of staring ahead. So that was quite a shock.'[33] Lord Moran, Churchill's doctor, confirmed that 'Everyone seemed to agree that the President has gone to bits physically.'[34] Looks did not deceive, because Roosevelt would die little more than two months later.

Sir Alexander Cadogan of the Foreign Office thought Stalin was 'the most impressive of the three men. He is very quiet and restrained. On the first day [of the talks] he sat for the first hour and a half or so without saying a word – there was no call for him to do so. The President flapped about and the P.M. boomed, but Joe just sat taking it all in and being rather amused. When he did chip in, he never used a superfluous word, and spoke very much to the point. He's obviously got a very good sense of humour – and a rather quick temper!'[35]

Even though Stalin was already in a powerful position at Yalta, he not only exploited his strength but made significant extra gains. The key to his triumph was his ability to distinguish between aspirations for the future and concrete achievements for the present. The former he could give away, the latter he would fight for ruthlessly. Consider, for example, how he endeared himself to the Allies, particularly Roosevelt, by his apparent concessions over the formation of the United Nations.

The Soviets had been arguing that each of their republics should receive a vote in the new assembly – which would allocate them sixteen votes to America's one.[36] This was blatantly an extreme position. After all, Roosevelt was not insisting that each American state had its own vote. But Stalin also knew that Roosevelt wanted the UN to be his legacy, and was desperate for the Soviets to commit. So he decided to use this leverage in the context of one of the thorniest issues of Yalta – the seemingly intractable problem of the governance of Poland.

Roosevelt wanted members of the two competing Polish regimes – Stalin's Lublin Poles and the Polish government in exile based in

38. Red Army soldiers during the battle of Stalingrad. In this close-quarter battle, the advantages the Germans possessed in mobile warfare counted for little.

39. Vasily Chuikov, commander of the Soviet 62nd Army in Stalingrad. His tough, sometimes brutal leadership style fitted well with the demands of this savage battle.

40. Friedrich Paulus, who led the German Sixth Army at Stalingrad, was an altogether different character to Chuikov. Paulus possessed a careful, almost scholarly personality and was ill-suited to the task he had been set.

41. By the time this photograph of Stalin was taken at the end of 1943, the Soviets had turned the corner in their fight against the Germans. After recapturing Stalingrad and thwarting the German advance at Kursk, the Soviet leader had every reason to be confident of future success.

42. Hitler, by the time this photo was taken in late 1942 or early 1943, knew that the chances of an eventual German victory were diminishing. He was also aware, as he sat here in his private plane, that he had promised that he would take his own life if Germany lost the war.

43. Resistance fighters of the Polish Home Army during the Warsaw uprising in the summer of 1944. Stalin's failure to support their action would cost many of them their lives.

44. A happy Joseph Stalin, resplendent in his marshal's uniform, stands next to Churchill at the Yalta conference in February 1945.

45. Victorious Red Army units during Operation Bagration in the summer of 1944. German Army Group Centre never recovered from the power and force of this Soviet assault.

46. Hitler talks to Luftwaffe officers towards the end of the war. By this time his charismatic authority was waning, but it was never fully extinguished until his death.

47. German soldiers examine the civilian victims of the Red Army attack on Nemmersdorf in East Prussia in October 1944. Nazi propaganda made a great deal of this atrocity, claiming that all Germans could expect similar treatment if Germany fell to the Soviets.

48. One of the last photographs taken of Adolf Hitler, just days before he killed himself on 30 April 1945.

49. The scene inside Hitler's bunker in Berlin after the Red Army had captured the city. Hitler dreamt of making a 'last stand', but he took his life underground, hiding from the enemy.

50. Winston Churchill, President Harry Truman and Joseph Stalin at the Potsdam conference in Germany in the summer of 1945. Behind their smiles was a great deal of disagreement about the way the post-war world should be shaped.

51. The Nazi concentration camp of Bergen-Belsen in the aftermath of its capture by the Allies. For all time the singular crime of the Holocaust would define Hitler's regime.

52. Inside a hut in a Soviet labour camp in 1945. Victory in the Second World War would not lead to Stalin relaxing his oppressive rule.

53. Stalin died on 5 March 1953 at the age of seventy-four. Present-day Russia still grapples with his legacy.

London – to come to Yalta so that the Allies could jointly force a compromise. This was not in Stalin's interest. He already had physical control not just of Poland, but also of the de facto government run by his puppets, the Lublin Poles. So he raised a number of problems with Roosevelt's plan. One of the most disingenuous was that he was unable to contact his own Polish government. Who could really believe that? But then, suddenly changing the subject, he suggested that the Allies should instead discuss the composition of the United Nations.

At this point the Soviets made a notable concession. They said they would be satisfied with two or three votes at the UN, not sixteen. Roosevelt immediately brightened. This was a 'great step forward which would be welcomed by all the peoples of the world'. Churchill offered Stalin and Molotov his 'heartfelt thanks'.[37]

In this atmosphere of gratitude towards Stalin, Molotov finally addressed the Polish question. Since 'time would not permit the carrying out of the President's suggestion to summon the Poles to the Crimea', he suggested that one solution would be 'to add to the Provisional Polish Government some democratic leaders from Polish *émigré* circles'.

In an instant the plan for the British and American leaders to have practical input into the formation of the new Polish government had disappeared. All that was left was Molotov's notion of 'adding' some members of the government in exile to the current puppet Polish regime. But, as later discussions at Yalta made clear, the Soviets would be in charge of that process.

As for elections in Poland, while Stalin agreed that the 'Polish government must be democratically elected', the Soviets were put in charge of making this happen. Allied ambassadors could only 'observe and report' events in Poland. For insightful observers what was happening here was obvious. Lord Moran had thought for months that 'Stalin means to make Poland a Cossack outpost of Russia' and concluded that 'he has not altered his intention here.'[38]

Hugh Lunghi, who served in the British embassy in Moscow and was part of the British delegation at Yalta, was astounded by the ease with which Stalin achieved his ends. Lunghi realized at once that the use of doublespeak by Soviet officials would enable them to circumvent any of the conditions the other allies placed on them. The Soviets argued, he remembered, that 'free elections meant one thing in certain countries and another thing in other countries. There was always the catchphrase of "These are bourgeois freedoms. They're not the same as our freedoms. Soviet Socialist Freedoms are the real freedoms." '[39]

Lunghi was 'impressed' by Stalin's 'clarity, his memory, his conciseness. He was a bit of a pedant because he insisted on the exact meaning of words.' Consequently Stalin knew exactly how concepts like 'democracy', 'freedom', 'fascist', and the notion that the new Polish regime must be 'friendly' to the Soviet Union, were all capable of vastly different interpretations. 'We knew by then', said Lunghi, 'they [the Soviets] called any opponent and particularly socialists, social democrats, they called them fascists, which meant that they could chop their heads off metaphorically speaking.'[40]

Admiral Leahy, Roosevelt's chief of staff, was also aware at Yalta of the problems caused by the Polish agreement, saying to Roosevelt that the deal was 'so elastic that the Russians can stretch it all the way from Yalta to Washington without even technically breaking it'.[41] On 17 February, just after the conference ended, *Pravda* seemed to confirm this judgement with an article explaining how 'democracy' had a number of different meanings and that each nation had a 'choice' as to the type that best fitted them.[42]

At Yalta, Stalin never made any concrete concession without getting something tangible in return. He agreed that the Soviets would declare war on Japan, for instance, but only after Germany had been defeated and in exchange for territory in the north of the Japanese archipelago. He also continued to exploit the fact that Churchill and Roosevelt liked his praise. Normally he had contempt for the honeyed words of flatterers, but by now he recognized the value of such sentiments in his relationship with his democratically elected colleagues. That is surely the explanation for his effusive tribute to Churchill at one of the dinners at Yalta. 'Stalin made [an] excellent speech last night in proposing Winston's health,' wrote Field Marshal Sir Alan Brooke in his diary on 5 February, 'stating that he alone had stood up against the might of Germany at the crucial moment and supported Russia when she was attacked, a thing he would never forget!!'[43]

Brooke, who disliked 'blah-flum' as much as Stalin, seems to have taken his words at face value. But how can Stalin have been sincere? Yes, Churchill had resisted the 'might of Germany' in 1940, but Brooke seems to have forgotten that Stalin was supplying Hitler's war machine with valuable raw materials at the same time, and that the very

Movement of Poland's borders, 1945

N

SWEDEN

Tallinn

Ventspils
Riga
Liepāja
Western Dvina

Baltic Sea

Kaunas
Vilnius
Kaliningrad
Minsk

GERMANY
Oder
Vistula
Bydgoszcz
Białystok
POLAND
Poznań
Berlin
Warsaw
Brest-Litovsk
SOVIET UNION
Oder
Łódź
Wrocław
Lublin
Prague
Kraków
Lwów
CZECHOSLOVAKIA
Stanisławów

Danube
Vienna
Bratislava
Miskolc
AUSTRIA
Budapest
HUNGARY
ROMANIA

Zagreb

| | Territory gained by Poland in 1945 |
| | Polish territory gained by the Soviet Union in 1945 |

0   100 miles
0   100 km

YUGOSLAVIA
Belgrade

existence of the Nazi–Soviet pact had given Hitler the security he needed to attack the British and French in the first place. Moreover, how could it be anything other than disingenuous for Stalin to say that he believed Churchill had 'supported Russia' after the launch of Barbarossa, when at the time he was furious at Churchill's refusal to do the one thing he craved, which was to open the second front?

Yet it wasn't just Brooke who was impressed by Stalin at Yalta; the cynical, world-weary Sir Alexander Cadogan was as well. 'I have never known the Russians so easy and accommodating,' he wrote in his diary on 11 February. 'In particular Joe [Stalin] has been extremely good. He *is* a great man, and shows up very impressively against the background of the other two ageing statesmen.'[44]

Churchill was also full of praise for the Soviet leader. On 19 February, after he had returned to London, he assured the cabinet that Stalin 'meant well to the world and to Poland'.[45] Four days later he went further and said: 'Poor Neville Chamberlain believed he could trust Hitler. He was wrong. But I don't think I'm wrong about Stalin.'[46] As for Roosevelt, he told a joint session of Congress on 1 March that the Yalta agreement 'ought to spell' the 'end of the system of unilateral action, the exclusive alliances, the spheres of influence, the balances of power, and all the other expedients that have been tried for centuries – and have always failed'.[47]

Stalin didn't get absolutely everything he wanted at Yalta. He sought clarity on the division of post-war Germany and agreement on the huge reparations that the Soviets were demanding from the Germans, and received neither. But he did make big gains – the biggest being that he finally got his way over the future of Poland. This victory was not inevitable. Even given that the Red Army already occupied Poland, the British and Americans could still have made Stalin's life difficult over his non-compliance with their wishes, had they chosen to.

For instance, given that the Soviet Union had been devastated by the conflict, the western Allies could have used their financial leverage aggressively. And if they hadn't wanted to go that far, Churchill and Roosevelt could at least have made public their disapproval of Stalin's actions, perhaps by openly condemning the arrest and imprisonment of leading figures in the Polish Home Army. Not only did they not follow either course, but both western leaders chose to speak positively about their relationship with Stalin in the aftermath of Yalta.

Roosevelt and Churchill, the two great charmers, gave every impression that they had been charmed. And very shortly, they would realize it.

While the Allies discussed the future of the world at Yalta, their bombers were inflicting horrendous damage on Germany. In one of the most devastating attacks, the Allies bombed Dresden for three successive days in the middle of February, killing at least 25,000 people.[48] Nora Lang, a young inhabitant of the city, remembered that 'there was fire everywhere. We had to walk along the middle of the street, to avoid being hit by flying roof tiles, or burned-out window-frames, or all the stuff that was flying around. It was like a hurricane made of fire.'[49]

Just ten days after this inferno, on 24 February, Hitler met his Gauleiters for what turned out to be the last time. It was an important anniversary – twenty-five years after the party programme had been first announced in Munich. Hitler greeted his Gauleiters at the Reich Chancellery in Berlin, but appeared 'stooped and older-looking than his visitors had seen him previously', and it seemed to one observer that 'the powers of suggestion he had employed in the past to mesmerize this circle were gone.'[50] Rudolf Jordan, Gauleiter of Halle-Merseburg, thought that Hitler's eyes were 'sad and tired', his 'back heavily bent' and his 'complexion pale and wan'.[51] Baldur von Schirach saw Hitler as 'a broken man' with an 'ash-coloured face'. This was 'not the Hitler with the charisma of before, this was a ghost standing in front of us . . .'.[52] Nonetheless, the Gauleiters did their best not to appear negative, creating an atmosphere that made it look, as one of them later wrote, that 'they all lived on the moon.' After a lacklustre speech, Hitler delivered a defiant monologue over lunch that seemed to perk up one or two of the assembled Nazi chiefs, with Rudolf Jordan later saying that 'Our depressed mood evaporates . . . We experience the old Hitler.'[53] But then, what else could he say? Of all the Nazi hierarchy, the Gauleiters were most tied to Hitler. Their future was chained, inexorably, to his.

Once again, with events going against him, Hitler refused to give an address in public. He had chosen not to travel to Munich for the anniversary and deliver a speech before an audience. Instead, he left it to one of his longest-serving party members, Hermann Esser, to perform that unenviable task. The proclamation Esser read out, written by Hitler, was full of the long-familiar ideas – only the strong can survive, the Jews are behind all of Germany's woes and Frederick the Great had managed to turn around a similarly terrible situation. But there was something new. Hitler said that he 'almost' wished his own house, the Berghof, had been bombed, as it would allow him to show solidarity with his fellow Germans.[54] Cold comfort indeed.

Yet even at this late stage of the war, with support for Hitler dropping, there was still no concerted effort to remove him. In part, as we have seen, this was because of both the fear of the advancing Red Army and the way the Nazi state was structured. The increasing use of terror to oppress the population of the Reich was also a factor. But there were other reasons, notably that a handful of Hitler's supporters remained committed to him until the last. Goebbels is the most blatant example, but others included the head of the navy, Karl Dönitz. After the war he attempted to present himself as a simple sailor who just happened to be chosen by Hitler to become President of Germany after his Führer's death. But the reality was that he was a fanatical believer in the Nazi cause. In a report on 4 March, he wrote: 'There is no need to explain to you that in our situation capitulation is suicide and means certain death; that capitulation will bring the death, the quick or slower destruction, of millions of Germans, and that, in comparison with this, the blood toll even of the harshest fighting is small. Only if we stand and fight have we any chance at all of turning round our fate. If we voluntarily surrender, every possibility of this is at an end. Above all, our honour demands that we fight to the last. Our pride rebels against crawling before a people like the Russians or the sanctimony, arrogance and lack of culture of the Anglo-Saxons.'[55]

Dönitz was entranced by Hitler. One U-boat commander, who saw him immediately after he met with the German leader, recalled that the Grand Admiral emerged from the encounter 'floating on a sea of emotion'.[56] By March 1945, Dönitz had lost both his sons in the war, and while one might imagine that this tragedy would make him doubt the wisdom of carrying on, it did not alter his commitment. Having lost so much, to admit he was wrong now would have meant accepting that his boys had died for nothing.

But for every Dönitz there were many other Nazis who were now wavering in their belief. The most notable was Albert Speer, currently Armaments Minister and formerly Hitler's treasured architect. The same month that Dönitz wrote his blistering support for a 'fight to the last', Speer listened to Hitler as he called for the destruction of German infrastructure in order to leave a scorched land for the invaders. 'If the war is lost,' said Hitler, 'the people will be lost also. It is not necessary to worry about what the German people will need for elemental survival. On the contrary, it is best for us to destroy even these things. For the nation has proved to be the weaker, and the future belongs solely to the stronger eastern nation. In any case only those who are inferior will remain after this struggle, for the good have already been killed.'[57]

After the war, Speer claimed that he had disagreed wholeheartedly with Hitler's words. 'I very naturally assumed', he wrote, 'that we wanted to end this war with the least possible devastation of the kind that would hamper future reconstruction.'[58] But why did Speer think this? As we have seen, Hitler was remarkably consistent in his thinking. His order to destroy German infrastructure was entirely compatible with his oft-stated worldview – only the strong deserved to live. Speer, together with millions of other Germans, had been happy to reap the benefits of a war of destruction, and now they had to face the negative consequences of such a bloodthirsty approach. Hitler had never hidden his belief that this was an existential fight for the future of Germany.

Nonetheless, Speer managed to use his considerable political and personal skills to get Hitler to agree that he, as Minister of Armaments, was in charge of the implementation of the destruction order. This did not prevent the military blowing up bridges, but it did stop extensive demolition of power plants and other utilities. Speer was also able to argue that merely to disable power and water installations temporarily 'fulfils the stated aim of the Führer'.[59] Speer, naturally enough, was well aware that actions like these would help him as he sought to survive in the post-war world.[60] His judgement was correct: despite his deep involvement in the regime, he subsequently escaped a death sentence at the Nuremberg trials.

As Speer sought to lessen the effects of Hitler's order, Stalin and his military commanders planned the final assault on Berlin. By mid-April they were ready, with Zhukov and his soldiers encamped by the River Oder, less than 50 miles from the German capital. His First Belorussian Front would attack through the centre, with Rokossovsky's Second Belorussian Front to the north and Konev's First Ukrainian Front to the south. Altogether, it was a force well in excess of two million people.

The previous year Stalin had told Zhukov that he would have the honour of taking Berlin. But now, with the end in sight, he changed his mind. He rubbed out the demarcation line between the First Belorus-sian and First Ukrainian Fronts less than 40 miles from Berlin.[61] He had deliberately left the question open – Zhukov might take Berlin, but so might Marshal Konev. It's likely that Stalin was thinking about more than just creating competition between the two marshals as he issued this challenge. He would also have been concerned about the popularity of Zhukov. Stalin was already focused on the post-war world. As we have seen, he knew his history, and would have been asking himself if Zhukov – brash and confident – might become another Napoleon.

Stalin's plan was not the best way to organize one of the biggest and most coordinated military operations in history. While creating this contest certainly injected urgency into the assault, it did nothing to improve the ability of the two marshals to cooperate. As Anatoly Mereshko, who took part in the Berlin offensive and was later deputy commander of all Warsaw Pact forces, confirmed: 'There was such competition for who would do it first [that is, take the German capital], who would [gain] the first place, and the relationship between Konev and Zhukov was tense.'[62]

Tension existed not just between the two marshals but between Sta-lin and the western Allies. One of the contentious issues was – yet again – Poland. The leaders of the western Allies had belatedly dis-covered that the Soviet 'interpretation' of certain words in the Yalta agreement differed from their own. The Soviets wanted to vet any potential additions to their puppet administration, and since their defin-ition of 'fascist' could be stretched to mean anyone they didn't like, the process was fraught. Roosevelt wrote to Stalin on 31 March expressing 'concern' about the way the Soviets were interpreting the Yalta agree-ment.[63] Churchill joined in the following day, registering his 'surprise and regret' that Molotov was not allowing 'observers' to enter Poland.[64]

Stalin's reply was characteristic. He immediately blamed the people accusing him. The reason for the difficulties over Poland, he said, was the inability of the Allies to stick to the Yalta agreement. The Allies appeared to want a totally new administration in Poland, whereas the agreement had merely called for the augmentation of the existing group. In his note of 7 April, he played his trump card. A necessary precondi-tion of any new Pole joining the government was that they 'are really striving to establish friendly relations between Poland and the Soviet Union'.[65] And who decided whether anyone lived up to this 'friendly' test? Why, of course, the Soviets themselves. Churchill and Roosevelt were trapped by their own previous acceptance of Stalin's vague formula.

By this time the inability – and, arguably, the unwillingness – of Britain and America to stop Stalin acting as he wished in the newly 'liberated' countries of eastern Europe had become all too apparent. Soviet repression in Romania prompted one British Foreign Office official to write that 'by a simple process of calling black white, democracy "fascism" and "fascism" (of left) "democracy" a legend is being built up which unless challenged will soon be accepted as [the] epitaph of an independent Romania.'[66] A few weeks before that, a British diplomat in Bulgaria had sent a note to London declaring, 'I am afraid we must reconcile ourselves to the fact that we cannot prevent the Russians victimising any Bulgarians they choose.'[67]

Churchill had contributed to the problem himself, because of his 'percentages' agreement. He recognized that his previous willingness to discuss with Stalin the extent of foreign influence to be permitted in various European countries now made it difficult for him to complain about the Soviet actions.[68] In a note he sent Roosevelt on 8 March he said that while he was 'distressed' by recent events in Romania where 'The Russians have succeeded in establishing the rule of a Communist minority by force and misrepresentation,' he 'nevertheless' was 'most anxious not to press this view to such an extent that Stalin will say "I did not interfere with your action in Greece [when the British had helped suppress Greek communists in December 1944], why do you not give me the same latitude in Roumania?"'[69]

This was the core of the problem. It was all very well for Churchill to talk, in the same message, about how Poland was the 'test case between us and the Russians of the meaning which is to be attached to such terms as Democracy, Sovereignty, Independence, Representative Government and free and unfettered elections', and speak in passionate terms of how Molotov 'wants to make a farce of consultations with the "Non-Lublin" Poles – which means that the new government in Poland would be merely the present one dressed up to look more respectable to the ignorant and also wants to prevent us from seeing the liquidations and deportations that are going on'. But the trouble was that Churchill had previously demonstrated via his 'percentages agreement' that he was prepared to do backroom deals with Stalin over the future of east

European countries. Morality is a concept that is difficult to apply selectively. Yet Churchill wanted to argue that while Romania and Bulgaria could – in effect – be given to Stalin, Poland was different. It was not an easy position to defend.

Roosevelt appeared more relaxed about Poland than Churchill. He had consistently cared less about the issue – apart from his temporary concern with Polish-American voters just prior to the 1944 presidential election. But he did have other anxieties about Stalin's behaviour. Not only was he concerned that Stalin had refused to give easy access to American POWs now on territory occupied by the Soviets, but it now looked as if he was reneging on a full commitment to the UN. The Soviet leader wouldn't let Molotov attend the forthcoming conference in San Francisco at which the structure of the United Nations was to be discussed. Even more difficult for Roosevelt, and perhaps the issue in his dealings with the Soviets that upset him most, was Stalin's allegation that the western Allies were secretly negotiating with the Germans.

In early March 1945 an SS general had contacted American agents in Switzerland about the prospect of the German Army surrendering in Italy. Though the western Allies had told the Soviets about the contacts – which eventually came to nothing – a squabble developed over the point at which Soviet representatives could attend any discussions with the Germans. The dispute culminated in a brutal message from Stalin to Roosevelt on 3 April which all but accused him of duplicity. 'You insist that there have been no negotiations yet,' wrote Stalin. 'It may be assumed that you have not been fully informed. As regards my military colleagues, they, on the basis of data which they have on hand, do not have any doubts . . .'[70] Roosevelt replied with 'astonishment' at the allegations. He denied the charge and ended the note with the words, 'Frankly, I cannot avoid a feeling of bitter resentment toward your informers, whoever they are, for such vile misrepresentations of my actions or those of my trusted subordinates.'[71] Even though Roosevelt's cables were often drafted for him by his staff, the raw hurt in this message is palpable.

Stalin responded, as he almost always did in such circumstances, with considerable coolness. While not doubting Roosevelt's or Churchill's 'honesty and dependability' he believed this quarrel highlighted a difference in opinion between the Allies about how they should negotiate with the Germans. His original position had not changed. He wanted the Soviets included at 'any' meeting with the Germans, no matter how preliminary.[72]

Stalin included an additional note in the copy of this message that he sent to Churchill. 'My messages are personal and strictly confidential,' he wrote to the British Prime Minister. 'This makes it possible to speak one's mind clearly and frankly. That is the advantage of confidential communications. If, however, you are going to regard every frank statement of mine as offensive, it will make this kind of communication very difficult.'[73]

Stalin's tone was that of a parent talking to an overemotional child. The subtext was 'calm down and grow up'. It's thus a remarkable message for one statesman to send to another, and it highlights once again the difference between Stalin and the British and American leaders. Both Roosevelt and Churchill had let themselves get into a dangerous pattern with Stalin. They thought their dealings would be easier if he liked them, but he didn't care if they liked him. It was this imbalance that resulted in Stalin's ability to reprimand Churchill. Stalin's dignity was never wounded. He was rarely emotional in his communications. He could express displeasure, but that was done in a calculated way. Extraordinarily, he seems hardly – if ever – to have revealed a vulnerable side. He never would have expressed the kind of personal feelings of upset that Roosevelt did in his note in early April. This gave the Soviet leader the most enormous strength in dealing with his allies.

Alongside this emotional coldness, Stalin possessed an ability to be deceitful with ease. On 1 April, for instance, after the meeting at which he engendered the rivalry between Konev and Zhukov over the taking of Berlin, Stalin sent a telegram to Eisenhower saying that 'Berlin has lost its former strategic importance' and that the Soviets were now focused not on taking the city but on linking up with the western Allies to the south. It was an out-and-out lie designed to allow his forces unfettered access to the German capital.[74]

It was also a sign of how, ultimately, Stalin considered himself in an alliance with no one.

While Stalin plotted the Soviet endgame, the Nazi regime – what was left of it – was under greater pressure than ever. On 21 March, Hitler appeared to Goebbels to be 'in some despair' though still asserting that the alliance between Stalin and the western powers would 'inevitably break up, so it is all about whether it breaks up before we are flat on the ground or after we have already been knocked down'.[75] A week later Goebbels admitted that there was now a fundamental disconnect between decisions made in the Führerbunker in Berlin and what was happening outside. 'We give orders in Berlin that in practice no longer arrive lower down, let alone can be carried out,' he wrote. 'I see in that the risk of an extraordinary loss of authority.'[76]

But for those who dealt with Hitler personally it was still, on occasion, possible to detect a positive attitude. On 12 April he met with Field Marshal Kesselring, who later wrote that the Führer 'was still optimistic. How far he was play-acting it is hard to decide. Looking back, I am inclined to think that he was literally obsessed with the idea of some miraculous salvation, that he clung to it like a drowning man to a straw.'[77]

According to Goebbels, part of that salvation appeared later that same day, when he brought Hitler the news that Franklin Roosevelt had suffered a cerebral haemorrhage and died. But Roosevelt's death would not lead to the longed-for splitting of the alliance and Hitler's deliverance. Harry Truman became President, and he was just as committed to the destruction of Nazism and to victory over Japan as Roosevelt had been. However, Truman's arrival marks an important moment of change in one respect. The new President, unlike his predecessor, was prepared to talk bluntly to the Soviets.

As well as clinging to the hope that the Allies would split apart, Hitler was indulging in his standard response to setbacks – blaming other people for his own mistakes. But by this point he was doing more than just blaming the Jews, he was also holding some of his most loyal followers responsible for the catastrophe facing Germany. Göring had been a focus of his opprobrium for some time, blamed for the inability of the Luftwaffe to prevent Allied air raids. Now Himmler became the subject of Hitler's rage, criticized for the inability of units under his command to hold back the Red Army in Pomerania in the north of Germany. SS General Sepp Dietrich, Hitler's former bodyguard, was another old comrade who endured his Führer's wrath. Dietrich had organized execution squads during the Night of the Long Knives in 1934, and was now an SS-Oberst-Gruppenführer in charge of the Sixth Panzer Army which included Hitler's own bodyguard, the elite SS Leibstandarte.

Hitler was furious with Dietrich because an offensive he had led in the Hungarian campaign in early March had failed. Consequently, he ordered that the armbands of the SS units that had participated should be taken from them. 'This will, of course, be the most severe humiliation for Sepp Dietrich,' wrote Goebbels. 'The Army generals take a mischievous pleasure at this blow to their rivals.' But in any case, 'the Leibstandarte is certainly not the Leibstandarte of old, since its leadership material and its men have been killed.'[78]

Although Hitler was enforcing a culture of blame, he had still not approached Stalin's vast capacity for personal retribution. While many ordinary Germans – soldiers and civilians – were now being executed for 'cowardice', the Führer had not yet called for his closest comrades to die. Even when it came to army officers, his most common method of removal was still to order retirement or sick leave. Guderian, for instance, was ordered to stand down as Chief of Staff of the Army at the end of March, and told he needed to take 'six weeks' convalescent leave'. This was after a fearsome row between the two earlier the previous month, during which, wrote Guderian, 'after each outburst of rage Hitler would stride up and down the carpet edge, then suddenly stop immediately before me and hurl his next accusation in my face. He was almost screaming, his eyes seemed about to pop out of his head and the veins stood out on his temples.'[79] Imagine what would have happened to a Red Army commander who so angered Stalin. A spell of convalescent leave would not, surely, have been the Soviet leader's response.

The start of the Red Army's assault on Berlin on 16 April was signalled by a gigantic Soviet artillery barrage. Konev's forces moved swiftly forward, but Zhukov was initially held at the Seelow Heights, a ridge next to marshy ground east of the city. It took three days for the massive forces at Zhukov's disposal to crush German resistance. But by 26 April – ten days after the launch of the offensive – Red Army soldiers were fighting in central Berlin.

Vladlen Anchishkin, commander of a mortar battery during the battle for the German capital, vividly remembered his feelings at the time. 'At last it was the end of the war,' he said. 'It was the triumph, and it was like a long-distance race, the end of the race. I felt really extreme – well, these words did not exist then – but I felt under psychological and emotional pressure . . . Behind me I had had four years of war . . . A war is not about map-making in the headquarters, but is a question of life or death. It's a question of who does it first, no matter whether it's a plane or a tank, or artillery. If the other man tries to kill me, what should I do? Shall I kiss him? I shall always try to kill him, but it's not very easy to kill . . . You shouldn't consider a soldier an intellectual. Even when an intellectual becomes a soldier and he sees the blood and the intestines and the brains then the instinct of self-preservation begins to work . . . He loses all the humanitarian features inside himself. A soldier turns into a beast . . . All the moral categories that the soldiers had, have been destroyed by their experience. War depraves a human being.'[80]

Gerda Steinke, a young secretary living in a Berlin apartment block with her mother, was about to witness first hand that depravity. She had seen the propaganda newsreels about Soviet atrocities and was 'afraid', but her mother told her, 'Oh, that's impossible, in a big city like Berlin, things like that can't happen.' But then, said Gerda, 'the first Russian arrived. And he filled the small entrance – it was only a little air-raid protection door – he filled this entrance completely. I'll never forget that, this first sight. It was a Mongolian with his sub-machine gun at readiness. He passed through, we all had to stretch out our hands in front of us. Then he took away our rings or wrist watches, and he left again.'[81]

Later that day more Soviet soldiers entered the room, but by now Gerda and her mother had managed to hide underneath a table, protected by a tablecloth which 'hung down almost to the floor'. She saw one soldier 'standing, his legs were right in front of me, it was a funny feeling. All I was thinking was, "Oh God, I hope he doesn't notice that we are sitting under here." That's when the first two or three women were asked to come with them. So they took them with them.'[82]

Gerda and her mother now sought refuge in a flat at the top of the building. They were fortunate. An elderly man on the floor below told the Soviet soldiers that there was an unexploded bomb in the roof, so Gerda and her mother were left undisturbed that night. But one of Gerda's friends, who had stayed in a flat lower down the building, was not so lucky. She was found by Red Army soldiers, and Gerda could hear what happened to her: 'So I had to listen to it all, how she was raped, and that was, for me, very, very terrible . . . I have felt it personally, as if it was me it was happening to. It was so horrible. At first it was just the screams, and then, groans. I shall never forget it in all my life. It was, for me, as if it was myself [being attacked] . . . We weren't in the same school but we were good friends. We celebrated our birthdays together, she was just exactly as old as me. Then, later, she never even greeted me any more, said hello, and we parted, the friendship was over. It wasn't my fault that I was upstairs on the fourth floor and not down there, with her.'

After listening to the suffering of her friend, Gerda moved out on to the balcony of the top-floor flat 'and sat in a corner, and I'd kind of finished with my life. If somebody had got in there, if a Russian had come in, I'd have jumped down. I was convinced it's all over, nobody's going to touch me and I'm going to jump down here. I was prepared, at any time, to jump down. There I was squatting in that position all that time, waiting, but nobody came upstairs.'

The next morning, she and her mother returned briefly to their own flat: 'I was in my room. Standing in front of the window, there was, on the street, a Russian female commissar. And she was, sort of, cracking a whip, and the Russians were driving around on the first bikes that they'd stolen. I looked down and I thought, it's all over, what else can happen now for me? How can things go on? I didn't have any feeling how it could possibly go on . . . Opposite there was a woman who, with her child, had thrown herself off the balcony. The boy was dead, but she wasn't, she'd broken both legs and afterwards was paralysed. These are all things that play a role in it. So you end up saying that you're not going to put up with it. I rather prefer to finish with everything, and jumping down from the fourth floor, I knew that that'll be it with you. There wouldn't be much left of me. I never thought, at that moment in time, that things would change again and I would be able to laugh again, I couldn't imagine that.'

Gerda moved with her mother later that day to live with friends. In that house the 'doors were still standing', and they managed to survive without being molested. She was aware, she said, that rapes 'happen in every army', but not 'in this concentrated way, not in this massive way, in this targeted concentrated way. I think it was meant to be a kind of humiliation for us, which is what it was. We were meant to be humiliated and that's what happened.'[83]

No one can ever know exactly how many women were raped by the Soviet conquerors. It's possible, however, that nearly two million women and girls in Germany alone endured this horror during the war and in its immediate aftermath.[84] The situation was so bad that women in Berlin did not ask each other whether they had been raped, but simply inquired 'how many?'

Vladlen Anchishkin, of the First Belorussian Front, had no sympathy: 'When you see this German beauty sitting and weeping about the savage Russians who were hurting her, why did she not cry when she was receiving parcels from the Eastern Front?'[85] Anchishkin would likely have approved of the sentiments of the Soviet propagandist Ilya Ehrenburg, who wrote, 'Soldiers of the Red Army. German women are yours!'[86]

Demonstrably, many Red Army soldiers had a craving for revenge together with a desire to commit acts of sexualized violence, but a number were also perplexed, posing to themselves overarching questions about the war. 'Millions of our men have now seen the rich farms in East Prussia,' wrote the Soviet war correspondent Vasily Grossman, 'the highly organised agriculture, the concrete sheds for livestock, spacious rooms, carpets, wardrobes full of clothes . . . And thousands of soldiers repeat these angry questions when they look around them in Germany: "But why did they come to us? What did they want?" '[87]

The answer was one the soldiers would have found outrageous, and would likely have provoked even greater fury. What the Nazis had wanted in the Soviet Union was not the people, not the buildings, not the culture, but the land and the resources it contained. In pursuit of Hitler's utopia, tens of millions of Soviet citizens were supposed to vanish – their lives erased.

But now, nearly four years after the German invasion of the Soviet Union, the architect of that utopian vision was about to meet his own end.

18. Victory and Defeat

Hitler's birthday on 20 April had previously been a day of celebration throughout Germany. On 20 April 1939, when he reached the age of fifty, Berlin in particular had been the scene of widespread festivities. Hitler, wrote Goebbels, had been 'hailed by the people like no mortal man has ever been hailed before. The audience is mad with enthusiasm. I never saw our people like this.'[1] Hitler had watched 'the biggest parade in the world' as the German Army marched past him in his honour – infantry, tanks, engineers, every branch of the service. In the sky above, Luftwaffe planes flew overhead in perfect formation. Hermann Göring, writing in the Nazi newspaper, the *Völkischer Beobachter*, promised that he and his Nazi comrades had 'dedicated ourselves' to Hitler 'until death, because we owe him everything'.[2]

The contrast between that day six years before and 20 April 1945 was stark. Hitler had journeyed from splendour to despair. Instead of watching a four-hour military parade, he climbed from his bunker into the garden of the Reich Chancellery to meet a handful of soldiers, including twenty boys from the Hitler Youth who had shown bravery in the fight against the Red Army.[3]

In 1939, when he had stood and acknowledged the vast parade in front of him, he had appeared fit and well. Now he was a shuffling, shaking wreck. As for his comrades, many of them in April 1945 couldn't wait to run away. Göring, who in 1939 had 'dedicated' himself to Hitler 'until death', told his Führer that he was urgently needed in southern Germany – an area safe from the Soviet advance. Nicolaus von Below, Hitler's Luftwaffe adjutant, had the 'impression that inwardly Hitler had rejected him. It was an unpleasant moment.'[4] Himmler and others hurried off as well. While Göring travelled south, Himmler suddenly found he had pressing business in north-west Germany – once again, far from the approaching Red Army.

Significantly, Hitler even dismissed Dr Morell, his personal physician. He no longer had need of his services and was frightened of being drugged. 'Next morning our ranks had thinned out,' wrote Traudl

Junge, one of Hitler's secretaries. 'The prominent people who had come with birthday wishes had left the sinking ship . . .'[5]

Two days after his birthday, on 22 April, Hitler almost broke down emotionally during an infamous meeting with his military commanders in the Führerbunker. Having learnt that an attack he had ordered on the Soviets hadn't taken place, he raged at four of his most senior military aides, including Keitel and Jodl. He screamed that he had been betrayed, and kept up the tirade for half an hour. None of these men who had worked so closely with him had ever witnessed anything like it before. As the outburst began to dissipate, they tried to convince him to leave for Berchtesgaden and the relative safety of the mountains of Bavaria, but he refused. He said he would die here, in Berlin. He was to spend the last eight days of his life in the German capital, where his belief that his formerly loyal paladins had betrayed him would grow almost to Stalin-like levels.

The next day, 23 April, Hitler received word from Göring that unless he heard news to the contrary he would assume Hitler was no longer alive and so he would take on the role of head of state himself. It wasn't that Göring was part of a conspiracy to usurp Hitler. He was almost certainly working on the basis that the German leader had likely killed himself by now. That's not, however, how Hitler saw it. He accused Göring of betraying him and ordered his arrest.

Shortly afterwards, Hitler experienced what he believed was another betrayal when news reached him that Himmler had been attempting to negotiate a surrender with the western Allies via Count Bernadotte, a Swedish official. 'The news hit the bunker like a bombshell,' remembered one officer who was with Hitler that day.[6] Hitler immediately threw Himmler out of the Nazi Party and stripped him of all his titles.

Hitler believed that Himmler and Göring had 'done untold damage to the country and to the whole nation, quite apart from their treachery towards me personally'.[7] But this was harsh. Hitler had given them permission to leave Berlin, and all they had subsequently done was to assume that he was dead – or shortly to die – and plan as best they could for a world without him.

The underlying reason why Hitler felt deceived reveals a great deal about how he differed from Stalin in the way he saw the world. As we have seen, at the time of Paulus' capture at Stalingrad Hitler had told those around him that in the event of imminent defeat they should gather 'together, build an all-round defence, and shoot yourself with the last cartridge'.[8] This was the dramatic end he imagined. But now Himmler and Göring had demonstrated they wanted no part of it. For Hitler, the idea that he was dispensable, while his acolytes went on with their lives, must have been almost impossible to accept. Why didn't all his followers want to die with him, just as the servants of ancient monarchs had accompanied their rulers into the next life?

Goebbels fully understood this aspect of Hitler's mentality. He, his wife and their six children all moved into the bunker to be close to Hitler in preparation for their own mass suicide. Goebbels had believed for months that if Germany couldn't win the war the next best alternative was dying heroically alongside Hitler, and he was prepared to sacrifice his wife and children to that end.

Goebbels had recently overseen the production of an expensive Agfacolor feature film entitled *Kolberg* which encapsulated his belief that an 'heroic' death could lead to immortality. As one of the German characters in this epic about a siege during the Napoleonic Wars says, 'Death is entwined with victory. The greatest achievements are always borne in pain . . .' Another declares, 'from the ashes and rubble a new people will rise like a Phoenix, a new Reich.'[9]

Goebbels was obsessed with *Kolberg*. He wrote, uncredited, many of the speeches in the film himself, and ensured that no expense was spared in the film's production with thousands of soldiers appearing as extras. 'Goebbels even said to me', said Wilfred von Oven, Goebbels' attaché, 'that it was more important that the soldiers act in his film rather than fight at the front, which was no longer worth doing since we were in the middle of a total collapse.' Goebbels also told Norbert Schultze, the film's composer, that 'the film *Kolberg* will survive us.'[10]

Kolberg opened in Berlin on 30 January 1945 – the twelfth anniversary of Hitler's appointment as Chancellor. And, in an indication of how precious he thought the film, Goebbels arranged via Göring to have a copy flown into the besieged city of La Rochelle so that it could be shown to the trapped soldiers on the same day as the film's premiere in Berlin. The linkage that Goebbels wanted the audience to feel – between the resistance featured in the film and the resistance required from Germans as the Allies came ever nearer – could not have been more explicit. Weeks later, Goebbels referred to *Kolberg* as an inspiration when he gave a speech to his staff at the Propaganda Ministry on 27 April: 'Gentlemen, in a hundred years' time they will be showing another fine colour film describing the terrible days we are living through. Don't you want to play a part in this film, to be brought back to life in a hundred years' time? Everybody now has a chance to choose the part which he will play in the film a hundred years hence. I can assure you that it will be a fine and elevating picture. And for the sake of that prospect it is worth standing fast. Hold out now, so that a hundred years hence the audience does not hoot and whistle when you appear on the screen.'[11]

In Goebbels' mind they were creating a myth to live alongside the most noble historical acts of self-sacrifice. In the ruins of Berlin they were Leonidas and the Spartans at the battle of Thermopylae, or Davy Crockett and Jim Bowie at the Alamo. And just as popular films have been made about both of these heroic last stands, so one day their deaths would be similarly exalted. 'He believed in himself,' said Hans-Otto Meissner, a German diplomat who knew Goebbels, 'and he believed that he would continue his life in history.'[12]

But Goebbels and Hitler were not Leonidas or Jim Bowie. Not only were they cowering in a reinforced concrete bunker beneath the streets of Berlin rather than fighting Red Army soldiers face to face, but they would inevitably be remembered for their legacy of crime, not for their self-imagined 'heroism'.

Nor, as the end neared, was the bunker filled with the atmosphere of devil-may-care courage that Goebbels would no doubt have wanted for his future film. Instead, the place was pervaded with a kind of indolence. One officer who served with Hitler in the bunker, Bernd Freytag von Loringhoven, remembered that it was 'absolutely macabre. The people there no longer had anything to do. They were hanging around the corridors, waiting for news. The enemy was close at hand. So the main topic in the bunker was "How do I kill myself?"'[13]

While Hitler largely supported Goebbels' fantasy of an heroic end in Berlin, in two significant ways he also demonstrated his inability to sustain the illusion. The first was in his terror of capture – something that meant he wasn't prepared to risk fighting in battle in case he survived. 'I do not wish to fall into the hands of the enemy', he wrote in the last hours of his life, 'who, for the amusement of its incited masses, needs a new spectacle directed by the Jews.'[14]

The second way in which Hitler failed to live up to his propaganda image was his decision, just before he took his own life, to marry his mistress, Eva Braun. In doing so he destroyed the fantasy that he was married 'to the nation'. He thus chose to reward her for her loyalty, over preserving the illusion of a leader who lived apart from normal mortals.

Nonetheless, until his last breath Hitler remained consistent in his ideological beliefs. In his political testament, which he signed just before he killed himself, he maintained that the war had been caused by 'those international statesmen who are either of Jewish origin or work for Jewish interests'. In the same document he made an oblique – yet obvious – reference to his pride at having murdered millions of Jews. He said that he had 'not left anybody in the dark about the fact that this time, millions of adult men would not die, and hundreds of thousands of women and children would not be burnt or bombed to death in the cities, without the actual culprit, albeit by more humane means, having to pay for his guilt'.[15] The words 'actual culprit' and 'humane means' – terms which were perversions of the truth – surely refer to the deaths of the Jews in the gas chambers.[16] Even at the very end, Hitler could not resist boasting about his infamous crime.

On the afternoon of Monday 30 April 1945, Adolf Hitler and his new wife, Eva Hitler, took their own lives in the Führerbunker. He shot himself and she took poison. The next day Goebbels and his wife presided over the murder of their six children and then killed themselves.

Stalin would almost certainly have looked with a cynical eye on Goebbels' and Hitler's attempt to create a mythic end to their lives. Not that he wasn't prepared to use historical parallels for his own benefit. During the war he had lauded past military greats in order to draw attention to Russia's victorious past, and he had a long-standing fascination with Ivan the Terrible, taking a keen interest in Eisenstein's multi-part film of the bloodthirsty sixteenth-century Tsar. But while Stalin saw Ivan the Terrible as the first in a direct line of leaders who sought to unify Russia – a route that passed from Ivan to Lenin to Stalin himself – his conception of Ivan was not as simplistic as Goebbels' or Hitler's view of their own hero, Frederick the Great.[17] He saw the infamous Tsar's faults as well as his triumphs. Incredibly, in his view the problem with Ivan the Terrible was that he had not been ruthless enough. According to Anastas Mikoyan, a member of the Politburo, 'Stalin said that Ivan Groznyi [known in the west as Ivan the Terrible] killed too few boyars [aristocrats], that he should have killed them all, and then he would have created a truly united and strong Russian state even earlier.' And to a writer who had praised Ivan the Terrible, Stalin said that 'the tsar had one shortcoming. When executing the boyars, between executions he for some reason suffered pangs of conscience and repented of his cruelty.'[18]

As we have seen, Hitler – unlike Stalin – took a romantic view of his own life, with all his talk of last stands and saving the last bullet for himself. 'In the last instance,' he had said in early 1944, 'if I should ever be deserted as supreme Leader, I must have as the last defence around me the entire officer-corps who must stand with drawn swords rallied round me.'[19] Stalin felt very differently. He looked at humanity with the deepest suspicion – distrustful of every person he met. He would never have wanted his 'entire officer-corps' to stand around him with 'drawn swords' because he'd be worried they would stab him.

Ultimately, for all of Hitler's desire for a mythic end, his final moments were distinctly squalid. After his suicide in a bleak underground bunker, his body was taken by his aides to the garden of the Reich Chancellery to be consumed by flames, as Soviet shells exploded near by.

The story of the relationship between Hitler and Stalin finished in Berlin on the afternoon of 30 April 1945. But this moment didn't mark the end of Stalin's interest in Adolf Hitler.

Despite the fact that Soviet commanders had learnt early in May that Hitler was dead, Stalin continued to insist he might be alive. A search by the Soviets had turned up a charred body in the Reich Chancellery gardens, and a forensic examination had proved the remains were those of the German leader.[20] The Soviet investigators also captured German eyewitnesses who outlined Hitler's last hours. But none of that made any difference to Stalin.

Accordingly, on 9 June, Zhukov appeared in person at a press conference and announced: 'Adolf Hitler's present whereabouts are a mystery . . . We have not identified Hitler's corpse. I cannot say anything definite about his fate.' Zhukov speculated that Hitler might currently be in Spain. The Soviet Commander of Berlin, Colonel General Berzarin, was happy to echo this bizarre claim, telling journalists: 'In my opinion Hitler went underground and is hiding somewhere in Europe, possibly with General Franco.'[21]

This ludicrous notion being spun by the concerted efforts of Zhukov and Berzarin can only have come from Stalin. He had decided, despite knowing that dental records proved Hitler was dead, to try and gain advantage by pretending otherwise. As a consequence of saying that the German leader was in Spain, Stalin heaped pressure on his hated enemy General Franco. What's more, the Soviets had only to allege that Hitler was 'hiding' in a particular country to embarrass the regime concerned. Even if the Soviets didn't claim to know exactly where he was, the idea that he was still alive and had not been apprehended by the western Allies was sufficient to cause controversy.

Despite the evidence in front of them that he was dead, the Soviet authorities did their best to get eyewitnesses to lie and say Hitler had escaped the German capital. Over the winter of 1945–6 and the following spring, Hitler's pilot Hans Baur was interrogated in Moscow and 'accused time and again of flying Hitler out of Berlin. During this [period] I was handled very roughly. An officer . . . frequently hit me with heavy blows to the head with his fists . . .'[22]

Stalin even brought his strange views about Hitler's continued existence to the final conference of the Big Three, held at Potsdam close to Berlin in the summer of 1945. He told the American Secretary of State, James Byrnes, that 'he believed that Hitler was alive and that it was possible he was then in either Spain or Argentina.'[23]

This deliberate attempt to mislead his allies was just one sign of how little Stalin had mellowed after the victory over Nazi Germany. He was as suspicious as ever, perhaps more so. And his distrust of his former wartime allies would play a crucial part in making the subsequent Cold War happen – something that should be considered as much a part of his legacy as the Soviet victory over the Nazis.

There were also policy reasons, of course, for the Cold War. The combination of Stalin's desire to squeeze as much reparations as possible out of the defeated nations and his continued insistence that the countries bordering the Soviet Union be 'friendly' to him had always made a split with the west likely.

At the Potsdam conference Stalin had even insisted that a major German city become part of the Soviet Union.[24] 'We consider it necessary to have at the expense of Germany one ice-free port in the Baltic. I think that this port must . . . [be] Königsberg. It is no more than fair that the Russians who have shed so much blood and lived through so much terror should want to receive some lump of German territory which would give some small satisfaction from this war.'[25] The western Allies agreed. So the ancient Prussian city of Königsberg – today called Kaliningrad – became part of the Soviet Union. Today it remains a Russian city, sitting in an island of territory more than 300 miles from the rest of modern Russia – a strange, isolated reminder of Stalin's post-war demands.

Both Truman and Churchill complained to Stalin at Potsdam that he was not living up to the promises made at Yalta that 'all satellite' governments be 'reorganized on democratic lines'. Churchill told the Soviet leader that in Romania and Bulgaria in particular 'we know nothing' because British representatives had not been allowed to check what was happening. An 'iron fence', he said, had come down around the British missions. These were words he would tweak the following year to 'iron curtain' in his famous speech at Fulton, Missouri. Stalin, in response to Churchill's accusation at Potsdam, simply replied: 'All fairy tales.'[26]

The Allies hadn't planned at Potsdam to split Germany apart, with East Germany becoming a wholly separate territory under Soviet dominance. But arguments about how much reparations could be taken from Germany led Stalin to make the suggestion that 'with regard to shares and foreign investments, perhaps the demarcation line between the Soviet and western zones of occupation should be taken as the dividing line [between the Soviets and the western Allies] and everything west of that line would go to the [western] Allies and everything east of that line to the Russians.'[27] This exchange epitomized the growing rift between Stalin and the western Allies. It foreshadowed the splitting of Germany into two separate countries – East and West – and was an early hint of the Cold War to come.

George Elsey, an American officer who attended the Potsdam conference, remembered that 'Soviet trucks, mostly American made, were hauling off anything that was haulable to be shipped back to the Soviet Union to help rebuild their economy. Even in the palace where the conference was being held, even when it was going on, the Soviets were stripping plumbing fixtures, stripping everything they could except from the small area where the conference itself was being held.'[28]

This impression that the Soviets in Germany were in a hurry to take whatever they could, both people and things, was shared by Sir Alexander Cadogan at Potsdam. 'The truth is that on any and every point, Russia tries to seize all that she can and she uses these meetings to grab as much as she can get,' he wrote in a minute to Churchill. 'I am deeply concerned at the pattern of Russian policy, which becomes clearer as they become more brazen every day.'[29]

Potsdam was never intended to be the last time the Allies met to discuss Germany. They believed that a future conference would be convened in order to agree a final peace treaty. They tasked a Council of Foreign Ministers to come up with a draft agreement, to be signed by the Germans 'when a government adequate for the purpose is established'.[30] But no such government came into being until after the reunification of Germany in 1990. So the peace treaty imagined by the Potsdam conference never happened. There was to be no new Versailles agreement to end the Second World War in Europe. Just a slow, acrimonious splitting apart of the Soviets from the British and Americans, symbolized by the slow splitting apart of Germany itself.

But even at this stage it was not certain that a fissure would develop between east and west. For two years after the war it was unclear exactly how Stalin would ensure that the countries of eastern Europe would remain 'friendly' to Moscow. The decisive split with the west came only in 1947 in the wake of the decision by the United States to launch a package of aid to selected European countries. This European Recovery Program – usually called the 'Marshall plan', after the American Secretary of State, George Marshall – was conditional on the countries receiving the assistance opening their markets to America.

Much as he wanted economic help delivered to eastern Europe, Stalin couldn't accept such a condition. He was particularly angry when he learnt that the government of Czechoslovakia was interested in attending a meeting in Paris to talk about the prospect of American aid. 'We were astonished that you had decided to participate in that gathering,' he told them. 'For us this question is a question about the friendship of the Soviet Union with the Czechoslovak republic. Whether you wish it or not, you are objectively helping to isolate the Soviet Union.' Every country that had 'friendly relations' with the Soviets, he said, was 'refraining from participation' in the American plan.[31]

At last, Stalin had arrived at his final definition of 'friendliness' in the context of the occupied countries bordering the Soviet Union. It meant becoming a vassal state. The formation by Stalin of the Council for Mutual Economic Assistance in January 1949 tied these countries still further to the Soviet Union.

Iron Curtain, 1949

N

NORWAY

SWEDEN

FINLAND

DENMARK

NETHERLANDS

Baltic Sea

SOVIET
UNION

BELGIUM

EAST
GERMANY

POLAND

LUXEMBOURG

WEST
GERMANY

CZECHOSLOVAKIA

SWITZERLAND

AUSTRIA

HUNGARY

ITALY

YUGOSLAVIA

ROMANIA

BULGARIA

ALBANIA

GREECE

TURKEY

Territory gained by the
Soviet Union in 1945

Countries under Soviet
control

Other communist
country

0		100 miles
0	100 km	

By the time of Stalin's death in 1953 the contrast between West and East Germany was remarkable in both economic and political terms. West Germany was a flourishing parliamentary democracy, basking in the 'economic miracle' that began in 1948.[32] East Germany, on the other hand, suffered economic hardship and political oppression – a state of affairs symbolized by the decision of the Soviet authorities to keep the former Nazi concentration camp of Buchenwald open until 1950.[33] It wasn't just those associated with Hitler's regime that the Soviets incarcerated behind the wire of Buchenwald, but anyone they thought opposed them – including some previous opponents of Nazism and even a handful of foreign nationals who had been living in Germany. Altogether more than 7,000 people perished under the Soviet administration of the camp.[34]

Stalin's decision to split so decisively with the west would lead directly to an arms race, and this in turn would mean that the Soviet economy was drained of resources. It's perhaps not going too far to say that his inability to reach a post-war accommodation with his former allies played a part in the subsequent collapse of the Soviet Union, because of this huge commitment to military expenditure at the expense of consumer goods. Stalin started down a road that subsequent Soviet leaders followed.

However, an arms race would not have been possible in the first place without Stalin's success in industrializing the Soviet Union. Soviet electrical output, for example, increased nearly tenfold between 1928 and 1940. This gigantic change in the structure of what had been primarily an agricultural economy was symbolized by the ability of Soviet scientists to develop and test a nuclear bomb by 1949. A necessary precondition of this achievement had been Stalin's ruthless commitment to industrialization.

As far back as 1931, Stalin had justified the rapid pace of industrialization by citing the need to defend the Soviet Union against the 'jungle law of capitalism', which he expressed as 'you are backward, you are weak – therefore you are wrong; hence, you can be beaten and enslaved. You are mighty – therefore you are right; hence, we must be wary of you. That is why we must no longer lag behind . . . There is no other way . . . We are 50 or a hundred years behind the advanced countries. We must make good this distance in 10 years. Either we do it, or they crush us.'[35]

In the wake of the Soviet victory, Stalin was not just focused on grand issues of state like building a nuclear bomb or the relationship with the west. He also spent time on something that was especially precious to him – his wartime reputation. And in his quest to seize the credit for defeating the Nazis, Stalin revealed an almost childlike boastfulness and overt lust for praise. He had previously been content for Soviet propaganda to develop a leadership cult around him, but had appeared never to lose his sense of cynicism about the process. Yet his desire to be seen now as the sole saviour of the Soviet Union seems to have been sincere. Molotov was surely correct when he said, 'Stalin struggled with his cult and then came to rather like it.'[36]

Before Hitler invaded, Stalin would, as we have seen, never wear military uniform. But not content with the Marshal's uniform he first donned in 1943, on 28 June 1945 he was promoted to 'generalissimo', a rank not seen in Russia since the Napoleonic Wars. He was now portrayed as the sole mastermind who had orchestrated the destruction of Nazi Germany. It was hard, however, for even the Soviet propaganda machine to sell this fiction. One problem was Marshal Zhukov. He had received a good deal of publicity in the Soviet press during the war for his military exploits and this was not an easy fact to unlearn – especially since it was Zhukov who had ridden through Red Square on a white horse to bask in the acclamation of the troops assembled for the victory parade on 24 June 1945. Stalin had merely watched as Zhukov trotted by. The rumour was that Stalin had decided not to take Zhukov's part in the celebrations because he wasn't confident that he could control his horse.

Given this background, it isn't surprising that Stalin turned on Zhukov. First Zhukov's colleague, Alexander Novikov, commander of the Soviet air force, was arrested in early 1946 and made to 'confess' that Zhukov was 'an exceptionally power-loving and narcissistic individual; he loves to be treated with honour, respect and servility and is intolerant of any opposition'. The grotesque irony was that if anyone was guilty of these charges it was Stalin.

In addition to these shortcomings, Novikov claimed that Zhukov had committed the ultimate sin in Stalin's eyes. He had tried to take credit for defeating the Nazis: 'Zhukov is not afraid of inflating his own role in the war as a senior commander, going so far as to declare that all the fundamental plans for military operations were developed by him.'[37]

In July 1946, the charges against Zhukov were discussed at a meeting chaired by Stalin. The problem with Zhukov, said Beria, was that he was not 'grateful, as he should be, to Comrade Stalin for all he has done'. So Beria thought that Zhukov 'should be put in his place'. Molotov and Malenkov agreed. But then something unusual happened. Zhukov's rival in the race for Berlin, Marshal Konev, gave a much more nuanced assessment. While Zhukov was 'difficult' he was nonetheless 'loyal' to the party and Stalin. Marshal Rybalko, who had commanded a Soviet Tank Army, echoed Konev's views, saying that Zhukov was a 'patriot'.[38]

Stalin decided not to send Zhukov to Beria's torture chambers, but to expel him from Moscow. He appointed him commander of the Odessa military district, 700 miles south of the Soviet capital. 'I understood that they were waiting for me to give up', Zhukov later told the war correspondent and poet Konstantin Simonov, 'and [were] expecting that I would not last a day as a district commander. I could not permit this to happen. Of course, fame is fame. At the same time it is a double-edged sword and sometimes cuts against you.'[39]

But just because Stalin had not acted immediately to destroy Zhukov, it didn't mean the marshal was safe. In the past Stalin had shown that he was prepared to let his victims suffer the agony of a slow and painful demolition of their reputation. For instance, the process of destroying Nikolai Bukharin, the prominent Bolshevik revolutionary, had taken years until his final pleading note to Stalin begging for his life – which Stalin never answered – and his execution in March 1938.

Like Bukharin, Zhukov was subjected to a campaign of harassment over several years. He was expelled from the Central Committee of the party; an investigation was started into how much plunder he had taken from Germany; and several officers who had been close to him during the war were arrested. In 1948 he suffered more humiliation when he was sent to command a remote military district in the Urals. Now he was 900 miles away from Moscow.[40]

Having broken the power of the most famous Soviet military commander of the war, Stalin now turned his attention to his own de facto deputy, Vyacheslav Molotov, who had loyally negotiated on his behalf with Hitler, Churchill and Roosevelt. Stalin attacked Molotov through his beloved wife, Polina Zhemchuzhina. She was Jewish, supported various Jewish causes and had relatives abroad – all factors that were sufficient to make Stalin suspicious, especially in the light of the formation of the

Jewish homeland of Israel in May 1948. Polina was accused in December that year of links with 'Jewish nationalists' and of conducting herself in a way that was 'politically inappropriate'.

When the resolution calling for Polina to be expelled from the party came before the Politburo, Molotov made what for him must have been an immense act of resistance. He abstained. This was merely a gesture, however, as the rest of the Politburo voted for her expulsion from the party. Shortly afterwards, in January 1949, Polina was sent into exile.[41]

Molotov brooded on his decision not to condemn his own wife. A few weeks after the Politburo meeting he wrote a fawning letter to Stalin confessing that he had made the wrong choice. It had been a 'mistake' to abstain, and he now wished to change his vote and support her expulsion from the party. Stalin had broken Molotov, as he had broken so many others.[42]

It's important as we consider these events to remember that there was no convincing evidence that either Zhukov or Molotov's wife was plotting against Stalin. Nonetheless, to Stalin's hyper-suspicious and prejudiced mind, the Jewish, independent-thinking wife of a close political colleague was a potential threat, as was a military hero like Zhukov. What mattered to him was not so much what they had already done, but what they might do in the future. And once someone starts thinking of attacking all *possible* threats, then the pool of individuals on which to focus becomes an ocean.

Stalin was attempting, in his own brutal way, to solve the problem of how to lead a Soviet Union that had changed radically as a result of the war. It wasn't just the obvious difficulties that concerned him – how to rebuild the infrastructure of a country devastated both physically and demographically – but how to resolve the psychological effects of the war on the Soviet people as well.

One leading Russian historian framed Stalin's challenge this way: 'Several million peasants who had never seen a railroad in their lives and had been born and bred in the middle of nowhere suddenly found themselves in the army. They found themselves in large towns, including ones in Europe. When he went there he was an ordinary obedient peasant, but now he had something in his head. He had his own opinion. You couldn't just shout at him. Stalin was concerned that there could be some "ideological loosening here", as he would say. "An incorrect reading of the situation." Things needed to be "tightened up".'[43]

The treatment Zhukov and Molotov's wife received was part of this process of post-war 'tightening'. So also was the attack on party officials in Leningrad in the late 1940s, culminating in 1950 in the execution of many of the key figures who had led the city during the siege. Stalin had worried since 1941 about the way in which, cut off from the rest of the country, Soviet officials inside the city might develop 'independent' thinking. Those killed in 1950 to prevent such heresy included Alexey Kuznetsov, deputy to Andrei Zhdanov, head of the city's wartime administration. Zhdanov himself had collapsed of heart problems in mysterious circumstances two years before.[44]

Stalin would continue seeking out enemies – real, potential and imaginary – until his dying breath. Three years after the attack on the Leningrad leaders, just before he died of a cerebral haemorrhage in March 1953, he was presiding over a search for 'traitors' among a collection of distinguished Soviet doctors. There was a strong anti-Semitic dimension to the persecution, with Jewish doctors accused of taking part in an Imperialist-Zionist conspiracy. Only his death brought the action to an end.

Stalin thus died as he had lived. Trusting no one but himself.

Afterword

I want to conclude with some brief words on the way in which Hitler and Stalin are perceived today – not least because these two individuals, almost more than any other historical figures, still live on in the consciousness of the public.

Since their criminal history is such a vital part of their legacy, we first need to confront the question of numbers, and look at the scale of suffering that each of them left behind. Here we must tread with extreme sensitivity. There can be no comparative balance sheet of horror. As the testimony in this book demonstrates, bare statistics cannot convey the true nature of the suffering. However, while always remaining mindful of that fact, it is surely also reasonable to pose the simple question – how many civilian deaths was each of these tyrants responsible for?

It's not an easy question to answer. One problem is the difficulty of gaining precise figures. Records are often fragmentary and those that exist deliberately falsified. Shifting borders, disputed nationalities and the distortion of figures for political purposes all compound the problem of working out the number who died. It is possible, however, to come to some broad conclusions.[1] The first is that Stalin and Hitler were each responsible for deaths on a scale that stuns the imagination.

One of Stalin's most notorious acts of destruction was undoubtedly the famine of the early 1930s in which at least five million people lost their lives, just under four million in Ukraine alone. Add to that between 1.6 million and three million who perished in the Gulag (this figure is one of the most difficult to calculate),[2] over a million who died as a consequence of forced deportations, around a million more who died as 'traitors' or 'enemies of the people', and a variety of other categories of deaths elsewhere, and one arrives at a total of more than nine million people killed. If one includes those who were released from the Gulag but who subsequently died of health problems caused by their imprisonment then the figure leaps even higher to well over thirteen million.[3]

How exactly does Hitler compare? As is well known, around six million Jews perished in the Holocaust, the majority of either Polish or Soviet nationality. Nearly two million non-Jewish Poles also died as a consequence of the Nazi occupation – a figure that has never received the publicity it should.[4] In addition, the Nazis planned on killing tens of millions of Soviet citizens – the majority non-Jews – under their occupation plans.[5] How many they actually killed is extremely hard to assess, but in excess of seven million non-combatants died on Soviet territory as a direct consequence of violence inflicted on them by German forces, of whom more than two million were Jews (a figure included as part of the six million estimate).[6] To this number must be added at least 200,000 Sinti and Roma, and all the other civilians from a variety of other persecuted groups killed across the Nazi empire in concentration camps and elsewhere. This gives us a total of about fourteen million non-combatants who perished under the Nazis.

This number is a low estimate, since it includes only those Soviet civilians killed by the Germans in direct and deliberate killing actions, in what some historians call 'hot or cold blood'.[7] In addition, large numbers of Soviet citizens died while working as forced labourers within the territory of the Reich, and several million more perished in the occupied Soviet Union of famine, disease or other causes attributable to the war. In total these deaths amount – at a minimum – to an additional six million. Added to the figure above of fourteen million, this gives an overall total of at least twenty million people.[8]

The six million Jews who died in the Holocaust fall into a separate category. As we have seen, Hitler had decided that the Jews as a group – men, women and children – would be 'exterminated', many in purpose-built factories of death. No one else in the history of the world has ever implemented such a plan. The Holocaust must rightly be considered the most infamous part of Hitler's legacy.

The distinctiveness of the Holocaust is especially relevant in any comparison between Hitler and Stalin because of the legacy of the *Historikerstreit* (Historians' Dispute) in Germany in the 1980s. This often fractious debate focused on the extent to which the Nazis' policy of extermination towards the Jews was different in kind to other atrocities, particularly those committed under Stalin. My own view – expressed not just in this book but previously in my histories of the Holocaust and Auschwitz – could not be clearer. I believe the Holocaust was singular, for the reasons I expressed in the previous paragraph and earlier in this work.[9]

There was also another key difference between the killings instigated by Hitler and the killings instigated by Stalin. The vast majority of those who died because of Stalin's actions were Soviet citizens, while the vast majority killed by Hitler were non-Germans. This difference follows from their respective ambitions. Stalin was focused on repression within Soviet territory for most of his time in power, while Hitler aimed at creating a vast new empire, within which there was no place for a whole variety of people that he deemed undesirable – chiefly the Jews. In that context it's a common misconception to think that German Jews made up substantial numbers of those who died. In fact, less than 1 per cent of Germans were Jews. It was the countries the Germans invaded – in particular Poland, Hungary and the Soviet Union – that contained large Jewish populations.

This geographical distribution of the deaths demonstrates one further difference between the two tyrants. Hitler's view was that Germany's only chance of long-term survival was to grow bigger – much bigger. As a result of his desire for German expansion, and his steadfast belief in racist ideology, he played the leading role in three of the most consequential decisions ever taken: the decision to invade Poland, which led to the Second World War; the decision to invade the Soviet Union and start the bloodiest single part of that conflict; and the decision to murder the Jews.[10]

Yet, incredibly, the appalling death toll for which Hitler was responsible represents the fulfilment of only a part of his ambition. Had his gigantic colonization plans ever been fully realized then tens of millions more would have died.[11]

As for Stalin, while he did not completely abandon the idea of exporting the revolution to other lands, he had no immense plan of conquest. The eastern European countries that came under his control after 1945 suffered this fate only in the wake of Hitler's defeat, and the territory he snatched in eastern Poland and elsewhere in 1939 he gained only because of his deal with the Nazis.

Of the two tyrants, therefore, it is Hitler who is more broadly seen as a symbol of evil today. Even those people I met who had once been committed Nazis, and were still sympathetic to the regime, had problems circumventing the Holocaust and Hitler's role in creating it. Nonetheless, a small minority tried. One tactic was to deny that the Holocaust had ever happened ('the photos are faked'); another was to say Hitler knew nothing about it ('Himmler kept all knowledge of the killings to himself'). But both excuses are easily demolished, as is the idea that there is somehow an equivalence between the mass murder of the Jews and the Allied bombing of civilians.[12] No matter how hard anyone attempted to spin the history, the truth remained the same. Hitler's personal legacy is that of a war criminal of the most loathsome kind.

Unfortunately, it does not follow that many of the ideas that underpinned Hitler's belief system have vanished from the earth. Fanatical and intolerant nationalism, for instance, is not just still with us but growing in many countries. Ever more strident political discourse and the scapegoating of different groups, whether Jews or others, are also on the increase. Just as worrying, the rule of law and the freedom of the press – two targets of attack by the Nazis – are under threat in countries that were once thought to be committed to democractic ideals. These developments ought to cause us grave concern.

As for the image of Stalin today, his popular reputation is more complex than Hitler's – especially in Russia. In 1956, Khrushchev, by then in charge of the Soviet Union, finally got his revenge on the man who had humiliated him on numerous occasions. Three years after Stalin's death, Khrushchev denounced the former Soviet leader in his famous 'secret speech' at the Twentieth Party Congress. He said Stalin had instigated the Great Terror against many honest people, had not prepared adequately for the war against Hitler, had unjustly deported entire ethnic groups and had pursued still more purges after the war.[13]

The speech did considerable damage to Stalin's reputation within the Communist Party and more broadly within the Soviet Union. So much so that Stalin's embalmed body, which since his death had lain next to Lenin's in the mausoleum on Red Square, was removed in 1961 and placed in the Kremlin Wall Necropolis. Stalin, overshadowed by Lenin in life, was now overshadowed by him in death.

Despite this posthumous humiliation, Stalin's reputation as the mighty leader who had defeated Hitler proved resilient. Even now, in the twenty-first century, Stalin's popularity among ordinary Russians remains high. One poll showed that 70 per cent of Russians view Stalin in a positive light,[14] another voted him the 'most outstanding public figure' in world history.[15] And many of the veterans I met who had lived through the Stalin years also saw this history with a nostalgic glow.

They missed Stalin's 'strong' leadership, and the feeling of security and purpose they had felt when living in the Soviet Union.

Vladimir Putin is partly responsible for the positive way that Stalin is seen in Russia today. His views on the former Soviet leader are distinctly ambivalent. In an interview in 2015, he said that 'it is impossible to put Nazism and Stalinism on the same plane because the Nazis directly, openly and publicly proclaimed one of their policy goals as the extermination of entire ethnic groups – Jews, Gypsies and Slavs. For all the ugly nature of the Stalin regime, for all the repressions and for all the deportations of entire peoples, the Stalin regime never set itself the goal of exterminating peoples, so the attempt to put the two [regimes] on the same footing is absolutely without foundation.'[16]

In part, Putin is correct. Stalin never 'openly and publicly' said he sought to exterminate an 'entire ethnic group', and the crime of the Holocaust undoubtedly remains a singular one, for all the reasons outlined previously in this book. But, as we also saw earlier, was not Stalin presiding over the slow extermination of a people such as the Kalmyks? And were they not an 'entire ethnic group'?[17]

In December 2019, during his annual news conference, Putin said that 'you can condemn Stalinism and totalitarianism as a whole, and in some ways these will be well-deserved reproaches.' But he later argued that 'Stalin did not stain himself with direct contact with Hitler whereas the French and British leaders met with him and signed some documents.' This, given the facts outlined in the first chapter of this book, is an utterly warped way of reading the history. When the British and French signed the Munich agreement in 1938 with Hitler – and presumably this is the meeting Putin is referring to – they did not come to a secret agreement with him to carve up eastern Europe between them, as Stalin did. The fact that Stalin never met with Hitler personally to fix up the deal does not mean he did not 'stain' himself in the process.

Putin subsequently made the incredible claim that Soviet troops never invaded Poland in September 1939. He alleged that the Poles had lost control of the country, and consequently 'there was no one to talk to about it [the Soviet incursion] . . . the Red Army did not invade those territories in Poland. German troops entered them and then left, and after that the Soviet troops entered.'[18] This idea would be laughable were it not such a disgraceful distortion of the history.

The reason why Putin was trying to sanitize the history of Stalin's pact with Hitler is obvious. This awkward period gets in the way of the heroic narrative of the Red Army's victory over Nazism. So Putin's solution to the problem was to twist and distort the actual version of events. And while it's disturbing to hear a powerful leader treat history in this way, at least his bizarre take on events demonstrates why understanding what genuinely happened is important.

I'll end with a final reflection, gained as a result of my experience of meeting hundreds of eyewitnesses from both sides. What struck me over the years was how many of them had done everything they could to rationalize what had been happening around them. So, for me, the story of Hitler and Stalin became about more than just the history of two individuals; it became over time a study of the malleability of the human mind.

A number of the eyewitnesses I met over the last thirty years illustrated this worrying aspect of human behaviour. But, in this context, the individual who had the most lasting effect on me was Tatiana Nanieva, a former nurse and member of the Communist Party who had thought before the war that 'everything was wonderful' in the Soviet Union. When I met her in the late 1990s in her cold, dilapidated flat in the suburbs of Kiev, she told of how despite her unwavering faith in Stalin she had been imprisoned after the war. Her 'crime' had been to allow herself to be captured by the Germans in October 1942, while tending wounded Red Army soldiers near the front line.

'Liberated' from German captivity by the advancing Soviet forces in January 1945, she was interrogated and sentenced to six years in a Soviet labour camp followed by a period in exile: 'For the [Soviet] guards, for the civilian labour force, we weren't people. We were whores. They only referred to us like that. As soon as one said it – then everyone did. They only called us that. "If you were there [in a German camp] and you survived then you can only be a whore." '[20]

Yet, despite all of this unjust suffering, she continued to think of Stalin as 'our God': 'Even when I was given a long prison sentence and branded a "Traitor of the Motherland" . . . when Stalin died in 1953, I cried. I cried less when my own father died than when Stalin died. I couldn't imagine that we would be able to live without him.'[21] Her desire to have faith in a redemptive leader was so intense that it survived even the systematic abuse she had received at the hands of the Soviet state.

Hitler and Stalin each possessed the power to inspire this kind of belief. They were both stern father-figures who sold their utopian dreams with absolute certainty. The dreams they offered were of a future that had meaning not just for you as an individual, but for your children and their children yet unborn. Buying into these dreams offered you hope and purpose. It meant you were not alone, but part of something of epic importance. Human beings are social animals, and the pressure to believe in these dreams was immense.

Moreover, because Hitler and Stalin promised their vast numbers of willing followers that there was a glorious world awaiting them in the future, the problems of the now could be brushed aside as the price of the utopia of tomorrow. But that tomorrow never came.

Ultimately – and despite their many differences – what united Hitler and Stalin was their readiness to kill millions of people in pursuit of their dreams. They were even prepared, for ideological reasons, to persecute people who were honest and compliant. It didn't matter if you were a Kalmyk like Aleksey Badmaev who had served bravely in the Red Army. You were still sent to a labour camp, starved of food and saw a number of your comrades die of mistreatment in front of you. And it didn't matter if you were a well-behaved German Jew. You were still sent to your death.

All of this horror should serve as a reminder – for all time – of the destruction that tyrants with utopian visions can inflict upon the world.

Acknowledgements

Over the last thirty years an enormous number of people have helped me in my work on Nazism, Stalinism and the Second World War. Space prevents me from naming every single one of them here, but crucial members of the various production teams have included: Valeri Azarianc, Martina Balazova, Valentina Galzanova, Marcel Joos, Maria Keder, SallyAnn Kleibel, Wanda Koscia, Tomasz Lasica, Michaela Lichtenstein, Teodor Matveev, Maria Mikushova, Anya Narinskaya, Stanislav Remizov, Elena Smolina, Dr Frank Stucke, Dominic Sutherland, Anna Taborska, Alexandra Umminger and Elena Yakovleva. In particular I need to mention two of my German colleagues, Tilman Remme and Detlef Siebert, who have been stalwart in their dedication to the work. I have hugely valued their friendship over these many years.

For this book in particular, Dr Elga Zalite conducted research at the Hoover Institution at Stanford University, and Julia Pietsch did valuable work in archives in Germany. Julia also read the book before publication and made a number of extremely useful comments. I also, of course, thank the BBC for permission to quote from the testimony gathered for the various television series that I wrote and produced.

Professor Sir Ian Kershaw, the world expert on Adolf Hitler, read the manuscript in draft and made many insightful suggestions. My debt to him for his advice and friendship over twenty-five years can never be repaid. Professor Robert Service, author of a brilliant biography of Stalin and a consultant on my series *World War Two: Behind Closed Doors* twelve years ago, also read the book before publication and gave me the benefit of his immense knowledge of Stalin and the Soviet state.

Julie Aldred, a friend of mine for many years, made a series of valuable criticisms of the work after reading it in draft. As did my daughter Camilla, a talented Oxford-educated historian.

The vast majority of the people I met who lived through these terrible times are no longer with us. But wherever they are now, I thank them in spirit.

I'm also grateful to Daniel Crewe, my publisher at Viking, for his faith in this project and for all of his editorial help. I must also mention his talented colleagues – Connor Brown, Rose Poole, Emma Brown and Olivia Mead. Not forgetting the team at my American publisher in New York, PublicAffairs, led by Clive Priddle. I thank them all. My copyeditor Peter James also made an important contribution. Andrew Nurnberg, my literary agent for nearly thirty years, remains an essential part of my working life.

My greatest personal debt is to my family, my wife Helena and my children Oliver, Camilla and Benedict (to whom this book is dedicated). How they manage to put up with me as I spend years working on a book like this, I just don't know. But I am so grateful they do.

Laurence Rees
London, May 2020

Notes

Preface

1 This meeting took place in February 2006.
2 Previously unpublished testimony. (This is the form of words used throughout this book to signify testimony which has not been published before, and which was obtained for the various television productions on Nazism, Stalinism and the Second World War that I have written and produced over the last thirty years.)
3 *Goebbels, Master of Propaganda*, written and produced by Laurence Rees, transmitted on BBC2 on 12 November 1992.
4 For example, when in 1934 Hitler ordered the murder of the leader of the Nazi stormtroopers, Ernst Röhm, together with other opponents, Stalin remarked, 'What a great fellow! How well he pulled this off!' See above p. 63. And on 8 May 1943 Hitler said that he envied Stalin for the way he had 'got rid of all opposition in the Red Army and thus ensured there is no defeatist tendency in the army'. See above p. 274.
5 Alan Bullock, *Hitler and Stalin: Parallel Lives*, HarperCollins, 1991. The most notable book since then has been Richard Overy's *The Dictators: Hitler's Germany and Stalin's Russia*, published by Allen Lane in 2004. That scholarly work takes a thematic, non-narrative approach to the subject.
6 Laurence Rees, *Their Darkest Hour*, Ebury Press, 2007, pp. viii–ix.
7 *A British Betrayal*, written and produced by Laurence Rees, transmitted on BBC2 on 11 January 1991.
8 Rees, *Their Darkest Hour*, pp. 225–8. Also see Nikolai Tolstoy, *The Minister and the Massacres*, Hutchinson, 1986, p. 133.
9 Rees, *Their Darkest Hour*, p. 229.
10 Ibid., p. ix.
11 See above pp. 45–6.

Introduction

1 August Kubizek, *The Young Hitler I Knew*, Greenhill Books, 2006, p. 34.

2 Ibid., p. 157.

3 Balthasar Brandmayer, *Meldegänger Hitler 1914–18*, Buchverlag Franz Walter, 1933, pp. 71–2.

4 He seems to have adopted the name 'Stalin' around 1911. Many Bolsheviks used pseudonyms, in part to help avoid detection by the authorities. Molotov, for instance, was born Vyacheslav Mikhailovich Skryabin but took the name 'Molotov', which means 'hammer' in Russian. And Vladimir Ilyich Ulyanov is better known today as 'Lenin' – a word that is derived from the Russian for 'large river'.

5 See Max Weber, *Essays in Sociology*, Routledge, 1998, pp. 245–64. Also Laurence Rees, *The Dark Charisma of Adolf Hitler*, Ebury Press, 2012.

6 Hans Frank, *Im Angesicht des Galgens*, Friedrich Alfred Beck, 1953, pp. 39–42. Rees, *Dark Charisma*, p. 33.

7 Rees, *Dark Charisma*, p. 37.

8 Moshe Lewin, 'Bureaucracy and the Stalinist State', in Ian Kershaw and Moshe Lewin (eds.), *Stalinism and Nazism: Dictatorships in Comparison*, Cambridge University Press, 1997, pp. 62–3.

9 Ronald Grigor Suny, 'Stalin and His Stalinism: Power and Authority in the Soviet Union, 1930–1953', in Kershaw and Lewin (eds.), *Stalinism and Nazism*, p. 32.

10 Frank, *Im Angesicht des Galgens*, pp. 335–6.

11 The number of Gauleiters expanded as more territory was taken into the Reich, such as Austria and the incorporated lands in Poland.

12 Bundesarchiv (henceforth BArch), NS 19/389, fol. 4.

13 Previously unpublished testimony.

14 Previously unpublished testimony.

15 *Diaries of William Lyon Mackenzie King*, entry for 29 June 1937, https://www.bac-lac.gc.ca/eng/discover/politics-government/prime-ministers/william-lyon-mackenzie-king/Pages/item.aspx?IdNumber=18112&. See Laurence Rees, *The Holocaust: A New History*, Viking, 2017, pp. 130–32.

16 Entry in Mackenzie King's diary for 29 March 1938, https://www.bac-lac.gc.ca/eng/discover/politics-government/prime-ministers/william-lyon-mackenzie-king/Pages/item.aspx?IdNumber=18924&. But after the pogrom of Kristallnacht, King wrote in his diary on 23 November 1938 that he had 'sympathy' for the Jews, https://www.bac-lac.gc.ca/eng/discover/politics-

government/prime-ministers/william-lyon-mackenzie-king/Pages/item. aspx?IdNumber=19622&.

17 Andrew Roberts, *'The Holy Fox': The Life of Lord Halifax*, Phoenix, 1997, p. 70.

18 John Julius Norwich (ed.), *The Duff Cooper Diaries*, Phoenix, 2006, entry for 17 September 1938, p. 260.

19 Kubizek, *Young Hitler*, p. 182.

20 Hugh Gibson (ed.), *The Ciano Diaries*, Simon Publications, 2001, entry for 30 April 1942, pp. 478–9.

21 Laurence Rees, *War of the Century*, BBC Books, 1999, pp. 20–21.

22 Previously unpublished testimony.

23 Robert Service, *Stalin: A Biography*, Macmillan, 2004, p. 53.

24 Previously unpublished testimony.

25 Konstantin M. Simonov, *Glazami cheloveka moego pokoleniia*, Novosti, 1989, pp. 422–3 (interview with Admiral Ivan Isakov conducted in 1962), quoted in Stephen Kotkin, *Stalin*, vol. 2: *Waiting for Hitler 1929–1941*, Allen Lane, 2017, p. 888.

26 Previously unpublished testimony.

27 Previously unpublished testimony.

28 George F. Kennan, *Memoirs 1925–1950*, Atlantic Monthly Press, 1967, p. 279.

29 Robert Gellately, *Lenin, Stalin and Hitler: The Age of Social Catastrophe*, Vintage, 2008, p. 544.

30 Until, towards the end of the Second World War, Stalin succumbed to the lure of uniform and dressed as a marshal. See above pp. 355–6.

31 *Hitler's Table Talk 1941–1944*, Phoenix, 2002, entry for 31 March 1942, p. 386.

32 Ibid., 13 December 1941, p. 144.

33 See above pp. 204–5.

34 Arthur de Gobineau, *Essai sur l'inégalité des races humaines* (1855), in English in *The Inequality of the Human Races*, William Heinemann, 1915. Rees, *Holocaust*, p. 6.

35 Alfred Ploetz, *Die Tüchtigkeit unsrer Rasse und der Schutz der Schwachen*, quoted in Peter Watson, *The German Genius*, Simon & Schuster, 2011, p. 434. Rees, *Holocaust*, p. 8.

36 Karl Binding and Alfred Hoche, *Die Freigabe der Vernichtung lebensunwerten Lebens. Ihr Maß und ihre Form*, Felix Meiner, 1920, pp. 49–50.

37 Rudolf von Sebottendorff, *Bevor Hitler kam. Urkundliches aus der Frühzeit der nationalsozialistischen Bewegung*, Deukula-Verlag Graffinger, 1933, pp. 44, 48.

38 Ibid., pp. 57–60.

39 Houston Stewart Chamberlain, *Foundations of the Nineteenth Century*, vol. I, Elibron Classics, 2005 (first published F. Bruckman, 1911), p. 350.

40 Adolf Hitler, *Mein Kampf*, Houghton Mifflin, 1971, p. 289.

41 Ibid., p. 305.

42 Ibid., p. 65.

43 Ibid., p. 288.

44 Gerhard L. Weinberg (ed.), *Hitler's Second Book: The Unpublished Sequel to Mein Kampf*, Enigma Books, 2003, pp. 113, 109.

45 Ibid., p. 113.

46 Ibid., p. 108.

47 Ibid., p. 130.

48 Hitler speech at the Nuremberg rally, in *Völkischer Beobachter*, Bayern-ausgabe, 7 August 1929, p. 1.

49 *Das Erbe* (1935), directed by Carl Hartmann.

50 BArch, R 9361 III/514455, SS-Führerpersonalakten, Joseph Altrogge, quoted in part in Tom Segev, *Soldiers of Evil: The Commandants of the Nazi Concentration Camps*, Diamond Books, 2000, p. 98.

51 See Karl Marx and Friedrich Engels, *Economic and Philosophic Manuscripts of 1844*, Wilder Publications, 2011.

52 But as Professor Service points out, Marx subsequently equivocated about the precise, uniform sequence of stages – one reason why Marxists can still argue about this to the present day.

53 *New Statesman*, special supplement to the magazine, 27 October 1934, H. G. Wells interview with Stalin, online at https://www.newstatesman.com /politics/2014/04/h-g-wells-it-seems-me-i-am-more-left-you-mr-stalin.

54 Service, *Stalin*, p. 98.

55 *New Statesman*, special supplement to the magazine, 27 October 1934.

56 N. H. Baynes (ed.), *Speeches of Adolf Hitler: Early Speeches 1922–1924, and Other Selections*, Howard Fertig, 2006, speech of 12 April 1922, pp. 15–16.

57 Joseph Stalin, *Selected Writing*, Greenwood Press, 1970, pp. 469–74.

58 Previously unpublished testimony.

59 Segev, *Soldiers of Evil*, interview with Johannes Hassebroek, p. 99.

1. The Pact

1 Previously unpublished testimony.

2 Hitler, *Mein Kampf*, pp. 660–61.

3　Ibid., p. 661.

4　Ibid.

5　Ibid.

6　Ibid., pp. 661–2.

7　Ibid., p. 654.

8　Alun Chalfont, *Montgomery of Alamein*, Weidenfeld & Nicolson, 1976, p. 318.

9　Stuart Andrews, *Lenin's Revolution*, Humanities-Ebooks, 2010, p. 67.

10　Dmitri Volkogonov, *Lenin: A New Biography*, Free Press, 1994, p. 230, quoting Lenin's pamphlet *'Left-wing' Communism: An Infantile Disorder*.

11　Borislav Chernev, *Twilight of Empire: The Brest-Litovsk Conference and the Remaking of Central Europe 1917–1918*, University of Toronto Press, 2017, p. 27.

12　In the treaty of Rapallo in 1922 the Soviets and the Germans reached an agreement that settled their territorial and financial differences. Both sides were aggrieved with others. The Germans had lost territory in the east as a result of the post-war treaties imposed by the Allies, and the Soviets had lost territory in the wake of Brest-Litovsk and their recent border war with Poland. The Germans and the Soviets were thus united by their sense that they had been wronged.

13　'Aufzeichnung ohne Unterschrift' (August 1936), in *Akten zur Deutschen Auswärtigen Politik 1918–1945*, Vandenhoeck & Ruprecht, 1977, Serie C: 1933–1936, Das Dritte Reich: Die Ersten Jahre, Band V, 2, 26. Mai bis 31. Oktober 1936, Dokumentnummer 490, pp. 793–801.

14　*International Military Tribunal (IMT)*, Der November 1945–1. Oktober 1946, Band XXXVI, Nürnberg, 1948, pp. 489ff.

15　Max Domarus, *Hitler. Reden und Proklamationen 1932–1945. Kommentiert von einem deutschen Zeitgenossen*, Band I: *Triumph, Zweiter Halbband 1935–1938*, R. Löwit, 1973, Hitler speech of 13 September 1937, pp. 728–9, 731.

16　Service, *Stalin*, p. 384.

17　Kotkin, *Stalin*, vol. 2: *Waiting for Hitler*, p. 682.

18　Harpal Brar, *Trotskyism or Leninism?*, H. Brar, 1993, p. 625, quoting a Trotsky essay in *Bulletin of the Opposition* of 1933.

19　Ibid.

20　Leon Trotsky, *The Stalin School of Falsification*, ed. Max Shachtman, Muriwai Books, 2018 (first published in English 1937), Kindle edn, location 2140.

21　Stalin, *Selected Writings*, p. 440.

22　Ibid., p. 441.

23　Ibid., p. 444.

24 Gabriel Gorodetsky (ed.), *The Maisky Diaries: The Wartime Revelations of Stalin's Ambassador in London*, Yale University Press, 2016, entry for 15 March 1939, p. 163.

25 Sir Frank Roberts interview in episode three of *Nazis: A Warning from History*, written and produced by Laurence Rees, first transmitted on BBC2 in 1997.

26 James Mace Ward, *Priest, Politician, Collaborator: Jozef Tiso and the Making of Fascist Slovakia*, Cornell University Press, 2013, pp. 181 and 177.

27 Ibid., p. 183.

28 Previously unpublished testimony.

29 Ian Kershaw, *Hitler 1936–1945: Nemesis*, Allen Lane, 2000, p. 171.

30 David Dilks (ed.), *The Diaries of Sir Alexander Cadogan, O.M., 1938–1945*, Cassell, 1971, entry for 20 March 1939, p. 161.

31 Frank McDonough, *Neville Chamberlain, Appeasement and the British Road to War*, Manchester University Press, 1998, p. 78.

32 Hansard, 31 March 1939, vol. 345, cols. 2415–20, online at https://api.par liament.uk/historic-hansard/commons/1939/mar/31/european-situation-1# S5CV0345P0_19390331_HOC_226. Chamberlain had first offered this Polish 'guarantee' at a speech in Birmingham on 17 March.

33 Ibid., at col. 2416.

34 Gorodetsky (ed.), *Maisky Diaries*, entry for 31 March 1939, p. 169.

35 Christopher Hill, *Cabinet Decisions on Foreign Policy: The British Experience, October 1938–June 1941*, Cambridge University Press, 1991, p. 49.

36 McDonough, *Chamberlain*, p. 82.

37 Ian Colvin, *The Chamberlain Cabinet*, Victor Gollancz, 1971, p. 200. The FO document is also quoted in Dilks (ed.), *Cadogan Diaries*, p. 175.

38 Richard Overy, *1939: Countdown to War*, Allen Lane, 2009, p. 13.

39 Hill, *Cabinet Decisions*, p. 53.

40 Anita Prazmowska, *Britain, Poland and the Eastern Front, 1939*, Cambridge University Press, 1987, pp. 142, 143.

41 Dilks (ed.), *Cadogan Diaries*, entry for 19 April 1939, p. 175.

42 Hill, *Cabinet Decisions*, p. 59.

43 Gorodetsky (ed.), *Maisky Diaries*, entry for 4 August 1939, p. 212.

44 *Documents on German Foreign Policy 1918–1945*, Series D: *1937–1945*, vol. VI: *The Last Months of Peace, March–August 1939*, United States Government Printing Office, 1956, Document 758, Ribbentrop to German Embassy in Moscow, 3 August 1939, p. 1048.

45 Chris Bellamy, *Absolute War: Soviet Russia in the Second World War*, Macmillan, 2007, p. 44.

46 Hitler did make the occasional comment in his lengthy speech about the dangers of 'Bolshevism', referring for example to 'Bolshevism's extermination of European culture'. Max Domarus, *Hitler. Reden und Proklamationen 1932–1945. Kommentiert von einem deutschen Zeitgenossen*, Band II: *Untergang, Erster Halbband 1939–1940*, R. Löwit, 1973, Hitler's speech to the Reichstag, 28 April 1939, p. 1164.

47 Ibid., pp. 1573, 1158.

48 Ibid., pp. 1574, 1159.

49 Ibid., pp. 1583, 1167.

50 Although the French were certainly much more keen to agree a deal than the British. See Louise Grace Shaw (ed.), *The British Political Elite and the Soviet Union 1937–1939*, Frank Cass, 2003, p. 139.

51 Ibid., p. 138.

52 Gibson (ed.), *Ciano Diaries*, entry for 11 August 1939, p. 119.

53 Ibid., entry for 12 August 1939, p. 119.

54 Andreas Hillgruber, *Germany and the Two World Wars*, Harvard University Press, 1981, p. 69.

55 *Documents on German Foreign Policy 1918–1945*, Series D, vol. VII: *The Last Days of Peace, August 9–September 3, 1939*, United States Government Printing Office, 1956, pp. 200–204.

56 Ibid., pp. 205–6.

57 V. N. Pavlov (the Soviet interpreter), 'Avtobiographicheskii Zametki', *Novaya i Noveyshaya Istoria*, 2000, pp. 98–9.

58 Gustav Hilger and Alfred G. Meyer, *The Incompatible Allies*, Macmillan, 1953, p. 304.

59 Andor Hencke interrogation and his memorandum of the conversation of 23 August in Politisches Archiv, Berlin, ADAP DVII DOK 213.

60 Albert Resis (ed.), *Molotov Remembers*, Ivan R. Dee, 1993, p. 12.

61 Sergei Khrushchev (ed.), *Memoirs of Nikita Khrushchev*, vol. 1: *Commissar (1918–1945)*, Pennsylvania State University Press, 2004, p. 225.

62 Nevile Henderson, *Failure of a Mission*, Hodder & Stoughton, 1940, p. 266.

2. Eliminating Poland

1 Alexander B. Rossino, *Hitler Strikes Poland: Blitzkrieg, Ideology, and Atrocity*, University Press of Kansas, 2003, pp. 16, 66–7 and 129.

2 Jürgen Matthäus, Jochen Böhler and Klaus-Michael Mallmann, *War, Pacification, and Mass Murder, 1939: The Einsatzgruppen in Poland*, Documenting Life and Destruction: Holocaust Sources in Context, Rowman & Littlefield, 2014, Document 18, Post-war interrogation of Bruno G, former member of Einsatzkommando 2/IV, in connection with 'reprisals' in Bydgoszcz, p. 59.

3 Robert Gerwarth, *Hitler's Hangman: The Life of Heydrich*, Yale University Press, 2012, p. 153. Five thousand of this total were Jews.

4 Gorodetsky (ed.), *Maisky Diaries*, entry for 17 September 1939, p. 225.

5 Jan Gross, *Revolution from Abroad*, Princeton University Press, 1988, p. 11.

6 For ease of understanding, throughout the book I refer to this city as Lwów. That's because this Polish version of the city's name was what the place was called before the war. Today the city is called Lviv – the name the Ukrainians know it by – and sits not in Poland but in an independent Ukraine. The Germans when they occupied the city referred to it as Lemberg and the Soviets called it Lvov. The city thus had four different names during the twentieth century. This variety of names is emblematic of the turbulent and often tragic history of this beautiful city.

7 Charles Burdick and Hans-Adolf Jacobsen (eds.), *The Halder War Diary 1939–1942*, Greenhill Books, 1988, entry for 20 September 1939, p. 58.

8 Previously unpublished testimony.

9 Previously unpublished testimony.

10 Previously unpublished testimony.

11 Previously unpublished testimony.

12 Ingeborg Fleischhauer, 'Der deutsch–sowjetische Grenz- und Freundschaftsvertrag vom 28. September 1939. Die deutschen Aufzeichnungen über die Verhandlungen zwischen Stalin, Molotov und Ribbentrop in Moskau', *Vierteljahrshefte für Zeitgeschichte*, vol. 39, no. 3, 1991, pp. 447–70. Gustav Hilger's notes, 'Aufzeichnung. Betr. Moskauer Besprechungen des Herrn Reichsaußenministers (Ende September 1939)', pp. 453–70, here p. 458.

13 Karl Schnurre, *Aus einem bewegten Leben, Heiteres und Ernstes*, 1986, pp. 90–95, unpublished memoirs, Politisches Archiv des Auswärtigen Amts Berlin, Nachlass Karl Schnurre.

14 Yosef Govrin, *The Jewish Factor in the Relations between Nazi Germany and the Soviet Union 1933–1941*, Vallentine Mitchell, 2009, p. 34.

15 See Nikolaus Wachsmann's introduction to Margarete Buber-Neumann, *Under Two Dictators: Prisoner of Stalin and Hitler*, Vintage, 2013, Kindle edn, location 176–94.

16 Buber-Neumann, *Under Two Dictators*, Kindle edn, p. 44.

17 Ibid., pp. 336–7.

18 Werner Präg and Wolfgang Jacobmeyer (eds.), *Das Diensttagebuch des deutschen Generalgouverneurs in Polen 1939–1945*, Deutsche Verlags-Anstalt, 1975, entry for 26/27 October 1939, p. 46.

19 Sergej Slutsch, '17. September 1939: Der Eintritt der Sowjetunion in den Zweiten Weltkrieg. Eine historische und völkerrechtliche Bewertung', *Vierteljahrshefte für Zeitgeschichte*, vol. 48, no. 2 (2000), pp. 219–54, here p. 231. Diary of the Soviet Delegation of the Russo-German Border Commission, in Foreign Policy Archive of the Russian Federation, Moscow, f. 011, op. 4, p. 27, d. 66, l. 22, entry for 27 October 1939.

20 Laurence Rees, *Auschwitz: The Nazis and the 'Final Solution'*, BBC Books, 2005, p. 44.

21 Jacob Sloan (ed.), *Notes from the Warsaw Ghetto: From the Journal of Emmanuel Ringelblum*, iBooks, 2006, entry for 12 February 1940, p. 19.

22 Previously unpublished testimony.

23 Michael Burleigh, *The Third Reich: A New History*, Pan Books, 2001, pp. 176–7.

24 Kotkin, *Stalin*, vol. 2: *Waiting for Hitler*, p. 595.

25 Elke Fröhlich (ed.), *Die Tagebücher von Joseph Goebbels*, Teil I: *Aufzeichnungen 1923–1941*, Band 7: *Juli 1939–März 1940*, K. G. Saur, 1998, entry for 23 January 1940, p. 282.

26 *Documents on German Foreign Policy 1918–1945*, Series D, vol. VIII: *The War Years, September 4, 1939–March 18, 1940*, United States Government Printing Office, 1954, Document 190, pp. 206–7.

27 Previously unpublished testimony.

28 Previously unpublished testimony, and Laurence Rees, *Nazis: A Warning from History*, BBC Books 2005, p. 120.

29 The German name for the city was Posen.

30 Peter Longerich, *Heinrich Himmler*, Oxford University Press, 2011, pp. 443–4.

31 Rees, *Nazis*, p. 121.

32 Ibid.

33 Previously unpublished testimony.

34 Jeannette von Hehn, 'Als Landfrau im Warthegau 1940–1945', *Jahrbuch des baltischen Deutschtums*, 1960, pp. 90–93.

35 Previously unpublished testimony.

36 Previously unpublished testimony, but see Rees, *Nazis*, pp. 122–3.

37 *Concise Statistical Year-Book of Poland, September 1939–June 1941*, Polish Ministry of Information, 2nd edn, June 1944 (first published December 1941), pp. 9–10.

38 Christopher Browning, *The Origins of the Final Solution*, William Heinemann, 2004, p. 57.

39 Jeremy Noakes and Geoffrey Pridham (eds.), *Nazism 1919–1945: A Documentary Reader*, vol. 3: *Foreign Policy, War and Racial Extermination*, Exeter University Press, 1991, pp. 932–4.

40 For further discussion on the Madagascar plan, see above pp. 310–11.

41 Joshua D. Zimmerman, *The Polish Underground and the Jews 1939–1945*, Cambridge University Press, 2015, p. 20.

42 Christopher Browning, *Nazi Policy, Jewish Workers, German Killers*, Cambridge University Press, 2000, Hans Frank speech, 25 November 1939, p. 8.

43 Anne Applebaum, *Gulag: A History of the Soviet Camps*, Penguin Books, 2004, p. 64.

44 Previously unpublished testimony, and Laurence Rees, *World War Two: Behind Closed Doors*, BBC Books, 2008, p. 29.

45 Applebaum, *Gulag*, p. 111.

46 Previously unpublished testimony.

47 Previously unpublished testimony.

48 Previously unpublished testimony. Also see Katherine Bliss Eaton, *Daily Life in the Soviet Union*, Greenwood Publishing, 2004, p. 69.

49 A similar point is also made by Gustaw Herling, *A World Apart*, Penguin Books, 1996 (first published 1951), p. 150.

50 Applebaum, *Gulag*, pp. 383–4, calculation of Aleksandr Guryanov.

51 Previously unpublished testimony, and Rees, *Behind Closed Doors*, p. 52.

52 Presidential Archive, Moscow, f. 17, op. 162, d. 26, l. 119, document from Beria to Stalin dated 2 December 1939.

53 Rees, *Behind Closed Doors*, pp. 47–9.

54 Previously unpublished testimony.

55 Herling, *A World Apart*, p. 11. Also see Thomas Lane, *Victims of Stalin and Hitler: The Exodus of Poles and Balts to Britain*, Palgrave, 2004, p. 102.

56 Herling, *A World Apart*, p. 22.

57 Ibid., p. 18.

58 Rees, *Auschwitz*, p. 40.

59 Quoted in Danuta Czech, 'The Auschwitz Prisoner Administration', in Yisrael Gutman and Michael Berenbaum (eds.), *Anatomy of the Auschwitz Death Camp*, Indiana University Press, 1998, p. 364.

60 See above p. 28.

61 Herling, *A World Apart*, p. 65.

62 Segev, *Soldiers of Evil*, p. 28.

63 Rudolf Hoess, *Commandant of Auschwitz*, Phoenix, 2000, pp. 70–71.

64 A small number of Poles were even released from Auschwitz. See, for example, the experiences of Władysław Bartoszewski, released from the camp at Easter 1941, detailed in Rees, *Auschwitz*, pp. 46–8.

65 Herling, *A World Apart*, p. 33.

66 Maren Röger, 'The Sexual Policies and Sexual Realities of the German Occupiers in Poland in the Second World War', *Contemporary European History*, vol. 23, issue 1, February 2014, pp. 1–21.

67 Polish Ministry of Information, *The German New Order in Poland*, Hutchinson, 1943, pp. 408–9.

68 Previously unpublished testimony.

69 Christopher Browning, *The Path to Genocide: Essays on Launching the Final Solution*, Cambridge University Press, 1992, p. 23.

70 *Hitler's Table Talk*, entry for night of 1–2 August 1941, pp. 18–19.

71 Rees, *Nazis*, p. 129.

72 Kotkin, *Stalin*, vol. 2: *Waiting for Hitler*, p. 705.

73 George Sanford, *Katyn and the Soviet Massacre of 1940*, Routledge, 2005, p. 297.

74 But Hitler did sign, in 1939, a document authorizing the killing of selected disabled people. Arguably, he subsequently recognized that associating himself too closely with the policy had been a mistake. Much better, from his point of view, to preside over the subsequent killings of the 'Final Solution', but keep his name off any written orders. See Rees, *Holocaust*, pp. 165–6.

3. Opposite Fortunes

1 The 1937 census calculated a Soviet population of 162 million, but this was too low for Stalin and so publication of the data was halted. In March 1939 he announced that the population was 170 million.

2 Overy, *Dictators*, p. 452.

3 H. G. Wells interview with Stalin, *New Statesman*, special supplement, 27 October 1934.

4 Kotkin, *Stalin*, vol. 2: *Waiting for Hitler*, p. 378.

5 Robert Gellately, *Stalin's Curse: Battling for Communism in War and Cold War*, Oxford University Press, 2013, p. 38.

6 William J. Spahr, *Stalin's Lieutenants: A Study of Command under Duress*, Presidio Press, 1997, p. 172.

7 Previously unpublished testimony.

8 Previously unpublished testimony, and 'Mark Lazarevich Gallay and the Mind of Josef Stalin', in Rees, *Their Darkest Hour*, pp. 197–203.

9 Dmitry Chernov and Didier Sornette, *Man-Made Catastrophes and Risk Information Concealment: Case Studies of Major Disasters and Human Fallibility*, Springer, 2016, p. 205. This episode is taken from the memoirs of Marshal Zhukov, and it is Zhukov who called Voroshilov a 'dilettante'.

10 Juho Kusti Paasikivi, *Meine Moskauer Mission 1939–41*, Holsten-Verlag, 1966, pp. 67–8.

11 Milovan Djilas, *Conversations with Stalin*, Penguin Books, 2014, pp. 50–51.

12 Väinö Tanner, *The Winter War: Finland against Russia 1939–1940*, Stanford University Press, 1957, pp. 67–8.

13 William R. Trotter, *The Winter War: The Russo-Finnish War of 1939–40*, Aurum Press, 2003, p. 17.

14 Khrushchev (ed.), *Khrushchev Memoirs*, vol. 1: *Commissar*, p. 249.

15 Gorodetsky (ed.), *Maisky Diaries*, entry for 27 November 1939, p. 240.

16 Kotkin, *Stalin*, vol. 2: *Waiting for Hitler*, p. 741.

17 Dmitri Volkogonov, *Stalin: Triumph and Tragedy*, Weidenfeld & Nicolson, 1991, p. 279. Beria's words were reported to Volkogonov by A. A. Yepishev.

18 Bellamy, *Absolute War*, p. 74. Voronov was told this by G. Kulik, a Commissar of Defence at a meeting also attended by General Meretskov.

19 Allen F. Chew, *The White Death: The Epic of the Soviet–Finnish Winter War*, KiwE Publishing, 2007, pp. 27–8.

20 Ibid., pp. 71–2.

21 Previously unpublished testimony.

22 Trotter, *Winter War*, p. 160.

23 Robert D. Lewallen, *The Winter War: The United States and the Impotence of Power*, Alyssiym Publications, 2010, p. 69.

24 Winston Churchill broadcast, 20 January 1940, online at https://winston churchill.org/resources/speeches/1940-the-finest-hour/the-war-situation-house-of-many-mansions/.

25 For example, the view of both Chamberlain and senior military figures in Britain about the deficiencies of the Red Army: see above p. 13.

26 Gorodetsky (ed.), *Maisky Diaries*, entry for 12 December 1939, pp. 244–5.

27 Ibid., entry for 21 February 1940, p. 257.

28 Khrushchev (ed.), *Khrushchev Memoirs*, vol. 1: *Commissar*, pp. 251–2.

29 Chew, *White Death*, p. 179.

30 Khrushchev (ed.), *Khrushchev Memoirs*, vol. 1: *Commissar*, p. 256.

31 Yuri Glazov, *The Russian Mind since Stalin's Death*, D. Reidel, 1985, p. 182.

32 Fröhlich (ed.), *Die Tagebücher von Joseph Goebbels*, Teil I, Band 7: *Juli 1939– März 1940*, entry for 11 November 1939, pp. 190–91.

33 Ibid., entry for 16 December 1939, pp. 233–4, here p. 233.

34 Ibid., entry for 6 December 1939, pp. 221–3, here pp. 221–2.

35 Heinz Boberach (ed.), *Meldungen aus dem Reich 1938–1945. Die geheimen Lageberichte des Sicherheitsdienstes der SS*, vol. 3, Pawlak, 1984, p. 524.

36 *Documents on German Foreign Policy*, Series D, vol. VIII: *The War Years, September 4, 1939–March 18, 1940*, Document 663, The Führer and Chancellor to Benito Mussolini, 8 March 1940, pp. 871–80, here p. 877.

37 *Völkischer Beobachter*, Norddeutsche Ausgabe, 9 December 1939, p. 2.

38 *Documents on German Foreign Policy*, Series D, vol. VIII: *The War Years, September 4, 1939–March 18, 1940*, Document 663, pp. 871–80, here p. 877.

39 Service, *Stalin*, p. 340.

40 *Völkischer Beobachter*, 3 July 1934.

41 *Deutsche Allgemeine Zeitung*, no. 302, 2 July 1934.

42 The Nazis did however enact legislation such as the Law for the Restoration of the Professional Civil Service in April 1933, which targeted Jews and communists for removal from the civil service. Under pressure from President von Hindenburg, exceptions were made for those who had served at the front in the First World War or had lost a relative in the war.

43 BArch, N 28/4, quoted in German in Klaus-Jürgen Müller, *General Ludwig Beck. Studien und Dokumente zur politisch-militärischen Vorstellungswelt und Tätigkeit des Generalstabschefs des deutschen Heeres 1933–1938*, Harald Boldt, 1980, pp. 498–501. Note that it is not certain who Beck intended this document for.

44 Hildegard von Kotze (ed.), *Heeresadjutant bei Hitler 1938–1943. Aufzeichnungen des Majors Engel*, Deutsche Verlags-Anstalt, 1974, pp. 67f. A copy of the diary is in the Institut für Zeitgeschichte, Munich (henceforth IfZ), ED 53.

45 Burdick and Jacobsen (eds.), *Halder War Diary*, entry for 3 November 1939, p. 76.

46 *Hitler's Table Talk*, entry for evening of 18 January 1942, p. 221.

47 Richard Giziowski, *The Enigma of General Blaskowitz*, Leo Cooper, 1997, p. 172.

48 Kershaw, *Nemesis*, pp. 269–70.

49 Domarus, *Hitler. Reden und Proklamationen*, Band II: *Untergang, Erster Halb-band 1939–1940*, Hitler speech of 23 November 1939, taken from notes subsequently found in the possession of the Wehrmacht High Command, pp. 1422–6.

50 Generalfeldmarschall Fedor von Bock, *The War Diary 1939–1945*, Schiffer, 1996, entry for 23 November 1939, p. 88.

51 Bericht zur innenpolitischen Lage (Nr. 15) 13 November 1939, in Boberach (ed.), *Meldungen aus dem Reich*, vol. 3, pp. 449–56.

52 Bock, *War Diary*, entry for 24 October 1939, p. 75.

53 Leonidas E. Hill (ed.), *Die Weizsäcker-Papiere 1933–1950*, Propyläen-Verlag, 1974, note from Ernst von Weizsäcker, 17 October 1939, p. 180.

54 Adam Tooze, *Wages of Destruction: The Making and Breaking of the Nazi Econ-omy*, Penguin Books, 2007, p. 368.

55 Ernest R. May, *Strange Victory: Hitler's Conquest of France*, I. B. Tauris, 2000, p. 413.

56 Winston S. Churchill, *The Second World War*, vol. II: *Their Finest Hour*, Penguin Books, 2005, p. 38.

57 Gorodetsky (ed.), *Maisky Diaries*, entry for 15 May 1940, p. 278.

58 Tooze, *Wages of Destruction*, p. 370.

59 Bock, *War Diary*, entry for 25 June 1940, p. 181.

60 Elke Fröhlich (ed.), *Die Tagebücher von Joseph Goebbels*, Teil I: *Aufzeichnungen 1923–1941*, Band 4: *März–November 1937*, K. G. Saur, 2000, entry for 10 July 1937, p. 214.

61 Kershaw, *Nemesis*, p. 300; Wolfgang Benz, *Die 101 wichtigsten Fragen. Das Dritte Reich*, C. H. Beck, 2013, Kindle edn, location 1267.

4. Dreams and Nightmares

1 Edward Crankshaw, *Khrushchev Remembers*, André Deutsch, 1974, pp. 156–7.

2 Khrushchev (ed.), *Khrushchev Memoirs*, vol. 1: *Commissar*, p. 266.

3 Sevket Akyildiz, ' "Learn, Learn, Learn!" Soviet Style in Uzbekistan: Implementation and Planning', in Sevket Akyildiz and Richard Carlson (eds.), *Social and Cultural Change in Central Asia: The Soviet Legacy*, Rout-ledge, 2014, p. 16.

4 Geoffrey Roberts, *Stalin's General: The Life of Georgy Zhukov*, Icon Books, 2013, Kindle edn, location 1471–8.

5 Carl Van Dyke, 'The Timoshenko Reforms: March–July 1940', *Journal of Slavic Military Studies*, vol. 9, no. 1 (March 1996), p. 87. Also quoted in Richard Overy, *Russia's War*, Allen Lane, 1997, p. 58.

6 Marius Broekmeyer, *Stalin, the Russians, and Their War*, University of Wisconsin Press, 2004, p. 55.

7 Van Dyke, 'Timoshenko', pp. 69–96.

8 Previously unpublished testimony.

9 Alex Danchev and Daniel Todman (eds.), *War Diaries 1939–1945: Field Marshal Lord Alanbrooke*, Phoenix, 2002, entry for 23 May 1940, p. 68.

10 Gorodetsky (ed.), *Maisky Diaries*, entries of 20 May and 10 July 1940, pp. 279 and 296.

11 Friedrich Kellner, *My Opposition: The Diary of Friedrich Kellner*, ed. Robert Scott Kellner, Cambridge University Press, 2018, p. 79. Kellner was a civil servant in southern Germany, a Social Democrat, who kept a secret diary.

12 Previously unpublished testimony.

13 Previously unpublished testimony.

14 Burdick and Jacobsen (eds.), *Halder War Diary*, entry for 13 July 1940, p. 227.

15 General Franz Halder, 'Spruchkammeraussage', 20 September 1948, IfZ, ZS 240/6, pp. 23–4.

16 Burdick and Jacobsen (eds.), *Halder War Diary*, entry for 3 July 1940, pp. 220–21.

17 Kershaw, *Nemesis*, p. 307.

18 Burdick and Jacobsen (eds.), *Halder War Diary*, entry for 13 July 1940, p. 227.

19 Domarus, *Hitler. Reden und Proklamationen*, Band II: *Untergang, Erster Halbband 1939–1940*, Hitler speech to Reichstag, 19 July 1940, pp. 1553, 1558.

20 Burdick and Jacobsen (eds.), *Halder War Diary*, entry for 31 July 1940, pp. 241–6.

21 Ibid., entry for 6 August 1940, p. 246.

22 Previously unpublished testimony.

23 Bock, *War Diary*, entry for 12–13 August 1940, p. 187.

24 William L. Shirer, *End of a Berlin Diary*, Rosetta Books, 2016, entry for 2 November 1946, p. 140.

25 Rees, *Nazis*, p. 85.

26 Ibid.

27 Gibson (ed.), *Ciano Diaries*, entry for 13 May 1941, p. 351.

28 Burdick and Jacobsen (eds.), *Halder War Diary*, entry for 1 November 1940, pp. 272–3.

29 Ibid., entry for 4 November 1940, p. 279.

30 Hitler, Directive no. 18, 12 November 1940, in Gerhard L. Weinberg, *Germany and the Soviet Union, 1939–1941*, E. J. Brill, 1954, p. 137.

31 Ivo Banac (ed.), *The Diary of Georgi Dimitrov 1933–1949*, Yale University Press, 2003, entry for 7 November 1940, p. 133.

32 Ibid., p. 134.

33 Valentin M. Berezhkov, *At Stalin's Side: His Interpreter's Memoirs from the October Revolution to the Fall of the Dictator's Empire*, Birch Lane Press, 1994, p. 7.

34 Ribbentrop and Molotov meeting, 12 November 1940, Memorandum of conversation, BArch, RM 41/40, online at http://www.worldfuturefund. org/wffmaster/Reading/Germany/Hitler-Molotov%20Meetings.htm.

35 Gabriel Gorodetsky, *Grand Delusion: Stalin and the German Invasion of Russia*, Yale University Press, 1999, p. 58.

36 Berezhkov, *At Stalin's Side*, p. 8.

37 Winston S. Churchill, *The Second World War*, vol. I: *The Gathering Storm*, Penguin Books, 2002, p. 121.

38 Kwok-sing Li, *A Glossary of Political Terms of the People's Republic of China*, The Chinese University of Hong Kong, 1995, p. 325.

39 Pavlov, 'Avtobiographicheskii Zametki', pp. 104–5.

40 Major Gerhard Engel, *At the Heart of the Reich: The Secret Diary of Hitler's Army Adjutant*, Frontline Books, 2017, entry for 15 November 1940, Kindle edn, location 1794.

41 Burdick and Jacobsen (eds.), *Halder War Diary*, entry for 16 November 1940, p. 283.

42 Jana Richter (ed.), *Die Tagebücher von Joseph Goebbels*, Teil I: *Aufzeichnungen 1923–1941*, Band 8: *April–November 1940*, K. G. Saur, 1998, entry for 18 November 1940, p. 425.

43 Ibid., entry for 14 November 1940, pp. 417–18.

44 Kotkin, *Stalin*, vol. 2: *Waiting for Hitler*, p. 764.

45 Ian Kershaw, *Fateful Choices: Ten Decisions that Changed the World, 1940–1941*, Allen Lane, 2007, p. 69.

46 *Documents on German Foreign Policy 1918–1945*, Series D, vol. XI: *The War Years, September 1, 1940–January 31, 1941*, United States Government Printing Office, 1960, Document 532, 18 December 1940, p. 899.

5. Hitler's War of Annihilation

1 International War Crimes Tribunal, Nuremberg, IMG, para 481 (statement of Erich von dem Bach-Zelewski, 7 January 1946), https://avalon. law.yale.edu/imt/01-07-46.asp. Bach-Zelewski wrongly dates the meeting to earlier in 1941, but Himmler's desk diary confirms that the meeting was in June just prior to the invasion. See Peter Witte et al. (eds.), *Der Dienstkalender Heinrich Himmlers 1941/42*, Christians, 1999, pp. 171–2. This figure of '30 million' was also used by Göring in late 1941, according to Count Ciano. See *Les Archives secrètes du Comte Ciano 1936–1942*, Librairie Plon, 1948, pp. 478–9. See also Peter Longerich, *Holocaust: The Nazi Persecution and Murder of the Jews*, Oxford University Press, 2010, p. 181.

2 Engel, *Diary*, entry for 18 December 1940, Kindle edn, location 1807.

3 Percy Ernst Schramm and Hans-Adolf Jacobsen (eds.), *Kriegstagebuch des Oberkommandos der Wehrmacht (Wehrmachtführungsstab)*, Band I: *1. August 1940–31. Dezember 1941*, Bernard & Graefe, 1965, entry for 9 January 1941, pp. 253–9, here p. 258.

4 Georg Thomas, *Geschichte der deutschen Wehr- und Rüstungswirtschaft (1918–1943/45)*, Harald Boldt Verlag, 1966, pp. 515–32. There is a great deal of academic discussion about this memo. See, for instance, Rolf-Dieter Müller, 'Von der Wirtschaftsallianz zum kolonialen Ausbeutung', in Militärgeschichtliches Forschungsamt (ed.), *Das Deutsche Reich und der Zweite Weltkrieg*, vol. 4.1: *Der Angriff auf die Sowjetunion*, Deutsche Verlags-Anstalt, 1983, pp. 98–326, here p. 126. Heinrich Uhlig, 'Das Einwirken Hitlers auf Planung und Führung des Ostfeldzuges', in *Vollmacht des Gewissens*, vol. 2, Alfred Metzner, 1965, pp. 147–286, here pp. 209–10. Christian Gerlach, *Kalkulierte Morde. Die deutsche Wirtschafts- und Vernichtungspolitik in Weißrußland 1941 bis 1944*, Hamburger Edition, 1999, p. 67.

5 Uhlig, 'Das Einwirken Hitlers auf Planung und Führung des Ostfeldzuges', pp. 210–11.

6 Kershaw, *Nemesis*, p. 345.

7 Bock, *War Diary*, entries for 31 January 1941 and 1 February 1941, pp. 196–8.

8 Ibid., entry for 3 December 1940, p. 193.

9 Max Domarus, *Hitler. Reden und Proklamationen 1932–1945. Kommentiert von einem deutschen Zeitgenossen*, Band II: *Untergang, Zweiter Halbband 1941–1945*, R. Löwit, 1965, Hitler speech 9 January 1941, p. 1653.

10 Gibson (ed.), *Ciano Diaries*, entry for 19 January 1941, p. 338.

11 Ibid., entry for 20 January 1941, p. 338.

12 David Stahel, *Operation Barbarossa and Germany's Defeat in the East*, Cambridge University Press, 2012, p. 73.

13 Kershaw, *Nemesis*, p. 146.

14 Bock, *War Diary*, entry for 14 December 1940, p. 195.

15 Winston S. Churchill, *The Second World War*, vol. III: *The Grand Alliance*, Penguin Books, 2005, p. 316.

16 Kotkin, *Stalin*, vol. 2: *Waiting for Hitler*, p. 841.

17 Gorodetsky, *Grand Delusion*, p. 53.

18 Bellamy, *Absolute War*, p. 141.

19 Previously unpublished testimony.

20 Evan Mawdsley, 'Crossing the Rubicon: Soviet Plans for Offensive War in 1940–1941', *International History Review*, vol. 25 (2003), p. 853. Also Kershaw, *Fateful Choices*, p. 280. And Roberts, *Stalin's General*, Kindle edn, location 1857–70.

21 Elke Fröhlich (ed.), *Die Tagebücher von Joseph Goebbels*, Teil I: *Aufzeichnungen 1923–1941*, Band 9: *Dezember 1940–Juli 1941*, K. G. Saur, 1998, entry for 7 May 1941, p. 296

22 Ibid., entry for 9 May 1941, p. 301.

23 Burdick and Jacobsen (eds.), *Halder War Diary*, entry for 30 March 1941, p. 346.

24 Note that General Warlimont subsequently said that those present had mostly accepted what Hitler said. Kershaw, *Nemesis*, p. 356.

25 Previously unpublished testimony.

26 Gerd R. Ueberschär and Wolfram Wette (eds.), *Der deutsche Überfall auf die Sowjetunion. 'Unternehmen Barbarossa' 1941*, Fischer Taschenbuch, 2011, p. 251. Original in BArch, RH 24-56/149.

27 Hans-Heinrich Wilhelm, *Rassenpolitik und Kriegführung: Sicherheitspolizei und Wehrmacht in Polen und in der Sowjetunion 1939–1942*, R. Rothe, 1991, pp. 133–40, here pp. 133–4, 138–9. Original in BArch, RH 20-18/71, AOK 18/Ia Nr. 406/41, g.Kdos.

28 Bock, *War Diary*, entry for 7 June 1941, pp. 219–20.

29 Field Marshal Erich von Manstein, *Lost Victories*, Zenith, 2004 (first published Athenaum-Verlag, 1955), p. 180.

30 Benoît Lemay, *Erich von Manstein: Hitler's Master Strategist*, Casemate, 2010, Kindle edn, pp. 251–3.

31 Manstein, *Lost Victories*, p. 179.

32 Michael Burleigh, *Moral Combat: A History of World War II*, HarperPress, 2010, p. 239.

33 Bock, *War Diary*, entry for 14 June 1941, pp. 220–22.

34 Alex J. Kay, 'Germany's Staatssekretäre, Mass Starvation and the Meeting of 2 May 1941', *Journal of Contemporary History*, vol. 41, no. 4 (2006), pp. 685–9. Also see the work of Gerlach, *Kalkulierte Morde*.

35 See above p. 91.

36 Stenographic report of the meeting of Reich Marshal Göring with the Reich commissioners for the occupied territories and military commanders on the food situation; at the Ministry of Aviation, Thursday 6 August 1942, 4 p.m., Léon Poliakov and Joseph Wulf, *Das Dritte Reich und seine Diener*, Ullstein, 1983, pp. 471ff. Also in Document 170-USSR, in *Der Prozess gegen die Hauptkriegsverbrecher vor dem Internationalen Militärgerichtshof, Nürnberg, 14. November 1945–1. Oktober 1946*, Band XXIX, Sekretariat des Gerichtshofs, 1949, pp. 385ff. (Translation here is the official one used at the Nuremberg trials.)

37 Götz Aly and Susanne Heim, *Architects of Annihilation: Auschwitz and the Logic of Destruction*, Weidenfeld & Nicolson, 2002, p. 239.

38 Ibid., p. 242.

39 Ibid., p. 237.

40 Fröhlich (ed.), *Die Tagebücher von Joseph Goebbels*, Teil I, Band 9: *Dezember 1940–Juli 1941*, entry for 29 March 1941, pp. 209–11.

41 See above p. xxx.

42 Rees, *Nazis*, p. 174.

43 Helmut Krausnick, Hans Buchheim, Martin Broszat and Hans-Adolf Jacobsen, *Anatomy of the SS State*, Collins, 1968, pp. 62–3.

44 Khrushchev (ed.), *Khrushchev Memoirs*, vol. 1: *Commissar*, p. 272.

45 Gorodetsky, *Grand Delusion*, p. 174.

46 Dilks (ed.), *Cadogan Diaries*, entry for 6 January 1941, p. 347.

47 Quoted in editorial comments in Gorodetsky (ed.), *Maisky Diaries*, pp. 361–2.

48 Ibid., entry for 18 June 1941, p. 363.

49 Presidential Archive, Moscow, f. 3, op. 50, d. 415, l. 1, 50–52. Here, Bellamy, *Absolute War*, pp. 146–7.

50 Broekmeyer, *Stalin, the Russians, and Their War*, p. 32.

51 Fröhlich (ed.), *Die Tagebücher von Joseph Goebbels*, Teil I, Band 9: *Dezember 1940–Juli 1941*, entry for 16 June 1941, pp. 376–80.

52 Previously unpublished testimony.

53 Bullock, *Hitler and Stalin: Parallel Lives*, p. 768.

54 Gibson (ed.), *Ciano Diaries*, entry for 21 June 1941, pp. 368–9.

55 Fröhlich (ed.), *Die Tagebücher von Joseph Goebbels*, Teil I, Band 9: *Dezember 1940–Juli 1941*, entry for 22 June 1941, pp. 395–6.

6. Invasion

1 Previously unpublished testimony.
2 Hilger and Meyer, *Incompatible Allies*, p. 336.
3 Service, *Stalin*, p. 410.
4 Previously unpublished testimony, and Rees, *Nazis*, p. 170.
5 Kershaw, *Nemesis*, p. 393. Bellamy, *Absolute War*, pp. 172–7.
6 Bernd Bonwetsch, 'Stalin, the Red Army and the "Great Patriotic War"', in Kershaw and Lewin (eds.), *Stalinism and Nazism*, pp. 185–6.
7 Simonov, *Glazami cheloveka moego pokoleniia*, pp. 291–306, discussed in ibid., p. 193.
8 Khrushchev (ed.), *Khrushchev Memoirs*, vol. 1: *Commissar*, p. 311.
9 Previously unpublished testimony.
10 Previously unpublished testimony.
11 Antony Beevor and Luba Vinogradova (eds.), *A Writer at War: Vasily Grossman with the Red Army 1941–1945*, Harvill Press, 2005, p. 12.
12 Previously unpublished testimony.
13 Anastas Mikoyan, *Tak Bylo*, Vagrius, 1999, pp. 390–92.
14 Khrushchev (ed.), *Khrushchev Memoirs*, vol. 1: *Commissar*, p. 304.
15 Overy, *Russia's War*, p. 78, and Service, *Stalin*, pp. 414–15, are two examples of works that explore the possibilities.
16 Mikoyan, *Tak Bylo*, p. 390.
17 Sergo Beria, *Beria, My Father: Inside Stalin's Kremlin*, ed. Françoise Thom, Duckworth, 2003, p. 71.
18 *Pravda*, 19 December 1939; in English in Overy, *Dictators*, p. 98.
19 Heinz Guderian, *Panzer Leader*, Penguin Books, 2009, p. 158.
20 Burdick and Jacobsen (eds.), *Halder War Diary*, entry for 3 July 1941, p. 446.
21 Friedrich Kellner, *My Opposition: The Diary of Friedrich Kellner*, ed. Robert Scott Kellner, Cambridge University Press, 2018, entries for 28 June 1941 and 30 June 1941, p. 127.
22 Gorodetsky (ed.), *Maisky Diaries*, entry for 27 June 1941, p. 368.
23 George Orwell, *Diaries*, ed. Peter Davison, Penguin Books, 2010, entry for 23 June 1941, p. 316.

24 Robert Sherwood, *Roosevelt and Hopkins: An Intimate History*, Enigma Books, 2001, Stimson to Roosevelt, 23 June 1941, pp. 204–5.

25 Online at https://www.jewishvirtuallibrary.org/secretary-of-state-welles-statement-on-germany-s-attack-on-the-soviet-union-june-1941.

26 Online at https://www.jewishvirtuallibrary.org/churchill-broadcast-on-the-soviet-german-war-june-1941.

27 Constantine Pleshakov, *Stalin's Folly: The Tragic First Ten Days of World War II on the Eastern Front*, Houghton Mifflin, 2005, p. 99.

28 Evan Mawdsley, *Thunder in the East: The Nazi–Soviet War 1941–1945*, Bloomsbury, 2nd edn, 2016, p. 61.

29 Oleh Romaniv and Inna Fedushchak, *Zakhidnoukrains'ka trahediia 1941*, Naukove tovarystvo im. Shevchenka, 2002, p. 155.

30 Previously unpublished testimony, and see Rees, *Behind Closed Doors*, p. 92.

31 Applebaum, *Gulag*, pp. 377–80.

32 This figure from Bellamy, *Absolute War*, p. 194. Also see Tomas Balkelis, 'Ethnicity and Identity in the Memoirs of Lithuanian Children Deported to the Gulag', in Violeta Davoliūtė and Tomas Balkelis (eds.), *Narratives of Exile and Identity: Soviet Deportation Memoirs from the Baltic States*, Central European University Press, 2018, pp. 41–64. Balkelis writes (p. 45) that around 5,500 children were deported from Lithuania by the Soviets in the first wave in June 1941, including more than 900 under the age of four.

33 Gellately, *Lenin, Stalin and Hitler*, p. 395.

34 https://www.jewishvirtuallibrary.org/stalin-speaks-to-the-people-of-the-soviet-union-on-german-invasion-july-1941.

35 Many of the interviewees I met who had lived through the war in the former Soviet Union certainly remembered.

36 https://www.jewishvirtuallibrary.org/stalin-speaks-to-the-people-of-the-soviet-union-on-german-invasion-july-1941.

37 Sarah Davies, *Popular Opinion in Stalin's Russia: Terror, Propaganda and Dissent 1934–1941*, Cambridge University Press, 1997, p. 81.

38 Steven Merritt Miner, *Stalin's Holy War: Religion, Nationalism, and Alliance Politics 1941–1945*, University of North Carolina Press, 2003, p. 217.

39 *Hitler's Table Talk*, night of 5–6 July 1941, p. 5.

40 Ibid., evening of 17 September and night of 17–18 September 1941, p. 33.

41 Ibid., p. 34.

42 Previously unpublished testimony.

43 Previously unpublished testimony, but also see Rees, *Their Darkest Hour*, pp. 35–40.

44 Anne Applebaum, *Red Famine: Stalin's War on Ukraine*, Allen Lane, 2017, pp. 132–4.

45 Ibid., p. 227.

46 The United States Holocaust Memorial Museum gives a figure of 4,000. Christopher Browning suggests 5,000: Browning, *Origins of the Final Solution*, p. 268.

47 Previously unpublished testimony.

48 Browning, *Origins of the Final Solution*, p. 268.

49 Rees, *Holocaust*, pp. 207–8.

50 Barry A. Leach, *German Strategy against Russia 1939–1941*, Oxford University Press, 1973, pp. 204–5.

51 Burdick and Jacobsen (eds.), *Halder War Diary*, entry for 11 August 1941, p. 506.

52 Schramm and Jacobsen (eds.), *Kriegstagebuch des Oberkommandos der Wehrmacht*, Band I: *1. August 1940–31 Dezember 1941*, pp. 1063–8.

53 Elke Fröhlich (ed.), *Die Tagebücher von Joseph Goebbels*, Teil II: *Diktate 1941–1945*, Band 1: *Juli–September 1941*, K. G. Saur, 1996, entry for 19 August 1941, pp. 261–2.

54 Ibid., p. 262.

55 See above p. xxiv.

56 Previously unpublished testimony.

57 Poul Grooss, *The Naval War in the Baltic 1939–1945*, Seaforth Publishing, 2018, p. 151.

58 Anna Reid, *Leningrad: Tragedy of a City under Siege 1941–44*, Bloomsbury, 2011, p. 70.

59 Korvettenkapitän Wehr, 'Die Minenschlacht vor Reval', *Marine Rundschau. Monatsschrift für Seewesen*, vol. 47 (October 1942), pp. 713–23.

60 Grooss, *Naval War*, p. 151.

61 Reid, *Leningrad*, p. 72.

62 Previously unpublished testimony, and Rees, *Nazis*, p. 185.

63 Roberts, *Zhukov*, Kindle edn, location 2088.

64 Ibid., location 2094–102.

65 Alexander Hill, *The Great Patriotic War of the Soviet Union 1941–45: A Documentary Reader*, Routledge, 2010, Document 33, Order of the Headquarters of the Supreme High Command of the Red Army Number 270, 16 August 1941, pp. 55–6.

66 Geoffrey Roberts, *Stalin's Wars: From World War to Cold War 1939–1953*, Yale University Press, 2006, p. 101.

67 Ibid., pp. 101–2.

68 Mawdsley, *Thunder in the East*, p. 78.

69 Khrushchev (ed.), *Khrushchev Memoirs*, vol. 1: *Commissar*, p. 315.

70 Ibid., p. 349.

71 Ibid., pp. 314–15.

72 Gorodetsky (ed.), *Maisky Diaries*, entry for 20 July 1941, p. 374.

73 Patrick J. Maney, *The Roosevelt Presence: The Life and Legacy of FDR*, University of California Press, 1992, p. 82.

74 Rees, *Behind Closed Doors*, pp. 128–9.

75 Ibid., p. 130.

76 Sherwood, *Roosevelt and Hopkins*, pp. 331–2. This quote is from an article Hopkins wrote after meeting Stalin.

77 Ibid., p. 317.

78 Ibid., p. 327.

79 Bellamy, *Absolute War*, p. 261.

80 Previously unpublished testimony.

81 Previously unpublished testimony.

82 Ernst Klee, Willi Dressen and Volker Riess (eds.), *'The Good Old Days': The Holocaust as Seen by Its Perpetrators and Bystanders*, Konecky & Konecky, 1991, pp. 66–7.

83 Anatoly Podolsky, 'The Tragic Fate of Ukrainian Jewish Women under Nazi Occupation, 1941–1944', in Sonja M. Hedgepeth and Rochelle G. Saidel (eds.), *Sexual Violence against Jewish Women during the Holocaust*, Brandeis University Press and University Press of New England, 2010, pp. 94–107, here p. 99. Also see Rees, *Holocaust*, p. 220.

84 Previously unpublished testimony.

85 Previously unpublished testimony.

7. Desperate Days

1 Fröhlich (ed.), *Die Tagebücher von Joseph Goebbels*, Teil II, Band 1: *Juli–September 1941*, entry for 24 September 1941, pp. 476–87, here pp. 481–2.

2 *Hitler's Table Talk*, evening of 17 September and night of 17–18 September 1941, p. 32.

3 Burdick and Jacobsen (eds.), *Halder War Diary*, entry for 17 May 1940, p. 149.

4 Also see Rees, *Dark Charisma*, pp. 271–4, for a discussion of this phenomenon.

5 Reid, *Leningrad*, p. 114.

6 Gorodetsky (ed.), *Maisky Diaries*, entry for 4 September 1941, p. 386.

7 Ibid., entry for 15 September 1941, p. 391.

8 Warren F. Kimball (ed.), *Churchill and Roosevelt: The Complete Correspondence*, 3 vols., Princeton University Press, 1984, vol. I, Churchill message of 5 September 1941, C–114x, p. 238.

9 David Stahel, *Operation Typhoon: Hitler's March on Moscow, October 1941*, Cambridge University Press, 2013, pp. 233–4.

10 Beevor and Vinogradova (eds.), *A Writer at War*, p. 43.

11 Niklas Zetterling and Anders Frankson, *The Drive on Moscow 1941: Operation Taifun and Germany's First Great Crisis of World War II*, Casemate, 2012, Kindle edn, location 1001–13.

12 Hans Schäufler (ed.), *Knight's Cross Panzers: The German 35th Tank Regiment in World War II*, Stackpole Books, 2010, p. 127.

13 Reid, *Leningrad*, p. 153.

14 Nicolaus von Below, *At Hitler's Side: The Memoirs of Hitler's Luftwaffe Adjutant 1937–1945*, Frontline Books, 2010, p. 114.

15 Domarus, *Hitler. Reden und Proklamationen*, Band II: *Untergang, Zweiter Halbband 1941–1945*, Hitler speech of 3 October 1941, pp. 1762–3.

16 Elke Fröhlich (ed.), *Die Tagebücher von Joseph Goebbels*, Teil II: *Diktate 1941–1945*, Band 2: *Oktober–Dezember 1941*, K. G. Saur, 1996, entry for 5 October 1941, pp. 57–63, here pp. 58, 60–62.

17 Rees, *Behind Closed Doors*, p. 108.

18 *Preussische Zeitung*, vol. 11, no. 281, 10 October 1941, p. 1.

19 *Völkischer Beobachter*, issue 283, vol. 54, 10 October 1941, pp. 1–2.

20 Fröhlich (ed.), *Die Tagebücher von Joseph Goebbels*, Teil II, Band 2: *Oktober–Dezember 1941*, entry for 10 October 1941, pp. 84–90, here pp. 87, 89–90.

21 Stahel, *Operation Typhoon*, pp. 77–8.

22 Previously unpublished testimony, but also see Rees, *Nazis*, pp. 186–7.

23 David M. Glantz, *Operation Barbarossa: Hitler's Invasion of Russia 1941*, The History Press, 2011, p. 145.

24 Previously unpublished testimony.

25 Beevor and Vinogradova (eds.), *A Writer at War*, entry for 4 October 1941, p. 48.

26 Rees, *War of the Century*, pp. 55–6.

27 Pavel Sudoplatov, *Special Tasks*, Warner Books, 1995, pp. 145–7.

28 Volkogonov, *Stalin: Triumph and Tragedy*, pp. 412–13.

29 Rees, *War of the Century*, Document 34 of the State Defence Committee, 15 October 1941, pp. 71–2.

30 Previously unpublished testimony.

31 Andrew Nagorski, *The Greatest Battle: Stalin, Hitler, and the Desperate Struggle for Moscow*, Simon & Schuster, 2007, Kindle edn, location 3176–82.

32 Mikhail M. Gorinov, 'Muscovites' Moods, 22 June 1941 to May 1942', in Robert W. Thurston and Bernd Bonwetsch (eds.), *The People's War: Responses to World War II in the Soviet Union*, University of Illinois Press, 2000, p. 124.

33 Previously unpublished testimony.

34 Banac (ed.), *Diary of Georgi Dimitrov*, entry for 15 October 1941, p. 197.

35 Previously unpublished testimony.

36 Beevor and Vinogradova (eds.), *A Writer at War*, p. 52.

37 Bock, *War Diary*, entry for 21 October 1941, pp. 337–8.

38 Ibid., entry for 31 October 1941, p. 347.

39 Klaus Schüler, 'The Eastern Campaign as a Transportation and Supply Problem', in Bernd Wegner (ed.), *From Peace to War: Germany, Soviet Russia, and the World 1939–1941*, Berghahn Books, 1997, p. 216.

40 Tooze, *Wages of Destruction*, pp. 498–9.

41 *Hitler's Table Talk*, evening of 17 October, pp. 69–70.

42 Ibid., night of 17–18 October 1941, p. 71.

43 Ibid., night of 21–22 October 1941, p. 83.

44 Ibid., p. 82.

45 See above pp. 194–5.

46 Richard Overy, 'Statistics', in I. C. B. Dear and M. R. D. Foot (eds.), *The Oxford Companion to the Second World War*, Oxford University Press, 1995, p. 1060.

47 Previously unpublished testimony.

48 *Voenno-istoricheskii Zhurnal*, no. 10 (1991), pp. 335–41. Also see Rees, *War of the Century*, p. 73.

49 See, for example, the conversation Nikolay Ponomariev witnessed between Stalin and Zhukov, Rees, *War of the Century*, pp. 70–71.

50 Roberts, *Zhukov*, Kindle edn, location 2494.

51 Lev Lopukhovsky, *The Viaz'ma Catastrophe, 1941: The Red Army's Disastrous Stand against Operation Typhoon*, Helion, 2013, p. 488.

52 Previously unpublished testimony.

53 Bellamy, *Absolute War*, p. 304.

54 Stalin speech on 7 November 1941, online at https://www.ibiblio.org/pha/timeline/411107awp.html.

55 Gorinov, 'Muscovites' Moods', p. 126.

56 Bock, *War Diary*, entry for 5 November 1941, p. 350.

8. A World War

1 Domarus, *Hitler. Reden und Proklamationen*, Band II: *Untergang, Zweiter Halbband 1941–1945*, Hitler speech at the Löwenbräukeller on the evening of Saturday 8 November 1941, p. 1772.

2 Ibid., pp. 1773–9.

3 Ibid., pp. 1776–81.

4 Jean Ancel, *The History of the Holocaust in Romania*, University of Nebraska Press and Yad Vashem, 2011, p. 325.

5 Ibid., p. 356.

6 Browning, *Origins of the Final Solution*, p. 293.

7 Radu Ioanid, *The Holocaust in Romania: The Destruction of Jews and Gypsies under the Antonescu Regime 1940–1944*, Ivan R. Dee, 2008, Kindle edn, pp. 120–21.

8 Ancel, *Romania*, p. 361.

9 Ibid., p. 353.

10 Nicholas Stargardt, *The German War: A Nation under Arms 1939–45*, Vintage, 2016, pp. 174–5. As Stargardt reminds us, Reichenau was 'one of the most Nazi of German generals' (p. 175) but this order was also reissued by Gerd von Rundstedt, commander of Army Group South, to all of the soldiers under his command.

11 Peter Longerich, *Heinrich Himmler*, Oxford University Press, 2012, pp. 552–3.

12 Browning, *Origins of the Final Solution*, pp. 323–4.

13 Overy, *Russia's War*, p. 233.

14 Guderian, *Panzer Leader*, p. 247.

15 Ueberschär and Wette (eds.), *Der deutsche Überfall auf die Sowjetunion*, pp. 308–9. Original in BArch, Alliierte Prozesse 9/NOKW-1535.

16 Fröhlich (ed.), *Die Tagebücher von Joseph Goebbels*, Teil II, Band 2: *Oktober–Dezember 1941*, entry for 22 November 1941, pp. 331–47, here pp. 336–8.

17 Ibid., entry for 30 November 1941, pp. 392–404, here pp. 398, 400, 403.

18 Konrad Heiden, *The Fuehrer*, Robinson, 1999, pp. 90–91.

19 Walter Rohland, *Bewegte Zeiten. Erinnerungen eines Eisenhüttenmannes*, Seewald, 1978, pp. 75–8.

20 Previously unpublished testimony, and testimony from Rees, *War of the Century*, pp. 77–8.

21 Bellamy, *Absolute War*, pp. 317–18.

22 Bock, *War Diary*, entry for 5 December 1941, p. 381.

23 Previously unpublished testimony.

24 Rees, *Behind Closed Doors*, p. 114, and previously unpublished testimony.

25 Previously unpublished testimony.

26 Bock, *War Diary*, entry for 7 December 1941, p. 383.

27 Kershaw, *Fateful Choices*, p. 396.

28 Kershaw, *Nemesis*, p. 442.

29 General Walter Warlimont, *Inside Hitler's Headquarters, 1939–1945*, Presidio Press, 1991, pp. 207–8.

30 Gibson (ed.), *Ciano Diaries*, entry for 8 December 1941, p. 416.

31 Domarus, *Hitler. Reden und Proklamationen*, Band II: *Untergang, Zweiter Halbband 1941–1945*, Hitler speech, 11 December 1941, pp. 1794–8.

32 Ibid., pp. 1801–8.

33 Ibid., pp. 1808–9.

34 Jeremy Noakes and Geoffrey Pridham (eds.), *Nazism 1919–1945: A Documentary Reader*, vol. 1: *The Rise to Power 1919–1934*, University of Exeter Press, 1991, p. 16.

35 Kershaw, *Nemesis*, p. 387.

36 Rees, *War of the Century*, quote from Goebbels diary, entry for 16 June 1941, on frontispiece.

37 Fröhlich (ed.), *Die Tagebücher von Joseph Goebbels*, Teil II, Band 2: *Oktober–Dezember 1941*, entry for 22 November 1941, pp. 331–47.

38 Below, *At Hitler's Side*, p. 120.

39 Bock, *War Diary*, entry for 16 December 1941, p. 396.

40 Guderian, *Panzer Leader*, p. 264.

41 Ibid., pp. 265–6, 268.

42 Previously unpublished testimony.

43 Fröhlich (ed.), *Die Tagebücher von Joseph Goebbels*, Teil II, Band 2: *Oktober–Dezember 1941*, entry for 13 December 1941, pp. 498–9.

44 Präg and Jacobmeyer (eds.), *Das Diensttagebuch des deutschen Generalgouverneurs in Polen*, pp. 452–9.

45 Georgii Kumanev, *Ryadom So Stalinym* (Next to Stalin): *Otkrovennye Svidetelstva*, Bilina, 1999, pp. 272–3.

46 Previously unpublished testimony.

47 Bernd Bonwetsch, 'War as a "Breathing Space": Soviet Intellectuals and the "Great Patriotic War"', in Thurston and Bonwetsch (eds.), *The People's War*, pp. 145–6.

48 *The Crime of Katyn: Facts and Documents*, Polish Cultural Foundation, 1989, p. 87.

49 David Reynolds and Vladimir Pechatnov (eds.), *The Kremlin Letters: Stalin's Wartime Correspondence with Churchill and Roosevelt*, Yale University Press, 2018, Stalin to Churchill, sent 8 November 1941, received 11 November 1941, pp. 67–8.

50 Gorodetsky (ed.), *Maisky Diaries*, entry for 11 November 1941, pp. 402–4.

51 Oleg A. Rzheshevsky (ed.), *War and Diplomacy: The Making of the Grand Alliance, from Stalin's Archives*, Routledge, 2016, Document 7, meeting of 17 December 1941, pp. 28–35.

52 Dilks (ed.), *Cadogan Diaries*, entry for 20 December 1941, p. 423.

53 Anthony Eden (Rt Hon the Earl of Avon, KG, PC, MC), *The Eden Memoirs: The Reckoning*, Cassell, 1965, p. 302.

54 Quoted in Ben Pimlott (ed.), *The Second World War Diary of Hugh Dalton 1940–45*, Jonathan Cape, 1986, entry for 13 January 1942, p. 348.

55 Dilks (ed.), *Cadogan Diaries*, entry for 17 December 1941, p. 422.

56 Gellately, *Stalin's Curse*, p. 103.

57 Eden telegram to Churchill, 5 January 1942, Public Record Office, Kew (PRO) PREM 3/399/7.

58 Churchill note to Eden, 7 January 1942 PRO FO 371/32864.

59 Eden, 17 December 1941, telegram to Churchill via Foreign Office, PRO FO 371/29655.

9. Hunger

1 For example, Reid, *Leningrad*, p. 3, suggests 750,000 as a single figure, and Cynthia Simmons and Nina Perlina, *Writing the Siege of Leningrad: Women's Diaries, Memoirs and Documentary Prose*, University of Pittsburgh Press, 2005, p. ix, suggest between 1.6 and 2 million in the 'Leningrad area' and 'no fewer than one million civilians' within the city.

2 *Stalin and the Betrayal of Leningrad*, produced by Martina Balazova, executive produced by Laurence Rees, transmitted on BBC TV in 2002.

3 Nadezhda Cherepenina, 'Assessing the Scale of Famine and Death in the Besieged City', in John Barber and Andrei Dzeniskevich (eds.), *Life and Death in Besieged Leningrad 1941–44*, Palgrave Macmillan, 2005, p. 52.

4 Reid, *Leningrad*, p. 106.

5 Antony Beevor, *The Second World War*, Weidenfeld & Nicolson, 2012, p. 203.

6 Militärgeschichtliches Forschungsamt (ed.), *Germany and the Second World War*, vol. IV: *The Attack on the Soviet Union*, Clarendon Press, 1998, pp. 644–6.

7 Burdick and Jacobsen (eds.), *Halder War Diary*, entry for 18 September 1941, p. 537.

8 Domarus, *Hitler. Reden und Proklamationen*, Band II: *Untergang, Zweiter Halbband 1941–1945*, letter from the Navy War Office to Army Group North, notifying them of Hitler's decision, 28 September 1941, p. 1755.

9 *Hitler's Table Talk*, night of 25–26 September 1941, p. 44.

10 Bellamy, *Absolute War*, letter to Leningrad authorities and Merkulov, 21 September 1941, pp. 356–7.

11 See above p. 18.

12 Reid, *Leningrad*, Lenin speech at All-Russian Food Conference in 1921, p. 166.

13 Sergey Yarov, *Leningrad 1941–1942: Morality in a City under Siege*, Polity Press, 2017, p. 43.

14 Ibid., p. 68. See also Alexis Peri, 'Queues, Canteens, and the Politics of Location in Diaries of the Leningrad Blockade, 1941–1942', in Wendy Z. Goldman and Donald Filtzer (eds.), *Hunger and War: Food Provisioning in the Soviet Union during World War II*, Indiana University Press, 2015, p. 196.

15 Simmons and Perlina, *Writing the Siege of Leningrad*, 'Diary of Anna Petrovna Ostroumova-Lebedeva, Artist', entry for 22 May 1942, p. 32.

16 Yarov, *Leningrad*, p. 231.

17 Elena Mukhina, *The Diary of Lena Mukhina: A Girl's Life in the Siege of Leningrad*, ed. and with a foreword by Valentin Kovalchuk, Aleksandr Rupasov and Aleksandr Chistikov, Pan Books, 2016, entry for 22 April 1942, p. 315.

18 *Stalin and the Betrayal of Leningrad*, BBC TV.

19 Simmons and Perlina, *Writing the Siege*, 'Diary of Vera Sergeevna Kostrovitskaia, Ballerina and Dance Teacher', April 1942, p. 51.

20 Reid, *Leningrad*, p. 287.

21 This figure from Reid, *Leningrad*, p. 288, but Bellamy, *Absolute War*, p. 380, quotes a figure of 1,500 arrested for cannibalism. Also note that there was

no specific offence of 'cannibalism' under Soviet law so offenders were charged with other crimes like 'banditry'.

22 Elena Kochina, *Blockade Diary: Under Siege in Leningrad 1941–1942*, Ardis, 2014, entry for 7 February 1942, p. 86.

23 Dmitry S. Likhachev, *Reflections on the Russian Soul: A Memoir*, Central European Press, 2000, p. 244. Also quoted in Reid, *Leningrad*, p. 194. But see also Likhachev's memories of the siege, in *Reflections*, pp. 216–62.

24 Kochina, *Blockade Diary*, entry for 3 October 1941, p. 42.

25 Ibid., entry for 2 January 1942, p. 68.

26 Ibid., entry for 28 January 1942, p. 82.

27 Previously unpublished testimony.

28 Armee-Befehl des Oberbefehlshabers der 6. Armee, 28 September 1941, quoted in Jeff Rutherford, *Combat and Genocide on the Eastern Front: The German Infantry's War 1941–1944*, Cambridge University Press, 2014, p. 170.

29 Previously unpublished testimony.

30 Karel C. Berkhoff, *Harvest of Despair: Life and Death in Ukraine under Nazi Rule*, Harvard University Press, 2004, p. 166.

31 Previously unpublished testimony.

32 Tooze, *Wages of Destruction*, pp. 482–3.

33 Christian Streit, 'Soviet Prisoners of War in the Hands of the Wehrmacht', in Hannes Heer and Klaus Naumann (eds.), *War of Extermination: The German Military in World War II 1941–1944*, Berghahn Books, 2009, p. 82. Also Ueberschär and Wette (eds.), *Der deutsche Überfall auf die Sowjetunion*, pp. 308–9. Original in BArch, Alliierte Prozesse 9/NOKW-1535.

34 Gibson (ed.), *Ciano Diaries*, entry for 25 November 1941, p. 411.

35 Previously unpublished testimony.

36 Previously unpublished testimony.

37 Omer Bartov, *The Eastern Front 1941–45: German Troops and the Barbarisation of Warfare*, Palgrave, 2001, pp. 116–17.

38 Rees, *War of the Century*, p. 67.

39 Previously unpublished testimony.

40 Rees, *Auschwitz*, p. 57.

41 Ibid., p. 80.

42 Previously unpublished testimony.

43 Hoess, *Commandant of Auschwitz*, pp. 121–3.

44 Previously unpublished testimony.

45 Isaiah Trunk, *Łódź Ghetto: A History*, Indiana University Press, 2008, p. 109.

46 Browning, *Path to Genocide*, pp. 31–42. There had been ghetto factories before this date, but it was only at this point that their capacity exponentially increased.

47 Alan Adelson and Robert Lapides (eds.), *Łódź Ghetto: Inside a Community under Siege*, Penguin Books, 1989, pp. 182–3.

48 Browning, *Origins of the Final Solution*, p. 321.

49 Guderian, *Panzer Leader*, p. 266.

50 See above p. 118.

51 Applebaum, *Gulag*, p. 118.

52 Golfo Alexopoulos, *Illness and Inhumanity in Stalin's Gulag*, Yale University Press, 2017, Kindle edn, p. 4.

53 Ibid., p. 19.

54 Gustaw Herling, *A World Apart*, pp. 136, 131–2.

55 Ibid., p. 135.

56 Ibid., p. 136.

57 Rees, *Behind Closed Doors*, p. 49.

58 See above p. 187.

59 Previously unpublished testimony.

10. *Stalin's Overreach*

1 Overy, *Dictators*, p. 497.

2 Overy, 'Statistics', in Dear and Foot (eds.), *Oxford Companion to the Second World War*, p. 1060.

3 David Stahel, *Kiev 1941: Hitler's Battle for Supremacy in the East*, Cambridge University Press, 2012, pp. 38–9.

4 Gellately, *Stalin's Curse*, p. 65, Stalin's speech, 6 November 1941.

5 E. A. Rees, *Iron Lazar: A Political Biography of Lazar Kaganovich*, Anthem Press, 2012, p. 236.

6 Rees, *Nazis*, p. 207.

7 Mawdsley, *Thunder in the East*, Stalin speech, 23 February 1942, p. 137.

8 Reid, *Leningrad*, p. 321.

9 David M. Glantz, *The Battle for Leningrad 1941–1944*, University Press of Kansas, 2002, pp. 204 and 325.

10 Ibid., pp. 180–88.

11 Reid, *Leningrad*, p. 329.

12 *Schlacht am Wolchow. Herausgegeben von der Propaganda-Kompanie einer Armee*, 3. Buchdruckerei Riga, 1942, pp. 14 and 16.

13 Ibid., General of the Cavalry Lindemann's note of 28 June 1942, p. 7.

14 K. K. Rokossovsky, *Soldatskiy dolg*, Olma Press, 2002, pp. 170, 172–4, quoted in Bellamy, *Absolute War*, pp. 348–9.

15 Hill, *Great Patriotic War*, Document 62, Order of the Headquarters of the Supreme High Command Number 57 of 22 January 1942, signed by both Stalin and Vasilevsky, p. 86.

16 David M. Glantz, *Kharkov: Anatomy of a Military Disaster through Soviet Eyes, 1942*, Ian Allan, 2010, p. 41.

17 Previously unpublished testimony.

18 Aleksandr Vasilevsky, *Delo vsei zhizni* (Life's Work), Political Literature, 1971, p. 92, quoted in Glantz, *Kharkov*, p. 198.

19 Glantz, *Kharkov*, p. 52.

20 Previously unpublished testimony.

21 Previously unpublished testimony.

22 Alan P. Donohue, 'Operation *KREML*: German Strategic Deception on the Eastern Front in 1942', in Christopher M. Rein (ed.), *Weaving the Tangled Web: Military Deception in Large-Scale Combat Operations*, Army University Press, 2018, pp. 79, 84. Also note that though Operation Kreml was signed off on 28 May, this deception plan was in operation before that date: see Glantz, *Kharkov*, p. 48.

23 Previously unpublished testimony.

24 H. Selle, 'Die Frühjahrsschlacht von Charkow: vom 12.–27. Mai 1942', *Allgemeine schweizerische Militärzeitschrift*, vol. 121, no. 8 (1955), pp. 581–602, here p. 602.

25 George Soldan, 'Zwischen zwei Schlachten', *Völkischer Beobachter*, no. 158, 7 June 1942, p. 3.

26 Kriegsberichter Herbert Rauchhaupt, 'Vom Abwehrkampf zur Vernichtungsschlacht. Kampfbilder aus der Schlacht um Charkow', *Völkischer Beobachter*, no. 168, 17 June 1942, p. 6; no. 169, 18 June 1942, p. 6; no. 170, 19 June 1942, p. 6.

27 Khrushchev (ed.), *Khrushchev Memoirs*, vol. 1: *Commissar*, pp. 372–80.

28 Roberts, *Zhukov*, Kindle edn, location 2671–736.

29 Previously unpublished testimony.

30 Sergei Shtemenko, *The Soviet General Staff at War 1941–1945*, Progress Publishers, 1986, p. 56, quoted in Earl F. Ziemke and Magna E. Bauer, *Moscow to Stalingrad: Decision in the East*, Center of Military History, United States Army, 1987, p. 282.

31 Khrushchev (ed.), *Khrushchev Memoirs*, vol. 1: *Commissar*, p. 383.

32 Ibid., p. 386.

33 Domarus, *Hitler. Reden und Proklamationen*, Band II: *Untergang, Zweiter Halbband 1941–1945*, New Year Proclamation to the German Volk, 1 January 1942, p. 1821.

34 Ibid., Hitler speech on 30 January 1942, at the Sportpalast in Berlin, pp. 1828–9.

35 *Hitler's Table Talk*, midday, 23 January 1942, pp. 235–6.

36 Ibid., midday, 27 January 1942, p. 257.

37 Hitler, *Mein Kampf*, pp. 96 and 248–9.

38 *Hitler's Table Talk*, midday, 8 February 1942, p. 304.

39 Ibid., at dinner, 9 April 1942, p. 419.

40 Ibid., midday, 23 April 1942, pp. 435.

41 Kershaw, *Nemesis*, p. 426.

42 Peter Löffler (ed.), *Bischof Clemens August Graf von Galen. Akten, Briefe und Predigten 1933–1946*, vol. 2: *1939–1946*, Matthias-Grünewald-Verlag, 1988, pp. 876–8.

43 Stargardt, *German War*, p. 162.

44 *Hitler's Table Talk*, midday, 8 February 1942, p. 304.

45 Robert Jay Lifton, *The Nazi Doctors*, Basic Books, 1986, p. 63.

46 Nikolaus Wachsmann, *Hitler's Prisons: Legal Terror in Nazi Germany*, Yale University Press, 2004, p. 210.

47 *Hitler's Table Talk*, midday, 8 February 1942, p. 303.

48 For example, the catalyst for the development of the child-euthanasia scheme was one case of a disabled child brought to Hitler's attention. See Rees, *Nazis*, pp. 72–4.

49 Wachsmann, *Hitler's Prisons*, p. 213.

50 Domarus, *Hitler. Reden und Proklamationen*, Band II: *Untergang, Zweiter Halbband 1941–1945*, Hitler's speech to the Reichstag, 26 April 1942, pp. 1874–5, 1877.

51 Elke Fröhlich (ed.), *Die Tagebücher von Joseph Goebbels*, Teil II: *Diktate 1941–1945*, Band 4: *April–Juni 1942*, K. G. Saur, 1995, entry for 27 April 1942, pp. 186–8.

52 Ibid., entry for 29 April 1942, pp. 198, 201.

53 Reynolds and Pechatnov (eds.), *Kremlin Letters*, pp. 111–12. This story was deleted by Churchill from his memoirs in the 1950s.

54 Rzheshevsky (ed.), *War and Diplomacy*, Document 15, record of talks with Churchill, 21 May 1942, p. 66.

55 Dilks (ed.), *Cadogan Diaries*, entry for 22 May 1942, p. 454.

56 Churchill note to Eden, 7 January 1942, PRO FO 371/32864. See above p. 174.

57 Reynolds and Pechatnov (eds.), *Kremlin Letters*, pp. 113–14.

58 See, for example, Stephen R. Rock, *Appeasement in International Politics*, University Press of Kentucky, 2000, p. 80.

59 Kimball (ed.), *Churchill and Roosevelt*, vol. I, FDR to Churchill, 18 March 1942, R–123/1, p. 421.

60 Just as they had at Chequers, Molotov's travel habits caused bemusement in the White House. When a valet unpacked his bag he discovered 'a large chunk of black bread, a roll of sausage and a pistol'. The President's wife, Eleanor Roosevelt, wrote that 'The secret service men did not like visitors with pistols but on this occasion nothing was said. Mr Molotov evidently thought he might have to defend himself, and also that he might be hungry.' (Eleanor Roosevelt, *This I Remember*, Greenwood Press, 1975, p. 251.) Molotov, like Stalin, was first and foremost a revolutionary. So the contents of his suitcase reflected his perception of the needs of a Bolshevik revolutionary on the road.

61 Rzheshevsky (ed.), *War and Diplomacy*, pp. 170–83.

62 Oleg A. Rzheshevsky, *Voina i Diplomatiia*, Nauka, 1997, p. 170. This version translated from the Russian. Also in Rzheshevsky (ed.), *War and Diplomacy*, pp. 179–80.

63 Hopkins memorandum, 29 May 1942, in Hopkins papers, FDR Presidential Library, Hyde Park, New York.

64 Rzheshevsky (ed.), *War and Diplomacy*, Document 72, talks on 30 May 1942, pp. 183–9.

65 Hopkins memorandum, 3 June 1942, in Hopkins papers, FDR Presidential Library, Hyde Park, New York.

66 Rzheshevsky, *War and Diplomacy*, Document 95, Molotov to Stalin, 4 June 1942, p. 220.

67 Kimball (ed.), *Churchill and Roosevelt*, vol. I, FDR to Churchill, 31 May 1942, R–152, pp. 503–4.

68 Rzheshevsky (ed.), *War and Diplomacy*, Document 99, Molotov to Stalin, received in Moscow 7 June 1942, p. 226.

69 Ibid., p. 221. Also see Professor S. H. Cross (the American interpreter), notes from 11 a.m. conference on Saturday 30 May 1942, Molotov Visit, Book 5, in FDR Presidential Library, Hyde Park, New York. Cross records that at this meeting, after questioning by Roosevelt, General Marshall

agreed to say that the Allies were 'preparing' a second front. Roosevelt then 'authorised Mr Molotov to inform Mr Stalin that we expect the formation of a Second Front this year'.

70 Hopkins memorandum, 3 June 1942, in Hopkins papers, FDR Presidential Library, Hyde Park, New York.

11. Across the Steppe

1 Previously unpublished testimony.

2 Previously unpublished testimony.

3 Testimony of Friedrich Paulus, Nuremberg War Trials, 11 February 1946, vol. 7, 56th day, https://avalon.law.yale.edu/imt/02-11-46.asp.

4 Previously unpublished testimony.

5 Stargardt, *German War*, p. 305.

6 Rees, *Nazis*, p. 248.

7 Previously unpublished testimony.

8 Previously unpublished testimony.

9 Previously unpublished testimony.

10 Burdick and Jacobsen (eds.), *Halder War Diary*, entry for 6 July 1942, p. 635.

11 Rees, *Nazis*, pp. 246–8.

12 Previously unpublished testimony.

13 Gorodetsky (ed.), *Maisky Diaries*, entry for 19 July 1942, p. 451.

14 Ibid., entry for 13 July 1942, p. 442.

15 Rees, *Nazis*, p. 94.

16 Bock, *War Diary*, entry for 31 July 1942, p. 539.

17 Domarus, *Hitler. Reden und Proklamationen*, Band II: *Untergang, Zweiter Halbband 1941–1945*, Directive Number 45, 23 July 1942, pp. 1899–900.

18 Burdick and Jacobsen (eds.), *Halder War Diary*, entry for 23 July 1942, p. 646.

19 Previously unpublished testimony.

20 Albert Speer, *Inside the Third Reich*, Phoenix, 1995, p. 332.

21 Hans Kehrl, *Krisenmanager im Dritten Reich. 6 Jahre Frieden – 6 Jahre Krieg. Erinnerungen. Mit kritischen Anmerkungen und einem Nachwort von Erwin Viefhaus*, Droste, 1973, p. 278. See also Speer's notes of the meeting. BArch, R 3/1505, minutes of the Führer meeting on 10, 11 and 12 August 1942.

22 Hill, *Great Patriotic War*, Document 74, Order of the People's Commissar of Defence of the USSR Number 227, 28 July 1942, Moscow, pp. 100–102.

23 Previously unpublished testimony.

24 See above p. 124.

25 Mawdsley, *Thunder in the East*, p. 152.

26 Previously unpublished testimony.

27 Martin Sixsmith, *Russia: A 1,000-Year Chronicle of the Wild East*, BBC Books, 2011, p. 344.

28 Antony Beevor, *Stalingrad*, Penguin Books, 1999, pp. 201–2.

29 Previously unpublished testimony.

30 Previously unpublished testimony. Also see Rees, *Behind Closed Doors*, pp. 151–2.

31 Prime Minister's minute to General Ismay, 17 May 1942, PRO D 100/2. Also see minutes of war cabinet meeting, 18 May 1942, PRO CAB 65/26.

32 Churchill Archive (CHAR) 20/78/26–8. Reynolds and Pechatnov (eds.), *Kremlin Letters*, pp. 124–7.

33 Stalin to Churchill, sent and received 23 July 1942, in Reynolds and Pechatnov (eds.), *Kremlin Letters*, p. 129.

34 Gorodetsky (ed.), *Maisky Diaries*, entries for 23 and 24 July 1942, pp. 453, 454.

35 Clark Kerr to Foreign Office, 25 July 1942, PRO FO 371/32911.

36 Lord Alanbrooke in BBC TV interview, broadcast 8 February 1957, https://www.bbc.co.uk/archive/the-alanbrooke-diaries/zf2f2sg.

37 PRO CAB 66/28/3, p. 19.

38 Churchill to Attlee, 13 August 1942, PRO FO 800/300.

39 Lord Tedder, *With Prejudice*, Cassell, 1966, p. 330.

40 PRO CAB 120/65.

41 Lord Moran, *Winston Churchill: The Struggle for Survival 1940–1965*, Heron Books, 1966, entry for 14 August 1942, pp. 60–61.

42 PRO FO 800/300. And Pavlov, 'Avtobiographicheskii Zametki', pp. 98–9.

43 Clark Kerr to Cripps, 26 April 1942, PRO FO 800/300. Martin Kitchen, *British Policy towards the Soviet Union during the Second World War*, Palgrave Macmillan, 1986, p. 125.

44 Tedder, *With Prejudice*, p. 332.

45 Ibid., p. 337.

46 Kitchen, *British Policy*, p. 126.

47 PRO FO 800/300.

48 Charles Richardson, *From Churchill's Secret Circle to the B B C: The Biography of Lieutenant General Sir Ian Jacob*, Brassey's, 1991, p. 139.

49 Danchev and Todman (eds.), *Alanbrooke War Diaries*, entry for 13 August 1942, pp. 299–300.

50 Ibid., entry for 14 August 1942, p. 301.

51 PRO FO 800/300.

52 Burdick and Jacobsen (eds.), *Halder War Diary*, entry for 30 August 1942, p. 664.

53 Kershaw, *Nemesis*, pp. 532–3.

54 Below, *At Hitler's Side*, pp. 151–2.

55 Ibid., p. 152.

56 Burdick and Jacobsen (eds.), *Halder War Diary*, entry for 24 September 1942, p. 670.

57 Bernhard R. Kroener, *'Der starke Mann im Heimatkriegsgebiet': Generaloberst Friedrich Fromm. Eine Biographie*, Ferdinand Schöningh, 2005, pp. 460–61. There were allegedly only four copies of Fromm's memo, none of which survived the war. Kroener reconstructed the content after testimony from three separate people who read it at the time.

58 IfZ, ZS 1747, Werner Kennes, 'Beantwortung der Fragen zur Geschichte des Chef H Rüst und BdE, Munich', 15 August 1949, pp. 7–8.

59 Fromm was arrested in the wake of the bomb plot of 22 July 1944. He was executed in March 1945.

60 Previously unpublished testimony.

61 Previously unpublished testimony.

12. *Struggle on the Volga*

1 Richard Overy, *The Bombing War: Europe 1939–1945*, Penguin, 2014, pp. 210–12. The previously accepted figure of 40,000 dead is now considered too high. This estimate of up to 25,000 dead is from Joel S. A. Hayward, *Stopped at Stalingrad: The Luftwaffe and Hitler's Defeat in the East, 1942–1943*, University of Kansas Press, 1998, p. 188. Hayward writes: 'Estimating fatalities is difficult because of a paucity of reliable statistical data. Yet this hellish attack caused at least as many deaths as similar-sized Allied raids on German cities. For example, it certainly claimed as many victims as the Allied attack on Darmstadt during the night of 11 and 12 September 1944, when the Royal Air Force unloaded almost 900 tons of bombs and killed

over 12,300 citizens. The Stalingrad death total may, in fact, have been twice that of Darmstadt, due to the fact that the Russian city was poorly provided with air-raid shelters.'

2 Previously unpublished testimony.

3 Previously unpublished testimony.

4 Rees, *Nazis*, p. 252.

5 Previously unpublished testimony.

6 Previously unpublished testimony.

7 Beevor, *Stalingrad*, p. 62.

8 Warlimont, *Inside Hitler's Headquarters*, p. 258.

9 Beevor, *Stalingrad*, p. 135.

10 Khrushchev (ed.), *Khrushchev Memoirs*, vol. 1: *Commissar*, p. 402.

11 Rees, *Nazis*, p. 255.

12 Beevor and Vinogradova (eds.), *A Writer at War*, p. 70.

13 Previously unpublished testimony.

14 Beevor, *Stalingrad*, p. 207.

15 Previously unpublished testimony.

16 Previously unpublished testimony.

17 Domarus, *Hitler. Reden und Proklamationen*, Band II: *Untergang, Zweiter Halbband 1941–1945*, p. 1909.

18 Rees, *Dark Charisma*, pp. 355–6.

19 Domarus, *Hitler. Reden und Proklamationen*, Band II: *Untergang, Zweiter Halbband 1941–1945*, Hitler speech, 30 September 1942, pp. 1916–17, 1919, 1922.

20 Sönke Neitzel (ed.), *Tapping Hitler's Generals: Transcripts of Secret Conversations 1942–45*, Frontline Books, 2013, words of General Ludwig Crüwell, p. 67.

21 Previously unpublished testimony.

22 Previously unpublished testimony.

23 Beevor and Vinogradova (eds.), *A Writer at War*, p. 120.

24 Testimony from *Timewatch: Mother of All Battles*, produced by Dai Richards, executive produced by Laurence Rees, transmitted on BBC2 in 1993.

25 Previously unpublished testimony.

26 Beevor and Vinogradova (eds.), *A Writer at War*, p. 223.

27 Previously unpublished testimony.

28 Beevor, *Stalingrad*, p. 197.

29 Roberts, *Stalin's Wars*, Stalin telegram to Maisky, 19 October 1942, pp. 141–2.

30 Previously unpublished testimony.

31 Rees, *Nazis*, p. 261, testimony of Joachim Stempel.

32 Below, *At Hitler's Side*, p. 156.

33 Hartmut Mehringer (ed.), *Die Tagebücher von Joseph Goebbels*, Teil II: *Diktate 1941–1945*, Band 6: *Oktober–Dezember 1942*, K. G. Saur, 1996, entry for 9 November 1942, p. 259.

34 Gibson (ed.), *Ciano Diaries*, entry for 9 November 1942, p. 541.

35 Domarus, *Hitler. Reden und Proklamationen*, Band II: *Untergang, Zweiter Halbband 1941–1945*, Hitler speech, 8 November 1942, pp. 1937–8, 1940, 1944.

36 Ibid.

37 Fritz Wiedemann, *Der Mann, der Feldherr werden wollte*, blick + bild Verlag für politische Bildung, 1964, p. 69, quoted in Jeremy Noakes and Geoffrey Pridham (eds.), *Nazism 1919–1945: A Documentary Reader*, vol. 2: *State, Economy and Society 1933–39*, Exeter University Press, 1984, pp. 207–8.

38 Bellamy, *Absolute War*, pp. 526–7. Also see Rees, *Nazis*, p. 269, testimony of Makhmut Gareev, and Beevor, *Stalingrad*, pp. 220–21.

39 Roberts, *Zhukov*, Kindle edn, location 2929.

40 Rees, *Nazis*, p. 272.

41 Previously unpublished testimony.

42 Hill, *Great Patriotic War*, Document 80, Memoirs of Georgii Zhukov, p. 106.

43 Rees, *Nazis*, pp. 273–4.

44 Previously unpublished testimony.

45 Below, *At Hitler's Side*, pp. 158–9.

46 Previously unpublished testimony.

47 Kershaw, *Nemesis*, p. 543.

48 Previously unpublished testimony.

49 Previously unpublished testimony.

50 Previously unpublished testimony.

51 Previously unpublished testimony.

52 Beevor, *Stalingrad*, p. 281.

53 The exact number trapped inside the ring versus the eventual number captured by the Soviets is a matter of debate, one that is analysed by Beevor in Appendix B of *Stalingrad*, pp. 439–40. Little more than 90,000 Germans and their allies were eventually taken prisoner by the Red Army at the time of surrender and though many were flown out by the Luftwaffe in the last weeks of the struggle, the death toll in the last days of the battle must have been enormous.

54 Rees, *Nazis*, pp. 278–9.

55 Beevor, *Stalingrad*, pp. 342–5.

56 Ibid., p. 345.

57 Below, *At Hitler's Side*, pp. 162–3.

58 Previously unpublished testimony, together with testimony from Rees, *Nazis*, p. 281.

59 Helmut Heiber and David M. Glantz (eds.), *Hitler and His Generals: Military Conferences 1942–1945*, Enigma Books, 2004, pp. 61–2, 66.

60 Ibid., pp. 59, 61.

61 Ibid., p. 59.

13. Fighting On

1 Domarus, *Hitler. Reden und Proklamationen*, Band II: *Untergang, Zweiter Halbband 1941–1945*, Göring speech, Reich Ministry of Aviation, 30 January 1943, pp. 1975–6.

2 UPI archives, dispatch by Robert Dawson of 30 January 1943.

3 Domarus, *Hitler. Reden und Proklamationen*, Band II: *Untergang, Zweiter Halbband 1941–1945*, Goebbels speech at the Berlin Sportpalast, 30 January 1943, pp. 1976–7.

4 'Nun, Volk steh auf, und Sturm brich los! Rede im Berliner Sportpalast', *Der steile Aufstieg*, Zentralverlag der NSDAP, 1944, pp. 167–204, Goebbels speech, 18 February 1943, online at https://research.calvin.edu/german-propaganda-archive/goeb36.htm.

5 Speer, *Inside the Third Reich*, p. 356.

6 Ibid., p. 358.

7 Louis Lochner (ed.), *The Goebbels Diaries 1942–1943*, Hamish Hamilton, 1948, entry for 2 March 1943, p. 197.

8 Ibid., p. 201.

9 Speer, *Inside the Third Reich*, p. 239.

10 Lochner (ed.), *Goebbels Diaries*, entry for 2 March 1943, pp. 197–8.

11 Ibid., entry for 9 March 1943, p. 214.

12 Ibid., entry for 9 March 1943, pp. 221–2. Also see Speer, *Inside the Third Reich*, pp. 362–3.

13 Speer, *Inside the Third Reich*, p. 366.

14 Lochner (ed.), *Goebbels Diaries*, entry for 2 March 1943, p. 200.

15 Elke Fröhlich (ed.), *Die Tagebücher von Joseph Goebbels*, Teil II: *Diktate 1941–1945*, Band 3: *Januar–März 1942*, K. G. Saur, 1994, entry for 27 March 1942, pp. 557–63.

16 Lochner (ed.), *Goebbels Diaries*, entry for 9 March 1943, p. 222.

17 Speer, *Inside the Third Reich*, pp. 362–3.

18 Elke Fröhlich (ed.), *Die Tagebücher von Joseph Goebbels*, Teil I: *Aufzeichnungen 1923–1941*, Band I/II: *Dezember 1925–Mai 1928*, K. G. Saur, 2005, entry for 15 February 1926.

19 Ibid., entry for 19 April 1926.

20 Rees, *Dark Charisma*, p. 377.

21 Uriel Tal, '*Political Faith*' of Nazism Prior to the Holocaust, Tel Aviv University, 1978, p. 30.

22 Guderian, *Panzer Leader*, p. 302.

23 Ibid., pp. 287–8.

24 Rees, *Dark Charisma*, p. 375.

25 Guderian, *Panzer Leader*, p. 304.

26 Stargardt, *German War*, German Foreign Office press and information unit, 2 February 1943, p. 338.

27 Ibid., p. 339.

28 Previously unpublished testimony.

29 Previously unpublished testimony.

30 Previously unpublished testimony.

31 Geoffrey Roberts, *Victory at Stalingrad: The Battle that Changed History*, Routledge, 2013, p. 135.

32 Rees, *Nazis*, p. 283.

33 Previously unpublished testimony.

34 Applebaum, *Gulag*, p. 391.

35 Tooze, *Wages of Destruction*, p. 482. Also see p. 185.

36 Roberts, *Victory at Stalingrad*, p. 135.

37 Mawdsley, *Thunder in the East*, p. 252.

38 James MacGregor Burns, *Roosevelt: The Soldier of Freedom*, Harvest Books, 2002, Stalin's telegram of 14 December 1942, p. 315.

39 Sherwood, *Roosevelt and Hopkins*, Stalin to Roosevelt and Churchill, 30 January 1943, p. 669.

40 Reynolds and Pechatnov (eds.), *Kremlin Letters*, Churchill to Stalin, sent 9 February 1943, received 12 February 1943, p. 211.

41 Gorodetsky (ed.), *Maisky Diaries*, entry for 5 February 1943, p. 475.

42 Ronald E. Powaski, *Toward an Entangling Alliance: American Isolationism, Internationalism, and Europe 1901–1950*, Greenwood Press, 1991, p. 100.

43 Thomas G. Paterson, *Meeting the Communist Threat: Truman to Reagan*, Oxford University Press, 1988, p. 7 (Paterson also uses the Truman quote, p. 8).

44 Kitchen, *British Policy*, p. 147.

45 Ibid., Oliver Harvey diary entry, 10 February 1943, p. 152.

46 Reynolds and Pechatnov (eds.), *Kremlin Letters*, Stalin to Churchill, sent and received 15 March 1943, pp. 220–21.

47 Gorodetsky (ed.), *Maisky Diaries*, entry for 31 March 1943, p. 502.

48 Reynolds and Pechatnov (eds.), *Kremlin Letters*, note by Christopher Warner, head of the Northern Department at the British Foreign Office, to Sir Archibald Clark Kerr, British Ambassador to the Soviet Union, 9 April 1943, p. 224.

49 Ibid., Churchill note to Eden, 18 March 1943, and cabinet meeting of the same day, p. 222.

50 Bellamy, *Absolute War*, p. 565.

51 Hartmut Mehringer (ed.), *Die Tagebücher von Joseph Goebbels*, Teil II: *Diktate 1941–1945*, Band 8: *April–Juni 1943*, K. G. Saur, 1993, entry for 9 April 1943, p. 81.

52 Ibid., entry for 17 April 1943, p. 115.

53 Ibid., entry for 9 April 1943, p. 81.

54 *War of the Century*, episode 3, *Crisis of Faith*, written and produced by Laurence Rees, first transmitted on BBC TV in 1999. Also see Rees, *War of the Century*, p. 182.

55 *Pravda*, 19 April 1943, front page.

56 Churchill to Eden, 28 April 1943, PRO FO 371/34571.

57 Churchill to Stalin, 24 April 1943, PRO CAB 66/36.

58 Stalin to Churchill, 25 April 1943, ibid.

59 Kitchen, *British Policy*, p. 156.

60 O'Malley report, 24 May 1943, PRO FO 371/34577.

61 Kimball (ed.), *Churchill and Roosevelt*, vol. II, Churchill to FDR, 13 August 1943, C–412/2, p. 389.

62 Alexander Etkind, Rory Finnin, Uilleam Blacker, Julie Fedor, Simon Lewis, Maria Mälksoo and Matilda Mroz, *Remembering Katyn*, Polity Press, 2012, report by Sir Alexander Cadogan, 18 June 1943, Kindle edn, p. 99.

63 Kitchen, *British Policy*, p. 154. Sir Archibald Clark Kerr, note to Foreign Office, 21 April 1943, PRO PREM 3, 354–8.

64 Rees, *Behind Closed Doors*, p. 394.

65 Mehringer (ed.), *Die Tagebücher von Joseph Goebbels*, Teil II, Band 8: *April–Juni 1943*, entry for 17 April 1943, pp. 115–16.

66 Ibid., entry for 8 May 1943, p. 233.

67　Stargardt, *German War*, p. 366.

68　*Mission to Moscow*, directed by Michael Curtiz, released in America by Warner Brothers, 22 May 1943.

69　William H. Standley, *Admiral Ambassador to Russia*, Henry Regnery, 1955, p. 368.

70　Joseph E. Davies papers, Manuscript Division, Library of Congress, Washington DC, entry for 20 May 1943.

71　*Foreign Relations of the United States* (henceforth *FRUS*), *The Conferences at Cairo and Tehran, 1943*, United States Government Printing Office, 1961, pp. 3–4.

72　Previously unpublished testimony. Also see Rees, *Behind Closed Doors*, p. 197.

73　Susan Butler (ed.), *My Dear Mr Stalin: The Complete Correspondence of Franklin D. Roosevelt and Joseph V. Stalin*, Yale University Press, 2005, dispatch of 2 June 1943, pp. 136–8.

74　Ibid., Stalin to Roosevelt, 11 June 1943, pp. 138–9.

75　Kitchen, *British Policy*, p. 161.

76　Kimball (ed.), *Churchill and Roosevelt*, vol. II, 20 June 1943, copy of telegram from Churchill to Stalin, sent to Roosevelt, C–322, pp. 266–8.

77　W. Averell Harriman and Elie Abel, *Special Envoy to Churchill and Stalin 1941–1946*, Random House, 1975, pp. 216–17.

78　Kimball (ed.), *Churchill and Roosevelt*, vol. II, Churchill to Roosevelt, 25 June 1943, C–328, pp. 278–9.

79　Ibid., Roosevelt to Churchill, 28 June 1943, R–297, pp. 283–4.

80　Ibid., Stalin's note of 24 June, forwarded by Churchill to Roosevelt on 29 June (though Stalin had separately copied Roosevelt in on the note on 24 June), C–335, pp. 285–90.

81　Rees, *Behind Closed Doors*, p. 200, report in *Nya Dagligt Allehanda*, 16 June 1943.

82　Kimball (ed.), *Churchill and Roosevelt*, vol. II, Churchill to Roosevelt, 28 June 1943, C–334, p. 285.

83　Joseph E. Davies papers, Library of Congress, entry for 20 May 1943.

84　Robert M. Citino, *The Wehrmacht Retreats: Fighting a Lost War, 1943*, University Press of Kansas, 2012, Kindle edn, pp. 122–6.

85　Guderian, *Panzer Leader*, p. 307.

86　Manfred Kittel (ed.), *Die Tagebücher von Joseph Goebbels*, Teil II: *Diktate 1941–1945*, Band 9: *Juli–September 1943*, K. G. Saur, 1993, entry for 27 July 1943, p. 179.

87 Guderian, *Panzer Leader*, p. 309.

88 Kershaw, *Nemesis*, p. 579.

89 Mehringer (ed.), *Die Tagebücher von Joseph Goebbels*, Teil II, Band 8: *April–Juni 1943*, entry for 25 June 1943, pp. 531–2.

90 Bellamy, *Absolute War*, p. 566.

91 Previously unpublished testimony.

92 Citino, *The Wehrmacht Retreats*, Kindle edn, p. 134.

93 Previously unpublished testimony.

94 Previously unpublished testimony.

95 Previously unpublished testimony.

96 *Mother of All Battles*, BBC2, 1993.

97 Ibid.

98 Ibid.

99 Bellamy, *Absolute War*, p. 583.

14. *Fiction and Reality*

1 Robert Citino calls the period from the early morning of 5 July and the launch of the battle of Kursk, to the end of 13 July and Hitler's decision to end the offensive as the result of the intense Soviet resistance, together with the new threat of the Allied invasion of Sicily, 'nine days that shook the world'. Citino, *The Wehrmacht Retreats*, Kindle edn, pp. 199–202.

2 Domarus, *Hitler. Reden und Proklamationen*, Band II: *Untergang, Zweiter Halbband 1941–1945*, p. 2023.

3 Philip Morgan, *The Fall of Mussolini: Italy, the Italians, and the Second World War*, Oxford University Press, 2007, p. 26.

4 Christopher Duggan, *Fascist Voices*, Bodley Head, 2012, pp. 387–8.

5 Kittel (ed.), *Die Tagebücher von Joseph Goebbels*, Teil II, Band 9: *Juli–September 1943*, entry for 27 July 1943, p. 169.

6 Overy, *Bombing War*, p. 329. Also see Max Hastings, *Bomber Command*, Pan Books, 1981, pp. 241–8.

7 Richard Holmes, *The World at War: The Landmark Oral History*, Ebury Press, 2008, p. 302.

8 Overy, *Bombing War*, pp. 334–5.

9 Kittel (ed.), *Die Tagebücher von Joseph Goebbels*, Teil II, Band 9: *Juli–September 1943*, entry for 29 July 1943, p. 190.

10 Holmes, *World at War*, p. 303.

11 Keith Lowe, *Inferno: The Devastation of Hamburg, 1943*, Penguin Books, 2012, Kindle edn, pp. 295–6.

12 Jeremy Noakes and Geoffrey Pridham (eds.), *Nazism 1919–1945: A Documentary Reader*, vol. 4: *The German Home Front in World War II*, University of Exeter Press, 2010, SD Report of 2 August 1943, p. 549.

13 Stargardt, *German War*, p. 374. See also Walter J. Boyne, *The Influence of Air Power upon History*, Pen and Sword, 2005, p. 219.

14 Kittel (ed.), *Die Tagebücher von Joseph Goebbels*, Teil II, Band 9: *Juli–September 1943*, entry for 25 July 1943, p. 160.

15 See, for example, the testimony of Karl Boehm-Tettelbach in Rees, *Their Darkest Hour*, pp. 236–8.

16 Stargardt, *German War*, pp. 375–6.

17 Ian Kershaw, 'The Persecution of the Jews and German Popular Opinion in the Third Reich', *Year Book of the Leo Baeck Institute*, vol. 26, 1981, p. 284.

18 Kershaw, *Nemesis*, p. 590. Also see Traudl Junge, *Until the Final Hour: Hitler's Last Secretary*, Weidenfeld & Nicolson, 2003, p. 88, and Erich Kempka, *I Was Hitler's Chauffeur*, Frontline Books, 2010, p. 174, Appendix 3 (extract from Christa Schroeder's *He Was My Chief*, Frontline Books, 2009).

19 Previously unpublished testimony.

20 Speer, *Inside the Third Reich*, p. 85.

21 Junge, *Until the Final Hour*, p. 63.

22 Speer, *Inside the Third Reich*, p. 145.

23 Ibid., p. 156.

24 Previously unpublished testimony.

25 Simon Sebag Montefiore, *Stalin: The Court of the Red Tsar*, Weidenfeld & Nicolson, 2010, Kindle edn, location 5559–84.

26 William J. Tompson, *Khrushchev: A Political Life*, Palgrave Macmillan, 1997, p. 86.

27 Kotkin, *Stalin*, vol. 2: *Waiting for Hitler*, pp. 108–10.

28 Peter Longerich, *Goebbels*, Vintage, 2015, pp. 157–60.

29 Svetlana Alliluyeva, *Twenty Letters to a Friend*, Harper Perennial, 2016, p. 166.

30 Service, *Stalin*, pp. 431–4.

31 Previously unpublished testimony.

32 Kershaw, *Nemesis*, p. 612.

33 Hill, *Great Patriotic War*, report of the Leningrad Headquarters of the Partisan Movement, 4 April 1944, Table 9.3, p. 210.

34 Karl-Heinz Frieser (ed.), *Germany and the Second World War*, vol. VIII: *The Eastern Front 1943–1944: The War in the East and on the Neighbouring Fronts*, Clarendon Press, 2017, p. 186.

35 Geoffrey P. Megargee, *War of Annihilation: Combat and Genocide on the Eastern Front, 1941*, Rowman & Littlefield, 2007, p. 65.

36 *Hitler's Table Talk*, evening of 8 August 1942, p. 621.

37 Timothy Patrick Mulligan, *The Politics of Illusion and Empire*, Praeger, 1988, p. 139.

38 Previously unpublished testimony.

39 Hill, *Great Patriotic War*, Document 134, Decree of the State Defence Committee 'On members of the families of traitors', No. GOKO-1926ss., 14 June 1942, p. 215.

40 Mawdsley, *Thunder in the East*, p. 211.

41 Rees, *Their Darkest Hour*, pp. 42–6.

42 Previously unpublished testimony.

43 Oleg V. Khlevniuk, *Stalin: New Biography of a Dictator*, Yale University Press, 2015, p. 227.

44 Butler (ed.), *My Dear Mr Stalin*, Stalin message to Roosevelt, 8 August 1943, pp. 150–51.

45 Ibid., Roosevelt to Stalin, 14 October 1943, p. 172.

46 Ibid., Roosevelt to Stalin, 8 November 1943, p. 181.

47 Churchill's doctor, the former Sir Charles Wilson, ennobled as Lord Moran in March 1943.

48 Moran, *Struggle for Survival*, entry for 25 November 1943, p. 131.

49 Ibid., p. 132.

50 *FRUS, The Conferences at Cairo and Tehran, 1943*, Bohlen minutes, pp. 482–6.

51 Moran, *Struggle for Survival*, entry for 28 November 1943, p. 134.

52 PRO CAB 99/25.

53 Brooke's views, quoted by Lord Moran, *Struggle for Survival*, entry for 28 November 1943, p. 135.

54 Danchev and Todman (eds.), *Alanbrooke War Diaries*, additional comments, later added by Brooke, to his entry for 28 November 1943, p. 483.

55 Charles E. Bohlen, *Witness to History 1929–1969*, W. W. Norton, 1973, p. 145.

56 PRO PREM 3/136/8, pp. 2–3 (also recorded in *FRUS, The Conferences at Cairo and Tehran, 1943*, Bohlen minutes, p. 512).

57 Churchill to Eden, 16 January 1944, PRO PREM 3/399/6.

58 Kitchen, *British Policy*, p. 177. Churchill to Eden, 7 January 1944, PRO PREM 3/355/7.

59 *FRUS, The Conferences at Cairo and Tehran, 1943*, pp. 594–6.

60 See above p. 174.

61 Bohlen, *Witness*, p. 152.

62 PRO PREM 3/136/9, pp. 12–13.

63 Dilks (ed.), *Cadogan Diaries*, entry for 17 January 1944, p. 597.

64 Moran, *Struggle for Survival*, entry for 29 November 1943, pp. 140–41.

15. *Mass Killing*

1 Nikolai Bougai, *The Deportation of Peoples in the Soviet Union*, Nova, 1996, p. 58.

2 Rolf-Dieter Müller, *The Unknown Eastern Front: The Wehrmacht and Hitler's Foreign Soldiers*, I. B. Tauris, 2012, p. 248. Also see J. Otto Pohl, 'The Loss, Retention, and Reacquisition of Social Capital by Special Settlers in the USSR, 1941–1960', in Cynthia J. Buckley, Blair A. Ruble and Erin Trouth Hofmann (eds.), *Migration, Homeland, and Belonging in Eurasia*, Woodrow Wilson Center Press, 2008, p. 209.

3 Norman M. Naimark, *Fires of Hatred: Ethnic Cleansing in Twentieth-Century Europe*, Harvard University Press, 2001, p. 89.

4 Ibid., pp. 91–2.

5 Previously unpublished testimony.

6 Previously unpublished testimony.

7 Elza-Bair Guchinova, *The Kalmyks*, Routledge, 2006, Kindle edn, location 755–62.

8 Previously unpublished testimony.

9 Previously unpublished testimony.

10 Browning, *Origins of the Final Solution*, words of Alexander Palfinger, deputy administrator of the Łódź Ghetto, in a report of 7 November 1940, p. 120. Palfinger explained that he was 'indifferent' to the fate of the Jews as long as their deaths did not affect Germans. He distinguished between Jews dying of an epidemic that could spread to Germans – which should be prevented – and Jews dying from 'non-infectious' diseases – which should be ignored: ibid., p. 460 n. 34. And BArch, R 138-II/18, kritischer Bericht, 7 November 1940, Palfinger.

11 Guchinova, *Kalmyks*, Kindle edn, location 990–97.

12 Ibid., location 872.

13 Previously unpublished testimony.

14 Guchinova, *Kalmyks*, Kindle edn, location 1041–66.

15 Browning, *Origins of the Final Solution*, pp. 69–70.

16 Yitzhak Arad, Yisrael Gutman and Abraham Margaliot (eds.), *Documents on the Holocaust*, University of Nebraska Press, 1999, Rademacher memo, 3 July 1940, pp. 216–18.

17 Ibid.

18 Browning, *Origins of the Final Solution*, pp. 69–70.

19 Previously unpublished testimony.

20 Rees, *Their Darkest Hour*, p. 19.

21 Previously unpublished testimony.

22 Previously unpublished testimony. But also see Rees, *Their Darkest Hour*, pp. 19–20.

23 Rees, *Auschwitz*, p. 171.

24 Previously unpublished testimony, and Rees, *Their Darkest Hour*, p. 19.

25 Previously unpublished testimony, but also see Rees, *War of the Century*, p. 195.

26 Previously unpublished testimony, but also see Rees, *War of the Century*, pp. 196–7.

27 Previously unpublished testimony.

28 Previously unpublished testimony.

29 There is ample testimony to demonstrate this in Rees, *Auschwitz*, and particularly in Jadwiga Bezwinska and Danuta Czech (eds.), *Amidst a Nightmare of Crime: Manuscripts of Prisoners in Crematorium Squads Found at Auschwitz*, Howard Fertig, 2013.

30 Previously unpublished testimony, and Rees, *Their Darkest Hour*, p. 21.

31 Previously unpublished testimony, and Rees, *Their Darkest Hour*, p. 21.

32 Testimony in episode 6 of *Auschwitz: The Nazis and the 'Final Solution'*, written and produced by Laurence Rees, transmitted on BBC TV in 2005, and Rees, *Their Darkest Hour*, p. 23.

33 Previously unpublished testimony.

34 Previously unpublished testimony.

35 Rees, *Behind Closed Doors*, p. 252.

36 Applebaum, *Gulag*, p. 388.

37 Previously unpublished testimony. But also see Rees, *Behind Closed Doors*, p. 254.

38 Danuta Czech, *Auschwitz Chronicle, 1939–1945: From the Archives of the Auschwitz Memorial and the German Federal Archives*, I. B. Tauris, 1990, p. 627.

39 Rees, *Holocaust*, p. 393.

40 Rees, *Auschwitz*, p. 206, and previously unpublished testimony.

41 Kershaw, *Nemesis*, pp. 627–8.

42 Rees, *Holocaust*, pp. 381–2.

43 Ibid., pp. 385–6.

44 Hitler's address to generals and officers, 26 May 1944, quoted in Hans-Heinrich Wilhelm, 'Hitlers Ansprache vor Generalen und Offizieren am 26. Mai 1944', *Militärgeschichtliche Mitteilungen*, vol. 20, no. 2 (1976), pp. 141–61, here p. 156. In English in Peter Longerich, *The Unwritten Order*, Tempus, 2005, p. 212.

45 St Petersburg was renamed Petrograd at the start of the First World War in 1914 in order to sound less German, and then Leningrad after the death of Lenin in 1924 and then turned back to St Petersburg in 1991 after the fall of the Soviet Union.

46 In his 'secret speech' in February 1956, Khrushchev alleged that Stalin would have deported the Ukrainians if he could, and was prevented from doing so only 'because there were too many of them and there was no place to which to deport them'. Online at https://www.marxists.org/archive/khrushchev/1956/02/24.htm.

47 Dieter Marc Schneider (ed.), *Die Tagebücher von Joseph Goebbels*, Teil II: *Diktate 1941–1945*, 11: *Januar–März 1944*, K. G. Saur, 1994, entry for 4 March 1944, pp. 396, 399–400.

16. Collapse of the Centre

1 See p. 306.

2 Overy, *Russia's War*, pp. 242–3.

3 Paul Adair, *Hitler's Greatest Defeat*, Arms and Armour, 1994, Hitler directive, 8 March 1944, p. 66.

4 Frieser (ed.), *Germany and the Second World War*, vol. VIII: *The Eastern Front*. Karl-Heinz Frieser makes the point at p. 520 that Hitler's idea of the Fortified Places was 'even more backward' than the thinking of the First World War.

5 Earl Ziemke, *Stalingrad to Berlin: The German Defeat in the East*, US Army Historical Series, Office of the Chief of Military History, 1987, General Hans Jordan, June 1944, p. 316.

6 Previously unpublished testimony.

7 Previously unpublished testimony.

8 Rees, *War of the Century*, p. 222.

9 Previously unpublished testimony.

10 Previously unpublished testimony.

11 Ian Kershaw, *The End: Hitler's Germany, 1944–1945*, Allen Lane, 2011, p. 27. Quote in German in Andreas Kunz, *Wehrmacht und Niederlage. Die bewaffnete Macht in der Endphase der nationalsozialistischen Herrschaft 1944 bis 1945*, Oldenbourg, 2007, p. 61.

12 Churchill, *The Second World War*, vol. III: *The Grand Alliance*, p. 615.

13 Stargardt, *German War*, p. 434.

14 Kershaw, *Nemesis*, p. 672.

15 Randall Hansen, *Disobeying Hitler: German Resistance after Valkyrie*, Oxford University Press, 2014, p. 58.

16 Ibid., pp. 53–7.

17 Ian Kershaw, *The 'Hitler Myth'*, Oxford University Press, 2001, pp. 215–19.

18 Stargardt, *German War*, p. 453.

19 Kershaw, *The End*, pp. 46–7.

20 Domarus, *Hitler. Reden und Proklamationen*, Band II: *Untergang, Zweiter Halbband 1941–1945*, 24 September 1944, p. 2150.

21 Previously unpublished testimony, and Rees, *Nazis*, pp. 348–9. After the war Fernau was sentenced to six years in prison for his part in a 'flying court martial' and the subsequent killing of a local farmer. See Rees, *Nazis*, pp. 350–53.

22 Keith Sword, *Deportation and Exile: Poles in the Soviet Union 1939–48*, Macmillan Press, 1994, p. 151.

23 Previously unpublished testimony.

24 See above p. 295.

25 Sword, *Deportation and Exile*, p. 154.

26 Bellamy, *Absolute War*, p. 617.

27 Rees, *Behind Closed Doors*, p. 273.

28 Previously unpublished testimony.

29 Previously unpublished testimony.

30 Previously unpublished testimony.

31 Yohanan Cohen, *Small Nations in Times of Crisis and Confrontation*, State University of New York Press, 1989, pp. 159–61. The meeting was held on 11 June 1944.

32 Jan Karski, *The Great Powers and Poland: From Versailles to Yalta*, Rowman & Littlefield, 2014, p. 409.

33 Cohen, *Small Nations*, p. 161.

34 Jan Ciechanowski, *The Warsaw Rising of 1944*, Cambridge University Press, 1974, p. 285.

35 General Sikorski Historical Institute (ed.), *Documents on Polish–Soviet Relations 1939–1945*, William Heinemann, 1967, vol. 2: *1943–1945*, Document 180, p. 313.

36 Bellamy, *Absolute War*, p. 618.

37 Roberts, *Zhukov*, Kindle edn, location 3545.

38 Norman Davies, *Rising '44: The Battle for Warsaw*, Pan Books, 2004, p. 321.

39 Previously unpublished testimony.

40 Jeremy Noakes and Geoffrey Pridham (eds.), *Nazism 1919–1945: A Documentary Reader*, vol. 3: *Foreign Policy, War and Racial Extermination*, University of Exeter Press, 2006, Document 715, p. 388.

41 Charles de Gaulle, *The Edge of the Sword*, Faber & Faber, 1960, p. 55.

42 Ibid., p. 62.

43 Moran, *Struggle for Survival*, entry for 22 September 1944, p. 185.

44 Danchev and Todman (eds.), *Alanbrooke War Diaries*, entries for 8 July 1943, 3 February 1942 and 19 August 1940, pp. 427, 227, 101.

45 Moran, *Struggle for Survival*, entry for 22 January 1943, p. 80.

46 Robert Dallek, *Franklin D. Roosevelt and American Foreign Policy 1932–1945*, Oxford University Press, 1995, p. 459.

47 Moran, *Struggle for Survival*, entry for 22 January 1943, p. 81.

48 Julian Jackson, *France: The Dark Years 1940–1944*, Oxford University Press, 2003, p. 551.

49 Ibid., p. 552.

50 Matthew Cobb, *Eleven Days in August: The Liberation of Paris in 1944*, Simon & Schuster, 2013, p. 43.

51 Jackson, *Dark Years*, pp. 561–7.

52 Domarus, *Hitler. Reden und Proklamationen*, Band II: *Untergang, Zweiter Halbband 1941–1945*, p. 2143.

53 Cobb, *Eleven Days*, Kindle edn, location 3201–22.

54 Jackson, *Dark Years*, p. 565.

55 Davies, *Rising '44*, p. 348.

56 Winston S. Churchill, *The Second World War*, vol. VI: *Triumph and Tragedy*, Penguin Books, 2005, p. 118.

57 Previously unpublished testimony.

58 *World War Two, Behind Closed Doors*, episode 5, written and produced by Laurence Rees, first transmitted on BBC2 in 2008.

59 PRO PREM 3/434/2, pp. 4–5.

60 PRO PREM 3/66/7.

61 Russian minutes from the meeting with the London Poles, 13 October 1944, published in Oleg A. Rzheshevsky, *Stalin and Churchill*, Navka, 2004, pp. 444–8. And translation of Polish transcript, General Sikorski Historical Institute (ed.), *Documents on Polish–Soviet Relations*, vol. 2: *1943–1945*, pp. 405–15.

62 Translation from Polish, General Sikorski Historical Institute (ed.), *Documents on Polish–Soviet Relations*, vol. 2: *1943–1945*, p. 423.

63 PRO PREM 3/66/7.

64 PM to war cabinet, 17 October 1944, CHAR 20/181 (CAC).

65 Mary Soames, *Clementine Churchill*, Houghton Mifflin, 1979, p. 361.

66 PM to war cabinet, 17 October 1944, CHAR 20/181 (CAC).

67 Sword, *Deportation and Exile*, p. 155.

68 Ibid., p. 157.

17. Dying Days

1 Stargardt, *German War*, pp. 470–72.

2 Kershaw, *The End*, pp. 114–18.

3 Domarus, *Hitler. Reden und Proklamationen*, Band II: *Untergang, Zweiter Halbband 1941–1945*, proclamation, 12 November 1944, p. 2164.

4 Kershaw, *Nemesis*, pp. 728–31.

5 Domarus, *Hitler. Reden und Proklamationen*, Band II: *Untergang, Zweiter Halbband 1941–1945*, pp. 2162–3.

6 Below, *At Hitler's Side*, p. 214.

7 Domarus, *Hitler. Reden und Proklamationen*, Band II: *Untergang, Zweiter Halbband 1941–1945*, p. 2171.

8 Below, *At Hitler's Side*, pp. 221–3.

9 Previously unpublished testimony.

10 Domarus, *Hitler. Reden und Proklamationen*, Band II: *Untergang, Zweiter Halbband 1941–1945*, pp. 2181–4, Hitler New Year Proclamation, 1 January 1945.

11 Tedder, *With Prejudice*, pp. 646–7.

12 Dilks (ed.), *Cadogan Diaries*, entry for 29 November 1943, p. 580.

13 Tedder, *With Prejudice*, p. 650.

14 David Reynolds, *From World War to Cold War*, Oxford University Press, 2006, Clark Kerr cable to Foreign Office, 13 August 1943, p. 243.

15 Tedder, *With Prejudice*, p. 649.

16 Jean Laloy (unofficial Russian–French interpreter), 'À Moscou: entre Staline et de Gaulle, Décembre 1944', *Revue des Études Slaves*, vol. 54, no. 1–2 (1982), p. 147.

17 Charles de Gaulle, *The Complete War Memoirs*, Carroll & Graf, 1998, pp. 756–7.

18 Ibid., p. 756.

19 Ibid., pp. 736–7.

20 Previously unpublished testimony.

21 Krisztián Ungváry, *Battle for Budapest*, I. B. Tauris, 2006, p. 286.

22 BFL XXV 4a 002645/1953, Budapest Capital Archive, and Ungváry, *Budapest*, p. 287.

23 Rees, *Behind Closed Doors*, pp. 326–7.

24 Previously unpublished testimony.

25 Milovan Djilas, *Conversations with Stalin*, Penguin Books, 1962, p. 76.

26 Beevor and Vinogradova (eds.), *A Writer at War*, p. 321.

27 Guderian, *Panzer Leader*, p. 383.

28 Ibid.

29 Ibid., p. 387.

30 Ibid., pp. 404–5.

31 Noakes and Pridham (eds.), *Nazism*, vol. 1: *The Rise to Power*, p. 16.

32 Rees, *Behind Closed Doors*, testimony of Hugh Lunghi, p. 334.

33 Ibid., p. 333.

34 Moran, *Struggle for Survival*, entry for 4 February 1945, p. 223.

35 Dilks (ed.), *Cadogan Diaries*, entry for 8 February 1945, p. 706.

36 David Reynolds, *Summits: Six Meetings that Shaped the Twentieth Century*, Allen Lane, 2007, p. 116, and Amos Yoder, *The Evolution of the United Nations System*, Taylor & Francis, 1997, p. 27.

37 *FRUS, The Conferences at Malta and Yalta, 1945*, United States Government Printing Office, 1955. Yalta discussions are at pp. 547–996.

38 Moran, *Struggle for Survival*, entry for 11 February 1945, p. 232.

39 Previously unpublished testimony.

40 Previously unpublished testimony.

41 Burns, *Roosevelt*, p. 572.

42 Fraser Harbutt, *The Iron Curtain: Churchill, America, and the Origins of the Cold War*, Oxford University Press, 1986, p. 93.

43 Danchev and Todman (eds.), *Alanbrooke War Diaries*, entry for 5 February 1945, p. 657.

44 Dilks (ed.), *Cadogan Diaries*, entry for 11 February 1945, pp. 708–9.

45 British war cabinet minutes, 19 February 1945, PRO WM (43) 22.1 CA.

46 Pimlott (ed.), *Dalton Diaries*, entry for 23 February 1945, p. 836.

47 George McJimsey (ed.), *Documentary History of the Franklin D. Roosevelt Presidency*, vol. 14: *The Yalta Conference, October 1944–March 1945*, University Publications of America, 2003, Document 144, p. 639.

48 The number of dead as a consequence of the bombing of Dresden remains a matter of debate. For a discussion of the issues see Appendix B in Frederick Taylor, *Dresden, Tuesday 13 February 1945*, Bloomsbury, 2004, pp. 503–9. After an exhaustive examination Taylor settled on a figure of 'between twenty-five thousand and forty thousand'. Sinclair McKay also gives a figure of 25,000 in Sinclair McKay, *Dresden: The Fire and the Darkness*, Penguin Books, 2020, Kindle edn, p. xx. But note that other historians arrive at estimates outside these parameters. For instance, Andrew Roberts, quoting German sources, posits a figure of 20,000 dead. See Andrew Roberts, *The Storm of War: A New History of the Second World War*, Allen Lane, 2009, p. 456.

49 Taylor, *Dresden*, p. 272.

50 Below, *At Hitler's Side*, p. 228.

51 Rudolf Jordan, *Erlebt und Erlitten. Weg eines Gauleiters von München bis Moskau*, Druffel, 1971, pp. 253–4.

52 Baldur von Schirach, *Ich glaubte an Hitler*, Mosaik, 1967, p. 307.

53 Jordan, *Erlebt und Erlitten*, pp. 257–8. Also see Kershaw, *The End*, p. 245.

54 Domarus, *Hitler. Reden und Proklamationen*, Band II: *Untergang, Zweiter Halbband 1941–1945*, proclamation of 24 February 1945, p. 2206.

55 Kershaw, *The End*, p. 264.

56 Rees, *Dark Charisma*, p. 377.

57 Speer, *Inside the Third Reich*, p. 588.

58 Ibid., p. 538.

59 Kershaw, *The End*, Speer message of 3 April, p. 477 n. 146.

60 Ibid., pp. 288–9, examines evidence of a second memo Speer wrote around this time that called for more 'drastic measures' of defence along the Oder and Rhine. Speer never referred to this memo after the war, for understandable reasons.

61 Antony Beevor, *Berlin: The Downfall, 1945*, Viking, 2002, pp. 146–7.

62 Previously unpublished testimony.

63 Butler (ed.), *My Dear Mr Stalin*, 31 March 1945, 299, p. 310.

64 Reynolds and Pechatnov (eds.), *Kremlin Letters*, Churchill to Stalin, 1 April 1945, p. 569.

65 Butler (ed.), *My Dear Mr Stalin*, Stalin to Roosevelt, 7 April 1945, 303, p. 319.

66 John Le Rougetel, UK Political Representative in Romania, to Foreign Office, 2 April 1945, PRO FO 371/48552, quoted in Kitchen, *British Policy*, p. 255.

67 William E. Houstoun-Boswall, UK Minister in Bulgaria, to Foreign Office, 28 February 1945, PRO FO 371/48123, quoted in Kitchen, *British Policy*, p. 255.

68 See above p. 348.

69 Kimball (ed.), *Churchill and Roosevelt*, vol. III, Churchill to Roosevelt, 8 March 1945, C–905, p. 547.

70 Butler (ed.), *My Dear Mr Stalin*, Stalin to Roosevelt, 3 April 1945, 300, p. 312.

71 Ibid., Roosevelt to Stalin, 4 April 1945, 301, pp. 313–15.

72 Ibid., Stalin to Roosevelt, 7 April 1945, 302, pp. 315–17.

73 Reynolds and Pechatnov (eds.), *Kremlin Letters*, Stalin to Churchill, 7 April 1945, p. 580.

74 Beevor, *Berlin*, pp. 146–7.

75 Maximilian Gschaid (ed.), *Die Tagebücher von Joseph Goebbels*, Teil II: *Diktate 1941–1945*, Band 15: *Januar–April 1945*, K. G. Saur, 1995, entry for 21 March 1945, pp. 566–7, 572.

76 Ibid., entry for 28 March 1945, pp. 612–13.

77 Kershaw, *Nemesis*, p. 792.

78 Gschaid (ed.), *Die Tagebücher von Joseph Goebbels*, Teil II, Band 15: *Januar–April 1945*, entry for 28 March 1945, pp. 613–14.

79 Guderian, *Panzer Leader*, pp. 428, 414.

80 Previously unpublished testimony, and also testimony from Rees, *Behind Closed Doors*, pp. 359–60.

81 *War of the Century*, episode 4, *Vengeance*, written and produced by Laurence Rees, transmitted on BBC2 on 26 October 1999.

82 Previously unpublished testimony.

83 Previously unpublished testimony.

84 Norman M. Naimark, *The Russians in Germany: A History of the Soviet Zone of Occupation 1945–1949*, Belknap Press, 1995, p. 133. See also Beevor, *Berlin*, p. 410. He writes that 'at least 2 million German women are thought to have been raped.'

85 Rees, *Behind Closed Doors*, p. 361.

86 Gregor Dallas, *Poisoned Peace: 1945 – The War that Never Ended*, John Murray, 2005, p. 7.

87 Beevor and Vinogradova (eds.), *Writer at War*, pp. 341–2.

18. Victory and Defeat

1 Jana Richter (ed.), *Die Tagebücher von Joseph Goebbels*, Teil I: *Aufzeichnungen 1923–1941*, Band 6: *August 1938–Juni 1939*, K. G. Saur, 1998, entry for 21 April 1939, p. 323.

2 *Völkischer Beobachter*, Norddeutsche Ausgabe, 20 April 1939, p. 1.

3 Kershaw, *Nemesis*, p. 798.

4 Below, *At Hitler's Side*, p. 235.

5 Junge, *Until the Final Hour*, p. 161.

6 Testimony of Bernd Freytag von Loringhoven in *Himmler, Hitler and the End of the Reich*, produced by Detlef Siebert, executive produced by Laurence Rees, transmitted on BBC2 on 19 January 2001.

7 Longerich, *Himmler*, p. 730. The quote is from Hitler's political testament.

8 Heiber and Glantz (eds.), *Hitler and His Generals*, p. 59. See above p. 254.

9 David Welch, *Propaganda and the German Cinema 1933–1945*, Oxford University Press, 1983, pp. 230–33.

10 *Goebbels, Master of Propaganda*, written and produced by Laurence Rees, transmitted on BBC2 on 12 November 1992.

11 Welch, *Propaganda*, p. 234.

12 *Goebbels, Master of Propaganda*, BBC2, 1992.

13 *Himmler, Hitler and the End of the Reich*, BBC2, 2001.

14 Max Domarus, *Hitler: Speeches and Proclamations 1932–1945*, vol. IV, Bolchazy-Carducci, 2004, Hitler's political testament, 29 April 1945, p. 3056.

15 Domarus, *Hitler. Reden und Proklamationen*, Band II: *Untergang, Zweiter Halbband 1941–1945*, pp. 2236–7, 2239.

16 The testimony of those who heard the screams of Jews crammed inside the gas chambers most certainly proves Hitler's claim that this was a 'humane' method of killing to be a lie. See testimony of Dario Gabbai in episode 1 of *Auschwitz: The Nazis and the 'Final Solution'*, written and produced by Laurence Rees, first transmitted on BBC2 in January 2005.

17 James Goodwin, *Eisenstein, Cinema and History*, University of Illinois Press, 1993, p. 184.

18 Maureen Perrie, *The Cult of Ivan the Terrible in Stalin's Russia*, Palgrave, 2001, p. 87.

19 Kershaw, *Nemesis*, pp. 618–19.

20 A dental bridge was discovered amid the charred remains, and this proved from dental records to be from Hitler's mouth. See ibid., p. 831.

21 Anton Joachimsthaler, *The Last Days of Hitler: The Legends, the Evidence, the Truth*, Arms and Armour, 1996, pp. 249–50.

22 Ibid., p. 242.

23 James Byrnes, *Speaking Frankly*, Harper & Brothers, 1947, p. 68. Also see Hugh Trevor-Roper, *The Last Days of Hitler*, Palgrave, 1995, p. xlviii, and Joachimsthaler, *Last Days*, p. 250.

24 Stalin had first made this demand back at the Tehran conference in 1943. *FRUS, The Conferences at Cairo and Tehran, 1943*, p. 604.

25 Roberts, *Stalin's Wars*, p. 275.

26 *FRUS, The Conference of Berlin, 1945*, United States Government Printing Office, 1960, vol. 2, pp. 359–62. Churchill's use of 'iron curtain' was not original. Goebbels, for example, used the term in *Das Reich* on 25 February 1945.

27 *FRUS, The Conference of Berlin, 1945*, pp. 566–7.

28 Rees, *Behind Closed Doors*, p. 370.

29 Dilks (ed.), *Cadogan Diaries*, p. 765, Cadogan minute of 17 July 1945 to Churchill.

30 Potsdam Agreement, 1 August 1945, clause A. 3 (i), https://www.nato.int /ebookshop/video/declassified/doc_files/Potsdam%20Agreement.pdf.

31 Service, *Stalin*, p. 505.

32 David R. Henderson, *German Economic Miracle*, https://www.econlib.org/ library/Enc/GermanEconomicMiracle.html.

33 Of the ten *Speziallager* (special camps) the Soviets established in occupied Germany, three were in former concentration camps: Buchenwald, Sachsenhausen and Jamlitz (former KZ Lieberose).

34 Rees, *Behind Closed Doors*, p. 385.

35 J. Stalin, *Problems of Leninism*, Foreign Language Publishing House, 1945, pp. 455–6, quoted in Martin McCauley, *Stalin and Stalinism*, Routledge, 4th edn, 2019, Kindle edn, pp. 139–40.

36 Sarah Davies, 'Stalin and the Making of the Leader Cult in the 1930s', in Balázs Apor, Jan C. Behrends, Polly Jones and E. A. Rees (eds.), *The Leader Cult in Communist Dictatorships: Stalin and the Eastern Bloc*, Palgrave Macmillan, 2004, p. 29.

37 A. N. Yakovlev and V. Naumov (eds.), *Georgii Zhukov: Stenogramma Oktiabr'skogo (1957 g.) Plenuma TsK KPSS i Drugie Dokumenty*, MFD, 2001.

38 Ibid.

39 Roberts, *Zhukov*, p. 247.

40 Ibid., pp. 247–50.

41 Rees, *Behind Closed Doors*, pp. 399–400. Y. Gorlizki and O. Khlevniuk, *Cold Peace: Stalin and the Soviet Ruling Circle, 1945–1953*, Oxford University Press, 2004, p. 198.

42 Rees, *Behind Closed Doors*, p. 400. Letter from Molotov to Stalin, 20 January 1949, in Russian State Archive of Social and Political History, f. 17, op. 163, d. 1518, l. 164. Stalin sacked Molotov as Foreign Minister in March 1949, though he kept his position as first deputy chairman of the council of ministers.

43 Interview with Professor Vladimir Naumov in *Stalin and the Betrayal of Leningrad*, produced by Martina Balazova, executive produced by Laurence Rees, transmitted on BBC2 on 9 August 2002.

44 See ibid.

Afterword

1 See Timothy Snyder, 'Hitler vs. Stalin: Who Was Worse?', *New York Review of Books*, 27 January 2011. Robert Gellately, *Lenin, Stalin and Hitler*, Knopf, 2007, pp. 253–6. Applebaum, *Red Famine*, p. xxiv. Also see Manfred Hildermeier, *Die Sowjetunion 1917–1991*, 3rd edn revised and enlarged, Oldenbourg, 2016, pp. 35–41 and 129–32. Also Dieter Pohl, 'Nationalsozialistische und stalinistische Massenverbrechen: Überlegungen zum wissenschaftlichen Vergleich', in Jürgen Zarusky (ed.), *Stalin und die Deutschen. Neue Beiträge der Forschung*, Oldenbourg, 2006, pp. 253–63. Gunnar Heinsohn, *Lexikon der Völkermorde*, Rowohlt Taschenbuch, 1998, p. 294. Christian Hartmann, *Unternehmen Barbarossa. Der deutsche Krieg im Osten 1941–1945*, C. H. Beck, 2012, p. 115. And https://encyclopedia.ushmm. org/content/en/article/documenting-numbers-of-victims-of-the-holocaust -and-nazi-persecution.

2 Assessing the number who died in the Gulag system is problematic. For example, Christian Gerlach and Nicolas Werth in their essay 'State Violence – Violent Societies', in Michael Geyer and Sheila Fitzpatrick (eds.), *Beyond Totalitarianism: Stalinism and Nazism Compared*, Cambridge University Press, 2009, write at p. 176, 'Between 16 and 17 million Soviet citizens were subject to imprisonment or forced labor; 10 percent of them died in the camps', while Timothy Snyder in his article 'Hitler vs. Stalin: Who Was Worse?', writes, 'The total figure for the entire Stalinist period

[of deaths in the Gulag] is likely between two million and three million'. And Anne Applebaum in *Gulag* writes at p. 520 that a number for the dead 'in the camps of the Gulag and in the exile villages in the Stalinist era, from 1929 to 1953 . . . based on archival sources is available, although even the historian who compiled it points out that it is incomplete, and does not cover all categories of prisoner in every year. Again, I reluctantly cite it: 2,749,163.' But Applebaum also reminds us (p. 521) of the limitations of mere numbers in aiding our understanding.

3 Golfo Alexopoulos in *Illness and Inhumanity in Stalin's Gulag*, Kindle edn, writes at p. 16, 'A conservative estimate, in my view, would place Gulag mortality in the range of six million at a minimum. I believe that it is reasonable to conclude from the Gulag's own health records that no fewer than one-third of all individuals who passed through Stalin's labor camps and colonies died as a result of their detention.'

4 The question of exactly how many non-Jewish Poles died in the Second World War is also difficult to assess. One overview of the question is provided by the United States Holocaust Memorial Museum: 'today scholars of independent Poland believe that 1.8 to 1.9 million Polish civilians (non-Jews) were victims of German occupation policies and the war. This approximate total includes Poles killed in executions or who died in prisons, forced labor, and concentration camps. It also includes an estimated 225,000 civilian victims of the 1944 Warsaw uprising, more than 50,000 civilians who died during the 1939 invasion and siege of Warsaw, and a relatively small but unknown number of civilians killed during the Allies' military campaign of 1944–45 to liberate Poland.' See p. 24 in https://www.ushmm.org/m/pdfs/2000 926-Poles.pdf.

5 See above pp. 91, 101.

6 John Barber and Mark Harrison, 'Patriotic War, 1941–1945', in Ronald Grigor Suny (ed.), *The Cambridge History of Russia*, vol. 3: *The Twentieth Century*, Cambridge University Press, 2006, pp. 217–42, here p. 226. Barber and Harrison are more specific and state that 7.4 million Soviet citizens died 'in hot or cold blood' during the German occupation.

7 The designation used by Barber and Harrison, ibid., p. 226.

8 Barber and Harrison give a specific estimate of 'premature deaths under [German] occupation' in the Soviet Union of 13.7 million, a total which includes 7.4 million killed in 'hot or cold blood' (see above): ibid.

9 See above p. 318.

10 Rees, *Dark Charisma*, p. 1.

11 See above p. 101.

12 See above p. 316.

13 Khrushchev's 'secret' speech to the Twentieth Party Congress of the Communist Party of the 25 February 1956, https://digitalarchive.wilsoncenter.org/document/115995.pdf?v=3c22b71b65bcbbe9fdfadead9419c995.

14 Reported in *Daily Telegraph*, 16 April 2019, https://www.telegraph.co.uk/news/2019/04/16/record-70-per-cent-russians-approve-stalin/.

15 Reported in *Moscow Times*, 26 June 2017, https://www.themoscowtimes.com/2017/06/26/stalin-named-worlds-most-remarkable-public-figure-poll-a58262.

16 Interview with Vladimir Putin on 'Direct Line' multichannel TV, 16 April 2015, quoted in Robert Service, *Kremlin Winter: Russia and the Second Coming of Vladimir Putin*, Picador, 2019, Kindle edn, location 704.

17 See above p. 309.

18 President Vladimir Putin's annual news conference, December 2019, http://en.kremlin.ru/events/president/news/62366.

19 Previously unpublished testimony, but also see Rees, *Their Darkest Hour*, pp. 101–6.

20 Rees, *War of the Century*, p. 235.

Index

Aachen 350
Abelesz, Israel 321
Alexopoulos, Golfo 463n3
Algeria 245
Alliluyeva, Kira xxvi
Alliluyeva, Nadezhda 291, 292
Alliluyeva, Svetlana 292
Altrogge, Joseph xxxii–xxxiii
Anchishkin, Vladlen 375–6, 378
Anders, Władysław 170–71, 345
Andreyeva, Nina 24–5
Anfilov, Viktor 138
anti-Semitism
  'Aryan' vs Jew narrative of H. S. Chamberlain
    xxx
  of Cadogan 303
  in Canada xxiv
  and Germany's defeat in First World War 2,
    151–2
  Lithuanian 119
  Nazi: and 'Aryan' purity xxxii–xxxiii, 259;
    and Babi Yar massacre 128–30; calumny that
    Jews were behind NKVD crimes 116; and
    civil service 417n42; against German Jews
    155, 156; ghetto confinement 36, 156,
    190–91, 308–9; and Goebbels' Total War
    speech 256; Hitler's desire for destruction of
    Jews 152, 168, 240–41, 289, 310–12, 319–22,
    383, 396; Hitler's racist doctrine and hatred
    of Jews xxx–xxxii, 1, 16, 64, 81, 130,
    150–52, 162–3, 167–8, 191–2, 203, 240–41,
    289, 311–12, 316, 319–22, 352, 354, 383; and
    Holocaust see Holocaust; and the Jewish
    'problem'/'question' 16, 36, 153, 154, 162–3,
    167–8, 203, 259, 310–11, 312, 314, 321–2, 354
    see also Holocaust; Kristallnacht xxxii;
    linking of Jews and 'partisans' 154; and
    'Madagascar' plan 35–6, 310–11; mass
    murder 39, 103, 128–30, 152, 168, 190–92,
    240–41, 259, 289, 310–11, 312, 313–14, 316,
    317, 319, 319–22, 330–31, 383, 395–6 see also
    Holocaust; and Operation Barbarossa see
    Jews: and Operation Barbarossa; against
    Polish Jews 24, 29, 34, 35–6, 103, 190–92,
    395–6, 397 see also Poland: concentration
    camps (Nazi) in; and starvation 190–92;

    unease of ordinary Germans hearing about
    persecution of Jews 288–9, 350–51; and
    yellow star 155
  Romanian anti-Semitism and mass murder of
    Jews 153–4
  of Sebottendorff xxix
  of Stalin 393
  Ukrainian 119, 128–30
Antonescu, Ion 152, 153
Antonov, Aleksei 356
Antwerp 352
Applebaum, Anne 463n2
Arctic convoys, British 224–6, 229
Ardennes forest offensive 352–3
arms race 389
Artem'ev, P. A. 147, 148–9
Astakhov, Georgii 15
atheism xxxiii
Atlantic Charter 174, 337–8
  and Soviet retention of eastern Poland after the
    war 300, 337–8
Augustów forest 27
Auschwitz 30, 43, 44, 188–90, 313–14, 315,
  316–17, 318
  Auschwitz Birkenau's construction 189, 190
  and Himmler 188–9
  Hungarian Jews sent to 318–19, 321
  Kapos 42, 316
  SS at 190, 319
Austria, Nazi invasion of 8
Avranches 343

Babi Yar massacre 128–30
Backe, Herbert 101
Badmaev, Aleksey 307–8, 402
Badoglio, Pietro 284
Bagration, Operation 324–9
Baibakov, Nikolai 223–4
Baku 91–2, 139, 230
Balkelis, Tomas 425n32
Baltic States 27, 30, 50, 51, 76, 86, 94, 116,
  127, 139, 172, 322 see also Estonia; Latvia;
  Lithuania
  Baltic Germans 30–32
  and Brest-Litovsk treaty 3, 81
  and Britain 172

Baltic States – *cont'd.*
  deportations from 116, 322
  Operation Bagration and Soviet takeover 329
  and Operation Barbarossa 94, 111
  and possible Soviet secret peace deal
    discussions with Germans 138–9
  and post-war borders 172
  Red Army in 27, 30–31, 50
Barbarossa, Operation, and German occupation
    of Soviet Union 109–283
  Babi Yar massacre 128–30
  and Baku/Caucasus oil 91–2, 94, 106, 139, 215,
    223–4, 230
  ber 295
  and Britain 104, 105–6, 113–15, 125–6, 134, 198
  Commissar Order 99, 185
  crisis in Soviet confidence witnessed by
    Grossman 134–5
  as 'decisive front' according to Hitler 279
  German officers' views and concerns before the
    start 98–101
  Hitler's confidence and boasting (autumn 1941)
    131–2
  Hitler's decision to hold out and continue
    fighting after Stalingrad defeat 256
  and Hitler's extremist views 163–4
  Hitler's 'master plan' and disappointment at
    progress (summer 1941) 120–21
  Hitler's vision, plans and
    discussions, and events leading to 78–94
  and Holocaust birth 103, 128–30, 168, 189–92,
    240–41, 259
  ideological nature of 98, 99, 106, 117, 132, 322,
    396–7
  initial offensive 107–30
  and Jews *see* Jews: and Operation Barbarossa
  Kharkov battle (May 1942) 198–202, 210,
    214, 235
  Kiev, 1941 battle of 124, 131
  Kursk offensive and battle 278–82
  and Leningrad 94, 131, 133, 221; siege 175–83
  mine-laying by Nazis at Tallinn, and Soviet
    naval disaster 122–3
  and Molotov 107, 108
  and Moscow *see* Moscow, and Operation
    Barbarossa
  Nazi expectations of deaths 91, 101
  Operation Blue's continuation of *see* Blue,
    Operation
  partisan opposition 293–5
  as a planned 'war of extermination' 18, 98,
    99–103, 131, 163
  Red Army's resistance and counter-attacks *see*
    Red Army: eastern front and German conflict
  and Russian steppes 132, 215–25
  Shlisselburg's fall 133

Smolensk battle 120
  and Soviet Council for Evacuation plans for
    restoring industrial capacities 194–5
  and Stalin 107–8, 127; and the Church 116–17;
    and Churchill 95, 114–15, 125–6, 134;
    finding scapegoats 115, 123, 133, 150, 202–3;
    and Kiev disaster 123–5, 144; leadership
    95–7, 108, 111–12, 115, 116–17, 121–7,
    195–202 *see also* Stalin, Joseph: leadership;
    mental state and decisions that shaped
    response to German invasion 95–8, 103–6,
    121; and military equipment production
    194–5; Order 270 to Red Army 123–5, 222;
    request for outside assistance 125–6, 134
  and Stalingrad 131, 132; and Operation Blue *see*
    Stalingrad: and Operation Blue; and
    Operation Ring 253; and Operation Saturn
    force availability 251–2; and Operation
    Uranus *see* Uranus, Operation; and
    Operation Winter Storm 251
  and starvation *see* starvation
  and Ukraine *see* Ukraine: and the Nazis
  and the US 114, 125–6, 134, 198
  and weather/temperature 142, 149, 157, 159,
    181, 184, 251
  Wehrmacht mission command (*Auftragstaktik*)
    111, 195
Bastogne 353
Baur, Hans 385
Bayeux 343
Beck, Ludwig 64, 330
Behnke, Carlheinz 102–3, 105, 117, 119, 129, 239
Behr, Winrich 252, 253
Belgium 69 *see also* Low Countries
  and Ardennes forest offensive 352, 353
Belorussia 138–9
Below, Günther von 167, 235
Below, Nicolaus von 135, 164, 231, 249, 253,
    353, 379
Berezhkov, Valentin 84, 85
Berghof, Hitler's mountain retreat 93, 246,
    289–91, 368
Beria, Lavrenti xxiii, 27, 39–40, 45, 76, 104–5,
    112, 140, 158
  and abandonment or defence of Moscow 145,
    146
  and Kalmyk deportations 308
  possible secret peace deal discussions with
    Germans 138–9
  and Zhukov 391
Berlin
  Führerbunker 350, 374, 379, 380, 381, 382,
    383, 384
  Hitler's fiftieth-birthday celebrations in 379
  Hitler's speech marking 1942 campaign for
    'winter relief' 239–41

Hitler's Sportpalast speeches 135–6, 203, 239
Hitler's talks with Hácha 9–10
Hitler's talks with Molotov 82–8
Jews 155
RAF bombing of 256
Red Army assault on 355, 369–71, 375–8
revolution (1919) 2, 98
Bernadotte, Folke 380
Berzarin, Nikolai 384–5
Berzina, Maya 38–9, 140
Bielecki, Jerzy 29, 42, 188
Blaskowitz, Johannes 65
Bletchley Park 279
Blomberg, Werner von 64
Blue, Operation 214–24, 230–45, 278
    and Caucasus resources 215, 220–21
    German October offensive 243, 244–5
    German POWs 262–4
    and Red Army *see* Red Army: eastern front
        and German conflict: and Operation Blue
    Riechel's battle plans 214–15
    and Stalin 214–15, 216, 221–4, 233, 243–4
    and Stalingrad *see* Stalingrad: and Operation
        Blue
Bobruisk 325–7
Bock, Fedor von 67, 72, 94, 99–100, 135, 142,
    149, 159
    and Hitler 92–3, 101, 142, 217
    and Paulus 235
Bodenschatz, Karl 258
Bohemia and Moravia, Protectorate of 8
Bohlen, Charles 300, 302
Bolshevism/Bolsheviks
    active member numbers xxiii
    anti-religious view of 98
    atheism of xxxiii
    and Brest-Litovsk treaty 3–4, 81
    British concerns about possible Bolshevik
        takeover 77
    and centralization of power xxi
    collectivization and agricultural restructuring
        118, 130, 188, 195
    commemorating 1941 anniversary of 1917
        revolution 141, 148–9
    economic-incompetence view of 98
    Hitler's hatred of xxxv, 1–2, 4–5, 81, 98, 117,
        131, 256, 351–2, 354
    inequality 179–80
    and the Jews *see* Jews: and Bolshevism/Marxism
    murder of Tsar Nicholas II and his family
        xxvii, 12
    and nationalism xxxv
    October Revolution xx
    Operation Barbarossa and Nazi aim to crush *see*
        Barbarossa, Operation, and German
        occupation of Soviet Union

Red Army *see entries at* Red Army
    rise of xxxiv, 125
    and Russian soldiers' discontent in First World
        War 125
Bór-Komorowski, Tadeusz 345
Borisov, Mikhail 281
Borisov, Vasily 160, 223
Bormann, Martin 257, 259, 291
Brandt, Nikolai 333, 346
Brauchitsch, Walther von 66–7, 82, 94, 106, 120,
    165, 166
Braun, Eva xxviii, 289–91
    marriage to Hitler xxviii, 382–3
Braunau am Inn xix
Bräutigam, Otto 155
Brest 113
Brest-Litovsk, treaty of 3–4, 81, 350
Bris, Aleksey 117–19
Britain
    air force *see* RAF
    army *see* British Army
    and Baltic States 172
    concerns about possible Bolshevik takeover 77
    and Finland 58–9, 60, 80
    Hess's flight to 103
    and Hitler/the Nazis: and Czechoslovakia's
        dismantling 10–11; and Hitler's 28 April
        1939 speech 15–16; Hitler's admiration of
        British Empire 78; Hitler's desire for
        alliance/friendship 15, 21, 79; Hitler's
        expectation that Britain would make peace
        93; Hitler's hesitation to attack 78, 79–80,
        82, 93; Munich agreement 9, 11, 13, 18, 399;
        Nazi attack plans 67–8, 79–80; Ribbentrop
        on Britain's 'defeat' 84; and Russia as
        'Britain's last hope' 80; and shelving of
        Madagascar plan 311
    naval power 78, 80
    and Poland 11–13, 21, 209, 270–74, 301–3, 337,
        346–9, 372
    and Soviet Union: and Arctic convoys 224–6,
        229; Chamberlain's distrust 12, 14; and
        Churchill's 'naughty' document on
        percentages of Allied influences 348, 371–2;
        and discovery of Polish mass graves 270–74;
        disdain of British elite for Soviet leadership
        103–4, 105–6; fear of Soviet alliance with
        Hitler 13, 14, 277; and Finland's attack by
        Red Army 58–9, 60, 80; First Protocol 134;
        and Hitler's view of Russia as 'Britain's last
        hope' 80, 102; Molotov's secret negotiations
        and treaty 208–11; and Operation
        Barbarossa 104, 105–6, 113–15, 125–6, 134,
        198; passing of intelligence to Soviets
        279–80; and Poland 11–13, 209, 270–74,
        301–3, 337, 346–9, 372; and post-war

Britain – *cont'd.*
  borders 171–2, 174, 209–11, 301–3, 337; and
    public opinion in 1938 9; Soviet proposal of
    military alliance with France and Britain
    12–15, 17, 21; Stalin and 'non-aggressive
    states' including 7–8; Stalin's congratulations
    for bombing campaign against Germany 268;
    and Stalin's desire for second front 125–6,
    209, 210, 225–6, 244, 266–9, 274–8, 298, 300;
    Stalin's request for British divisions to fight
    alongside Red Army 134
  and the US 80; American resources behind
    British war effort 144, 161; Atlantic Charter
    see Atlantic Charter; Cairo conference 298;
    Churchill and Roosevelt relations *see*
    Churchill, Winston: and Roosevelt; First
    Protocol 134; strained relationship around
    time of Tehran conference 298–9
  and Versailles treaty *see* Versailles, treaty of
  War Office 105
British Army 77
  Stalin's request for divisions to fight alongside
    Red Army 134
  tanks 134
British Empire 15, 16, 78, 87
Brooke, Sir Alan 230, 300, 342, 364–5
Bryansk 136, 142
Brygidki prison, Lwów 115–16, 119
Bubenchikov, Fyodor 221–2, 248, 296–7, 327
Buber-Neumann, Margarete 28
Buchenwald concentration camp 389
Budapest 320
  declared by Hitler as 'fortified place' 357
  fall to Red Army 357–8, 359
Bukharin, Nikolai 391
Bukovina 76, 86
Bulgaria 89, 348
  declaration of war on Germany 351
  Hitler on reason for 'collapse' of 355
  Soviet occupation/repression 351, 371; and
    British exclusion 386
Bullock, Alan: *Hitler and Stalin: Parallel Lives* xvi
Burckhardt, Carl 17
Burkovski, Albert 234, 243
Busch, Ernst 329
Büttner, Gretl 286
Byrnes, James 385

Cadogan, Sir Alexander 10–11, 12, 14, 104,
    172–3, 209, 273, 303, 355, 362, 366, 386–7
Cairncross, John 279–80
Cairo conference 298
Canada, King's fight against admitting Jews
    xxiv
cannibalism 181–2, 190

capitalism
  vs socialism xxxiv, xxxv, 389
  Stalin at war with xxxv–xxxvi, 389
Caucasus 82, 91–2, 94, 106
  and Operation Blue *see* Blue, Operation
  resources 215, 220–21; oil 82, 91–2, 94, 106,
    139, 215, 223–4, 230
Chamberlain, Houston Stewart: *Foundations of the
    Nineteenth Century* xxx
Chamberlain, Neville xxiv, 366
  and deal with Soviets 12, 14, 17
  distrust of Soviets 12, 14
  and Munich agreement 11, 13
  and Nazi takeover of Czech lands 11
  and Poland 11
  and Red Army 13
Choltitz, Dietrich von 344, 345
Christianity and the Church
  Catholic Church 205–6
  Hitler's hatred of xxviii, 204–6
  Orthodox Church 116–17
  and Stalin: hatred of Christianity xxviii; and
    Operation Barbarossa 116–17; suffering
    under 116
Christie, Malcolm 15
Chuikov, Vasily 237, 238, 243
Churchill, Winston
  and Arctic convoy losses 224–6
  and Cripps 103
  and de Gaulle 341, 342–3
  and democratic 'principles' 174
  ego 229
  on Finland 58–9
  Fulton speech 386
  and Hitler 203, 240
  and the 'iron fence'/'iron curtain' 386
  and the Jews, in Hitler's eyes 203, 240–41, 352
  and Katyn massacre discovery 271–2
  and Maisky 8, 125–6, 134, 171, 217, 226,
    244, 268
  and Mikołajczyk 347, 348
  and Molotov 209, 213
  and Nazi western offensive 69
  and Operation Barbarossa 95, 114–15, 125–6, 134
  rallying attempt on British following defeat of
    France 77
  and Roosevelt 80, 134, 211, 212–13, 275; and
    Atlantic Charter *see* Atlantic Charter;
    criticism of Churchill 337; and Katyn
    massacre 273; and Russian repression in
    Romania 348; and second-front question
    274–8, 298, 300; and Stalin and Yalta
    conference/agreement 361–7, 370–71; and
    Stalin's meeting with Davies 275–8; and
    Stalin's Tehran conference 297–304

and Soviet swallowing of Baltic States 329
and Stalin 105–6, 171, 225–30, 244, 269, 272,
  297, 366, 372–3; and Arctic convoys 224–6;
  and Churchill's self-delusion 348–9, 366–7;
  and Cripps 103; and democratic elements of
  Yalta agreement 386; and 'London Poles'
  347; and 'naughty' document on percentages
  of Allied influences 348, 371–2; and
  Operation Barbarossa 95, 114–15, 125–6,
  134; at Potsdam 386; and Roosevelt, and
  Yalta conference/agreement 361–7, 370–71;
  and Roosevelt, in Tehran 299–304; and
  second-front question 125–6, 225–30, 244,
  266–9, 274–8, 298, 300; and Soviet retention
  of eastern Poland after the war 301–3,
  337–8, 346–9, 372; and Stalin's foreign
  policy speech (spring 1939) 8; and Stalin's
  meeting with Davies 275–8
and Yalta conference/agreement 361–2, 363,
  364–7, 370–71, 386
Ciano, Galeazzo, Count xxiv–xxv, 17, 83, 93,
  105, 161, 185
Clark Kerr, Sir Archibald 226, 228, 229, 273, 356
coal 220–21
Cold War 385, 386
Comintern 6, 301
commissars 76, 95, 98, 99–100, 124, 151, 185, 223,
  274, 377
  Commissar Order 99, 185
  Jewish 151
concentration camps *see individual camps by name*
Crimean Tatars 306, 317–18
Cripps, Sir Stafford 103, 104, 228
Curzon Line 337–8
Czechoslovakia
  dismantled by Hitler 8–11
  Stalin and its interest in Marshall plan 387
  Sudetenland 8–9

D-Day 210, 324, 337
Dachau concentration camp 43
Darges, Fritz xxiii
Davies, Joseph 275–6, 277
de Gaulle, Charles 341–5, 356–7
death camps *see individual camps by name*
democracy
  and Atlantic Charter 174, 300, 337–8
  Churchill and democratic 'principles' 174
  Hitler's hatred of xxii, xxxvii–xxxviii
  Stalin's opposition to xxxvii–xxxviii
  and Yalta agreement 363, 364, 386 *see also* Yalta
    conference/agreement
Desert Victory 268
Dietrich, Otto 136
Dietrich, Sepp 374–5

Dimitrov, Georgi 83, 84, 141
disabled people, Nazi 'euthanasia' of 39, 205, 206,
  396, 415n74, 437n48
Djilas, Milovan 51, 359
Dlanic 153
Domobranci xvii
Dönitz, Karl 368
Döring, Herbert 290–91, 292
Dragunov, Georgy 25–6, 39
Drax, Sir Reginald Aylmer Ranfurly Plunkett-
    Ernle-Erle- 14–15, 17
Dresden bombing 367, 458n48
Dunkirk 69
  evacuation 77
Dyukarev, Nikolai 40, 44–5
Dzhugashvili, Vasily (son of Stalin) 292
Dzhugashvili, Yakov (son of Stalin) 292

Eden, Anthony 104, 171–2, 173–4, 179, 209, 210,
  271, 273, 275–6, 301, 302
Ehrenburg, Ilya 378
Eichmann, Adolf 36, 191, 320–21
Eigi, Irma 31, 32
Eigi family 31, 32
Einsatzgruppen 24, 103, 119
Eisenhower, Dwight D. 345, 373
Ekart, Antoni 192
Elbrus, Mount 220
Elser, Georg 67
Elsey, George 126, 276, 386
Endre, László 320
Engel, Gerhard 88, 91
Engels, Frederick xxxiii, xxxvi–xxxvii, 291
  portrait in Stalin's office 355, 356
English Channel 69, 77, 79
Erbe, Das xxxii
Esser, Hermann 367–8
Estonia 27, 30, 31 *see also* Baltic States
  Tallinn naval disaster 122–3
European Recovery Program (Marshall)
  plan 387

famine *see* starvation
Ferenczy, László 320
Fernau, Walter 332
Feste Plätze (fortified places) 325, 328, 357
Fiedler, Heinz 325–7
Filipkowski, Władysław 339
Finland
  armed forces 47, 52, 54, 55, 58–9, 60
  arms supplies from Germany 88
  and Britain 58–9, 60, 80
  Civil War 62
  and France 60
  Hitler on reason for 'collapse' of 355

Finland – *cont'd.*
　Hitler's concern that Red Army should not
　　extend occupation of 86–7
　Karelo-Finnish Republic 61
　and League of Nations 62
　and the Nazis 61–2, 86–7, 88, 89
　peace treaty with Soviets 60
　sham 'democratic' government 59, 61
　Soviet campaign against *see*
　　Winter War
　under Soviet 'sphere of influence' 62, 86–7,
　　88, 89
　Stalin's ignoring of Finns' views (1939) 357
　US national Finland Day 58
First World War xix–xx, 72, 350
　anti-Semitism and Germany's defeat in 2,
　　151–2
　and Brest-Litovsk treaty 3–4, 81, 350
　food-supply collapse 101
　German Jews in 156
　and Hitler xix, xx, 151–2, 156, 178
　hunger 175
　Russian soldiers' discontent as enabler of
　　Bolshevik Revolution 125
　and Stalin xix–xx
　and Versailles treaty 2, 5–6, 65
Forster, Albert xxiii, 27, 45
Fosdick, Henry Emerson 58
France
　and Americans in First World War 245
　Avranches breakthrough and
　　counter-attack 343
　and Finland 60
　Free French movement 343
　Munich agreement 9, 11, 18, 399
　and the Nazis: 1940 armistice 73; fall of Paris
　　74, 94; and French 2nd Armoured Division
　　345; initial Allied advance in France 324;
　　May 1940 defeat 69–72, 74, 86, 94; plans and
　　preparations for conquest 65, 67–8
　Paris *see* Paris
　and Soviet Union: Soviet proposal of
　　military alliance with France and Britain
　　12–15, 17, 21; Stalin and 'non-aggressive
　　states' including 7–8
　and Versailles treaty *see* Versailles, treaty of
Franco, Francisco 6, 384–5
Frank, Hans xxi, xxiii, 28–9, 34, 35, 36, 168, 171
Fromm, Friedrich 232–3, 329–30, 441n59
Funk, Walther 90
Fyodorov, Veniamin 327–8

Galen, Clemens August von 205–6
Gallay, Mark 49, 54, 96
Gareev, Makhmut 202–3

Gauleiters xxiii, 44, 45, 156, 367, 406n11
Gavrilchenko, Inna 184, 185
Gehlen, Reinhard 293
Georges, Alphonse-Joseph 69
Georgia xix, xx, xxxv
Germany
　air force *see* Luftwaffe
　Allied 1944 advance into 350–55
　Allied bombing campaign in 227, 244, 256, 258,
　　286, 367; attempts to compare Holocaust
　　with 316, 398; Berlin 256; Dresden 367,
　　458n48; Hamburg 285–6; Nuremberg 258;
　　RAF *see* RAF: bombing campaign against
　　Germany
　anti-Semitism at end of First World War
　　xxix, 2
　armed forces, unified under Nazis *see*
　　Wehrmacht
　and Brest-Litovsk treaty 3–4, 81
　and Bukovina 86
　'classless' xxxvi, 241
　Communist Party 5
　contrast between West and East 389
　East 389
　Historikerstreit (Historian's Dispute) 396
　Hitler's attack on legal profession and judicial
　　system 206–8
　Hitler's doubts about loyalty of German
　　people, and view that those losing faith
　　deserved to 'disappear' 203–4
　and Japan *see* Japan: and Germany/the Nazis
　Jews 155, 156
　navy under Nazis *see* Kriegsmarine
　Nazi *see* Nazism/National Socialists
　Potsdam and the splitting of 386–7
　rationing 208
　Reich population oppressed by Nazi terror
　　tactics 368
　Soviet agreement in treaty of Rapallo
　　409n12
　tripartite pact with Japan and Italy 87, 88,
　　160–61
　Versailles treaty 2, 5–6, 65
　Volga Germans 155, 168–9, 306
　West 389
　and world wars *see* First World War; Second
　　World War theatres and major events
Gersdorff, Rudolf Christoph Freiherr von 288
Gestapo 28, 262
　NKVD and Lwów Gestapo HQ 334–5
ghettos 36, 156, 190–91, 308–9
Gobineau, Arthur de: *Essai sur l'inégalité des races
　　humaines* xxix
Goebbels, Joseph 30, 61, 62, 89, 97, 68, 207–8,
　　245, 256–8, 259–60, 331, 374, 379

and Allied 1944 advance into Germany: and
    Nemmersdorf murders and rapes 350; and
    possible peace deal with Stalin 351
and Bormann 257
and discovery of Polish mass graves 270
and German Jews 155, 156
and Göring 257–8, 259, 286
on Hitler's 3 October 1941 Sportpalast
    speech 136
and Italy 285
and Katyn massacre 273
and *Kolberg* 381–2
loyalty to Hitler 368; and determination to die
    with wife and children alongside him 3
    81, 382
and Operation Barbarossa 102, 105, 106,
    120–21, 131, 132, 136, 157
and RAF bombing 285–7
regaining confidence in Hitler 259–60
rising scepticism 323
suicide 383
Total War speech 256
Goebbels, Magda 291, 292
Golokolenko, Ivan 248, 249–50
Göring, Hermann 4, 9, 34, 43, 83, 92, 101,
    164–5, 185–6, 195, 207, 257–8,
    259, 379
failure as head of Luftwaffe 256, 374
and Goebbels 257–8, 259, 286
and Guderian 261
Hitler's feeling of betrayal by 380–81
Hitler's order of arrest 380
speech following German defeat at Stalingrad
    255–6
Gorky 156
Great Britain *see* Britain
Great Terror 48–9, 54, 63, 67, 73, 81–2, 179, 274,
    331, 398
Greece 13, 97, 348, 372
Greenwood, Arthur 11
Greiser, Arthur 44, 45, 190–91
Groeben, Peter von der 111, 261
Groening, Oskar 312–14, 315, 316–17, 319
Grossman, Vasily 111, 134–5, 137–8, 142, 237,
    242, 243, 359, 378
Gryniv, Boguslava and family 37–8
Guderian, Heinz 68, 113, 156, 232, 278–9, 331,
    360–61
and Göring 261
and Hitler 68, 165–6, 167, 192, 261, 279,
    360–61, 375
and Kursk offensive 279, 280
Gulag camps 39, 41–2, 44, 118, 192, 193, 295, 296,
    395, 462–3n2, 463n3
Gutterer, Leopold 89

Hácha, Emil 9–10
Haeften, Werner von 330
Halder, Franz 24, 65, 79, 81, 82, 83, 88–9, 106,
    113, 120, 133, 156, 177, 216, 218, 231, 236
Halifax, Edward Frederick Lindley Wood, 1st
    Earl of xxiv, 11–12, 53, 77
Hamburg bombing 285–6
Harriman, Averell xxvii, 276, 340
Harris, Sir Arthur 285
Harvey, Oliver 268
Hassebroek, Johannes xxxvii
Hehn, Jeannette von 32–3
Heiden, Konrad 157
Heim, Ferdinand 249
Heinrichs, Erik 60
Henderson, Sir Nevile 21
Herling, Gustaw 41–3, 44, 192–3
Hess, Rudolf 103, 244
Heydrich, Reinhard 103
Himmler, Heinrich xxiii, 30, 31–2, 34, 42, 91,
    101, 203, 261, 287
and Auschwitz 188–9
Beer Hall Putsch anniversary speech (1944)
    351–2
and destruction of Warsaw 341
expelled from Nazi Party and stripped of titles
    380
and Jews to be treated as partisans 154
and 'Madagascar' plan 35, 310, 311
'Some Thoughts on the Treatment of the Alien
    Population in the East' memo 35
and Soviet advance on Germany 360, 374
Hindenburg, Paul von xxii, 63, 64, 417n42
Hindenlang, Gerhard 235, 262
Historikerstreit (Historian's Dispute) 396
Hitler, Adolf
anti-Semitism xxx–xxxii, 1, 16, 64, 81, 130,
    150–52, 162–3, 167–8, 191–2, 203, 240–41,
    289, 310–11, 316, 319–22, 352, 354, 383; and
    fear of American Jews 352
appearance xxiv; in 1945 367; eyes xxiii, xxiv
appointed Chancellor of Germany xxii
appointed head of state and Führer xxii, 287
Ardennes forest offensive 352–3
assassination attempts xxvi, 64, 67, 288, 329–31
authorizing violent/destructive acts:
    decimation of Leningrad and its citizens
    177–8; destruction/mass murder of Jews 152,
    168, 241, 289, 310, 312, 319–22, 383, 395–6 *see
    also* Holocaust; with invasion of Poland
    22–4, 30, 397; killing of selected disabled
    Germans 415n74 *see also* disabled people,
    Nazi 'euthanasia' of; Röhm murder and
    'Night of the Long Knives' 62–3, 405n4;
    scorched-land policy 368–9; torture 29

Hitler, Adolf – *cont'd.*
Berghof mountain retreat 93, 246, 289–91, 368
birth and family background xix
and Bock 92–3, 101, 142, 217
and Bormann 257, 259, 291
and Braun xxviii, 289–91; marriage xxviii, 382–3
and Britain *see* Britain: and Hitler/the Nazis
character: blaming scapegoats/creating blame culture xix, 150–51, 203, 207, 249, 352, 375; bombastic 17–18, 20; as 'charismatic leader' xx–xxi, 135–6, 352; contempt 9, 361; contrasting impressions on people who knew or met him xix, xxiii–xxv, 85; extremist views 18, 163–4, 361, 369, 380–81; exuding trust and confidence xxiii, 135–6, 239, 259–60; hatred of democracy xxii, xxxvii–xxxviii; inability to listen to others' points of view xxii; intransigence xxii, 166; living in own alternative reality 106, 165–6, 252–3; megalomania 3, 17–18; overconfidence/absolute conviction 101, 143, 167, 323; perceived as unbalanced oddity xix; persuasiveness 65, 135–6, 259–60; propaganda image xxvi, 121, 289, 383; ruthlessness xvii, 18, 63–4, 69, 177–8; suspicion of institutional attempt to restrict him xxiii; temper xix, 218, 236, 238–9, 258; trust xxvi; uncompromising xxii
and Christianity xxviii, 204–6
and Churchill 203, 240
and a 'classless' Germany xxxvi, 241
and collapse of his allies 351, 355
coup attempt in Munich xxx
Czechoslovakia's dismantling by 8–11
and demand/myth of self-sacrifice 254, 361, 380–81, 382, 383, 384
despair and mental state in April 1945 379–83
doubts about loyalty of German people, and view that those losing faith deserved to 'disappear' 203–4
dress xxvii
and Feste Plätze 325, 328, 357
fiftieth-birthday celebrations 379
and Finland 62
and First World War xix, xx, 151–2, 156, 178
Frederick the Great references 166, 353, 368
and Gauleiters xxiii, 45, 367
and Magda Goebbels, before her marriage 292
and Guderian 68, 165–6, 167, 192, 261, 278–9, 360–61, 375
and Hácha 9–10
health problems 292

and Himmler 34, 287, 351–2, 360; and Hitler's feeling of betrayal 380–81
and Horthy 319–20, 351
and Hungary 319–21, 351
infrastructure destruction order 368–9
and Knight's Cross 241
and Kursk offensive 278–82
last days in Berlin bunker 380–84
leadership 63–73, 132–3, 143, 168; charismatic xx–xxi, 135–6, 352; in comparison with Stalin's 47–73, 91, 120–27, 133, 143–6, 196, 215, 324; dismissing accurate intelligence 360–61; inadequacies/mistakes with Operation Bagration 325–7, 328; 'leadership/ Leader crisis' and Goebbels' and Göring's attempt to influence him 257–9; multiple leadership roles of armed forces 232; and retreat from public view to avoid association with failure 255; tensions with generals 64, 65–7, 79, 94, 120, 131–2, 202, 217, 218
Lebensraum policy 64, 81, 90, 102, 239
legal profession and judicial system attacked by 206–8
and Manstein 252, 261; plan 68
Mein Kampf xxx, 1–2, 3, 6, 102, 204
modern perceptions in comparison with Stalin 395–401
and Molotov: and Nazi–Soviet pact *see* Nazi–Soviet pact; talks in Berlin 82–8
in Munich's German Workers' Party xx
and Mussolini xxiv–xxv, 62–3, 88, 93, 163–4, 283–4
'Nazification' of armed forces 331–2
negotiating tactics 86–7
obstacles to deposing 287
and oil *see* Nazism/National Socialists: and oil
Operation Barbarossa *see* Barbarossa, Operation, and German occupation of Soviet Union
and Operation Blue 215, 217–18, 220–21, 230–33, 236, 238–40, 245, 255, 256, 261–2 *see also* Blue, Operation
and Operation Uranus 249, 250–51, 252–3, 254
pact with Stalin *see* Nazi–Soviet pact
as a painter xix
and Paris 344
and Pearl Harbor bombing 161, 162
and Poland *see* Poland: and Hitler/the Nazis
popular idolization of 84, 239, 379
in prison xxx
racial ideology xxviii–xxxiii, 1, 5, 81, 130, 191–2, 203–4, 322
and RAF bombing 286–7
rhetorical tactics 18, 163, 203, 240, 246
and Roosevelt 16, 162–3, 240, 245

Second Book xxx–xxxi
and Slavs 81, 117
Slovakia's creation by 8, 9–10
soldiers' oaths to 288, 330
and Soviet advance on Germany 353, 360,
374–5; loss of confidence 353; scorched-land
policy 368–9
Soviet invasion *see* Barbarossa, Operation, and
German occupation of Soviet Union
speeches: Beer Hall Putsch 1941 anniversary,
Löwenbräukeller 150–52; Beer Hall Putsch
1942 anniversary, Löwenbräukeller 245–6;
Beer Hall Putsch 1944 anniversary,
Löwenbräukeller, read out by Himmler
351–2; launch of Nazi Party programme 1945
anniversary, Löwenbräukeller, read out by
Esser 367–8; Berchtesgaden (22 August 1939
to military commanders) 17–19; Berlin
speech marking 1942 campaign for 'winter
relief' 239–41; broadcast on radio 135–6,
162, 354; on classless Germany (April 1922)
xxxvi; either/or tactics 18, 163, 203, 246;
New Year 1942 message 203; New Year 1945
message 354–5; Nuremberg (September 1937)
4; Reich Chancellery (23 November 1939 to
military commanders) 66–7; to Reichstag
1939 (28 April) 15–16; to Reichstag 1940 (19
July) 79; to Reichstag 1941 (11 December)
162–3, 164, 167; to Reichstag 1942 (26 April)
207–8; Sportpalast (3 October 1941) 135–6;
Sportpalast (30 January 1942) 203;
triumphant happy ending of 151–2, 157, 163
SS loyalty to 287
on Stalin: and his Great Terror 73, 274; and his
introduction of commissars to Red Army
274; as instrument in hands of Jewry 151;
ridiculing his claims about German war
losses 151
Stalin's admiration for Röhm murder 63,
405n4
Stalin's and Hitler's areas of similarity:
approving torture xxii, 29, 311;
authorizing violent acts *see* Hitler, Adolf:
authorizing violent/destructive acts; Stalin,
Joseph: authorizing violent/destructive
acts; blaming scapegoats/creating blame
culture xix, 49, 115, 123, 133, 150–51,
202–3, 207, 249, 352, 375; choosing a
subservient sexual partner 290–91; in
concern about loyalty of people near
borders with other states 322; contempt 9,
87, 171, 339, 361; dismissing accurate
intelligence 96, 104, 214–15, 360–61;
emotional insulation from suffering caused
by their actions 192, 297; family

backgrounds xix; health problems during
the war 292; with ideologies as drivers
xxviii–xxxv, 1, 5, 81, 98, 99, 106, 117, 130,
132, 191–2, 203–4, 322, 396–7 *see also* Hitler,
Adolf: anti-Semitism; intransigent
negotiating tactics 86–7; living in own
alternative reality 106, 165–6, 252–3; as
loners xxviii, 158, 291; mass deportation
use 30, 31, 32–3, 34, 35–40, 116, 155–6, 168,
305–11, 313, 314–16, 317–18, 320–21, 322,
398; popular idolization of both leaders 84,
239, 379, 401; as profoundly post-
Enlightenment figures xxviii–xxix;
ruthlessness xvii, 18, 63–4, 69, 125, 130,
169, 177–9, 332–6 *see also* Great Terror;
targeting whole groups of people 305–23
see also Hitler, Adolf: anti-Semitism;
Holocaust; in understanding power of
hunger 175; utopianism xxxvi, xxxvii,
239, 241, 378, 401; as war criminals 46,
311, 398
Stalin's attitude in 1930s to 5–6
stress from wartime working hours after life of
a dilettante 246
suicide 383; and Stalin's doubts about his death
384–5
suicides of people connected with xxviii
as Supreme Head of Army and all Armed
Forces 232
Supreme Law Lord appointment 207–8
as symbol of evil 397
tensions with generals 64, 65–7, 79, 94, 120,
131–2, 202, 217, 218, 230–32, 258
torture approved/ordered by 29
total number of deaths attributable to 395–6
Ukrainians subject to scathing comments by
117
and the US *see* United States of America: and
Hitler/the Nazis
utopian vision xxxvii, 239, 241, 378, 401
in Vienna as young man xix
view of Soviet Union: as 'Britain's last hope'
80; hatred of Bolshevism xxxv, 1–2, 4–5, 81,
98, 117, 131, 256, 351–2, 354; as place for new
German Empire 3, 16, 73, 81, 91, 397; as
primary target 78; theories and opinions
before Nazi–Soviet pact xxxi, 1–2
at Vinnitsa 230, 231, 236, 258, 259
as war criminal 398
and weapon development 195
at Wolf's Lair 117, 167, 329–30
worldview and thoughts about death
xxxi–xxxii
Hitler, Eva *see* Braun, Eva
Hitler Youth 239, 379

Hoche, Alfred xxix
Hoepner, Erich 99, 159
Hoffmann, Heinrich 289, 290
Hoffmann, Max 3–4
Holocaust 305, 310–11, 313–14, 316, 318, 319–22,
    354, 383, 395–8, 399
    attempts to compare with Allied bombing of
        German cities 316, 398
    and death camps see *individual camps by name*
    denial 397
    German invasion of Soviet Union and
        birth of 103, 128–30, 168, 189–92,
        240–41, 259
    and *Historikerstreit* (Historian's Dispute) 396
    lack of paper trail to Hitler 311–12
Hong Kong 162
Hopkins, Harry 126–7, 298–9
    and Molotov 211–12
Höppner, Rolf-Heinz 191–2
Horn, Wolfgang 187
Horthy, Miklós 319–20, 331
    blackmailed by Nazis through kidnapping of
        son 351
Höss, Rudolf 43, 189–90, 191–2, 316
Huczyńska, Anna 33, 34
Huczyńska, Irena 33–4
Hungary
    German occupation of 320–21
    and Hitler 319–21, 351
    Horthy and recall of Hungarian soldiers from
        eastern front 319–20, 331
    Jews 319–21, 397; sent to Auschwitz 318–19,
        321
    as member of Axis alliance 319; and Red Army
        accusations of murder and rape 358
    rapes by Red Army soldiers in 357–8
    Red Army taking Budapest 357–8, 359
    and Slovakia 9
hunger see starvation

industrialization
    Industrial Revolution xxxiii–xxxiv
    Stalin and Soviet 194, 389
iron 220
Ismay, Hastings, 1st Baron 225
Istomina, Valentina 291
Italy 283–5
    and Allied landing in Sicily 283
    anti-fascist demonstrations following fall of
        Mussolini 284–5
    Fascist Grand Council 284
    Hitler on reason for 'collapse' of 355
    Stalin and 'aggressive states' including 7
    tripartite pact with Germany and Japan 87, 88
Ivanova, Viktoria 128, 129–30

Jacob, Ian 229
Jagiellonian University, Kraków 40–41
Japan
    and Germany/the Nazis: and Pearl Harbor
        bombing 161, 162; tripartite pact with
        Germany and Italy 87, 88, 160–61
    Hong Kong's fall to 162
    Pearl Harbor attack 160–61, 162
    Singapore's fall to 162
    and Soviet Union: Stalin and 'aggressive states'
        including 7; Stalin's message in Tehran
        concerning 300; and Yalta conference/
        agreement 364
Jeschonnek, Hans 286
Jews
    American 352
    anti-Semitism see anti-Semitism
    and Bolshevism/Marxism xxx, 1–2, 5, 16, 98,
        99, 102–3, 150–52, 154, 167–8, 352, 354; and
        Goebbels' Total War speech 256
    and Canada xxiv
    and Churchill, in Hitler's eyes 203, 240–41, 352
    commissars 151
    deported from Baltic States 116
    German 155, 156
    in Germany in First World War 156
    ghetto confinement 36, 156, 190–91, 308–9
    Hungarian 320–21, 397; sent to Auschwitz
        318–19, 321
    linked with 'partisans' by Germans 154
    Lithuanian 119
    Nazi Jewish 'problem'/'question' 16, 36, 153,
        154, 162–3, 167–8, 203, 259, 310–11, 312, 314,
        321–2, 354 see also Holocaust
    and Nazi 'Madagascar' plan 35–6, 310–11
    and Operation Barbarossa 102–3, 119, 128–30,
        150–52; and Babi Yar massacre 128–30; and
        starvation 190–92; unease of ordinary
        Germans hearing about persecution of Jews
        288–9, 350–51
    Polish 24, 29, 34, 35–6, 103, 190–91, 395–6, 397
    and Roosevelt, in Hitler's and the Nazis' eyes
        162–3, 177, 352
    in Ukraine 119, 330–31; sent from Kiev to Babi
        Yar 128–30
    US, Hitler, and the 'Jewish question' 16,
        162–3, 167–8
Jodl, Alfred 79, 93–4, 230, 231, 329, 380
Jordan, Hans 325
Jordan, Rudolf 367
Junge, Traudl 379–80

Kaganovich, Lazar 194, 195
Kalinin, Ekaterina xxii
Kalinin, Mikhail xxii

Kaliteyev, Vyacheslav 123
Kalmykova, Tamara 242
Kalmyks
    in German Kalmyk Cavalry Corps 305
    in Red Army 305, 310, 402
    Stalin's ethnic cleansing of 305–10, 313,
        314–16, 399
Kantovski, Vladimir 295–6
Kapos 42, 316
Karelia
    Eastern 51
    Karelian Isthmus 55
    Karelo-Finnish Republic 61
Katyn massacre 46, 270–74, 304
    and German propaganda 270, 272–3
    O'Malley report 273
    and Stalin's attack on Polish government in
        exile 271, 302
Kaufmann, Karl 156, 286
Kaunas 119
Kazakhstan 37–8, 39
Kazakhstan (troopship) 123
Keitel, Wilhelm 73, 106, 166, 261, 380
Kellner, Friedrich 77, 113
Kennan, George xxvii
Kesselring, Albert 374
Kharkov 184–5, 186
    battle of 198–202, 210, 214, 235
    Soviet capture and German recapture 266
Khropatiy, Fiodor 358–9
Khrushchev, Nikita 110
    and Hess 103
    and Kharkov campaign 198, 201–3
    and Stalin 20, 52, 59, 74, 103, 112, 125, 198,
        202–3, 291–2, 398
Khudykh, Dmitry 270–71
Kiev
    Babi Yar massacre of Jews of 128–30
    under German occupation 127–8, 129–30;
        Soviet forces in November 1943
        closing on 298
    Soviet booby traps left in 127
    Stalin's Order 270 and Soviet disaster at 123–5,
        131, 144
King, Ernest 212
King, Mackenzie xxiv
Kirponos, Mikhail 124
Kirshin, Viktor 181
Klein, Joseph 214
Klimmer, Otto 77–8, 353–4
Kluge, Günther von 167, 330
Kochina, Elena 182
Kolberg (film) 381–2
Konev, Ivan Stepanovich 370, 373, 391
Königsberg (now Kaliningrad) 385–6

Kostrovitskaia, Vera 181
Krankemann, Ernst 42
Krause, Karl Wilhelm xxiii–xxiv
Kriegsmarine 78, 80, 81
    and Tallinn naval disaster 122–3
    U-boats 161, 164, 214
Kristallnacht xxxii
Kroener, Bernhard R. 441n57
Krüger, Friedrich-Wilhelm 34
Krutova, Valentina 234, 251
Kubizek, August xxiv
Küchler, Georg von 99
kulaks (rich peasants) 33, 37, 53, 118, 228
Kulish, Nikolai 170
Kursk offensive and battle 278–82
Kutaisi Prison xxv
Kutuzov, Mikhail 222–3, 306, 356
Kutuzov, Operation 292–3
Kuusinen, Otto 53, 59, 61
Kuvakova, Evdokiya 308, 317
Kuznetsov, Alexey 393
Kuznetsov, Nikolay Gerasimovich 122

La Rochelle 381
labour camps, Soviet 28, 308, 400
    Gulag *see* Gulag camps
Lagarde, Paul de 35
Landsberg, Otto 2
Lang, Nora 367
Latvia 19, 27, 30–31, 196 *see also* Baltic States
League of Nations 62
Leahy, William Daniel 364
Leclerc, Philippe 345
Lemelsen, Joachim 186–7
Lend-Lease 266
Lenin, Vladimir Ilyich xx, xxi
    and Brest-Litovsk treaty 3, 81
    and Stalin xxxiv–xxxv, 48
    What is to be Done? xxxiv
Leningrad (now St Petersburg) 50, 51
    churches 116
    and Operation Barbarossa 94, 131, 133, 175–83,
        221; and starvation 131, 175, 179–83
    partisans' headquarters 293
    siege of 175–83, 393
    and Stalin 175–7, 178; attack on party officials
        393; remembering revolution on streets of
        Petrograd 322
    starvation at 131, 175, 179–83
Levitska, Anna 25, 335–6
Likhachev, Boris 357
Likhachev, Dmitry 182
Lindemann, Georg 197
List, Wilhelm 230–31, 236
literacy, Soviet 75

Lithuania 27, 30, 116, 329 *see also* Baltic States
children deported from 425n32
Jews murdered 119
Lloyd George, David, 1st Earl 69
Łódź ghetto 36, 156, 190–91, 309
Loringhoven, Bernd Freytag von 382
Low Countries 65, 67, 69, 97 *see also* Belgium;
Luxembourg; Netherlands
Lublin 86, 334, 338, 339
Lublin Poles (Soviet government in Poland) 339,
357, 362–3, 372
Luftwaffe 81, 165
failure in provisions for Sixth Army at
Stalingrad 252
planes 89, 196, 214
reconnaissance inadequacies with Kursk
offensive 280–81
Stalingrad bombing 234
Lukin, Lieutenant General 137
Lunghi, Hugh xxvi–xxvii, 273, 362, 363–4
Luxembourg 69 *see also* Low Countries
Lwów (now Lviv) 25, 29, 37, 337, 338, 412n6
Brygidki prison 115–16, 119
Gestapo HQ 334–5
Home Army officers 334, 338
Levitska's experiences under Soviet and
German occupation compared 335–6
liberation 334
pogroms by Ukrainians 119
and Roosevelt 336

Maisky, Ivan 8, 11, 14–15, 24, 53, 59, 77, 267
and Churchill 8, 125–6, 134, 171, 217, 226,
244, 268
and Operation Barbarossa 104, 113, 134
and Operation Blue 217
Maiziere, Ulrich de 260
Malenkov, Georgi 112, 145, 176, 391
Mannerheim, Carl Gustaf 52, 55, 59, 60
Mannerheim Line 55, 58
Manstein, Erich von 68, 100–101, 251–2, 261, 266
Mao Zedong 87
Marshall, George 212, 213, 276, 387
Marshall plan 387
Marx, Karl xxxiii–xxxiv, xxxvi, 2
Communist Manifesto (with Engels) xxxiii
Das Kapital xxxiii–xxxiv
portrait in Stalin's office 355, 356
Marxism xxxiii–xxxv
inadequacies for Soviet Union xxxvi
Jews and *see* Jews: and Bolshevism/Marxism
and Stalin xxviii, xxxiii–xxxv
Mauth, Maria 78
Mauth, Walter 264–5
Meissner, Hans-Otto 382

Mekhlis, Lev 110
Mensheviks xxxiv
Menzel, Hubert 81–2, 215, 250, 251
as prisoner of war 263–4
Mercader, Ramón 7
Mereshko, Anatoly 216, 237, 370
Meretskov, Kirill 75–6, 98
Merkulov, Vsevolod (Boris) 104
Mikołajczyk, Stanisław 336–9, 347–8
Mikoyan, Anastas 112, 383–4
Mikoyan, Stepan xxv, 48–9
Milani, Milena 284–5
Minsk 111–12, 113, 325, 327
Model, Walter 329
Mogilev 327
Moldavia 138–9
Molotov, Polina 291
Molotov, Vyacheslav 2, 19, 20, 27, 46, 50, 51, 96,
176, 291, 438n60
Berlin talks with Hitler 82–8
and Churchill 209, 213
and defence of Moscow 145
and Hopkins 211–12
and Mikołajczyk 339
negotiations with Allies: in America 211–13,
347; in Britain 208–11, 213
and Operation Barbarossa 107, 108
possible secret peace deal discussions with
Germans 138–9
refusing entry of 'observers' to Poland 370
and Roosevelt 211–13, 298, 347
on Stalin and his cult 390
Stalin's post-war attack on him through his
wife, Polina 391–2, 393
at Yalta 363
and Zhukov 391
Molotov–Ribbentrop pact *see* Nazi–Soviet pact
Montgomery, Bernard Law, 1st Viscount 3
Moran, Charles Wilson, 1st Baron 298–9, 303–4,
342, 343, 362, 363
Morell, Theodor 10, 292, 379
Morocco, French 245
Moscow, and Operation Barbarossa 94, 117,
120
and Operation Typhoon 135–49, 156–9
Red Army counter-attack outside Moscow
159–60
siege and security measures 147–9
Stalin and defence of Moscow 145–9, 169
Moskalenko, Kirill 138–9
Mukhina, Elena 179, 180
Müller, Karl-Hermann 1
Münch, Gerhard 233, 238, 244, 250,
252, 253–4
Münchener Beobachter xxix

Munich
  agreement 9, 11, 13, 18, 399
  Beer Hall Putsch anniversaries, and speeches
    by Hitler *see under* Hitler, Adolf: speeches
  German Workers' Party xx
  Hitler as young painter in xix
  Hitler's coup attempt xxx
  Nazi Party programme revealed in Hofbräuhaus
    beer hall (1920) 163, 361
  revolution (1919) 2
  Thule Society xxix
Muslimova, Musfera 318
Mussolini, Benito 284
  fall of 284, 286
  and Hitler xxiv–xxv, 62–3, 88, 93, 163–4,
    283–4
  and Pearl Harbor bombing 161
  on Ribbentrop 83

Nanieva, Tatiana 400
nationalism
  and Bolshevism xxxv
  and Imperial Russia xxxv
  National Socialism *see* Nazism/National
    Socialists
  and Stalin xxxv
  today's fanatical and intolerant nationalism
    398
Nazi–Soviet pact 1–21, 108, 364–6
  background 1–19
  contribution to German defeat of France 86
  Nazis' enthusiasm for 15
  negotiations 15, 19–20
  perceived illogicality of 1
  Poland and 'sphere of interests' agreement
    changes 26–7
  and Putin 399–400
  signing 20
  as Stalin's personal decision 14
Nazism/National Socialists
  air force *see* Luftwaffe
  Allied bombing campaign against Nazi
    Germany *see* Germany: Allied bombing
    campaign in
  anti-Semitism *see* anti-Semitism: Nazi
  armed forces, unified under *see* Wehrmacht
  and 'Aryan' purity xxxii–xxxiii, 259
  Austria invaded by Nazis 8
  Beer Hall Putsch anniversaries: 18th 150; 19th
    245; 21st 351
  and Britain *see* Britain: and Hitler/
    the Nazis
  and Caucasus resources 215, 220–21; oil 82,
    91–2, 94, 106, 139, 215, 223–4, 230
  and the Church 204–6

and a 'classless' Germany xxxvi, 241
and coal supplies 220–21
concentration/death camps *see individual camps
  by name*
Czechoslovakia's dismantling by 8–11
Economic Four Year Plan 195
'euthanasia' of the disabled 39, 205, 206, 396,
  415n74, 436n47
and Finland 61–2, 86–7, 88, 89
and France *see* France: and the Nazis
Gauleiters xxiii, 44, 45, 156, 367, 406n11
gender inequality women's roles under
  241, 242
and German arrogance, pride and faith in
  weaponry 77–8
Gestapo *see* Gestapo
Greece's fall to 97
Hitler and the disposability of xxiii
Holocaust *see* Holocaust
Hungary's occupation by 319–21
and Japan *see* Japan: and Germany/the Nazis
Kapos 42
Kesselschlachten ('cauldron battles') 72
Kristallnacht xxxii
Law for the Restoration of the Professional
  Civil Service 417n42
and leaders' declaration of willingness for
  self-sacrifice 163, 361
Lebensraum policy 64, 81, 90, 102, 239
and Low Countries 65, 67, 69, 97
Manstein plan 68
membership xxiii
and motherhood/the German
  mother 241
Munich agreement 9, 11, 13, 18, 399
navy *see* Kriegsmarine
'Night of the Long Knives' 63–4, 374
and oil 76, 82, 91–2, 94, 106, 139, 215,
  223–4, 230
and Poland *see* Poland: and Hitler/
  the Nazis
propaganda *see* propaganda: Nazi
as renamed German Workers' Party xx
Second World War *see* Second World War
  theatres and major events
Slovakia's creation by 8, 9–10
and Soviet campaign in Finland 61–3
Soviet invasion *see* Barbarossa, Operation, and
  German occupation of Soviet Union
Soviet pact *see* Nazi–Soviet pact
Soviet trade relationship 89
'sphere of influence' 86
SS *see* SS (Schutzstaffel)
Stalin and *see* Stalin, Joseph: and the Nazis
sterilization regime xxxii

Nazism/National Socialists – *cont'd.*
  stormtroopers 63–4
  twenty-five-point 1920 programme revealed at
    Hofbräuhaus beer hall 163, 361
  and Ukraine *see* Ukraine: and the Nazis
  and the US *see* United States of America: and
    Hitler/the Nazis
  use of terror to oppress Reich population 368
  Wehrmacht *see* Wehrmacht
  western offensive 66–73
  Yugoslavia's fall to 97
Nemmersdorf 350
Netherlands 69
Neumann, Franz 5
Neurath, Konstantin Hermann von xxiv
Nevsky, Alexander 222–3, 306
Nicholas II of Russia
  abdication xx
  murdered with family by Bolsheviks xxvii, 12
NKVD xxii, xxxvii, 38, 45, 76, 138, 140, 193,
    270, 280, 316, 338 *see also* Beria, Lavrenti
  arrests of Polish officers 338
  deportations by 116; Kalmyks 306–8, 313,
    314–16, 317, 320; Osadniks 40; Poles 37–8,
    44; Tatars 318
  files 181–2
  imprisonment of Polish Home Army soldiers
    and leading Poles 349
  and Katyn massacre 272 *see also* Katyn
    massacre
  and Lwów Gestapo HQ 334–5
  murders of prisoners at Brygidki prison
    115–16, 119
  and Perevalov xxxvii, 312, 313, 316
  secret police 22, 28, 29, 112, 311
  securing Moscow 147–8
  and Tatars 317–18
North Africa
  Allied campaign in 266, 274; and British defeat
    214, 217; and *Desert Victory* 268; invasion of
    Algeria and French Morocco 245
  Rommel and the Afrika Korps in 214, 268
Novikov, Alexander 390
Novocherkassk 221
Novosibirsk 37, 307, 309
nuclear bomb 389
Nuremberg
  bombing 258
  trials 369

Obozny, Grigory 141
Odessa, anti-Semitism and massacre of Jews
    153–4
Ogryzko, Vladimir 147–8
Öhquist, Harald 52, 60

oil 76, 82, 91–2, 94, 106, 139, 215, 223–4, 230
Olbricht, Friedrich 330
O'Malley, Sir Owen 272–3
Operations, named military *see* Bagration,
    Operation; Barbarossa, Operation, and
    German occupation of Soviet Union; Blue,
    Operation; Kutuzov, Operation; Rail War,
    Operation; Ring, Operation; Saturn,
    Operation; Typhoon, Operation; Uranus,
    Operation; Winter Storm, Operation
Orel 135, 293
Oreshin, Politruk 55
Orgburo xxi–xxii
Orthodox Church 116–17
Orwell, George 114
Osadniks 39–40
Osipovna, Anastasia 180
Ostroumova-Lebedeva, Anna Petrovna 180
Oven, Wilfred von 381

Palfinger, Alexander 451n10
Papen, Franz von 63
Paris
  fall of 74, 94
  uprising and liberation 341–5
Parodi, Alexandre 344
partisans, Soviet xvi, 100, 187, 293–5
  Jews to be treated as partisans by Nazis 154
  Ukrainian partisans fighting Red Army
    partisans 322
Patton, George Smith Jr 353
Paulus, Friedrich 233, 235–6, 237, 251, 252, 254
Pavlov, Dmitry 115
Pearl Harbor attack 160–61, 162
Peenemünde, RAF raid 286
Perevalov, Nikonor xxxvii, 312–13,
    314–16, 317
Petluk, Ekatarina 242–3, 281
Petrograd 322, 453n45 *see also*
    Leningrad
Pfannmüller, Hermann 206
Pleiger, Paul 220–21, 224
Ploetz, Alfred xxix, xxxi
Poland 22–46
  armed forces 25; Home Army 40, 334, 338–41,
    345, 346, 347, 349, 366, 372; Stalin's 333,
    345, 346
  and Britain *see* Britain: and Poland
  deportations from 30, 31, 32–3, 34, 35–40
  ghettos 36, 156, 190–91, 308–9
  government in exile: and Roosevelt's meeting
    with Mikołajczyk 336–8; Stalin's attack on
    271, 302; Stalin's demand for change in 338;
    Stalin's ignoring of views of 357; and Yalta
    conference/agreement 362–3

and Hitler/the Nazis 6, 11, 14, 17–18, 21, 66,
335–6; brutal treatment of Poles 65; and
Nazi concentration camps 29, 41, 44 *see also*
Auschwitz; cooperation between, and
comparison of the Nazi and Soviet invasions
22–46, 209; and Einsatzgruppen 24; and
General Government 30, 33–4, 35, 36; and
Hitler's Berchtesgaden speech 17–19;
invasion and elimination of Poland 22–4,
28–36, 397; at Jagiellonian University 41;
and Jews 24, 29, 34, 35–6, 103, 190–92,
395–6, 397; non-Jewish death totals under
Nazi occupation 396, 463n4; and the
Osadniks 39–40; and racism 24, 30, 44, 45;
and Warsaw uprising 338, 339–41, 347,
463n4; and Warthegau 31–2, 44, 45, 191
Jews 24, 29, 34, 35–6, 103, 190–91, 395–6, 397
'London Poles' 347
(Nazi) concentration camps in 29, 41, 44 *see also*
Auschwitz
Osadniks 39–40
and Soviet Union 11–13, 170, 209, 301–3,
332–40; and 1st Polish Army 333, 346; and
Allied discovery of mass graves 270–74;
cooperation between, and comparison of the
Nazi and Soviet invasions 22–46, 209; and
Curzon Line 337–8; deportations 37–8, 44;
Katyn massacre *see* Katyn massacre; and
Lublin Poles 339, 357, 362–3, 372; Molotov
refusing entry of 'observers' to Poland 370;
murder of Polish prisoners 115–16, 119, 270;
NKVD arrests of Polish officers 338; NKVD
imprisonment of Polish Home Army soldiers
and leading Poles 349; NKVD murder of
leading Polish figures 270; and 'Polish
Committee of National Liberation' 332–3;
and Putin 399–400; rape by Red Army
soldiers 359–60; Red Army access question
13, 21; Red Army invasion, and elimination
of Poland 22–7, 28–30, 36–46, 82, 170,
270–74, 332–40, 399; as Soviet–German
barrier 6; Soviet retention of eastern Poland
after the war 301–3, 337–8, 346–9, 372, 397;
and Stalin *see* Stalin, Joseph: and Poland; and
western Allied concerns about Stalin's
interpretation of Yalta agreement 370; and
Yalta conference/agreement 362–4, 366, 370
Warsaw *see* Warsaw
and Yalta conference 362–4, 366
Politburo xxi–xxii, 113, 158
Ponomarenko (railwayman from Kiev) 44
Ponomariev, Nikolay 121–2, 123, 141–2
Popadyn, Olga 29, 115–16
Popov, Markian 176
Porunca Vremii 153

Posen *see* Poznań
Potsdam conference 385–7
Poznań 31, 32, 33, 191
Prague 11
Pravda 53, 113, 146, 271, 303, 364
Preussische Zeitung 136
Pripet Marshes 325
Pronicheva, Dina 129
Pronin, V. S. 145
propaganda
Allied 270, 277, 289, 348
films xxvi, xxxii
Nazi xxxv, 18, 52, 121, 183, 185, 192, 204, 241,
253, 262, 272, 273, 289, 350, 353, 376;
Hitler's propaganda image xxvi, 121, 289, 383
Soviet xv, 26, 97, 113, 264, 338, 390; Stalin's
propaganda image xxvi
Putin, Vladimir 399–400

racism
anti-Semitic *see* anti-Semitism
and 'Aryan' purity xxxii–xxxiii, 259
Hitler's ideology xxviii–xxxiii, 1, 5, 64, 81,
130, 191–2, 203–4, 322 *see also* Hitler, Adolf:
anti-Semitism
Holocaust driven by racial hatred 316 *see also*
Holocaust
killing 'racially unwanted' children xxix,
xxxi–xxxii
of Nazis in Poland 24, 30, 44, 45
and Operation Barbarossa 99, 102–3, 119,
128–30, 132
Stalin's ethnic cleansing of Kalmyks 305–10,
314–16, 399
Raeder, Erich 79, 82, 161
RAF 77
bombing campaign against Germany 227, 256,
286; Allied attack on Nuremberg 258;
Berlin 256; Churchill's promises about
Berlin 244; and Goebbels 285–7; Hamburg
285–6; and Hitler 286–7; Peenemünde raid
286; Stalin's congratulations for 268
Rail War, Operation 293
Rapallo, treaty of 409n12
rape
by German soldiers 129, 341
by Hungarians in Soviet Union 358
by Red Army soldiers 357–9; in Germany 350,
376–8; in Hungary 357–8; in Poland 359–60;
Stalin's views 359; in Yugoslavia 359
and venereal disease 358
Raubal, Geli xxviii
Rauchhaupt, Herbert 201
Ravensbrück concentration camp 28
Razumovsky, Lev 175

Red Air Force 8, 49, 58, 346
Red Army: eastern front and German conflict *see also* Barbarossa, Operation, and German occupation of Soviet Union
  backstop units to shoot any retreating soldiers 178–9, 222
  and Budapest 357–8, 359
  and 'campaign wives' 242
  counter-attacks to Barbarossa and German occupation: battle of Kharkov (May 1942) 198–202, 210, 214, 235; encirclement attempt on Second Panzers 265–6; outside Moscow (December 1941) 159–60; Operation Bagration 324–9; Operation Kutuzov 292–3; Operation Ring 253; Operation Saturn 251–2; Operation Uranus *see* Uranus, Operation; wide-ranging disastrous offensive (January 1942) 196–203
  counter-offensive towards and into Germany 350; Berlin assault 355, 369–71, 375–8; and friendly fire 370; Hitler's responses 353, 360–61; and murders by Red Army soldiers 350; and Nemmersdorf 350; and rape *see* rape: by Red Army soldiers; and rivalry between Marshals 369, 370, 375; and Stalin's demeanour 355; Vistula–Oder offensive 346, 360–61
  defeat and crushing at Kiev 124, 131, 144
  draconian discipline 178–9, 222, 238, 295–7
  equipment production for 194–5
  German underestimation of Red Army 120–21
  under initial advance 108–12; caught by surprise 107
  interference from 'military illiterates' 110, 196–201 *see also* Stalin, Joseph: Red Army interference by
  and Kursk offensive 280–82
  leadership inadequacies/mistakes 111–12, 115, 121, 122–5, 144–6, 196–203, 265–6
  mass murders by retreating army 119
  and military equipment production safeguarded through Council for Evacuation 194–5
  officers killed on Commissar Order 99, 185
  and Operation Blue 215, 216–17, 236–8, 243; disciplinary killing of soldiers during battle of Stalingrad 238; and Order 227 not to retreat 221–2
  and Operation Typhoon 135–7, 142, 158, 159–60
  and partisans xvi, 100, 187, 293–5, 323
  and penal battalions 295–7
  POWs 107, 108, 142, 185–90, 193, 200, 241–2, 265

  prevention of surrendering (by Order 270) 123–5, 222
  women's roles 241–3
Red Army: the fighting force
  2nd Tank Army 338
  4th Army 76
  6th Army 200
  13th Guards Rifle Division 237
  32nd Army 137
  44th Division 55–8
  62nd Army 237
  77th Guards Regiment 327
  163rd Division 55, 58
  artillery 60, 108–10, 194, 198, 248, 253, 375
  in Baltic States 27, 30, 50
  Belorussian Front: First 332, 369, 378; Second 369
  and Bonapartists 47
  and Chamberlain 13
  and commissars *see* commissars
  comparisons with Wehrmacht: assessments of relative strength prior to conflict 74, 105, 120–21; decision-making on front line 110–11, 195–6; equipment and supplies 61, 108–10, 125, 144, 158, 159–60, 194–5, 216–17, 239, 258, 280, 281, 282, 329; leadership 61, 67, 110–12, 120–21, 143–6, 195–7, 199–200, 215, 324; numbers 282, 329, 360; women's roles 241–3
  disparaged by Nazis after Finnish campaign 61
  draconian discipline 178–9, 222, 238, 295–7
  expansion during 1930s 47
  Finnish campaign 47, 50–63, 67, 74, 75–6, 80, 81–2
  Great Terror and destruction of officer corps 48, 63, 67, 73, 81–2, 274, 331
  Kalmyks in 305, 310, 402
  mass release of commanders from prison 74
  military testing accidents 48–9
  modernization 48, 108–10
  officer medals created by Stalin 222–3, 306
  peasants enlisted in 392
  penal battalions 295–7
  and Poland 13, 21, 22–7, 28–30, 36–46, 82, 170, 332–40, 399; and 1st Polish Army 333, 346; and Home Army 40, 334, 338–40, 345, 346, 347; Stalin's authorization of mass killing of Polish officers xvii, 45–6, 170–71, 270 *see also* Katyn massacre
  Political Administration 110
  proactive reaction to attack 96–7
  as sclerotic 110
  Second Shock Army 197
  suspicion of radio 48, 110

tanks 60, 110, 125, 144, 159–60, 194, 195, 198, 201, 239, 247, 248, 281–2, 325; T34 159–60, 241
and Trotsky 47
Ukrainian Front: First 334, 369; Second 358
unprepared for major conflict after Winter War 74, 97, 107
wargames 98
women in 241–3, 282
Red Army News 146
Reichel, Joachim 214
Reichenau, Walther von 127, 154, 165, 184, 430n10
Reichert, Rüdiger von 98–9
Reiter, Maria xxviii
Reva, Anatoly 186
Reynaud, Paul 69
Ribbentrop, Joachim von 15, 17, 19, 21, 26–7, 34–5, 82–3, 174, 361
    Molotov–Ribbentrop pact *see* Nazi–Soviet pact
    and the Molotov Berlin talks 82, 84–5, 87–8
    and Operation Barbarossa 93
    and Pearl Harbor bombing 161
Richter, Herbert xxi
Ring, Operation 253
Ringelblum, Emmanuel 29
Roberts, Sir Frank 9
Roes, Wilhelm 241–2, 280–81
Rohland, Walter 157–8
Röhm, Ernst 63–4, 405n4
Rokossovsky, Konstantin 74–5, 136, 197–8, 265–6, 325, 340
Roma 396
Romania 13, 76, 87, 348
    anti-Semitism, and murder of Jews by Romanian Army 153–4
    as anti-Slavic buffer for Germany 152
    declaration of war on Germany 351
    Hitler on reason for 'collapse' of 355
    oil fields 76
    and Soviet Union: and British exclusion 386; occupation/repression by Soviets 351, 371, 372; Romanian invasion of Soviet Union 152–3
Rommel, Erwin 214, 232
Roosevelt, Eleanor 438n60
Roosevelt, Franklin D. 161
    arrogance 299
    and Churchill *see* Churchill, Winston: and Roosevelt
    and de Gaulle 341, 342
    death 374
    and Hitler 16, 162–3, 240, 245
    and Hopkins 126–7

and the Jews, in Hitler's and the Nazis' eyes 162–3, 177, 240, 352
    and Mikołajczyk 336–8, 347–8
    and Molotov 211–13, 298, 347
    Nazi idea for him to look after Leningrad citizens 177
    and O'Malley report into Katyn massacre 273
    and Stalin 126–7, 134, 211, 213, 229, 230, 266–7, 275–8, 372–3; and American POWs 372; and Churchill in Tehran 297–300; and Soviet retention of eastern Poland after the war 302–3, 337–8, 347–8, 372; and Stalin's allegations of secret Allied negotiations with Germans 372–3; and United Nations 362, 363, 372; and Yalta conference/agreement 361–3, 364, 366–7, 370–71
    and United Nations 211, 362, 372
    and Yalta conference 361–3, 364, 366–7, 370–71
Rosenberg, Alfred 101–2, 155, 156
Rosenfeld, Oskar 191
Rostov 157, 165, 218, 221
Royal Navy 78, 80
    Arctic convoys 224–6, 229; PQ17 loss 224, 225, 226
Rubbel, Alfred 159–60, 218–20, 280, 281
Ruman, Tadeusz 40–41
Rundstedt, Gerd von 165, 430n10
Russia
    Bolshevism *see* Bolshevism/Bolsheviks
    Brest-Litovsk treaty 3–4, 81, 350
    and Churchill's 'naughty' document on percentages of Allied influences 348, 371–2
    Mensheviks xxxiv
    murder of Russian Imperial Family xxvii, 12
    nationalism and Imperial Russia xxxv
    October Revolution xx
    portrayal as dominant member of Soviet family 306
    Soviet *see* Soviet Union
    Stalin and imperial history/glory of 222–3, 306, 324, 355, 356
    steppes 132, 215–16, 218, 225; and Operation Blue *see* Blue, Operation
Russian Social Democratic Labour Party xxxiv
Rybalko, Pavel 391
Rzhev 197, 297

Sachsenhausen concentration camp 42, 188, 292
Sagun, Ivan 281
St Petersburg *see* Leningrad
Saternus, Wiesława 193
Saturn, Operation 251–2

Schaefer-Kehnert, Walter 136–7, 158–9
Schirach, Baldur von 289, 367
Schirach, Henrietta von 289
Schlegelberger, Franz 207
Schleicher, Kurt von 64
Schlitt, Ewald 207
Schmückle, Gerd 282
Schneider, Albert 107, 183
Schröder, Manfred von 10
Schulenburg, Friedrich-Werner Count von der 26, 107
Schultze, Norbert 381
SD (intelligence arm of SS) 61–2, 274
    reports 67, 286, 288, 331, 350
Sebottendorff, Rudolf von xxix–xxx
Second Shock Army 197
Second World War theatres and major events
    Allied advance into Germany 350–55; and Hitler's Ardennes forest offensive 352–3; Red Army in Germany *see* Red Army: eastern front and German conflict: counter-offensive towards and into Germany
    Allied bombing campaign against Germany *see* Germany: Allied bombing campaign in
    Allied invasion of Algeria and French Morocco 245
    Allied landing in Sicily 283
    Allies shaken by discovery of Polish mass graves 270–74
    beginning, with German attack on Poland 22, 397
    Berlin *see* Berlin
    British defeat in North Africa 217
    British loss of PQ17 Arctic convoy 224, 225, 226
    Bulgaria's declaration of war on Germany 351
    D-Day 210, 324, 337
    Dunkirk evacuation 77
    eastern front: Baltic States *see* Baltic States; as 'decisive front' according to Hitler 279; effects of war on Soviet citizens 170; Horthy and recall of Hungarian soldiers 319–20, 331; Leningrad siege 175–83; Nazi invasion and occupation of Soviet Union *see* Barbarossa, Operation, and German occupation of Soviet Union; Blue, Operation; Kursk offensive and battle; Rail War, Operation; Typhoon, Operation; Winter Storm, Operation; Poland *see* Poland; Red Army's defence of Soviet Union and counter-offensives against Germans *see* Red Army: eastern front and German conflict; and Stalingrad *see* Stalingrad; Ukraine *see* Ukraine; Warsaw *see* Warsaw
    Finland's invasion by Soviets 53–63
    France's fall and occupation 69–72, 74, 86, 94
    Hitler's declaration of war on USA 161, 162
    Holocaust *see* Holocaust
    Hungary's occupation by Germans 320–21
    Japanese attack on Pearl Harbor 160–61
    Kalmykia *see* Kalmyks
    and level of suffering due to ruthlessness of leaders 178–83
    Nazi May 1940 western attack 69–72
    North Africa *see* North Africa
    and Paris *see* Paris
    Potsdam and the splitting of Germany 386–7
    rationing in Germany 208
    Romania's declaration of war on Germany 351
    and Stalin's desire for second front 125–6, 209, 210, 211–13, 225–6, 244, 266–9, 274–8, 298, 300
    starvation *see* starvation
    Tehran conference 297–304
    US invasion with Allies of Algeria and French Morocco 245
Selle, Herbert 201
Semenyak, Georgy 108, 186
Sergius, Patriarch 116
Service, Robert 408n51
sex
    between German soldiers and Ukrainian women 129
    rape *see* rape
    and Red Army 'campaign wives' 242
    and venereal disease 358
Shaposhnikov, Boris Mikhaylovich 124
Shevenok, Captain 54
Shirer, William 83
Shlisselburg 133
Shostakovich, Dmitri 170
Siberia 37, 50, 118
    Kalmyk deportations to 306–8, 313, 314–16
    Stalin's exile in xx, 37
Sicily 283
Sikorski, Władysław 170, 171
Simonov, Konstantin 110, 391
Singapore 162
Sinti 396
Slavs 81, 99, 117, 129, 399
Slovakia 8, 9–10
    and Hungary 9
Smoleń, Kazimierz 189
Smolensk 120, 288
    Polish mass graves near 270–74
Snyder, Timothy 462–3n2

socialism
 vs capitalism xxxiv, xxxv, 389
 and a 'classless' Germany xxxvi, 241
 German national *see* Nazism/National
  Socialists
 revolts in Berlin and Bavaria 98
Soldan, Lieutenant Colonel 201
Soviet Communist Party
 Congress: Eleventh xxi; Eighteenth xxxvi, 7;
  Twentieth 398
 Stalin's appointment as leader xxi
 Stalin's attitude to xxii–xxiii
Soviet Union
 administrative concealment policy 38–9
 air force 8, 49, 58, 346; planes 194
 and Allied Lend-Lease 266
 arms race 389
 Baltic States taken over by 329
 Bolshevism *see* Bolshevism/Bolsheviks
 and Britain *see* Britain: and Soviet Union
 and Bukovina 76, 86
 Bulgaria's occupation/repression by 351, 371
 Caucasus *see* Caucasus
 centralization of power 194–5
 as a closed country 26
 Cold War 385, 386
 collapse of 389
 collectivization and agricultural restructuring
  118, 130, 188, 195
 Comintern 6, 301
 commissars *see* commissars
 Communist Party *see* Soviet Communist Party
 Council for Evacuation 194–5
 and Council for Mutual Economic
  Assistance 387
 education 75
 effects of war on citizens 170
 Finnish campaign *see* Winter War
 and France *see* France: and Soviet Union
 German agreement in treaty of Rapallo
  409n12
 Great Terror 48–9, 54, 63, 67, 73, 81–2, 179,
  274, 331, 398
 Gulag system *see* Gulag camps
 Hitler's view of *see* Hitler, Adolf: view of
  Soviet Union
 industrialization 194, 389
 intelligence gathering under Stalin 95–6
 and Japan *see* Japan: and
  Soviet Union
 Kalmyk ethnic cleansing 305–10, 313,
  314–16, 399
 and Karelo-Finnish Republic 61
 and Königsberg 385–6
 kulaks 33, 37, 53, 118, 228

labour camps *see* labour camps, Soviet
literacy 75
Nazi invasion of *see* Barbarossa, Operation, and
 German occupation of Soviet Union
Nazi pact with *see* Nazi–Soviet pact
Nazi trade relationship 89
NKVD *see* NKVD
nuclear bomb 389
Orgburo xxi–xxii
partisans *see* partisans, Soviet
patriotism 74, 149, 223, 224, 248
peasants enlisted in army 392
penal system 37, 43 *see also* Gulag camps;
 labour camps, Soviet
and Poland *see* Poland: and Soviet Union; Red
 Army: the fighting force: and Poland;
 Stalin, Joseph: and Poland
Politburo xxi–xxii, 113, 158
population in late 1930s 47, 415n1
post-war leadership of a people psychologically
 devastated by war 392
POW camps 263–5
propaganda *see* propaganda: Soviet
Red Army *see entries at Red Army*
and Romania *see* Romania: and Soviet Union
and Second World War *see* Red Army: eastern
 front and German conflict; Second World
 War theatres and major events
secret police 22, 28, 29, 112, 311 *see also* Beria,
 Lavrenti; NKVD
'sphere of influence' 19, 62, 86–7, 88, 89
split with west 386–9
Stalin on inadequacies of Marxist doctrine for
 Soviet Union xxxvi
Stalin's view of Soviet involvement in foreign
 conflicts 6, 7–8
starvation *see* starvation
State Defence Committee *see* Stavka
Tallinn naval disaster 122–3
and the tripartite pact 87, 88
Ukraine's suffering under Soviet rule 118
Urkas 41–2
and the US *see* United States of America: and
 Soviet Union
and Volga Germans 155, 168–9, 306
weather and climate 142, 149, 157, 159, 181,
 184, 251
Winter War against Finland *see* Winter War
Spain 6, 384–5
Speer, Albert 220, 257, 258, 259, 290, 368–9,
 458n60
Spitzy, Reinhard 83, 217
SS (Schutzstaffel) xxxvii, 28, 29, 43, 261, 312, 372
 see also Himmler, Heinrich
 at Auschwitz 190, 319

SS (Schutzstaffel) – *cont'd.*
  brutal treatment of Poles 65
  intelligence arm *see* SD
  and Kapos 42
  loyalty to Hitler 287
  murdering Jews in Ukraine 330–31
  in Warsaw uprising 340
Stalin, Joseph
  admiration for Hitler over Röhm murder 63,
    405n4
  agricultural collectivization 118, 130, 195
  and Allied 1940 defeat in France 74
  anti-Semitism 393
  appearance xxvi–xxvii, 173
  appointed General Secretary of the
    Communist Party xxi
  appointed head of the People's Commissariat
    for Nationalities xxxv
  and Arctic convoys 224–6, 229
  and August 1939, courted by British and
    Germans 16–17
  authorizing violent/destructive acts: ethnic
    cleansing 305–10, 313, 314–16, 317–18;
    Great Terror 48–9, 63, 67, 73, 81–2, 179,
    274, 331, 398; against Kalmyks 305–10,
    313, 399; Katyn massacre 46, 270–74, 304;
    mass killing of Polish officers/elite xvii,
    45–6, 170–71, 270 *see also* Katyn massacre;
    with millions of deaths through famine
    118, 395; torture xxii, 29, 311
  birth and family background xix, 2
  and Cadogan 14, 172–3
  character: anger, and difficulties of telling
    him bad news 49; blaming scapegoats/
    creating blame culture 49, 115, 123, 133,
    150, 202–3; as bureaucrat xxi, 45; concern
    for reputation 390; contempt/scorn 9, 87,
    171, 339, 361; deceitfulness/insincerity 116,
    170–71, 303, 373, 385; emotional coldness
    373; fondness of using vague concepts 53;
    hatred of democracy xxxvii–xxxviii;
    imperturbability xxv; inscrutability
    xxvii; insistence/certainty he was right
    215, 289; intimidating others to tell him
    what he wanted to hear 104–5, 145–6, 158,
    210; kindness seen by Ponomariev 122;
    lack of compassion 169; lack of desire to
    impress or be liked 85, 171, 373; listening
    attention 75; lust for praise 390;
    overconfidence 135, 196, 198, 265;
    propaganda film persona xxvi; rationalism
    260; ruthlessness xvii, 63, 125, 130, 169,
    178–9, 332–6 *see also* Great Terror;
    self-presentation as modest worker 355;
    shrewdness 173; suspiciousness xxv–xxvi,

  7, 26, 47, 48, 95, 96, 210, 214, 244, 322, 384,
    385, 392; watchfulness 20, 299, 300
  children xxviii, 292
  and Christianity *see* Christianity and the
    Church: and Stalin
  and Churchill *see* Churchill, Winston: and
    Stalin
  and the Cold War 385
  commemorating 1941 anniversary of 1917
    revolution 141, 148–9
  comrades' fear of 112–13, 158, 202, 270,
    291–2
  and Council for Mutual Economic
    Assistance 387
  and danger of contact between Soviet citizens
    and foreigners 26
  and Davies 275–6, 277
  and de Gaulle 356–7
  death 393; and posthumous
    humiliation with moving of embalmed
    body 398
  dress: grey workers' tunic xxvii; military
    uniform 355–6, 390
  drinking 108, 172–3, 228, 292
  and Eden 171–2, 173–4, 179
  Eighteenth Congress of the Communist Party
    address xxxvi
  Finnish campaign 47, 50–63, 67, 74, 75–6, 80,
    81–2
  and First World War xix–xx
  and Franco 6, 384–5
  Georgian accent xxvi–xxvii
  and German Communist Party 5
  Great Terror 48–9, 54, 63, 67, 73, 81–2, 179,
    274, 331, 398
  as head of Stavka 115
  health problems 292
  Hitler on *see* Hitler, Adolf: on Stalin
  Hitler's death questioned by 384–5
  and Hitler's *Mein Kampf* 6
  Hitler's similarities *see* Hitler, Adolf: Stalin's
    and Hitler's areas of similarity
  and Hopkins 126–7
  and imperial history/glory of Russia 222–3,
    306, 324, 355, 356, 383
  and industrialization 194, 389
  and intelligence gathering 95–6
  and Istomina 291
  and Ivan the Terrible 112, 383–4
  and Kalmuk deportations/ethnic cleansing
    305–10, 313, 314–16
  and Khrushchev 20, 52, 59, 74, 103, 112, 125,
    198, 202–3, 291–2, 398
  and Königsberg 385–6
  in Kutaisi Prison xxv

leadership 144–6, 398–9; appealing to
patriotism 223, 224, 248; and attack on party
officials in Leningrad 393; of a changed
post-war Soviet Union 392; in comparison
with Hitler's 47–73, 91, 120–27, 133, 143–6,
196, 215, 324; cult 390; dismissing accurate
intelligence 96, 104, 214–15; in failed
offensive in centre of eastern front 265–6;
and Finnish campaign 47, 50–61; and
interference with Red Army *see* Stalin,
Joseph: Red Army interference by; and
Operation Barbarossa 95–7, 108, 111–12, 115,
116–17, 121–7, 195–202 *see also* Barbarossa,
Operation: and Stalin; and Operation Blue
214–15, 216, 221–4, 243–4; and Operation
Uranus 246–54; Order 227 not to retreat
221–2; paralysis 112; and power of
ambiguity 339–40; and 'tightening' 390–93;
visit to the front (August 1943) 297
and Lenin xxxiv–xxxv, 48
and Leningrad *see* Leningrad (now St
Petersburg): and Stalin
marriages xxviii
and the Marshall plan 387
Marxism and the National Question xxxv
Marxist ideology xxviii, xxxiii–xxxv; and its
inadequacies for Soviet Union xxxvi
and Mikołajczyk 347–8
military uniform 355–6, 390
modern perceptions in comparison with Hitler
395–401
and nationalism xxxv
and the Nazis: attitudes in 1930s 5–6;
conviction they would not attack 106; and
defence of Moscow 145–9, 169; hatred of
Nazism xxxv; incorrect theory of his
intention to make pre-emptive strike 96–7;
mental state and decisions that shaped
response to German invasion 95–8, 103–6,
121; non-provocative stance 97; and
Operation Barbarossa *see* Barbarossa,
Operation, and German occupation of
Soviet Union: and Stalin; and Operation
Blue 214–15, 216, 221–4, 233, 243–4; and
Operation Typhoon 138, 141, 145–9
negotiating tactics/expertise 87, 173, 299–302,
361–7
office medals created by 222–3, 306
as Orgburo member xxi–xxii
and Poland: arguments with western Allies
concerning interpretation of Yalta
agreement 370; demand for change in
government in exile 338; and his
authorizing murder of thousands of Polish
officers/elite xvii, 45–6, 170–71, 270 *see also*
Katyn massacre; and Lublin Poles 339, 357,
362–3; and Soviet retention of eastern
Poland after the war 301–3, 337–8, 346–9,
372, 397; Stalin's own armed forces in
Poland 333, 346; subject to personal hatred/
cynicism of 22, 170, 346; and Warsaw
uprising 338, 345–6, 347; and Yalta
conference/agreement 362–4, 366, 370
as Politburo member xxi–xxii
and post-war borders 171–2, 174, 209–11, 337;
and eastern Poland 301–3, 337–8, 346–9,
372, 397
at Potsdam conference 385–6
propaganda adoration of 113, 297
Putin and reputation of 398–400
rape by Red Army soldiers in Stalin's
view 359
Red Army interference by 110, 196–8;
destruction of officer corps in Great Terror
48, 63, 67, 73, 81–2, 274, 331; Order 270 and
disaster at Kiev 123–5, 131, 144, 222
rejection of birth name Iosif Jughashvili xx
revolutionary roots xix–xx
and Roosevelt *see* Roosevelt, Franklin D.: and
Stalin
and second-front question 125–6, 209, 210,
211–13, 225–6, 229, 244, 266–9, 274–8, 298,
300
service to Communist Party xxii–xxiii
Siberian exile xx, 37
and Soviet assault on Berlin 355, 369–70
and Soviet involvement in foreign conflicts
6; foreign policy speech (spring 1939)
7–8
split with west 386–9
and the splitting of Germany 386–7
and Tallinn naval disaster 122–3
and Tatar deportations 318
as Tiflis robbery organizer xx, xxxiv–xxxv
torture approved/authorized by xxii, 29, 311
total number of deaths attributable to 395
training as priest xix–xx
and Trotsky 6–7, 47
and Truman 374, 386
and Ukraine 118, 183, 192
and United Nations 362, 363, 372
utopian vision xxxvii, 401
and Volga Germans 155, 168–9, 306
and Voroshilov 49–50, 60–61, 73, 74
as war criminal 46, 311
and war with capitalism xxxv–xxxvi, 389
wives xxviii
and Yalta conference 361–7, 370, 386
Zhukov's treatment after the war
390–91, 393

Stalingrad 131, 132
    and Operation Blue 218, 233, 234–40; battle as
        emblematic for Germans 240; disciplinary
        killing of Red Army soldiers during battle of
        238; German Sixth Army defeat 246–54,
        255–6, 261–2; Göring's speech following
        German defeat 255–6; Hitler's and Goebbels'
        lies about Sixth Army defeat 256–7, 261–2;
        Luftwaffe bombing 234; and Red Army
        counter-attack, Operation Uranus *see* Uranus,
        Operation; Red Army defence 236–8
    and Operation Ring 253
    and Operation Saturn force availability 251–2
    and Operation Uranus *see* Uranus, Operation
    and Operation Winter Storm 251
    as symbol of Soviet resistance 235
    Tsaritsyn renamed as 235
Standley, William 275
Stargardt, Nicholas 430n10
starvation 175–93, 328, 396
    among Soviet POWs 185–90, 193
    breaking people by 193
    and cannibalism 181–2, 190
    and children 180
    of deported Kalmyks 308–9, 317
    in First World War 175
    in ghettos 308; Łódź 190–91
    in Gulag 192, 193
    and hunger in a Soviet prison camp 264–5
    and inequality 179–80
    of Jews 190–92
    at Leningrad 131, 175, 179–83
    and Nazi Hunger Plan 101–2; and Leningrad
        131, 175, 179–85
    and the power of hunger 175, 192–3
    while Soviet Communist Party leadership ate
        well 179–80
    in Ukraine 118, 179, 183, 184–5, 192, 395
Stauffenberg, Claus von xxvi, 329, 330–31
Stavka (Soviet State Defence Committee) 115,
    140, 147, 198, 295
steel 220
Steinke, Gerda 376–7
Stempel, Joachim 198–9, 201, 215–16, 233,
    234–5, 238
Stenkin, Pavel 187–8, 189, 190, 193
Stepanov, Army Commissar 169
sterilization xxxii
Strazdovski, Viktor 137
Sudetenland 8–9
Sudoplatov, Pavel 138, 139
Suomussalmi, battle of 58
Suvorov, Alexander 222–3, 306, 355, 356
Sverdlov, Fyodor 110–11, 169–70
Sweden 50, 60
Szálasi, Ferenc 351

Tachieva, Vera 306–7
Tallinn naval disaster 122–3
Talvela, Paavo Juho 60
Tatars 306, 317–18
Tedder, Arthur 227, 228–9, 355, 356
Tehran conference 297–304
Thomas, Georg 92
Thule Society xxix
Tiflis (now Tbilisi) xx, xxxiv–xxxv
Timoshenko, Mikhail 26, 55–7, 58, 76, 111, 294–5
Timoshenko, Semyon 60, 75, 76, 97, 107
    and Kharkov campaign 198, 201–2
Tiso, Jozef 9
Todt, Fritz 158
torture xxii, 29, 48, 74, 262, 271, 311, 335
Tosno 176
Treblinka death camp 318
Tresckow, Henning von 329, 330
Trotsky, Leon 2
    in exile 6–7
    murder 7
    and Red Army 47
    and Stalin 6–7, 47
    The Stalin School of Falsification 7
Truman, Harry 267, 374, 386
Tsessarsky, Tatyana 140
Tsymbaliuk, Olha 118
Tukhachevsky, Mikhail 48, 49, 74, 274
Tupikov, Vasily Ivanovich 124
Turkey/Turks 89, 105
    'Turks in front of Vienna' 98
Typhoon, Operation 135–49, 156–9
    Red Army counter-attack 159–60

U-boats 161, 164, 214
Udet, Ernst 164–5
Ukraine
    anti-Semitism 119, 128–30
    and Brest-Litovsk treaty 3, 81
    Communist Party 20
    famine and starvation 118, 179, 183, 184–5,
        192, 395
    Jews 119, 128–30, 330–31
    Kharkov *see* Kharkov
    Kiev *see* Kiev
    and the Nazis: Babi Yar massacre 128–30;
        collaboration with Germans 117–19, 128,
        130, 322–3; Hitler on Ukraine/Ukrainians
        17, 117; Hitler's field headquarters *see*
        Vinnitsa; and Operation Barbarossa 117–19,
        123–5; sex between German soldiers and
        Ukrainian women 129; viewed as 'a good
        bread-basket' 102
    peasant deportation 37, 118
    and possible Soviet secret peace deal
        discussions with Germans 138–9

and Stalin 118, 183, 192
suffering under Soviet rule 118
Ukrainian partisans fighting Red Army
partisans 322
United Kingdom *see* Britain
United Nations 211, 362, 363, 372
United States of America
and Allied 1944 advance into Germany 350
and Britain *see* Britain: and the US
and First World War 245
and Hitler/the Nazis: Hitler's declaration of
war 161, 162; Hitler's speech to Reichstag
1941 (11 December) 162–3, 164; Hitler's
view of US xxx–xxxi, 16, 162–3, 164; and
'Jewish question' 16, 162–3, 167–8; and
Operation Barbarossa 114, 125–6, 134, 198;
and Pearl Harbor bombing 160–61, 162
Japan's attack on Pearl Harbor 160–61, 162
Jews 352
Marshall plan 387
national Finland Day 58
navy 161
Second World War invasion with Allies of
Algeria and French Morocco 245
and Soviet Union: and discovery of Polish
mass graves 273; First Protocol 134;
Molotov's talks and understanding with
Roosevelt 210–13, 280, 347; and Operation
Barbarossa 114, 125–6, 134, 198; Soviet
expectations of US launching an invasion of
western Europe 213; and Soviet retention of
eastern Poland after the war 302–3, 337–8;
Stalin and 'non-aggressive states' 7–8;
Stalin and Roosevelt relations *see* Roosevelt,
Franklin D.: and Stalin; and Stalin's desire
for second front 211–13, 229, 266–8, 274–8,
298, 300
and Versailles treaty *see* Versailles, treaty of
Uranus, Operation 246–54, 255–6, 265
German POWs 262–4
Uratadze, Grigol xxv
Urkas 41–2
utopianism xxxvii, 239, 312, 378, 401
classless Nazi utopia xxxvi, 241
Uzbekistan 75, 318

Vasilevsky, Aleksandr 202, 246–7, 248, 265
venereal disease 358
Versailles, treaty of 2, 5–6, 65
Verzhbitskii, N. K. 140
Victor Emmanuel III of Italy 284
Vienna 36
Vilnius 329
Vinnitsa 230, 231, 236, 258, 259
Vinogradov, Alexei 57–8
Vitman, Boris 198–9

Volga, River 234–5, 237, 245
Volga Germans 155, 168–9, 306
Völkischer Beobachter 62, 136, 201, 379
Volkogonov, Dmitri 138–9
Voronov, Nikolai 54
Voroshilov, Kliment 49–50, 60–61, 73, 74,
173, 176
Vyazma 136–7, 142, 187, 197

Wagner, Eduard 185
Wall Street Journal 267
Walz, Helmut 214, 216, 243
Warlimont, Walter 161, 236
Warsaw
civilian deaths in 1939 invasion and siege of
463n4
destruction ordered by Himmler 341
Germans tormenting Poles in 29
ghetto 309
liberated ruins 346
uprising 338, 339–41, 345–6, 347, 463n4
weather/climate, Soviet Union 142, 149, 157, 159,
181, 184, 251
Weber, Max xx
Wehr, Lieutenant Commander 123
Wehrmacht 13, 66–73, 80–81
6th Army 201, 233, 235–7, 238, 239, 250, 255,
262; POWs 262, 264; and Red Army's
Operation Uranus 246–54, 255–6
9th Army 278
18th Army 99, 197
Afrika Korps 214, 268
air force *see* Luftwaffe
Ardennes forest offensive 352–3
Army Group Centre 94, 99, 110–11, 113, 115,
120, 123, 136, 142–3, 156, 158, 165, 197, 288,
293, 324, 329
Army Group North 175, 196
Army Group South 94, 165, 214, 215, 217–18;
Group A 218, 230–32, 236, 239, 252; Group B
218, 233
and British Army 77
and Einsatzgruppen 24, 103, 119
flexible leadership 67, 200
High Command 99, 177, 215
Hitler's multiple leadership roles 232
Hitler's tensions with generals 64, 65–7, 79, 94,
120, 131–2, 202, 217, 218, 230–32
Hungary's invasion by 320–21
infantry divisions: 30th 264; 71st 215, 238;
305th 243
and Knight's Cross 241
Luftwaffe *see* Luftwaffe
mission command (*Auftragstaktik*) 111, 195
navy *see* Kriegsmarine
'Nazification' demanded by Hitler 331–2

Wehrmacht – *cont'd.*
  Operation Barbarossa *see* Barbarossa,
    Operation, and German occupation of
    Soviet Union
  Operation Blue *see* Blue, Operation
  Operation Typhoon *see* Typhoon, Operation
  Panzer armies/groups: 2nd 124, 135, 166, 265;
    3rd 160; 4th 99, 159; 5th 353; 6th 374
  Panzer divisions: 1st 139; 4th, 6th Company
    135; 7th 282; 11th 136–7; 14th 199, 215, 233;
    16th 250; 48th 249; Leibstandarte 266; SS
    divisions 266
  and Poland 24, 66 *see also* Poland: and Hitler/
    the Nazis
  POWs 262–5
  rape by soldiers 129, 341
  Red Army comparisons *see* Red Army: the
    fighting force: comparisons with
    Wehrmacht
  Red Army conflicts *see* Red Army: eastern
    front and German conflict
  sex between soldiers and Ukrainian women 129
  soldiers' oaths to Hitler 288, 330
  and stormtroopers 63–4
  supply and resource problems 142–3, 144, 157
  tanks 68–9, 111, 119–20, 124, 132, 135, 139, 144,
    159, 280, 282; Panther 278; Tiger 278, 281
  trucks 110
  and weapon development 195
  women auxiliaries 241
Welles, Sumner 114
Wells, H. G. xxx
Werner, Kurt 128

Wiedemann, Fritz 246
Wilhelm II of Germany xxvii, 65, 72
Wilson, Sir Charles 228
Winter Storm, Operation 251
Winter War 47, 50–63, 67, 74, 75–6, 80, 81–2
Witter, Ben 286
Wolak, Zbigniew 340–41
Wollschlaeger, Arthur 135
world wars *see* First World War; Second World
    War theatres and major events

Yablonsky, Vyacheslav 144–5, 334–5
Yalta conference/agreement 361–7, 370, 386
Yefimov, Boris xv
Yerofeyev, Vladimir xxv
Yevtushenko, Yevgeny 170
Yugoslavia 97, 359

Zeitzler, Kurt 231, 249
Zelenskaia, Irina 180
Zhdanov, Andrei 175, 393
Zhemchuzhina, Polina 391–2, 393
Zhukov, Georgy 75, 97, 98, 107, 108, 111, 123, 138,
    194, 269–70, 373
  and Berlin assault 369–70, 375
  and defence of Moscow 146, 147
  First Deputy Commissar of Defence
    appointment 223
  and Kharkov campaign 198, 201, 202
  and Operation Uranus 246–7, 248, 265
  publicity given by Stalin to 146, 147
  and Stalin's doubts about Hitler's death 384–5
  Stalin's post-war treatment of 390–91, 393